PRINCIPLES OF Macroeconomics

About the Authors

John B. Taylor is one of the field's most inspiring teachers. As the Raymond Professor of Economics at Stanford University, his distinctive instructional methods have made him a legend among introductory economics students and have won him both the Hoagland and Rhodes prizes for teaching excellence. As described by the *Wall Street Journal,* Taylor's "sober appearance . . . belies a somewhat zany teaching style." Few of his students forget how he first illustrated a shift of the demand curve (by dressing up as a California raisin and dancing to "Heard It Through the Grapevine"), or how he proved that the supply and demand model actually works (by having student buyers and sellers call out live bids to him in the classroom). It is this gift for clear explanations and memorable illustrations that makes his textbook so useful to students around the country.

Professor Taylor is also widely recognized for his research on the foundations of modern monetary theory and policy. One of his well-known research contributions is a rule—now widely called the Taylor Rule—used at central banks around the world. *U.S. News and World Report* wrote about his rule, "Amaze Your Friends! Predict the Fed's Next Move!" His latest research focuses on international monetary policy.

Taylor has had an active career in public service, recently completing a four-year stint as the head of the International Affairs division at the United States Treasury, where he had responsibility for currency policy, international debt, and oversight of the International Monetary Fund and the World Bank and worked closely with leaders and policymakers from countries throughout the world. He has also served as economic adviser to the governor of his state (California), to the U.S. Congressional Budget Office, and to the President of the United States and has served on several boards and as a consultant to private industry.

Professor Taylor began his career at Princeton, where he graduated with highest honors in economics. He then received his Ph.D. from Stanford and taught at Columbia, Yale, and Princeton before returning to Stanford.

Akila Weerapana is an Associate Professor of Economics at Wellesley College. He was born and raised in Sri Lanka and came to the United States to do his undergraduate work at Oberlin College, where he earned a B.A. with highest honors in Economics and Computer Science in 1994. Inspired by his professors at Oberlin, he went on to graduate school at Stanford University. He received his Ph.D. in Economics from Stanford in 1999, writing his dissertation on monetary economics under the mentorship of John Taylor. Having taught several classes at Stanford while he was a graduate student, Akila was determined to pursue a career as a liberal arts college professor, combining his research interests with the opportunity to teach economics to gifted college students. Since 1999, Akila has taught more than 800 students in the Economics Department at Wellesley College.

Akila's teaching interests span all levels of the department's curriculum, including introductory and intermediate macroeconomics, international finance, monetary economics, and mathematical economics. He was awarded Wellesley's Pinanski Prize for Excellence in Teaching in 2002. He also enjoys working with thesis students, having advised more than a dozen of these students at Wellesley. The projects that these students have worked on range from a study of the economic benefits of eradication of river blindness in Ghana to the impact of joining the European Union on the Spanish economy to analyzing the determinants of enterprise performance in Russia. He has advised many students who have pursued graduate study in economics or have gone on to work in economic research at the Federal Reserve.

In addition to teaching, Akila has research interests in macroeconomics, specifically in the areas of monetary economics, international finance, and political economy. In the area of monetary economics, his work focuses on the international dimensions of monetary policy, including the potential for gains from coordination and the importance of asymmetric relationships between countries. On the political economy side, his work examines the macroeconomic implications of political institutions and policy stances; examples include how the South African government's attitude towards the AIDS pandemic may affect exchange rates, how domestic economic growth responds to political institutions such as redistricting mechanisms and voter initiatives, and how political and economic variables can increase or decrease violent conflict.

Sixth Edition

PRINCIPLES OF Macroeconomics

JOHN B. TAYLOR

AKILA WEERAPANA

Houghton Mifflin Company

Boston New York

Executive Publisher: George Hoffman
Executive Editor: Lisé Johnson
Sponsoring Editor: Kathleen Swanson
Senior Marketing Manager: Nicole Hamm
Associate Editor: Megan Hoar
Senior Project Editor: Carol Merrigan
Art and Design Manager: Jill Haber
Cover Design Director: Tony Saizon
Senior Photo Editor: Jennifer Meyer Dare
Senior Composition Buyer: Chuck Dutton
New Title Project Manager: James Lonergan
Editorial Assistant: Angela Lang
Marketing Assistant: Lauren Foye

Cover photography: Harold Burch, New York City

Printed in the U.S.A.

Library of Congress Control Number: 2007934818

Instructor's examination copy:
ISBN-10: 0-547-00496-6
ISBN-13: 978-0-547-00496-9

For orders, use student text ISBNs:
ISBN-10: 0-618-96763-X
ISBN-13: 978-0-618-96763-6

2 3 4 5 6 7 8 9-VH-11 10 09 08

Brief Contents

Contents

CHAPTER 12 The Economic Fluctuations Model 298

CHAPTER 13 Using the Economic Fluctuations Model 320

CHAPTER 14 Fiscal Policy 336

PART 4 Trade and Global Markets 401

CHAPTER 17 Economic Growth and Globalization 402

CHAPTER 18 The Gains from International Trade 418

CHAPTER 19 International Trade Policy 444

Preface

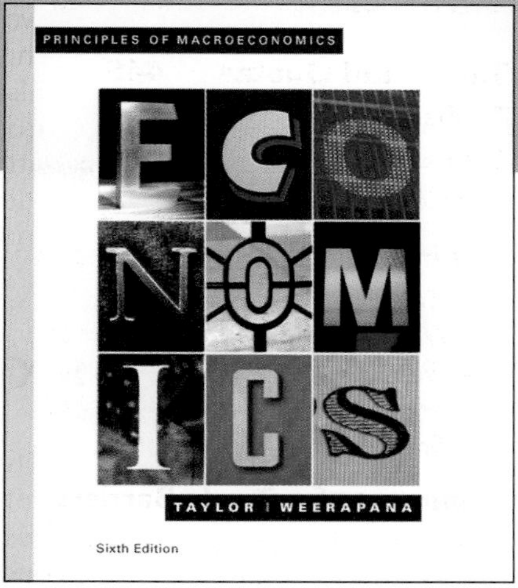

Our goal in this book is to present modern economics in a form that is intuitive, relevant, and memorable to students who have had no prior exposure to the subject. We enjoy teaching introductory economics, and we have enjoyed working on this book. Other teachers of introductory economics have added to our enjoyment by their enthusiastic responses to our approach. Students in our classes, and also email messages from other students around the country and around the world, have rewarded us with their interesting questions and comments. We aim for clarity and for a one-on-one teacher-student focus in the writing, often imagining that we are talking with students as we write.

THE NEW ECONOMICS FROM GENERATION TO GENERATION

We both took introductory economics ourselves—one of us in the 1960s, and the other in the 1990s. People called 1960s-vintage economics the "new economics," because many new ideas, including those put forth by John Maynard Keynes, were being applied to public policy for the first time. But by the 1990s there was a "new" new economics, stressing incentives, expectations, long-run fundamentals, institutions, and the importance of stable, predictable economic policies, that another generation of economists used to improve on the earlier tradition. Now, as we near the end of the first decade of the twenty-first century, there are even newer ideas, many of them dealing with globalization, that are rightfully part of modern economics.

The world economy has also changed radically. The United States and many other countries have experienced far fewer recessions in recent years, and those recessions have been relatively short and mild. The recession in 2001 was one of the shortest recessions on record in the United States. Market economies are now the preferred choice of virtually all countries around the world. The two most populous countries of the world, India and China, have opened up their economies and are experiencing rapid economic growth. Billions of people are linked together through international trade in this new economy. These changes have made economics more fascinating and more relevant than ever.

In this book, we give these recent developments a prominent, clearly explained place within the basic tradition of economics. We emphasize the central idea of economics: that people make purposeful choices with scarce resources and interact with other people when they make these choices. We explain this idea using examples of choices that students actually face. We give real-world examples of how markets work, and we explain why markets are efficient when the incentives are right and inefficient when the incentives are wrong. We stress long-run fundamentals, but we also discuss current public policy issues where the short run matters. Big policy questions that are being debated by economists and others today receive special attention. We know from our teaching experience that examples of how economic ideas are used in practice make economics more interesting to students, thereby making learning economics easier.

CHANGES TO THE SIXTH EDITION

The Sixth Edition has been thoroughly revised, streamlined, and simplified. Introductions, data, case studies, newspaper articles, and boxes discussing academic research have been updated to keep the book topical. Over 50 percent of the articles included in the retitled Economics in the News are new and more attention is given to the explanations within each news feature. Many of the Economics in Action boxes are new, providing both instructors and students with fresh applications to discuss. Our hallmark, yellow "conversation boxes" have been retained and extended throughout the text to enhance students' understanding of the material. The Case Study and Point/Counterpoint features from the Fifth Edition have either been removed or incorporated into the text as new features.

In addition to reworking pedagogical elements, many of the more difficult topics have been revised to help make the text more student-friendly. These changes are outlined below.

Content Changes

A detailed account of the chapter-by-chapter changes in the text can be found in the Transition Guide available in the *Instructor's Resource Manual* or on the instructor website. Here are just a few highlights:

- The gasoline market is used as a new example to illustrate the discussion in Chapter 2, "Observing and Explaining the Economy." Attention is also focused on the research work of young economists in the news, to provide students with a glimpse of the possibilities that await someone with a good grasp of economic concepts.
- Chapter 3, "The Supply and Demand Model," now focuses purely on the basics of the supply and demand model, while Chapter 4 has been retitled "Subtleties of the Supply and Demand Model" and now tackles subtler extensions such as price ceilings, price floors, and elasticity.
- The macroeconomics section has been revised to incorporate the economic developments of the last 25 years, including the rapid growth of China and India and the simultaneous continued growth and stabilizing of the U.S. economy.
- The discussion in Chapter 7, "The Spending Allocation Model," has been revised to better illustrate how different sectors of the economy affect one another in the long run.
- Chapter 9, "Productivity and Economic Growth," has been refined to reflect the changes occurring in the twenty-first century. The discussion of Malthusian issues has been eliminated and the material on deriving the growth accounting

formula is now completely in the appendix, simplifying the discussion significantly.

- The section on how the Fed controls the money supply in Chapter 10, "Money and Inflation," has been replaced by a more intuitive and less complex explanation that better describes actual monetary policy today.
- Chapters 14 and 15, "Fiscal Policy" and "Monetary Policy," have been updated to include a new discussion of the growing U.S. budget deficit and its potential implications for the U.S. economy (Chapter 14) and new coverage of the economic impact of the Volcker disinflation of the 1980s (Chapter 15).
- A new section on the challenges that fiscal policy faces because of the rapid growth of unfunded entitlements, including social security and Medicare, has been added to Chapter 14, "Fiscal Policy."
- In Chapter 16, the discussion of financial markets has been expanded to cover corporate governance issues. The discussion of foreign exchange markets has been removed to keep the focus on capital markets.
- Chapter 20, "Transition Economies," has been removed from the Sixth Edition, and Chapter 19, "International Trade Policy," has been updated to function as the new capstone chapter.
- The end-of-chapter questions for each chapter have been thoroughly revised and updated with new figures, data, and examples.

A BRIEF TOUR

Principles of Macroeconomics is designed for a one-term course. Recognizing that teachers use a wide variety of sequences and syllabi, the text allows for alternative plans of coverage. International economic issues are considered throughout the text, with separate chapters on international economic policy.

The basic workings of markets and the reasons they improve people's lives are the subjects of Part One. Chapter 1 outlines the unifying themes of economics: scarcity, choice, and economic interaction. The role of prices, the inherent international aspect of economics, the importance of property rights and incentives, and the difference between central planning and markets are some of the key ideas in this chapter. Chapter 2 introduces the field of economics through a case study showing how economists observe and explain economic puzzles. Chapters 3 and 4 cover the basic supply and demand model and elasticity. Here, the goal is to show how to use the supply and demand model to make sense of the world—and to learn how to "think like an economist." The concept of elasticity is now wholly contained in Chapter 4.

The study of macroeconomics begins with Chapter 5. This chapter gives an overview of the facts, emphasizing that macroeconomics is concerned with the growth and fluctuations in the economy as a whole. Chapter 6 shows how GDP and other variables are measured.

Chapter 7 starts with the first macro model to determine the long-run shares of GDP. Chapter 8 gives an analysis of how the level of unemployment in the economy as a whole is determined. Labor, capital, and technology are then presented in Chapter 9 as the fundamental determinants of the economy's growth path. One clear advantage of this approach is that it allows students to focus first on issues about which there is general agreement among economists. Moreover, this ordering helps students better understand short-term economic fluctuations. Similarly, the long-run treatment of money, presented in Chapter 10, sets the stage for the discussion of economic fluctuations.

As shown in the six chapters of Part Three (Chapters 11 through 16), the economy does fluctuate as it grows over time. Declines in production and increases in unemployment (characteristics of recessions) have not vanished from the landscape as long-term growth issues have come to the fore. Part Three delves into the causes of these fluctuations and proposes an analysis of why they end. It begins by explaining why shifts in aggregate demand may cause the economy to fluctuate and ends by showing that price adjustment plays a significant role in the end of recessions. Chapter 16 discusses financial markets.

Ever-increasing global economic linkages will be one of the hallmarks of the world that today's students of economics will grow up to live in. Part Four (Chapters 17 through 19) aims to equip students with a better understanding of the economic relationships among countries. With issues about which there are many differing opinions about, the text tries to explain these opinions as clearly and as objectively as possible; it also stresses the areas of agreement.

PEDAGOGICAL FEATURES

The following pedagogical features are designed to help students learn economics.

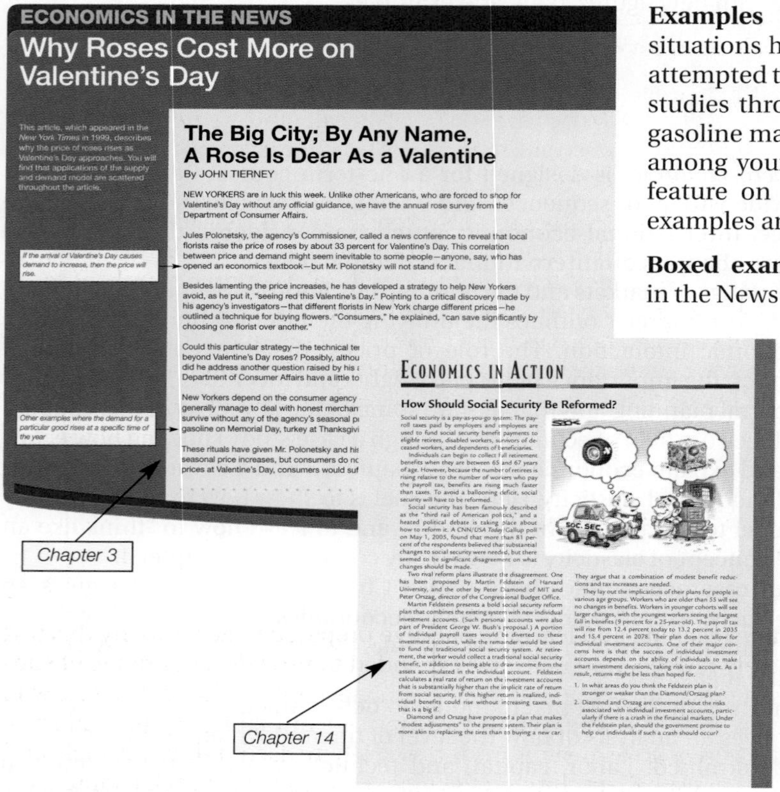
ECONOMICS IN THE NEWS

Why Roses Cost More on Valentine's Day

This article, which appeared in the *New York Times* in 1999, describes why the price of roses rises as Valentine's Day approaches. You will find that applications of the supply and demand model are scattered throughout the article.

The Big City; By Any Name, A Rose Is Dear As a Valentine

By JOHN TIERNEY

NEW YORKERS are in luck this week. Unlike other Americans, who are forced to shop for Valentine's Day without any official guidance, we have the annual rose survey from the Department of Consumer Affairs.

Jules Polonetsky, the agency's Commissioner, called a news conference to reveal that local florists raise the price of roses by about 33 percent for Valentine's Day. This correlation between price and demand might seem inevitable to some people—anyone, say, who has opened an economics textbook—but Mr. Polonetsky will not stand for it.

If the arrival of Valentine's Day causes demand to increase, then the price will rise.

Besides lamenting the price increases, he has developed a strategy to help New Yorkers avoid, as he put it, "seeing red this Valentine's Day." Pointing to a critical discovery made by his agency's investigators—that different florists in New York charge different prices—he outlined a technique for buying flowers. "Consumers," he explained, "can save significantly by choosing one florist over another."

Could this particular strategy—the technical te
beyond Valentine's Day roses? Possibly, althou
did he address another question raised by his
Department of Consumer Affairs have a little to

New Yorkers depend on the consumer agency
generally manage to deal with honest merchan
survive without any of the agency's seasonal p
gasoline on Memorial Day, turkey at Thanksgivi

Other examples where the demand for a particular good rises at a specific time of the year

These rituals have given Mr. Polonetsky and his
seasonal price increases, but consumers do no
prices at Valentine's Day, consumers would suf

ECONOMICS IN ACTION

How Should Social Security Be Reformed?

Social security is a pay-as-you-go system: The payroll taxes paid by employers and employees are used to fund social security benefit payments to eligible retirees, disabled workers, survivors of deceased workers, and dependents of beneficiaries.

Individuals can begin to collect full retirement benefits when they are between 65 and 67 years of age. However, because the number of retirees is rising relative to the number of workers who pay the payroll tax, benefits are rising much faster than taxes. To avoid a ballooning deficit, social security will have to be reformed.

Social security has been famously described as the "third rail of American politics," and a heated political debate is taking place about how to reform it. A CNN/*USA Today*/Gallup poll on May 1, 2005, found that more than 81 percent of the respondents believed that substantial changes to social security were needed, but there seemed to be significant disagreement on what changes should be made.

Two rival reform plans illustrate the disagreement. One has been proposed by Martin Feldstein of Harvard University, and the other by Peter Diamond of MIT and Peter Orszag, director of the Congressional Budget Office.

Martin Feldstein presents a bold social security reform plan that combines the existing system with new individual investment accounts. (Such personal accounts were also part of President George W. Bush's proposal.) A portion of individual payroll taxes would be diverted to these investment accounts, while the remainder would be used to fund the traditional social security system. At retirement, the worker would collect a traditional social security benefit, in addition to being able to draw income from the assets accumulated in the individual account. ...

Examples within the text. Illustrations of real-world situations help explain economic ideas and models. We have attempted to include a wide variety of brief examples and case studies throughout the text. Examples include a look at the gasoline market in Chapter 2, a case study on unemployment among young people around the world in Chapter 8, and a feature on the 2001 recession in Chapter 13. Many other examples are simply woven into the text.

Boxed examples to give real-life perspectives. Economics in the News boxes explain how to decipher recent news stories about economic activities and policy, such as "Why Roses Cost More on Valentine's Day" in Chapter 3 and "The Fed Raises and Then Lowers the Interest Rate" in Chapter 12. Economics in Action boxes examine current issues and debates, such as "Measuring the Quality of Life Across Nations" in Chapter 6 and "How Should Social Security Be Reformed?" in Chapter 14.

Stimulating vignettes at the beginning of each chapter. Examples of opening vignettes include the opportunity costs of college for Tiger Woods in Chapter 1 and debates over minimum-wage increases and rising oil prices in Chapter 4. Chapter 7 begins with a look at the potential impact of a large budget deficit on the investment share of GDP.

Functional use of full color. Color is used to distinguish between curves and to show how the curves shift dynamically over time. An example of the effective use of multiple colors can be found in the equilibrium price and equilibrium quantity figure in Chapter 3 (Figure 8).

Chapter 3, Figure 8

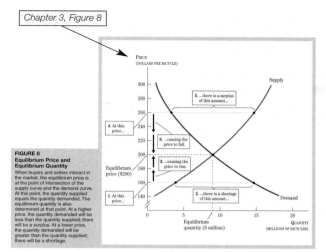

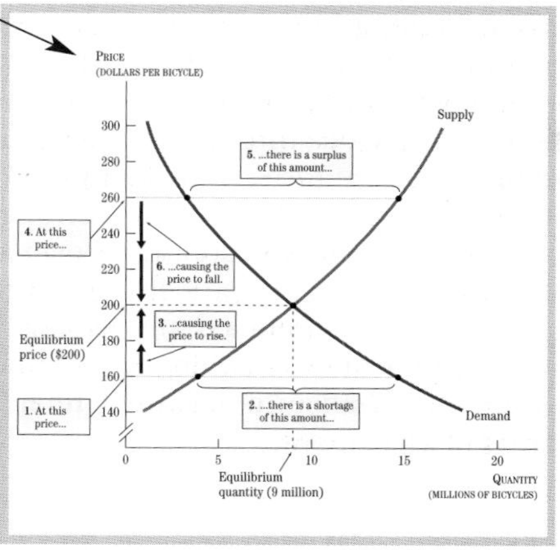

FIGURE 8
Equilibrium Price and Equilibrium Quantity
When buyers and sellers interact in the market, the equilibrium price is at the point of intersection of the supply curve and the demand curve. At this point, the quantity supplied equals the quantity demanded. The equilibrium quantity is also determined at that point. At a higher price, the quantity demanded will be less than the quantity supplied; there will be a surplus. At a lower price, the quantity demanded will be greater than the quantity supplied; there will be a shortage.

Complete captions and small conversation boxes in graphs. The captions and small yellow-shaded conversation boxes make many of the figures completely self-contained. In some graphs, sequential numbering of these conversation boxes stresses the dynamic nature of the curves. Again, Figure 8 in Chapter 3 provides a good example.

Conversation boxes in text margins. These appear when an additional explanation or reminder might help students grasp a new concept more easily.

Use of photos and cartoons to illustrate abstract ideas. Special care has gone into the search for and selection of photos and cartoons to illustrate difficult economic ideas, such as inelastic supply curves or opportunity costs. Many text photos and photo spreads have short titles and captions to explain their relevance to the text discussion.

Key term definitions. Definitions of key terms appear in the margins and in the alphabetized glossary at the end of the book. The key terms are listed at the end of every chapter and appendix.

Brief reviews at the end of each major section. These reviews summarize the key points in abbreviated form as the chapter evolves; they are useful for preliminary skim reading as well as for review.

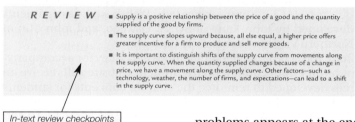

REVIEW

- Supply is a positive relationship between the price of a good and the quantity supplied of the good by firms.
- The supply curve slopes upward because, all else equal, a higher price offers greater incentive for a firm to produce and sell more goods.
- It is important to distinguish shifts of the supply curve from movements along the supply curve. When the quantity supplied changes because of a change in price, we have a movement along the supply curve. Other factors—such as technology, weather, the number of firms, and expectations—can lead to a shift in the supply curve.

In-text review checkpoints

Questions for review at the end of every chapter. These are tests of recall and require only short answers; they can be used for oral review or as a quick self-check.

Problems. An essential tool in learning economics, the problems have been carefully selected, revised, and tested for this edition. An ample supply of these problems appears at the end of every chapter and appendix. Some of the problems ask the reader to work out examples that are slightly different from the ones given in the text; others require a more critical thinking approach. A second set of problems that parallel those in the textbook has been included in our course management systems.

ENHANCED TEACHING AND LEARNING PACKAGE FOR STUDENTS AND INSTRUCTORS

The highly effective teaching and learning package prepared to accompany this text has been completely revised, updated, and expanded to provide a full range of support for students and instructors. It includes several new options for instructors who wish to take full advantage of the online environment in managing their courses. Students, too, will derive great benefit from the newly revised online tutorials and quizzing that will help walk them through the main concepts from each chapter.

Student Resources

Micro and Macro Study Guides. Revised and updated by David Papell of the University of Houston, Wm. Stewart Mounts, Jr., of Mercer University, and John Solow of the University of Iowa, these study guides provide a wonderful learning opportunity that many students will value. Each chapter contains an overview, an informal chapter review, and a section called Zeroing In that harnesses students' intuition to explain the chapter's most important concepts. The study guides also provide ample means for practice in using the economic ideas and graphs introduced in each text chapter and address a variety of learning needs through graph-based questions and problems as well as multiple-choice practice tests. A section called Working It Out provides worked problems that take the student step-by-step through the analytical process needed for real-world application of the core concepts covered in the chapter. These are followed by practice problems that require students to use the same analytical tools on their own. Detailed answers are provided for all review and practice questions. End-of-part quizzes offer students yet another chance to test their retention of material before taking in-class exams.

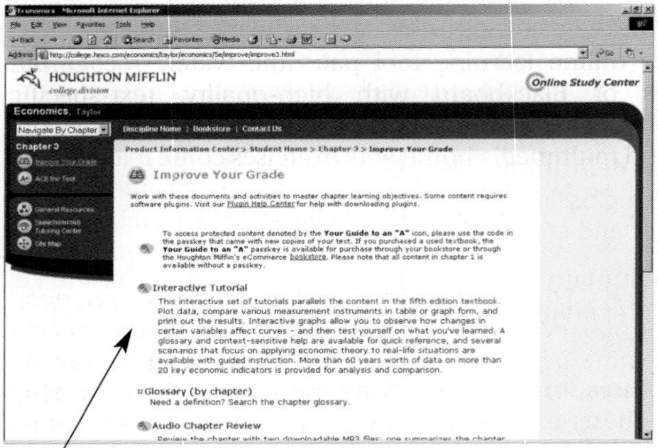

Check out the Internet Exercises, Economics W.I.R.E.D., Parallel Problems, and HM NewsNow news feeds and videos powered by the Associated Press, to practice and apply economic concepts.

HM EconSPACE
Powerful online tools. Premium content.

HM EconSpace™ Student Website. The student website (found at college.hmco.com/pic/taylor6e) provides an extended learning environment for students where materials are carefully developed to complement and supplement each chapter. Students will find key economic links as well as numerous opportunities to test their mastery of chapter content—including glossary terms; brief, objective-type quizzes (ACE); and extended Web-based assignments developed by John Kane of SUNY, Oswego, and John Min of Northern Virginia Community College.

Students who purchase the text package that includes a passkey for accompanying course management or premium content on the student website will receive an additional set of resources developed to reinforce the chapter concepts for students with a variety of learning styles. Included here are step-by-step online tutorials with interactive graphs, audio summary and quiz MP3 files for downloading, and additional online (ACE+) practice quizzes. Students can also utilize electronic flashcards, hangman games, and crossword puzzles to test their knowledge of key terms and definitions.

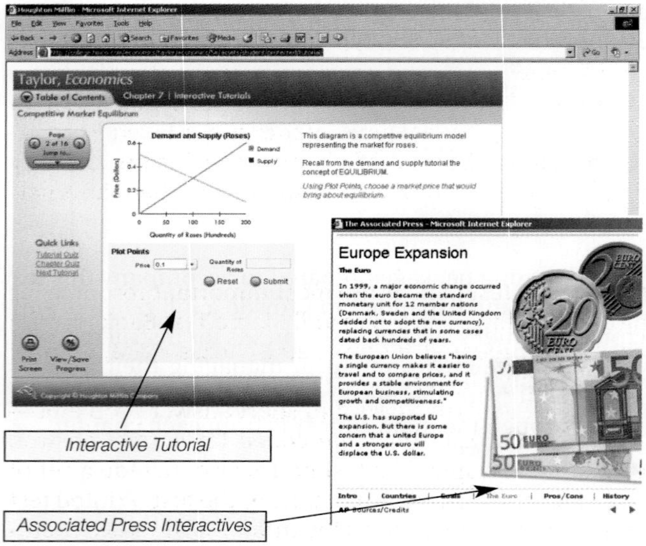

Interactive Tutorial

Associated Press Interactives

Instructor Resources

Aplia. Founded in 2000 by economist and professor Paul Romer in an effort to improve his own economics courses at Stanford, Aplia is the leading online learning platform for economics. Houghton Mifflin has partnered with Aplia to provide a rich online experience that gets students involved and gives instructors the tools and support they need. The integrated Aplia courses offered for Taylor/Weerapana include math reviews/tutorials, news analyses, and online homework assignments correlated with the relevant Taylor/Weerapana text. In addition, a digital version of the text is embedded in the course, to make it easy for students to access the text when completing assignments. Instructors should consult

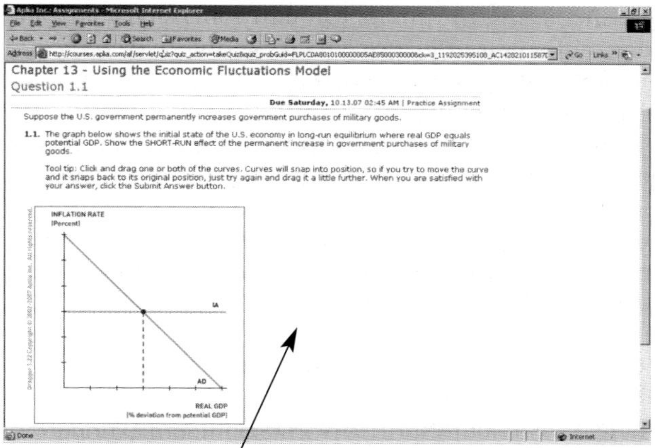

Aplia provides problem sets, news analyses, math and graphing tutorials, experiments, assessment and grading functionality and more.

their Houghton Mifflin sales representative for more information on how to use Aplia with this text.

Course Management Systems. The content found on the Eduspace online learning tool is also available on Blackboard course cartridges and WebCT ePacks for instructors who wish to use these systems to create distance-learning or hybrid courses.

Eduspace®. One of the most challenging aspects of teaching a Principles course is providing students with ample opportunity for practice and review. The Eduspace online learning tool pairs the widely recognized resources of Blackboard with high-quality, text-specific content from Houghton Mifflin. Auto-graded homework problems that parallel the text and multimedia homework exercises come ready to use for online assignments and grading. Students will find a wealth of chapter review material as well, including tutorials with interactive graphs developed for each chapter.

Smarthinking™ Online Tutoring Service. Students who need more individualized, one-on-one tutorial help will have access to the Smarthinking Online Tutoring Service. This live tutoring service allows students to interact online with an experienced Smarthinking e-structor (online tutor) between 3:00 P.M. and 1:00 A.M. ET every Sunday through Thursday and between 12:00 P.M. and 6:00 P.M. ET every Friday and Saturday. Smarthinking provides state-of-the-art communication tools, such as chat technology and virtual whiteboards designed for easy rendering of economic formulas and graphs, to help students absorb key concepts and learn to think economically.

Multimedia eBook. In addition, a multimedia eBook combines the text with interactive elements such as Houghton Mifflin videos, Associated Press Interactive clips, audio chapter reviews, tutorials, and more, to go beyond the typical learning experience. Content is correlated with the Table of Contents so that students can use a particular asset to enhance their understanding as they read. For example, students can listen to chapter-specific summaries when they read the end-of-chapter conclusion and key points. Students can also highlight text and take virtual notes to help them internalize key concepts.

Micro and Macro Test Banks. A reliable test bank is the most important resource for efficient and effective teaching and learning. The Micro and Macro Test Banks for the Sixth Edition have been revised and prepared by Jim Lee of Texas A&M, Corpus Christi, and Eugenio D. Suarez of Trinity University. They contain more than 5,000 test questions—including multiple-choice, true/false, and short answer problems—many of which are based on graphs. The questions are coded for correct answer, question type, level of difficulty, and text topic. The test banks also include a set of parallel problems that match the end-of-chapter problems from the text. Printed test banks are available on demand; please contact your Houghton Mifflin sales representative for more information on how to obtain a printed copy.

HMTesting CD, powered by Diploma. HM Testing allows instructors to generate and edit tests easily. The program includes an online testing feature that instructors can use to administer tests via their local area network or over the Web. It also has a gradebook feature that lets users set up classes, record and track grades from tests or assignments, analyze grades, and produce class and individual statistics. The program prints graphs and tables in addition to the text part of each question. HMTesting provides a complete testing solution, including classroom administration and online testing features in addition to test generation.

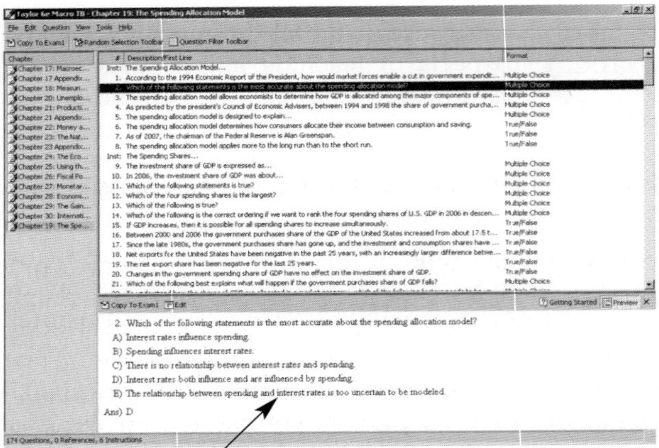

With HMTesting, instructors can scramble the questions and answer choices, edit questions, add their own questions to the pool, and customize their exams in various other ways.

Instructor's Resource Manual. Prepared and revised by John Taylor, Wm. Stewart Mounts, Jr., of Mercer University, and Sarah E. Culver of the University of Alabama at Birmingham, the *Instructor's Resource Manual* provides both first-time and experienced instructors with a variety of additional resources for use with the text. Each chapter contains a brief overview, teaching objectives, key terms from the text, a section that orients instructors to the text's unique approach, and a suggested lecture outline with teaching tips that provide both additional examples not found in the text and hints for teaching more difficult material. Discussion topics and solutions to end-of-chapter text problems are also provided.

PowerPoint Slides. Created by Brian Rosario of the University of California, Davis, the Premium PowerPoint Lecture Slides provide a complete lecture for each chapter, including animations and key figures and tables from the text. Both these presentations and slides of the Main Text Figures and Tables are available to download through the instructor website or through our course management systems. Instructors can use these presentations as is or can delete from and add to them to suit specific class needs.

Overhead Transparencies. Overhead transparencies of the Premium PowerPoint Lecture Slides and the Main Text Figures and Tables are available to adopters of *Economics, Principles of Microeconomics,* and *Principles of Macroeconomics.*

Check out the PowerPoint Slides that accompany HM NewsNow news feeds and videos from the Associated Press on the instructor website.

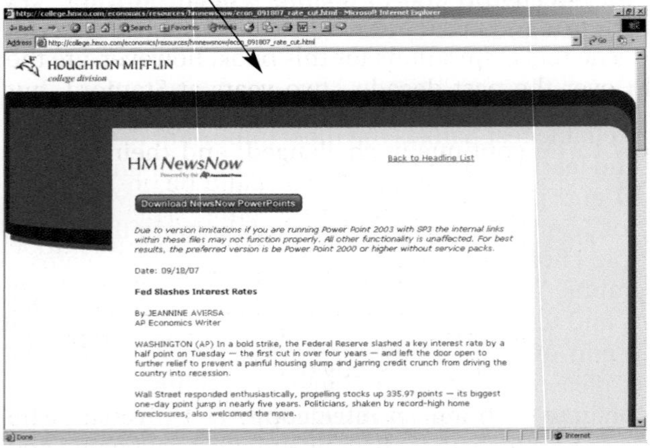

Classroom Response System (CRS). Using state-of-the art wireless technology and text-specific content, a Classroom Response System provides a convenient way to gauge student comprehension, deliver quizzes or exams, and provide "on-the-spot" assessment. Various answering modes, question types, and display options mean that the CRS is as functional as you want it to be. The content is customizable and available on the instructor website or through our course management systems.

HM EconSpace™ Instructor Website. The instructor website (found at college.hmco.com/pic/taylor6e) provides guided Web activities related to the key concepts of each chapter of the textbook. These include, among other materials, Internet Assignments (with solutions) prepared by John Kane of SUNY, Oswego, and Economics W.I.R.E.D. Web links developed by John S. Min of Northern Virginia Community College. Brief tips to the instructor on how the material might best be used in the classroom along with discussion questions or exercises for assessing student learning accompany the W.I.R.E.D. exercises. The instructor website also contains all of the instructor materials found in the *Instructor's Resource Manual* and a complete set of parallel questions (and solutions) that match the end-of-chapter problems from the text. Additionally, we offer HM NewsNow news feeds and videos from the Associated Press with PowerPoints that include discussion, polling, and multiple-choice questions.

ACKNOWLEDGMENTS

Completing a project like this is a team effort, and we both have been blessed with good students and colleagues who have given us advice and encouragement.

John B. Taylor. I am grateful to my colleagues at Stanford, whom I have consulted hundreds of times over the years, including Don Brown, Tim Breshanan, Anne Kreuger, Tom McCurdy, Paul Milgrom, Roger Noll, John Pencavel, Paul Romer, Nate Rosenberg, and Frank Wolak. I must acknowledge with very special gratitude Akila's willingness to join this project. Akila first demonstrated his extraordinary teaching and writing skills even before completing his Ph.D. at Stanford. After receiving his Ph.D., Akila joined the faculty at Wellesley College, where he has taught the Principles course for many semesters and further established his reputation for teaching excellence, and where, in 2002, he received the Anna and Samuel Pinanski Teaching Award. His ability to get complex topics across to his students and his enthusiasm for bringing policy implications alive is clearly reflected in our new coauthored book.

Akila Weerapana. I am exceedingly grateful to John for giving me the opportunity to communicate my enthusiasm for teaching economics to a broader audience than the students in my classes at Wellesley. My passion for economics stems from the inspiration I received from my economics professors: Barbara Craig and Peter Montiel at the undergraduate level, and John Taylor, Frank Wolak, and Chad Jones at the graduate level. I too have benefited immensely from working with my colleagues. The faculty members in the Economics Department at Wellesley live up to the liberal arts ideal that I aspire to, combining excellent teaching with active research. Special thanks are owed to Courtney Coile and David Lindauer for the time they spent helping me understand how best to pitch topics in microeconomics that I am less familiar with teaching than they are. The real inspirations for this book, however, are the students that I have taught over the past decade—two years at Stanford, but especially, the last eight years at Wellesley. Without their enthusiasm for economics, their willingness to be continually challenged, and their need to better understand an ever-changing world, none of this would be possible. My contributions to this book are shaped by countless hours spent talking economics with my students. Through this book, I hope that this conversation extends to many others. Along these lines, special thanks go to Helena Steinberg, Class of 2008 at Wellesley. She served as an invaluable and patient resource for how students would react to and understand economic concepts, examples, newspaper articles, photographs, cartoons, and study questions.

We would also like to thank William B. Stronge of Florida Atlantic University, who provided wonderful end-of-chapter problems that are conceptually challenging and require students to think more deeply about the concepts. Bill's efforts helped us meet an incredibly demanding schedule, and we are grateful for his contributions.

Numerous reviewers provided insights, suggestions, and feedback along the way—often at critical points in product and supplement development. These individuals include Mohsen Bahmani-Oskooee, University of Wisconsin, Milwaukee; Erik Craft, University of Richmond; David H. Eaton, Murray State University; Lewis Freiberg, Northeastern Illinois University; Wang Fuzhong, Beijing University of Aeronautics & Astronautics; Janet Gerson, University of Michigan; Lisa Grobar, California State University, Long Beach; Ritika Gugnani, Jaipuria Institute of Management (Noida); Gautam Hazarika, University of Texas, Brownsville; Aaron Johnson, Missouri State University; Jacob Kurien, Rockhurst University; Babu Nahata, University of Louisville; Soloman Namala, Cerritos College; Sebastien Oleas, University of Minnesota, Duluth; Greg Pratt, Mesa Community College; Virginia Reilly, Ocean County College; Brian Rosario, University of California, Davis; William B. Stronge, Florida Atlantic University; Della Lee Sue, Marist College; J. S. Uppal, State University of New York, Albany; Michele T. Villinski, DePauw University; and Laura Wolff, Southern Illinois University, Edwardsville.

We are grateful to Sarah L. Stafford of the College of William and Mary and Robert J. Rossana of Wayne State University for their detailed and timely accuracy checks of the main texts and several key supplements.

We are especially appreciative of the contributions of the Sixth Edition supplements authors for their creativity, dedication, and careful coordination of content; this group includes Sarah E. Culver, University of Alabama, Birmingham; David H. Eaton, Murray State University; John Kane, State University of New York, Oswego; Jim Lee, Texas A&M University, Corpus Christi; John S. Min, Northern Virginia Community College; Wm. Stewart Mounts, Jr., Mercer University; David H. Papell, University of Houston; Virginia Reilly, Ocean County College Center for Economic Education; Brian Rosario, University of California, Davis; John Solow, University of Iowa; William B. Stronge, Florida Atlantic University; Eugenio D. Suarez, Trinity University; and Laura Wolff, Southern Illinois University, Edwardsville. We would also like to thank Edward Gullason of Dowling College for reviewing many of these supplements and Matthew Berg and Julia Ong for copyediting them.

Finally, we would like to thank the team at Houghton Mifflin who labored over this Sixth Edition, including Ann West, Kathleen Swanson, Carol Merrigan, James Hamilton, Angela Lang, and Megan Hoar.

Reviewers

This book would not exist without the help of all the reviewers and readers who have provided suggestions incorporated into each revision.

Mark D. Agee
Pennsylvania State University, Altoona

James Alm
University of Colorado, Boulder

Lee J. Alston
University of Illinois

Christine Amsler
Michigan State University

Lisa Anderson
College of William and Mary

Charles Andrews
Mercer University

Mohsen Bahmani-Oskooee
University of Wisconsin, Milwaukee

Dean Baim
Pepperdine University

R.J. Ballman, Jr.
Augustana College

Samiran Banerjee
Georgia Institute of Technology

Raymond S. Barnstone
Northeastern University and Lesley College

Laurie Bates
Bryant College

Kari Battaglia
University of North Texas

Klaus G. Becker
Texas Tech University

Valerie R. Bencivenga
Cornell University

Sidney M. Blumner
California Polytechnic University

William M. Boal
Drake University

Brian Boike
Boston University

Roger Bowels
University of Bath

Paula Bracy
University of Toledo

Jozell Brister
Abilene Christian University

Robert Brown
Texas Tech University

Robert Buchele
Smith College

Mark L. Burkey
North Carolina A&T State University

Michael R. Butler
Texas Christian University

Richard Call
American River College

Leonard A. Carlson
Emory University

Michael J. Carter
University of Massachusetts, Lowell

William F. Chapel
University of Mississippi

Chiuping Chen
American River College

Kenneth Chinn
Southeastern Oklahoma State University

Marcelo Clerici-Arias
Stanford University

Stephen L. Cobb
University of North Texas

Mike Cohick
Collin County Community College

Kathy L. Combs
California State University, Los Angeles

Joyce Cooper
Boston University

Erik Craft
University of Richmond

Steven Craig
University of Houston

Sarah Culver
University of Alabama, Birmingham

Michael A. Curme
Miami University

Ward S. Curran
Trinity College

Joseph Daniels
Marquette University

Audrey Davidson
University of Louisville

Gregg Davis
Marshall University

Gregory E. DeFreitas
Hofstra University

Mary E. Deily
Lehigh University

David N. DeJong
University of Pittsburgh

David Denslow
University of Florida

Enrica Detragiache
Johns Hopkins University

Michael Devereux
University of British Columbia

Michael Dowd
University of Toledo

Douglas Downing
Seattle Pacific University

Dean Dudley
United States Military Academy

David H. Eaton
Murray State University

Mary E. Edwards
St. Cloud State University

Ken Farr
Georgia College

David Figlio
University of Oregon

Lewis Freiberg
Northeastern Illinois University

Gerald Friedman
University of Massachusetts, Amherst

Edwin T. Fujii
University of Hawaii

Wang Fuzhong
Beijing University of Aeronautics & Astronautics

Mary Gade
Oklahoma State University

Charles Geiss
University of Missouri

Janet Gerson
University of Michigan

J. Robert Gillette
University of Kentucky

Donna Ginther
Southern Methodist College

David Gleicher
Adelphi University

Mark Glick
University of Utah

Stuart M. Glosser
University of Wisconsin, Whitewater

Abbas Grammy
California State University

Phil Graves
University of Colorado, Boulder

Gregory Green
Idaho State University

Paul W. Grimes
Mississippi State University

Lisa Grobar
California State University, Long Beach

Lorna S. Gross
Worcester State College

Shoshana Grossbard-Shechtamn
San Diego State University

Ritika Gugnani
Jaipuria Institute of Management (Noida)

Robin Hahnel
American University

Alan Haight
Bowling Green State University

David R. Hakes
Linfield College

Greg Hamilton
Marist College

Mehidi Harian
Bloomsburg University

Richard Harper
University of West Florida

Mitchell Harwitz
State University of New York, Buffalo

Gautam Hazarika
University of Texas, Brownsville

Mary Ann Hendryson
Western Washington University

James B. Herendeen
University of Texas, El Paso

Pershing J. Hill
University of Alaska, Anchorage

Denise Hixson
Midlands Technical College

Gail Mitchell Hoyt
University of Richmond

James M. Hvidding
Kutztown University

Beth Ingram
University of Iowa

Murat F. Iyigun
University of Colorado, Boulder

Joyce Jacobsen
Wesleyan University

Syed Jafri
Tarleton State University

David Jaques
California Polytech University, Pomona

John Jascot
Capital Community College

Allan Jenkins
University of Nebraska at Kearney

Aaron Johnson
Missouri State University

David Johnson
Wilfred Laurier University

Charles W. Johnston
University of Michigan, Flint

Nake Kamrany
University of Southern California

John Kane
State University of New York, Oswego

Manfred Keil
Claremont McKenna College

Kristen Keith
University of Alaska

Elizabeth Kelly
University of Wisconsin, Madison

Jongsung Kim
Bryant University

John Klein
Georgia State University

Harry T. Kolendrianos
Danville Community College

Jacob Kurien
Rockhurst University

Margaret Landman
Bridgewater State College

Phillip J. Lane
Fairfield University

William Lang
Rutgers University

William D. Lastrapes
University of Georgia

Lawernce A. Leger
Loughborough University

David Li
University of Michigan

Susan Linz
Michigan State University

John K. Lodewijks
University of New South Wales

R. Ashley Lyman
University of Idaho

Bridget Lyons
Sacred Heart University

Craig MacPhee
University of Nebraska, Lincoln

Michael Magura
University of Toledo

Robert A. Margo
Vanderbilt University

John D. Mason
Gordon College

Robert McAuliffe
Babson College

Henry N. McCarl
University of Alabama, Birmingham

Laurence C. McCulloch
Ohio State University

Rob Roy McGregor
University of North Carolina, Charlotte

Richard McIntyre
University of Rhode Island

Mark McLeod
Virginia Tech

Gaminie Meepagala
Howard University

Frederick Menz
Clarkson University

Micke Meurs
American University

Khan A. Mohabbat
Northern Illinois University

Norma Morgan
Curry College

Peter Morgan
State University of New York, Buffalo

W. Douglas Morgan
University of California, Santa Barbara

Wm. Stuart Mounts
Mercer University

Vai-Lam Mui
University of Southern California

David C. Murphy
Boston College

Babu Nahata
University of Louisville

Soloman Namala
Cerritos College

Andrew Narwold
University of San Diego

Ronald C. Necoechea
Ball State University

John Neri
University of Maryland

Rebecca Neumann
University of Colorado, Boulder

Hong V. Nguyen
University of Scranton

Edd Noell
Westmont College

Lou Noyd
Northern Kentucky University

Rachel Nugent
Pacific Lutheran University

Anthony Patrick O'Brien
Lehigh University

William C. O'Connor
Western Montana College

Sebastien Oleas
University of Minnesota, Duluth

Eliot S. Orton
New Mexico State University

Jan Palmer
Ohio University

David Papell
University of Houston

Walter Park
American University

Charles Parker
Wayne State College

A. Cristina Cunha Parsons
Trinity College, Washington, D.C.

James Payne
Eastern Kentucky University

David Petersen
American River College, Sacramento

E. Charles Pflanz
Scottsdale Community College

William A. Phillips
University of Southern Maine

Glenn J. Platt
Miami University

Charles Plott
California Institute of Technology

Lidija Polutnik
Babson College

Salena Porca
University of South Carolina

Greg Pratt
Mesa Community College

David L. Prychitko
State University of New York, Oswego

Salim Rashid
University of Illinois, Urbana-Champaign

Margaret A. Ray
Mary Washington College

Virginia Reilly
Ocean County College

Geoffrey Renshaw
University of Warwick

John Ridpath
York University

Brian Rosario
University of California, Davis

B. Peter Rosendorff
University of Southern California

Robert J. Rossana
Wayne State University

Greg Rose
Sacramento City College

Marina Rosser
James Madison University

Kartic C. Roy
University of Queensland

Daniel Rubenson
Southern Oregon State College

Jeffrey Rubin
Rutgers University

Robert S. Rycoft
Mary Washington College

Jonathan Sandy
University of San Diego

Jeff Sarbaum
State University of New York, Binghamton

Gary Saxonhouse
University of Michigan

Edward Scahill
University of Scranton

James Byron Schlomach
Texas A&M University

Torsten Schmidt
University of New Hampshire

Thomas J. Shea
Springfield College

William J. Simeone
Providence College

Michael Smitka
Washington & Lee University

Ronald Soligo
Rice University

John Solow
University of Iowa

Clifford Sowell
Berea College

Michael Spagat
Brown University

David Spencer
Brigham Young University

Sarah L. Stafford
College of William and Mary

J.R. Stanfield
Colorado State University

Ann B. Sternlicht
University of Richmond

Richard Stevenson
Liverpool University

James Stodder
Rensselaer Polytechnic Institute

Leslie S. Stratton
University of Arizona

William B. Stronge
Florida Atlantic University

Robert Stuart
Rutgers University

Della Lee Sue
Marist College

Dave Surdam
Loyola University, Chicago

James Swoffard
University of South Alabama

Bette Lewis Tokar
Holy Family College

Paul Turner
University of Leeds

J. S. Uppal
State University of New York, Albany

Lee J. Vanscyoc
University of Wisconsin, Oshkosh

Michele T. Villinski
DePauw University

Gerald R. Visgilio
Connecticut College

Manhar Vyas
University of Pittsburgh

Shaianne T.O. Warner
Ithaca College

William V. Weber
Eastern Illinois University

Karl Wesolowski
Salem State College

Jospeh Wesson
State University of New York, Potsdam

Geoff Whittam
University of Glasgow

Kenneth P. Wickman
State University of New York, Cortland

Catherine Winnett
University of Bath

Jennifer P. Wissink
Cornell University

Laura Wolff
Southern Illinois University, Edwardsville

Simon Wren-Lewis
University of Strathclyde

Peter R. Wyman
Spokane Falls Community College

Yung Y. Yang
California State University, Sacramento

Ali Zaker Shahrak
University of Santa Clara

PRINCIPLES OF
Macroeconomics

Part 1

Introduction to Economics

Chapter 1

The Central Idea

This is a true story. In the spring of 1996, a 19-year-old college sophomore who had just finished taking introductory economics was faced with a *choice:* to continue college for an additional two years or to leave college and begin devoting all his time to a job. The job was being a professional golfer on the PGA Tour—a job for which that sophomore was uniquely qualified, having already won three U.S. amateur titles. Doing both college and the PGA Tour was not an option because time is *scarce*. Since there are only 24 hours in a day, that sophomore simply did not have the time for both activities, so he had to make a choice. But in choosing one activity, he would incur a cost by giving up the other activity. Choosing golf would mean passing up the job opportunities that would inundate a college senior who was well trained in economics; choosing college would mean passing up the potential tournament winnings and the guarantees of advertising endorsements that awaited a professional golfer. The golfer—a young guy named Tiger Woods—had to make a choice, and he did. He became a professional golfer.

A decade later, it seems that Tiger Woods made the right choice. He was selected to be the Sportsman of the Year in 1996, he won the venerable Masters Tournament in 1997, and by the end of 2006 he had won 54 tournaments, 12 major championships, and almost $65 million in prize money. His endorsement income was even greater; he had earned almost $500 million over his first decade of play and was predicted to be the first athlete to make over a billion dollars in endorsement income.

Tiger Woods was able to reap such rich rewards from his golf talents because of the opportunities he had to *interact with people*. Golf fans enjoyed watching him play. They were willing to pay money to interact with him by sitting in the gallery as he played in tournaments. Executives who ran companies like Nike, American Express, and General Motors interacted with him and paid him to endorse their products. And Tiger's family, friends, and teachers interacted with him, conveying basic skills, enhancing his confidence, and helping him remain cool under pressure. Tiger gained from these interactions with different groups of people, and they gained from interacting with Tiger, too.

The story of Tiger Woods is a story about economics, and not simply because of all the money that he has earned. His story illustrates the idea that lies at the center of economics: that people make *purposeful choices* with *scarce resources* and *interact with others* when they make these choices. More than anything else, **economics** is the study of how people deal with scarcity.

economics: the study of how people deal with scarcity.

scarcity: the situation in which the quantity of resources is insufficient to meet all wants.

choice: a selection among alternative goods, services, or actions.

Scarcity is a situation in which people's resources are limited. People always face a scarcity of something—even someone as rich as Tiger Woods faces a scarcity of time. Scarcity implies that people must make a **choice** to forgo, or give up, one thing in favor of another. Most of the time the choices are far more difficult than the one Tiger Woods faced: A student may have to find a job to support her family instead of going to college; a worker may have to delay his retirement to hold on to a job that has health benefits; a parent may have to decide between staying at home with a child and working. As you read this, you may find yourself reflecting on decisions that you have had to make in your life—which college to attend, whether to take economics or biology, whether you should take all your classes after 10 A.M. or try to have them all done before noon.

economic interactions: exchanges of goods and services between people.

market: an arrangement by which economic exchanges between people take place.

Economic interactions between people occur every time they trade or exchange goods with each other. For example, a college student will buy education services from a university in exchange for tuition. A teenager may sell labor services to Taco Bell in exchange for cash. Within a household, one member may agree to cook dinner in exchange for the other person agreeing to wash the dishes. Economic interactions typically take place in a **market.** A market is simply an arrangement by which buyers and sellers can interact and exchange goods and services with each other. There are many markets in the United States, ranging from the New York stock market to a local flea market. Interactions do not have to take place with the buyer and seller in close physical proximity to each other; the telephone, radio, television, and the Internet all help enhance the opportunities for economic interactions to take place.

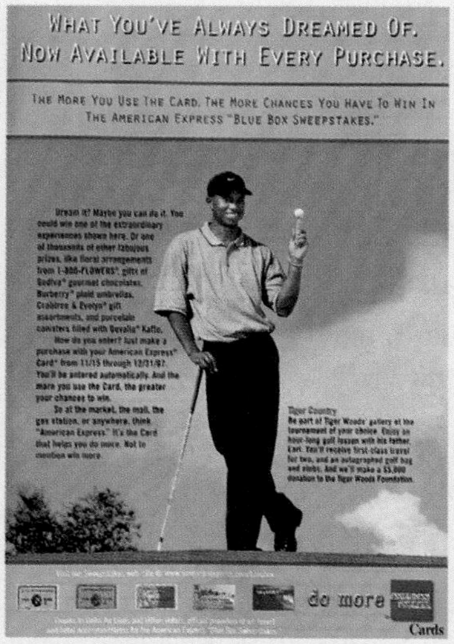

The choice was to continue college or join the Pro Tour. What would you have done?

The purpose of this book is to introduce you to the field of economics, to provide you with the knowledge that will help you understand how so much of what happens in the world today is shaped by the actions of people who had to make choices when confronted by scarcity. A better understanding of economics will equip you to understand the opportunities and challenges that you face as an individual—should you take out a student loan to continue your studies in graduate school? It will also leave you better able to be a more informed citizen about the challenges that the nation faces—should the government provide affordable health care for everyone in the economy? Soon you will find yourself viewing the world through the lens of economics. Your friends may tell you that you are "thinking like an economist." You should take that as a compliment!

The first step toward this goal is for you to get an intuitive feel for how pervasive scarcity, choice, and economic interactions are in the real world. That is the purpose of this chapter.

SCARCITY AND CHOICE FOR INDIVIDUALS

It is easy to find everyday examples of how people make purposeful choices when they are confronted with a scarcity of time or resources. A choice that may be on your mind when you study economics is how much time to spend on it versus other activities. If you spend all your time on economics, you may get a 100 on the final exam, but that might mean you get a zero in biology. If you spend all your time on biology, then you may get a 100 in biology and a zero in economics. Most people resolve the choice by *balancing* out their time to get a decent grade in both subjects. If you are premed, then biology will probably get more time. If you are interested in business, then more time on economics might be appropriate.

Now let us apply this basic principle to two fundamental economic problems: individual choices about what to *consume* and what to *produce*. For each type of economic problem, we first show how scarcity forces one to make a choice, then show how people gain from interacting with other people.

Consumer Decisions

Consider Maria, who is going for a walk in a park on a sunny day. Maria would love to wear a hat (baseball style with her school logo) and sunglasses on the hike, but she has brought neither with her. Maria has brought $20 with her, however, and there is a store in the park that is having a "two for one" sale. She can buy two hats for $20 or two pairs of sunglasses for $20. She would prefer to buy one hat and one pair of sunglasses, but that is not possible. Her scarcity of funds causes her to make a choice. The $20 limit on her spending is an example of a *budget constraint*, a scarcity of funds that limits her to spending no more than this amount. Her choice will depend on her tastes. Let us assume that when she is forced by scarcity to make a choice, she will choose the sunglasses.

Opportunity Cost. Maria's decision is an example of an economic problem that all people face: A budget constraint forces them to make a choice between different items that they want. Choosing one item means that you have to give up other items. The **opportunity cost** of a choice is the value of the next-best forgone alternative that was not chosen. The opportunity cost of the hats is the loss from not being able to wear the sunglasses. An opportunity cost occurs every time there is a choice. For example, the opportunity cost of going to an 8 A.M. class rather than sleeping in is the sleep you lose when you get up early. The opportunity cost of Tiger Woods's staying in college was

opportunity cost: the value of the next-best forgone alternative that was not chosen because something else was chosen.

millions of dollars in prize money and endorsement income. In many cases involving choice and scarcity, there are many more than two things to choose from. If you choose vanilla ice cream out of a list of many possible flavors, then the opportunity cost is the loss from not being able to consume the *next-best* flavor, perhaps strawberry.

Now, suppose Maria is not the only hiker. Also in the park is Adam, who also has $20 to spend. Adam also loves both hats and sunglasses, but he likes hats more than sunglasses. When forced to make a choice, he buys the hats. His decision is shaped by scarcity just as Maria's is: Scarcity comes from the budget constraint. He must make a choice, and there is an opportunity cost for each choice.

Gains from Trade: A Better Allocation. Now suppose that Adam and Maria meet each other in the park. Let's consider the possibility of economic interaction between them. Maria has two pairs of sunglasses and Adam has two hats, so Maria and Adam can trade with each other. Maria can trade one of her pairs of sunglasses for one of Adam's hats, as shown in Figure 1. Through such a trade, both Maria and Adam can improve their situation. There are **gains from trade** because the trade reallocates goods between the two individuals in a way that they both prefer. Trade occurs because Maria is willing to exchange one pair of sunglasses for one hat, and Adam is willing to exchange one hat for one pair of sunglasses. Because trade is mutually advantageous for both Maria and Adam, they will voluntarily engage in it if they are able to. In fact, if they do not gain from the trade, then neither will bother to make the trade.

gains from trade: improvements in income, production, or satisfaction owing to the exchange of goods or services.

This trade is an example of an economic interaction in which a reallocation of goods through trade makes both people better off. There is no change in the total quantity of goods produced. The number of hats and sunglasses has remained the same. Trade simply reallocates existing goods.

The trade between Maria and Adam is typical of many economic interactions that we will study in this book. Thinking like an economist in this example means recognizing that a voluntary exchange of goods between people must make them better off. Many economic exchanges are like this, even though they are more complicated than the exchange of hats and sunglasses.

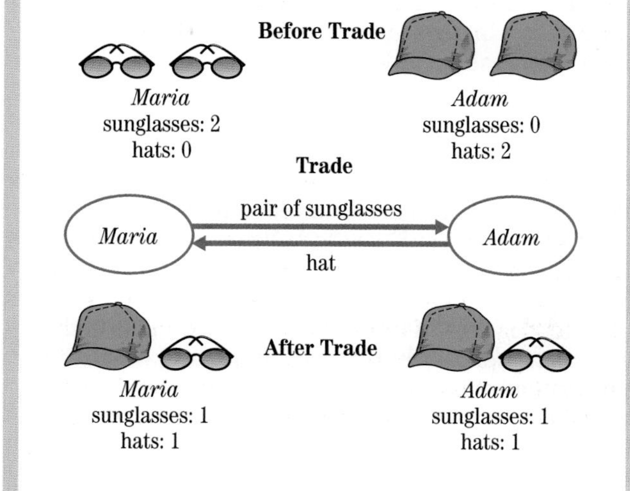

FIGURE 1
Gains from Trade Through a Better Allocation of Goods
Without trade, Maria has more pairs of sunglasses than she would like, and Adam has more hats than he would like. By trading a hat for a pair of sunglasses, they both gain.

Producer Decisions

Now consider two producers—Emily, a poet, and Johann, a printer. Both face scarcity and must make choices. Because of differences in training, abilities, or inclination, Emily is much better at writing poetry than Johann is, but Johann is much better at printing greeting cards than Emily is.

If Emily writes poetry full time, she can produce 10 poems in a day; but if she wants to make and sell greeting cards with her poems in them, she must spend some time printing cards and thereby spend less time writing poems. However, Emily is not very good at printing cards; it takes her so much time to do so that if she prints 1 card, she has time to write only 1 poem rather than 10 poems during the day.

If Johann prints full time, he can produce 10 different greeting cards in a day. However, if he wants to sell greeting cards, he must write poems to put inside them. Johann is so poor at writing poems that if he writes only 1 poem a day, his production of greeting cards drops from 10 to 1 per day.

The following is a summary of the choices Emily and Johann face because of a scarcity of time and resources.

	Emily, the Poet		Johann, the Printer	
	Write Full Time	*Write and Print*	*Print Full Time*	*Write and Print*
Cards	0	1	10	1
Poems	10	1	0	1

If Emily and Johann cannot interact, then each can produce only 1 greeting card with a poem on the inside in a day. Alternatively, Emily could produce 10 poems without the cards and Johann could produce 10 cards without the poems, but then neither would earn anything. We therefore assume that when confronted with this choice, both Emily and Johann will each choose to produce 1 greeting card with a poem inside. In total, they produce 2 greeting cards.

Gains from Trade: Greater Production. Now consider the possibility of economic interaction. Suppose that Emily and Johann can trade. Johann could sell his printing services to Emily, agreeing to print her poems on nice greeting cards. Then Emily could sell the greeting cards to people. Under this arrangement, Emily could spend all day writing poetry, and Johann could spend all day printing. In total, they could produce 10 different greeting cards together, expending the same time and effort it took to produce 2 greeting cards when they could not trade.

Note that in this example the interaction took place in a market: Johann sold his print jobs to Emily. Another approach would be for Emily and Johann to go into business together, forming a firm, Dickinson and Gutenberg Greetings, Inc. Then their economic interaction would occur within the firm, without buying or selling in the market.

Whether in a market or within a firm, the gains from trade in this example are huge. By trading, Emily and Johann can increase their production of greeting cards fivefold, from 2 cards to 10 cards.

Specialization, Division of Labor, and Comparative Advantage. This example illustrates another way in which economic interaction improves people's lives. Economic interaction allows for **specialization:** people concentrating their production efforts on what they are good at. Emily specializes in poetry, and Johann specializes in printing. The specialization creates a division of labor. A **division of labor** occurs when some workers specialize in one task while others specialize in another task. They divide the overall production into parts, with some workers concentrating on one part (printing) and other workers concentrating on another part (writing).

specialization: a concentration of production effort on a single specific task.

division of labor: the division of production into various parts in which different groups of workers specialize.

comparative advantage: a situation in which a person or group can produce one good at a lower opportunity cost than another person or group.

The poetry/printing example of Emily and Johann also illustrates another economic concept, **comparative advantage.** In general, a person or group of people has a comparative advantage in producing one good relative to another good if that person or group can produce that good with comparatively less time, effort, or resources than another person or group can produce that good. For example, compared with Johann, Emily has a comparative advantage in writing relative to printing. And compared with Emily, Johann has a comparative advantage in printing relative to writing. As this example shows, production can be increased if people specialize in the skill in which they have a comparative advantage[1]—that is, if Emily specializes in writing and Johann in printing.

[1] Other examples are explored in Chapter 29, where you can see that comparative advantage can also occur when one person is absolutely better at both activities.

Economics in Action

Gains from Trade on the Internet

The Internet has created many new opportunities for gains from trade. Internet auction sites like eBay allow sellers a way to offer their goods for sale and buyers a way to make bids on sale items. The gains are similar to those of Maria and Adam as they trade sunglasses for hats. Hundreds of different types of sunglasses and baseball hats (and millions of other things) can be bought and sold on eBay—nearly 39,000 types of sunglasses and 5,900 types of baseball hats were for sale at last count.

If you—like Maria—want to sell a pair of sunglasses and buy a baseball hat, you can simply go to www.ebay.com, offer a pair of sunglasses to sell, and search for the hat you would like to buy. The computer screen will show photos of some of the sunglasses and baseball hats that are offered. You may also find yourself looking through other categories, like baseball cards or beachwear, and decide to enter into another economic transaction, simply because eBay is an extremely large marketplace that lets you interact with more individuals than you had intended to when you first decided to look for a baseball hat.

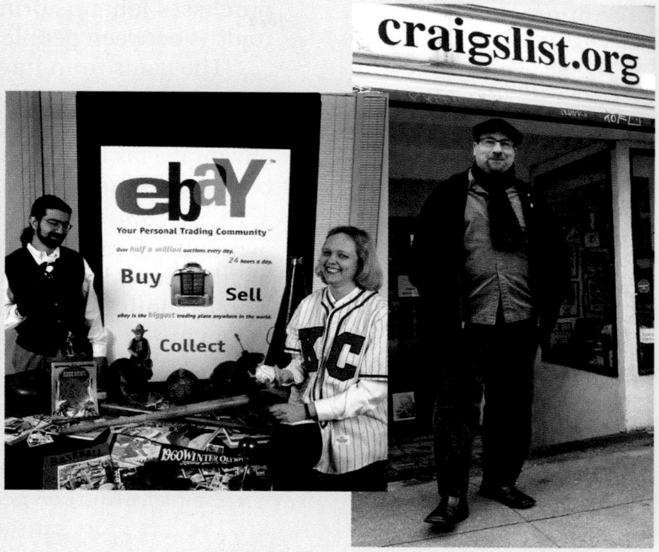

Even though many of the Internet-related businesses that started in the mid-1990s failed to make it through the tech implosion of the early part of this decade, eBay has remained hugely successful—it is a $40 billion company with offshoots, imitators, and competitors all over the world. Today there are nearly 100 million registered users, with millions of sales of items, ranging from sunglasses and baseball hats to antiques and cars, transacted in a single day.

Another site that has been phenomenally successful at bringing individuals together to gain from trade is Craigslist. Craig Newmark, the founder of Craigslist, saw the power of the Internet for bringing together buyers and sellers who previously had typically interacted through classified advertisements in the back pages of newspapers. Craigslist has become one of the first places that people go when they are looking for an apartment to rent or a used car to buy (or, for that matter, looking to rent out their apartment or to sell their used car). Furthermore, Craigslist was quick to exploit the fact that for certain goods and services (apartment sublets, secondhand furniture, used cars), it was more important to reach a group of buyers and sellers who lived in geographical proximity to the person initiating the transaction than it was to reach millions of people all over the world, as eBay did. The success of Craigslist has been such that a 2005 article in *SF Weekly* estimated that Bay Area newspapers were losing more than $50 million a year in classified advertising revenue as a result of economic transactions switching over to Craigslist.

Perhaps the main reason for the success of these online marketplaces is their underlying simplicity. They provide information and a means for buyers and sellers to interact with each other, just as markets have done throughout history, but the scale of these virtual flea markets dwarfs what was possible before the Internet. The Internet will only continue to grow as a technology that enhances economic interactions. Social networking sites like Facebook and MySpace are already extremely popular with young people today. The vast sums of money that companies are prepared to pay to own these sites indicates that they too will become important online locations for economic interactions to take place in the future.

QUESTIONS TO PONDER

1. Can you think of potential gains from trade for you (or for a friend or a family member) that can be realized by using eBay or Craigslist?
2. Craigslist was able to successfully distinguish itself from eBay in the types of transactions that took place on it. How can social networking sites like Facebook or Myspace best distinguish themselves from other Internet trading sites?

International Trade

international trade: the exchange of goods and services between people or firms in different nations.

Thus far, we have said nothing about where Emily and Johann live or work. They could reside in the same country, but they could also reside in different countries. Emily could live in the United States; Johann, in Germany. If this is so, when Emily purchases Johann's printing service, **international trade** will take place because the trade is between people in two different countries.

The gains from international trade are thus of the same kind as the gains from trade within a country. By trading, people can better satisfy their preferences for goods (as in the case of Maria and Adam), or they can better utilize their comparative advantage (as in the case of Emily and Johann). In either situation, there is a gain to both participants from trade.

REVIEW

- All individuals face scarcity in one form or another. Scarcity forces people to make choices. When a choice is made, there is also an opportunity cost of not doing one thing because another thing has been chosen.
- People benefit from economic interactions—trading goods and services—with other people.
- Gains from trade occur because goods and services can be allocated in ways that are more satisfactory to people.
- Gains from trade also occur because trade permits specialization through the division of labor. People should specialize in the production of goods in which they have a comparative advantage.

SCARCITY AND CHOICE FOR THE ECONOMY AS A WHOLE

Just as individuals face scarcity and choice, so does the economy as a whole. The total amount of resources in an economy—workers, land, machinery, factories—is limited. Thus, the economy cannot produce all the health care, crime prevention, education, or entertainment that people want. A choice must be made. Let us first consider how to represent scarcity and choice in the whole economy and then consider alternative ways to make the choices.

Production Possibilities

To simplify things, let us suppose that production in the economy can be divided into two broad categories. Suppose the economy can produce either computers (laptops, desktops, servers) or movies (thrillers, love stories, mysteries, musicals). The choice between computers and movies is symbolic of one of the most fundamental choices individuals in any society must face: how much to invest in order to produce more or better goods in the future versus how much to consume in the present. Computers help people produce more or better goods. Movies are a form of consumption. Other pairs of goods could also be used in our example. Another popular example is guns versus butter, representing defense goods versus nondefense goods.

ECONOMICS IN ACTION

Teaching Jobs and Graduate School Applications—Two Sides of the Same Coin

Dozens of new teachers join schools in Silicon Valley, California. Applications to MBA programs at Chicago and MIT soar. Do these two seemingly unrelated events have anything in common? Actually, they do. Behind them we find the same economic phenomenon at work: opportunity costs.

For years, California and other parts of the United States have experienced teacher shortages. During the economic boom of the 1990s, college graduates who might have been interested in teaching had better-paying alternatives in the private sector. In 2000, a teaching job in Silicon Valley paid an average salary of $50,000, while a job in the computer industry paid an average of $80,000, not counting possible gains from stock options—at least a $30,000 differential.

At the same time, college graduates who were considering advancing their education faced a similar decision: "Should I get an MBA and improve my career and future salaries, or should I accept an immediate, high-paying job at a start-up or consulting firm?"

As the recession hit the United States in 2001, many workers were laid off, and others saw their salaries reduced. The U.S. unemployment rate grew from 4.7 percent in January 2001 to 5.6 percent in January 2002, and in Santa Clara County—the heart of Silicon Valley—the increase in the unemployment rate was more dramatic: from 1.7 percent to 7.7 percent. Hewlett-Packard, for example, laid off 6,000 workers—almost 7 percent of its work force—while one of its spinoffs, Agilent, reduced salaries 10 percent for all its 48,000 employees in 2001.

With lower salaries and fewer jobs in the private sector, the opportunity cost of teaching and studying fell. Business schools reported a barrage of applications, with increases of between 50 and 100 percent over the previous year. School districts witnessed a sharp decrease in the number of vacancies available, with many new teachers willing to undergo months of training and substantial pay cuts relative to their old high-tech jobs.

Think of the options you will be facing when you graduate. Given the jobs and salaries currently available, what career do you think you would like to pursue? What would your opportunity cost be?

production possibilities: alternative combinations of production of various goods that are possible, given the economy's resources.

With a scarcity of resources such as labor and capital, there is a choice between producing some goods, such as computers, versus other goods, such as movies. If the economy produces more of one, then it must produce less of the other. Table 1 gives an example of the alternative choices, or the **production possibilities,** for computers and movies. Observe that there are six different choices, some with more computers and fewer movies, others with fewer computers and more movies.

Table 1 tells us what happens as available resources in the economy are moved from movie production to computer production or vice versa. If resources move from producing movies to producing computers, then fewer movies are produced. For example, if all resources are used to produce computers, then 25,000 computers and zero movies can be produced, according to the table. If all resources are used to produce movies, then no computers can be produced. These are two extremes, of course. If 100 movies are produced, then we can produce 24,000 computers rather than 25,000 computers. If 200 movies are produced, then computer production must fall to 22,000.

TABLE 1
Production Possibilities

	Movies	Computers
A	0	25,000
B	100	24,000
C	200	22,000
D	300	18,000
E	400	13,000
F	500	0

Increasing Opportunity Costs

The production possibilities in Table 1 illustrate the concept of opportunity cost for the economy as a whole. The opportunity cost of producing more movies is the value of the forgone computers. For example, the opportunity cost of producing 200 movies rather than 100 movies is 2,000 computers.

An important economic idea about opportunity costs is demonstrated in Table 1. Observe that movie production increases as we move down the table. As we move from row to row, movie production increases by the same number: 100 movies. The decline in computer production between the first and second rows—from 25,000 to 24,000 computers—is 1,000 computers. The decline between the second and third rows—from 24,000 to 22,000 computers—is 2,000 computers. Thus, the decline in computer production gets greater as we produce more movies. As we move from 400 movies to 500 movies, we lose 13,000 computers. In other words, the opportunity cost, in terms of computers, of producing more movies increases as we produce more movies. Each extra movie requires a loss of more and more computers. What we have just described is called **increasing opportunity costs,** with emphasis on the word *increasing*.

increasing opportunity cost: a situation in which producing more of one good requires giving up an increasing amount of production of another good.

Why do opportunity costs increase? You can think about it in the following way. Some of the available resources are better suited for movie production than for computer production, and vice versa. Workers who are good at building computers might not be so good at acting, for example, or moviemaking may require an area with a dry, sunny climate. As more and more resources go into making movies, we are forced to take resources that are much better at computer making and use them for moviemaking. Thus, more and more computer production must be lost to increase movie production by a given amount. Adding specialized computer designers to a movie cast would be very costly in terms of lost computers, and it might add little to movie production.

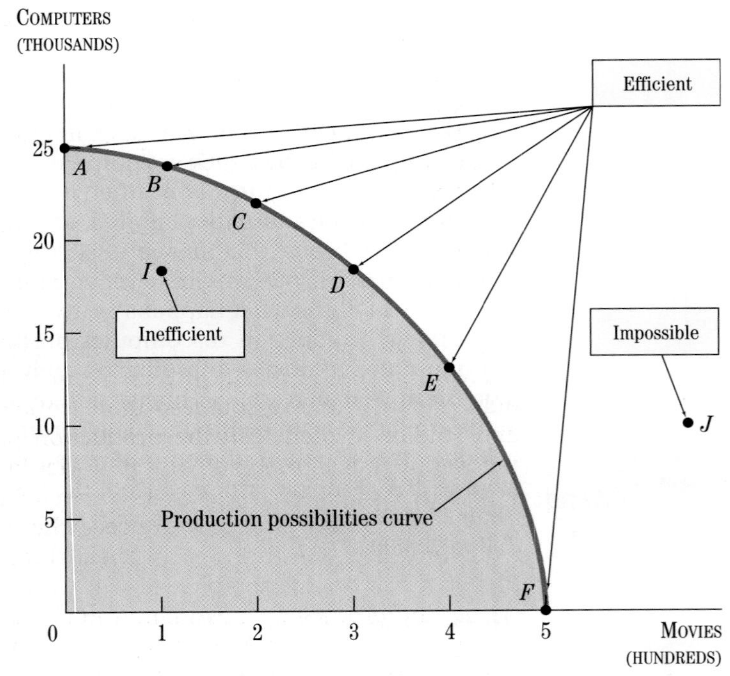

FIGURE 2
The Production Possibilities Curve

Each point on the curve shows the maximum number of computers that can be produced when a given amount of movies is produced. The points with letters are the same as those in Table 1 and are connected by smooth lines. Points in the shaded area inside the curve are inefficient. Points outside the curve are impossible. For the efficient points on the curve, the more movies that are produced, the fewer computers that are produced. The curve is bowed out because of increasing opportunity costs.

The Production Possibilities Curve

Figure 2 is a graphical representation of the production possibilities in Table 1 that nicely illustrates increasing opportunity costs. We put movies on the horizontal axis and computers on the vertical axis of the figure. Each pair of numbers in a row of the table becomes a point on the graph. For example, point *A* on the graph is from row A of the table. Point *B* is from row B, and so on.

production possibilities curve: a curve showing the maximum combinations of production of two goods that are possible, given the economy's resources.

When we connect the points in Figure 2, we obtain the **production possibilities curve.** It shows the maximum number of computers that can be produced for each quantity of movies produced. Note that the curve in Figure 2 slopes downward and is bowed out from the origin. That the curve is bowed out indicates that the opportunity cost of producing movies increases as more movies are produced. As resources move from computer making to moviemaking, each additional movie means a greater loss of computer production.

Inefficient, Efficient, or Impossible?

The production possibilities curve shows the effects of scarcity and choice in the economy as a whole. Three situations can be distinguished in Figure 2, depending on whether production is in the shaded area, on the curve, or outside the curve.

First, imagine production at point *I*. This point, with 100 movies and 18,000 computers, is inside the curve. But the production possibilities curve tells us that it is possible to produce more computers, more movies, or both with the same amount of resources. For some reason, the economy is not working well at point *I*. For example, a talented movie director may be working on a computer assembly line because her short film was not yet been seen by studio executives, or perhaps frequent power outages have disrupted all production of computer chips. Points inside the curve, like point *I*, are *inefficient* because the economy could produce a larger number of movies, as at point *D*, or a larger number of computers, as at point *B*. Points inside the production possibilities curve are possible, but they are inefficient.

Second, consider points on the production possibilities curve. These points are *efficient*. They represent the maximum amount that can be produced with available resources. The only way to raise production of one good is to lower production of the other good. Thus, points on the curve show a *tradeoff* between one good and another.

Third, consider points to the right and above the production possibilities curve, like point *J* in Figure 2. These points are *impossible*. The economy does not have the resources to produce those quantities.

Shifts in the Production Possibilities Curve.

The production possibilities curve is not immovable. It can *shift* out or in. For example, the curve is shown to shift out in Figure 3. More resources—more workers, for example, or more cameras, lights, and studios—would shift the production possibilities curve out. A technological innovation that allowed one to edit movies faster would also shift the curve outward. When the production possibilities curve shifts out, the economy grows because more goods and services can be produced. The production possibilities curve need not shift outward by the same amount in all directions. There can be more movement up than to the right, for example.

As the production possibilities curve shifts out, impossibilities are converted into possibilities. Some of what was impossible for the U.S. economy in 1975 is possible now. Some of what is impossible now will be possible in 2035. Hence, the economists' notion of possibilities is a temporary one. When we say that a certain

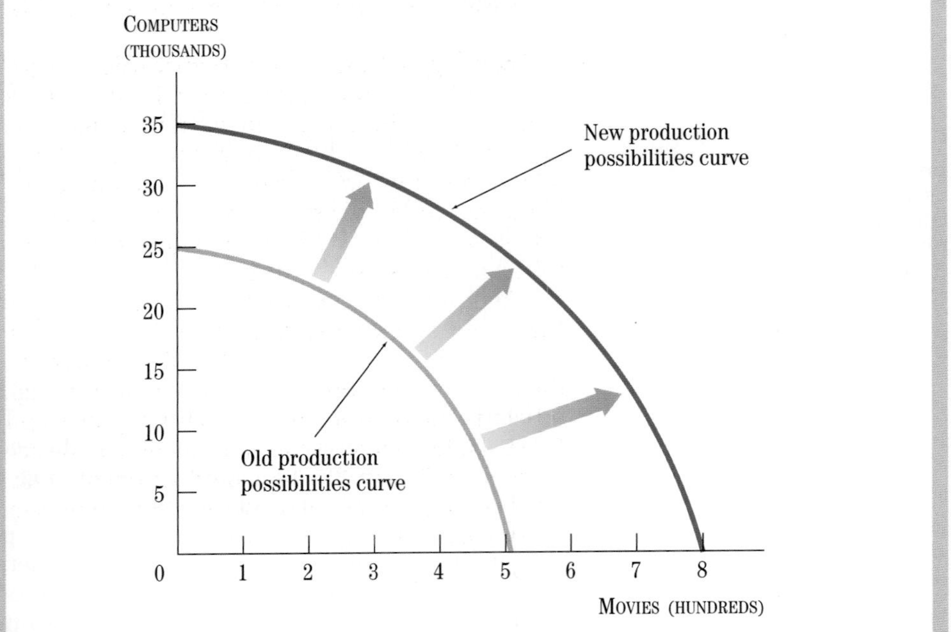

FIGURE 3
Shifts in the Production Possibilities Curve
The production possibilities curve shifts out as the economy grows. The maximum numbers of movies and computers that can be produced increase. Improvements in technology, more machines, or more labor permit the economy to produce more.

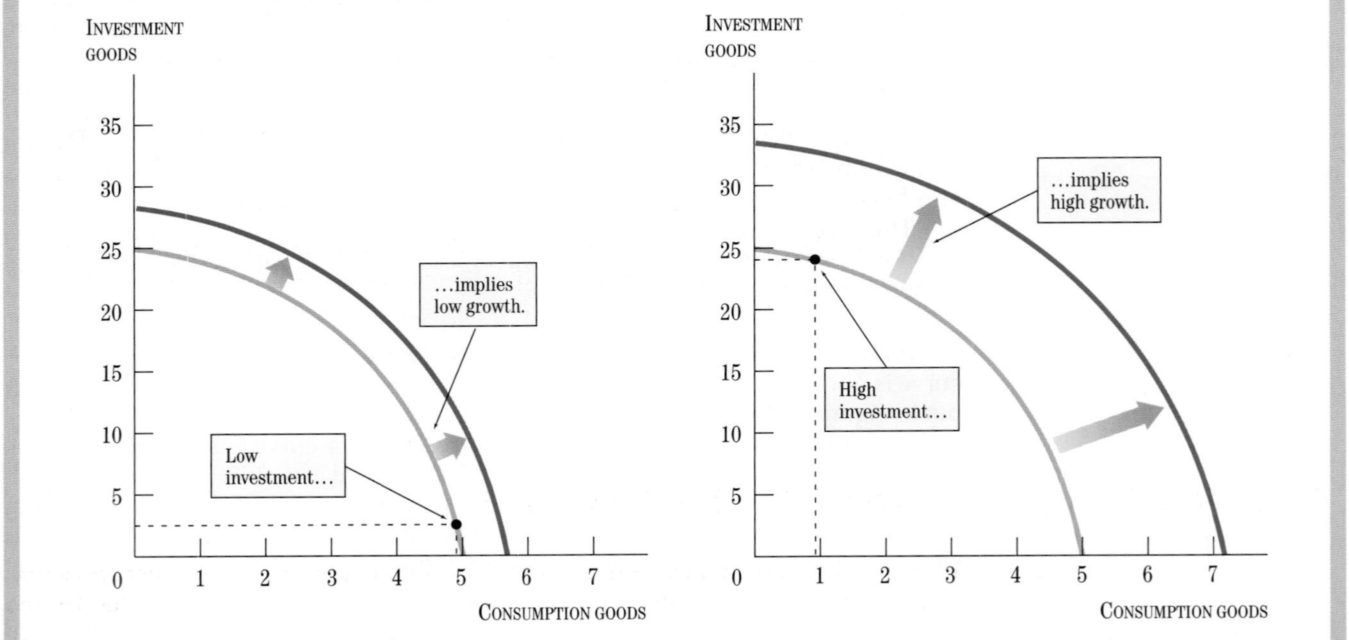

FIGURE 4
Shifts in the Production Possibilities Curve Depend on Choices

On the left, few resources are devoted to investment for the future; hence, the production possibilities curve shifts only a little over time. On the right, more resources are devoted to investment and less to consumption; hence, the production possibilities curve shifts out by a larger amount over time.

combination of computers and movies is impossible, we do not mean "forever impossible," we only mean "currently impossible."

Scarcity, Choice, and Economic Progress. However, the conversion of impossibilities into possibilities is also an economic problem of choice and scarcity: If we invest less now—in machines, in education, in children, in technology—and consume more now, then we will have less available in the future. If we take computers and movies as symbolic of investment and consumption, then choosing more investment will result in a larger outward shift of the production possibilities curve, as illustrated in Figure 4. More investment enables the economy to produce more in the future.

The production possibilities curve represents a *tradeoff*, but it does not mean that some people win only if others lose. First, it is not necessary for someone to lose in order for the production possibilities curve to shift out. When the curve shifts out, the production of both items increases. Although some people may fare better than others as the production possibilities curve is pushed out, no one necessarily loses. In principle, everyone can gain. Second, if the economy is at an inefficient point (like point I in Figure 2), then production of both goods can be increased with no tradeoff. In general, therefore, the economy is more like a win-win situation, where everyone can achieve a gain.

REVIEW

- The production possibilities curve represents the choices open to a whole economy when it is confronted with a scarcity of resources. As more of one item is produced, less of another item must be produced. The opportunity cost of producing more of one item is the reduced production of another item.
- The production possibilities curve is bowed out because of increasing opportunity costs.
- Points inside the curve are inefficient. Points on the curve are efficient. Points outside the curve are impossible.
- The production possibilities curve shifts out as resources increase.
- Outward shifts of the production possibilities curve or moves from inefficient to efficient points are the reasons why the economy is not a zero-sum game, despite the existence of scarcity and choice.

MARKET ECONOMIES AND THE PRICE SYSTEM

There are three essential questions or problems that every economy must find a way to solve, whether it is a small island economy or a large economy like the United States.

- *What* is to be produced: movies, computers, guns, butter, greeting cards, Rollerblades, health care, or something else? In other words, where on the production possibilities curve should an economy be?

The Three Fundamental Economic Questions
Any economic system has to answer three questions: What goods and services should be produced—cars, televisions, or something else? How should these goods or services be produced—in what type of factory, and with how much equipment and labor? And for whom should these goods be produced?

- *How* are these goods to be produced? In other words, how can an economy use the available resources so that it is not at an inefficient point inside the production possibilities curve?
- *For whom* are the goods to be produced? We know from the hat/sunglasses example that the allocation of goods in an economy affects people's well-being. An economy in which Maria could not trade her sunglasses for a hat would not work as well as one in which such trades and reallocations are possible. Moreover, an economy in which some people get everything and others get virtually nothing is also not working well.

market economy: an economy characterized by freely determined prices and the free exchange of goods and services in markets.

command economy: an economy in which the government determines prices and production; also called a centrally planned economy.

Broadly speaking, the **market economy** and the **command economy** are two alternative approaches to answering these questions. In a market economy, most decisions about what, how, and for whom to produce are made by individual consumers, firms, governments, and other organizations interacting in markets. In a command, or centrally planned, economy, most decisions about what, how, and for whom to produce are made by those who control the government, which, through a central plan, commands and controls what people do.

Command economies are much less common today than they were in the mid-twentieth century, when nearly half the world's population, including the residents of Eastern Europe, the Soviet Union, and China, lived in centrally planned economies. After many decades of struggling to make this system work, leaders of the command economies gradually grew disillusioned with the high degree of inefficiency resulting from the planned approach, which required that the state, or central planners, make critical detailed production decisions; this often resulted in shortages or surplus of products and, as a by-product, in political unrest. Since

1990, most command economies have, with varying degrees of success, tried to convert from a command to a market system. The difficulties are partly due to the fact that these economies had none or few of the social, legal, or political fixtures critical to the market system. China has been by far the most successful of these economies at making the transition, developing a model that the Chinese term "socialism with Chinese characteristics." Beginning in the 1970s, elements of both the command and market economies coexisted in China; in the mid-1990s, market mechanisms grew more dominant. Today, while its political system is still highly centralized, China's economy is much more decentralized. Many people credit China's rapid economic growth in recent years to its successful transition away from a decentralized economic system.

Key Elements of a Market Economy

Let's take a closer look at some of the ingredients critical to a market economy.

freely determined prices: prices that are determined by the individuals and firms interacting in markets.

Freely Determined Prices. In a market economy, most prices—such as the price of computers—are freely determined by individuals and firms interacting in markets. These **freely determined prices** are an essential characteristic of a market economy. In a command economy, most prices are set by government, and this leads to inefficiencies in the economy. For example, in the Soviet Union, the price of bread was set so low that farmers fed bread to the cows. Feeding bread to livestock is an enormous waste of resources. Livestock could eat plain grain. By feeding the cows bread, farmers added the cost of the labor to bake the bread and the fuel to heat the bread ovens to the cost of livestock feed. This is inefficient, like point *I* in Figure 2.

In practice, not all prices in market economies are freely determined. For example, some cities control the price of rental apartments. We will look at these exceptions later. But the vast majority of prices are free to vary.

property rights: rights over the use, sale, and proceeds from a good or resource.

Property Rights and Incentives. Property rights are another key element of a market economy. **Property rights** give individuals the legal authority to keep or sell property, whether land or other resources. Property rights are needed for a market economy because they give people the ability to buy and sell goods. Without property rights, people could take whatever they wanted without paying. People would have to devote time and resources to protecting their earnings or goods.

incentive: a device that motivates people to take action, usually so as to increase economic efficiency.

Moreover, by giving people the rights to the earnings from their work, as well as letting them suffer some of the consequences or losses from their mistakes, property rights provide an **incentive.** For example, if an inventor could not get the property rights to an invention, then the incentive to produce the invention would be low or even nonexistent. Hence there would be few inventions, and we would all be worse off. If there were no property rights, people would not have incentives to specialize and reap the gains from the division of labor. Any extra earnings from specialization could be taken away.

Freedom to Trade at Home and Abroad. Economic interaction is a way to improve economic outcomes, as the examples in this chapter indicate. Allowing people to interact freely is thus another necessary ingredient of a market economy. Freedom to trade can be extended beyond national borders to other economies.

International trade increases the opportunities to gain from trade. This is especially important in small countries, where it is impossible to produce everything. But the gains from exchange and comparative advantage also exist for larger countries.

A Role for Government. Just because prices are freely determined and people are free to trade in a market economy does not mean that there is no role for government. For example, in virtually all market economies, the government provides defense and police protection. The government also helps establish property rights. But how far beyond that should it go? Should the government also address the "for whom" question by providing a safety net—a mechanism to deal with the individuals in the economy who are poor, who go bankrupt, who remain unemployed? Most would say yes, but what should the government's role be? Economics provides an analytical framework to answer such questions. In certain circumstances—called **market failure**—the market economy does not provide good enough answers to the "what, how, and for whom" questions, and the government has a role to play in improving on the market. However, the government, even in the case of market failure, may do worse than the market, in which case economists say there is **government failure.**

market failure: any situation in which the market does not lead to an efficient economic outcome and in which there is a potential role for government.

government failure: the situation where the government fails to improve on the market or even makes things worse .

The Role of Private Organizations. It is an interesting feature of market economies that many economic interactions between people take place in organizations—firms, families, charitable organizations—rather than in markets. Some economic interactions that take place in an organization also take place in a market. For example, many large firms employ lawyers as part of their permanent staff. Other firms simply purchase the services of such lawyers in the market; if the firm wants to sue someone or is being sued by someone, it hires an outside lawyer to represent it.

Economic interactions in firms differ from those in the market. Staff lawyers inside large firms are usually paid annual salaries that do not depend directly on the number of hours worked or their success in the lawsuits. In contrast, outside lawyers are paid an hourly fee and a contingency fee based on the number of hours worked and how successful they are.

Incentives within an organization are as important as incentives in markets. If the lawyers on a firm's legal staff get to keep some of the damages the firm wins in a lawsuit, they will have more incentive to do a good job. Some firms even try to create marketlike competition between departments or workers in order to give more incentives.

Why do some economic interactions occur in markets and others in organizations? Ronald Coase of the University of Chicago won the Nobel Prize for showing that organizations such as firms are created to reduce market *transaction costs*, the costs of buying and selling, which include finding a buyer or a seller and reaching agreement on a price. When market transaction costs are high, we see more transactions taking place within organizations. For example, a firm might have a legal staff rather than outside lawyers because searching for a good lawyer every time there is a lawsuit is too costly. In a crisis, a good lawyer may not be available.

The Price System

The previous discussion indicates that in market economies, freely determined prices are essential for determining what is produced, how, and for whom. For this reason, a market economy is said to use *the price system* to solve these problems. In this section, we show that prices do a surprising amount of work: (1) Prices serve as *signals* about what should be produced and consumed when there are changes in tastes or changes in technology, (2) prices provide *incentives* to people to alter their production or consumption, and (3) prices affect the *distribution of income*, or who gets what in the economy.

Let's use an example. Suppose that there is a sudden new trend for college students to ride bicycles more and drive cars less. How do prices help people in the economy decide what to do in response to this new trend?

Signals. First, consider how the information about the change in tastes is signaled to the producers of bicycles and cars. As students buy more bicycles, the price of bicycles rises. A higher price will signal that it is more profitable for firms to produce more bicycles. In addition, some bicycle components, like lightweight metal, will also increase in price. Increased lightweight metal prices signal that production of lightweight metal should increase. As the price of metal rises, wages for metalworkers may increase. Thus, prices are a signal all the way from the consumer to the metalworkers that more bicycles should be produced. This is what is meant by the expression "prices are a signal."

It is important to note that no single individual knows the information that is transmitted by prices. Any economy is characterized by limited information, where people cannot know the exact reasons why prices for certain goods rise or fall. Hence, it is rather amazing that prices can signal this information.

Incentives. Now let's use this example to consider how prices provide incentives. A higher price for bicycles will increase the incentives for firms to produce bicycles. Because they receive more for each bicycle, they produce more. If there is a large price increase that is not merely temporary, new firms may enter the bicycle business. In contrast, the reduced prices for cars signal to car producers that production should decrease.

Distribution. How do prices affect the distribution of income? On the one hand, workers who find the production of the good they make increasing because of the higher demand for bicycles will earn more. On the other hand, income will be reduced for those who make cars or who have to pay more for bicycles. Local delivery services that use bicycles will see their costs increase.

REVIEW

- The market economy and the command economy are two alternative systems for addressing the questions any economy must face: what to produce, how to produce, and for whom to produce.
- A market economy is characterized by several key elements, such as freely determined prices, property rights, and freedom to trade at home and abroad.
- For a market economy to work well, markets should be competitive and the government should play a role.
- Prices are signals, they provide incentives, and they affect the distribution of income.

Gains from Trade on the Radio

Even in today's Internet-connected world, economic interactions that use older technologies like the radio are very common. Tradio helps potential buyers and sellers learn about each other in a virtual market, realizing gains from trade that would not be possible without the exchange of information. All you need is someone who wants to sell something and someone else who wants to buy. Even though radio stations do not charge buyers and sellers, you will notice that tradio is not just a public service. Tradio is very low-cost programming that attracts a large audience and many paid ads from local businesses—a win-win situation for individual buyers and sellers, radio stations, and local businesses. Gains from trade in action!

Who Needs eBay? For Towns Across U.S., Tradio Is Real Deal

By REID J. EPSTEIN, Staff Reporter | The Wall Street Journal
September 11, 2002

GLASGOW, Mont.—It was a little after nine one recent morning, and local residents were already on the line to Lori Mason's radio show.

One caller wanted to unload a riding lawnmower ($500). Another tried to sell an irrigation pump ($100), and four offered up washing machines, including one that "leaks a little bit" ($10). Others still were looking to buy eight bales of straw, fresh dill and a large dog house.

When one young woman phoned in to put her '79 GMC pickup on the block, the 54-year-old Ms. Mason not only recognized her voice but urged her to loosen up.

"Oh, sorry," said the caller, 23-year-old day-care provider Jamie Seyfert. "We're willing to trade for guns, jet skis or anything fun."

This is the sound of "tradio" (pronounced TRADE-ee-o), a kind of on-air swap meet that has been a fixture of small-town stations from Florida to Alaska for decades. Far from being rendered obsolete by the Internet, many tradio shows are doing surprisingly well these days. They are the top moneymakers for some stations, often commanding a premium from local advertisers. And the format may be pushing into bigger markets. In April, WCCO in Minneapolis introduced "The WCCO Great Garage Sale" and saw its ratings jump 29% in the time slot.

Three-Stoplight Town

Here in Glasgow, a three-stoplight railroad town of 3,253 people on the lonely plains of northeastern Montana, the half-hour show is simulcast three mornings a week from the second-floor studio of locally owned stations KLTZ and KLAN. Virtually everyone in town, from the mayor to the editor of the weekly paper, has bought or sold something on the show.

Here's how it works: Callers announce they're selling something—a gas heater that "would be good in your garage, your huntin' shack or whatever," a "very large collection of Fiestaware dishes in all the new colors" or some "very friendly young goats"—and leave their phone number. Anyone interested calls the seller, and the transaction is negotiated face-to-face.

Internet Connection

While it may sound archaic in the age of eBay, the tradio format seems to be benefiting from the buzz generated by the popular Web auction site. Some tradio shows are using the Internet to their advantage—allowing listeners to submit items for sale via e-mail and posting items called into the show on their Web sites.

The tradio format first took hold in the early 1950s when powerful nationwide radio networks cut back on programming. To fill the void, small-town stations began broadcasting obituaries, birthdays and anniversaries. An appliance-store owner in Seguin is believed by many in the industry to have started the first tradio show. He began buying air time to read notices of items for sale that customers had posted on a bulletin board inside his store.

In small towns that don't have daily newspapers—the closest daily to Glasgow is the *Herald* in Williston, N.D., 144 miles away—tradio takes the place of classifieds and, perhaps more important, gossip. When Ms. Mason heard a caller say he was selling his $100 irrigation pump, she exclaimed, "You're on the new water line!" and quizzed him about the difference that had made in his water supply.

Another big attraction is the price. A classified ad in the weekly *Glasgow Courier* costs $5.25 per column inch, while calls to "Tradio" are free. And eBay, which exacts a sliding fee based on the price of the item sold, also requires a hookup to the Internet.

Alicia Sibley, a 24-year-old hay farmer, is a regular listener to the Glasgow show. She was driving her tractor a few weeks ago when she heard a caller offering to sell a 6-foot freezer. She phoned the seller—who had bought the freezer to stock up on frozen foods for fear of a catastrophe at the turn of the millennium—and made a deal for $200. "It's a real nice one, too," Ms. Sibley said. "I saved around $200."

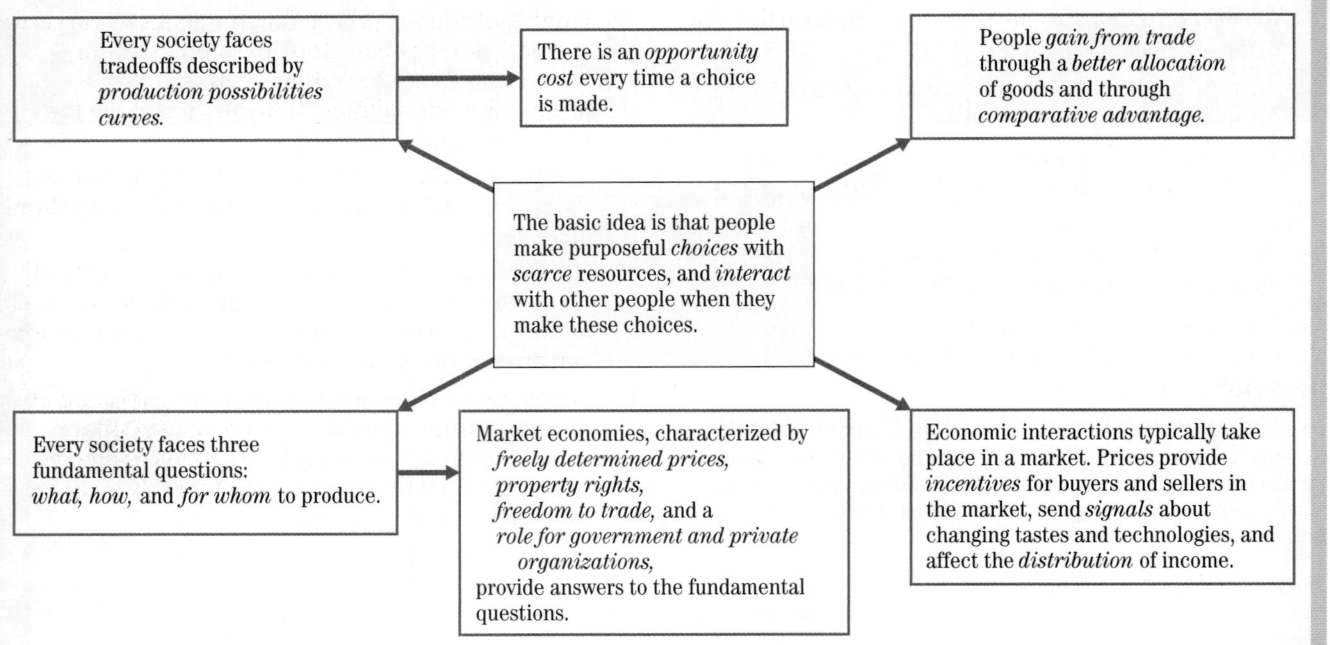

FIGURE 5
From One Central Idea, Many Powerful Ideas Follow

As you study economics, you will see the same central idea again and again. This figure illustrates how many powerful economic ideas are connected to the one in the center.

CONCLUSION

One basic idea lies at the center of economics: People make purposeful choices with scarce resources, and interact with other people when they make these choices.

This introductory chapter illustrates this idea, starting with Tiger Woods's decision whether to leave school and continuing with simple examples of people making choices about what to consume or produce.

From this central idea, many other powerful ideas follow, as summarized visually in Figure 5. There is an *opportunity cost* every time a choice is made. People *gain from trade,* both through a *better allocation* of goods and through *comparative advantage.* Every society faces tradeoffs described by *production possibilities curves.* Every society faces three fundamental questions: *what, how,* and *for whom* to produce. Market economies—characterized by *freely determined prices, property rights, freedom to trade,* and *a role for both government and private organizations*—give an answer to these three questions. The price system helps a market economy work by providing *incentives,* sending *signals,* and affecting the *distribution* of income.

You will see this central idea again and again as you study economics.

KEY POINTS

1. Everyone faces a scarcity of something, usually time or resources.
2. Scarcity leads to choice, and choice leads to opportunity costs.
3. Trade leads to gains because it allows goods and services to be reallocated in a way that improves people's well-being.
4. Trade also leads to gains because it permits people to specialize in what they are relatively good at.
5. The production possibilities curve summarizes the tradeoffs in the whole economy due to scarcity.
6. Economic production is efficient if the economy is on the production possibilities curve. Production is inefficient if the economy is inside the production possibilities curve.
7. Points outside the production possibilities curve are currently impossible. More investment, more workers, or better technology can shift the production possibilities curve out and make the impossible possible.
8. The three basic questions that any economy must face are what, how, and for whom production should take place.
9. A well-functioning market system, involving freely determined prices, property rights, freedom to trade, and a role for government and private organizations, can answer these basic questions.
10. Prices transmit signals, provide incentives, and affect the distribution of income in a market economy. If prices are set at the wrong levels by government, waste and inefficiency—such as feeding bread to livestock—will result.

KEY TERMS

economics
scarcity
choice
economic interactions
market
opportunity cost
gains from trade
specialization
division of labor
comparative advantage
international trade
production possibilities
increasing opportunity cost
production possibilities curve
market economy
command economy
freely determined prices
property rights
incentive
market failure
government failure

QUESTIONS FOR REVIEW

1. What is the basic idea at the center of economics?
2. Why does scarcity imply a choice among alternatives?
3. What is the opportunity cost of making a choice?
4. How can there be gains from trade even when total production of goods and services doesn't change?
5. How can specialization lead to gain from trade?
6. What is the principle of increasing opportunity costs?
7. Why is the production of a combination of goods that is located inside the production possibilities curve considered to be inefficient?
8. What are the key ingredients of a market economy?
9. What are the three basic questions that any economic system must address?
10. What roles do prices play in a market economy?

PROBLEMS

1. Suppose that you are president of the student government, and you have to decide how to allocate a $20,000 fund for guest speakers for the year. Conan O'Brien and Will Ferrell each cost $10,000 per appearance, Stephen Colbert costs $20,000 per appearance, and former economic advisers to the government charge $1,000 per lecture. Explain the economic problem of choice and scarcity in this case. What issues would you consider in arriving at a decision?

2. Michelle Wie, a teenage golf prodigy who earned $16 million in endorsements and $4 million in prize money and appearance fees in 2006, announced that she would enroll as a student at Stanford University in the fall of 2007. What is her opportunity cost of a year of college? How does it compare to your opportunity cost of a year of college?

3. Allison will graduate from high school next June. She has ranked her three possible postgraduation plans in the following order: (1) Work for two years at a consulting job in her hometown paying $20,000 per year, (2) attend a local community college for two years, spending $5,000 per year on tuition and expenses, and (3) travel around the world tutoring a rock star's child for pay of $5,000 per year. What is the opportunity cost of her choice?

4. Suppose you have two boxes of chocolate chip cookies and a friend of yours has two 2 gallons of milk. Explain how you can both gain from trade. Is this a gain from trade through *better allocation* or *greater production?*

5. Suppose Tina and Julia can produce brownies and romantic poems (which can be combined to make a lovely gift) in the following combinations in a given week:

Tina		Julia	
Brownies	*Poems*	*Brownies*	*Poems*
50	0	25	0
40	1	20	1
30	2	15	2
20	3	10	3
10	4	5	4
0	5	0	5

   a. If Tina and Julia are each currently producing 2 poems per week, how many brownies are they producing? What is the total production of brownies and poems between them?
   b. Is there a possibility for increasing production? Why or why not?
   c. Suppose Julia completely specializes in producing poems and Tina completely specializes in producing brownies. What will be their total production of brownies and poems?

6. Suppose you must divide your time between studying for your math final and writing a final paper for your English class. The fraction of time that you spend studying math and its relation to your grade in the two classes is given in the table below.

Fraction of Time Spent on Math	Math Grade	English Grade
0	0	97
20	45	92
40	65	85
60	75	70
80	82	50
100	88	0

   a. Draw a tradeoff curve for the math grade versus the English grade.
   b. What is the opportunity cost of increasing the time spent on math from 80 to 100 percent? What is the opportunity cost of increasing the time spent on math from 60 to 80 percent?
   c. Are there increasing opportunity costs from spending more time on math? Explain.
   d. Suppose your parents want you to get a 92 in both subjects. What would you tell them?

7. A small country produces only two goods, cars and cakes. Given its limited resources, this country has the following production possibilities:

Cars	Cakes
0	200
25	180
50	130
75	70
100	0

   a. Draw the production possibilities curve.
   b. Suppose car production uses mainly machines and cake production uses mainly labor. Show what happens to the curve when the number of machines increases, but the amount of labor remains unchanged.

8. Tracy tells Huey that he can improve his economics grade without sacrificing fun activities or his grades in other courses. Can you imagine ways in which this might be possible? What does that imply about the initial situation? If Huey is taking just two courses and he can improve his economics grade without hurting his math grade, how could you represent this situation graphically?

9. Suppose decreased production of oil in the Middle East causes the price of oil to rise all over the world. Explain how this change in the price signals information to U.S. producers of various goods, provides incentives to U.S. producers of various goods, and affects the distribution of income.

10. "When you look at the economies of the United States, Europe, or Japan, you see most of the ingredients of a market economy. For example, consider bicycles. Prices in the bicycle market are free to vary; people have property rights to the bicycles they buy; many people sell bicycles; many bicycles sold in the United States, Europe, and Japan come from other countries; the government regulates bicycle use (no bicycles on the freeways, for example); and bicycle production takes place within firms with many workers." Replace bicycles with another good or service of your choosing in this quotation and comment on whether the quotation is still true.

Chapter 2

Observing and Explaining the Economy

Mark McClellan and Jim Hamilton are two of the best economists in the world. Yet, they are hardly household names here in the United States. It turns out that very few economists are widely known outside the profession; this anonymity was sadly deepened in 2006 with the passing away of Milton Friedman and John Kenneth Galbraith, perhaps the two individuals with the highest public name recognition in the discipline. It is unfortunate that so many people are unfamiliar with the work of Mark McClellan and Jim Hamilton because they are experts at observing and explaining trends in the two markets—health care and oil—whose fluctuations have the biggest impact on the budgets of ordinary individuals. The research and policy work that they do sheds light on why these markets behave as they do, and what kind of policies would be most effective at keeping the costs of health care and the price of gasoline down.

Mark McClellan's economic expertise and insights on health-care policy led him to Washington, D.C., where, in 2001 and 2002, he served as one of the three members of President Bush's Council of Economic Advisers. From 2002 to 2004, Mark served as Commissioner of the Food and Drug Administration before going on to a position as an administrator of the Centers for Medicare and Medicaid Services, where he was instrumental in launching the new prescription drug benefit component of the Medicare program. Jim Hamilton is a prolific economist, currently at the University of California at San Diego, who is well known for his work on oil price shocks and monetary policy. He also disseminates his research to a wider audience using an economics weblog at _www.econbrowser.com_. On a recent day, he had posted on his blog articles and opinions about the rising price of oil, the use of subsidies for ethanol production, the implications of oil prices for the trade deficit of the United States, and the macroeconomic implications of an expansion of the war in Iraq into Iran.

The purpose of this chapter is to give you a broad overview of what economists such as Mark McClellan and Jim Hamilton actually do. Even though you are just beginning your foray into economics, for some of you this may be the first step in a journey to becoming an expert on an important industry in the economy. If you reach that goal, you should follow in the footsteps of Mark McClellan and Jim Hamilton and use your knowledge to design policies that improve people's lives and communicate your ideas to a broader audience so that they can become more informed citizens. Who knows, star economists may one day be as famous as star golfers!

WHAT DO ECONOMISTS DO?

Economics is a way of thinking. It entails accurately *describing* economic events, *explaining* why the events occur, *predicting* under what circumstances such events might take place in the future, and *recommending* appropriate courses of action. To make use of economics, you will want to learn to do the describing, the explaining, and even the predicting and recommending yourself—that is, to reason and think like an economist. By making use of economics in this way, you can better understand the economic challenges and opportunities you face, and thereby make improvements in your own life or the lives of those around you.

Just as physicists try to explain the existence of black holes in outer space and biologists try to explain why dinosaurs became extinct, economists try to explain puzzling observations and facts about the economy. Many of these observations come from everyday life. Are there some economic observations—from your own experience, from recent news stories, or from your history or political science courses—that you find puzzling? Some of your questions might be like these:

- Why is college tuition so high?
- Why have the wages of college graduates increased much more rapidly than the wages of high school dropouts since the 1970s?
- Why are there so many different types of toothpaste?
- Why is the average income of people in the United States about 35 times higher than that of people in China?
- Why is unemployment much higher in Europe than in the United States?
- Why has health-care spending increased faster than the rest of the U.S. economy?
- Will the price of gas reach $4 a gallon before it reaches $2 a gallon?

All these questions are based on observations about the economy. Some, like the question about college tuition, are fairly obvious and are based on casual observation. Others, like the question about the historical trends in the wages of high school and college graduates, would become evident in the course of reading a book or talking to a parent or a relative. In order to answer such questions, economists, like physicists or biologists, need to systematically document and quantify their observations and look for patterns. If we can establish the date when dinosaurs became extinct, then we may be able to test our hunch that a cataclysmic event such as an asteroid hitting the earth caused their extinction. To illustrate how economists document and quantify their observations, let us briefly focus on the last of the preceding questions, the one about the price of a gallon of gasoline.

THE FLUCTUATING PRICE OF GASOLINE

Describing an Economic Event

Observation 1: The price of gasoline has risen sharply in the past five years compared to the preceding decade.

Few prices affect the lives of as many people as does the price of gasoline. In the summer of 2006, the average price of a gallon of gasoline in the United States reached $3 a gallon, according to data gathered by the Department of Energy. Just a few months later, in early 2007, the average price of a gallon of gasoline was close to $2 a gallon. The difference between $3 a gallon and $2 a gallon has a substantial impact on many people. If you own a car, filling your gas tank at the higher price would cost you $60 instead of $40. The more you spend on gas, the less you have to spend on other things—food at the grocery store, for example. The price of food itself will rise because the cost of transporting food will increase. It will cost you more to fly home to visit your family at Thanksgiving because airlines will raise their ticket prices. And if the reason for the increase in the price of gasoline was an increase in the price of crude oil, then millions of low-income families will face serious financial strain as they pay to heat their homes during the winter. Rising oil prices are always a hot-button issue in congressional and presidential elections. But let's focus first on how an economist would go about understanding fluctuations in the price of gasoline.

The first task is to collect some historical data so we understand how gasoline prices have changed over time. With relatively little effort, you can track down an online data series from the Department of Energy that provides month-by-month information on the movement of gasoline prices in the United States since 1990.

Graphs are a helpful way to present data like this series on gasoline prices. Figure 1 plots the average price of a gallon of gasoline in the United States between

FIGURE 1
Retail Price of Gasoline in the United States, 1991–2006

For each month from 1991 to 2006, the average price of a gallon of gasoline in the United States is plotted; the line connects all the points.

Source: Department of Energy: *U.S. Retail Gasoline Prices.*

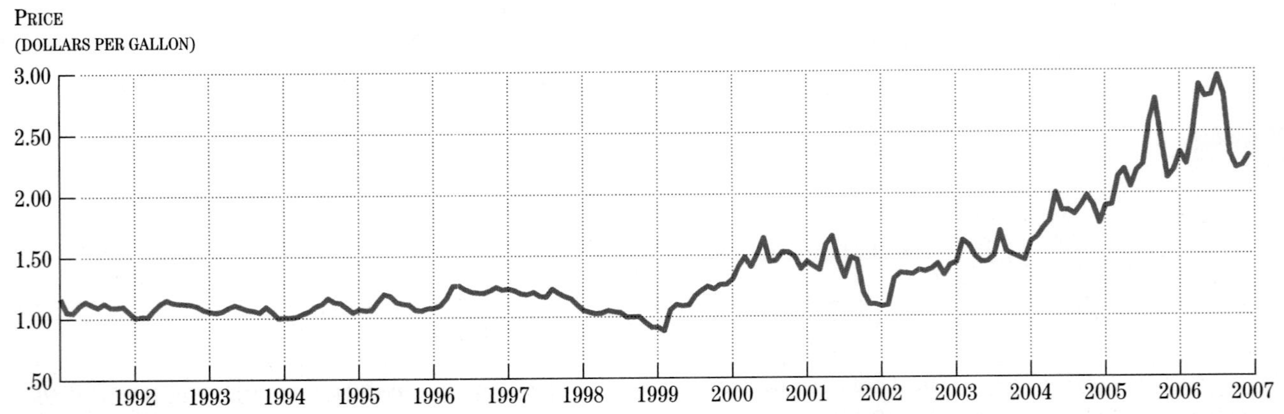

1991 and 2006. The vertical axis is measured in dollars per gallon; the horizontal axis measures the date, in years. How would you characterize the behavior of the average price of gasoline in the United States?

In describing a data series, you should focus on both the long-run movements (any trends you can see in the data) and the short-run movements (how volatile the series is) in the data series. Gasoline prices did not exhibit much of a trend between 1991 and 1998, even though they did fluctuate. Prices were more volatile in the period from 1998 to 2002, first rising smoothly and then dropping sharply. Since mid-2002, gasoline prices show a sharp upward trend, reaching almost $3 in the summers of 2005 and 2006 before cooling off a bit.

relative price: the price of a particular good compared to the price of other things.

To understand how these fluctuations in the price of gasoline affect consumer behavior, economists would be more interested in the **relative price** of gasoline (the price of gasoline compared to the prices all other goods and services in the economy). Even if the $1.10 price of a gallon of gasoline in December of 1991 was similar to the price of gasoline in December 1997, the prices of all other goods and services would have increased between 1991 and 1997. A typical consumer would find it financially less onerous to buy $1.10 gasoline in 1997 than it was for her to buy $1.10 gasoline in 1991; she would have to give up fewer purchases of other goods and services to fill her car's gas tank. In other words, the relative price of gasoline decreased between 1991 and 1997, even though the actual price of gasoline did not. Economists often adjust the price of a good to take into account changes in overall prices before they do comparisons over time.

$$\text{Relative price of gasoline} = \frac{\text{price of gasoline}}{\text{average price of all other goods and services}}$$

The relative price of gasoline is plotted in Figure 2. Observe that the relative price of gasoline fell between 1991 and 1999; it cost less in terms of other goods and services to buy a gallon of gas in 1999. The relative price rose between 2002 and 2006; it cost more in terms of other goods and services to buy a gallon of gas. This indicates that the price of gasoline increased at a faster rate than did the prices of other goods and services. Notice also that the increase in gasoline prices in the last five years is not quite as dramatic when we look at the relative prices. In other words, even though the price of gasoline was rising, the price of other goods and services was rising as well, so $3 per gallon gasoline in 2006 was not as costly in terms of what you had to give up to fill the tank as similarly priced gasoline would have been in the past.

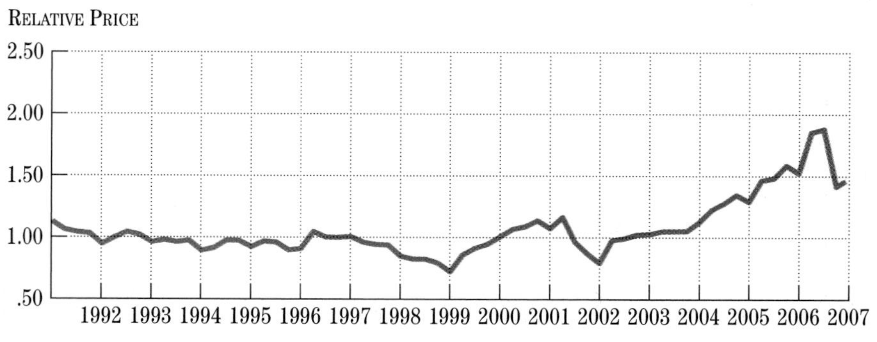

FIGURE 2
Relative Price of Gasoline
Gasoline prices rose by less than did other prices in the early 1990s, and then again in the late 1990s; relative prices fell during this time. Between 2002 and mid-2006, gasoline prices rose much faster than did other prices.

Note: The relative price is a ratio of the price of gasoline to the average price of all goods and services. The ratio is set to 1 in January 2000. This is arbitrary; using another year would not change the conclusions.

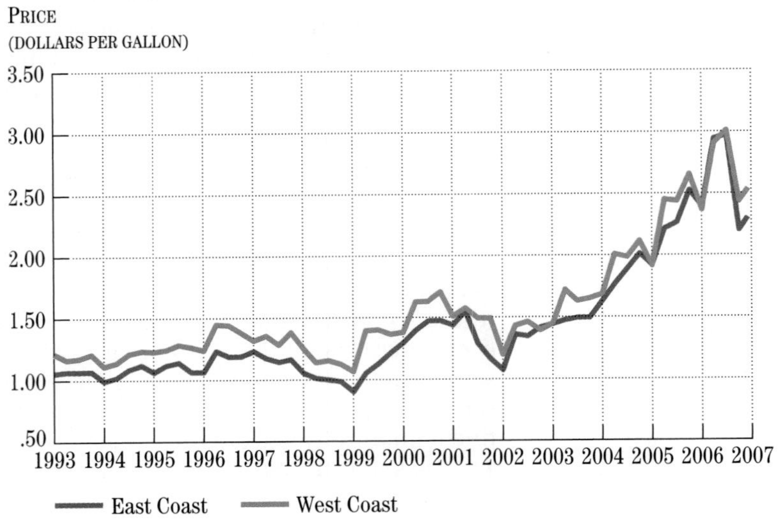

FIGURE 3
Regional Variations in the Retail Price of Gasoline
The two lines show the price of a gallon of gasoline on the East Coast and the West Coast of the United States. The price on the West Coast is typically higher.

Data Limitations. Economic data are not always accurate. Data that are collected via survey methods can be inaccurate because people sometimes do not understand the survey questions, are too busy to answer them carefully, or do not have the correct information. Sometimes the data may be more aggregated than you would like them to be—the average price of a gallon of gasoline in the United States conceals the substantial regional variation in gasoline prices, as you can see in Figure 3. By not having regional data and focusing only on the national average, you may end up missing a potentially important pattern in the data or fail to identify a potential explanation for the movements in gasoline prices.

REVIEW

- Economics is a way of thinking about the world that aims to find the right variables to describe an economic event, to identify what factors may have brought about that event, to predict how changes elsewhere in the economy will affect the variable of interest, and to recommend policies that can improve outcomes.
- Economists have to think carefully about the limitations of the data they use. For example, when studying changes over time, it is important to correct for changes in the overall price level, which can otherwise lead you to misleading conclusions.

EXPLAINING AN ECONOMIC EVENT

What factors can explain the changes we have observed in the price of gasoline in the United States? If you had read Jim Hamilton's thoughts on the subject on his weblog, you would immediately hone in on the price of a barrel of crude oil in the world market. Gasoline is produced from crude oil in oil refineries; the more expensive crude oil is, the more costly it will be to produce a gallon of gasoline. So, we can use these

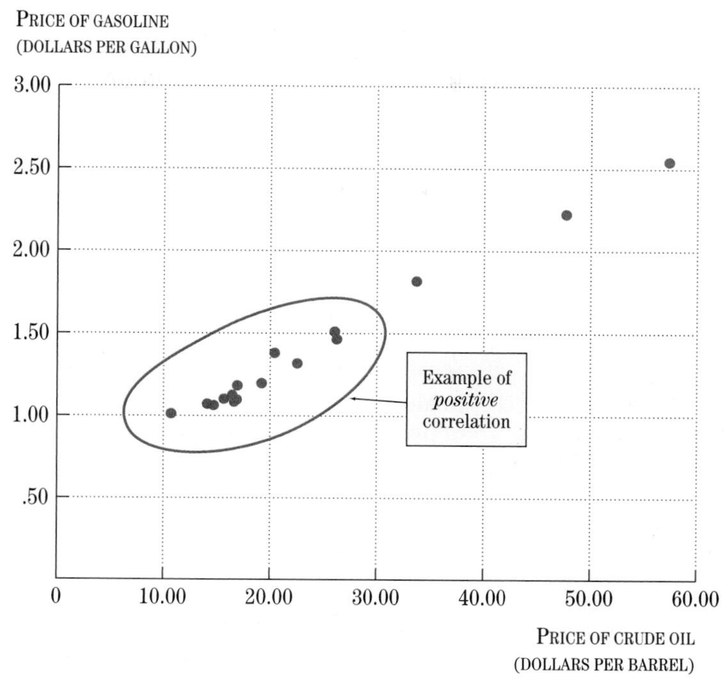

FIGURE 4
Price of Gasoline versus Price of Crude Oil
The figure plots pairs of points: the price of a gallon of gasoline on the vertical axis and the price of a barrel of crude oil on the horizontal axis. These two series show a very strong positive correlation.

economic variable: any economic measure that can vary over a range of values.

two economic variables to quantify our observations about the gasoline market in the United States. An **economic variable** is any economic measure that can vary over a range of values. Are there any obvious patterns in how the prices of these two variables have moved over time?

Figure 4 is useful for determining whether the price of crude oil and the price of gasoline are correlated. Two variables are said to be *correlated* if they tend to move up or down at the same time. There is a *positive correlation* if the two variables move in the same direction—when one goes up, the other goes up. There is a *negative correlation* if the two variables move in opposite directions—when one goes up, the other goes down. Each point in the figure corresponds to the price of crude oil and the price of gasoline in a particular month. The price of gasoline is on the vertical axis, and the price of crude oil is on the horizontal axis.

The points in Figure 4 trace out a very clear pattern: The two variables show a very strong positive correlation. As the price of crude oil rises, the price of gasoline also rises. Conversely, as the price of crude oil falls, the price of gasoline also falls. The price of crude oil will, as you might expect, be an important determinant of gasoline prices. You can already see, though, that the price of crude oil alone will not suffice as an explanation of the price of gasoline because of the differences in gasoline prices between the West Coast and the East Coast of the United States. These regional differences are mostly due to differences in regulations concerning automobile emissions, which mean that the gasoline sold on the West Coast is somewhat different from the gasoline sold elsewhere in terms of the various additives needed to influence how cleanly it burns. The cost of these additives and the presence of state regulations are potential explanatory variables for the regional variation in gasoline prices.

Correlation versus Causation. Just because there is a correlation between two variables does not necessarily mean that one caused the other. There is a difference between *causation* and *correlation*. *Correlation* means that one event is usually observed to occur along with another. *Causation* means that one event brings about another event. But correlation does not imply causation. For example, high readings on a thermometer are correlated with hot weather (high readings occur when it is hot outside). But the thermometer readings do not cause the hot weather. In fact, the causation is the other way around: Hot weather causes the reading on the thermometer to be high.

Similarly, in the example we looked at, gasoline prices and crude oil prices are positively correlated. However, gasoline prices do not cause the high crude oil prices. Here too we would have good reason to believe that causation ran from crude oil prices to gasoline prices. In many instances, determining causation is very difficult. For example, spending on health care and the price of health care both rose in the last five years. It's very difficult to conclude whether spending on health care increased because health care was expensive or whether the price of health care was higher because lots of people were spending money on health care and using up scarce medical resources. Economists are often faced with situations where causation is difficult to determine.

The Lack of Controlled Experiments in Economics. In many sciences—certainly psychology, medicine, and biology—investigators perform **controlled experiments** to determine whether one event causes another event. An example of a controlled experiment is the clinical trial of a new drug. New drugs are tested by trying them out on two groups of individuals. One group gets the drug; the other group gets a placebo (a pill without the drug). If the experiment results in a significantly greater number of people being cured among the group taking the drug than among the control group not taking the drug, investigators conclude that the drug causes the cure.

controlled experiments: empirical tests of theories in a controlled setting in which particular effects can be isolated.

Unfortunately, such controlled experiments are rare in economics. When faced with a situation with limited data (say, data for one country over a particular time period), causation is hard to determine. In these circumstances, we can try to look at other countries' experience, or we can look at the experience of different states within the United States. But, unfortunately, no two countries or states are alike in all respects. Thus, attempting to control for other factors is not as easy as in the case of clinical trials.

In recent years, economists have adapted some of the methods of experimental science and have begun to conduct economic experiments in laboratory settings that are similar to the real world. These experiments can be repeated, and various effects can be controlled for. **Experimental economics** is a growing area of economics. The findings of experimental economics have affected economists' understanding of how the economy works. Experiments in economics also provide an excellent way to *learn* how the economy works, much as experiments in science courses can help one learn about gravity or the structure of plant cells. But because it is difficult to replicate real-world settings exactly in such experiments, they have not yet been applied as widely as the clinical or laboratory experiments in other sciences.

experimental economics: a branch of economics that uses laboratory experiments to analyze economic behavior.

REVIEW

- One of the most significant challenges for an economist is to identify whether one variable has a causal impact on another. Even though two variables may be strongly correlated, correlation does not imply causation.
- In the natural sciences, controlled experiments are used to establish causation. Because controlled experiments are rare in economics, establishing causation is more difficult in economics.

ECONOMICS IN ACTION

An Economic Experiment to Study Discrimination

As you know by now, economists are hampered by their inability to run controlled experiments. Without controlled experiments, it is always a challenge to definitively establish whether one variable has a causal impact on another. However, even though good experiments are rare in economics, they are by no means nonexistent. In 2004, economists Marianne Bertrand and Sendhil Mullainathan published a paper[1] that described a labor market experiment they ran to study discrimination patterns in labor markets.

The title of Bertrand and Mullainathan's paper, "Are Emily and Greg More Employable than Lakisha and Jamal?," gives an idea of what their experiment was about. They wanted to test whether résumés that were attached to African American–sounding names (like Lakisha Washington and Jamal Jones) got fewer callbacks for interviews than did identical-quality résumés attached to names that were more typically associated with whites (like Emily Walsh and Greg Baker). This was a controlled experiment in that the only difference between the two résumés was the name of the candidate. If the résumés with African American names got fewer callbacks than the résumés with white names, that would be evidence of differential treatment simply on the basis of race.

A controlled labor market experiment like this is a much better way to test for differential treatment than looking at the observed labor market outcomes of whites and African Americans. After all, in many cases a researcher would not be able to get data on applicants for a position; even if he did get the data, the applicants will have very different profiles and qualifications; and furthermore, it would be very difficult for the researcher to know how to judge whether one candidate was more qualified than another across a variety of job types.

An overview of their project is given here; you can find the complete version of the paper online if you are interested.

- Bertrand and Mullainathan sent out nearly 5,000 résumés in response to 1,300 help wanted advertisements in Boston and Chicago.
- The résumés were of two types: one containing education and work experience for a highly qualified worker, and the other containing information for a less-qualified worker.
- Each position received four résumés, two high-quality ones and two low-quality ones. One résumé of each type was randomly assigned one of a set of names commonly associated with whites, and the other was assigned a name from a set of names commonly associated with African Americans.
- The results of the experiment showed that applicants with white-sounding names had to send out about 10 résumés before getting a callback, whereas applicants with African American–sounding names had to send out around 15 résumés.
- The researchers found that white names with a higher-quality résumé had a much higher probability of being called back (almost 30 percent) for an interview than whites with a lower-quality résumé. The gap between African Americans with high-quality résumés and African Americans with low quality résumés was smaller, implying that the gap between the races is even wider at the top end of the quality distribution.
- The results held true across different industries and different occupations.
- The researchers also looked at the issue of class by choosing white and African American names that are associated with relatively low levels of parental education and names associated with high levels of education. The differences in perceived class were nowhere near as important as the differences in perceived race.

This paper is an example of how creative, interesting, and influential good economics research can be. The results provided compelling evidence of labor market access differentials across race. Because this was an experiment, we can be much surer that the causal factor behind the differential treatment was the perceived race. Furthermore, the pernicious effect of this lack of equal access is quite substantial: Mullainathan and Bertrand estimate that it takes eight years of extra experience on a résumé to make up for having an African American–sounding name! They also point out that standard policy recommendations for minority unemployment, which include better training and education programs, will not necessarily be the solution here, since the rewards for having more experience and skills seem to be smaller for African American workers than for white workers. While you may be dismayed by the results of the paper, keep in mind that the insights it provides may represent an important step in making people aware of the extent of unequal access to labor markets, and encourage more people to work toward bettering the situation.

[1]Marianne Bertrand and Sendhil Mullainathan, "Are Emily and Greg More Employable than Lakisha and Jamal? A Field Experiment on Labor Market Discrimination," *American Economic Review,* 94(4), September 2004.

Predicting the Impact of Future Changes

Having figured out how to describe the economic event, the rise in gasoline prices, and armed with a better understanding of what might explain why gasoline prices have risen, we move on to the next challenge for the economist: predicting what will happen to gasoline prices in the future.

economic model: an explanation of how the economy or part of the economy works.

Economic Models. In order to explain economic facts and observations, one needs an economic theory, or a *model*. An **economic model** is an explanation of how the economy or a part of the economy works. In practice, most economists use the terms *theory* and *model* interchangeably, although sometimes the term *theory* suggests a general explanation and the term *model* suggests a more specific explanation. The term *law* is also typically used interchangeably with the terms *model* and *theory* in economics.

Economic models are always abstractions, or simplifications, of the real world. They take very complicated phenomena, such as the behavior of people, firms, and governments, and simplify them. Economists like to draw an analogy between a model and a road map—both are abstractions of a much more complex reality. Some maps (like some models) can be very detailed; others are just broad abstractions. There is no single "correct" model, just as there is no single "correct" map. If you wanted to drive from New York to California, you would need an interstate map, one that ignores the details of individual streets within a city to show the main highways. In contrast, if you were headed from one neighborhood of Chicago to another, an interstate map would be of no use; instead, you would need a map that showed city streets in greater detail.

Microeconomic versus Macroeconomic Models. There are two types of models corresponding to the two main branches of economics: microeconomics and macroeconomics. They each have their purpose.

microeconomics: the branch of economics that examines individual decision-making at firms and households and the way they interact in specific industries and markets.

macroeconomics: the branch of economics that examines the workings and problems of the economy as a whole–GDP growth and unemployment.

gross domestic product (GDP): a measure of the value of all the goods and services newly produced in an economy during a specified period of time.

Microeconomics studies the behavior of individual firms and households or specific markets like the health-care market or the college graduate market. It looks at variables such as the price of a college education or the reason for increased wages of college graduates. Microeconomic models explain why the price of gasoline varies from station to station and why there are discount airfares. The analogy in the map world is to the city street map.

Macroeconomics focuses on the whole economy—the whole national economy or even the whole world economy. The most comprehensive measure of the size of an economy is the **gross domestic product (GDP).** GDP is the total value of all goods and services made in the country during a specific period of time, such as a year. GDP includes all newly made goods such as cars, shoes, gasoline, airplanes, and houses; it also includes services like health care, education, and auto repair. Macroeconomics tries to explain the changes in GDP over time rather than the changes in a part of the GDP, like health-care spending. It looks at questions such as what causes the GDP to grow and why many more workers are unemployed in Europe than in the United States. The analogy in the map world is to the interstate map.

Do not be critical of economic models just because they are simplifications. In every science, models are simplifications of reality. Models are successful if they explain reality reasonably well. In fact, if they were not simplifications, models would be hard to use effectively. Economic models differ from those in the physical sciences because they endeavor to explain human behavior, which is complex and often unpredictable. It is for this reason that the brilliant physicist Max Planck said that economics was harder than physics.

Economic models can be described with words, with numerical tables, with graphs, or with algebra. To use economics, it is important to be able to work with these different descriptions. Figures 5 and 6 show how models can be illustrated with graphs. By looking at a graph, we can see quickly whether the model has an inverse or

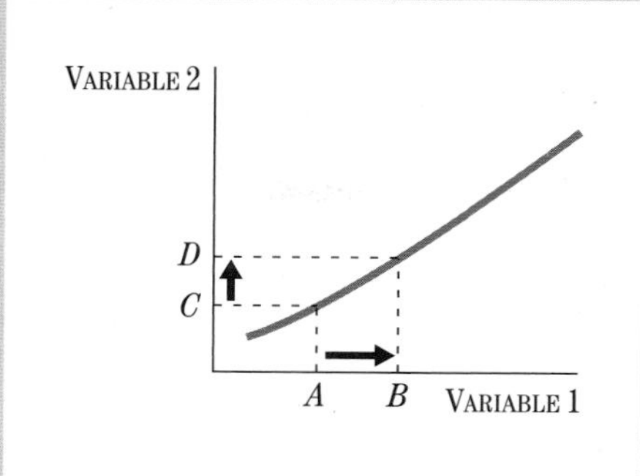

FIGURE 5
A Model with Two Positively Related Variables
The upward-sloping line shows how the variables are related. When one variable increases from *A* to *B*, the other variable increases from *C* to *D*. If one variable declines from *B* to *A*, the other variable declines from *D* to *C*. We say that variable 1 is positively related to variable 2, or that variable 1 varies directly with variable 2.

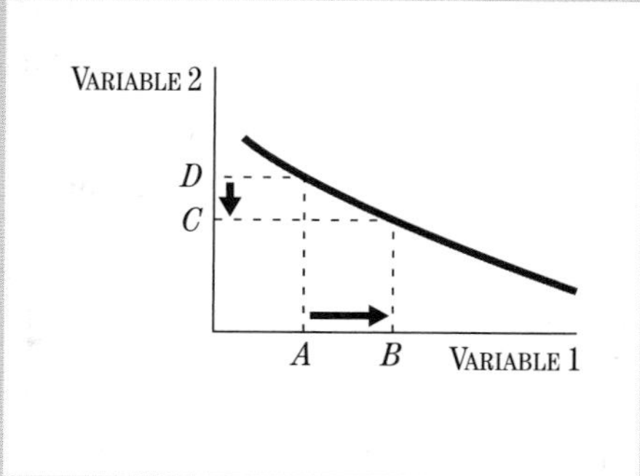

FIGURE 6
A Model with Two Negatively Related Variables
When one variable increases from *A* to *B*, the other variable decreases from *D* to *C*. Likewise, when one variable decreases from *B* to *A*, the other variable increases from *C* to *D*. We say that variable 1 is negatively related to variable 2, or that variable 1 varies inversely with variable 2.

a direct relationship. If a model says that one variable varies inversely with the other, this means that if the first variable rises, then the second falls. If a model says that one variable varies directly with another, this means that if one variable rises, the other also rises. In economics, the expression "is positively related to" is frequently used in place of the phrase "varies directly with," which is more common in other sciences. Similarly, the expression "is negatively related to" is frequently used in place of "varies inversely with."

positively related: a situation in which an increase in one variable is associated with an increase in another variable; also called *directly related.*

negatively related: a situation in which an increase in one variable is associated with a decrease in another variable; also called *inversely related.*

In Figure 5, two variables are shown to be **positively related.** In other words, when variable 1 increases from *A* to *B*, variable 2 increases from *C* to *D* by the specific amount given by the curve. Likewise, when variable 1 decreases from *B* to *A*, variable 2 decreases from *D* to *C*. In Figure 6, a model with two variables that are **negatively related** is shown. Here, when variable 1 increases from *A* to *B*, variable 2 decreases from *D* to *C*. Likewise, when variable 1 decreases from *B* to *A*, variable 2 increases from *C* to *D*. Models have *constants* as well as variables. The constants in the models in Figures 5 and 6 are the positions and shapes of the curves.

An Example: A Model with Two Variables. Figure 7 shows a model describing how doctors employed in a health maintenance organization provide physical examinations. The model states that the more doctors who are employed at the HMO, the more physical exams can be given. The model is represented in four different ways: (1) with words, (2) with a numerical table, (3) with a graph, and (4) with algebra.

On the lower right of Figure 7, we have the verbal description: more doctors mean more physical exams, but additional doctors increase the number of exams by smaller amounts, presumably because the diagnostic facilities at the HMO are limited; for example, there are only so many rooms available for physical exams.

On the upper left, we have a table with numbers showing how the number of examinations depends on the number of doctors. Exactly how many examinations can be given by each number of doctors is shown in the table. Clearly this table is much more

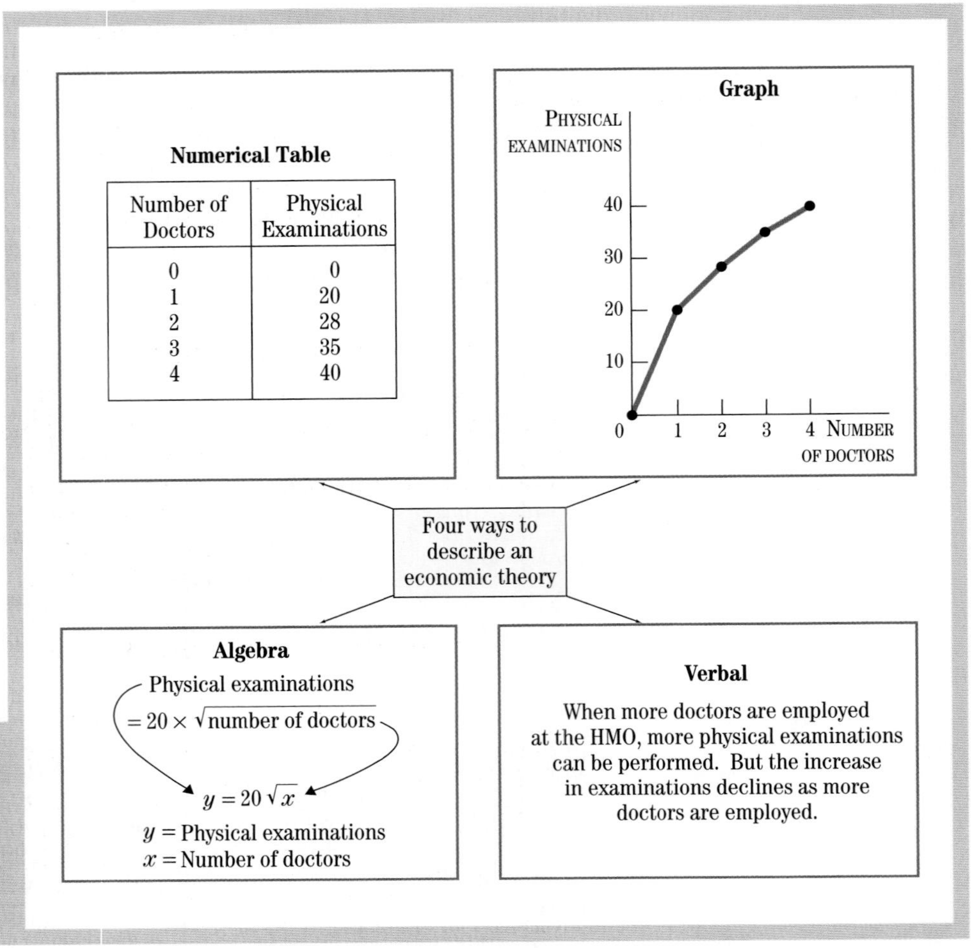

Number of Doctors	Physical Examinations
0	0
1	20
2	28
3	35
4	40

FIGURE 7
Economic Models in Four Ways
Each way has advantages and disadvantages; this book focuses mostly on verbal descriptions, graphs, and numerical tables, but occasionally some algebra will be used to help explain things.

specific than the verbal description. Be sure to distinguish between the meaning of a table that presents a model and a table that presents data. They look similar, but one is a model of the real world and the other represents observations about the real world.

On the upper right, we have a curve showing the relationship between doctors and physical examinations. The curve shows how many exams each number of doctors can perform. The points on the curve are plotted from the information in the table. The vertical axis has the number of examinations; the horizontal axis has the number of doctors. The points are connected with a line to help visualize the curve.

Finally, in the lower left we show the doctor-examination relationship in algebraic form. In this case, the number of exams is equal to the square root of the number of doctors times 20. If we use the symbol y for the number of exams and x for the number of doctors, the model looks a lot like the equations in an algebra course.

All four ways of representing models have advantages and disadvantages. The advantage of the verbal representation is that we usually communicate with people in words, and if we want our economic models to have any use, we need to communicate with people who have not studied economics. However, the verbal representation is not as precise as the other three. In addition to verbal analysis, in this book we will focus on tabular and graphical representations and, when appropriate, algebraic descriptions as well.

The *Ceteris Paribus* Assumption

ceteris paribus: "all other things being equal"; refers to holding all other variables constant or keeping all other things the same when one variable is changed.

In order to use models for prediction, economists use the assumption of ***ceteris paribus,*** which means "all other things being equal." For example, the prediction that variable 2 will fall from *D* to *C* assumes that the curve in Figure 6 does not shift: The position of the curve when variable 1 is at *A* is *equal* to the position of the curve when variable 1 is at *B*. If other things were not equal—if the curve shifted—then we could not predict that variable 2 would fall from *D* to *C* when variable 1 rose from *A* to *B*. Similarly, predicting that more doctors can produce more physical exams assumes that there is no power outage that would cause the diagnostic equipment to stop operating.

The Use of Existing Models

Because economics has been around for a long time, there are many existing models that can be applied to explain observations or make predictions that are useful to decision-makers. Much of what economists do in practice, whether in government or business or universities, is use models that are already in existence.

The models are used in many different types of applications, from determining the effects of discrimination in the workplace to evaluating the gains from lower health-care prices. Frequently the models are applied in new and clever ways.

The Development of New Models

Like models in other sciences, economic models change and new models are developed. Many of the models in this book are very different from the models in books published 40 years ago. New economic models evolve because some new observations cannot be explained by existing models.

The process of the development of new models or theories in economics proceeds much like that in any other science. First one develops a *hypothesis,* or a hunch, to explain a puzzling observation. Then one tests the hypothesis by seeing if its predictions of other observations are good. If the hypothesis passes this test, then it becomes accepted. In practice, however, this is at best a rough description of the process of scientific discovery in economics. Existing models are constantly being reexamined and tested. Some economists specialize in testing models; others specialize in developing them. There is an ongoing process of creating and testing of models in economics.

In the following chapter, you will be introduced to the supply and demand model, and how it can be applied to understanding the gasoline market.

REVIEW

- Economists use models to describe economic phenomena and to understand how changes in some variables affect the variable of interest. Economic models are abstractions, or simplifications, of a more complex reality. They can be extremely detailed or rather abstract, depending on the purpose of use.
- Economic models are different from models in the physical sciences because they must deal with human behavior. Models can be represented verbally, with numerical tables, with graphs, and with algebra.
- Economists also have a long-standing interest in improving the economic policy of governments. Economics can be used in a positive sense, to understand why government policies are the way they are, or in a normative sense, to identify what government policies should be enacted.

RECOMMENDING APPROPRIATE POLICIES

Ever since the birth of economics as a field—around 1776, when Adam Smith published the *Wealth of Nations*—economists have been concerned about and motivated by a desire to improve the economic policy of governments. In fact, economics was originally called *political economy*. Much of the *Wealth of Nations* is about what the government should or should not do to affect the domestic and international economy.

Adam Smith argued for a system of *laissez faire*—little government control—where the role of the government is mainly to promote competition, provide for national defense, and reduce restrictions on the exchange of goods and services. One hundred years later, Karl Marx brought a new perspective to Smith's (and other classical economists') view of political economy, arguing against the laissez-faire approach. His analysis of market economies, or **capitalism,** centered on the contradictions that he saw arising out of such a system, particularly the conflict between the owners of production and the laborers. He argued that these contradictions would result in the inevitable collapse of capitalism and the emergence of a new economic system, called **socialism,** in which government would essentially own and control all production. While Marx actually wrote very little about what a socialist or communist economy would look like, the centrally planned economies that arose in the Soviet Union, Eastern Europe, and China in the twentieth century can be traced to Marx's ideas.

capitalism: an economic system based on a market economy in which capital is individually owned, and production and employment decisions are decentralized.

socialism: an economic system in which the government owns and controls all the capital and makes decisions about prices and quantities as part of a central plan.

Most countries today have rejected the command economy and have moved toward market economies, but the debate about the role of government continues. In many modern market economies, the government plays a large role, and for this reason, such economies are sometimes called **mixed economies.** How great should the role of government be in a market economy? Should the government provide health-care services? Should it try to break up large firms?

mixed economy: a market economy in which the government plays a very large role.

Positive versus Normative Economics

In debating the role of government in the economy, economists distinguish between positive and normative economics. **Positive economics** is about what is; **normative economics** is about what should be. For example, positive economics endeavors to explain why health-care spending slowed down in the mid-1990s or why the price of gasoline increased so rapidly in late 2005. Normative economics aims to develop and recommend policies that might prevent health-care spending or gasoline prices from rising rapidly in the future. In general, normative economics is concerned with making recommendations about what the government should do—whether it should control the price of electricity or health care, for example. Economists who advise governments spend much of their time doing normative economics. In the United States, the president's **Council of Economic Advisers** has legal responsibility for advising the president about which economic policies are good and which are bad.

positive economics: economic analysis that explains what happens in the economy and why, without making recommendations about economic policy.

normative economics: economic analysis that makes recommendations about economic policy.

Council of Economic Advisers: a three-member group of economists appointed by the president of the United States to analyze the economy and make recommendations about economic policy.

Positive economics can also be used to explain *why* governments do what they do. For example, why did the U.S. government break up AT&T into regional phone companies in 1984? Why were tax rates cut in the 1980s, increased in the 1990s, then cut again in the 2000s? Positive analysis of government policy requires a mixture of both political science and economic science, with a focus on what motivates voters and the politicians they elect.

Economics as a Science versus a Partisan Policy Tool

Although economics, like any other science, is based on facts and theories, it is not always used in a purely scientific way.

In political campaigns, economists put forth arguments in favor of one candidate, emphasizing the good side of their candidate's ideas and de-emphasizing the

ECONOMICS IN ACTION

Science or Persuasion?

In a recent court case, a grocery store chain, Lucky Stores, was sued for discriminating against female workers. The case illustrates how economics can be used in a partisan as well as a scientific way.

Economists were called as expert witnesses for both sides. Labor economist John Pencavel testified for the plaintiffs, the women who brought the suit. He found that women at Lucky earned between 76 and 82 percent of what Lucky's male workers earned. Pencavel found that women were regularly placed in jobs that paid less than jobs given male coworkers, although there was no significant difference between them in terms of education and experience. There was little difference in the wages of the male and female workers within each type of job, but some jobs paid more than others, and women happened to be assigned to the lower-paying jobs.

Joan Haworth, another labor economist, was an expert witness for the defendant, Lucky Stores. She reported survey evidence showing that Lucky's assignment of women and men to different jobs reflected differences in the work preferences of men and women. Thus, Lucky justified its job assignments by arguing that there was a gender difference in attitudes toward work. Lucky argued that its employment policies were based on observed differences in the career aspirations of male and female employees. For example, one manager at Lucky testified that women were more interested in cash register work and men were more interested in floor work.

After weighing the facts and economic arguments, the judge decided the case in favor of the plaintiffs. Although male and female employees received equal pay for equal work, the judge concluded that Lucky's employment policies involved discrimination. The judge wrote: "The court finds defendant's explanation that the statistical disparities between men and women at Lucky are caused by differences in the work interests of men and women to be unpersuasive."

The decision is a landmark because of the economic analysis that showed that discrimination could exist even if men and women were being paid the same wage for equal work. Of course, not all sex discrimination cases are decided in favor of the plaintiffs. But whoever wins a given case, economics is almost always a key consideration in the judge's decision.

You be the judge. Would you have been persuaded by the economic argument used by Lucky Stores or by the defendants?

bad side. In a court of law, one economist may help a defendant—making the best case possible—and another economist may help the plaintiff—again, making the best case possible. In other words, economics is not always used objectively. A good reason to learn economics for yourself is to see through fallacious arguments.

But economics is not the only science that is used in these two entirely different modes. For example, there is currently a great controversy about the use of biology and chemistry to make estimates of the costs and benefits of different environmental policies. This is a politically controversial subject, and some on both sides of the controversy have been accused of using science in nonobjective ways.

Economics Is Not the Only Factor in Policy Issues

Although economics can be very useful in policy decisions, it is frequently not the only factor. For example, national security sometimes calls for a recommendation on a policy issue different from one based on a purely economic point of view. Although most economists recommend free exchange of goods between countries, the U.S.

ECONOMICS IN THE NEWS

Young Economists at Work

This article which appeared in the *New York Times* describes the work of Emily Oster, one of the young stars in the field of economics. This article appeared just as she embarked on a career as an economics professor. The article also talks about other young economists who are doing important and interesting work. You will be able to easily find most of the work done by Emily and other young economists online.

Emily's research begins with an observation about the economy.

How the scope of economic analysis has expanded in recent years

Emily Oster's explanation for why some African countries had very high rates of HIV

The policy conclusions that follow from Emily Oster's research

The Future of Economics Isn't So Dismal

By DAVID LEONHARDT—Chicago

On a summer day a few years ago, a recent college graduate named Emily Oster was talking to her boyfriend about the research that was, and wasn't, being done on the spread of AIDS. She was an aspiring economist at the time, getting ready to go to graduate school, and she was struck by the fact that her field had little to say about why some countries had such high H.I.V. rates.

To most people, that may not sound like a question an economist needs to be asking. It's more the domain of epidemiologists or public health workers, and they were already doing good work on it.

But economists have been acting a lot like intellectual imperialists in the last decade or so. They have been using their tools—mainly the analysis of enormous piles of data to tease out cause and effect—to examine everything from politics to French wine vintages.

As the daughter of two economists, Ms. Oster probably understood this better than most 22-year-olds. Her father, Ray Fair, invented a semi-famous economic formula that has an impressive track record of predicting presidential elections. Her mother, Sharon Oster, studies business strategy.

So during her time as a Ph.D. student at Harvard, the younger Ms. Oster took on AIDS in Africa. Her most provocative finding was that Africans didn't really behave so differently from people in countries with much lower H.I.V. rates. They did not have many more sexual partners than Americans on average. And, like Americans, Africans had cut back on unsafe sex in response to AIDS—or at least relatively well-off, healthy Africans had.

Poorer Africans, who of course make up the continent's overwhelming majority, had made fewer changes. They had less of an incentive to practice safe sex, Ms. Oster concluded, because many of them could not expect to reach old age, whether or not they contracted H.I.V. Any attack on AIDS should therefore include an attack on poverty.

"This is not the kind of thing epidemiologists would do. It's not the way they would have framed it," Ms. Oster, now 26, said. "It's an idea only an economist would love."

Whatever you think of her conclusions, there's no denying that her subject is more interesting—and, yes, more important—than the esoteric fiscal and monetary models that once dominated economics. Ms. Oster is studying death, not taxes.

Last weekend, hundreds of economists gathered in Chicago for their annual conference, where they interviewed one another for job openings, presented new research papers and had the occasional glass of wine. This was my sixth such conference, and I have often been stunned by how much of the research here, like Ms. Oster's work, would interest non-economists.

As "The Soulful Science," a new book by Diane Coyle, puts it, there has been a "remarkable creative renaissance in how economics is addressing the most fundamental questions—and how it is starting to help solve problems." The reams of data that computers can now crunch have ushered the field into a new golden age, Ms. Coyle writes, yet most of its accomplishments are not widely known.

Other young economists whose work has been deemed interesting by the economics profession

So before this year's conference, I did an informal poll of about 20 senior economists around the country and asked a single question: who are the young (untenured) economists doing work that is both highly respected among experts and relevant to the rest of us? Who, in other words, is the future of economics?

Thirteen names came up more than once, and I'm sure a scientific survey would have produced a longer list. As it is, though, the list is incredibly diverse. It includes Justin Wolfers, who once worked for an Australian bookie and is now an expert on online prediction markets, and Raj Chetty, who grew up in both India and Milwaukee and studies antipoverty policy.

Emily Oster, an Assistant Professor at the University of Chicago, is one of a group of young economists whose research has attracted considerable attention.

Ms. Oster is on the list, and so is the boyfriend with whom she first discussed her AIDS ideas: Jesse Shapiro, now her husband. He has done innovative work on, among other things, the benefits of television for some toddlers. The two of them are the inaugural fellows at a University of Chicago research center run by Gary Becker (a Nobel laureate), Steven Levitt (co-author of "Freaknomics") and Kevin Murphy (winner of a MacArthur genius award).

In the end, this new era of economics matters because it has a chance to influence the world that is its subject matter. Ms. Oster, for example, has presented her work to the President's Commission on AIDS and others, and her findings seem to be one small part of the recent push for better H.I.V. prevention measures.

A reminder about why the study of economics matters

In Massachusetts, a 41-year-old economist named Jonathan Gruber helped design the new state program to provide health insurance for every resident, which is a model for the California plan announced on Monday. The new federal pension law, meanwhile, encourages employers to sign up workers automatically for 401(k) plans largely because academic research has shown just how costly procrastination is.

For all this success, though, there are still two big obstacles holding back the economics revolution. The first is that the field remains too narrow in its approach. As David Colander, an economist at Middlebury College, notes, researchers are rewarded—with job offers, endowed chairs and prizes—for finding statistically significant patterns that can be published in prestigious journals. They're generally not rewarded for collaborating with experts in other fields to put those patterns into better context.

As a result, there is too much "cleverness for cleverness's sake," Mr. Colander says, and not enough "judgment and wisdom."

The second obstacle is that when economists do uncover a nugget of true wisdom, they're often hesitant to follow it to its natural conclusion and to become principled advocates for better policy. Theirs is not to judge, they insist, only to report what they find. Otherwise, they may risk their reputation for impartial research.

Which is a fair point. But it's a risk worth taking, because the alternative is frankly much worse.

When David Hume, the philosopher and friend of Adam Smith, called for the establishment of a "science of human nature" in the 18th century, he helped invent modern economics. The new generation of researchers will probably come closer to realizing his vision, and to making economics a true science, than any of their predecessors.

But think about what scientists do when they uncover a problem: they try to solve it. To do otherwise is to let an impressive piece of research turn into a scientifically rigorous piece of trivia.

government restricted exports of high-technology goods such as computers during the cold war because defense specialists worried that the technology could help the military in the Soviet Union, and this was viewed as more important than the economic argument. There are still heavy restrictions on trade in nuclear fuels for fear of the proliferation of nuclear weapons.

Disagreement Between Economists

Watching economists debate issues on television or reading their opinions in a newspaper or magazine certainly gives the impression that they rarely agree. There are major controversies in economics, and we will examine them in this book. But when people survey economists' beliefs, they find a surprising amount of agreement.

Why, then, is there the popular impression of disagreement? Because there are many economists, and one can always find some economist with a different viewpoint. When people sue other people in court and economics is an issue, it is always possible to find economists who will testify for each side, even if 99 percent of economists would agree with one side. Similarly, television interviews or news shows want to give both sides of public policy issues. Thus, even if 99 percent of economists agree with one side, the producers are able to find at least one on the other side.

Economists are human beings with varying moral beliefs and different backgrounds and political views that are frequently unrelated to economic models. For example, an economist who is very concerned about the importation of drugs into the United States might appear to be more willing to condone a restriction on coffee exports from Brazil and other coffee-exporting countries in order to give Colombia a higher price for its coffee to offset a loss in revenue from cocaine. Another economist, who felt less strongly about drug imports, might argue strongly against such a restriction on coffee. But if they were asked about restrictions on trade in the abstract, both economists would probably argue for government policies that prevent them.

CONCLUSION: A READER'S GUIDE

In Chapter 1, we explored the central idea of economics: scarcity, choice, and economic interaction. In this chapter, we discussed how economists observe economic events and use economic models to explain these phenomena. It is now time to move on and learn more about the models and application of the central idea. As you study economic models in the following chapters, it will be useful to keep three points in mind. They are implied by the ideas raised in this chapter.

First, *economics—more than other subjects—requires a mixture of verbal and quantitative skills*. Frequently, those who come to economics with a good background in physical science and mathematics find the mix of formal models with more informal verbal descriptions of markets and institutions unusual and perhaps a little difficult. If you are one of these people, you might wish for a more cut-and-dried, or mathematical, approach.

In contrast, those who are good at history or philosophy may find the emphasis on formal models and graphs difficult and might even prefer a more historical approach that looked more at watershed events and famous individuals and less at formal models of how many individuals behave. If you are one of these people, you might wish that economic models were less abstract.

In reality, however, economics is a mixture of formal modeling, historical analysis, and philosophy. If you are very good at math and you think the symbols and graphs of elementary economics are too simple, think of Max Planck's comment about economics and focus on the complexity of the economic phenomena that these simple models and graphs are explaining. Then when you are asked an open-ended question about government policy that does not have a simple yes or no answer, you will not be caught off guard. Or if your advantage is in history or philosophy, you should spend more time honing your skills at using models and graphs. Then when you are asked to solve a cut-and-dried economic problem with an exact answer requiring graphical analysis, you will not be caught off guard.

Second, *economics is a wide-ranging discipline*. When your friends or relatives hear that you are taking economics, they may ask you for advice about what stock to buy. Economists' friends and relatives are always asking them for such advice. Some topics that you study in economics will help you answer questions about whether to invest in the stock market or put your money in a bank or how many stocks to buy. But even these areas of economics will not offer any predictions about the success of particular companies. Rather, what economics gives you is a set of tools that you can use to obtain information about companies, industries, or countries and to analyze them yourself. Furthermore, the scope of economics is vast. Even among the faculty in a small college, you will find economists who study childhood obesity, trade barriers, real estate markets, abortion policy, the formation of American corporations, economic growth, international lending agencies, social security, agricultural pollution, and school choice.

Third, and perhaps most important, *the study of economics is an intellectually fascinating adventure in its own right*. Yes, economics is highly relevant, and it affects people's lives. But once you learn how economic models work, you will find that they are actually fun to use. Every now and then, just after you have learned about a new economic model, put the book down and think of the economic model independent of its message or relevance to society—try to enjoy it the way you would a good movie. In this way, too, you will be learning to think like an economist.

KEY POINTS

1. Economics is a way of thinking that requires observation (describing economic events), explanation (identifying variables that are potential explanatory variables of the event), prediction (building and using economic models to predict future events), and policy recommendations (courses of action for government—and business—to follow, based on these observations and models).
2. Finding the appropriate data series to explain economic events is a challenge because data can often be hard to find or incomplete, or can be misleading if they are not appropriately transformed.
3. Finding explanations for why an economic event occurred is challenging because even if you can find variables that are correlated with the variable you are interested in, correlation does not imply causation. The inability to run controlled experiments also makes it difficult for economists to definitively establish a causal explanation for an economic event.
4. Economists have to explain the complex behavior of humans in economic situations. They often use models that are abstractions, or simplifications, of reality in their work. Economic models, like models in other sciences, can be described with words, with tables, with graphs, or with mathematics. All four ways are important and complement one another.
5. Economists use the tools of economic analysis to come up with policy insights concerning what the government is doing, or what the government should be doing, with regard to the economist's area of interest. Improving economic policy has been a goal of economists since the time of Adam Smith.
6. Economics is a discipline that requires a combination of analytical, mathematical, and verbal skills. You can apply the tools of economics to almost any problem that involves decision-making by individuals. Many students are interested in studying economics because they find it very relevant to events that occur in the world, but the study of economics can be an intellectually stimulating exercise in its own right.

KEY TERMS

relative price
economic variable
controlled experiments
experimental economics
economic model
microeconomics
macroeconomics
gross domestic product (GDP)
positively related
negatively related
ceteris paribus
capitalism
socialism
mixed economy
positive economics
normative economics
Council of Economic Advisers

QUESTIONS FOR REVIEW

1. How do economists typically approach an economics-related problem?
2. What are the challenges that economists face in trying to describe an economic event?
3. What is meant by a relative price, and why is it important in certain situations to look at the relative price of a good instead of the actual price of that good?
4. What does it mean for two variables to be correlated? What is the difference between positive and negative correlation?
5. Why doesn't correlation imply causation? Can you come up with your own example of why correlation does not imply causation?
6. Why do economists use economic models? Can you come up with some reasons why economists should be careful in using models?
7. What is the *ceteris paribus* assumption? Why is it so important in economics?
8. What is the difference between macroeconomics and microeconomics? Between positive and normative economics?
9. What academic disciplines do you think of as being more scientific than economics? Why do you think so? Which disciplines do you consider to be less scientific, and why?
10. Look through the research and teaching interests of the economics faculty members in your department. Collectively, how wide-ranging are those interests? Are there any areas that you were surprised to find that the tools of economics could be applied to?

PROBLEMS

1. Which of the following variables are studied as part of microeconomics, and which are studied as part of macroeconomics?
   a. The U.S. unemployment rate
   b. The amount of tips earned by a waiter
   c. The national rate of inflation
   d. The number of hours worked by a student
   e. The price paid to obtain this economics textbook
2. Consider the following table, which provides the price of chicken and the price of all foods from 1991 to 2006.
   a. Calculate the relative price of chicken for each year.
   b. Plot the relative price of chicken as in Figure 2.
   c. What can you say about how the price of chicken has varied in comparison to the price of all foods in the decade from 1996 to 2006?

Year	Price of All Foods	Price of Chicken	Relative Price
1996	92	95	
1997	93	98	
1998	96	98	
1999	97	99	
2000	100	100	
2001	103	103	
2002	104	105	
2003	108	106	
2004	111	114	
2005	113	116	
2006	116	114	

3. A change in the relative price of a good matters more than the change in the price of a good in analyzing

the change in spending on that good. Show that the relative price of a good can fall on occasions when the price of that good is rising, falling, or remaining unchanged, using numerical examples from the table in problem 2.

4. Indicate whether you expect positive or negative correlation for the following pairs of variables, labeled *X* and *Y*. For each pair, state whether *X* causes *Y*, *Y* causes *X*, or both.
   a. Sunrise (*X*) and crowing roosters (*Y*)
   b. The use of umbrellas (*X*) and a thunderstorm (*Y*)
   c. The price of theater tickets (*X*) and the number of theatergoers (*Y*)
   d. Weekly earnings of a worker (*X*) and the number of hours a week she works at her job (*Y*)
   e. The number of children who were vaccinated against a disease (*X*) and the number of children who currently suffer from that disease (*Y*)

5. Consider an economic model of donut production. Show how to represent this model graphically, algebraically, and verbally, as in Figure 6.

Number of Workers	Number of Donuts Produced
0	0
1	100
4	200
9	300
16	400

6. Suppose you decide to build a model to explain why the average worker in a particular occupation works more hours during some weeks than during others.
   a. What data would you collect to describe this phenomenon?
   b. What variable do you believe would supply the major part of the explanation of the variation in hours worked?
   c. If you graph the data with hours worked on the vertical axis and your explanatory variable on the horizontal axis, will the relationship be upward-sloping or downward-sloping?
   d. What does your answer to part c imply for whether the data on hours worked and the data on your explanatory variable are positively or negatively correlated?

7. Why is it typical for economists to make the *ceteris paribus* assumption when making predictions? Now consider the statement: "If the local McDonald's restaurant reduces the price of a Big Mac hamburger, it will sell a lot more hamburgers." What other variables are most likely being held fixed under the *ceteris paribus* assumption when this statement is being made?

8. Suppose you wanted to modify the Bertrand and Mullainathan study to focus on gender discrimination. Describe the "experiment" that you would run. Also be sure to explain how the *ceteris paribus* assumption is involved in terms of the names you would choose for the men and for the women.

9. Identify whether the following policy statements are positive or normative. Explain.
   a. "The price of gasoline is too high."
   b. "The average price of gasoline rose to a record high of $3.07 in May 2007."
   c. "Forty-four million Americans lack access to health insurance."
   d. "The government needs to provide basic health care to the uninsured."
   e. "The collapse in the real estate market will affect many Americans."

10. Suppose an economic study shows that increasing the tax rate on cigarettes will reduce the amount of smoking. Which of the following statements can be validly made on the basis of the study because they are positive statements, and which cannot be validly made because they are normative statements?
   a. Increasing the cigarette tax rate is a method of reducing smoking.
   b. If the government wishes to reduce smoking, it ought to raise the cigarette tax.
   c. If the government wishes to reduce smoking, it can raise the cigarette tax.
   d. The government ought to reduce smoking by raising the cigarette tax.
   e. The government should not raise the cigarette tax on low-income smokers.

Reading, Understanding, and Creating Graphs

Whether you follow the stock market, the health-care market, or the whole economy, graphs are needed to understand what is going on. That is why the financial pages of newspapers contain so many graphs. Knowing how to read, understand, and even create your own graphs is part of learning to "think like an economist." Graphs help us see correlations, or patterns, in economic observations. Graphs are also useful for understanding economic models. They help us see how variables in the model behave. They help us describe assumptions about what firms and consumers do.

Computer software to create graphs is now widely available. A graphing program with many examples is provided with the software that accompanies this text. To understand how helpful graphs can be, you might want to create a few of your own graphs using the time-series data in the "Explore" section of the software. Here we provide an overview of basic graphing techniques.

Visualizing Observations with Graphs

Most economic graphs are drawn in two dimensions, like the surface of this page, and are constructed using a **Cartesian coordinate system.** The idea of Cartesian coordinates is that pairs of observations on variables can be represented in a plane by designating one axis for one variable and the other axis for the other variable. Each point, or coordinate, on the plane corresponds to a pair of observations.

Time-Series Graphs

In many instances, we want to see how a variable changes over time. Consider the federal debt held by the public—all the outstanding borrowing of the federal government that has not yet been paid back. Table A.1 shows observations of the U.S. federal debt. The observations are for every 10 years. The observations in Table A.1 are graphed in Figure A.1. The graph in Figure A.1 is called a **time-series graph** because it plots a series—that is, several values of the variable—over time.

Observe the scales on the horizontal and vertical axes in Figure A.1. The seven years are put on the horizontal axis, spread evenly from the year 1950 to the year 2010. The last year is a forecast. For the vertical axis,

TABLE A.1
U.S. Federal Government Debt

Year	Debt (billions of dollars)
1950	219
1960	237
1970	283
1980	712
1990	2,412
2000	3,410
2010 (Projected)	5,949

Source: Congressional Budget Office.

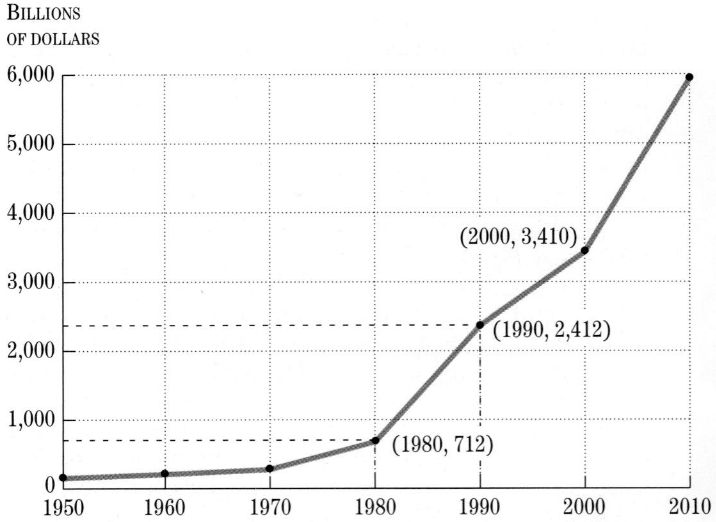

FIGURE A.1
U.S. Federal Debt
Each point corresponds to a pair of observations—the year and the debt—from Table A.1.

FIGURE A.2
Stretching the Debt Story in Two Ways
The points in both graphs are identical to those in Figure A.1, but by stretching or shrinking the scales, the problem can be made to look either less dramatic or more dramatic.

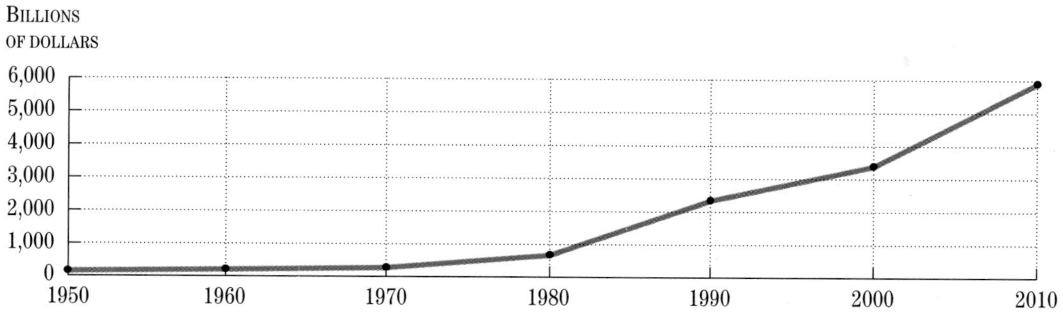

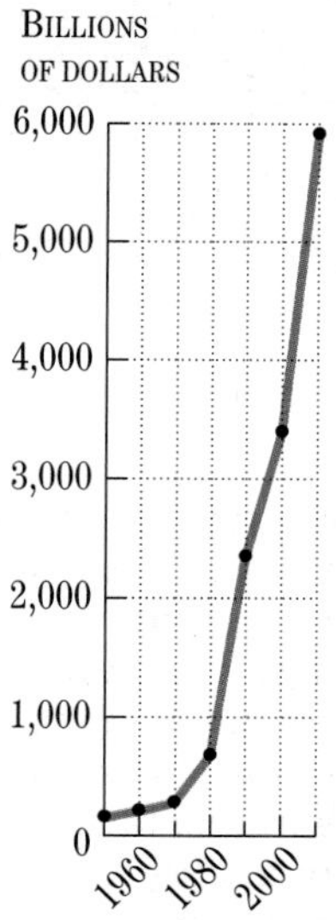

one needs to decide on a scale. The range of variation for the debt in Table A.1 is very wide—from a minimum of $219 billion to a maximum of $5,949 billion. Thus, the range on the vertical axis—from $0 to $6,000 billion in Figure A.1—must be wide enough to contain all these points.

Now observe how each pair of points from Table A.1 is plotted in Figure A.1. The point for the pair of observations for the year 1950 and the debt of $219 billion is found by going over to 1950 on the horizontal axis, then going up to $219 billion and putting a dot there. The point for 1960 and $237 billion and all the other points are found in the same way. In order to better visualize the points, they can be connected with lines. These lines are not part of the observations; they are only a convenience to help in eyeballing the observations. The points for 1980, 1990, and 2000 are labeled with the pairs of observations corresponding to Table A.1, but in general there is no need to put in such labels.

One could choose scales different from those in Figure A.1, and if you plotted your own graph from the data in Table A.1 without looking at Figure A.1, your scales would probably be different. The scales determine how much movement there is in a time-series graph. For example, Figure A.2 shows two ways to stretch the scales to make the increase in the debt look more or less dramatic. So as not to be fooled by graphs, therefore, it is important to look at the scales and think about what they mean.

As an alternative to time-series graphs with dots connected by a line, the observations can be shown on a bar graph, as in Figure A.3. Some people prefer the visual look of a bar graph, but, as is clear from a comparison of Figures A.1 and A.3, they provide the same information as time-series graphs.

The debt as a percentage of GDP is given in Table A.2 and graphed in Figure A.4. Note that this figure makes the debt look very different from the way it looks in the first one. As a percentage of GDP, the debt fell from the end of

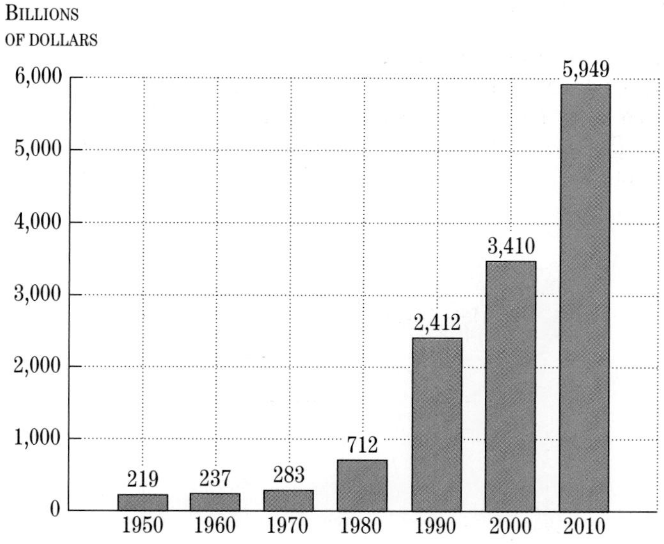

FIGURE A.3
U.S. Federal Debt in Bars
The observations are identical to those in Figure A.1.

TABLE A.2
U.S. Federal Debt as a Percentage of GDP

Year	Debt (percent of GDP)
1950	82.5
1960	46.8
1970	28.2
1980	25.7
1990	42.3
2000	35.9
2010 (Projected)	37.8

Source: U.S. Department of Commerce and Table A.1.

World War II (when it was very large because of the war debt) until around 1980. It increased during the 1980s and declined in the 1990s, but has started to increase again in the 2000s.

Sometimes the data to be graphed have no observations close to 0, in which case including 0 on the vertical axis would leave some wasted space at the bottom of the graph. To eliminate this space and have more room to see the graph itself, we can start the range near the minimum value and end it near the maximum value. This is done in Figure A.5, where the debt as a percentage of GDP is shown up to 1980. Note, however, that cutting off the bottom of the scale could be misleading to people who do not look at the axis. In particular, 0 percent is no longer at the point where the horizontal and vertical axes intersect. To warn people about the missing part of the scale, a little cut is sometimes put on the axis, as is done in Figure A.5, but you have to look carefully at the scale.

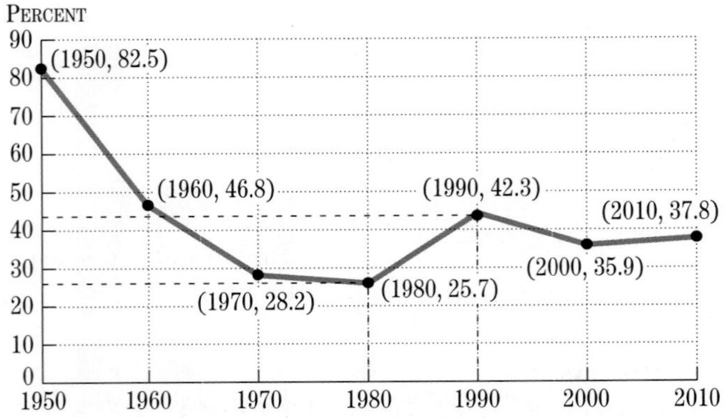

FIGURE A.4
U.S. Federal Debt as a Percentage of GDP
Each point corresponds to a pair of observations from Table A.2.

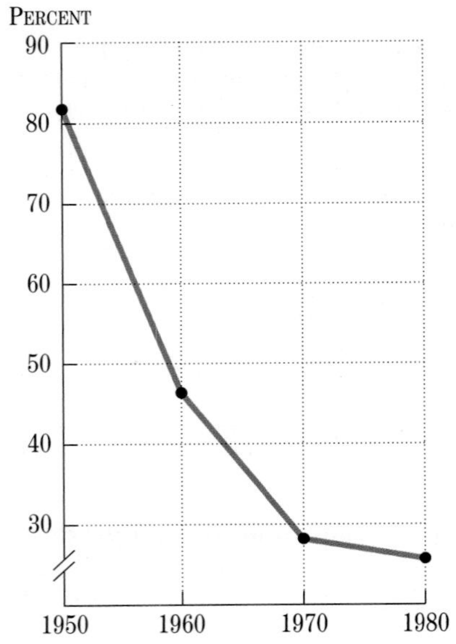

FIGURE A.5
A Look at Debt as a Percentage of GDP from 1950 to 1980
(*Note:* To alert the reader that the bottom part of the axis is not shown, a break point is sometimes used, as shown here.)

Time-Series Graphs Showing Two or More Variables

So far, we have shown how a graph can be used to show observations on one variable over time. What if we want to see how two or more variables change over time together? Suppose, for example, we want to look at how observations on debt as a percentage of GDP compare with the interest rate the government must pay on its debt. (The interest rate for 2010 is, of course, a forecast.) The two variables are shown in Table A.3.

TABLE A.3
Interest Rate and Federal Debt as a Percentage of GDP

Year	Debt (percent of GDP)	Interest Rate (percent)
1950	82.5	1.2
1960	46.8	2.9
1970	28.2	6.5
1980	25.7	11.5
1990	42.3	7.5
2000	35.9	5.5
2010 (Projected)	37.8	5.5

Source: Federal Reserve Board and Table A.2.

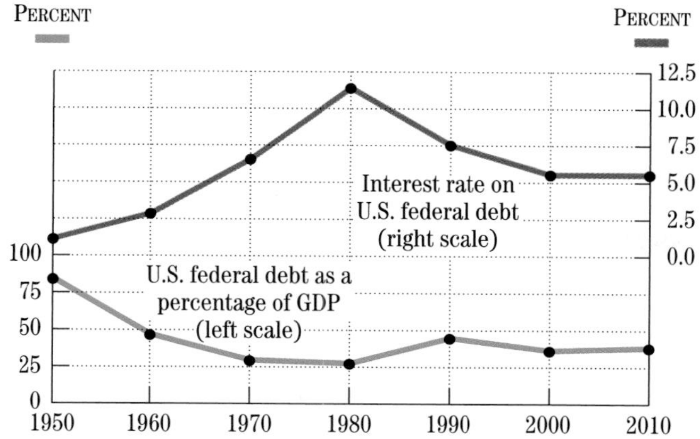

FIGURE A.6
Comparing Two Time Series with a Dual Scale
When two variables have different scales, a dual scale is useful. Here the interest rate and the debt as a percentage of GDP are plotted from Table A.3.

The two sets of observations can easily be placed on the same time-series graph. In other words, we can plot the observations on the debt percentage and connect the dots and then plot the interest rate observations and connect the dots. If the scales of measurement of the two variables are much different, however, it may be hard to see both. For example, the interest rate ranges between 1 and 12 percent; it would not be very visible on a graph going all the way from 0 to 100 percent, a range that is fine for the debt percentage. In this situation, a **dual scale** can be used, as shown in Figure A.6. One scale is put on the left-hand vertical axis, and the other scale is put on the right-hand vertical axis. With a dual-scale diagram, it is very important to be aware of the two scales. In Figure A.6 we emphasize the different axes by the color line segment at the top of each vertical axis. The color line segment corresponds to the color of the curve plotted using that scale.

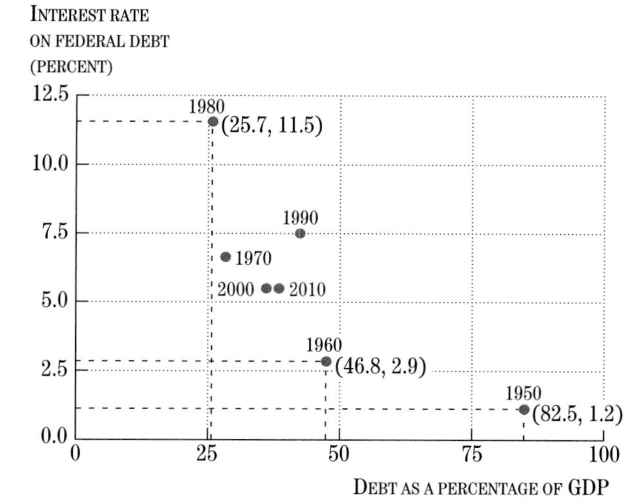

FIGURE A.7
Scatter Plot
Interest rate and debt as a percentage of GDP are shown.

Scatter Plots

Finally, two variables can be usefully compared with a **scatter plot.** The Cartesian coordinate method is used, as in the time-series graph; however, we do not put the year on one of the axes. Instead, the horizontal axis is used for one of the variables and the vertical axis for the other variable. We do this for the debt percentage and the interest rate in Figure A.7. The interest rate is on the vertical axis, and the debt percentage is on the horizontal axis. For example, the point at the upper left is 25.7 percent for the debt as a percentage of GDP and 11.5 percent for the interest rate.

Pie Charts

Time-series graphs, bar graphs, and scatter plots are not the only visual ways to observe economic data. For example, the *pie chart* in Figure A.8 is useful for

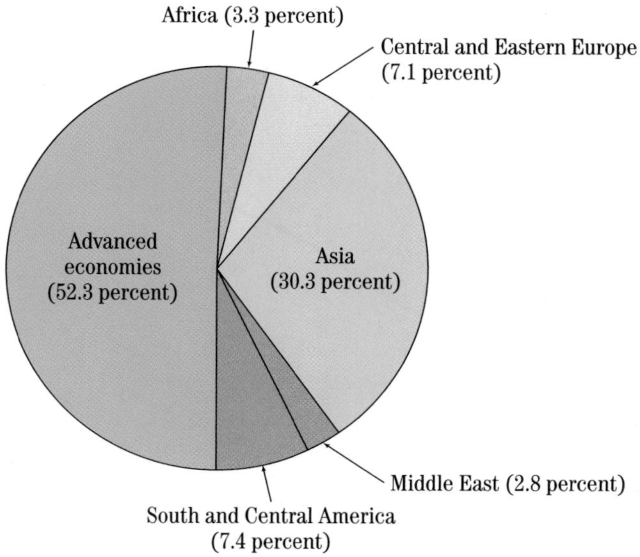

FIGURE A.8
Pie Chart Showing the Shares of the World's GDP
The pie chart shows how the world's GDP in 2005 is divided up into that produced by different groups of countries, including the industrial (advanced) economies, Asia, Africa, South America, Central and Eastern Europe, and the Middle East.

comparing percentage shares for a small number of different groups or a small number of time periods. In this example, the pie chart is a visual representation of how the industrial countries produce more than half of the world's GDP, while the developing countries in Asia, Africa, South and Central America, and the Middle East produce 40 percent and the former communist countries in Eastern Europe and the former Soviet Union, now in transition toward market economies, produce about 7 percent.

Visualizing Models with Graphs

Graphs can also represent models. Like graphs showing observations, graphs showing models are usually restricted to curves in two dimensions.

Slopes of Curves

Does a curve slope up or down? How steep is it? These questions are important in economics, as in other sciences. The **slope** of a curve tells us how much the variable on the vertical axis changes when we change the variable on the horizontal axis by one unit.

The slope is computed as follows:

$$\text{Slope} = \frac{\text{change in variable on vertical axis}}{\text{change in variable on horizontal axis}}$$

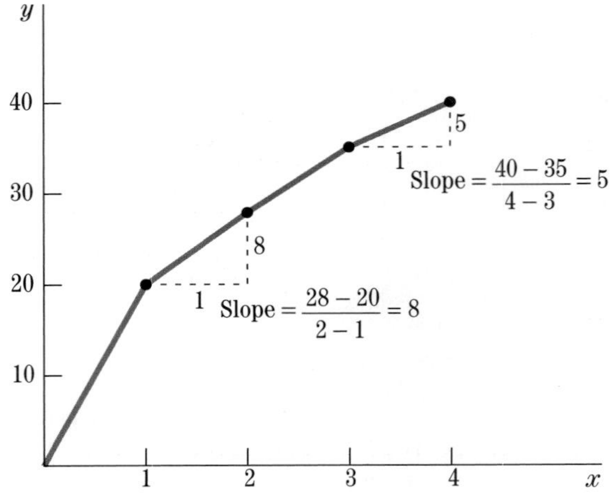

FIGURE A.9
Measuring the Slope
The slope between two points is given by the change along the vertical axis divided by the change along the horizontal axis. In this example, the slope declines as *x* increases. Since the curve slopes up from left to right, it has a positive slope.

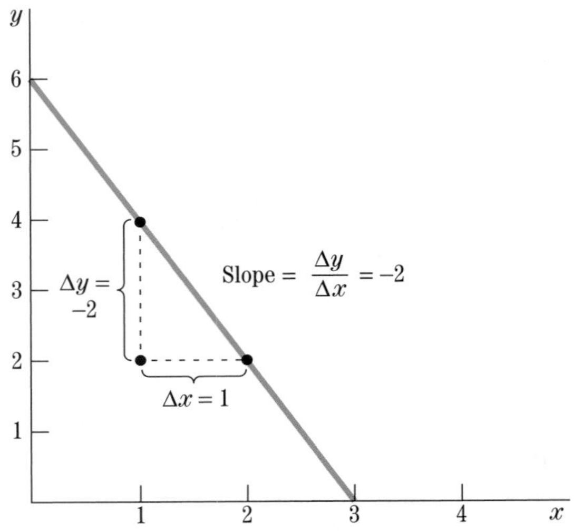

FIGURE A.10
A Relationship with a Negative Slope
Here the slope is negative: $(\Delta y)/(\Delta x) = -2$. As *x* increases, *y* falls. The line slopes down from left to right. In this case, *y* and *x* are inversely, or negatively, related.

In most algebra courses, the vertical axis is usually called the *y*-axis and the horizontal axis is called the *x*-axis. Thus, the slope is sometime described as

$$\text{Slope} = \frac{\text{change in } y}{\text{change in } x} = \frac{\Delta y}{\Delta x}$$

where the Greek letter Δ (delta) means "change in." In other words, the slope is the ratio of the "rise" (vertical change) to the "run" (horizontal change).

Figure A.9 shows how to compute the slope. In this case, the slope declines as the variable on the *x*-axis increases.

Observe that *the steeper the curve, the larger the slope*. When the curve gets very flat, the slope gets close to zero. Curves can either be upward-sloping or downward-sloping. If the curve slopes up from left to right, as in Figure A.9, it has a **positive slope,** and we say that the two variables are positively related. If the curve slopes down from left to right, it has a **negative slope,** and we say that the two variables are negatively related. Figure A.10 shows a case where the slope is negative. When *x* increases by 1 unit ($\Delta x = 1$), *y* declines by 2 units ($\Delta y = -2$). Thus, the slope equals -2; it is negative. Observe how the curve slopes down from left to right.

If the curve is a straight line, then the slope is a constant. Curves that are straight lines—like that in Figure A.10—are called **linear.** But economic relationships do not

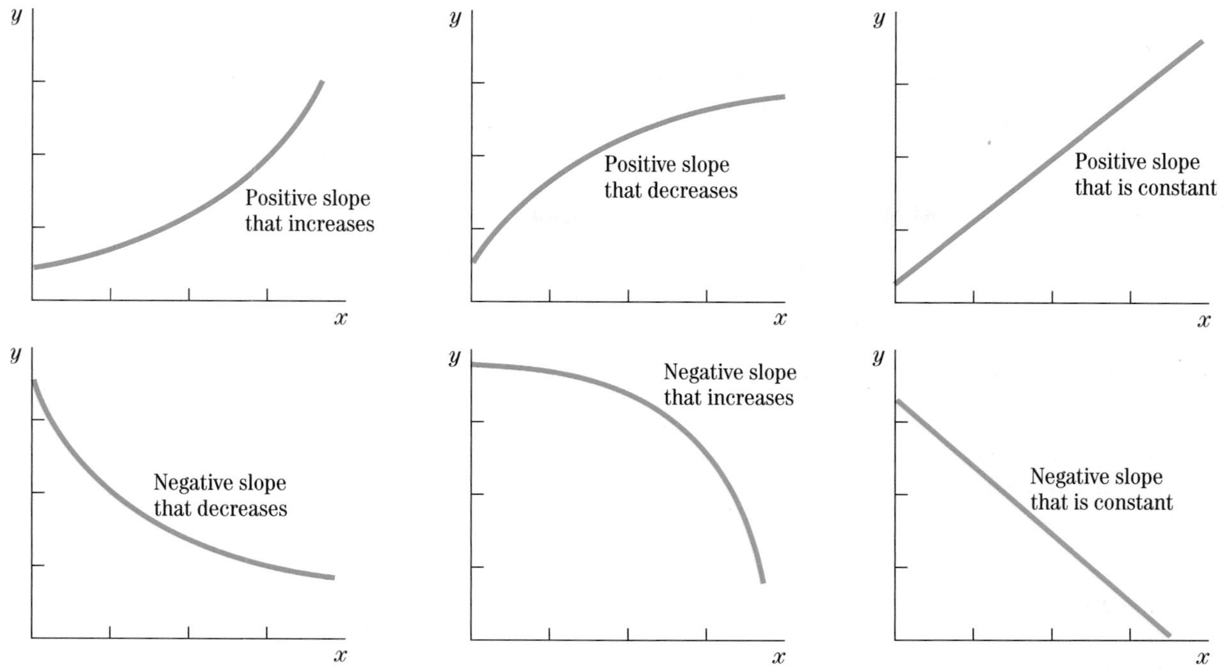

FIGURE A.11
Six Types of Relationships
In the top row, the variables are positively related. In the bottom row, they are negatively related.

need to be linear, as the example in Figure A.9 makes clear. Figure A.11 shows six different examples of curves and indicates how they are described.

Graphs of Models with More than Two Variables

In most cases, economic models involve more than two variables. For example, the number of physical examinations could depend on the number of nurses as well as the number of doctors. Or the amount of lemonade demanded might depend on the weather as well as on the price.

Economists have devised several methods for representing models with more than two variables with two-dimensional graphs. Suppose, for example, that the relationship between y and x in Figure A.10 depends on a third variable z. For a given value of x, larger values of z lead to larger values of y. This example is graphed in Figure A.12. As in Figure A.10, when x increases, y falls. This is a **movement along the curve.** But what if z changes? We represent this as a **shift of the curve.** An increase in z shifts the curve up; a decrease in z shifts the curve down.

Thus, by distinguishing between shifts of and movements along a curve, economists represent models with more than two variables in only two dimensions.

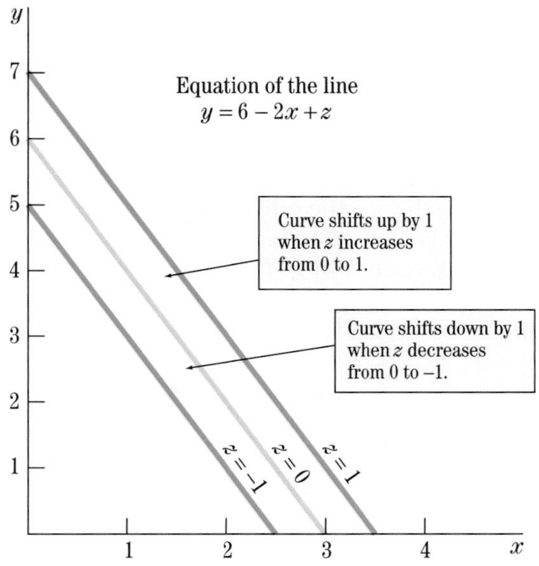

FIGURE A.12
A Third Variable Shifts the Curve
In order to represent models with three variables (x, y, and z) on a two-dimensional graph, economists distinguish between movements along the curve (when x and y change, holding z unchanged) and shifts of the curve (when z changes).

Only two variables (x and y) are shown explicitly on the graph, and when the third (z) is fixed, changes in x and y are movements along the curve. When z changes, the curve shifts. The distinction between "movements along" and "shifts of" curves comes up many times in economics.

KEY TERMS AND DEFINITIONS

Cartesian coordinate system: a graphing system in which ordered pairs of numbers are represented on a plane by the distances from a point to two perpendicular lines, called axes.

time-series graph: a graph that plots a variable over time, usually with time on the horizontal axis.

dual scale: a graph that uses time on the horizontal axis and different scales on the left and right vertical axes to compare the movements of two variables over time.

scatter plot: a graph in which points in a Cartesian coordinate system represent the values of two variables.

slope: a characteristic of a curve that is defined as the change in the variable on the vertical axis divided by the change in the variable on the horizontal axis.

positive slope: a slope of a curve that is greater than zero, representing a positive or direct relationship between two variables.

negative slope: a slope of a curve that is less than zero, representing a negative or inverse relationship between two variables.

linear: a situation in which a curve is straight, with a constant slope.

movement along the curve: a situation in which a change in the variable on one axis causes a change in the variable on the other axis, but the position of the curve is maintained.

shift of the curve: a change in the position of a curve, usually caused by a change in a variable not represented on either axis.

QUESTIONS FOR REVIEW

1. What is the difference between a scatter plot and a time-series graph?
2. Why are dual scales sometimes necessary?
3. What is the advantage of graphs over verbal representations of models?
4. What does a curve with a negative slope look like?
5. What is the difference between a shift in a curve and a movement along a curve?

PROBLEMS

1. The table below presents data on the debt and the debt to GDP ratio predicted by the Congressional Budget Office for the United States for each year through 2015.

Year	Debt	Debt to GDP Ratio
2005	4,656	38.1
2006	4,965	38.5
2007	5,246	38.6
2008	5,506	38.5
2009	5,737	38.2
2010	5,949	37.8
2011	6,054	36.7
2012	6,004	34.8
2013	5,941	33.0
2014	5,847	31.1
2015	5,726	29.1

Source: Congressional Budget Office.

   a. Construct a time-series plot of the ratio of government debt to GDP.
   b. Construct a time-series plot of the debt.
   c. Construct a scatter plot of the debt ratio and the debt.

2. The following table shows the number of physical examinations given by doctors at an HMO with three different-size clinics: small, medium, and large. The larger the clinic, the more patients the doctors can handle.

Exams per Small Clinic	Exams per Medium Clinic	Exams per Large Clinic	Number of Doctors
0	0	0	0
20	30	35	1
28	42	49	2
35	53	62	3
40	60	70	4

   a. Show the relationship between doctors and physical exams given with *three* curves, where the number of doctors is on the horizontal axis and the number of examinations is on the vertical axis.
   b. Describe how the three relationships compare with one another.
   c. Is a change in the number of doctors a shift of or a movement along the curve?
   d. Is a change in the size of the clinic a shift of or a movement along the curve?

3. Consider two variables that change over time, which we will denote as Numerator and Denominator. Consider also a combination of the two variables, denoted as Ratio, formed by the formula:

$$\text{Ratio} = \frac{\text{Numerator}}{\text{Denominator}}$$

a. If both Numerator and Denominator are increasing over time, what must be true if Ratio is to rise over time?

b. If both Numerator and Denominator are decreasing over time, what must be true if Ratio is to rise over time?

c. If Ratio is not changing over time, what must be true about the behavior of Numerator and Denominator over time, and relative to each other?

4. A tradeoff is a situation in which more of one variable is obtained along with less of another. Which of the six relationships in Figure A.11 can represent a tradeoff situation?

5. Consider an upward-sloping straight line that has a slope of 1. It bisects the positive *xy* quadrant. Select any point on the line. What must be true about the distances between the origin and the *x* coordinate and between the origin and the *y* coordinate?

Chapter 3

The Supply and Demand Model

It's called "March Madness" for a reason! Every March, four college basketball teams travel to a neutral city, where they compete in the Final Four, the last round of college basketball's national championship. Each college receives a limited allotment of tickets; if you were a student at one of these colleges, and you were lucky enough to have the opportunity to buy one of these tickets, you would most likely pay about $100 to $200 to get a seat at the game. But when you reached the city where the Final Four is being played, you would find people on the street willing to pay staggering amounts of money for those tickets—as much as $5,000. The temptation to sell the tickets and watch the game on TV would be quite high, even for a fairly devoted fan. On the other hand, if you were a devoted fan of your team, but you did not have the opportunity to buy one of the allotted tickets, then you would find yourself having to pay several thousand dollars for a Final Four ticket, either to an online ticket broker or to a seller on an online auction site or on the street.

Why does a Final Four ticket cost so much? Who decides what price to charge for a Final Four ticket? Why does the college sell its allotment of tickets at a much lower price than that charged by a street seller or by an online ticket broker? How does the college decide who gets its limited allotment of tickets? Who ends up going to the Final Four game, and who ends up selling their ticket and watching the game on television? The purpose of this chapter is to show how to find the answers to such questions using the *supply and demand model.*

Recall from Chapter 2 that a model is a simplified description of a more complex reality. The supply and demand model is what economists use to explain how prices are determined in a market. We can use this model to understand the market for Final Four tickets or Super Bowl tickets, as well in a variety of other settings. What causes the price of gasoline to fluctuate? What causes the price of computers to fall over time, even though the prices of most other goods seem to rise over time? Why do roses cost

Supply and Demand in the Final Four
The model of supply and demand can explain why tickets to the NCAA Final Four cost so much more in the broader market than what the participating schools charge a few lucky buyers. It also explains more routine buyer and seller interactions, describing the behavior of sellers and buyers and how they connect in markets.

more on Valentine's Day? Once you understand how the model works, you will find yourself using it over and over again to understand the markets that you come across in your everyday life.

The supply and demand model consists of three elements: *demand*, describing the behavior of consumers in the market; *supply*, describing the behavior of firms in the market; and *market equilibrium*, connecting supply and demand and describing how consumers and firms interact in the market. Economists like to compare the supply and demand model to a pair of scissors. Demand is one blade of the scissors, and supply is the other. Either blade alone is incomplete and virtually useless; but when the two blades of a pair of scissors are connected to form the scissors, they become an amazingly useful, yet simple, tool. So it is with the supply and demand model.

DEMAND

demand: a relationship between **price** and **quantity demanded.**

price: the amount of money or other goods that one must pay to obtain a particular good.

quantity demanded: the quantity of a good that people want to buy at a given price during a specific time period.

To an economist, the term *demand*—whether the demand for tickets or the demand for roses—has a very specific meaning. **Demand** is a relationship between two economic variables: (1) *the price of a particular good* and (2) *the quantity of that good that consumers are willing to buy at that price during a specific time period*, all other things being equal. For short, we call the first variable the **price** and the second variable the **quantity demanded.** The phrase *all other things being equal*, or *ceteris paribus*, is appended to the definition of demand because the quantity that consumers are willing to buy depends on many other things besides the price of the good; we want to hold these other things constant, or equal, while we examine the relationship between price and quantity demanded.

Demand can be represented by a numerical table or by a graph. In either case, demand describes how much of a good consumers will purchase at each price. Consider the demand for bicycles in a particular country, as presented in Table 1. Of course, there are many kinds of bicycles—mountain bikes, racing bikes, children's bikes, and inexpensive one-speed bikes with cruiser brakes—so you need to simplify and think about this table as describing demand for an average, or typical, bike.

Observe that as the price rises, the quantity demanded by consumers goes down. If the price goes up from $180 to $200 per bicycle, for example, the quantity demanded goes down from 11 million to 9 million bicycles. On the other hand, if the price goes down, the quantity demanded goes up. If the price falls from $180 to $160, for example, the quantity demanded rises from 11 million to 14 million bicycles.

demand schedule: a tabular presentation of demand showing the price and quantity demanded for a particular good, all else being equal.

law of demand: the tendency for the quantity demanded of a good in a market to decline as its price rises.

The relationship between price and quantity demanded in Table 1 is called a **demand schedule**. The relationship shows price and quantity demanded moving in opposite directions, and this is an example of the law of demand. The **law of demand** says that the higher the price, the lower the quantity demanded in the market; and the lower the price, the higher the quantity demanded in the market. In other words, the law of demand says that the price and the quantity demanded are negatively related, all other things being equal.

TABLE 1
Demand Schedule for Bicycles (millions of bicycles per year)

Price	Quantity Demanded	Price	Quantity Demanded
$140	18	$240	5
$160	14	$260	3
$180	11	$280	2
$200	9	$300	1
$200	7		

The Demand Curve

Figure 1 represents demand graphically. It is a graph with the price of the good on the vertical axis and the quantity demanded of the good on the horizontal axis. It shows the demand for bicycles given in Table 1. Each of the nine rows in Table 1 corresponds to one of the nine points in Figure 1. For example, the point at the lower right part of the graph corresponds to the first row of the table, where the price is $140 and the quantity demanded is 18 million bicycles. The resulting curve showing all the combinations of price and quantity demanded is the **demand curve.** It slopes downward from left to right because the quantity demanded is negatively related to the price.

demand curve: a graph of demand showing the downward-sloping relationship between price and quantity demanded.

Why does the demand curve slope downward? The demand curve tells us the quantity demanded by all consumers. Consumers have scarce resources and need to choose between bicycles and other goods. It is important to remember that when economists draw a demand curve, they hold constant the price of other goods: running shoes, in-line skates, motor scooters, and so on. If the price of bicycles falls, then bicycles become more attractive to people in comparison with these other goods—some consumers who previously found the price of bicycles too high may decide to buy a bicycle rather than buy other goods. Conversely, when the price of bicycles increases, then bicycles become less attractive to people in comparison with other goods—some consumers may decide to buy in-line skates or motor scooters instead of bicycles. As a result, quantity demanded declines when the price rises and vice versa.

There's plenty of evidence in the real world that demand curves are downward-sloping. In June of 2004, vehicle sales at General Motors were slowing. In July, General Motors increased the cash-back offer on most of its trucks and cars. You might (correctly) speculate that this reduction in the price of vehicles was intended to increase vehicle sales. Policies designed to reduce smoking by teenagers or to cut down on drinking on college campuses often aim to do this by raising the price of cigarettes and alcohol. The idea, of course, is that teens would buy fewer cigarettes and students would buy less alcohol if these goods were more expensive.

Shifts in Demand

Price is not the only thing that affects the quantity of a good that people buy. Weather conditions, concerns about the environment, or the availability of bike lanes on roads can influence people's decisions to purchase bicycles, for example. If climate change brought on an extended period of warm weather, people would have more opportunities to ride their bicycles. As a result, more bicycles would be purchased at any given price. Or perhaps increased awareness of the health benefits of exercise might lead people to ride their bicycles to work rather than drive their cars. This would also lead to more purchases of bicycles at any given price. Alternatively, if bike

Price	Quantity Demanded
$140	18
$160	14
$180	11
$200	9
$220	7
$240	5
$260	3
$280	2
$300	1

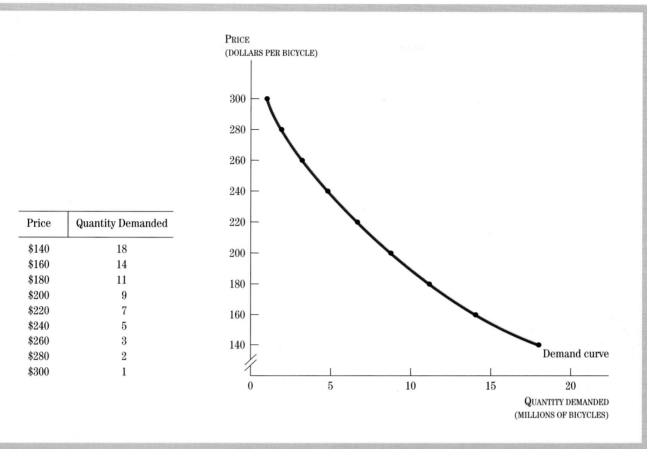

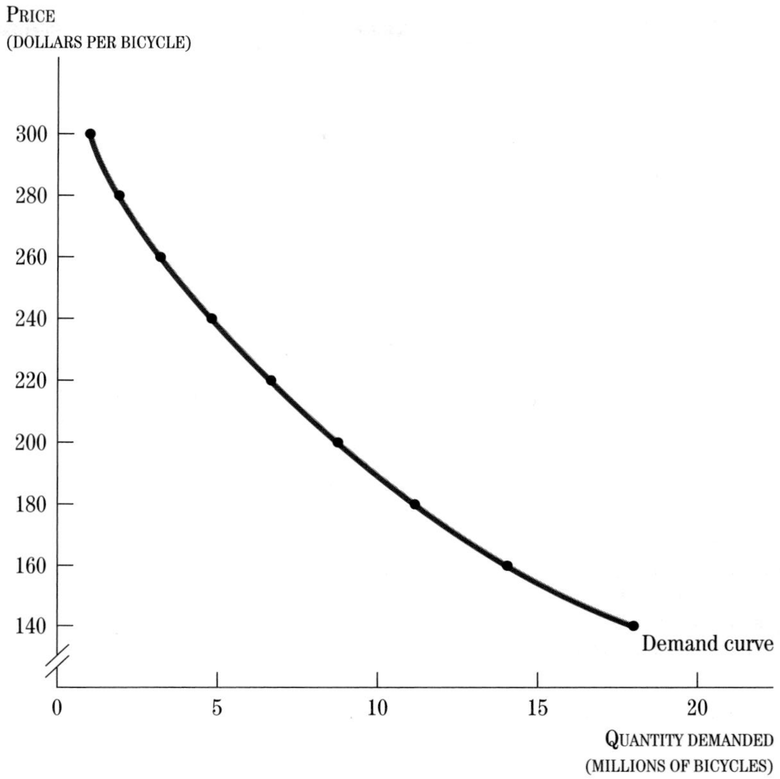

FIGURE 1
The Demand Curve

The demand curve shows that the price of a good and the quantity demanded by consumers are negatively related—the curve slopes down. For each price, the demand curve gives the quantity demanded, or the quantity that consumers are willing to buy at that price. The points along the demand curve for bicycles shown here are the same as the pairs of numbers in Table 1.

lanes are taken away to allow for an extra lane of cars on the road, there will be fewer bicycles purchased at any given price.

The demand curve is drawn assuming that all other things are equal, except the price of the good. A change in any one of these other things, therefore, will shift the demand curve. An increase in demand shifts the demand curve to the right—at every price, quantity demanded will increase. A decrease in demand shifts the demand curve to the left—at every price, quantity demanded will decrease.

An increase in demand is illustrated in Figure 2. The lightly shaded curve labeled "old demand curve" is the same as the demand curve in Figure 1. An extended period of warm weather will increase demand and shift the demand curve to the right. The arrow shows how this curve has shifted to the right to the more darkly shaded curve labeled "new demand curve." When the demand curve shifts to the right, more bicycles are purchased than before at any given price. For example, before the shift in demand, a $200 price led to 9 million bicycles being purchased. But when the demand curve shifts to the right because of warmer weather, that same price leads to 13 million bicycles being purchased. On the other hand, if bicycle lanes were taken away from roads, then the demand curve would shift to the left because people's purchases of bicycles would now be less at any given price.

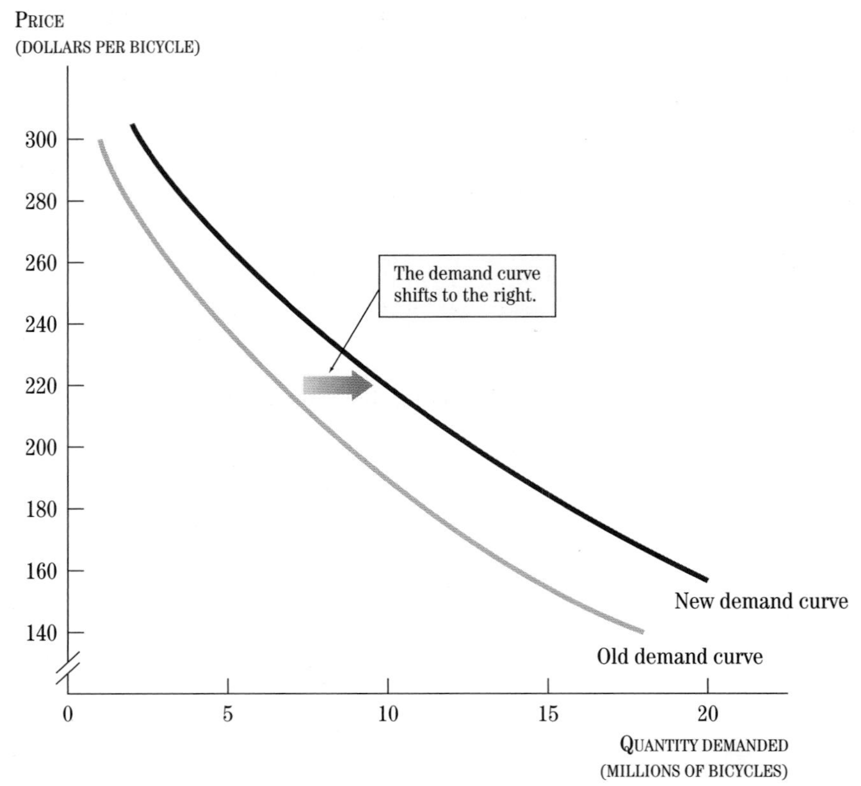

FIGURE 2
A Shift in the Demand Curve
The demand curve shows how the quantity demanded of a good is related to the price of the good, all other things being equal. A change in one of these other things—the weather or people's tastes, for example—will shift the demand curve, as shown in the graph. In this case, the demand for bicycles increases; the demand curve for bicycles shifts to the right.

There are many reasons the demand curve may shift. Most of them can be attributed to one of several sources: *consumers' preferences, consumers' information, consumers' incomes, the number of consumers in the market, consumers' expectations of future prices,* and *the price of related goods.* Let us briefly consider each source of shifts in demand.

Consumers' Preferences. In general, a change in people's tastes or preferences for a product compared to other products will change the amount of the product they purchase at any given price. On many college campuses, there has been an increase in demand for clothing that is certified as not having produced in "sweatshops." Also, over the last couple of decades, consumers have shown a great deal of interest in buying "organically grown" fruits and vegetables, which are produced without using artificial pesticides or fertilizers.

Consumers' Information. A change in information relating to a product can also cause the demand curve to shift. For example, when people learned about the dangers of smoking, the demand for cigarettes declined. Shortly after an outbreak of *E. coli* in parts of the United States was linked to contaminated spinach, there was a decrease in demand for spinach at grocery stores. After a number of fatal car accidents led to a mass recall of Firestone tires in 2000, the demand for Firestone tires fell fairly dramatically.

Consumers' Incomes. If people's incomes change, then their purchases of goods usually change. An increase in income increases the demand for most goods, while a decline in income reduces the demand for these goods. Goods for which demand increases when income rises and decreases when income falls are called **normal goods** by economists. Many of the goods that people typically purchase—shoes, clothing, jewelry—fall into the category of normal goods.

normal good: a good for which demand increases when income rises and decreases when income falls.

inferior good: a good for which demand decreases when income rises and increases when income falls.

However, the demand for some goods may decline when income increases. Such goods are called **inferior goods** by economists. The demand for inferior goods declines when people's income increases because they can afford more attractive goods. For example, instant noodles form the basis of many college students' diets. However, after these students leave college and start working and earning a salary, many of them will switch over to eating microwavable meals or to eating out in restaurants. Thus, the demand for instant noodles will fall as income rises. Another example of an inferior good that is familiar to many college students in Boston and New York is the cheap bus service that runs between the "Chinatowns" in the two cities; a bus ticket may cost as little as $10, whereas a plane ticket between the two cities may cost $150. However, as students graduate and start earning money, they often end up buying more of the $150 plane tickets and fewer of the $10 bus tickets. In that case, the plane ticket can be categorized as a normal good, while the bus ticket is categorized as an inferior good.

Number of Consumers in the Market. Demand is a relationship between price and the quantity demanded by *all* consumers in the market. If the number of consumers increases, then demand will increase. If the number of consumers falls, then demand will decrease. For example, the number of teenagers in the U.S. population expanded sharply in the late 1990s. This increased the demand for *Seventeen* magazine, for Rollerblades, for Clearasil, and for other goods that teenagers tend to buy. As the baby-boom generation in the United States ages, the demand for health care, hair coloring kits and luxury skin care products is increasing.

Consumers' Expectations of Future Prices. If people expect the price of a good to increase, they will want to buy it before the price increases. Conversely, if people expect the price to decline, they will purchase less and wait for the decline. One sees this effect of expectations of future price changes often. "We'd better buy before the price goes up" is a common reason for purchasing items during a clearance sale. Or, "Let's put off buying that flat-screen TV until the postholiday sales."

In general, it is difficult to forecast the future, but sometimes consumers know quite a bit about whether the price of a good will rise or fall, and they react accordingly. Thus, demand increases if people expect the *future* price of the good to rise. And demand decreases if people expect the *future* price of the good to fall.

In 1995, President Clinton threatened a 100 percent tariff (tax) on some luxury cars produced in Japan. This resulted in an immediate increase in demand for these cars, since buyers were afraid they would become too expensive after the tariff was imposed.

Prices of Closely Related Goods. A change in the price of a closely related good can increase or decrease demand for another good, depending on whether the good is a substitute or a complement. A **substitute** is a good that provides some of the same uses or enjoyment as another good. Butter and margarine are substitutes. In general, the demand for a good will increase if the price of a substitute for the good rises, and the demand for a good will decrease if the price of a substitute falls. Sales of CDs and downloaded music are substitutes. You would therefore expect a decrease in the price of downloaded music to decrease the demand for CDs. This may help

substitute: a good that has many of the same characteristics as, and can be used in place of, another good.

Substitutes and Complements
Music CDs and downloaded music are examples of substitutes; they share similar characteristics. You would expect, therefore, that a rise in the price of CDs would result in an increase in the sale of downloaded music—and vice versa. SUVs and gasoline are examples of complements; they tend to be consumed together. With an increase in gasoline prices in 2004 and 2005, consumers were less eager to purchase SUVs, and their sales declined.

explain why the recording industry filed lawsuits against users of online file-sharing software in 2003.

A **complement** is a good that tends to be consumed together with another good. Gasoline and SUVs are complements. The rapid increase in gasoline prices in 2004 and 2005 led to a decrease in demand for SUVs.

complement: a good that is usually consumed or used together with another good.

Movements Along versus Shifts of the Demand Curve

We have shown that the demand curve can shift, and we have given many possible reasons for such shifts. As you begin to use demand curves, it is very important that you be able to distinguish *shifts* of the demand curve from *movements along* the demand curve. This distinction is illustrated in Figure 3.

A *movement along* the demand curve occurs when the quantity demanded changes as a result of a *change in the price of the good.* For example, if the price of bicycles rises, causing the quantity demanded by consumers to fall, then there is a movement along the demand curve. You can see in Figure 3 that at point *A*, the price is $200 and the quantity demanded is 9 million. Now suppose the price rises to $220. Then the quantity demanded falls from 9 million to 7 million. This can be shown as a movement along the demand curve for bicycles from point *A* to point *B*. Conversely, if the price of a bicycle falls to $180, then the quantity demanded will increase to 11 million bicycles. This can be shown as an increase from point *A* to point *C* in Figure 3. Economists refer to a movement along the demand curve as a *change in the quantity demanded.*

A *shift* of the demand curve, on the other hand, occurs if there is a change that is due to *any source except the price.* Remember, the term *demand* refers to the entire curve or schedule relating price and quantity demanded, while the term *quantity demanded* refers to a single point on the demand curve. As we discussed earlier, if there was an increase in warm weather, people would be more likely to buy bicycles at any given price. This means that the entire demand curve would shift to the right. On the other hand, the elimination of bicycle lanes would make people less likely to buy bicycles at any given price. The entire demand curve would shift to the left. When the demand curve shifts, economists say that there is a *change in demand.*

You should be able to tell whether an economic event causes (1) a change in demand or (2) a change in the quantity demanded; or, equivalently, (1) a shift in the demand curve or (2) a movement along the demand curve. Here's an example to test your understanding of demand shifts and movement along the demand curve. In 2001, Disney's theme park attendance was lower than in previous years as a result of

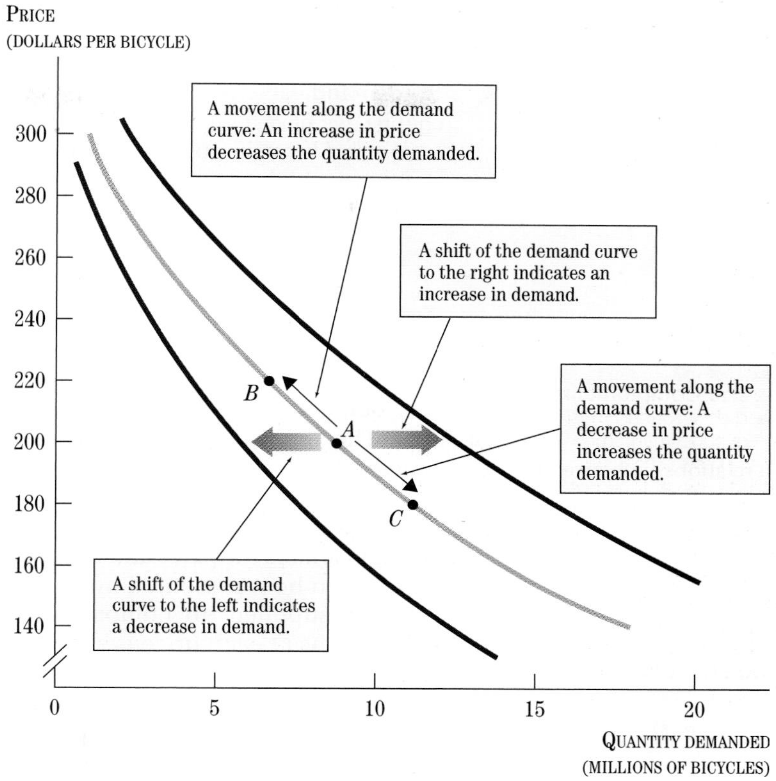

FIGURE 3
Shifts of versus Movements Along the Demand Curve
A *shift* of the demand curve occurs when there is a change in something (other than the good's own price) that affects the quantity of a good that consumers are willing to buy. An increase in demand is a shift to the right of the demand curve. A decrease in demand is a shift to the left of the demand curve. A *movement along* the demand curve occurs when the price of the good changes, causing the quantity demanded to change, as, for example, from point *A* to point *B* or *C*.

the weak economy. Because of the fall in attendance, Disney lowered the adult admission price at its California Adventure park, which helped increase attendance. Which of these was a *change in demand* and which was a *change in the quantity demanded* in the market for theme parks?

The decrease in attendance caused by the weak economy in 2001 was a decrease in demand—fewer people were going to theme parks in 2001 than in prior years for any given ticket price. The demand curve for theme park visits thus shifted to the left. When Disney lowered its admission price, it hoped to entice more people to spend their money on a trip to its California Adventure park instead of on other goods. This is an increase in the quantity demanded—the park management anticipated more attendance at a lower price. This was a movement along the demand curve for theme park visits.

REVIEW

- Demand is a negative relationship between the price of a good and the quantity demanded, all other things being equal.
- The demand curve slopes down because when the price of a good rises, consumers are less likely to use their scarce resources to buy that good. Conversely, when the price of a good falls, some consumers who previously had

not chosen to buy the good because the price was too high may decide to buy the good.

- It is important to distinguish shifts of the demand curve from movements along the demand curve. When the quantity demanded changes as a result of a price change, we have a movement along the demand curve. When there is a change in demand brought about by something other than a price change, there is a shift in the demand curve.

SUPPLY

supply: a relationship between **price** and **quantity supplied.**

quantity supplied: the quantity of a good that firms are willing to sell at a given price.

Whereas demand refers to the behavior of consumers, supply refers to the behavior of firms. The term *supply*—whether it is the supply of tickets or the supply of computers—has a very specific meaning for economists. **Supply** is a relationship between two variables: (1) *the price of a particular good* and (2) *the quantity of the good that firms are willing to sell at that price,* all other things being the same. For short, we call the first variable the **price** and the second variable the **quantity supplied.**

Supply can be represented by a numerical table or by a graph. An example of the quantity supplied (in millions of bicycles) in the entire market by bicycle-producing firms at each price is shown in Table 2. For example, at a price of $180, the quantity supplied is 7 million bicycles. Observe that as the price increases, the quantity supplied increases, and that as the price decreases, the quantity supplied decreases. For example, if the price rises from $180 to $200, the quantity supplied increases from 7 to 9 million bicycles. The relationship between price and quantity supplied in Table 2 is called a **supply schedule.** The relationship shows price and quantity supplied moving in the same direction, and this is an example of the law of supply. The **law of supply** says that the higher the price, the higher the quantity supplied; and the lower the price, the lower the quantity supplied. In other words, the law of supply says that the price and the quantity supplied are positively related, all other things being equal.

TABLE 2
Supply Schedule for Bicycles (millions of bicycles per year)

Price	Quantity Supplied
$140	1
$160	4
$180	7
$200	9
$220	11
$240	13
$260	15
$280	16
$300	17

The Supply Curve

supply schedule: a tabular presentation of supply showing the price and quantity supplied of a particular good, all else being equal.

law of supply: the tendency for the quantity supplied of a good in a market to increase as its price rises.

supply curve: a graph of supply showing the upward-sloping relationship between price and quantity supplied.

We can represent the supply schedule in Table 2 graphically by plotting the price and quantity supplied on a graph, as shown in Figure 4. The scales of each axis in Figure 4 are exactly the same as those in Figure 1, except that Figure 4 shows the quantity supplied, whereas Figure 1 shows the quantity demanded. Each pair of numbers in Table 2 is plotted as a point in Figure 4. The resulting curve showing all the combinations of prices and quantities supplied is the **supply curve.** Note that the curve slopes upward: At a price of $280, the quantity supplied is high—16 million bicycles. If the price were $160 a bicycle, then firms would be willing to sell only 4 million bicycles.

Why does the supply curve slope upward? Imagine yourself running a firm that produces and sells bicycles. If the price of the bicycles goes up from $180 to $280, then you can earn $100 more for each bicycle you produce and sell. Given your production costs, if you earn more from each bicycle, you will have a greater incentive to produce and sell more bicycles. If producing more bicycles increases the costs of producing each bicycle, perhaps because you must pay the bike assembly workers a higher wage for working overtime, the higher price will give you the incentive to incur these costs. Other bicycle firms will be thinking the same way. Thus, firms are

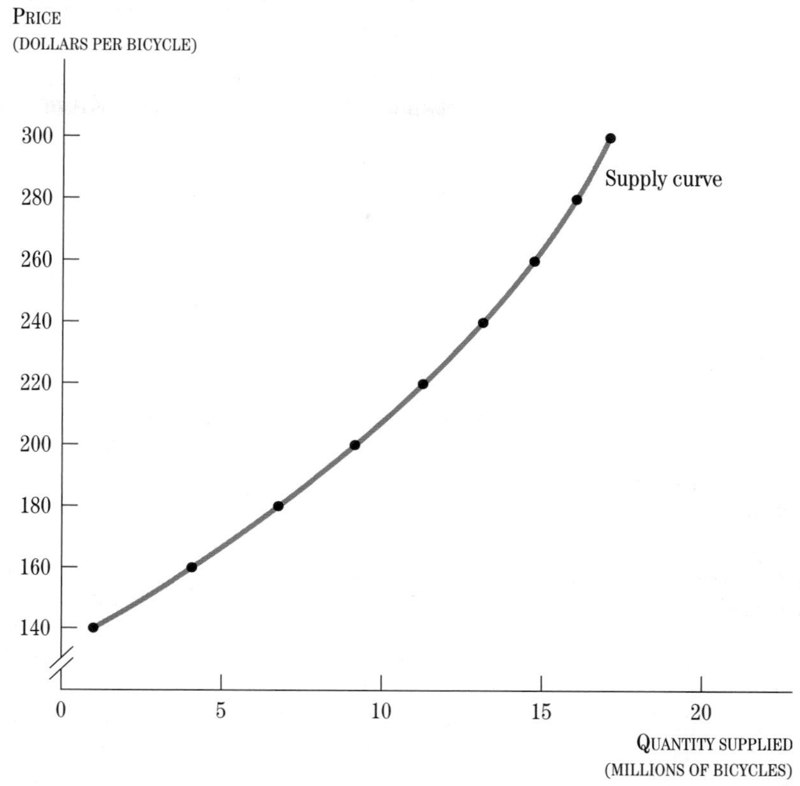

FIGURE 4
The Supply Curve
The supply curve shows that the price and the quantity supplied by firms in the market are positively related. The curve slopes up. For each price on the vertical axis, the supply curve shows the quantity that firms are willing to sell along the horizontal axis. The points along the supply curve for bicycles match the pairs of numbers in Table 2.

willing to sell more bicycles as the price rises. Conversely, the incentive for firms to sell bicycles will decline as the price falls. Basically, that is why there is a positive relationship between price and quantity supplied.

When formulating economic policy, it is important to remember this supply relationship. When the price of a good increases, it leads to an increase in the quantity supplied. If U.S. agricultural policy results in the U.S. government offering to pay farmers a higher price for their corn, then the farmers will respond by increasing their production of corn. If there is a collapse in coffee prices on the world market, some coffee farmers in developing countries will switch to producing other crops instead of coffee.

Shifts in Supply

The supply curve is a relationship between price and the quantity supplied drawn on the assumption that all other things are held constant. If any one of these other things changes, then the supply curve shifts. For example, suppose a new machine is invented that makes it possible to produce bicycle frames at less cost; then firms would have more incentive at any given price to produce and sell more bicycles. Supply would increase; the supply curve would shift to the right.

Figure 5 shows that the supply curve for bicycles would shift to the right because of a new cost-reducing machine. The supply curve would shift to the left if there were

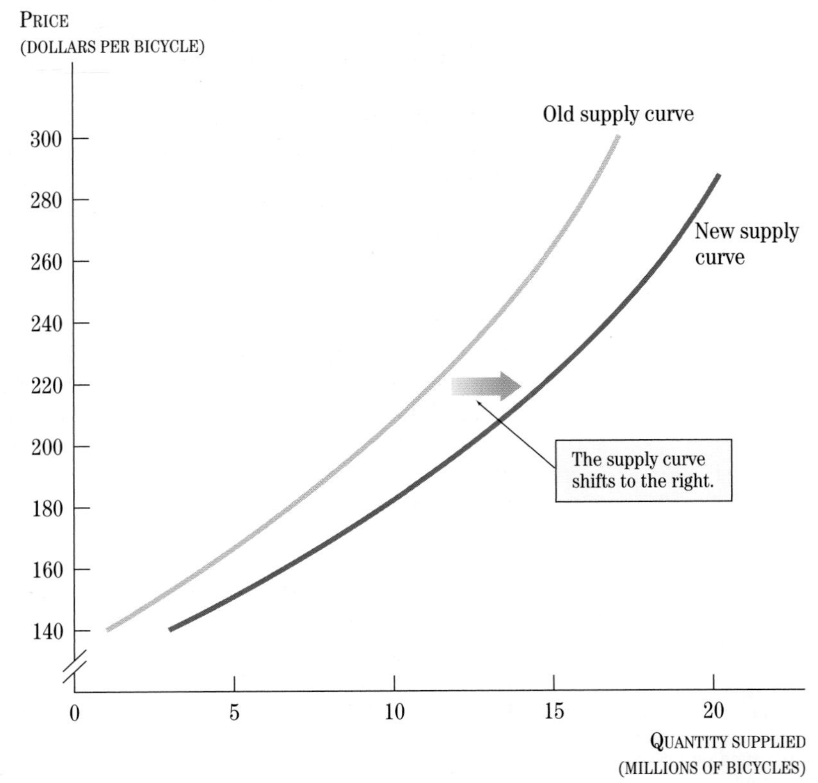

FIGURE 5
A Shift in the Supply Curve
The supply curve is a relationship between the quantity supplied of a good and the price of the good, all other things being equal. A change in one of these other things (other than the good's price) will shift the supply curve, as shown in the graph. In this case, the supply of bicycles increases; the supply curve for bicycles shifts to the right.

a decrease in supply. Supply would decrease, for example, if bicycle-producing firms suddenly found that their existing machines would break down unless they were oiled with an expensive lubricant each time a bicycle was produced. This would raise costs, lower supply, and shift the supply curve to the left.

Many things can cause the supply curve to shift. Most of these can be categorized by the source of the change in supply: *technology, weather conditions, the price of inputs used in production, the number of firms in the market, expectations of future prices,* and *government taxes, subsidies, and regulations.* Let us briefly consider the sources of shifts in supply.

Technology. Anything that changes the amount a firm can produce with a given amount of inputs to production can be considered a change in technology. The Harbour Report, a study that examines the number of labor hours needed to produce an automobile, calculated that in 2005, General Motors needed 34 hours per vehicle, while Toyota needed only 28 hours per vehicle. Suppose an improvement in technology enabled General Motors to reduce the time it took to produce a car by 6 hours per vehicle. This improvement in technology would correspond to an increase in supply, a shift in the supply curve to the right. Another way of viewing an increase in supply is that producers are willing to sell any given quantity at a lower price than before. This makes sense, since production costs are lower with the improvement in technology.

Weather Conditions. Droughts, earthquakes, and hurricanes also affect how much of certain types of goods can be produced with given inputs. A drought can reduce the amount of wheat that can be produced on a farm in the Midwest. An unusually cold winter in 2006 destroyed over a billion dollars worth of citrus fruit in California. Hurricanes Katrina and Rita disrupted oil drilling and refining activities in Texas and Louisiana. Because such events change the amount that can be produced with a given amount of inputs, they are similar to changes in technology. In the examples just given, the supply curve shifted to the left, although you could have favorable weather conditions that would shift the supply curve for a particular good to the right.

The Price of Inputs Used in Production. If the prices of the inputs to production—raw materials, labor, and capital—increase, then it becomes more costly to produce goods, and firms will produce less at any given price; the supply curve will shift to the left. When the U.S government imposed trade restrictions that caused the price of imported steel to rise in 2002, firms that used imported steel to produce household appliances were unwilling to produce the same quantity of appliances at existing price levels. So an increase in production costs causes the supply curve to shift to the left, and a decrease in production costs causes the supply curve to shift to the right.

The Number of Firms in the Market. Remember that the supply curve refers to *all* the firms producing the product. If the number of firms increases, then more goods will be produced at each price; supply increases, and the supply curve shifts to the right. A decline in the number of firms, on the other hand, would shift the supply curve to the left. For example, if a country removes barriers that prevent foreign car manufacturers from selling cars to the domestic market, then the number of firms producing cars for that country's domestic market will increase, and the supply curve for cars in that economy will shift to the right.

Expectations of Future Prices. If firms expect the price of the good they produce to rise in the future, then they will hold off selling at least part of their production until the price rises. For example, farmers in the United States who anticipate an increase in wheat prices because of political turbulence in Russia may decide to store more wheat in silos and sell it later, after the price rises. Thus, expectations of *future* price increases tend to reduce supply. Conversely, expectations of *future* price decreases tend to increase supply.

Government Taxes, Subsidies, and Regulations. The government has the ability to affect the supply of particular goods produced by firms. For example, the government imposes taxes on firms to pay for such government services as education, police, and national defense. These taxes increase firms' costs and reduce supply. The supply curve shifts to the left when a tax on what firms sell in the market increases.

The government also makes payments—subsidies—to firms to encourage those firms to produce certain goods. Such subsidies have the opposite effect of taxes on supply. An increase in subsidies reduces firms' costs and increases the supply. If the U.S. government provided subsidies for corn production to encourage the use of ethanol, an alternative fuel for cars that is produced from corn, this would increase the production of corn. On the other hand, when the U.S. government imposes a tax on cigarettes, there will be a decrease in the supply of cigarettes.

Governments also regulate firms. In some cases, such regulations can change the firms' costs of production or their ability to produce goods and thereby affect supply. For example, if a city government decides that only vendors who successfully

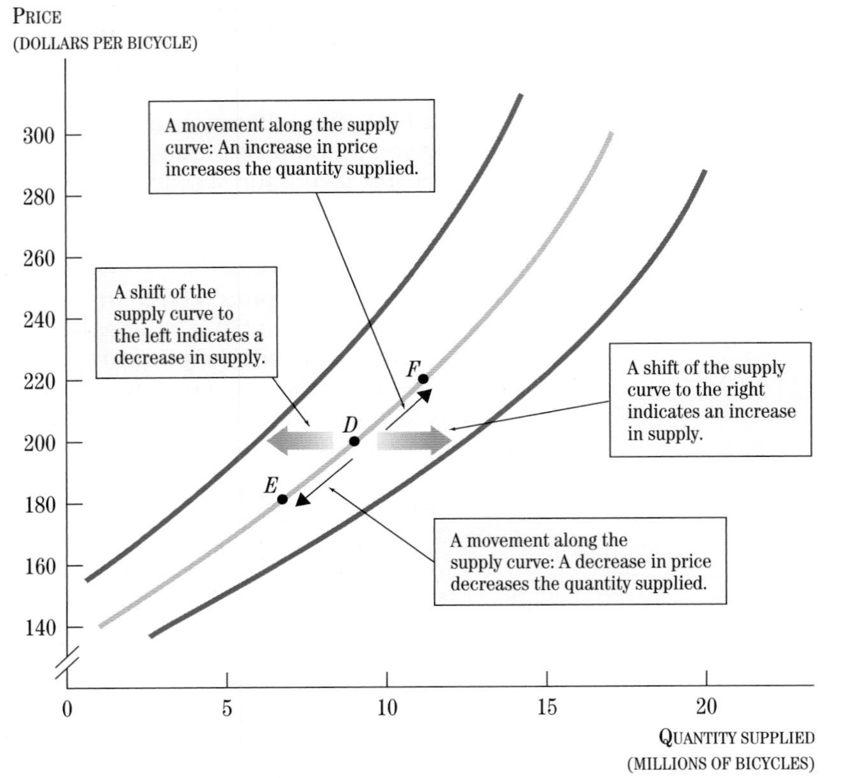

FIGURE 6
Shifts of versus Movements Along the Supply Curve
A *shift* of the supply curve occurs when there is a change in something (other than the price) that affects the amount of a good that firms are willing to supply. An increase in supply is a shift to the right of the supply curve. A decrease in supply is a shift to the left of the supply curve. A movement along the supply curve occurs when the price of the good changes, causing the quantity supplied by firms to change—for example, from point *D* to point *E* or *F*.

pass a health and sanitation inspection are allowed to sell food from street carts, the supply curve for street-vendor food will shift to the left.

Movements Along versus Shifts of the Supply Curve

As with the demand curve, it is very important that you understand how to distinguish between *shifts* of the supply curve and *movements along* the supply curve. This distinction is illustrated in Figure 6.

A *movement along* the supply curve occurs when the quantity supplied changes as a result of a *change in the price of the good.* For example, if a copper mine in Zambia increases its production because the price of copper has increased on the world market, that is a movement along the supply curve. In our bicycle example, an increase in the price of bicycles from $200 to $220 would increase the quantity supplied from 9 million bicycles to 11 million bicycles. This can be shown as a movement along the supply curve for bicycles from point *D* to point *F*. Conversely, if the price of a bicycle were to fall from $200 to $180, then the quantity supplied would decrease to 7 million bicycles. This can be shown as movement from point *D* to point *E* in Figure 6. Economists refer to a movement along the supply curve as a *change in the quantity supplied.*

A *shift* of the supply curve, on the other hand, occurs if there is a change due to *any source except the price.* An unexpected winter freeze in California will mean that farmers will be able to produce fewer oranges at any given price. This means that the supply curve of oranges will shift to the left. When the supply curve shifts, economists say that there is a *change in supply*.

You should be able to tell whether a change in something causes (1) a change in supply or (2) a change in the quantity supplied; or, equivalently, (1) a shift in the supply curve or (2) a movement along the supply curve. Here's an example to test your ability to distinguish between movement along a supply curve and a shift in the supply curve. Suppose that U.S. agricultural policy guarantees farmers a specific price on certain crops. An economist suggested that the government should instead pay farmers to not plant some of their fields. Which policy is describing a *change in supply* and which is describing a *change in the quantity supplied* in the market for corn?

A policy that pays farmers to leave cornfields unplanted describes a decrease in supply. The amount of corn supplied will be lower at any price. When the U.S. government guarantees the price of corn, this describes an increase in the quantity supplied—more corn will be grown in anticipation of the higher price. The increase in price leading to an increase in quantity supplied corresponds to movement along the supply curve.

REVIEW

- Supply is a positive relationship between the price of a good and the quantity supplied of the good by firms.
- The supply curve slopes upward because, all else equal, a higher price offers greater incentive for a firm to produce and sell more goods.
- It is important to distinguish shifts of the supply curve from movements along the supply curve. When the quantity supplied changes because of a change in price, we have a movement along the supply curve. Other factors—such as technology, weather, the number of firms, and expectations—can lead to a shift in the supply curve.

MARKET EQUILIBRIUM: COMBINING SUPPLY AND DEMAND

Figure 7 summarizes what you have learned thus far about consumers' demand for goods in a market and firms' supply of goods in a market. Now we put supply and demand together to complete the supply and demand model. Consumers who want to buy goods and firms that want to sell goods interact in a market. When consumers and firms interact, a price is determined at which the transaction occurs. Recall that a market does not need to be located at one place; the U.S. bicycle market consists of all the bicycle firms that sell bicycles and all the consumers who buy bicycles.

Fascinatingly, no single person or firm determines the price in the market. Instead, the market determines the price. As buyers and sellers interact, prices may go up for a while and then go down. Alfred Marshall, the economist who did the most to develop the supply and demand model in the late nineteenth century, called this process the "higgling and bargaining" of the market. The assumption underlying the supply and demand model is that, in the give and take of the marketplace, prices adjust until they settle down at a level where the quantity supplied by firms equals the quantity demanded by consumers. Let's see how.

SUPPLY

Supply describes firms.

The supply curve looks like this:

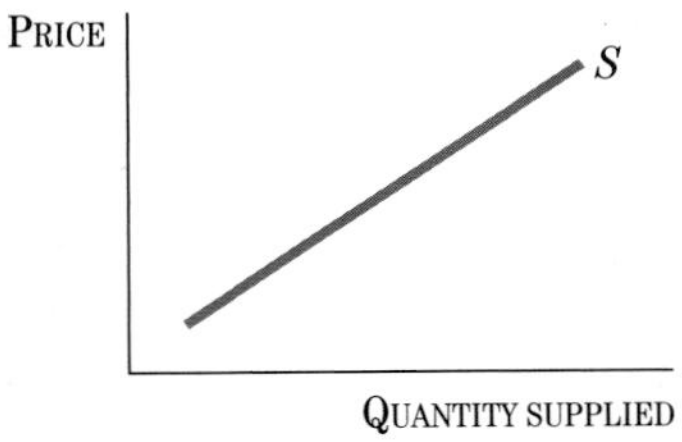

Law of Supply

Price and quantity supplied are positively related.

Movements along supply curve occur

when price rises and quantity supplied rises
or
when price falls and quantity supplied falls.

Shifts in supply are due to:

Technology (new inventions)

Weather (especially for agricultural products)

Number of firms in market

Price of goods used in production (inputs such as fertilizer, labor)

Expectations of future prices (firms will sell less now if prices are expected to rise; for example, farmers may store goods to sell next year)

Government taxes, subsidies, regulations (commodity taxes, agricultural subsidies, safety regulations)

DEMAND

Demand describes consumers.

The demand curve looks like this:

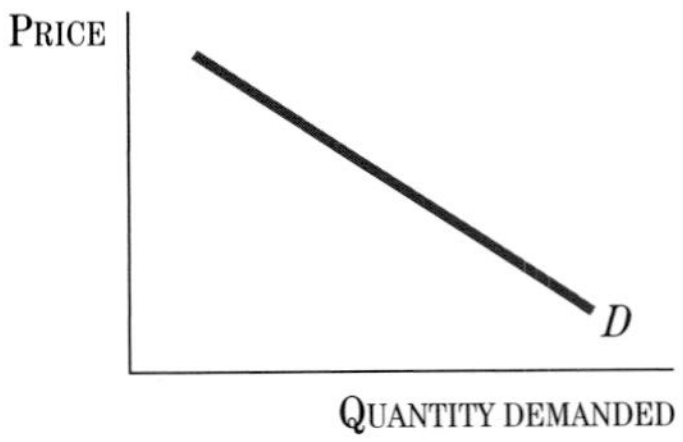

Law of Demand

Price and quantity demanded are negatively related.

Movements along demand curve occur

when price rises and quantity demanded falls
or
when price falls and quantity demanded rises.

Shifts in demand are due to:

Preferences (changes in consumers' tastes)

Number of consumers in market

Consumers' information (about smoking, or faulty products, for example)

Consumers' income (normal goods versus inferior goods)

Expectations of future prices (consumers will buy more now if prices are expected to rise in the future)

Price of related goods (both substitutes, like butter and margarine, and complements, like gasoline and SUVs)

FIGURE 7
Overview of Supply and Demand

Determination of the Market Price

To determine the market price, we combine the demand relationship with the supply relationship. We can do this using either a table or a diagram. First consider Table 3, which combines the demand schedule from Table 1 with the supply schedule from Table 2. The price is in the first column, the quantity demanded by consumers is in the second column, and the quantity supplied by firms is in the third column. Observe that the quantity that consumers are willing to buy is shown to decline with the price, while the quantity that firms are willing to sell is shown to increase with the price.

TABLE 3
Finding the Market Equilibrium

Quantity supplied equals quantity demanded. → $200 row

Price	Quantity Demanded	Quantity Supplied	Shortage, Surplus, or Equilibrium	Price Rises or Falls
$140	18	1	Shortage = 17	Price rises
$160	14	4	Shortage = 10	Price rises
$180	11	7	Shortage = 4	Price rises
$200	9	9	Equilibrium	No change
$220	7	11	Surplus = 4	Price falls
$240	5	13	Surplus = 8	Price falls
$260	3	15	Surplus = 12	Price falls
$280	2	16	Surplus = 14	Price falls
$300	1	17	Surplus = 16	Price falls

Finding the Market Price. Pick a price in Table 3, any price. Suppose the price you choose is $160. Then the quantity demanded by consumers (14 million bicycles) is greater than the quantity supplied by firms (4 million bicycles). In other words, there is a shortage of 14 − 4 = 10 million bicycles. A **shortage,** or **excess demand,** is a situation in which the quantity demanded is greater than the quantity supplied. With a shortage of bicycles, buyers who really need a bicycle will start to offer to pay more to acquire a bicycle, while firms that are faced with an abundance of potential customers wanting to buy their bicycles will begin to charge higher prices. Thus, $160 cannot last as the market price. Observe that as the price rises above $160, the quantity demanded falls and the quantity supplied rises. Thus, as the price rises, the shortage begins to decrease. Suppose the price increases to $180. At that price, the quantity demanded falls to 11 million bicycles and the quantity supplied rises to 7 million bicycles. There is still a shortage and the price will still rise, but the shortage is now much less, at 11 − 7 = 4 million bicycles. The shortage will disappear only when the price rises to $200, as shown in Table 3.

shortage (excess demand): a situation in which quantity demanded is greater than quantity supplied.

Suppose instead that you had picked a price above $200, let's say $260. Then the quantity demanded by consumers (3 million bicycles) is less than the quantity supplied by firms (15 million bicycles). In other words, there is a surplus of 12 million bicycles. A **surplus,** or **excess supply,** is a situation in which the quantity supplied is greater than the quantity demanded. With a surplus of bicycles, buyers who really need a bicycle have an abundance of sellers who are eager to sell them a bicycle, while firms have to compete with one another to entice buyers for their products. Therefore, the price of bicycles will fall: Firms that are willing to sell bicycles for less than $260 will offer to sell to consumers at lower prices. Thus, $260 cannot be the market price either. Observe that as the price falls below $260, the quantity demanded rises and the quantity supplied falls. Thus, the surplus decreases. If you choose any price above $200, the same thing will happen: There will be a surplus, and the price will fall. The surplus disappears only when the price falls to $200.

surplus (excess supply): a situation in which quantity supplied is greater than quantity demanded.

Thus, we have shown that for any price below $200, there is a shortage, and the price rises; while for any price above $200, there is a surplus, and the price falls. What if the market price is $200? Then the quantity supplied equals the quantity demanded; there is neither a shortage nor a surplus, and there is no reason for the price to rise or fall. This price of $200 is called the **equilibrium price** because at this price the quantity supplied equals the quantity demanded, and there is no tendency for the

equilibrium price: the price at which quantity supplied equals quantity demanded.

ECONOMICS IN THE NEWS

Why Roses Cost More on Valentine's Day

This article, which appeared in the *New York Times* in 1999, describes why the price of roses rises as Valentine's Day approaches. You will find that applications of the supply and demand model are scattered throughout the article.

The Big City; By Any Name, A Rose Is Dear As a Valentine

By JOHN TIERNEY

NEW YORKERS are in luck this week. Unlike other Americans, who are forced to shop for Valentine's Day without any official guidance, we have the annual rose survey from the Department of Consumer Affairs.

Jules Polonetsky, the agency's Commissioner, called a news conference to reveal that local florists raise the price of roses by about 33 percent for Valentine's Day. This correlation between price and demand might seem inevitable to some people—anyone, say, who has opened an economics textbook—but Mr. Polonetsky will not stand for it.

If the arrival of Valentine's Day causes demand to increase, then the price will rise.

Besides lamenting the price increases, he has developed a strategy to help New Yorkers avoid, as he put it, "seeing red this Valentine's Day." Pointing to a critical discovery made by his agency's investigators—that different florists in New York charge different prices—he outlined a technique for buying flowers. "Consumers," he explained, "can save significantly by choosing one florist over another."

Could this particular strategy—the technical term is "shopping"—have applications even beyond Valentine's Day roses? Possibly, although the Commissioner did not elaborate. Nor did he address another question raised by his agency's research: do the investigators at the Department of Consumer Affairs have a little too much time on their hands?

New Yorkers depend on the consumer agency to enforce laws against fraud, but they generally manage to deal with honest merchants all by themselves. They could probably survive without any of the agency's seasonal price surveys—roses on Valentine's Day, gasoline on Memorial Day, turkey at Thanksgiving, gefilte fish at Passover.

Other examples where the demand for a particular good rises at a specific time of the year

These rituals have given Mr. Polonetsky and his predecessors publicity as they wail against seasonal price increases, but consumers do not necessarily benefit. If florists didn't raise prices at Valentine's Day, consumers would suffer in two ways.

equilibrium quantity: the quantity traded at the equilibrium price.

market equilibrium: the situation in which the price is equal to the equilibrium price and the quantity traded equals the equilibrium quantity.

price to change. There is no other price for which quantity supplied equals quantity demanded. If you look at all the other prices, you will see that there is either a shortage or a surplus, and thus there is a tendency for the price to either rise or fall.

The quantity bought and sold at the equilibrium price is 9 million bicycles. This is the **equilibrium quantity.** When the price equals the equilibrium price and the quantity bought and sold equals the equilibrium quantity, we say that there is a **market equilibrium.**

First, many cost-conscious New Yorkers who now order other flowers for Valentine's Day—because their partners aren't fanatical about getting roses—would start ordering them, so there wouldn't be enough roses to meet the increased demand. As a result, some rose fanatics would have to do without.

As price rises, the quantity demanded falls. Only those who really value giving roses, instead of other flowers or chocolate, to their Valentine will end up buying roses at the higher price.

Second, the customers who buy roses at other times of the year would end up paying artificially high prices to subsidize the customers on Valentine's Day. There's a good reason that prices are higher this week: the roses cost extra to grow and ship.

To meet this annual peak in demand, growers in the United States, Colombia, Ecuador and Holland must prune their bushes in the late fall to start new growth in time for Valentine's Day. "By pruning, you're cutting off a lot of roses that would have bloomed before Valentine's Day," Jim Lebberes, the president of Kiamos and Tooker, a flower wholesaler in the Bronx, explained. "So you're sacrificing a lot of production, and you need to recover that lost income somehow."

A higher price increases the quantity supplied as growers reorganize their production schedule to get roses to market in early February.

Then there's the cost of shipping. "Let's say there are five regularly scheduled cargo planes that leave Bogota for Miami and New York every night," Mr. Lebberes said. "They fly north with flowers and return south with other cargo. Now suddenly for Valentine's Day you need to charter another 15 planes, and those planes fly back empty, because there's no corresponding increase in demand for southbound cargo. So each one of those roses is costing you a round-trip ticket."

February is not a good time of the year to grow roses in North America—the roses have to be shipped in from South America. The high transportation cost means that supply can't rise to meet all of the increased demand.

When you add these wholesale costs to the extra expenses at the retail level, like overtime pay for employees, the 33-percent increase doesn't sound unreasonable. In fact, it may reflect a phenomenon that economists call the "good-will factor." This phenomenon was demonstrated after Hurricane Andrew hit Miami in 1992 and created a shortage of plywood. Lumber companies refused to raise their prices, forgoing an easy profit because they were afraid they'd offend their long-term customers.

New York's florists presumably show some of the same restraint on Valentine's Day to maintain their customers' good will. With more careful investigation next year, Mr. Polontesky could probably call a press conference the week of Valentine Day's and announce that rose prices are too low. That may not sound immediately appealing to him. But it would definitely be newsworthy.

Our discussion of the determination of the equilibrium price shows how the market price coordinates the buying and selling decisions of many firms and consumers. We see that the price serves a *rationing function*. When there is a shortage, a higher price reduces the quantity demanded and increases the quantity supplied to eliminate the shortage. Similarly, when there is a surplus, a lower price increases the quantity demanded and decreases the quantity supplied to eliminate the surplus. Thus, both shortages and surpluses are eliminated by the forces of supply and demand.

Two Predictions. By combining supply and demand, we have completed the supply and demand model. The model can be applied to many markets, not just the example of the bicycle market. One prediction of the supply and demand model is that *the equilibrium price in the market will be the price for which the quantity supplied equals the quantity demanded.* Thus, the model provides an answer to the question of what determines the price in the market. Another prediction of the model is that *the equilibrium quantity bought and sold in the market is the quantity for which the quantity supplied equals the quantity demanded.*

Finding the Equilibrium with a Supply and Demand Diagram

The equilibrium price and quantity in a market can also be found with the help of a graph. Figure 8 combines the demand curve from Figure 1 and the supply curve from Figure 4 in the same diagram. Observe that the downward-sloping demand curve intersects the upward-sloping supply curve at a single point. At that point of intersection, the quantity supplied equals the quantity demanded. Hence, the *equilibrium price is at the intersection of the supply curve and the demand curve.* The equilibrium price of $200 is shown in Figure 8. At that price, the quantity demanded is 9 million bicycles, and the quantity supplied is 9 million bicycles. This is the equilibrium quantity.

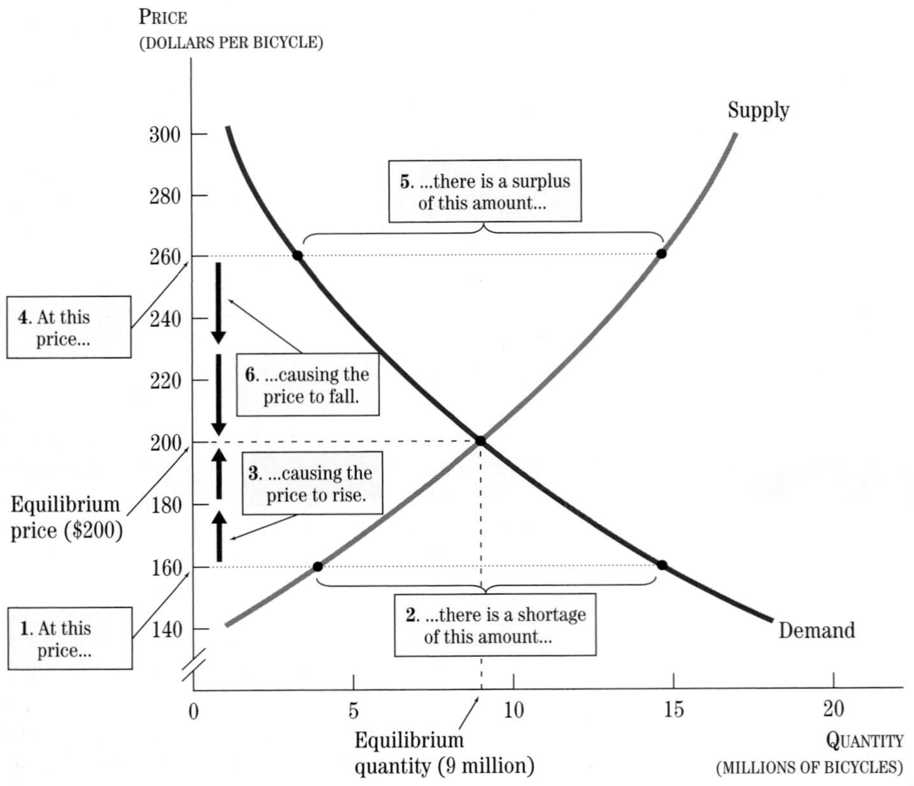

FIGURE 8
Equilibrium Price and Equilibrium Quantity
When buyers and sellers interact in the market, the equilibrium price is at the point of intersection of the supply curve and the demand curve. At this point, the quantity supplied equals the quantity demanded. The equilibrium quantity is also determined at that point. At a higher price, the quantity demanded will be less than the quantity supplied; there will be a surplus. At a lower price, the quantity demanded will be greater than the quantity supplied; there will be a shortage.

If the price were lower than this equilibrium price, say, $160, then the quantity demanded would be greater than the quantity supplied. There would be a shortage, and there would be pressure on the price to increase, as shown in the graph. The increase in gasoline prices in 2004 and 2005 led to an increase in demand for hybrid automobiles. With a shortage of hybrid vehicles and long waiting lists, some automobile sellers increased the price of the hybrids.

On the other hand, if the price were above the equilibrium price, say, $260, then the quantity supplied would be greater than the quantity demanded. There would be a surplus, and there would be pressure on the price to fall. After September 11, 2001, a large number of vacationers cancelled vacation plans that involved air travel. Caribbean hotels, with a surplus of vacant hotel rooms following this decrease in demand, began to offer big discounts.

Thus, the market price will tend to move toward the equilibrium price at the intersection of the supply curve and the demand curve. We can calculate exactly what the equilibrium price is in Figure 8 by drawing a line over to the vertical axis. And we can calculate the equilibrium quantity by drawing a line down to the horizontal axis.

Market Outcomes When Supply or Demand Changes

Now that you know how to find the equilibrium price and quantity in a market, we can use the supply and demand model to analyze the impact of factors that change supply or demand on equilibrium price and quantity. We first consider a change in demand and then a change in supply.

Effects of a Change in Demand. Figure 9 shows the effects of a shift in the demand curve for bicycles. Suppose that a shift occurs because of a fitness craze that increases the demand for bicycles. The demand curve shifts to the right, as shown in graph (a) in Figure 9. The demand curve before the shift and the demand curve after the shift are labeled the "old demand curve" and the "new demand curve," respectively.

If you look at the graph, you can see that something must happen to the equilibrium price when the demand curve shifts. The equilibrium price is determined at the intersection of the supply curve and the demand curve. With the new demand curve, there is a new intersection and, therefore, a new equilibrium price. The equilibrium price is no longer $200 in Figure 9(a); it is up to $220 per bicycle. Thus, the supply and demand model predicts that the price in the market will rise if there is an increase in demand. Note also that there is a change in the equilibrium quantity of bicycles. The quantity of bicycles sold and bought has increased from 9 million to 11 million. Thus, the equilibrium quantity has increased along with the equilibrium price. The supply and demand model predicts that an increase in demand will raise both the price and the quantity sold in the market.

We can use the same method to find out what happens if demand decreases, as shown in graph (b) in Figure 9. Suppose that the elimination of dedicated bicycle lanes on roads shifts the demand curve for bicycles to the left. At the new intersection of the supply and demand curves, the equilibrium price is lower, and the quantity sold is also lower. Thus, the supply and demand model predicts that a decrease in demand will both lower the price and lower the quantity sold in the market.

Note in these examples that when the demand curve shifts, it leads to a movement along the supply curve. First, the demand curve shifts to the right or to the left. Then there is movement along the supply curve because the change in the price affects the quantity of bicycles that firms will sell.

Effects of a Change in Supply. Figure 10 shows what happens when there is a change in the market that shifts the supply curve. Suppose a new technology reduces

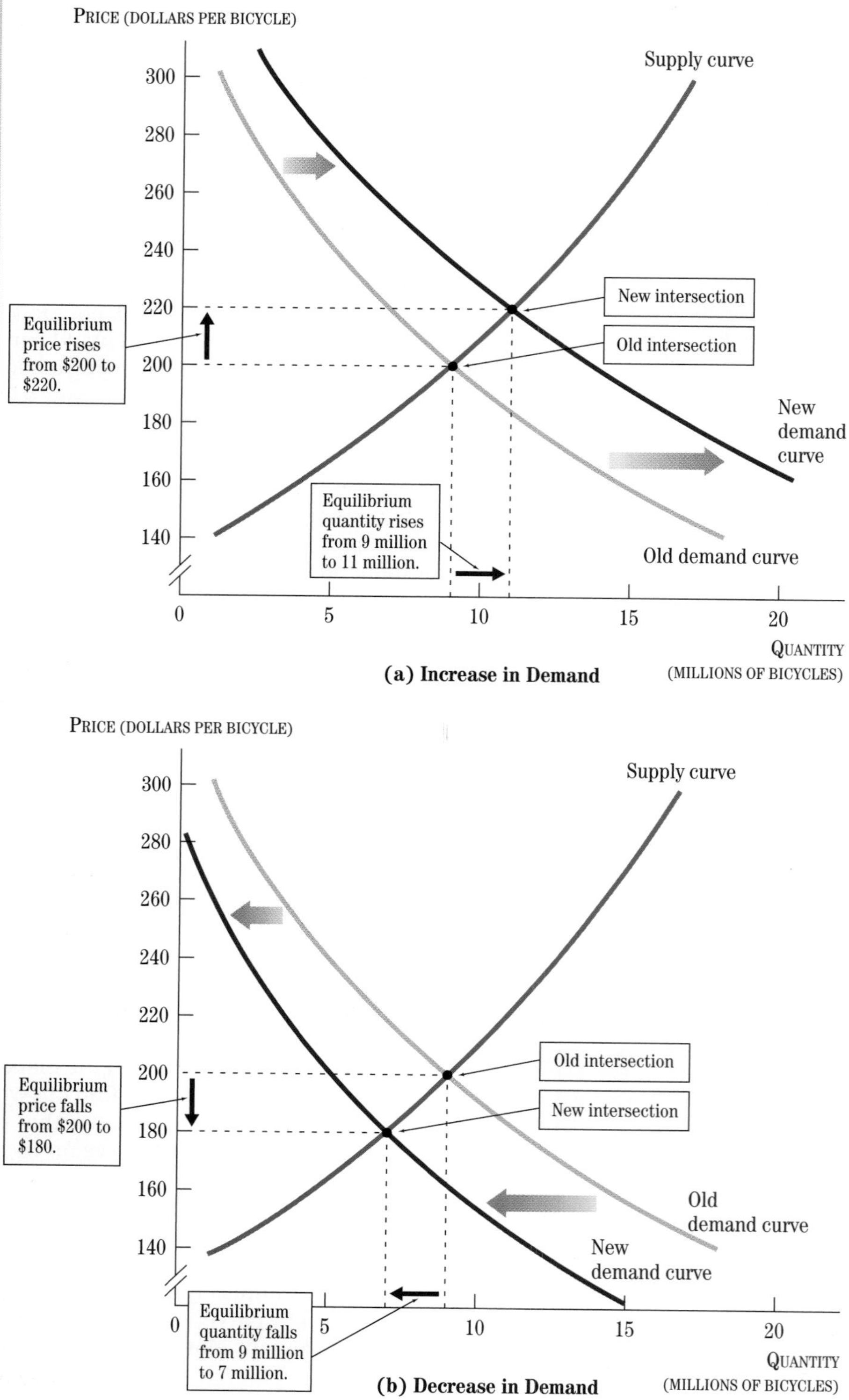

FIGURE 9
Effects of a Shift in Demand
When demand increases, as in graph (a), the demand curve shifts to the right. The equilibrium price rises, and the equilibrium quantity also rises. When demand decreases, as in graph (b), the demand curve shifts to the left. The equilibrium price falls, and the equilibrium quantity also falls.

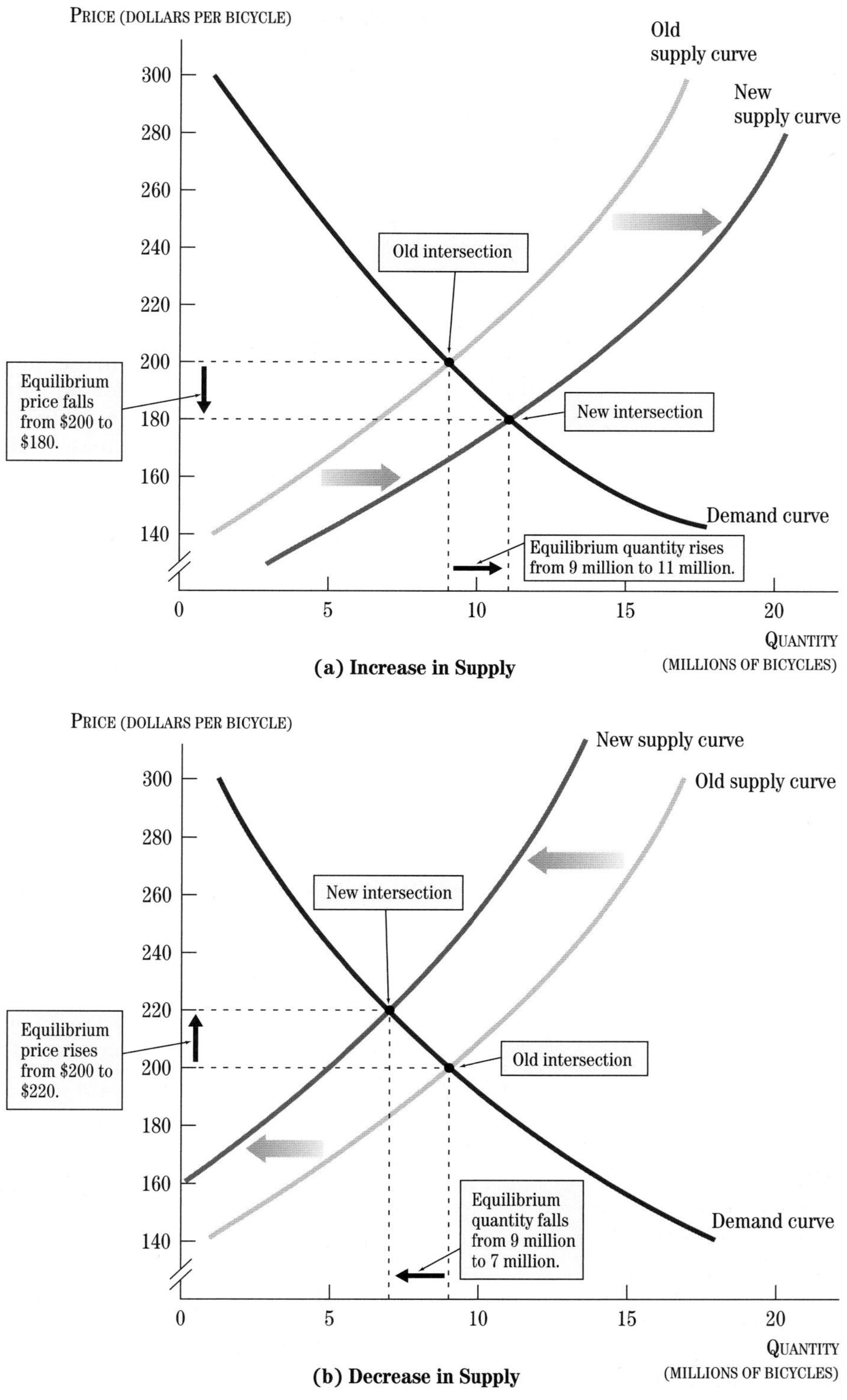

FIGURE 10
Effects of a Shift in Supply
When supply increases, as in graph (a), the supply curve shifts to the right; the equilibrium price falls, and the equilibrium quantity rises. When supply decreases, as in graph (b), the supply curve shifts to the left; the equilibrium price rises, and the equilibrium quantity falls.

TABLE 4
Effects of Shifts in Demand and Supply Curves

Shift	Effect on Equilibrium Price	Effect on Equilibrium Quantity
Increase in demand	Up	Up
Decrease in demand	Down	Down
Increase in supply	Down	Up
Decrease in supply	Up	Down

the cost of producing bicycles, resulting in the supply curve for bicycles shifting to the right. Figure 10(a) shows that there is a new equilibrium price, which is lower than the old equilibrium price. In addition, the equilibrium quantity rises. Thus, the supply and demand model predicts that an increase in the supply of bicycles will lower the price and raise the quantity of bicycles sold.

Suppose instead that an increase in the cost of bicycle tires increases the cost of producing bicycles, resulting in the supply curve for bicycles shifting to the left. Figure 10(b) shows that the equilibrium price rises, and the equilibrium quantity falls. Thus, the model predicts that a decrease in the supply of bicycles will raise the price of bicycles and lower the quantity of bicycles sold.

Table 4 summarizes the results of this analysis of shifts in the supply and demand curves.

When Both Curves Shift. The supply and demand model is easiest to use when you are analyzing a factor that shifts either demand or supply, but not both. However, in reality, it is possible for something or several different things to simultaneously shift both supply and demand. To predict whether the price or the quantity rises or falls in such cases, we need to know whether demand or supply shifts by a larger amount. Dealing with the possibility of simultaneous shifts in demand and supply curves is important in practice, as we show in the following example.

REVIEW

- The supply and demand model is used to predict the price and the quantity that result from interactions of consumers and producers in a market.
- In a market, the price will adjust upward or downward until the quantity supplied equals the quantity demanded. This price is called the equilibrium price, and the corresponding quantity is called the equilibrium quantity.
- Changes in the economy that cause the demand curve to shift to the right will raise both the equilibrium price and the equilibrium quantity. Changes that cause the demand curve to shift to the left will lower both the equilibrium price and the equilibrium quantity.
- Changes in the economy that cause the supply curve to shift to the right will lower the equilibrium price and raise the equilibrium quantity. Changes that cause the supply curve to shift to the left will raise the equilibrium price and lower the equilibrium quantity.

ECONOMICS IN ACTION

Using the Supply and Demand Model to Analyze Real-World Issues

Between January and October of 2005, a period of eight months, the average price of a gallon of gasoline in the United States rose from $1.75 to $2.92 a gallon, an increase of almost 60 percent, according to data gathered by the Department of Energy. Rising gasoline prices are of critical importance to the American people. If you own a car, rising gasoline prices have a direct impact on you—you may have to cut back on driving, or ask your parents for more money to buy gasoline, or spend less on other things because you are spending more on gasoline. Even if you do not own a car yourself, rising gasoline prices can affect you. The prices of goods and services will rise because the cost of transportation increases. Bus fares, taxi fares, and airplane tickets may all rise in price because of the high price of gasoline.

Why did the price of gasoline go up so rapidly in 2005? How long did the high price of gasoline last? What could policymakers do to lower the price of gasoline? The model of supply and demand gives us a tool to model the market for gasoline, to examine the causes of the high price, to understand the impact on the American people and American businesses, and to focus on what policymakers can do to lower the price of gasoline.

One key factor in the rising price of gasoline is that people tend to drive more as the weather gets nicer and winter turns into spring and then into summer. Furthermore, as President Bush pointed out in an April 2005 press conference, "Over the past decade, America's energy consumption has been growing about 40 times faster than our energy production." Demand for gasoline had been increasing, as more Americans were driving gas-guzzling SUVs and people were driving more miles. These factors shifted the demand curve for gasoline to the right.

On the supply side, the destruction caused by Hurricane Katrina disrupted drilling on oil rigs and shut down refineries along the Gulf Coast. This reduction in supply added to a longer-term trend whereby the supply of gasoline was being lowered as a result of a reduction in U.S. refining capacity. In addition, both stricter environmental regulations for refining gasoline and the increasing price of oil led to an increase in production costs for gasoline. All these factors combined to cause the supply of gasoline to shift to the left.

Figure 11 illustrates the events that led to the rapid increase in gasoline prices, using a supply and demand model. The equilibrium price will unambiguously be higher,

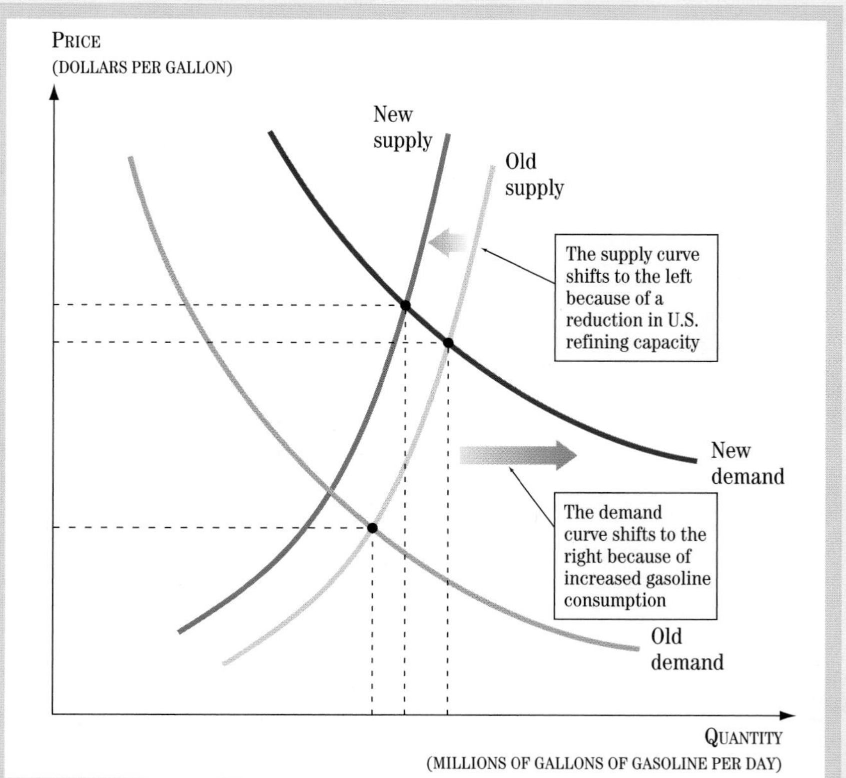

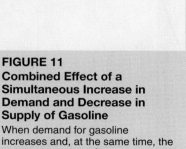

FIGURE 11
Combined Effect of a Simultaneous Increase in Demand and Decrease in Supply of Gasoline
When demand for gasoline increases and, at the same time, the supply of gasoline *decreases* because of decreased refining capacity, the supply curve will shift to the left; the equilibrium price increases, and the equilibrium quantity also increases. In this situation, the increase in demand is larger than the decrease in supply.

since the increase in demand and the decrease in supply will both tend to push the price higher. The impact on equilibrium quantity will be ambiguous, since the increase in demand would push the equilibrium quantity higher, but the decrease in supply would push equilibrium quantity lower. Figure 11 illustrates one possible outcome, where the increase in demand is larger than the decrease in supply, leading to a rise in equilibrium quantity.

How did the high price of gasoline hurt American businesses and the American people? Here are a few examples. When its earnings were lower than expected in May 2005, Wal-Mart speculated that its customers had less money to spend because of the high price of gasoline. The rising cost of gasoline caused SUV sales to be lower in 2005. Many Americans had to cut back on their summer travel plans, or cut back their spending on things other than summer travel, because of the rising price of gasoline.

What could policymakers have done to lower the price of gasoline? President Bush stressed in his press conference that Congress needed to pass an energy bill to address the high price of energy. President Bush stated, "You can't wave a magic wand. I wish I could." A magic wand won't work, but the model of supply and demand can predict what will. Policies that encourage the development of new technologies for conservation of energy and the development of new sources of energy that would reduce the demand for gasoline can help eventually decrease the equilibrium price of oil. President Bush pointed out that the best way to get the price of gasoline to fall quickly would be to encourage oil-producing nations to increase their supply of oil. An increase in the supply of oil would lead to an increase in the supply of gasoline and a reduction in its price.

Figure 12 illustrates the gasoline market with a simultaneous decrease in demand and increase in supply. Both the decrease in the demand for gasoline and the increase in the supply of gasoline would lead to a decrease in the equilibrium price of gasoline. This is a prediction that policymakers could easily make. What if they wanted to also predict the change in the consumption of gasoline resulting from this energy bill? A decrease in demand would decrease equilibrium consumption, while an increase in supply

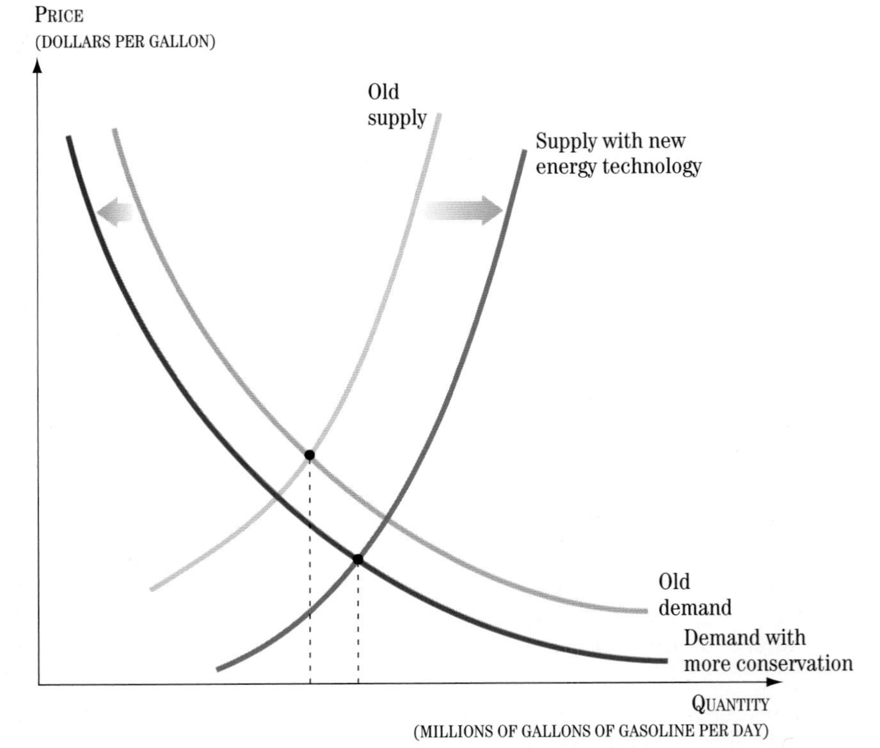

FIGURE 12
Predicted Effects of Energy Policy
The supply and demand model can also be used to predict what would happen with a successful energy policy that promoted the development of new sources of energy and energy conservation. Here, demand decreases slightly due to the effects of energy conservation, and supply increases due to the development of new technology for energy development. When demand decreases and supply increases, the equilibrium price goes down and the equilibrium quantity increases.

would increase equilibrium consumption. Policymakers therefore could not predict whether gasoline consumption would rise or fall without knowing whether demand or supply would shift by a larger amount. Figure 12 shows a resulting increase in the consumption of gasoline because the supply increase is greater in magnitude than the demand decrease.

Draw a graph yourself, but make the demand decrease larger than the supply increase. You will see a resulting decrease in the consumption of gasoline. If policymakers want an energy bill that both reduces the price of gasoline and reduces the quantity of gasoline consumed, they need to be sure that conservation efforts are the primary focus of the plan.

CONCLUSION

This chapter has shown how to use the supply and demand model to find out how equilibrium price and quantity are determined in markets where buyers and sellers interact freely. The supply and demand model is probably the most frequently used model in economics, and it has been in existence for over a hundred years in pretty much the same form as economists use it now. You will come to appreciate it more and more as you study economics.

A key feature of the model is that the equilibrium price and quantity are found at the intersection of the supply and demand curves. We can use the model to analyze how a change in factors that shift either the supply curve or the demand curve (or both) will affect equilibrium price and quantity in the market.

In later chapters we will take a closer look at the supply and demand model to understand issues like by how much equilibrium price or quantity changes when the demand curve or the supply curve shifts. We can also look at whether a market where buyers and sellers interact freely can deliver the best outcomes for society, or if there is some way to improve on those outcomes.

We will also look at the impact of price floors and price ceilings on market outcomes. This will enable you to better understand policy debates about minimum wages and rent controls.

KEY POINTS

1. Demand is a negative relationship between the price of a good and the quantity demanded by consumers. It can be shown graphically by a downward-sloping demand curve.
2. A movement along the demand curve occurs when a higher price reduces the quantity demanded or a lower price increases the quantity demanded.
3. A shift of the demand curve occurs when something besides a change in price changes the quantity of a good that people are willing to buy.
4. Supply is a positive relationship between the price of a good and the quantity supplied by firms. It can be shown graphically by an upward-sloping supply curve.
5. A movement along the supply curve occurs when a higher price increases the quantity supplied or a lower price decreases the quantity supplied.
6. A shift of the supply curve occurs when something besides a change in price changes the quantity of a good that firms are willing to sell.
7. The equilibrium price and equilibrium quantity are determined by the intersection of the supply curve and the demand curve. At this intersection point, the quantity supplied equals the quantity demanded—there are no shortages or surpluses.
8. The adjustment of prices moves the market into equilibrium. In situations where there is a shortage or an excess demand for goods, price will rise,

increasing the quantity supplied and reducing the quantity demanded. In situations where there is a surplus or an excess supply of goods, price will fall, decreasing the quantity supplied and increasing the quantity demanded.

9. We can use the supply and demand model to analyze the impact of changes in factors that move the supply curve or the demand curve or both. By shifting either the supply curve or the demand curve, observations of prices can be explained and predictions about prices can be made.
10. When the demand curve shifts to the right (left), both equilibrium price and equilibrium quantity will increase (decrease). When the supply curve shifts to the right (left), the equilibrium price will fall (rise), and the equilibrium quantity will rise (fall).

KEY TERMS

demand	demand curve	supply	shortage (excess demand)
price	normal good	quantity supplied	surplus (excess supply)
quantity demanded	inferior good	supply schedule	equilibrium price
demand schedule	substitute	law of supply	equilibrium quantity
law of demand	complement	supply curve	market equilibrium

QUESTIONS FOR REVIEW

1. Why does the demand curve slope downward?
2. Why does the supply curve slope upward?
3. What is the difference between a shift in the demand curve and a movement along the demand curve?
4. What are four things that cause a demand curve to shift?
5. What is the difference between a shift in the supply curve and a movement along the supply curve?
6. What are four things that cause a supply curve to shift?
7. How can one find the equilibrium price and equilibrium quantity?
8. What happens to the equilibrium price if the supply curve shifts to the right?
9. What happens to the equilibrium price if the demand curve shifts to the right?
10. If both the supply curve and the demand curve shift to the right, what happens to the equilibrium quantity? What about the equilibrium price?

PROBLEMS

1. For each of the following markets, indicate whether the stated change causes a shift in the supply curve, a shift in the demand curve, a movement along the supply curve, and/or a movement along the demand curve.
   a. The housing market: Consumers' incomes fall.
   b. The tea market: The price of sugar goes down.
   c. The coffee market: There is a freeze in Brazil that severely damages the coffee crop.
   d. The fast-food market: The number of fast-food restaurants in an area decreases.
   e. The peanut market in the U.S. southeast: A drought lowers supply.
2. Determine which of the following four sentences use the terminology of the supply and demand model correctly.
   a. "The price of bicycles rose, and therefore the demand for bicycles went down."
   b. "The demand for bicycles increased, and therefore the price went up."
   c. "The price of bicycles fell, decreasing the supply of bicycles."
   d. "The supply of bicycles increased, and therefore the price of bicycles fell."
3. Use the supply and demand model to explain what happens to the equilibrium price and the

equilibrium quantity for frozen yogurt in the following cases:

a. There is a large expansion in the number of firms producing frozen yogurt.
b. It is widely publicized in the press that frozen yogurt isn't more healthy for you than ice cream.
c. It is widely publicized in the press that people who eat a cup of frozen yogurt a day live to be much happier in their retirement years.
d. There is a sudden increase in the price of milk, which is used to produce frozen yogurt.
e. Frozen yogurt suddenly becomes popular because a movie idol promotes it in television commercials.

4. Suppose a decrease in consumers' incomes causes a decrease in the demand for chicken and an increase in the demand for potatoes. Which good is inferior and which is normal? How will the equilibrium price and quantity change for each good?

5. Consider the following supply and demand model of the world tea market (in billions of pounds).

Price per Pound	Quantity Supplied	Quantity Demanded
$.38	1,500	525
$.37	1,000	600
$.36	700	700
$.35	600	900
$.34	550	1,200

a. Is there a shortage or a surplus when the price is $.38? What about $.34?
b. What are the equilibrium price and the equilibrium quantity?
c. Graph the supply curve and the demand curve.
d. Show how the equilibrium price and quantity can be found on the graph.
e. If there is a shortage or surplus at a price of $.38, calculate its size in billions of pounds and show it on the graph.

6. Consider problem 5. Suppose that there is a drought in Sri Lanka that reduces the supply of tea by 400 billion pounds at every price. Suppose demand does not change.

a. Write down in a table the new supply schedule for tea.
b. Find the new equilibrium price and the new equilibrium quantity. Explain how the market adjusts to the new equilibrium.
c. Graph the new supply curve along with the old supply curve and the demand curve.
d. Show the change in the equilibrium price and the equilibrium quantity on the graph.
e. Did the equilibrium quantity change by more or less than the change in supply? Show how you arrived at your answer using both the table and the supply and demand diagram that you drew.

7. Suppose you notice that the prices of fresh fish have been rising while the amounts sold have been falling in recent years. Which of the following is the best explanation for this?

a. Consumer preferences have shifted in favor of fish because it is healthier than red meat.
b. Fishermen are prevented from using the most advanced equipment because of concerns about overfishing.
c. Consumers' incomes have risen faster than inflation.
d. Consumers have become worried about mercury levels in fish.

8. Suppose the prices of illegal drugs fall in your community at the same time that police drug seizures increase. Which is the best explanation for this?

a. Fewer drugs are being supplied locally.
b. Police arrests are removing more drug dealers.
c. Police arrests are reducing drug consumption sharply.
d. More drugs are being supplied locally.

9. In the United States, corn is often used as an ingredient in animal feed for livestock. Why does an increase in the use of corn to make ethanol, an additive that is used in gasoline, raise the price of meat? Use supply and demand curves for the corn market and the meat market to explain your answer.

10. Using the demand and supply diagrams (one for each market), show what short-run changes in price and quantity would be expected in the following markets if terrorism-related worries about air safety cause travelers to shy away from air travel. Each graph should contain the original and new demand and supply curves, and the original and new equilibrium prices and quantities. For each market, write one sentence explaining why each curve shifts or does not shift.

a. The market for air travel
b. The market for rail travel
c. The market for hotel rooms in Hawaii
d. The market for gasoline

Chapter 4

Subtleties of the Supply and Demand Model: Price Floors, Price Ceilings, and Elasticity

When the 110th Congress convened in early January of 2007, one of the first items on the legislative agenda of congressional Democrats was to pass an increase in the minimum wage from $5.15 an hour to $7.25 an hour. Supporters argued that an increase in the legally mandated minimum wage was needed to help low-income workers. Without this intervention, some workers would earn a wage that was "too low"; the higher wage would boost the incomes of these workers and help improve their lives. Opponents of the plan and skeptics argued that intervening in the labor market would not help these workers and might even end up hurting them. They pointed out that raising the minimum wage would result in some low-income workers losing their jobs. They also argued that a minimum-wage increase was a poorly targeted policy—most of the benefits would not in fact accrue to those who were truly in need. Were the supporters of the plan correct in their claim that many poor people's lives could be improved by instituting a higher minimum wage? Or were the opponents correct to claim that a higher minimum wage could end up hurting more people than it helped?

In the run-up to the election that brought the 110th Congress into office, another issue that attracted a lot of attention was the rise in gasoline prices. Oil prices had been rising steadily since 2000 and had reached almost $60 a barrel in September of 2005 in the aftermath of Hurricanes Rita and Katrina. Oil prices had risen sharply several times before—in 1990, in 1980, and in the early 1970s. In the previous chapter, you looked at a case study that examined how rising energy consumption and disruptions in supply can lead to sharp increases in the price of oil. The supply and demand model tells us that an increase in oil supply or a decrease in oil demand will decrease the price of oil. But by how much? For example, by how much would an increase in fuel efficiency standards reduce the price of oil? And how much would the price fall if the U.S. government managed to persuade the oil-producing countries to increase production by 5 percent?

In this chapter, we look at more sophisticated aspects of the supply and demand model that are helpful in understanding policy debates, like the minimum-wage increase or how best to combat the rise in oil prices. We will first look at how to use the supply and demand model in situations where government policies do not allow price to be freely determined in a market. These interventions can take the form of a *price ceiling*, a maximum price imposed by the government when it feels that the equilibrium price is "too high," or a *price floor*, a minimum price imposed by the government when it feels that the equilibrium price is "too low," as in the case of the minimum wage. This extension of the supply and demand model will also be very helpful in solidifying your understanding of the important role played by prices in the allocation of resources.

Then we will move on to discussing an elegant, and remarkably useful, economic concept called *elasticity* that economists use when they work with the supply and demand model. In economics, elasticity is a measure of how sensitive one variable is to another. In the case of the supply and demand model, elasticity measures how sensitive the quantity of a good that people demand, or that firms supply, is to the price of the good. In this chapter we show how the concept of elasticity can be used to answer the questions raised earlier about how changes in the demand for and supply of oil affect the price of oil, and how much unemployment is caused when the minimum wage is raised. You will learn a formula that shows how elasticity is calculated and then learn how to work with and talk about elasticity.

INTERFERENCE WITH MARKET PRICES

Thus far, we have used the supply and demand model in situations in which the price is freely determined without government control. But at many times throughout history, and around the world today, governments have attempted to control market prices. The usual reasons are that government leaders were not happy with the outcome of the market or were pressured by groups who would benefit from price controls.

price control: a government law or regulation that sets or limits the price to be charged for a particular good.

price ceiling: a government price control that sets the maximum allowable price for a good.

price floor: a government price control that sets the minimum allowable price for a good.

Price Ceilings and Price Floors

In general, there are two broad types of government **price controls.** Controls can stipulate either a **price ceiling,** a maximum price at which a good can be bought and sold, or a **price floor,** a minimum price at which a good can be bought and sold. Why would a government choose to intervene in the market and put in a price floor or a price ceiling? What happens when such an intervention is made?

Ostensibly, the primary purpose of a price ceiling is to help consumers in situations where the government thinks that the equilibrium price is "too high" or is inundated with consumer complaints that the equilibrium price is too high. For example, the United States government controlled oil prices in the early 1970s, stipulating that firms could not charge more than a stated maximum price of $5.25 per barrel of crude oil at a time when the equilibrium price was well over $10 per barrel. As another example, some cities in the United States place price controls on rental apartments; landlords are not permitted to charge a rent higher than the maximum stipulated by the **rent control** law in these cities. Tenants living in rent-controlled units pay less than the market equilibrium rent that would prevail in the absence of the price ceiling.

rent control: a government price control that sets the maximum allowable rent on a house or apartment.

Conversely, price floors are imposed by governments in order to help the suppliers of goods and services in situations where the government feels that the equilibrium price is "too low" or is influenced by complaints from producers that the equilibrium price is too low. For example, the U.S. government requires that the price of sugar in the United States not fall below a certain amount. Another example is in the labor market, where the U.S. government requires that firms pay workers a wage of at least a given level, called the **minimum wage.**

minimum wage: a wage per hour below which it is illegal to pay workers.

Side Effects of Price Ceilings

Even though price ceilings are typically implemented with the idea of helping consumers, they often end up having harmful side effects that hurt the consumers that the ceiling was put in place to help. If the price ceiling that the government puts in place to prevent firms from charging more than a certain amount for their products is lower than the equilibrium price, then a shortage is likely to result, as illustrated in Figure 1. The situation of a persistent shortage, where sellers are unwilling to supply as much as buyers want to buy, is illustrated for the general case of any good in the top graph in Figure 1 and for the specific case of rent control in the bottom graph.

Dealing with Persistent Shortages. Because higher prices are not allowed, the shortage must be dealt with in other ways. Sometimes the government issues a limited amount of ration coupons, which do not exceed the quantity supplied at the restricted maximum price, to people to alleviate the shortage. This was done in World War II; people had to present these ration coupons at stores in order to buy certain goods, and only those who had ration coupons could buy those goods. If the price ceiling had not been in place, the shortage would have driven prices higher, and those who were willing and able to pay the higher price would have been able to buy the goods without the need for a ration coupon.

Alternatively, if there are no ration coupons, then the shortage might result in long waiting lines. In the past, in centrally planned economies, long lines for bread were frequently observed because of price controls on bread. Sometimes black markets develop, in which people buy and sell goods outside the watch of the government and charge whatever price they want. In the past, this was typical in command economies. Black markets are also common in less-developed countries today when the governments in these countries impose price controls.

Another effect of price ceilings is a reduction in the quality of the good sold. By lowering the quality of the good, the producer can reduce the costs of producing it. A frequent criticism of rent control is that it can lower the quality of housing—landlords are more reluctant to paint the walls or to repair the elevator since they are prevented from charging a higher price.

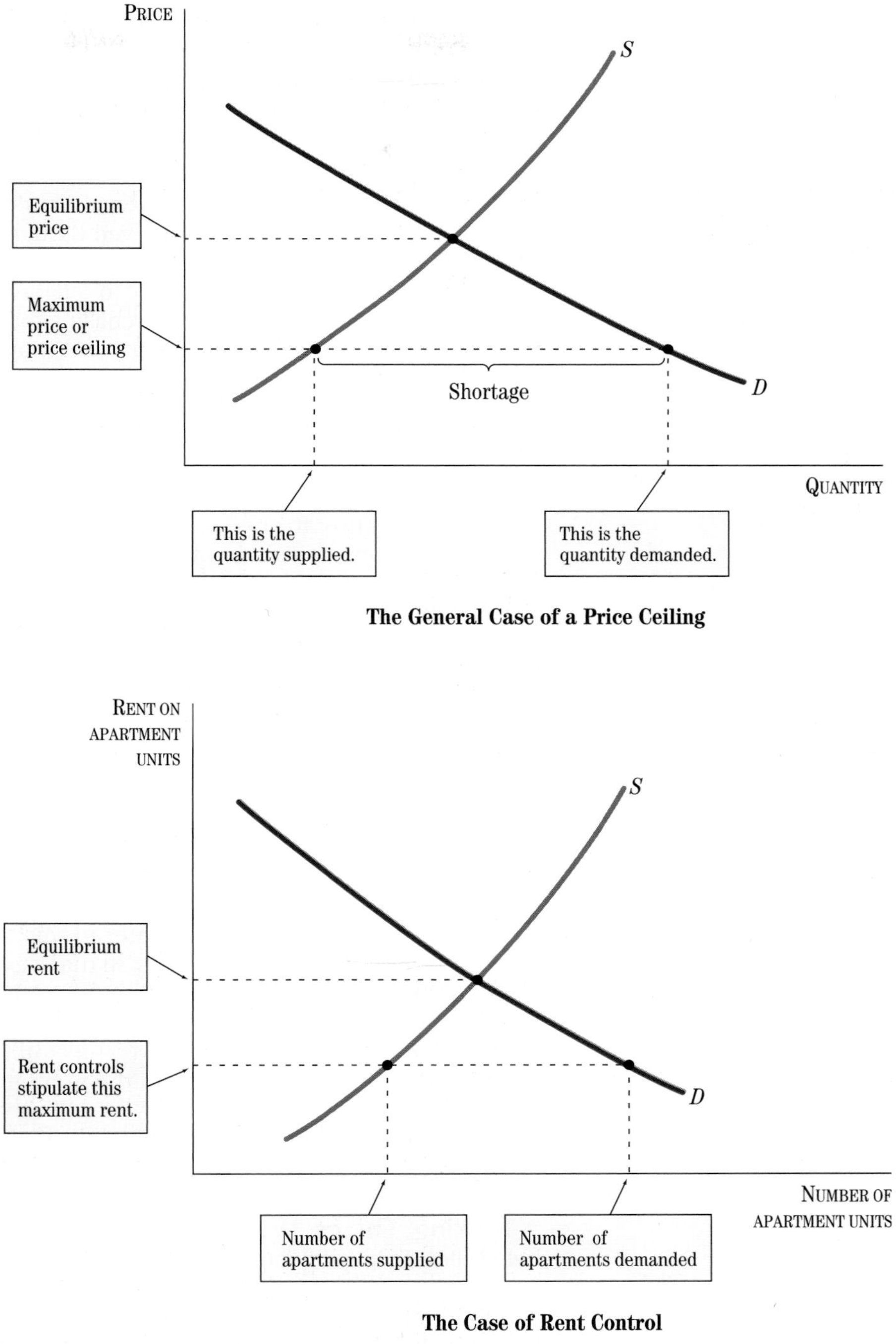

FIGURE 1
Effects of a Maximum-Price Law

The top diagram shows the general case when the government prevents the market price from rising above a particular maximum price, or sets a price ceiling below the equilibrium price. The lower diagram shows a particular example of a price ceiling, rent controls on apartment units. The supply and demand model predicts that there will be a shortage. The shortage occurs because the quantity supplied is less than consumers are willing to buy at that price. The shortage leads to rationing, black markets, or lower product quality.

Making Things Worse. Although the stated purpose of price ceilings is to help people who have to pay high prices, the preceding examples indicate how price ceilings can make things worse. Issuing ration coupons raises difficult problems about who gets the coupons. In the case of a price ceiling on gasoline, for example, should the government give more coupons to those who commute by car than to those who do not? Rationing by waiting in line is also a poor outcome. People who are waiting in line could be doing more enjoyable or more useful things. Similarly, black markets, being illegal, encourage people to go outside the law. People transacting in black markets may also be more vulnerable to theft or fraud. Lowering the quality of the good is also a bad way to alleviate the problem of a high price. This simply eliminates the higher-quality good from production; both consumers and producers lose. Price ceilings are also not particularly well targeted. Even though the goal of a price ceiling may be to ensure that someone who can't afford to pay the equilibrium price can still end up purchasing the good, there is no way to guarantee that only those who can't afford to pay the equilibrium price end up purchasing the good. For instance, many people who end up living in rent-controlled apartments may not be poor at all.

Side Effects of Price Floors

Like price ceilings, price floors are typically enacted with the goal of helping out producers who are facing low market equilibrium prices, but they often end up having harmful side effects that hurt the people that the floor was put in place to help. If the price floor that the government puts in place exceeds the equilibrium price, then a surplus will occur. The situation of a persistent surplus, where sellers are willing to supply more output than buyers want to buy, is illustrated for the general case of any good in the top graph of Figure 2 and for the specific case of the minimum wage in the bottom graph.

Dealing with Persistent Surpluses. How is this surplus dealt with in actual markets? In markets for farm products, the government usually has to buy the surplus and, perhaps, put it in storage. Buying farm products above the equilibrium price costs taxpayers money, and the higher price raises costs to consumers. For this reason, economists argue against price floors on agricultural goods. As an alternative, the government sometimes reduces the supply by telling firms to plant fewer acres or to destroy crops. But government requirements that land be kept idle or crops destroyed are particularly repugnant to most people.

As we will see in more detail later in this book, the supply and demand model can also be applied to labor markets. In that case, the price is the price of labor, or the wage. What does the supply and demand model predict about the effects of a minimum wage? In the case of labor markets, a minimum wage can cause unemployment. If the minimum wage exceeds the equilibrium wage, the number of workers demanded at that wage is less than the number of workers who are willing to work. Even though some workers would be willing to work for less than the minimum wage, employers are not permitted to pay them less than the minimum wage. Therefore, there is a surplus of unemployed workers at the minimum wage.

Making Things Worse. Even though the stated purpose of price floors is to help sellers by paying them a higher price, the preceding examples indicate how price floors can make things worse. The resources allocated to building grain silos to store surplus grain could have been used to hire doctors or teachers or to build low-income houses. The land that farmers are encouraged to keep in an undeveloped, yet unfarmed state could have been used for a housing development or as a high school athletic field. Price floors, like price ceilings, are also not particularly well targeted. Even though the goal of a price floor may be to ensure that a poor farmer does not suffer because crop prices are too low, the benefits of the higher price will typically

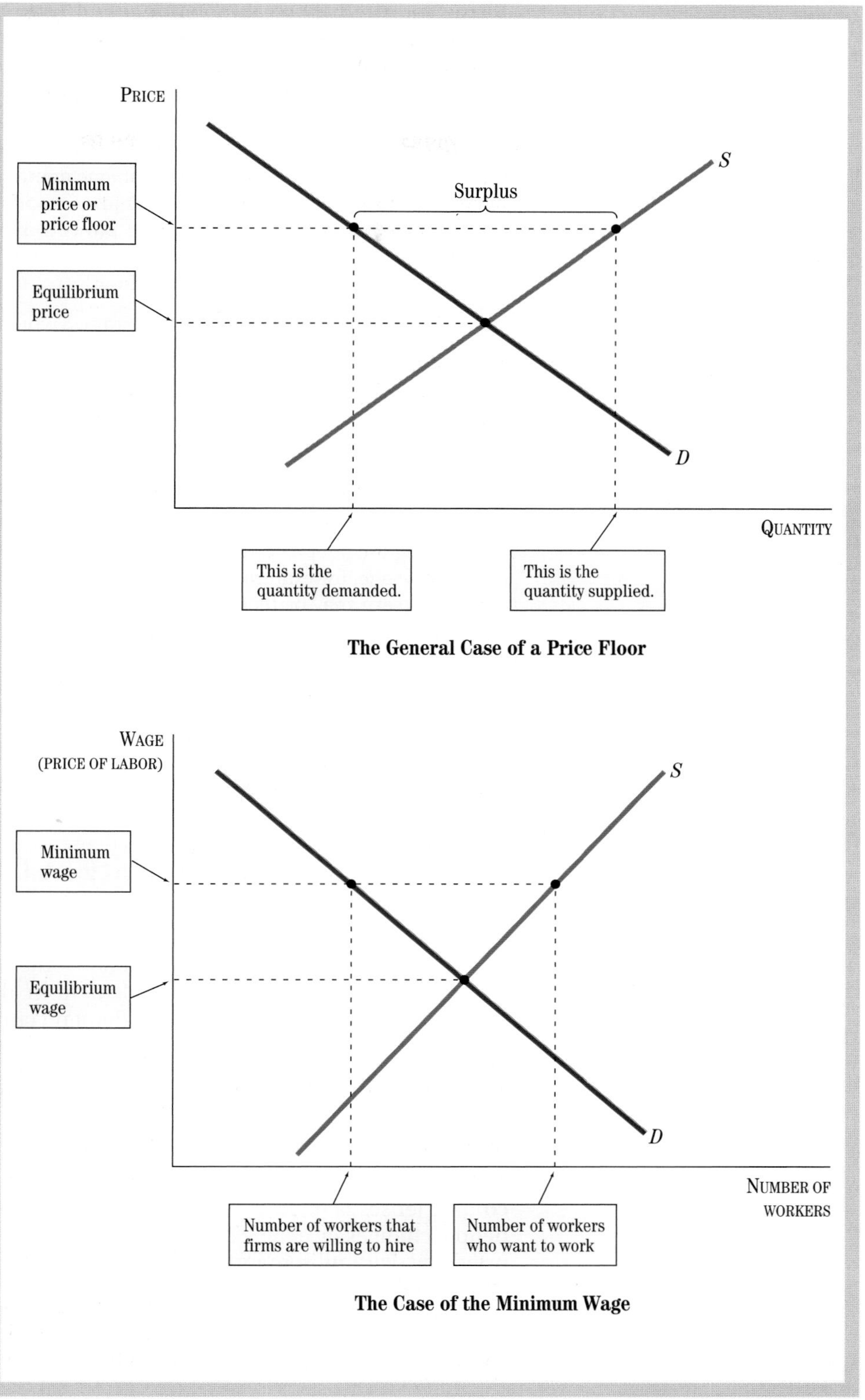

FIGURE 2
Effects of a Minimum-Price Law

The top diagram shows the general case when the government prevents the market price from falling below a particular minimum price, or sets a price floor above the equilibrium price. The lower diagram shows a particular example when the price of labor—the wage—cannot fall below the minimum wage. The supply and demand model predicts that sellers are willing to sell a greater quantity than buyers are willing to buy at that price. Thus, there is a surplus of the good or, in the case of labor, unemployment for some of those who would be hired only at a lower wage.

accrue to extremely wealthy farmers and large agricultural businesses with lots of resources. In the case of the minimum wage, teenagers from relatively well-off families may end up earning a higher salary as a result of the minimum wage, but a poor parent may end up losing his or her job and joining the ranks of the unemployed.

REVIEW

- Governments will occasionally intervene in markets because they think that the equilibrium price is too high or too low. In some instances where the government thinks the price that buyers have to pay is too high, it may impose a price ceiling. In some instances where the government thinks the price that sellers are receiving is too low, it may impose a price floor.
- Price ceilings cause persistent shortages, which, in turn, cause rationing, black markets, and a reduced quality of goods and services. Price ceilings also may not end up helping the people that the policy was designed to benefit. In the case of rent control, for example, the people who end up in rent-controlled apartments may be more affluent than the individuals who are unable to find an apartment because of the persistent shortages.
- Price floors cause persistent surpluses, which, in turn, result in resources being diverted away from other productive activities. Price floors also may not end up helping the people that the policy was designed to benefit. In the case of a minimum wage, for example, the workers who end up in jobs earning the higher minimum wage may be teenagers from relatively well-off families, while a poor worker may be unable to find a job because of the surplus of unemployed workers.

ELASTICITY OF DEMAND

Defining the Price Elasticity of Demand

The price elasticity of demand is a measure of the sensitivity of the *quantity demanded* of a good to the *price* of the good. “Price elasticity of demand” is sometimes shortened to “elasticity of demand,” the “demand elasticity,” or even simply “elasticity” when the meaning is clear from the context. The price elasticity of demand always refers to a particular demand curve or demand schedule, such as the world demand for oil or the U.S. demand for bicycles. Since the demand curve slopes downward, as the price increases, the quantity demanded by consumers declines, and as the price decreases, the quantity demanded by consumers increases, all else held equal. The price elasticity of demand is a measure of *how much* the quantity demanded changes when the price changes.

For example, when economists report that the price elasticity of demand for contact lenses is high, they mean that the quantity of contact lenses demanded by people changes by a large amount when the price changes. Or if they report that the price elasticity of demand for bread is low, they mean that the quantity of bread demanded changes by only a small amount when the price of bread changes.

price elasticity of demand: the percentage change in the quantity demanded of a good divided by the percentage change in the price of that good.

We can define the price elasticity of demand clearly with a formula: **Price elasticity of demand** is the percentage change in the quantity demanded divided by the percentage change in the price. That is,

$$\text{Price elasticity of demand} = \frac{\text{percentage change in quantity demanded}}{\text{percentage change in price}}$$

ECONOMICS IN ACTION

How Policymakers Use Price Elasticity of Demand to Discourage Underage Drinking

Policymakers use information about the price elasticity of demand in many ways. Take the government's efforts to reduce underage drinking. In a 2003 study on underage drinking, the National Academy of Sciences recommended that one way to reduce underage drinking would be to increase the tax on alcohol. To implement this policy effectively, it would be important for policymakers to know which demand curve most accurately represents the demand for alcohol by underage drinkers. The amount that a tax would reduce the quantity of alcohol consumed by underage drinkers depends on their price elasticity of demand.

Recall that a new tax is modeled as a decrease in supply. You can see how this works by drawing this supply shift and a demand curve with high price elasticity of demand and then drawing the same supply shift and a demand curve with a low price elasticity of demand, as in Figure 3. Alcohol consumption responds more to the tax when the price elasticity of demand is high. If the price elasticity of demand for alcohol by underage drinkers is low (that is, if the quantity of alcohol demanded by underage drinkers changes by only a small amount when the price of alcohol changes), then a new tax on alcohol must be large to accomplish the goal of a reduction in underage drinking. If the price elasticity of demand for alcohol by underage drinkers is high (that is, if the quantity of alcohol demanded by underage drinkers changes by a large amount when the price of alcohol changes), then the tax might not need to be very big to accomplish the policymakers' goal. Which do you think is more likely?

We emphasize that the price elasticity of demand refers to a particular demand curve; thus, the numerator of this formula is the percentage change in quantity demanded when the price changes by the percentage amount shown in the denominator. All the other factors that affect demand are held constant when we compute the price elasticity of demand.

For example, the price elasticity of demand for gasoline is about .2. Thus, if the price of gasoline increases by 10 percent, the quantity of gasoline demanded will fall by 2 percent ($.2 \times 10$). The price elasticity of demand for alcoholic beverages is about 1.5; thus, if the price of alcoholic beverages rises by 10 percent, the quantity demanded will fall by 15 percent (1.5×10). As you can see from these examples, knowing the elasticity of demand enables us to determine by how much the *quantity demanded* changes when the price changes.

The Size of the Elasticity: High versus Low

There are two graphs in Figure 3, each showing a different possible demand curve for oil in the world. We want to show why it is important to know which of these two demand curves gives a better description of economic behavior in the oil market. Each graph has the price of oil on the vertical axis (in dollars per barrel) and the quantity of oil demanded on the horizontal axis (in millions of barrels of oil a day).

Both of the demand curves pass through the same point *A*, where the price of oil is $20 per barrel and the quantity demanded is 60 million barrels per day. But observe that the two curves show different degrees of sensitivity of the quantity demanded to the price. In the top graph, where the demand curve is relatively flat, the quantity demanded of oil is very sensitive to the price; in other words, the demand curve has a high elasticity. For example, consider a change from point *A* to point *B:* When the price rises by $2, from $20 to $22, the quantity demanded falls by 12 million, from 60 million to 48 million barrels a day. In percentage terms, when the price rises by 10 percent ($2/20 = .10$, or 10 percent), the quantity demanded falls by 20 percent ($12/60 = .20$, or 20 percent).

On the other hand, in the bottom graph, the quantity demanded is not very sensitive to the price; in other words, the demand curve has a low elasticity. It is relatively steep. When the price rises by $2 from point *A* to point *C*, the quantity demanded falls by 3 million barrels. In percentage terms, the same 10 percent increase in price reduces the quantity demanded by only 5 percent (3/60 = .05, or 5 percent). Thus, the sensitivity of the quantity to the price, or the size of the elasticity, is what distinguishes these two graphs.

The Impact of a Change in Supply on the Price of Oil

Now consider what happens when there is a decline in supply in the world oil market. In Figure 4 we combine the supply curve for oil with the two demand curves for oil from Figure 3. Initially the oil market is in equilibrium in Figure 4; in both

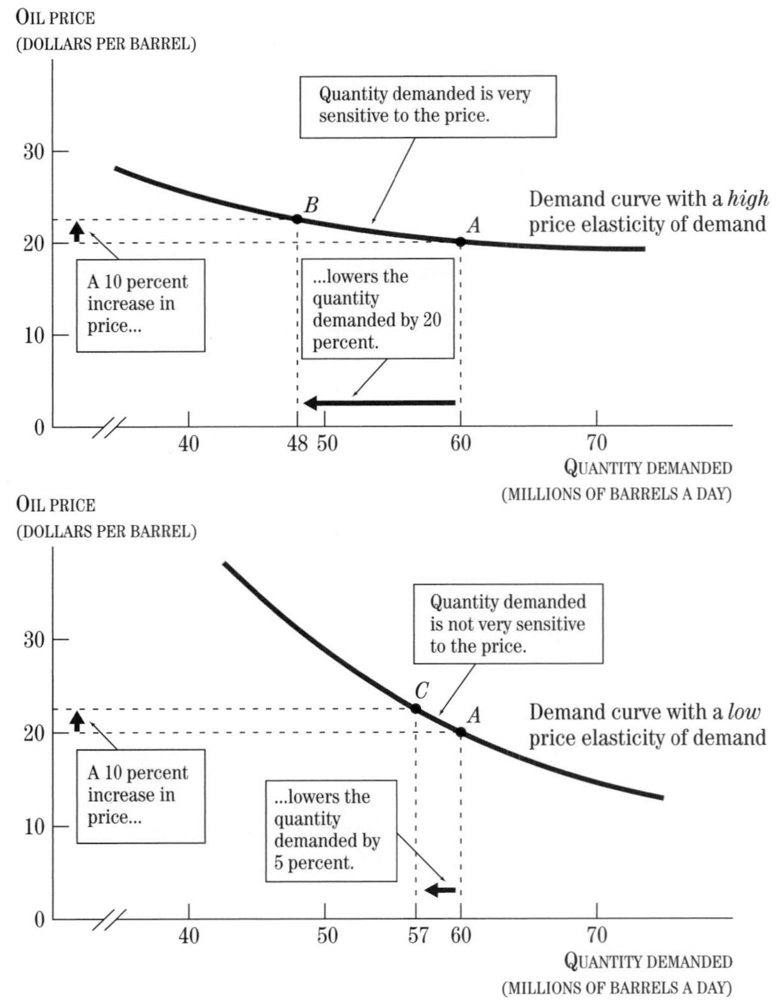

FIGURE 3
Comparing Different Sizes of the Price Elasticity of Demand
Both sets of axes have exactly the same scale. In the top graph, the quantity demanded is very sensitive to the price; the elasticity is high. In the bottom graph, the quantity demanded is not very sensitive to the price; the elasticity is low. Thus, the same increase in price ($2, or 10 percent) reduces the quantity demanded much more when the elasticity is high (top graph) than when it is low (bottom graph).

graphs, the quantity demanded equals the quantity supplied. The equilibrium price is $20 per barrel, and the equilibrium quantity is 60 million barrels a day, just like at point *A* in Figure 3. A reduction in the supply of oil—perhaps because of the reduction in Iraqi oil production or the shutdown of refineries following Hurricane Katrina—is also shown. The exact same leftward shift in supply is shown in the top and bottom graphs of Figure 4.

Now, observe how the equilibrium price changes in the two graphs. Recall that this change is our prediction—using the supply and demand model—of what would happen to the price of oil if the supply declined. We know that a decrease in supply will lead to an increase in the equilibrium price and a decrease in the equilibrium quantity. However, as the two graphs show, there is a huge difference in the size of the predicted price increase. In the top graph, the oil price increases only a little. If the

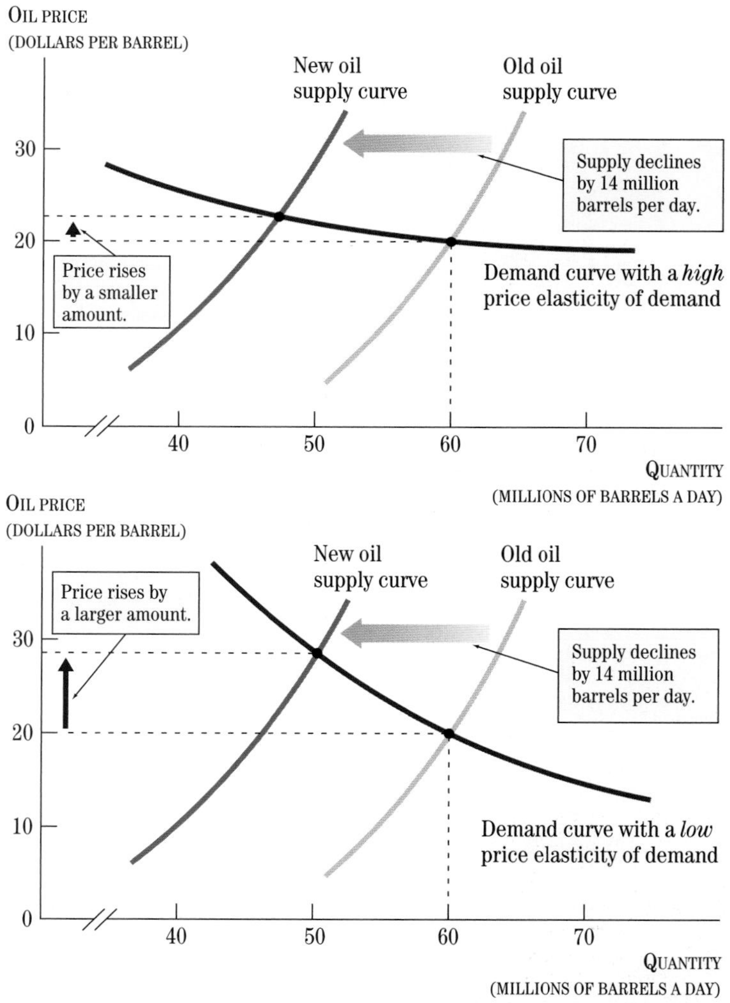

FIGURE 4
The Importance of the Size of the Price Elasticity of Demand
The impact on the oil price of a reduction in oil supply is shown for two different demand curves. The reduction in supply is the same for both graphs. When the price elasticity of demand is high (top graph), there is only a small increase in the price. When the price elasticity of demand is low (bottom graph), the price rises by much more.

ECONOMICS IN THE NEWS

Increasing School Enrollment in Africa

The economic weakness of many sub-Saharan African countries can be attributed to myriad factors, including lack of education, civil wars, corruption, resource exploitation, disease, and a lack of adequate institutions. While these problems may seem intractable, sometimes only a small change in policy and a small increase in resources are all it takes, as this article from the *Christian Science Monitor* about how to increase school enrollment shows.

Even though $42 may not seem like a lot to you, this represents about 25% of the average income in some African countries.

For poor families with serious income constraints, the demand for education becomes extremely sensitive to price. Why do you think this effect is especially pronounced for female children?

Lowering the price of education dramatically increased the quantity of students demanding that education. What does that say about the elasticity of demand for education?

Easing the Burden of School Fees in Africa

By STEPHANIE HANES | Correspondent of The Christian Science Monitor

SOWETO, SOUTH AFRICA—Orison Makhaluza leans back on the cracked leather sofa and watches his young grandnieces scurry through the small cement house. They look tiny in their gray school jumpers and knee socks, which they are still wearing, even though school ended hours ago.

Last month, Mr. Makhaluza wasn't sure if the girls would ever wear the uniforms. He wasn't sure if they would go to school at all. The problem, he explains, was school fees. His sister, the girls' grandmother, started taking care of the four children, ages 5 to 11, when their mother died last year. But she couldn't afford to pay the school fees—$42 per student—required by the girls' primary school. So the school told the children they could not attend classes.

"Education, it's the key of the future," says Makhaluza, who has been unemployed for five years and lives at his sister's house. "But our kids, they are told they cannot go to school." Although South African law says that no student should be denied an education and that impoverished students should be exempt from paying fees, children's advocates say that schools often do not understand or follow these regulations. The government pays for teachers' salaries and buildings, but schools need extra money to pay for basics such as water, electricity, and pencils. School officials and education-rights advocates say schools have incentive to take harsh measures, such as keeping a child out of the classroom, to convince parents to pay. Parents, many of whom are uneducated, often don't understand the law well enough to challenge schools. In Makhaluza's case, a grass-roots group called the Education Rights Project talked to the school about his grandnieces, and the girls were admitted. The school said there had been a misunderstanding.

Across Africa and in other developing regions, organizations such as UNICEF and the World Bank, along with children's rights groups, are encouraging countries to provide free education. They worry that school fees are keeping hundreds of thousands of children—particularly girls—from school. Other expenses, such as the cost of books, transportation, and uniforms, can also keep schools out of reach for poor families, many of whom live on less than a dollar a day.

These organizations point to countries like Kenya, where President Mwai Kibaki, fulfilling a campaign promise, declared in 2003 that all primary schools would be free of fees. In just a few months, primary school enrollment increased from about 6 million to 7.2 million. Although the move has put unprecedented strains on Kenya's education system—the government had not budgeted for the huge increase in students—international observers say it proves that fees have kept poor children out of the classroom.

Last year, the United Nations announced that universal free primary education was one of its top priorities. But many countries say they simply cannot afford to lift school fees, adding that parents have a responsibility to contribute to their children's education. About 80 percent of the countries in East Asia and the Pacific have mandatory fees, according to a 2001 World Bank study, as do many Middle Eastern and North African countries, such as Egypt, Jordan, and Tunisia. This year, the Botswana government reintroduced school fees after 20 years of free education, saying it could no longer afford to subsidize schools.

Besides Kenya, a handful of countries in eastern and southern Africa have done away with primary school fees, including Tanzania, Malawi, and Uganda. The efforts are bolstered in part by populist politics and in part by money donated from wealthy countries such as the United States. Yet South Africa, the richest nation in the region, still allows schools to charge. Although South African law says that the government must fund all public schools, the education department says that there is also "a responsibility on all public school governing bodies to do their utmost to improve the quality of education in their schools by raising additional resources to supplement those which the state provides." "All parents," it says, "are thereby encouraged to increase their own direct financial and other contributions." Parents are supposed to vote on the fee level for their children's school. While no school is required to charge fees, in practice, many would go without electricity and water if they did not raise extra funds.

How wealthy countries can assist poor countries to make an important policy change

But school officials say they are getting better at preventing poor children from slipping through the cracks. Regarding fees, the balance of power has shifted to parents, says Rej Brijraj, chief executive officer of the South African Council for Educators, a statutory body charged with maintaining professional standards.The onus is now on schools to prove that parents can pay, rather than parents having to prove to school boards that they cannot afford fees. Last year, the South African Parliament passed the Education Laws Amendment Bill, which makes a certain percentage of South Africa's approximately 28,000 schools "fee free." That bill, however, has not yet been signed into law.

"By and large, I must say that school governing bodies have shown great responsibility in setting school fees, and the state has been very vigilant to make sure that learners are not disadvantaged," Mr. Brijraj says. Recently there have been a number of grass-roots efforts designed to educate both schools and parents about the law and children's rights. But Makhaluza still has concerns. Children who don't pay or can't conform to school rules can face ridicule. His own son was called a "hooligan" by a teacher because he was not wearing a school uniform—a luxury that Makhaluza said he could not afford.

In many African countries, school uniforms are required, which imposes an additional cost.

Sharon September, education project coordinator at South Africa's Alliance for Children's Access to Social Security, says she still hears of schools retaliating against families who cannot pay. "We hear stories where students are refused entry to school," she says. "Or where children attend, and don't get their report at the end of the year because they didn't pay. There have been cases where mothers have been told to clean the toilets to make up for the fact they can't pay." Lerato Mokgadi, a 22-year-old 12th-grader, says her high school in the Soweto township, just outside Johannesburg, refused to release her end-of-year report because her mother had not paid fees."I never paid the school fees because I wasn't working," says her mother, Maria Mokgadi.

The younger Mokgadi's report was crucial. She knew that she had not passed the countrywide exam necessary for university entrance. But without her report, she didn't know which subject she had failed, so she could not register for additional classes. A local representative of the Education Rights Project spoke with the school on Mokgadi's behalf, and returned with the report card."If this were an equal society, school fees would be fine," Ms. September says. "Nobody has a problem contributing. But if fees serve as an exclusionary measure, because every child has a right to an education, it should be altered."

ECONOMICS IN ACTION

Predicting the Size of a Price Increase

Economists used a numerical value of elasticity to predict the size of the oil price rise caused by the Iraqi invasion of Kuwait in 1990. Here are the steps they took:

- First, they determined—after looking at historical studies of oil prices and quantities—that the price elasticity of the demand for oil was .1. In other words, $e_d = .1$.
- Second, they calculated—after consulting with oil producers—that the invasion of Kuwait would reduce the world oil supply by 7 percent. They assumed that this 7 percent would also be the percentage decline in the quantity of oil demanded because other sources of oil could not increase in a short period of time. In other words, $\Delta Q_d/Q_d = .07$, or 7 percent.
- Third, they plugged these numbers into the formula for elasticity to calculate that the oil price would rise by 70 percent. Here is the exact calculation behind this step: Rearrange the definition of elasticity, $e_d = (\Delta Q_d/Q_d)/(\Delta P/P)$, to put the percentage change in the price on the left. That is, $\Delta P/P = (\Delta Q_d/Q_d)/e_d$. Now plug in $\Delta Q_d/Q_d = .07$ and $e_d = .1$ to get $.07/(.1) = .70$, or 70 percent.

The 70 percent price rise predicted might seem large. In fact, the actual rise in the price of oil in 1990 was large, even larger than 70 percent: The price of oil rose from $17 per barrel in July 1990 to $36 in October 1990, or about 112 percent. (The larger-than-predicted price increase may have been due to worries that Iraq would also invade Saudi Arabia and reduce the oil supply even further.)

This type of calculation—showing that a huge oil price increase could be caused by the 7 percent reduction in oil supply—was a factor in the decision by the United States and its allies to send troops to the Middle East to halt the Iraqi invasion of Saudi Arabia and to eventually force Iraq out of Kuwait.

Could you use the same type of reasoning to determine how much the price of oil would fall if oil producers increased supply? Suppose the increase was 4 percent.

elasticity is very high, then only a small increase in the price is enough to get people to reduce their use of oil and thereby bring the quantity demanded down to the lower quantity supplied. On the other hand, in the bottom diagram, the price rises by much more. Here the elasticity is very low, and so a large increase in price is needed to get people to reduce their use of oil and bring the quantity demanded down to the quantity supplied.

Thus, in order to determine how much the price will rise in response to a shift in oil supply, we need to know how sensitive the quantity demanded is to the price, or the size of the elasticity of demand.

REVIEW

- We know that an increase in price will lower the quantity demanded, whereas a decrease in price will increase the quantity demanded. The price elasticity of demand is a number that tells us by how much the quantity demanded changes when the price changes.
- The price elasticity of demand, which we also refer to as "elasticity of demand" or just as "elasticity," is defined as the percentage change in the quantity demanded divided by the percentage change in the price.
- A given change in price has a larger impact on quantity demanded when the elasticity of demand is higher.
- A given shift of the supply curve will have a larger impact on equilibrium quantity (and a smaller impact on equilibrium price) when the elasticity of demand is higher.

WORKING WITH DEMAND ELASTICITIES

Having demonstrated the practical importance of elasticity, let us examine the concept in more detail and show how to use it. Some symbols will be helpful.

If we let the symbol e_d represent the price elasticity of demand, then we can write the definition as

$$e_d = \frac{\Delta Q_d}{Q_d} \div \frac{\Delta P}{P} = \frac{\Delta Q_d / Q_d}{\Delta P / P}$$

where Q_d is the quantity demanded, P is the price, and Δ means "change in." In other words, the elasticity of demand equals the "percentage change in the quantity demanded" divided by the "percentage change in the price." Observe that to compute the percentage change in the numerator and the denominator, we need to divide the change in the variable (ΔP or ΔQ_d) by the variable (P or Q_d).

Because the quantity demanded is negatively related to the price along a demand curve, the elasticity of demand is a negative number: When $\Delta P/P$ is positive, $\Delta Q_d / Q_d$ is negative. But when economists write or talk about elasticity, they usually ignore the negative sign and report the absolute value of the number. Because the demand curve always slopes downward, this nearly universal convention need not cause any confusion, as long as you remember it.

It is easy to do back-of-the-envelope computations of price elasticity of demand. Suppose a study shows that when the price of Australian wine fell by 8 percent, the quantity of Australian wine sold increased by 12 percent. The price elasticity of demand for Australian wine is

$$e_d = \frac{\Delta Q_d / Q_d}{\Delta P / P} = \frac{12}{8} = 1.5$$

Suppose your university raises student season ticket prices from $50 to $60, which results in the quantity of season tickets sold falling from 2,000 to 1,800. The price elasticity of demand for season ticket prices would be

$$e_d = \frac{\Delta Q_d / Q_d}{\Delta P / P} = \frac{200/2{,}000}{10/50} = \frac{.1}{.2} = .5$$

Notice that measured in percentage changes, the demand for Australian wine is responsive to changes in the price, and the demand for season tickets is not very responsive to changes in the price.

The Advantage of a Unit-Free Measure

unit-free measure: a measure that does not depend on a unit of measurement.

An attractive feature of the price elasticity of demand is that it does not depend on the units of measurement of the quantity demanded—whether barrels of oil or pounds of peanuts. It is a **unit-free measure** because it uses percentage changes in price and quantity demanded. Thus, it provides a way to compare the price sensitivity of the demand for many different goods. It even allows us to compare the price sensitivity of less expensive goods—like rice—with that of more expensive goods—like steak.

For example, suppose that when the price of rice rises from 50 cents to 60 cents per pound, the quantity demanded falls from 20 tons to 19 tons: That is a decline of 1 ton for a 10 *cent* price increase.

In contrast, suppose that when the price of steak rises by $1, from $5 to $6 per pound, the quantity demanded falls by 1 ton, from 20 tons to 19 tons of steak. That would be a decline of 1 ton for a 1 *dollar* price increase.

Using these numbers, the price sensitivity of the demand for steak and the demand for rice might appear to be very different: 10 cents to get a ton of reduced purchases versus \$1 to get a ton of reduced purchases. Yet the elasticities are the same. The percentage change in price is 20 percent in each case (\$1/\$5 = \$.10/\$.50 = .20, or 20 percent), and the percentage change in quantity is 5 percent in each case: 1 ton of rice/20 tons of rice = 1 ton of steak/20 tons of steak = .05, or 5 percent. Hence, the elasticity is 5/20 = 1/4 in both cases.

Elasticity allows us to compare the price sensitivity of different goods by looking at ratios of percentage changes regardless of the units for measuring either price or quantity. With millions of different goods and hundreds of different units of measurement, this is indeed a major advantage.

Elasticity versus Slope

After looking at Figure 3, you might be tempted to say that demand curves that are very steep have a low elasticity, and demand curves that are very flat have a high elasticity. That turns out not to be the case, so you have to be careful not to simply look at a flat demand curve and say that it has a high elasticity. You need to understand why the *elasticity of the demand curve* is not the same as the *slope of the demand curve.* Remember that the slope of a curve is the change in the y variable over the change in the x variable; in the case of the demand curve, the slope is defined as the change in price divided by the change in quantity demanded. The slope is not a unit-free measure—it depends on how the price and quantity are measured. Elasticity, on the other hand, is a unit-free measure.

To illustrate the difference between slope and elasticity, we show in Figure 5 a demand curve for rice and a demand curve for steak. The two demand curves have different slopes because the prices are so different. When the price of rice increases by 10 cents, the quantity demanded of rice falls by 1 ton; whereas when the price of steak increases by \$1 (or 100 cents), the quantity demanded of steak falls by 1 ton. The slope of the steak demand curve is (−100 cents a ton), which is 10 times greater than the slope of the rice demand curve (−10 cents a ton). Yet the elasticity is the same for the change from A to B for both demand curves—the price of rice and the price of steak both increased by 20 percent, while the quantity demanded of rice and the quantity demanded of steak both decreased by 5 percent.

Calculating the Elasticity with a Midpoint Formula

To calculate the elasticity, we need to find the percentage change in the quantity demanded and divide it by the percentage change in the price. As we have already illustrated with examples, to get the percentage change in the price or quantity, we need to divide the change in price (ΔP) by the price (P) or the change in quantity demanded (ΔQ_d) by the quantity demanded (Q_d). But when price and quantity demanded change, there is a question about what to use for P and Q_d. Should we use the old price and the old quantity demanded before the change, or should we use the new price and the new quantity demanded after the change?

The most common convention that economists use is a compromise between these two alternatives. They take the *average,* or the *midpoint,* of the old and new quantities demanded and the old and new prices. That is, they compute the elasticity using the following formula, called the *midpoint formula:*

$$\text{Price elasticity of demand} = \frac{\text{change in quantity}}{\text{average of old and new quantities}} \div \frac{\text{change in price}}{\text{average of old and new prices}}$$

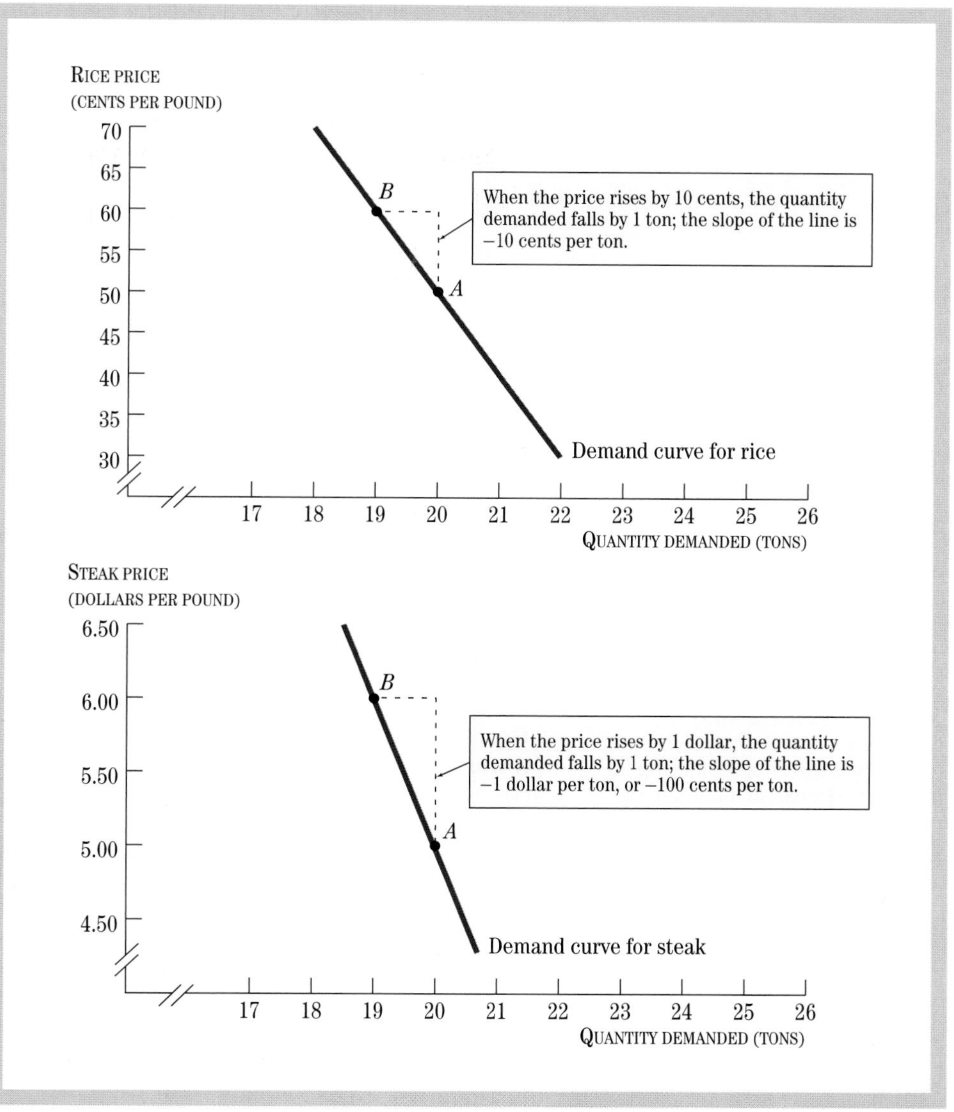

FIGURE 5
Different Slopes and Same Elasticities
The slope of the steak demand curve in the bottom graph is greater than the slope of the rice demand curve in the top graph. The price elasticity of demand for rice and steak from point *A* to point *B* is the same, however. From point *A* to point *B*, the price rises by 20 percent and the quantity demanded decreases by 5 percent. Thus, the elasticity is 1/4 for both rice and steak at these points.

For example, if we use the midpoint formula to calculate the price elasticity of demand for oil when the price changes from \$20 to \$22 and the quantity demanded changes from 60 million to 48 million barrels a day, we get

$$\left[\frac{12}{(60 + 48)/2}\right] \div \left[\frac{2}{(20 + 22)/2}\right] = 0.2222 \div 0.0952 = 2.33$$

That is, the price elasticity of demand is 2.33 using the midpoint formula. When we originally calculated the elasticity using the old price and the old quantity demanded, we came up with an elasticity of

$$\left[\frac{12}{60}\right] \div \left[\frac{2}{20}\right] = 0.2 \div 0.1 = 2$$

If we had used the new price and the new quantity, we would have calculated the elasticity to be

$$\left[\frac{12}{48}\right] \div \left[\frac{2}{22}\right] = 0.25 \div 0.0909 = 2.75$$

So the elasticity calculated using the midpoint formula turns out to be in between these two values, as you would expect.

Talking about Elasticities

Economists classify demand curves by the size of the price elasticities of demand, and they have developed a very precise terminology for doing so.

elastic demand: demand for which the price elasticity is greater than 1.

inelastic demand: demand for which the price elasticity is less than 1.

perfectly inelastic demand: demand for which the price elasticity is zero, indicating no response to a change in price and therefore a vertical demand curve.

perfectly elastic demand: demand for which the price elasticity is infinite, indicating an infinite response to a change in price and therefore a horizontal demand curve.

Elastic versus Inelastic Demand. Goods for which the price elasticity is greater than 1 have an **elastic demand.** For example, the quantity of foreign travel demanded decreases by more than 1 percent when the price rises by 1 percent because many people tend to travel at home rather than abroad when the price of foreign travel rises.

Goods for which the price elasticity of demand is less than 1 have an **inelastic demand.** For example, the quantity of eggs demanded decreases by less than 1 percent when the price of eggs rises by 1 percent because many people do not want to substitute other things for eggs at breakfast.

Perfectly Elastic versus Perfectly Inelastic Demand. A demand curve that is vertical is called **perfectly inelastic.** Figure 6 shows a perfectly inelastic demand curve. The elasticity is zero because when the price changes, the quantity demanded does not change at all. No matter what the price, the same quantity is demanded. People who need insulin have a perfectly inelastic demand for insulin. As long as there are no substitutes for insulin, they will pay whatever they have to in order to get the insulin.

A demand curve that is horizontal is called **perfectly elastic.** Figure 6 also shows a perfectly elastic demand curve. The elasticity is infinite. The perfectly flat demand curve is sometimes hard to imagine because it entails infinitely large movements of quantity for tiny changes in price. In order to better visualize this case, you can imagine that the curve is tilted ever so slightly. Goods that have a lot of comparable substitutes are likely to have high elasticities of demand.

Table 1 summarizes the terminology about elasticities.

FIGURE 6
Perfectly Elastic and Perfectly Inelastic Demand

A perfectly inelastic demand curve is a vertical line at a certain quantity. The quantity demanded is completely insensitive to the price: Whatever happens to the price, the quantity demanded does not change. A perfectly elastic demand curve is a flat line at a certain price. An increase in price reduces the quantity demanded to zero; a small decrease in price raises the quantity demanded by a huge (literally infinite) amount.

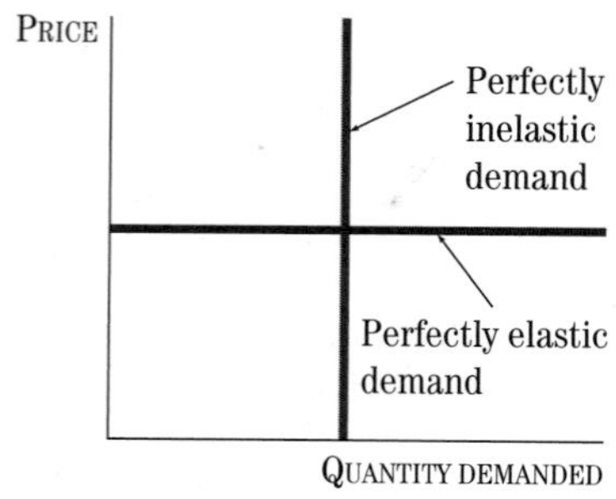

TABLE 1
Terminology for Price Elasticity of Demand

Term	Value of Price Elasticity of Demand (e_d)
Perfectly inelastic	0 (vertical demand curve)
Inelastic	Less than 1
Elastic	Greater than 1
Perfectly elastic	Infinity (horizontal demand curve)

Revenue and the Price Elasticity of Demand

When people purchase 60 million barrels of oil at \$20 a barrel, they must pay a total of \$1,200 million (\$20 × 60 million). This is a payment to the oil producers and is the producers' revenue. In general, revenue is the price (*P*) times the quantity (*Q*), or *P* × *Q*. A change in price will therefore affect revenue. While this seems obvious, it is important that you understand exactly how price affects revenue. In fact, a change in price has two opposite effects on revenue. For instance, when the price increases, people pay more for each item, which increases revenue; but they buy fewer items, which in turn reduces revenue. The price elasticity of demand determines which of these two opposite effects dominates, because elasticity is a measure of how much the quantity demanded changes when price changes.

Figure 7, which is a replica of Figure 3 with the scales changed, illustrates the effects on revenue. In the top graph, revenue went from \$1.2 billion (60 million × \$20 = \$1,200 million) to \$1.056 billion (48 million × \$22 = \$1,056 million). In other

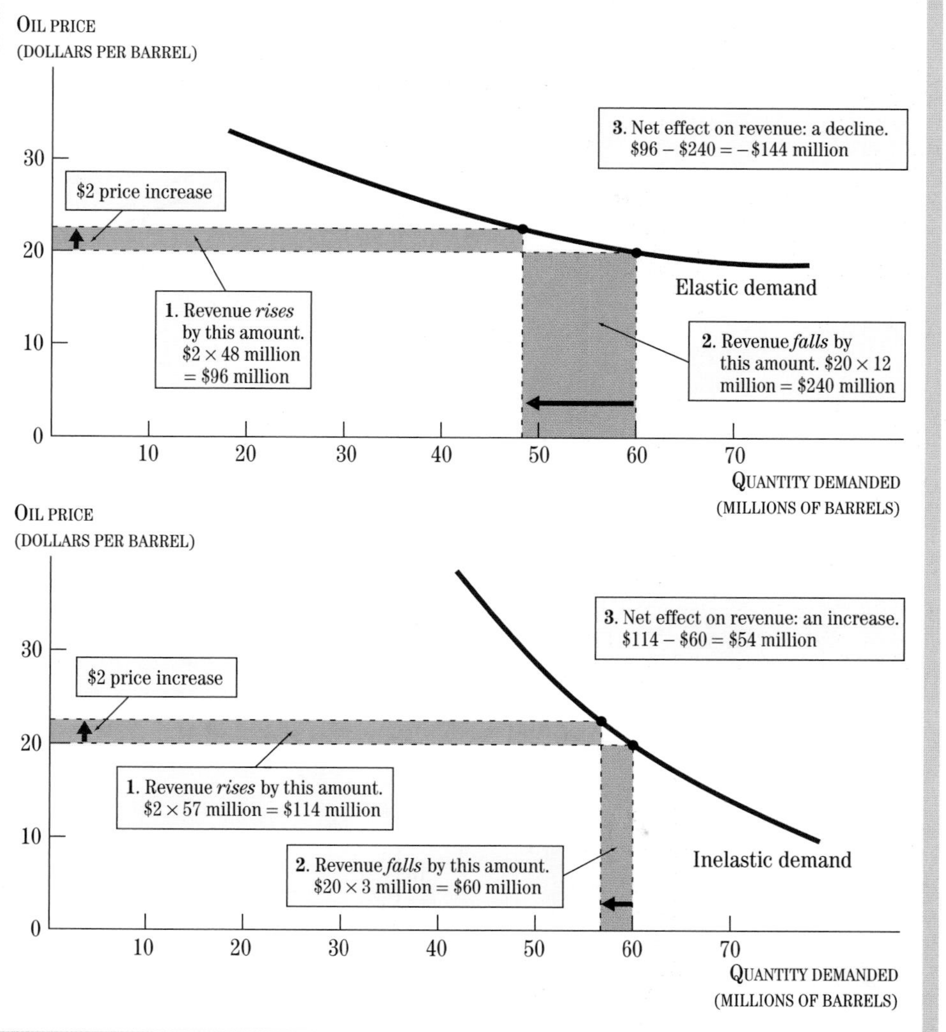

FIGURE 7
Effects of an Increase in the Price of Oil on Revenue
These graphs are replicas of the demand curves for oil shown in Figure 3, with the scale changed to show the change in revenue when the price of oil is increased. An increase in the price has two effects on revenue, as shown by the gray- and pink-shaded rectangles. The increase in revenue (gray rectangle) is due to the higher price. The decrease in revenue (pink rectangle) is due to the decline in the quantity demanded as the price is increased. In the top graph, where elasticity is greater than 1, the net effect is a decline in revenue; in the bottom graph, where elasticity is less than 1, the net effect is an increase in revenue.

words, revenue declined by $144 million even though price increased. Now compare this to the revenue changes in the bottom graph. There revenue went from $1.2 billion to $1.254 billion (57 million × $22 = $1,254 million), an increase of $54 million. Using the old price and the old quantity demanded, you can show that the elasticity of demand in the top graph is 2 while the elasticity of demand in the bottom graph is 0.5. We can see from this example that, following a price increase, revenue fell in the case where the elasticity was greater than 1, and revenue rose when elasticity was less than 1.

Is this always the case? We can illustrate the relationship between elasticity and revenue better by using a simple straight-line demand curve, as shown in Figure 8. Because this is a straight line, the slope is identical at all points on the demand curve—a $1 change in price will change quantity demanded by 2 units.

If you calculate the elasticity of demand at each point along the line, what you will find is that the elasticity of demand is equal to 1 at a price of $5 and a quantity

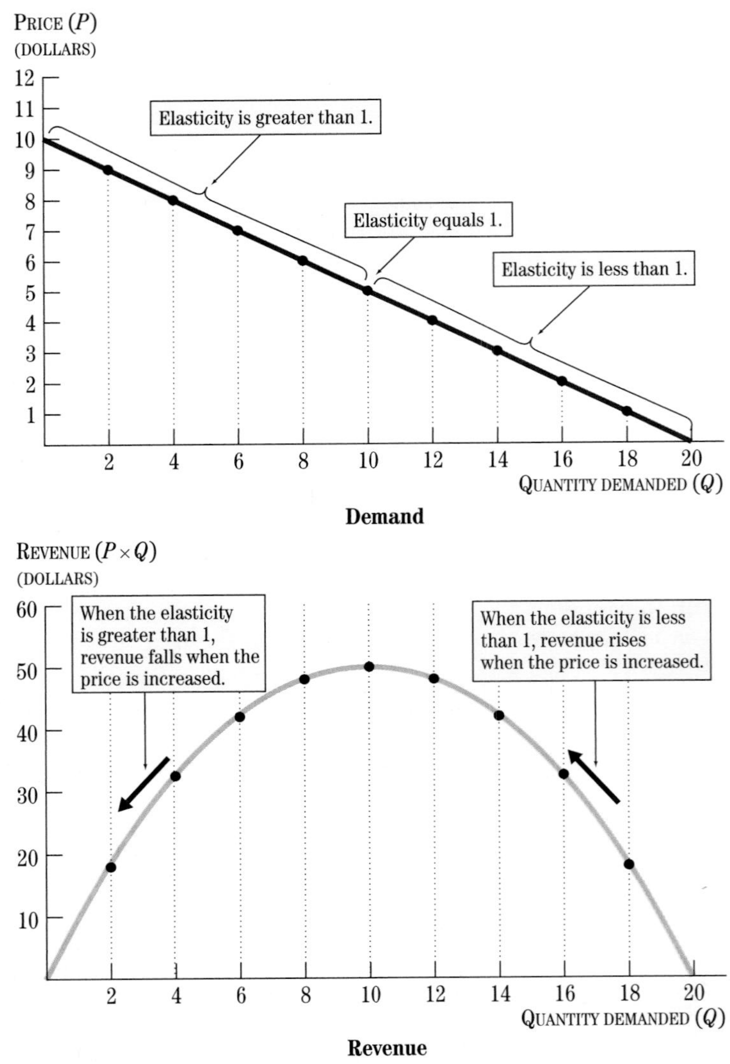

FIGURE 8
Revenue and Elasticity of a Straight-Line Demand Curve
Along the straight-line demand curve at the top, the price elasticity ranges from above 1 (to the left) to below 1 (to the right). When the price elasticity is greater than 1, an increase in the price will reduce revenue, as shown in the lower panel.

demanded of 10. At this point, a $1 change in price (which is equivalent to a 20 percent change in the price) results in a 2-unit change in quantity demanded (which is also equivalent to a 20 percent change in the quantity demanded). To the left of this point, the elasticity of demand is greater than 1. You can see this by considering what happens at a price of $6 and a quantity demanded of 8. A $1 change in price will continue to bring about a 2-unit change in quantity demanded, but the percentage change in price is smaller ($1/$6 = 16.66 percent instead of 20 percent), while the percentage change in quantity is larger (2/8 = 25 percent instead of 20 percent). Thus, the elasticity will now be greater than 1. To the right of this point, the elasticity of demand is less than 1. You can see this by considering what happens at a price of $4 and a quantity demanded of 12. A $1 change in price will continue to bring about a 2-unit change in quantity demanded, but the percentage change in price is larger ($1/$4 = 25 percent instead of 20 percent), while the percentage change in quantity is smaller (2/12 = 16.67 percent instead of 20 percent). Thus, the elasticity will now be less than 1.

For each point along the demand curve, you can calculate revenue by simply multiplying price and quantity. The bottom panel of Figure 8 shows how revenue changes as the quantity demanded changes. Revenue begins at $0 (at a price of $10, quantity demanded is zero), increases for a while as quantity demanded increases, then starts decreasing again, ending up at $0 (because quantity demanded of 20 corresponds to a price of zero). Interestingly, you can see that the range over which revenue is rising with quantity demanded corresponds exactly with the range where the elasticity is greater than 1. Similarly, the range over which revenue is falling corresponds with the region of the demand curve where the elasticity is less than 1. Table 2 summarizes the relationship between revenue and the price elasticity of demand. An increase in price will raise revenue if the elasticity is less than 1 and will lower revenue if the elasticity is greater than 1.

This relationship between the elasticity of demand and the revenue impact of a price change is a very important one. Businesses need to know the price elasticity of demand for their products to understand the implications of raising or lowering prices. For instance, in 2003, United Airlines announced 40 percent cuts in some one-way business fares in the hope of increasing revenue. Would more business travelers decide to fly with lower fares? If so, would the increase in customers lead to an increase or a decrease in United Airlines' revenue? The answer depends on the price elasticity of demand for business air travel. Similarly, the recent increase in the use of wireless phones and prepaid phone cards has resulted in a decrease in the demand for pay phones. In 2001, because of this decrease in demand, SBC Communications Inc. increased the price of a pay phone call. Could this increase in price lead to an increase in revenue? The answer depends on the price elasticity of demand for pay phone calls.

If demand for business air travel is price elastic and demand for pay phones is price inelastic, then both United Airlines and SBC changed prices to increase revenue—United Airlines cut business fares to increase revenue, taking advantage of price-elastic demand, and SBC increased the price of using a pay phone call to increase revenue, taking advantage of price-inelastic demand. How would United or

TABLE 2
Revenue and the Price Elasticity of Demand

Elasticity Is	Effect of a Price Increase on Revenue	Effect of a Price Decrease on Revenue
Less than 1 (< 1)	Revenue increases	Revenue decreases
Equal to 1 (= 1)	No change in revenue	No change in revenue
Greater than 1 (> 1)	Revenue decreases	Revenue increases

TABLE 3
Estimated Price Elasticities of Demand

Type of Good or Service	Price Elasticity
Jewelry	2.6
Eggs	0.1
Telephone (first line)	0.1
Telephone (second line)	0.4
Foreign travel	1.2
Cigarettes (18–24)	0.6
Cigarettes (25–39)	0.4
Cigarettes (40–older)	0.1
Gasoline (short run)	0.2
Gasoline (long run)	0.7

SBC know whether demand would be elastic or inelastic? The next section discusses the determinants of price elasticity of demand. You should judge as you read this chapter whether demand for business air travel and demand for pay phone calls are likely to be price elastic or price inelastic.

What Determines the Size of the Price Elasticity of Demand?

Table 3 shows price elasticities of demand for several different goods and services. The price elasticity for jewelry, for example, is 2.6. This means that for each percentage increase in the price of jewelry, the quantity demanded will fall by 2.6 percent. Compared with other elasticities, this is large. On the other hand, the price elasticity of eggs is very small. For each percentage increase in the price of eggs, the quantity of eggs demanded falls by only .1 percent.

Why do these elasticities differ in size? Several factors determine a good's elasticity.

The Degree of Substitutability. A key factor is whether there are good substitutes for the item in question. Can people easily find a substitute when the price goes up? If the answer is yes, then the price elasticity will be high. Foreign travel has a high elasticity because there is a reasonably good substitute: domestic travel.

On the other hand, the low price elasticity for eggs can be explained by the lack of good substitutes. As many fans of eggs know, these items are unique; synthetic eggs are not good substitutes. Hence, the price elasticity of eggs is small. People will continue to buy them even if the price rises a lot.

The degree of substitutability depends in part on whether a good is a necessity or a luxury. There are no good substitutes for a refrigerator if you want to easily preserve food for more than a few hours. However, a fancy refrigerator with an exterior that blends in with the rest of your kitchen is more of a luxury and is likely to have a higher price elasticity.

Big-Ticket versus Little-Ticket Items. If a good represents a large fraction of people's income, then the price elasticity will be high. If the price of foreign travel doubles, many people will not be able to afford to travel abroad. On the other hand, if the good represents a small fraction of income, the elasticity will be low. For example, if the price of eggs doubles, most people will still be able to afford to buy as many eggs as before the price rise.

Temporary versus Permanent Price Changes. If a change in price is known to be temporary, the price elasticity of demand will tend to be high because many people can easily shift their purchases either later or earlier. For example, suppose a sewing machine store announces a discount price that will last only one day. Then people will shift their purchase of the sewing machine they were thinking about buying to the sale day.

On the other hand, if the price cut is permanent, the price elasticity will be smaller. People who expect the price decrease to be permanent will not find it advantageous to buy sooner rather than later.

Differences in Preferences. Different groups of consumers may have different levels of elasticity. For example, young cigarette smokers, whose habit of smoking may not be entrenched, are more sensitive to changes in prices than older smokers. Table 3 shows that the price elasticity of demand for cigarettes for young adults between 18 and 24 years old is much higher than the very low price elasticity for people older than 40.

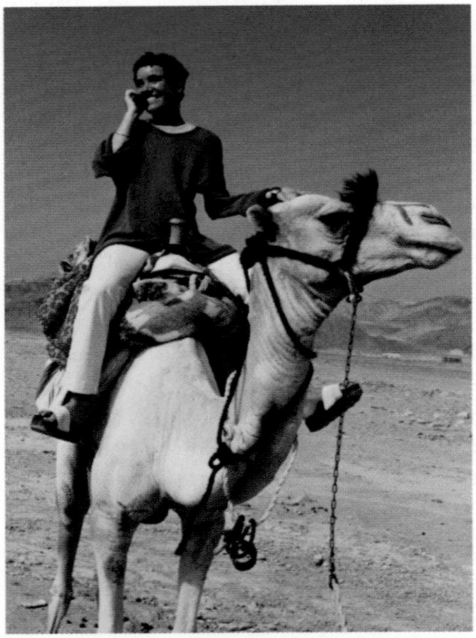

Price Elasticity of Cell Phone Service in the Desert
There's probably not much of a substitute available for long-distance communication in the desert, which would make the price elasticity of the cell phone used here quite low. Do you think the caller in this picture would be equally insensitive to an increase of $.10 per minute in the price of her calls if she were seated in her apartment in Chicago?

What Is the Price Elasticity of Demand for Star Wars Movies?
For these fans, the prospect of attending the May 2005 opening of *Star Wars: Episode III—Revenge of the Sith* is price inelastic (i.e., they will pay almost anything for a ticket to this opening); but for moviegoers in general, the answer to that question may say a lot about the future of the movie industry. If purchases of movie tickets fall off as the price of a general admission ticket goes up, and at the same time revenue from ticket sales increases, then demand for movie tickets is price inelastic.

Long-Run versus Short-Run Elasticity. Frequently the price elasticity of demand is low immediately after a price change but then increases after a period of time has passed. In order to analyze these changes, economists distinguish between the *short run* and the *long run.* The short run is simply a period of time before people have made all their adjustments or changed their habits; the long run is a period of time long enough for people to make such adjustments or change their habits.

Many personal adjustments to a change in prices take a long time. For example, when the price of gas increases, people can reduce the quantity demanded in the short run only by driving less and using other forms of transportation more, or by reducing the heating in their homes. This may be inconvenient or impossible. In the long run, however, when it comes time to buy a new car or a new heating system, they can buy a more fuel-efficient one, or one that uses an alternative energy source. Thus, the quantity of gas demanded falls by larger amounts in the long run than in the short run (Table 3).

Habits that are difficult to break also cause differences between short-run and long-run elasticity. Even a large increase in the price of tobacco may have a small effect on the quantity purchased because people cannot break the smoking habit quickly. But after a period of time, the high price of cigarettes may encourage them to break the habit, while discouraging potential new users. Thus, the long-run elasticity for tobacco is higher than the short-run elasticity.

Here are a few examples to test your understanding of the determinants of the price elasticity of demand. The movie industry reported that its summer 2004 revenue was 3 percent higher than the previous year. A closer analysis reveals that ticket sales were down 1 percent. How could ticket revenue increase at the same time that the number of tickets sold decreased? The ticket price must have increased. Demand for movies must also be price inelastic, so that the reduction in ticket sales was more than offset by the increase in the price of the movie tickets. Does this make sense for the movie industry? It is plausible that some people feel that they *must see* the newest release and that the cost of the movie is a little-ticket item for many people who go to the movies. This would make the price elasticity of demand low and demand plausibly price inelastic.

General Motors Corporation reported that in 2002 its revenue rose by 5.4 percent. At the same time, General Motors offered large discounts to customers purchasing cars. How could revenue increase while the price of cars was going down? It must be that more cars were sold at the lower price and that demand for these cars is price elastic. The reduction in price was therefore offset by the increase in cars sold, and revenue increased. Does this make sense for General Motors cars? It is plausible that customers feel there are close substitutes and that this is a big-ticket purchase for many customers. This would make the price elasticity of demand high and demand plausibly price elastic.

Income Elasticity and Cross-Price Elasticity of Demand

Recall that the price elasticity of demand refers to movements along the demand curve. We emphasized in Chapter 3 the difference between a shift in the demand curve and a movement along the demand curve. A *shift* in the demand curve occurs when there is a change in the quantity that people are willing to buy due to a change in anything except the price—for example, a change in income.

income elasticity of demand: the percentage change in quantity demanded of a good divided by the percentage change in income.

The concept of elasticity can be applied to changes in the quantity that consumers are willing to buy caused by changes in income. This elasticity must be distinguished from the price elasticity of demand. The **income elasticity of demand** is

TABLE 4
Estimated Income Elasticities of Demand

Type of Good or Service	Income Elasticity
Food	.58
Clothing/footwear	.88
Transport	1.18
Medical care	1.35
Recreation	1.42

the percentage change in the quantity of a good demanded at any given price divided by a percentage change in income. That is,

$$\text{Income elasticity of demand} = \frac{\text{percentage change in quantity demanded}}{\text{percentage change in income}}$$

For example, if incomes rise by 10 percent and, as a result, people purchase 15 percent more health care at a given price, the income elasticity of health care is 1.5. Table 4 lists income elasticities of demand for several different goods and services.

As discussed in Chapter 3, the demand for most goods increases when people's incomes increase. If you have more income, your demand for movies will probably increase at each price. Recall that a normal good is a good or service whose demand increases as income increases. But not every good is a normal good; if the demand for a good declines when income increases, the good is called an inferior good. The income elasticity of demand for an inferior good is negative and is reported as a negative number by economists.

cross-price elasticity of demand: the percentage change in the quantity demanded of one good divided by the percentage change in the price of another good.

Another type of elasticity relating to shifts in the demand curve is the **cross-price elasticity of demand,** which is defined as the percentage change in the quantity demanded divided by the percentage change in the price of another good. For example, an increase in the price of Rollerblades would *increase* the quantity demanded of bicycles at every price as people shifted away from Rollerblading to bicycle riding. Rollerblades are a substitute for bicycles. A cross-price elasticity can also go in the other direction. An increase in the price of bicycle helmets may *reduce* the demand for bicycles. Bicycle helmets and bicycles are complements. For a complement, the cross-price elasticity of demand is negative.

REVIEW

- The price elasticity of demand, or elasticity, is used to measure how much the quantity demanded changes when the price changes. Elasticity also helps determine how large a price increase will occur as a result of a shift in supply, and by how much revenue will change when the price rises.
- Elasticity is a unit-free measure—it is the ratio of the percentage change in quantity demanded to the percentage change in price. In other words, it measures by what percentage quantity demanded changes when the price changes by 1 percent.
- Horizontal demand curves have infinite price elasticity. Vertical demand curves have zero price elasticity. Most products have a price elasticity between these two extremes. We use the term *elastic demand* to refer to an elasticity of demand that is greater than 1 and *inelastic demand* to refer to an elasticity of demand that is less than 1.
- Other than the horizontal and vertical cases, elasticity is different from the slope of the demand curve, however. A demand curve that is a straight line has a different elasticity of demand at each point.
- The size of the price elasticity of demand depends on the availability of substitutes for the item, whether the item represents a large fraction of income, and whether the price change is temporary or permanent.
- Whereas the price elasticity of demand refers to movements along the demand curve, the income elasticity of demand refers to shifts in the demand curve caused by changes in income. Most goods are normal and have a positive income elasticity of demand. Inferior goods have a negative income elasticity of demand.
- The cross-price elasticity of demand also relates to shifts in the demand curve, in this case, a change in the price of a complement or substitute good.

ECONOMICS IN ACTION

Will an Increase in the Minimum Wage Benefit Poor Workers?

When the 110th Congress took office in January 2007, the first bill brought to the floor by the newly elected Democratic majority was an increase in the federal minimum wage from $5.15 to $7.25. The *Washington Post*[1] reported that the plan "could begin the process of ending Congress's longest stretch without a minimum-wage increase since the mandatory minimum was created in 1938. In the past decade, inflation has depleted the value of the minimum wage to the lowest level in more than 50 years." The proponents of the bill argued that a boost in the minimum wage would be an important source of additional income for millions of poor workers (according to the *Washington Post*, almost 6 million workers earning the $5.15 minimum wage and 7 million earning just above that level). Opponents and skeptics argued that the bill would impose too great a burden on employers, would lead to many minimum-wage workers losing their jobs, and would not do as much to help poor people as proponents seemed to claim.

Below, we discuss the policy debate (and provide links to online sources) surrounding the arguments for and against a minimum-wage increase. We also discuss how these arguments relate to the material you have covered, or will cover, in this book.

WHAT IS THE FEDERAL MINIMUM WAGE?

The federal minimum wage is a floor on wages that applies to all "covered non-exempt" workers. In other words, with a few exceptions discussed later, a worker cannot be paid less than the minimum wage—essentially, a floor is placed on the price of labor. If a covered worker resides in a state where the state minimum wage exceeds the federal minimum wage, then the worker has to be paid the higher state minimum. The Department of Labor[2] provides a concise summary of who is a "covered non-exempt worker." Essentially, anyone who works for an enterprise that has more than two employees and does more than $500,000 of business a year is covered. Any individual working in a company that operates interstate is covered, as are domestic workers like nannies and cooks. Exemptions are granted to various categories of workers like farm workers, sailors on non-U.S. registered ships, workers who earn tips (provided tip income + wage income exceeds the minimum wage), teenagers (in the first 90 days of a new job), and workers with disabilities that affect their production.

WHAT ARE THE ARGUMENTS FOR INCREASING THE FEDERAL MINIMUM WAGE?

A nice summary[3] of the arguments in support of an increase in the minimum wage has been provided by the Economic Policy Institute (EPI) a think tank located in Washington, D.C. According to the EPI, an increase in the minimum wage would raise the hourly wage rate of almost 11 percent of the work force, either directly because they earn the minimum wage or indirectly because they earn a wage that is just above the current minimum wage or is tied to the minimum wage. The EPI also argued that the average minimum-wage worker earns more than 50 percent of the family's earnings and that almost 1.5 million single mothers would benefit from the higher minimum wage. The benefits would also accrue more to women, minorities, and working households at the bottom of the income distribution. In addition, because so many years have elapsed since the last minimum-wage increase, even with the benefit of the Earned Income Tax Credit, another program designed to increase the incomes of the working poor, a single parent with two children working 40 hours a week ends up earning below the poverty line. The EPI pointed out that inflation had reduced the real minimum wage—the $5.15 minimum wage that was implemented in 1995 was worth $3.95 in inflation-adjusted terms. Finally, and perhaps most importantly, the EPI argued that there is no evidence of job loss from the last increase in the minimum wage.

To put it simply, the arguments are that the minimum wage has been unchanged for too long, it is now time to increase it to give a boost to the earnings of minimum-wage earners, few workers will lose their jobs because firms will refuse to pay a higher wage, and many minimum-wage workers who will benefit from this increase are extremely dependent on their job to support their families. The EPI also issued a statement of support for increasing the minimum wage signed by 650 leading economists, including five Nobel Prize winners.[4]

WHAT ARE THE ARGUMENTS AGAINST INCREASING THE FEDERAL MINIMUM WAGE?

Not everyone agreed with the arguments made by the proponents of the plan. Opposition in Congress and the Senate-centered around the cost imposed on business

[1] "House Passes Increase in Minimum Wage to $7.25," *Washington Post*, January 11, 2007.

[2] http://www.dol.gov/esa/minwage/q-a.htm.

[3] "Minimum Wage, Facts at a Glance," http://www.epi.org/content.cfm/issueguides_minwage_minwage facts.

[4] "Hundreds of Economists Say: Increase the Minimum Wage," http://www.epi.org/content.cfm/minwagestmt2006.

owners who had to pay the salaries. Opponents claimed that the hardships imposed by having to pay $7.25 an hour would force small business owners to lay off workers or even put them out of business. They agreed to be more supportive of the proposal if it was linked with tax relief for business owners to compensate them for the additional costs that were being imposed on them. The general economic arguments against an increase in the minimum wage are nicely summarized by the economist David Neumark.[5] Professor Neumark was not writing about the increase in the federal minimum wage, his focus was on an increase in the minimum wage in the state of Missouri. Nonetheless, the arguments he makes are applicable to this policy as well.

Professor Neumark provides three arguments for why a minimum wage increase may not work the way its proponents intend. First, he points out that in response to a higher price for labor, the quantity demanded of workers (especially low-skilled, low-paid ones) by firms would decrease. In other words, workers making the current minimum wage may lose their jobs and end up earning zero dollars instead of the higher minimum wage. Second, low-income workers losing their jobs would be especially harmful to the poorest families, who depend on these workers' incomes. Third, the higher minimum wage would make it hard for young workers to find jobs, thus denying them the experience and training needed to eventually obtain a higher-paying position. He also points out that many minimum-wage workers are not poor, they are teenagers from relatively well-off families. Hence, he argues, an increase in the minimum wage is not a particularly well-targeted policy in terms of helping the poor.

The Congressional Budget Office (CBO) picked up on this theme of how to best help the poor. The CBO, in a letter dated January 9, 2007, addressed to the outgoing Republican chair of the Senate Finance Committee,[6] pointed out that only 18 percent of minimum-wage workers lived in families who earned an income below the poverty line. Similarly, only 15 percent of the increase in wages would go to families earning below the poverty line. In contrast, the CBO argued, an increase in the Earned Income Tax Credit program, which provides additional income to working poor families through the income tax system, would provide similar amounts of income to poor families for about 20 percent of the cost of the minimum-wage increase.

In essence, the arguments against the minimum-wage increase were that it would lead to job losses, would hurt poor families that were the least able to afford job losses, would benefit mostly workers in families above the poverty line, and was more expensive and less well targeted than other programs designed to boost the incomes of the working poor.

THE KEY ECONOMIC QUESTION

The arguments for and against the minimum-wage increase rest on an economic concept that is familiar to you: the elasticity of demand. If the elasticity of demand for labor is large, then the imposition of a higher minimum wage that increases the price of hiring workers will lead to a substantial decrease in the demand for workers. On the other hand, if the demand for labor is relatively inelastic, then an increase in the price of labor will not lead to much of a decrease in the demand for labor. In essence, you could simplify the argument to say that supporters of the minimum wage increase believed that the demand for labor was not very elastic (more workers would earn a higher wage, and very few would lose their jobs), whereas the skeptics and the opponents believed that the demand was very elastic (many workers would lose their jobs, and only a few would earn the higher wage). How do economists settle disputes like this? Once the theory behind the opposing sides of an argument is understood, the best way to settle the debate is to use data to settle it empirically. In other words, use past experiences with minimum-wage increases, along with the tools of statistical and economic analysis, to estimate the magnitude of the elasticity of demand for minimum-wage labor.

THE EMPIRICAL EVIDENCE

There have been a plethora of empirical studies estimating the impact of a minimum-wage increase on the labor market. Perhaps the work that has had the most impact in recent years is a study by David Card and Alan Krueger,[7] who showed that an increase in the state minimum wage in New Jersey had no impact on the employment of minimum-wage workers in the fast-food industry. Their study surveyed fast-food establishments located along the New Jersey/Pennsylvania border, comparing the response by employers in New Jersey (where wages went up) to the response by employers in Pennsylvania (who did not have to pay higher wages). One interesting explanation for their results was that they found that the price of fast food went up in New Jersey following the change. In other words, employers seemed to be passing on their higher wage costs

[5] David Neumark, "The Economic Effects of Minimum Wages," http://showmeinstitute.org/smi_study_2.pdf

[6] www.cbo.gov/ftpdoc.cfm?index=7721&type=1.

[7] David Card and Alan B. Krueger, "Minimum Wages and Employment: A Case Study of the Fast-Food Industry in New Jersey and Pennsylvania," *American Economic Review*, 84(4), 1994.

to their customers, which in turn would explain why the elasticity of demand was not apparently very high. An earlier, more broad-based study by David Neumark and William Wascher[8] concluded that the elasticity of demand was between −0.1 and −0.2 for teenagers (a 10 percent increase in wages would reduce teenage employment by between 1 and 2 percent).

A more recent paper by the same authors provides a comprehensive survey (more than 150 pages in length) of the empirical literature on the minimum wage.[9] After looking at the evidence for the United States and for other countries, they conclude that recent increases in the minimum wage had indicated an elasticity of demand for teenage labor of between −0.1 and −0.3 and of around −0.1 for workers who made close to the existing minimum wage. They also find generally larger effects on hours (firms are more likely to cut back on the number of hours in response to a higher minimum wage) and more long-term effects (over time, firms are more likely to substitute away from minimum-wage workers to more productive, higher-paid workers or to invest in machines and equipment that do the job that minimum-wage workers do).

[8]David Neumark and William Wascher, "Employment Effects of Minimum and Sub-Minimum Wages: Panel Data on State Minimum Wage Laws," *Industrial and Labor Relations Review*, 46(1), 1992.
[9]David Neumark and William Wascher, "Minimum Wages and Employment: A Review of Evidence from the New Minimum Wage Research," *NBER* Working Paper No. 12663, November 2006.

THE DECISION

An increase in the federal minimum wage from \$5.15 to \$7.25 represents a 40 percent increase in the minimum wage, which, if you go by the estimates above, would reduce teenage employment by between 4 and 12 percent (with higher wages for the remaining 88 to 96 percent of workers) and reduce low-wage employment by between 0 and 4 percent (for the remaining 96 percent of workers). Some questions for you to ponder:

1. If you were in Congress, would you support this increase?
2. Would your answer change if you looked beyond the elasticities and focused on how many minimum-wage workers came from poor households?
3. Is the opportunity cost of implementing a minimum-wage increase, instead of, say, expanding the Earned Income Tax Credit program, worth it?
4. Do you think that legislators who oppose a minimum-wage bill and argue for an expansion of the Earned Income Tax Credit (EITC) program would in fact have supported an EITC program expansion in the absence of the minimum-wage bill?
5. Should Congress continue to have divisive battles over the minimum wage every few years, or should it instead come up with an agreeable number that is automatically indexed to inflation?

ELASTICITY OF SUPPLY

Knowing how sensitive the quantity supplied is to a change in price is just as important as knowing how sensitive the quantity demanded is. The price elasticity of supply measures this sensitivity. "Price elasticity of supply" is sometimes shortened to "supply elasticity" or "elasticity of supply." Supply describes the behavior of firms that produce goods. A high price elasticity of supply means that firms raise their production by a large amount if the price increases. A low price elasticity of supply means that firms raise their production only a little if the price increases.

price elasticity of supply: the percentage change in quantity supplied divided by the percentage change in price.

The **price elasticity of supply** is defined as the percentage change in the quantity supplied divided by the percentage change in the price. That is,

$$\text{Price elasticity of supply} = \frac{\text{percentage change in quantity supplied}}{\text{percentage change in the price}}$$

The price elasticity of supply refers to a particular supply curve, such as the supply curve for gasoline or video games. All other things that affect supply are held constant when we compute the price elasticity of supply. For example, suppose the price elasticity of supply for video games is .5. Then, if the price of video games rises by 10 percent, the quantity of video games supplied will increase by 5 percent (.5 × 10).

Working with Supply Elasticities

All the attractive features of the price elasticity of demand also apply to the price elasticity of supply. To see this, let us first take a look at the definition of the price elasticity of supply using symbols. If we let the symbol e_s be the price elasticity of supply, then it can be written as

$$e_s = \frac{\Delta Q_s}{Q_s} \div \frac{\Delta P}{P} = \frac{\Delta Q_s / Q_s}{\Delta P / P}$$

where Q_s is the quantity supplied and P is the price. In other words, the price elasticity of supply is the percentage change in the quantity supplied divided by the percentage change in price. Observe the similarity of this expression to the analogous expression for the price elasticity of demand on page 93: The only difference is the use of quantity supplied (Q_s) rather than quantity demanded (Q_d). This means that the concepts and terminology for supply elasticity are very similar to those for demand elasticity. For example, if you go to Table 1 and replace "Demand" with "Supply," you have the terminology of price elasticity of supply. Moreover, like the price elasticity of demand, the price elasticity of supply is a unit-free measure, and the elasticity of supply and the slope of the supply curve are not the same thing.

Because of this similarity, our discussion of supply elasticity can be very brief. It is useful to consider the extreme cases of perfectly elastic supply and perfectly inelastic supply, and then to go through an example illustrating the importance of knowing the size of the price elasticity of supply.

Perfectly Inelastic Supply
The paintings of Leonardo da Vinci provide an example of a good with a perfectly inelastic supply. The supply curve is vertical because no matter how high the price, no more *Mona Lisas* can be produced. However, what about the demand to see the *Mona Lisa?* Is it perfectly inelastic? Will raising the price of admission charged by the Louvre Museum in Paris reduce the number of people coming to see the painting?

perfectly elastic supply: supply for which the price elasticity is infinite, indicating an infinite response of quantity supplied to a change in price and therefore a horizontal supply curve.

perfectly inelastic supply: supply for which the price elasticity is zero, indicating no response of quantity supplied to a change in price and therefore a vertical supply curve.

Perfectly Elastic and Perfectly Inelastic Supply. As in the case of demand, there can be **perfectly elastic supply** or **perfectly inelastic supply,** as shown in Figure 9. The vertical supply curve is perfectly inelastic; it has zero elasticity. Such supply curves are not unusual. For example, there is only one *Mona Lisa.* A higher price cannot bring about a higher quantity supplied, not even one more *Mona Lisa.* But the supply curve for most goods is not vertical. Higher prices will encourage coffee producers to use more fertilizer, hire more workers, and eventually plant more coffee trees. Thus the quantity supplied increases when the price rises.

The horizontal supply curve is perfectly elastic. In this case, the price does not change at all. It is the same regardless of the quantity supplied. It is easier to understand the horizontal supply curve if you view it as an approximation to a supply curve that is *nearly* horizontal, one with a very high elasticity. Then only a small increase in price brings forth a huge increase in the quantity supplied by firms.

Why the Size of the Price Elasticity of Supply Is Important. Now let us look at the importance of knowing the size of the supply elasticity even if it is not at one of these two extremes. Figure 10 shows two different supply curves for coffee. The horizontal axis shows the quantity of coffee supplied around the world in billions of pounds; the vertical axis shows the price in dollars per pound of coffee. For the supply curve in the top graph, the quantity supplied is very sensitive to the price; the price elasticity of supply is high. For the supply curve in the bottom graph, the price elasticity of supply is much lower.

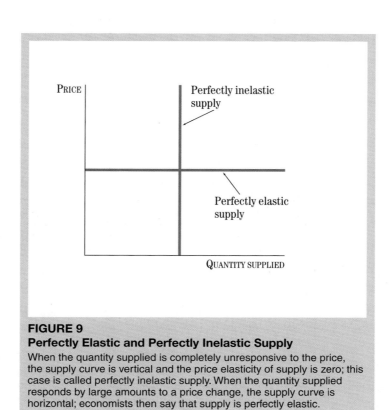

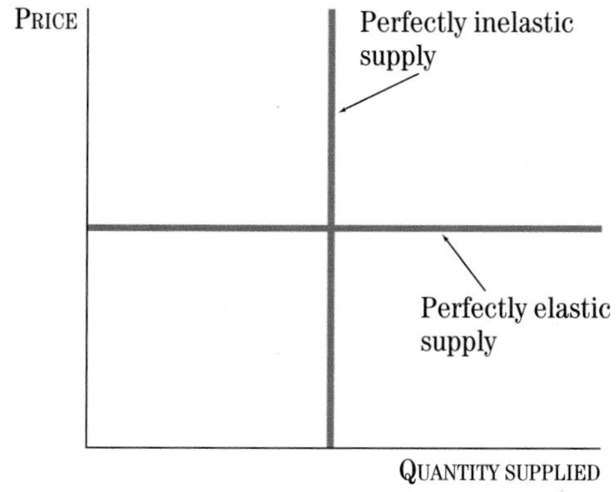

FIGURE 9
Perfectly Elastic and Perfectly Inelastic Supply
When the quantity supplied is completely unresponsive to the price, the supply curve is vertical and the price elasticity of supply is zero; this case is called perfectly inelastic supply. When the quantity supplied responds by large amounts to a price change, the supply curve is horizontal; economists then say that supply is perfectly elastic.

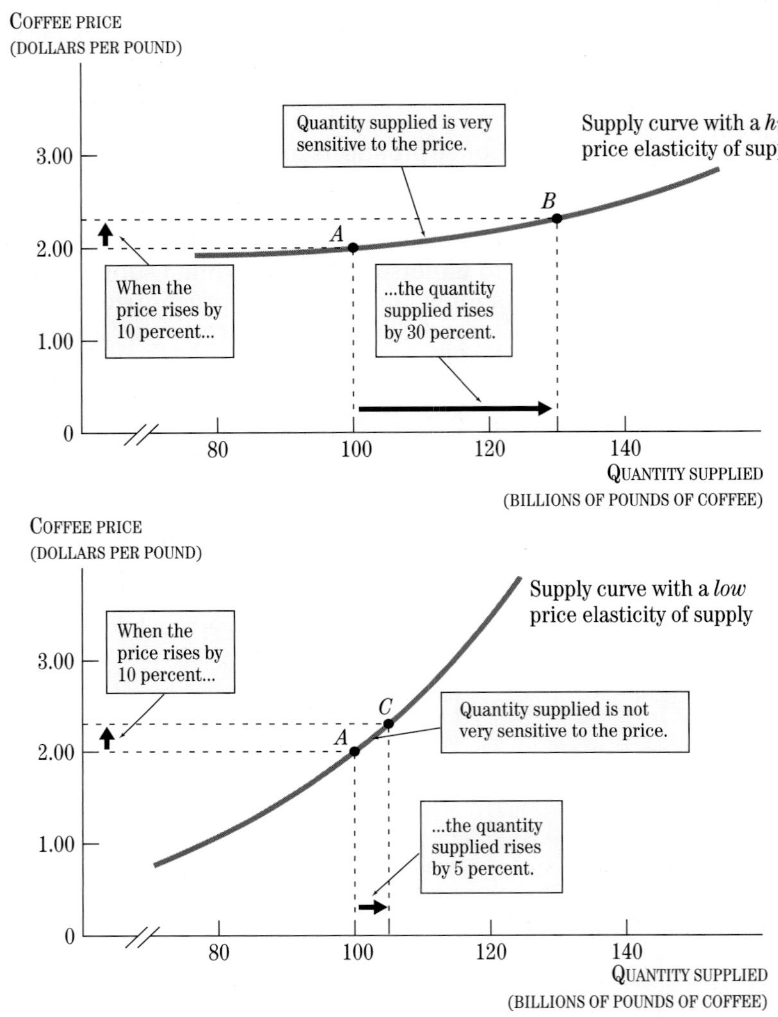

FIGURE 10
Comparing Different Sizes of the Price Elasticities of Supply
In the top graph, the quantity supplied is much more sensitive to price than in the bottom graph. The price elasticity of supply is greater between points *A* and *B* at the top than between points *A* and *C* at the bottom.

The price elasticity of supply is important for finding the response of price to shifts in demand. This is shown in Figure 11, where the demand for coffee declines, perhaps because of concerns about the effect of the caffeine in coffee or because of a decrease in the price of caffeine-free substitutes for coffee. In any case, if the price elasticity of supply is high, as in the top graph, the price does not change as much as when the price elasticity of supply is low, as in the bottom graph. With a high price elasticity, a small change in price is enough to get firms to bring the quantity supplied down to the lower quantity demanded.

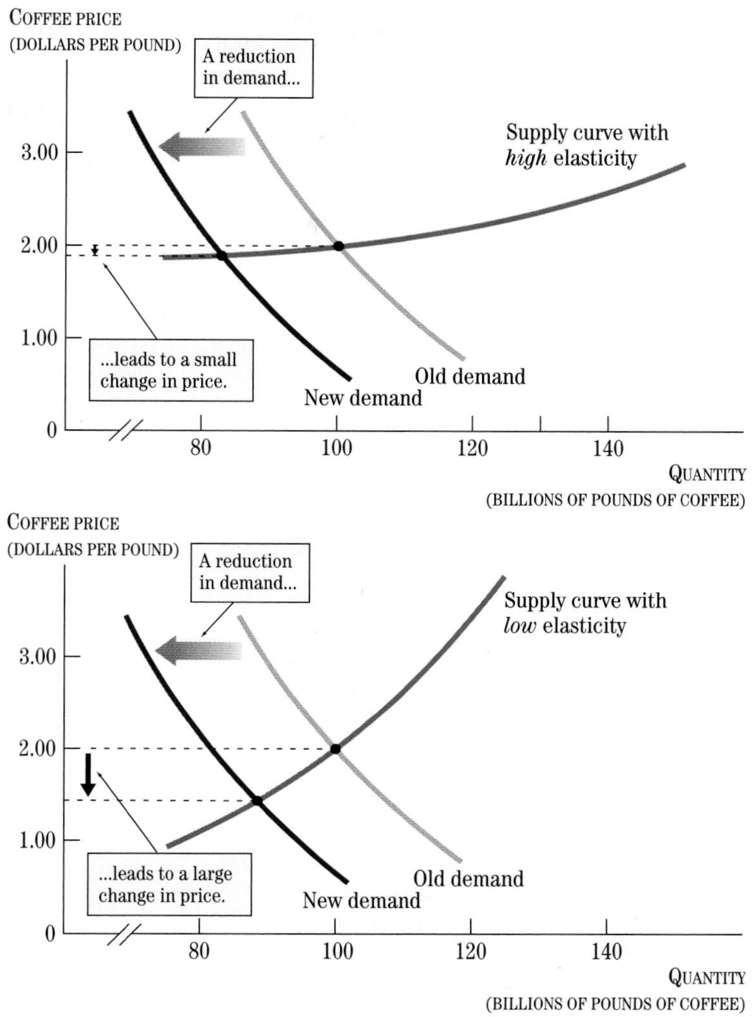

FIGURE 11
Importance of Knowing the Size of the Price Elasticity of Supply
When demand changes, the price will also change. If the price elasticity of supply is high, there will be a small change in price. If the price elasticity of supply is low, there will be a large change in price.

REVIEW

- The price elasticity of supply is a number that tells us how sensitive the quantity supplied is to the price. It is defined as the percentage change in the quantity supplied divided by the percentage change in the price.
- The attractive features of the price elasticity of demand are also true for the price elasticity of supply. Its size does not depend on the units of measurement of either price or quantity.
- The price elasticity of supply is useful for determining how much prices will change when there is a change in demand.

CONCLUSION

In this chapter, we have extended our analysis of the supply and demand model in two directions. We first learned about what happens when the government intervenes to put a price ceiling or a price floor into the economy. Understanding how to use the supply and demand model with price floors and ceilings enables us to better understand policy debates such as the one surrounding the increase in the minimum wage.

The second extension was to develop an understanding of *how much* the equilibrium price and quantity change in response to changes in supply or demand. The concept of price elasticity of demand helps us understand what happens to the quantity demanded when there is a change in price or when there is a change in the supply of a good. We can also predict whether revenue will increase or decrease when prices are cut or raised. The related concept of the elasticity of supply is also useful in understanding what happens to the quantity supplied when there is a change in price or when there is a change in the demand for a good. We also discussed the concept of an income elasticity of demand, which can help clarify how the quantity demanded for various goods will change as incomes rise, and the cross-price elasticity of demand, which tells us how much the quantity demanded of a good changes as prices for substitute or complementary goods change.

KEY POINTS

1. Governments will occasionally intervene in markets because they think that the equilibrium price is too high or too low. When they act to impose a maximum price on a market, because they think the price that buyers have to pay is too high, they are said to be imposing a price ceiling. When they act to impose a minimum price on a market, because they think the price that sellers are receiving is too low, they are said to be imposing a price floor.
2. Price ceilings cause shortages, with the quantity supplied being less than the quantity demanded. Shortages lead to rationing or black markets. Price floors cause surpluses, with the quantity supplied being greater than the quantity demanded. Surpluses lead to resources being diverted away from other productive activities to deal with the extra output that needs to be stored or disposed of.
3. Rent controls are a classic application of a price ceiling, and minimum wages are a classic application of a price floor. The supply model helps us understand some basic issues related to these policies, which frequently appear in the news today. We will go on to develop the supply and demand model further, which will allow us to do a more sophisticated analysis of minimum-wage laws, for example, than we have done so far in this chapter.
4. Elasticity is a measure of the sensitivity of one economic variable to another. For example, the price elasticity of demand measures how much the quantity demanded changes when the price changes.
5. Elasticity is a unit-free measure. The price elasticity of demand is the percentage change in the quantity demanded divided by the percentage change in price. It refers to changes in price and quantity demanded along the demand curve, all other things being equal.
6. Demand is said to be elastic if the price elasticity of demand is greater than 1 and inelastic if the price elasticity of demand is less than 1.
7. When the elasticity is greater than 1, an increase in the price reduces the quantity demanded by a percentage greater than the percentage increase in the price, thereby reducing revenue. When the elasticity is less than 1, an increase in the price reduces the quantity demanded by a percentage less than the percentage increase in the price, thereby increasing revenue.

8. The elasticity of demand for a good depends on whether the good has close substitutes, whether its value is a large or a small fraction of total income, and the time period of the change.
9. Whereas the price elasticity of demand refers to movements along the demand curve, the income elasticity of demand refers to shifts in the demand curve caused by changes in income, and the cross-price elasticity of demand refers to shifts in the demand curve caused by changes in the price of other goods. Most goods are normal and have a positive income elasticity of demand. Inferior goods have a negative income elasticity of demand.
10. The price elasticity of supply is defined as the percentage change in the quantity supplied divided by the percentage change in the price. If a good has a high price elasticity of supply, then a change in price will cause a big change in the quantity supplied. Conversely, if a good has a low price elasticity of supply, then a change in price will have only a small impact on the quantity supplied.

KEY TERMS

price control
price ceiling
price floor
rent control
minimum wage
price elasticity of demand
unit-free measure
elastic demand
inelastic demand
perfectly inelastic demand
perfectly elastic demand
income elasticity of demand
cross-price elasticity of demand
price elasticity of supply
perfectly elastic supply
perfectly inelastic supply

QUESTIONS FOR REVIEW

1. Why is the price elasticity of demand a unit-free measure of the sensitivity of the quantity demanded to a price change?
2. What factors determine whether the price elasticity of demand is high or low?
3. What is the difference between elastic and inelastic demand?
4. Why is the price elasticity of demand useful for finding the size of the price change that occurs when supply shifts?
5. If the price elasticity of demand for textbooks is 2 and the price of textbooks increases by 10 percent, by how much does the quantity demanded fall?
6. Why is the price elasticity of demand lower in the short run than in the long run?
7. For what values of the price elasticity of demand do increases in the price increase revenue?
8. What is the income elasticity of demand?
9. What is the difference between the price elasticity of demand and the income elasticity of demand?
10. What is the slope of a perfectly elastic supply curve?

PROBLEMS

1. Consider the market for automatic teller machine services in a city. The price is the fee for a cash withdrawal.
    a. Sketch the demand curve and the supply curve for ATM transactions.
    b. How is the equilibrium price determined?
    c. If the town council imposes a ban on ATM fees—equivalent to a price ceiling in this market—what happens to quantity supplied and quantity demanded?
    d. Economists frequently argue against price controls because of the shortages and associated problems that they create. What are some of the potentially negative side effects of interference in the ATM market?

2. In 1991 the price of milk fell 30 percent. Senator Leahy of Vermont, a big milk-producing state, supported a law in the U.S. Congress to put a floor on the price. The floor was $13.09 per hundred pounds of milk. The market price was $11.47.
  a. Draw a supply and demand diagram for milk and show how the equilibrium price and quantity would be determined in the absence of the price floor.
  b. Using the diagram you just drew, explain the effects of the legislation.
  c. The dairy farmers supported the legislation, while consumer groups opposed it. Why?
  d. Economists frequently argue against price floors because of the surpluses and associated problems that they create. What are some of the potentially negative side effects of interference in the milk market?

3. More than twenty states have laws outlawing price gouging during a state of emergency, which might be declared after a hurricane or an earthquake. These laws prohibit price increases on basic necessities, such as gasoline. Which of the arguments against price ceilings might not be very significant during a state of emergency?

4. Donors of organs for transplantation or medical research are prohibited from charging a price for these organs (there is a price ceiling of zero). Will this result in a shortage? How will the market cope with the shortage?

5. Consider the following data for a demand curve:

Price	Quantity
11	10
10	20
9	30
8	40
7	50
6	60
5	70
4	80
3	90

  a. Use the midpoint formula to calculate the elasticity between a price of $10 and $11.
  b. Use the midpoint formula to calculate the elasticity between a price of $3 and $4.
  c. Since this is a linear demand curve, why does the elasticity change?
  d. At what point is price times quantity maximized? What is the elasticity at that point?

6. Consider the following data for a supply curve:

Price	Quantity Supplied
2	10
3	20
4	30
5	40
6	50
7	60
8	70
9	80

  a. Use the midpoint formula to calculate the price elasticity of supply between a price of $7 and $8.
  b. Use the midpoint formula to calculate the price elasticity of supply between a price of $3 and $4.
  c. How does supply elasticity change as you move up the supply curve?
  d. Why does the supply elasticity change even though the slope of the supply curve is unchanged as you move up the supply curve?

7. Given the following income elasticities of demand, would you classify the following goods as normal or inferior goods?
  a. Potatoes: elasticity = 0.5
  b. Pinto beans: elasticity = −0.1
  c. Bottled water: elasticity = 1.1
  d. Video cameras: elasticity = 1.4

8. Calculate the cross-price elasticity for the following goods. Are they substitutes or complements?
  a. The price of movie theater tickets goes up by 10 percent, causing the quantity demanded for video rentals to go up by 4 percent.
  b. The price of computers falls by 20 percent, causing the quantity demanded of software to increase by 15 percent.
  c. The price of apples falls by 5 percent, causing the quantity demanded of pears to fall by 5 percent.
  d. The price of ice cream falls by 6 percent, causing the quantity demanded of frozen yogurt to fall by 1 percent.

9. Food items often have low elasticities of demand. Suppose excellent weather leads to bumper yields of agricultural crops. Why might farmers complain about market conditions?

10. The board of directors of an airline wishes to increase revenue. One group favors cutting airfares, and the other group favors raising airfares. What are the assumptions each group is making about the price elasticity of demand?

11. Compare a market in which supply and demand are very (but not perfectly) inelastic to one in which supply and demand are very (but not perfectly) elastic. Suppose the government decides to impose a price floor $1 above the equilibrium price in each of these markets. Compare, diagrammatically, the surpluses that result. In which market is the surplus larger?

12. In 1992, the federal government placed a tax of 10 percent on goods like luxury automobiles and yachts. The yacht-manufacturing industry had huge declines in orders for yachts and laid off many workers, whereas the reaction in the auto industry was much milder. (The tax on yachts was subsequently removed.) Explain this situation using two supply and demand diagrams. Compare the elasticity of demand for luxury autos with that for yachts based on the experience with the luxury tax.

Part 2

Principles of Macroeconomics

Chapter 5

Macroeconomics: The Big Picture

The quarter century from 1980 to 2005 is filled with remarkable economic developments. Perhaps the most significant of these stories is the rapid economic growth of China. According to data collected by the International Monetary Fund, production per person in China in 2005 was fifteen times as large as it had been in 1980. The economy of the second most populous nation in the world, India, also grew at a rapid pace. Production per person in India in 2005 was almost five times as large as it had been in 1980. Such rapid rates of economic growth in China, India, and several other countries meant a better quality of life for hundreds of millions of people. The World Bank calculated that the number of people living on an income of less than $1 a day fell by almost 200 million even as the world population increased by more than a billion people over this period.

In stark contrast to China and India, sub-Saharan African countries like Sierra Leone, Togo, and Niger had economies that were essentially producing as much output per person in 2005 as they had produced back in 1980. Understanding why China and India grew so fast, and why these sub-Saharan African countries (and other poor countries like Haiti) were unable to bring about even moderate rates of growth is vital for anyone who wants to improve the living conditions of the world's poor.

In the United States, the economy has changed dramatically from the high inflation rates and unemployment rates experienced in the 1970s. The U.S. economy experienced a serious economic downturn in 1981–1982, but in the two decades since then it has experienced almost continuous economic growth, accompanied by declining rates of inflation and unemployment. The two downturns, or recessions, that occurred in the United States during this period (in 1990–1991 and in 2001) lasted only eight months each and were much milder than previous recessions had been. The U.S. economy also became much more stable—less likely to experience significant ups and downs—over this period. Some economists refer to this period as "the Great Moderation." Is this Great Moderation the result of better policymaking by the Federal Reserve and by our elected leaders? Or is it because we have benefited from technological advances like more effective pharmaceuticals, the invention of the personal computer, and the creation of the Internet? Or is it simply the result of "good luck" in terms of the economy being hit by less disruptive shocks than in the turbulent decade of the 1970s? These are also questions that a student of economics should want to, and be able to, answer.

The study of macroeconomics will give you the knowledge you need to address such questions. Macroeconomics is the study of the *whole market economy.* Like other parts of economics, macroeconomics uses the central idea that people make purposeful decisions with scarce resources. However, instead of focusing on the workings of one market—whether the market for peanuts or the market for bicycles—macroeconomics focuses on the economy as a whole. Macroeconomics looks at the big picture: Economic growth, recessions, unemployment, and inflation are among its subject matter. You should accordingly put on your "big picture glasses" when you study macroeconomics.

By studying macroeconomics, you can better understand the changes that are taking place in the economy, better understand the role of good economic policies in driving economic growth and reducing unemployment, and become a more informed and educated citizen. Hopefully, you will be inspired by the study of macroeconomics to do your part to help bring about strong economic growth, which in turn can help alleviate poverty, free up resources to clean up the environment, and lead to a brighter future for your generation.

This chapter summarizes the overall workings of the economy, highlighting key facts to remember. It also provides a brief preview of the macroeconomic theory designed to explain these facts. The theory will be developed in later chapters.

MEASURING THE "SIZE" OF AN ECONOMY

To understand why some economies have done so much better than others, we first need to understand how macroeconomists measure the size of an economy. Gross domestic product (GDP) is the economic variable that is of most interest to macroeconomists. GDP is the total value of all new goods and services produced in the economy during a specified period of time, usually a year or a quarter. The total value of goods and services can change either because the quantities of goods and services are changing or because their prices are changing. As a result, economists often

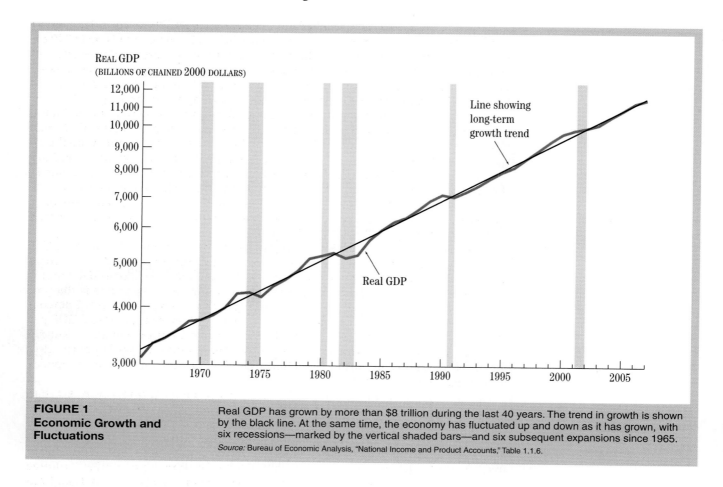

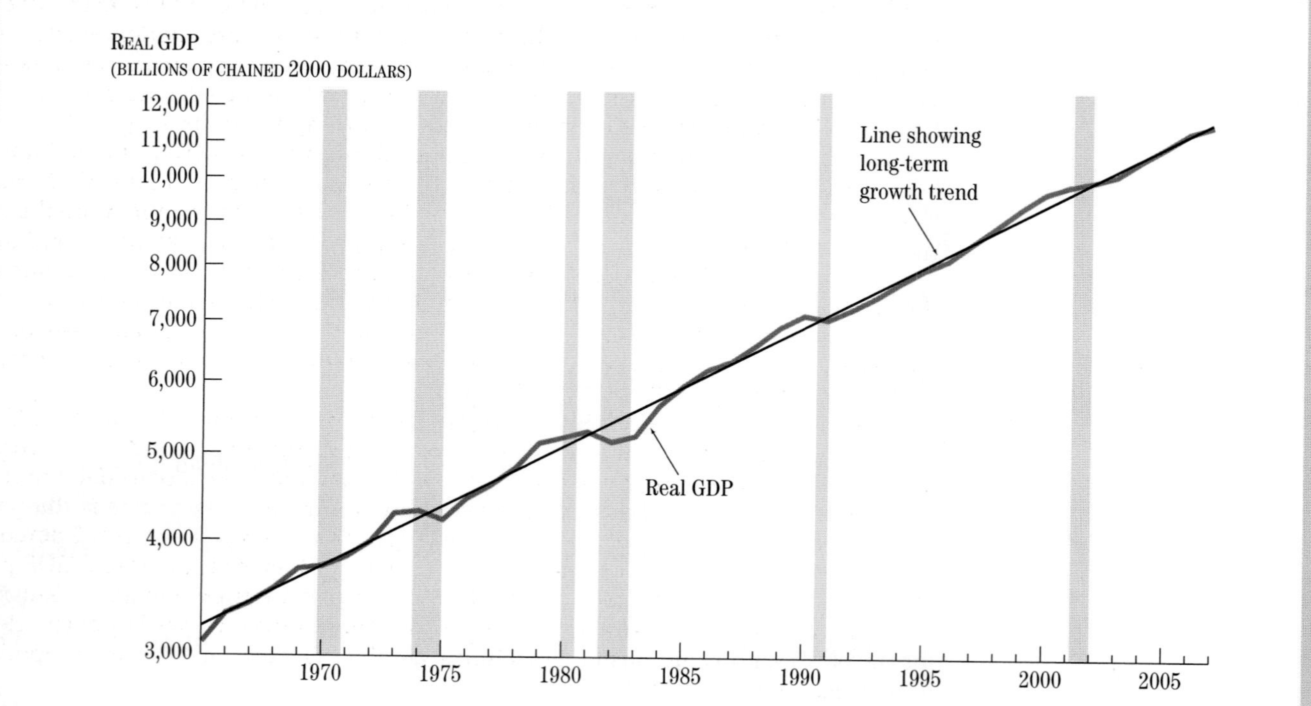

FIGURE 1
Economic Growth and Fluctuations

Real GDP has grown by more than $8 trillion during the last 40 years. The trend in growth is shown by the black line. At the same time, the economy has fluctuated up and down as it has grown, with six recessions—marked by the vertical shaded bars—and six subsequent expansions since 1965.
Source: Bureau of Economic Analysis, "National Income and Product Accounts," Table 1.1.6.

real gross domestic product (real GDP): a measure of the value of all the goods and services newly produced in a country during some period of time, adjusted for changes in prices over time.

economic growth: an upward trend in real GDP, reflecting expansion in the economy over time.

economic fluctuations: swings in real GDP that lead to deviations of the economy from its long-term growth trend.

prefer to use **real gross domestic product (real GDP)** as the measure of production; the adjective *real* means that we adjust the measure of production to account for changes in prices over time. Real GDP, also called *output* or *production,* is the most comprehensive measure of how well the economy is doing.

Figure 1 shows the changes in real GDP in recent years in the United States. When you look at real GDP over time, as in Figure 1, you notice two simultaneous patterns emerging. Over the long term, increases in real GDP demonstrate an upward trend, which economists call long-term **economic growth.** In the short term, there are **economic fluctuations**—more transient increases or decreases in real GDP. These short-term fluctuations in real GDP are also called *business cycles.* The difference between the long-term economic growth trend and the economic fluctuations can be better seen by drawing a relatively smooth line between the observations on real GDP. Such a smooth trend line is shown in Figure 1. Sometimes real GDP fluctuates above the trend line, and sometimes it fluctuates below the trend line. In this section we look more closely at these two patterns: economic growth and economic fluctuations.

Economic Growth: The Relentless Uphill Climb

The large increase in real GDP shown in Figure 1 means that people in the United States now produce a much greater amount of goods and services each year than they did 40 years ago. Improvements in the economic well-being of individuals in any society cannot occur without such an increase in real GDP. To get a better measure of how individuals benefit from increases in real GDP, we consider average production per person, or *real GDP per capita.* Real GDP per capita is real GDP divided by the number of people in the economy. It is the total production of all food, clothes, cars, houses, CDs, concerts, education, computers, and so on, per person. When real GDP per capita is increasing, then the well-being—or the standard of living—of individuals in the economy, at least on average, is improving.

How much economic growth has there been during the last 40 years in the United States? The annual *economic growth rate*—the percentage increase in real GDP each year—provides a good measure. On average, for the last 40 years, the annual economic growth rate has been a little over 3 percent per year. This may not sound like much, but it means that real GDP has more than tripled. The increase in production in the United States over the past 40 years is larger than what Japan and Germany together now produce. It is as if all the production of Japan and Germany—what is made by all the workers, machines, and technology in these countries—were annexed to the U.S. economy, as illustrated in Figure 2.

How much did real GDP *per capita* increase during this period? Because the U.S. population grew by about almost 100 million people during this period, the increase in real GDP per capita has been less dramatic than the increase in real GDP, but it is impressive nonetheless. The annual growth rate of real GDP per capita is the percentage increase in real GDP per capita each year. It has averaged just over 2 percent per year. Again, this might not sound like much, but it has meant that real GDP per capita more than doubled, from about $16,000 per person in 1965 to about $37,500 per person in 2005. That extra $21,500 per person represents increased opportunities for travel, TVs, housing, washing machines, aerobics classes, health care, antipollution devices for cars, and so on.

Over long spans of time, small differences in economic growth—even less than 1 percent per year—can transform societies. For example, economic growth in the southern states was only a fraction of a percent greater than that in the North in the 100 years after the Civil War. Yet this enabled the South to rise from a real income per capita about half that of the North after the Civil War to one about the same as that of the North today. Economic growth is the reason that fast-growing countries like Korea can catch up with and even surpass slow-growing countries like Mexico. Data from the International Monetary Fund show that in 1980, Korea had a real GDP per capita

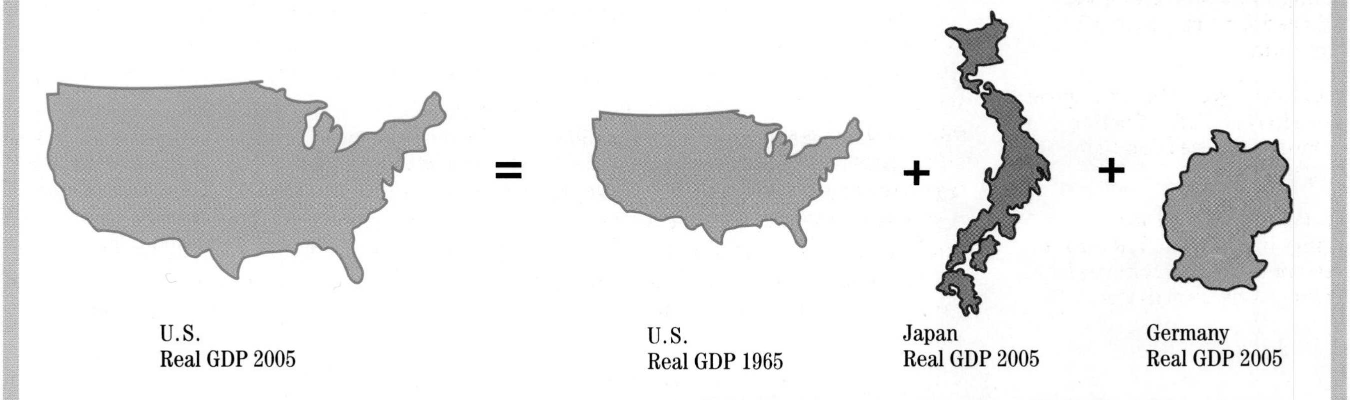

FIGURE 2
Visualizing Economic Growth

Over the last 40 years, production in the U.S. economy has increased by more than the total current production of the Japanese and German economies combined. It is as if the United States had annexed Germany and Japan.

ECONOMICS IN THE NEWS

How Economic Growth Can Transform an Economy

This article, which appeared in *The Economist* in August of 2006, describes the process of rapid economic growth in Vietnam. The growth rate that Vietnam is experiencing in 2006 is similar to what China experienced beginning in the 1980s. If Vietnam is able to sustain such high growth rates for the next decade or two, then Vietnamese society will be transformed dramatically, much like Chinese society was over the past two decades.

Good Morning At Last

From *The Economist* print edition

HANOI—Signs of rapid development are visible everywhere around Hanoi: from the flashy sport-utility vehicles on the city's roads to the dormitory villages of smart "executive" homes rising among the fields on the capital's outskirts. George Bush and other world leaders will see it for themselves when Hanoi hosts the Asia-Pacific economic summit in November. That meeting will take place in a new satellite-city, Tu Liem, which is now being built on Hanoi's south-western edge. The futuristic conference centre, with a distinctive wavy glass roof, looks almost finished. Nearby, a huge five-star hotel is getting a final coat of paint. Along Tu Liem's broad, four-lane avenues, some apartment blocks are already occupied, others are just steel skeletons. Between the building sites, cows and buffalo still graze in what was open pasture only recently.

Before starting its doi moi market-oriented reforms in the mid-1980s, the Socialist Republic of Vietnam flirted with real communism and came close to famine. Since then, a reform process that was uneven at first has gathered momentum. Recent economic growth, though not quite as stellar as China's, has been remarkable. In 2001–05 it averaged over 7.5%, reaching a peak of 8.4% last year. This year the government is going all out to hit an 8% target.

Highlights the recent growth performance of Vietnam

Since 1990, Vietnam's exports have increased faster than China's. Their growth shows no signs of slackening. Between January and July they amounted to $22 billion, a year-on-year rise of over 25%. Having alarmed the Brazilians by becoming their main competitor in coffee growing, Vietnam is now ramping up its exports of everything from shrimps to ships to shoes (the last prompting the European Union to announce anti-dumping tariffs last month). It has just become the world's largest exporter of pepper and aims soon to overtake Thailand in rice. It is even selling tea to India.

Foreign-owned factories are chalking up the fastest gains. The government's aim of increasing electronics exports by 27% annually should be boosted by Intel's recent decision to build a $605m microchip plant in Ho Chi Minh City. Though farmers' harvests are still rising, industry's still-higher growth rate means that agriculture's share of economic output continues to shrink—from about 25% in 2000 to 21% last year. By 2010 it may be down to 15%.

This economic revolution is being accompanied by a social one. Though Vietnam is still, overall, one of Asia's poorest countries, with income per head behind India's, its recent growth has been impressively egalitarian. The Asian Development Bank (ADB) reckons that deep poverty in Vietnam—defined as a daily income equivalent to under $1—is now only slightly more prevalent than the average for South-East Asia, whereas in 1990 Vietnam's figure was more than twice the regional average. By this measure, Vietnam has overtaken China, India and the Philippines and now has only slightly more poverty than Indonesia.

How economic growth has helped alleviate poverty in Vietnam

Life expectancy has jumped and infant mortality plunged since the 1990s. Vietnam does better on both these counts than Thailand, a far richer country. Almost three-quarters of Vietnamese children of secondary-school age are in class, up from about a third in 1990. Again, Vietnam has overtaken China, India and Indonesia.

Economic growth can also lead to improved health and living standards.

The new five-year plan, approved at April's congress of the ruling Communist Party, is laden with targets for increasing output and improving infrastructure, with the objective of making Vietnam a modern, industrial nation by 2020. Of course, other Asian countries' leaders, from Malaysia to the Philippines, declare similar objectives. The difference is that Vietnam's rulers seem to mean it—and their recent record suggests they might pull it off.

The April congress was preceded by a purge of high officials suspected of corruption—most notably at a road-building agency where some staff stole millions of dollars to bet on football matches. While Nong Duc Manh, the party's general secretary, has survived, the other two members of the ruling triumvirate—the president and prime minister—have since been dropped in favour of youngish, southern Vietnamese officials, seen as supporters of continued economic reform.

Good Times, Bad Times

Vietnam is on a roll and its prospects look good. But much could still go wrong. As Vietnam joins the global economy (it should become a member of the World Trade Organisation in the coming year or so) it is becoming more vulnerable to volatile commodity prices and fickle bond-market investors, whose gyrations are largely outside its control. The recent export surge has been helped by strong global demand and high prices for the things Vietnam sells, from rice to crude oil, but a world recession—or an economic bust in China—could cause a big slowdown. The government is racing to build enough power stations, roads and railways to keep the economy moving. Any delays in these would spell trouble.

The challenges that lie ahead for Vietnam

The communist government's continuing acceptance by ordinary Vietnamese rests largely on its success in delivering prosperity and better public services. If it fails to reduce corruption or produce jobs for the more than 1m young Vietnamese who join the labour force each year and the 1m villagers migrating to the cities, the country's social cohesion and sense of purpose would be in danger.

That makes it vital to accelerate the government's programme to restructure and sell thousands of state-owned firms. They are more graft-prone than private companies, and devour the lion's share of scarce land and credit while creating few new jobs. The private sector provides most of the growth in jobs and exports, but would do better still if it was not crowded out by the public sector. Le Dang Doanh, an economic adviser to the government, reckons that, but for the vested interests slowing down privatisation, Vietnam could now be growing at 11%, just like China.

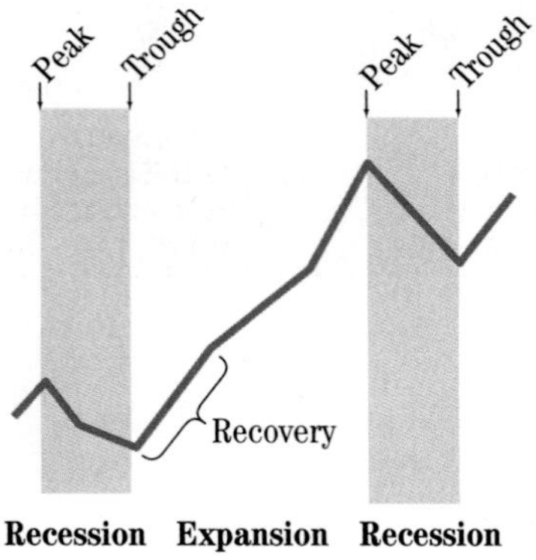

that was about 60 percent of Mexico's real GDP per capita, but by 2005, Korea's real GDP per capita was almost twice as large as Mexico's. Economic growth is also key to improvements in the less-developed countries in sub-Saharan Africa, South Asia, and Latin America. Because economic growth has been lagging in many of these countries, their real GDP per capita is considerably less than that of the United States.

Economic Fluctuations: Temporary Setbacks and Recoveries

Clearly, real GDP grows over time, but every now and then real GDP stops growing, falls, and then starts increasing rapidly again. These ups and downs in the economy—that is, economic fluctuations or business cycles—can be seen in Figure 1.

One of these business cycles, the one in 1991, is blown up for closer examination in Figure 3. No two business cycles are alike. Certain phases are common to all business cycles, however. These common phases are shown in the diagram in the margin. When real GDP falls, economists say that there is a **recession;** a rule of thumb says that the fall in real GDP must last for a half year or more before the decline is considered a recession. The highest point before the start of a recession is called the **peak.** The lowest point at the end of a recession is called the **trough,** a term that may cause you to imagine water accumulating at the bottom of one of the dips.

recession: a decline in real GDP that lasts for at least six months.

peak: the highest point in real GDP before a recession.

trough: the lowest point of real GDP at the end of a recession.

expansion: the period between the trough of a recession and the next peak, consisting of a general rise in output and employment.

recovery: the early part of an economic expansion, immediately after the trough of the recession.

The period between recessions—from the trough to the next peak—is called an **expansion,** as shown for a typical fluctuation in the margin. The early part of an expansion is usually called a **recovery** because the economy is just recovering from the recession.

The peaks and troughs of the six recessions since the late 1960s are shown by vertical bars in Figure 1. The shaded areas represent the recessions. The areas between the shaded bars show the expansions. The dates of all peaks and troughs back to 1920 are shown in Table 1. The average length of each business cycle from peak to peak is slightly more than five years, but it is clear from Table 1 that business cycles are not regularly occurring ups and downs, like sunup and sundown. Recessions occur irregularly. There were only 12 months between the back-to-back recessions of the early

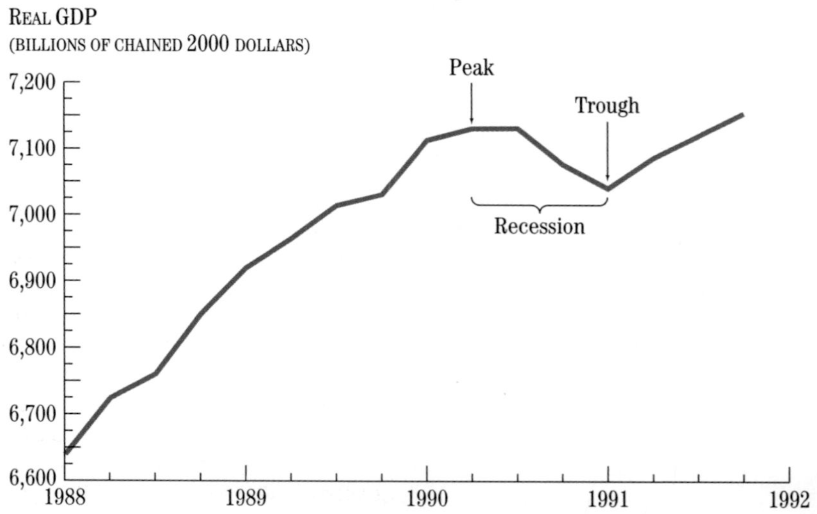

FIGURE 3
The Phases of Business Cycles
Although no two business cycles are alike, they have common features, including the *peak, recession,* and *trough,* shown here for the 1991 recession.

Source: Bureau of Economic Analysis, "National Income and Product Accounts," Table 1.1.6; National Bureau of Economic Research, "Business Cycle Expansions and Contractions."

TABLE 1
Comparison of Recessions

Recession *Peak* *Trough*	Duration of Recession (months from peak to trough)	Decline in Real GDP (percent from peak to trough)	Duration of Next Expansion (months from trough to peak)
Jan 1920–Jul 1921	18	8.7	22
May 1923–Jul 1924	14	4.1	27
Oct 1926–Nov 1927	13	2.0	21
Aug 1929–Mar 1933	43	32.6	50
May 1937–Jun 1938	13	18.2	80
Feb 1945–Oct 1945	8	11.0	37
Nov 1948–Oct 1949	11	1.5	45
Jul 1953–May 1954	10	3.2	39
Aug 1957–Apr 1958	8	3.3	24
Apr 1960–Feb 1961	10	1.2	106
Dec 1969–Nov 1970	11	1.0	36
Nov 1973–Mar 1975	16	4.9	58
Jan 1980–Jul 1980	6	2.5	12
Jul 1981–Nov 1982	16	3.0	92
Jul 1990–Mar 1991	8	1.4	120
Mar 2001–Nov 2001	8	0.0	61*

*As of December 2006.

Source: National Bureau of Economic Research.

1980s, while 58 months of uninterrupted growth occurred between the 1973–1975 recession and the 1980 recession. The recession phases of business cycles also vary in duration and depth. The 1990–1991 recession, for example, was not nearly as long or as deep as the 1973–1975 recession.

Table 1 illustrates how much less volatile the U.S. economy has been in recent times. The 1990–1991 recession and the 2001 recession were among the shortest recessions in U.S. history, lasting about eight months. Both of these recessions were preceded by very long economic expansions lasting between seven and ten years. The most recent economic expansion surpassed the five-year mark in late 2006. Increasingly, almost uninterrupted economic growth has seemed to be the norm for the U.S. economy.

Economists debate whether economic policies were responsible for the length of the recent expansions and the brevity of the recent recessions. We will examine these debates in later chapters. Economists are also interested in understanding the factors that cause a recession, even though they don't always agree on what those factors were. The factors to which the 2001 recession has been ascribed include a fall in spending on equipment and buildings by firms and a sharp decline in the stock market. The first month of the 1990–1991 recession occurred just after Iraq invaded Kuwait, causing a disruption in the oil fields and a jump in world oil prices, so some argue that this jump in oil prices was a factor in the recession.

A Recession's Aftermath. After a recession, the economy usually takes several years to return to its pre-recession state. Thus, a period of bad economic times always follows a recession while the economy recovers. Technically, economists define recessions as periods in which real GDP is declining, and recoveries as periods in which real GDP is rising again. However, despite this technical distinction between bad economic times when things are getting worse (recession) and bad economic times when things are improving (recovery), many people still associate the word *recession* with bad economic times in general. Furthermore, not all economic indicators move in lockstep with real GDP. For example, although the 2001 recession ended in November 2001, the unemployment rate kept rising for another year. Technically speaking, though, the recession was over in November 2001 when GDP began to grow again—well before the effects of an improving economy were felt by most people.

Recessions versus Depressions. Recessions have been observed for as long as economists have tracked the economy. Some past recessions lasted so long and were so deep that they are called *depressions*. There is no formal definition of a depression. A depression is a huge recession.

Fortunately, we have not experienced a depression in the United States for a long time. Figure 4 shows the history of real GDP for about 100 years. The most noticeable decline in real GDP occurred in the 1929–1933 recession. Real GDP fell by 32.6 percent in this period. This decline in real GDP was so large that it was given its own designation by economists and historians—the *Great Depression*. The recessions of recent years have had much smaller declines.

Table 1 shows how much real GDP fell in each of the sixteen recessions since the 1920s. The 1920–1921 recession and the 1937–1938 recession were big enough to be classified as depressions, but both are small compared to the Great Depression. Real GDP also declined substantially after World War II, when war production declined.

Clearly, recent recessions have not been even remotely comparable in severity to the Great Depression or the other huge recessions of the 1920s and 1930s. The 1990–1991 recession, for example, had only one-twentieth the decline in real GDP that occurred during the Great Depression. But because any recession rivets attention on people's hardship and suffering, there is always a tendency to view a current recession as worse than all previous recessions. Some commentators reporting on the 1990–1991 recession wondered whether it should be compared with the Great Depression. For example, in September 1992, Louis Uchitelle of the *New York Times* wrote, "Technically, the recession is over, but spiritually, it continues. . . . The question is, what to call these hard times. What has been happening in America since 1989 seems momentous enough to enter history as a major economic event of the 20th century."[1]

REVIEW

- The behavior of real GDP in the United States is characterized by a long-term upward trend (economic growth) and more transient increases and decreases around that trend (economic fluctuations).
- Economic growth provides lasting improvements in the well-being of people. Small differences in economic growth, sustained over long spans of time, can transform societies.
- Periodically, real GDP stops growing and begins to decline. A decline that lasts for at least six months is known as a recession. Recessions vary in length and intensity, but have become less severe since the 1980s.
- A recession that is very severe is called a depression. The Great Depression of the 1930s was about twenty times more severe than the 1990–1991 recession when measured by the decline in real GDP.

[1] Louis Uchitelle, "Even Words Fail in This Economy," *New York Times*, September 8, 1992, p. C2.

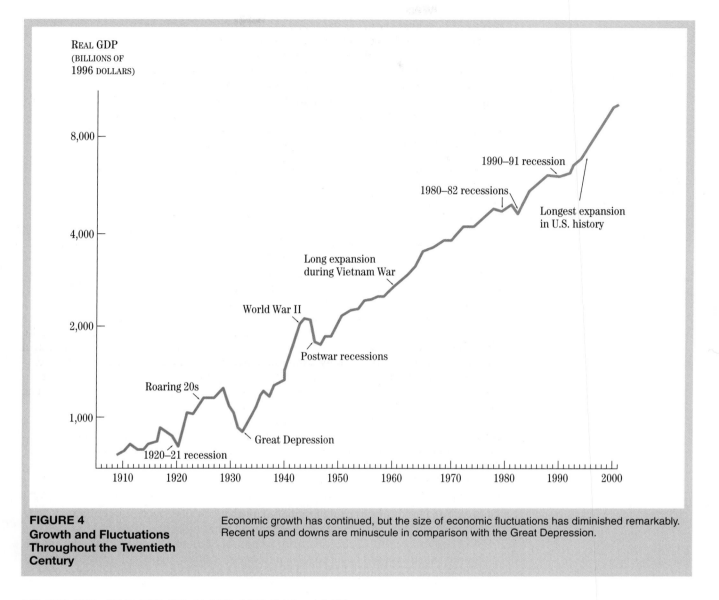

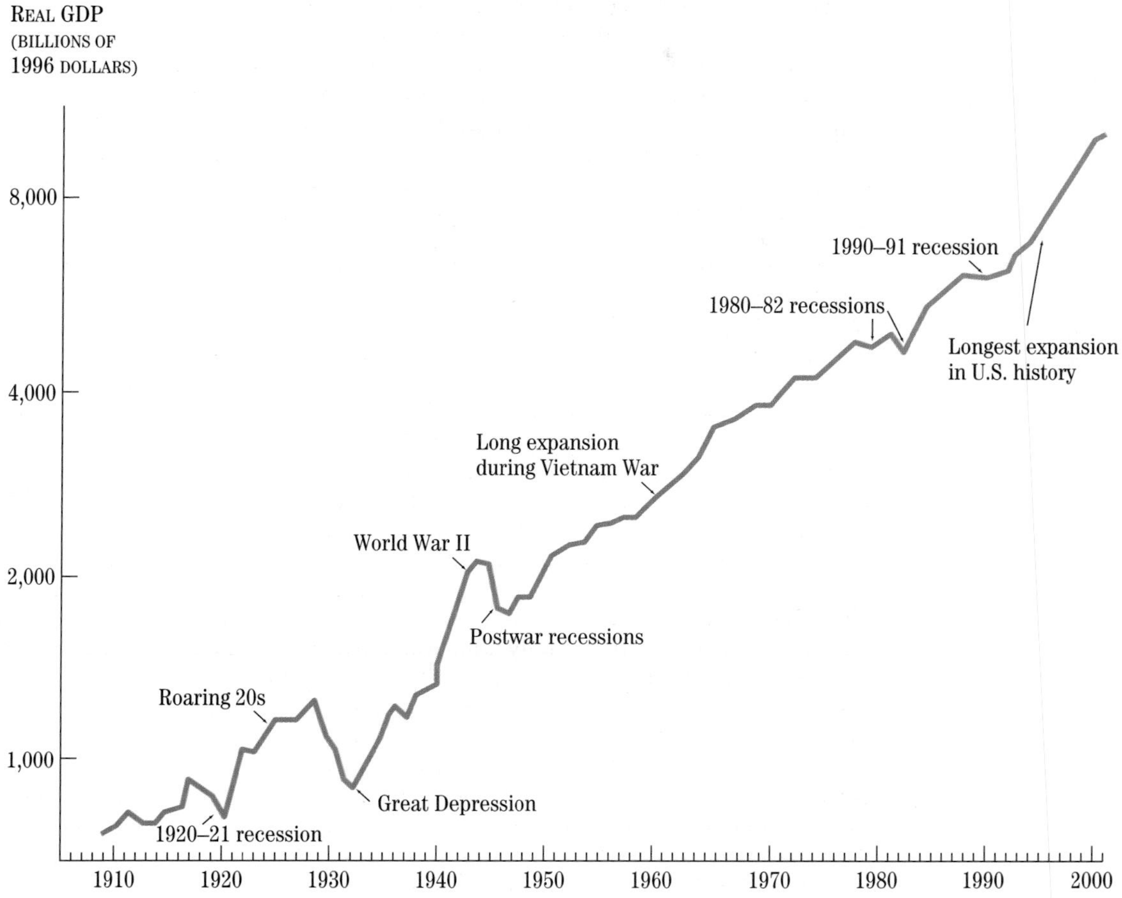

FIGURE 4
Growth and Fluctuations Throughout the Twentieth Century

Economic growth has continued, but the size of economic fluctuations has diminished remarkably. Recent ups and downs are minuscule in comparison with the Great Depression.

UNEMPLOYMENT, INFLATION, AND INTEREST RATES

As real GDP changes over time, so do other economic variables, such as unemployment, inflation, and interest rates. Looking at these other economic variables gives us a better understanding of the human story behind the changes in real GDP. They also provide additional information about the economy's performance—just as a person's pulse rate or cholesterol level gives information different from the body temperature. No one variable is sufficient.

Unemployment During Recessions

unemployment rate: the percentage of the labor force that is unemployed.

There are fluctuations in unemployment just as there are fluctuations in real GDP. The **unemployment rate** is the number of unemployed people as a percentage of the labor

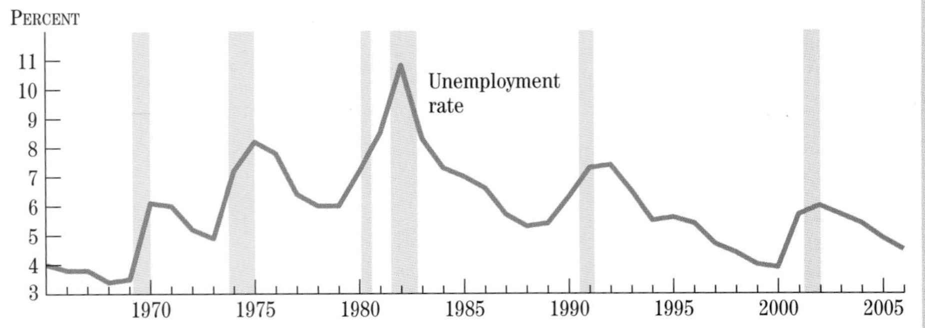

FIGURE 5
The Unemployment Rate
The number of unemployed workers as a percentage of the labor force—the unemployment rate—increases during recessions because people are laid off and it is difficult to find work. Sometimes the unemployment rate continues to increase for a while after the recession is over, as in 1991 and 2001. But eventually unemployment declines during the economic recovery.
Source: Bureau of Labor Statistics, "Unemployment Rate—Civilian Labor Force."

inflation rate: the percentage increase in the overall price level over a given period of time, usually one year.

force; the labor force consists of those who are either working or looking for work. Every time the economy goes into a recession, the unemployment rate rises because people are laid off and new jobs are difficult to find. The individual stories behind the unemployment numbers frequently represent frustration and distress.

Figure 5 shows what happens to the unemployment rate as the economy goes through recessions and recoveries. The increase in the unemployment rate during a recession is eventually followed by a decline in unemployment during the recovery. Note, for example, how unemployment rose during the recessions of 1973–1975 and 1981–1982. Around the time of the 2001 recession, the unemployment rate rose from 3.9 percent to 5.7 percent.

Figure 6 shows how high the unemployment rate got during the Great Depression. It rose to nearly 25 percent; one in four workers was out of work. Fortunately, recent increases in unemployment during recessions have been much smaller. The unemployment rate reached 10.4 percent in the early 1980s, the highest level since World War II.

Even though the most recent recession pales in comparison to the Great Depression, it still caused a lot of pain and hardship across the country. Figure 7 illustrates how rapidly unemployment rose, even in what most economists described as a mild recession. In the 12 months from March of 2001 to March of 2002, the unemployment rate increased by almost 1.5 percentage points. To put this number in more human terms, the number of unemployed workers across the country increased by about 2.1 million.

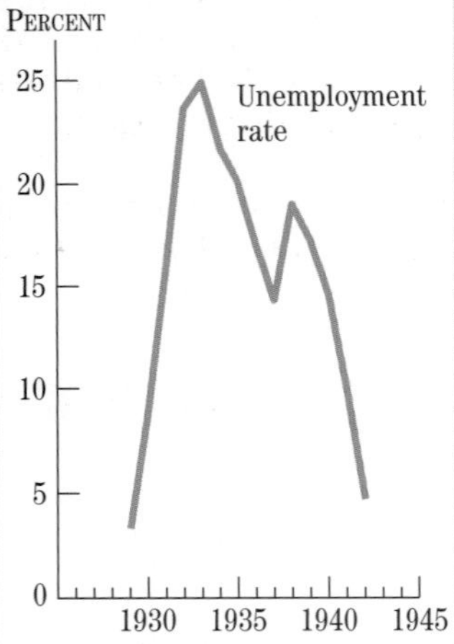

FIGURE 6
Unemployment During the Great Depression
The increase in unemployment in the United States during the Great Depression was huge compared with the increases in unemployment during milder downturns in the economy. Almost one in four workers were unemployed during the Great Depression.
Source: Bureau of Labor Statistics, "Compensation from Before World War I Through the Great Depression," Robert Van Giezeu and Albert E. Schwenk.

Inflation

Just as output and unemployment have fluctuated over time, so has inflation. The **inflation rate** is the percentage increase in the average price of all goods and services from one year to the next. Figure 8 shows the inflation rate for the same 40-year period we have focused on in our examination of real GDP and unemployment. Clearly, a low and stable inflation rate has not been a feature of the United States during this period. There are several useful facts to note about the behavior of inflation.

First, inflation is closely correlated with the ups and downs in real GDP and employment: Inflation increased prior to every recession in the last 40 years and then subsided during and after every recession. We will want to explore whether this close correlation between the ups and downs in inflation and the ups and downs in the economy helps explain economic fluctuations.

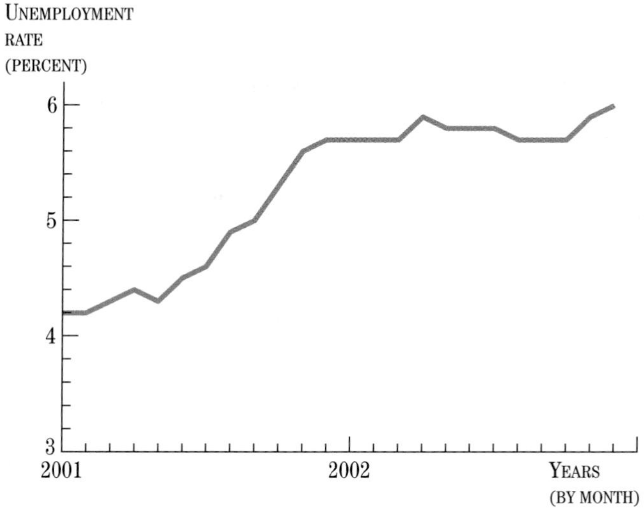

FIGURE 7
The Rapid Rise of Unemployment in 2001
When the economy moves from expansion into recession, unemployment can climb very rapidly over a period of a few months, as we saw at the end of the long expansion in 2001.
Source: Bureau of Labor Statistics.

Second, there are longer-term trends in inflation. For example, inflation rose from a low point during the 1970s to a high point of double-digit inflation in 1980. This period of persistently high inflation until 1980 is called the *Great Inflation.* The Great Inflation ended in the early 1980s, when the inflation rate declined substantially. Such a decline in inflation is called *disinflation.* (When inflation is negative and the average price level falls, economists call it *deflation.*)

Third, judging by history, there is no reason to expect the inflation rate to be zero, even on average. The inflation rate has averaged around 2 or 3 percent in the United States since 1990.

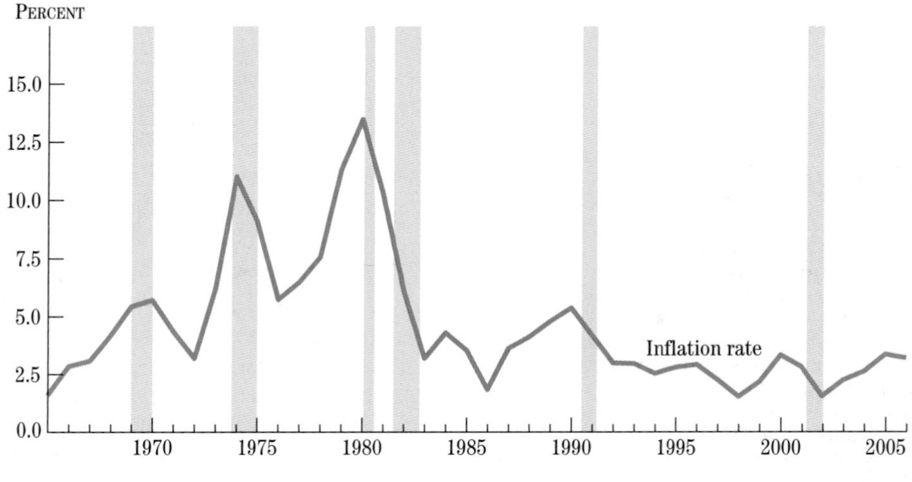

FIGURE 8
The Ups and Downs in Inflation
Inflation has increased before each recession and then declined during and immediately after each recession. In addition, a longer-term upward trend in inflation reached a peak in 1980. Since 1981, America has experienced a disinflation—a decline in the rate of inflation.
Source: Bureau of Labor Statistics, "Percent Change in CPI for All Urban Consumers".

Why does inflation increase before recessions? Why does inflation fall during and after recessions? What caused the Great Inflation? Why is inflation not equal to zero even in more normal times, when the economy is neither in recession nor in a boom? What can economic policy do to keep inflation low and stable? These are some of the questions and policy issues about inflation addressed by macroeconomics.

Interest Rates

interest rate: the amount received per dollar loaned per year, usually expressed as a percentage (e.g., 6 percent) of the loan.

The **interest rate** is the amount that lenders charge when they lend money, expressed as a percentage of the amount loaned. For example, if you borrow $100 for a year from a friend and the interest rate on the loan is 6 percent, then at the end of the year you must pay your friend back $6 in interest in addition to the $100 you borrowed. The interest rate is another key economic variable that is related to the growth and change in real GDP over time.

Different Types of Interest Rates and Their Behavior. There are many different interest rates in the economy: The *mortgage interest rate* is the rate on loans to buy a house; the *savings deposit interest rate* is the rate people get on their savings deposits at banks; the *Treasury bill rate* is the interest rate the government pays when it borrows money from people for a year or less; the *federal funds rate* is the interest rate banks charge each other on very short-term loans. Interest rates influence people's economic behavior. When interest rates rise, for example, it is more expensive to borrow funds to buy a house or a car, so many people postpone such purchases.

Figure 9 shows the behavior of a typical interest rate, the federal funds rate, during the last 40 years. First, note how closely the ups and downs in the interest rate are correlated with the ups and downs in the economy. Interest rates rise before each recession and then decline during and after each recession. Second, note that, as with the inflation rate, there are longer-term trends in the interest rate. The interest

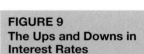

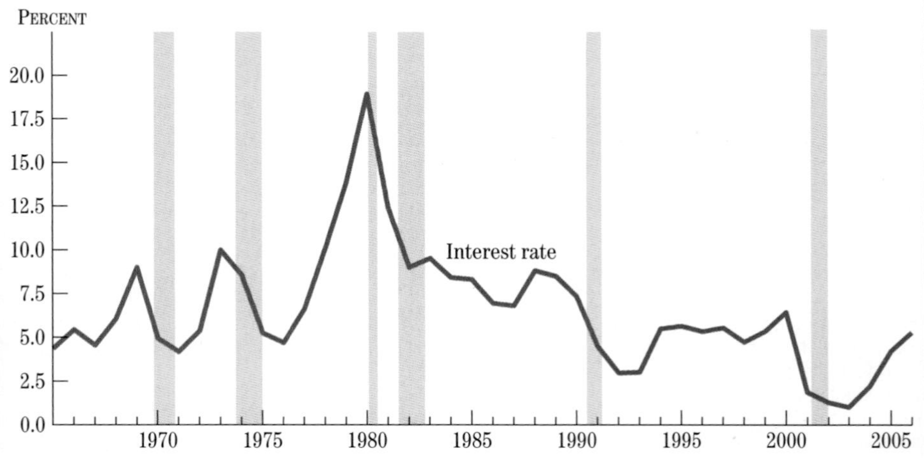

FIGURE 9
The Ups and Downs in Interest Rates
Interest rates generally rise just before a recession and then decline during and just after the recession. There was also a longer-term trend upward in interest rates in the 1970s and a downward trend after the 1980s. (The interest rate shown here is the federal funds interest rate.)

Source: Board of Governors of the Federal Reserve, "Selected Interest Rates—Federal Funds Rate."

rate rose in the 1970s and early 1980s. Each fluctuation in interest rates during this period brought forth a higher peak in interest rates. Then, in the 1980s, the interest rate began a downward trend; each peak was lower than the previous peak.

The Concept of the Real Interest Rate. As we will see, the trends and fluctuations in interest rates are intimately connected with the trends and fluctuations in inflation and real GDP. In fact, the long-term rise in interest rates in the 1960s and 1970s was partly due to the rise in the rate of inflation. When inflation rises, people who lend money will be paid back in funds that are worth less because the average price of goods rises more quickly. To compensate for this decline in the value of funds, lenders require a higher interest rate. For example, if the inflation rate is 20 percent and you lend someone $100 for a year at 6 percent, then you get back $106 at the end of the year. However, the *average* price of the goods you can buy with your $106 is now 20 percent higher. Thus, your 6 percent gain in interest has been offset by a 20 percent loss. It is as if you receive *negative* 14 percent interest: 6 percent interest less 20 percent inflation. The difference between the stated interest rate and the inflation rate is thus a better measure of the real interest rate. Economists define the **real interest rate** as the interest rate less the inflation rate that people expect. The term **nominal interest rate** is used to refer to the interest rate on a loan, making no adjustment for inflation. For example, the real interest rate is 2 percent if the nominal interest rate is 5 percent and inflation is expected to be 3 percent ($5 - 3 = 2$). To keep the real interest rate from changing by a large amount as inflation rises, the nominal interest rate has to increase with inflation. Thus, the concept of the real interest rate helps us understand why inflation and interest rates have moved together. We will make much more use of the real interest rate in later chapters.

real interest rate: the interest rate minus the expected rate of inflation; it adjusts the nominal interest rate for inflation.

nominal interest rate: the interest rate uncorrected for inflation.

REVIEW

- The unemployment rate rises during recessions and falls during recoveries.
- Inflation and interest rates rise prior to recessions and then fall during and just after recessions.
- There was a long-term increase in interest rates and inflation in the 1970s. Interest rates and inflation were lower in the 1990s and into the 2000s.

MACROECONOMIC THEORY AND POLICY

Because strong economic growth raises the living standards of people in an economy, and because increases in unemployment during recessions cause hardship, two goals of economic policy are to raise long-term growth and to reduce the size of short-term economic fluctuations. However, the facts—summarized above—about economic growth and fluctuations do not give economists a basis for making recommendations about economic policy. Before one can be confident about recommending a policy, one needs a coherent theory to explain the facts.

Macroeconomic theory is divided into two branches. *Economic growth theory* aims to explain the long-term upward rise of real GDP over time. *Economic fluctuations theory* tries to explain the short-term fluctuations in real GDP. Economic growth theory and economic fluctuations theory combine to form *macroeconomic theory,* which explains why the economy both grows and fluctuates over time.

Aggregate Supply and the Production Function
The theory of economic growth is based on the production function, which is a model of how labor, capital, and technology jointly determine the aggregate supply of output in the economy. Here the workers at the automobile plant are part of the economy's **labor** (left), the tools that the workers are using to assemble the cars are the economy's **capital** (middle), and computer programming skills are part of the economy's **technology** (right), which raises the value of output for a given amount of labor and capital.

The Theory of Long-Term Economic Growth

Economic growth theory starts by distinguishing the longer-term economic growth trend from the short-term fluctuations in the economy. This is not as easy as it may seem because the long-term growth trend itself may change.

It will be useful to give a name to the upward trend line in real GDP shown in Figure 1. We will call it **potential GDP.** Potential GDP represents the long-run tendency of the economy to grow. Real GDP fluctuates around potential GDP. No one knows exactly where potential GDP lies and exactly what its growth rate is, but any trend line that has the same long-term increase as real GDP and intersects real GDP in several places is probably a good estimate.

Note that potential GDP as defined here and as used by most macroeconomists is not the maximum amount of real GDP. As Figure 1 shows, sometimes real GDP goes above potential GDP. Thus, potential GDP is more like the average or trend level of real GDP.

Economic growth theory postulates that the potential GDP of an economy is given by its **aggregate supply.** *Aggregate* means total. Aggregate supply is all goods and services produced by all the firms in the economy using the available labor, capital, and technology. **Labor** is the total number of hours workers are available to work in producing real GDP. **Capital** is the total number of factories, cultivated plots of land, machines, computers, and other tools available for the workers to use to produce real GDP. **Technology** is all the available know-how—from organizational schemes to improved telecommunications to better computer programming skills—that workers and firms can use when they produce real GDP. Labor, capital, and technology jointly determine aggregate supply.

potential GDP: the economy's long-term growth trend for real GDP, determined by the available supply of capital, labor, and technology. Real GDP fluctuates above and below potential GDP.

aggregate supply: the total value of all goods and services produced in the economy by the available supply of capital, labor, and technology (also called potential GDP).

labor: the number of hours people are available to work in producing goods and services.

capital: the factories, improvements to cultivated land, machinery and other tools, equipment, and structures used to produce goods and services.

technology: anything that raises the amount of output that can be produced with a given amount of labor and capital.

The Production Function.

We can summarize the relationship between the three determinants and the aggregate supply of real GDP as

$$\text{Real GDP} = F(\text{labor, capital, technology})$$

which we say in words as "real GDP is a function, *F*, of labor, capital, and technology." The function *F* means that there is some general relationship between these variables. For this relationship, we assume that higher capital, higher labor, and higher technology all mean higher real GDP; and lower capital, lower labor, and lower technology all

production function: the relationship that describes output as a function of labor, capital, and technology.

mean less real GDP. We call this relationship the **production function** because it tells us how much production (real GDP) of goods and services can be obtained from a certain amount of labor, capital, and technology inputs. A higher long-term economic growth rate for the economy requires a higher growth rate for one or more of these three determinants. A lower long-term economic growth rate may be due to a slower growth rate for one or more of these three determinants.

The production function applies to the entire economy, but we also have production functions for individual firms in the economy. For example, consider the production of cars. The car factory and the machines in the factory are the capital. The workers who work in the factory are the labor. The assembly-line production method is the technology. The cars coming out of the factory are the output. The production function for the economy as a whole has real GDP as output, not just cars, and all available labor, capital, and technology as inputs, not just those producing cars.

Government Policy and Economic Growth

Most governments have been interested in finding ways to increase economic growth. Economic policies that aim to increase long-term economic growth are sometimes called *supply-side policies* because they concentrate on increasing the growth of potential GDP, which is the aggregate supply of the economy.

Fiscal Policy. Our preview of growth theory already tells us where policies to increase growth should focus: on increasing the available supply of labor, capital, and technology. The growth rate of capital depends on how much businesses invest in new capital each year. The amount that businesses choose to invest depends in part on the incentives they have to invest. We will see that the incentive to invest depends on the amount of taxing, spending, and borrowing by government. Hence, government policy can affect the incentive to invest and thereby stimulate long-term economic growth. Government policy concerning taxing, spending, and borrowing is called *fiscal policy.*

Labor supply also depends on incentives. In the case of labor, it is the incentive for firms to hire workers, for people to work harder or longer, for workers who are not in the labor force to come into the labor force, or for people to retire later in life. Again, government policy toward taxing, spending, and borrowing affects these incentives.

Finally, technology growth can also be affected by government policy if the government gives incentives for researchers to invent new technologies or provides funds for education so that workers can improve their skills and know-how.

Monetary Policy. Keeping inflation low and stable is another part of government policy to stimulate long-term economic growth. We will see that the government has an important role to play in determining the inflation rate, especially over the long term, because the inflation rate in the long term depends on the growth rate of the money supply, which can be controlled by the government. Government policy concerning the money supply and the control of inflation is called *monetary policy.* The institution of government assigned to conduct monetary policy is the central bank. In the United States the central bank is the Federal Reserve System.

Why should low and stable inflation be part of an economic growth policy? An examination of inflation and economic growth in a number of countries indicates that inflation is negatively correlated with long-term economic growth. The reason for this negative correlation over the long term may be that inflation raises uncertainty and thereby reduces incentives to invest in capital or improve technology. The theory of economic growth tells us that lower capital growth and lower technological growth reduce economic growth.

ECONOMICS IN ACTION

The Economic Impact of September 11

The tragic events of September 11, 2001, left a trail of human destruction that was hitherto almost unimaginable. In the days and months following September 11, people all over the United States tried to assess the human and economic toll of the events of that fateful day. The assessment that many macroeconomists were asked to make was to calculate the economic impact of the events of September 11. As the economist Paul Krugman, who is also a regular columnist for the *New York Times,* said in his Op-Ed column a few days after September 11, "It seems almost in bad taste to talk about dollars and cents after an act of mass murder. Nonetheless, we must ask about the economic aftershocks from Tuesday's horror." Macroeconomic theory can help us understand the long- and short-term economic impact of this and other such tragedies.

In the case of September 11, the most obvious short-term costs were the destruction of life and property in New York, Washington, D.C., and Pennsylvania; the disruption of financial markets, given that many large financial institutions were located in and around the World Trade Center; and the costs to airlines from disruptions in air travel in the days following the tragedy. However, the theory of economic fluctuations, presented in Chapters 11 and 12, tells us that spending shocks have feedback effects that aggravate the initial direct effects. In the case of New York, the disruption to the economy was substantially greater than the destruction of property and clean-up costs would indicate because of drastic cutbacks in tourism, which led to a sharp falloff in hotel stays, dining out in restaurants, and shopping for expensive goods in Manhattan. The lack of spending by consumers led firms in the hotel, restaurant, and retail industries to lay off thousands of workers. According to a study done by the New York City Chamber of Commerce in September 2001, the cost in terms of reduced economic activity was expected to be almost $40 billion, and the cost in terms of employment was expected to be almost 25,000 jobs. Financial markets were severely disrupted in the short run: They were closed for the remainder of the week, and when they opened the following week, the Dow Jones Industrial Average fell from 9605.5 to 8920.7, a decline of about 7 percent. At the end of the first week of trading, the Dow had fallen to 8235.8, a decline of about 14 percent. The airline industry was hit hard: In the weeks following September 11, airlines announced plans to lay off tens of thousands of workers—20,000 apiece at American Airlines and United Airlines.

The theory of economic fluctuations states that when faced with an economic shock that reduces spending, policymakers can respond by putting into place specific measures designed not only to stop the fall in spending, but indeed to try to restore both confidence and spending by consumers and firms. The president promised $20 billion in federal aid to New York to help the city rebuild. As fears mounted that one or more airlines would have to go into bankruptcy, both the House and Senate sought to provide relief for the beleaguered airline industry by overwhelmingly approving a bill that provided $5 billion in federal funds and $10 billion in loan guarantees. The response of monetary policymakers to the events of September 11 was equally swift: On September 17, the Federal Reserve cut interest rates from 3.5 percent to

The Theory of Economic Fluctuations

Our review of the performance of the economy showed some of the hardships that come from economic fluctuations, especially recessions and unemployment. Can government economic policy improve economic performance by reducing the size of these fluctuations? To answer these questions, we need a theory to interpret the facts of economic fluctuations.

Aggregate Demand and Economic Fluctuations. The theory of economic fluctuations emphasizes fluctuations in the demand for goods and services as the reason for the ups and downs in the economy. Because the focus is on the sum of the demand for all goods and services in the economy—not just the

3 percent, making it cheaper for firms and individuals to borrow money, and also announced its willingness to take steps to restore normalcy to financial markets. Help was offered not only by the government and the Federal Reserve; millions of people all over the United States contributed hundreds of millions of dollars to charities that helped the victims and their families make payments on their rent, school tuition, and health care, doing their part to keep the negative effects from deepening.

The theory of economic growth tells us that the long-term growth of an economy depends on its ability to produce goods and services, which in turn depends on the economy's stocks of labor, capital, and technology. While the destruction of life and property in New York and Washington, D.C., was substantial—"more than we can bear," in the words of Mayor Giuliani—the loss of labor and capital was small relative to the size of the entire U.S. population and the entire U.S. capital stock. In the same Op-Ed piece mentioned earlier, Paul Krugman speculated that the long-term effects would not be substantial: "Nobody has a dollar figure for the damage yet, but I would be surprised if the loss is more than 0.1 percent of U.S. wealth—comparable to the material effects of a major earthquake or hurricane." While such calculations may seem a little too cold-blooded at first glance, it is important that macroeconomists make such assessments so that we can develop a more complete understanding of the impacts of such tragedies, and also so that we can come up with appropriate policy responses to these events.

The prediction that the events of September 11 would not have a long-term effect seems to have been vindicated. In the weeks following September 11, the financial markets seemed to stabilize and then recover: By November 9 the Dow had reached the level it was at on September 10, and it ended the year almost 6 percent higher, at 10,021. GDP grew rapidly in the fourth quarter of 2001, and the unemployment rate seemed to stabilize and then improve as well.

The economy has recovered in the ensuing years. Between December of 2001 and December of 2005, GDP increased at an average annual growth rate of 3 percent, the unemployment rate declined from 5.7 percent to 5.2 percent, and the Dow increased from 10,021 to 10,718.

demand for peanuts or bicycles—we use the term *aggregate demand.* More precisely, **aggregate demand** is the sum of the demands from the four groups that contribute to demand in the whole economy: consumers, business firms, government, and foreigners.

aggregate demand: the total demand for goods and services by consumers, businesses, government, and foreigners.

According to this theory, the declines in real GDP below potential GDP during recessions are caused by declines in aggregate demand, and the increases in real GDP above potential GDP are caused by increases in aggregate demand. For example, the decrease in real GDP in the 1990–1991 recession may have been due to a decline in government demand. In fact, government military spending did decline sharply. Or the recession may have been due to a decline in demand by consumers as they learned about Iraq's invasion of Kuwait in August 1990, saw oil and gasoline prices rise, and worried about the threat of war.

Thus, a key assumption of the theory of economic fluctuations is that real GDP fluctuates around potential GDP. Why is this a good assumption? How do we know that the fluctuations in the economy are not due solely to fluctuations in potential GDP, that is, in the economy's aggregate supply? The rationale for the assumption is that most of the determinants of potential GDP usually change rather smoothly. Clearly, population grows relatively smoothly. We do not have a sudden drop in the U.S. population every few years, nor is there a huge migration of people from the United States during recessions. The same is true with factories and equipment in the economy. Unless there is a major war at home, we do not suddenly lose equipment or factories in the economy on a massive scale. Even disasters such as the deadly Gulf Coast hurricanes of 2005 (Katrina and Rita), the 1994 earthquake in California, or the attacks of September 11, 2001, although devastating for those hit, take only a tiny fraction out of the potential GDP of the entire U.S. economy. Finally, technological know-how does not suddenly decline; we do not suddenly forget how to produce things. The steady upward movement of potential GDP thus represents gradual accumulations—growth of population, growth of capital, and growth of technology. However, although many economists place more emphasis on the role of aggregate demand in short-run economic fluctuations than on that of fluctuations in potential GDP, it is too extreme to insist that there are absolutely no fluctuations in potential GDP.

Macroeconomic Policy and Economic Fluctuations

Macroeconomic policy can have substantial effects on economic fluctuations. Many governments would like to implement policies that either help to avoid recessions or minimize the impact of recessions when they do occur. Monetary policymakers typically prefer to implement policies that minimize fluctuations in GDP. Policies used to influence economic fluctuations are sometimes called *demand-side policies* because they aim to influence aggregate demand in the economy.

Fiscal Policy. On the fiscal side, the primary tools that the government uses to influence demand are government purchases and taxes. If the economy shows signs of entering a recession, the government can try to increase demand by implementing tax cuts and/or spending increases. A good example was the tax cuts implemented by Congress in 2001 when the economy was showing signs of sliding into recession. Often these policies are intended to mitigate the negative impact on aggregate demand of other factors, such as a fall in consumer or investor confidence or a fall in our exports because of a recession in one of the countries that is among our major trading partners.

Monetary Policy. To keep inflation low and stable, the Federal Reserve will also implement policies that influence demand. The primary tools that the Federal Reserve uses to influence demand are changes in interest rates. If there are signs that inflation is on the rise because aggregate demand is growing faster than potential output, the Federal Reserve may step in and raise interest rates, which will slow down spending, as you will soon learn in Chapter 7. In addition to keeping inflation low and stable, the Federal Reserve is also concerned with minimizing the adverse impact of recessions. When the economy goes into recession, the Federal Reserve will try to increase demand by lowering interest rates. A good example of this type of behavior was seen in 2001 and 2002 when the Federal Reserve lowered interest rates twelve times—going from an interest rate of 6.5 percent to an interest rate of 1.25 percent.

REVIEW

- Economic growth theory concentrates on explaining the long-term upward path of the economy.
- Economic growth depends on three factors: the growth of capital, labor, and technology.
- Government policy can influence long-term economic growth by affecting these three factors. To raise long-term economic growth, government policies can provide incentives for investment in capital, for research and development of new technologies, for education, and for increased labor supply. A monetary policy of low and stable inflation can also have a positive effect on economic growth.
- Economic fluctuations theory assumes that fluctuations in GDP are due to fluctuations in aggregate demand.
- Monetary policy and fiscal policy can reduce the fluctuations in real GDP. Finding good policies is a major task of macroeconomics.

CONCLUSION

This chapter started with a brief review of the facts of economic growth and fluctuations. The key facts are that economic growth provides impressive gains in the well-being of individuals over the long term, that economic growth is temporarily interrupted by recessions, that unemployment rises in recessions, and that inflation and interest rates rise before recessions and decline during and after recessions. These are the facts on which macroeconomic theory is based and about which macroeconomic policy is concerned. Remembering these facts helps you understand theory and make judgments about government policy.

After showing how we measure real GDP and inflation in Chapter 6, we go on to look at explanations for the facts and proposals for macroeconomic policies in Chapters 7 through 15.

KEY POINTS

1. Macroeconomics is concerned with economic growth and fluctuations in the whole economy.
2. China, India, Korea, and many other economies have grown dramatically in recent years.
3. Economic growth occurs because of increases in labor, capital, and technological know-how.
4. Economic policies that provide incentives to increase capital and resources devoted to improving technology can increase growth rates.
5. Economic fluctuations consist of recessions (when real GDP falls and unemployment increases) followed by recoveries (when real GDP rises rapidly and unemployment falls).
6. Recent recessions have been much less severe than the Great Depression of the 1930s, when real GDP fell by over 30 percent.
7. Inflation and interest rates rise before recession and fall in the aftermath.
8. The most popular theory of economic fluctuations is that they occur because of fluctuations in aggregate demand.
9. Macroeconomic policies include monetary and fiscal policies that are aimed at keeping business cycles small and inflation low.
10. Economic growth theory and economic fluctuations theory combine to form macroeconomic theory, which explains why the economy grows and fluctuates over time.

KEY TERMS

real gross domestic product (real GDP)
economic growth
economic fluctuations
recession
peak
trough
expansion
recovery
unemployment rate
inflation rate
interest rate
real interest rate
nominal interest rate
potential GDP
aggregate supply
labor
capital
technology
production function
aggregate demand

QUESTIONS FOR REVIEW

1. What are the two broad branches of macroeconomic theory?
2. What is the difference between economic growth and economic fluctuations?
3. What is the difference between a recession period and a recovery period?
4. How do unemployment, inflation, and interest rates behave during recessions?
5. How many recessions have there been since the Great Depression?
6. How do the two most recent recessions compare to past recessions?
7. What is potential GDP?
8. What is aggregate demand?
9. What are the primary determinant of economic growth?
10. Describe how monetary policy and fiscal policy can affect economic growth and economic fluctuations?

PROBLEMS

1. The graph below shows a period of back-to-back recessions that occurred in the United States in the 1980s. Show the peaks, recessions, troughs, and recovery phases of this unusual period.

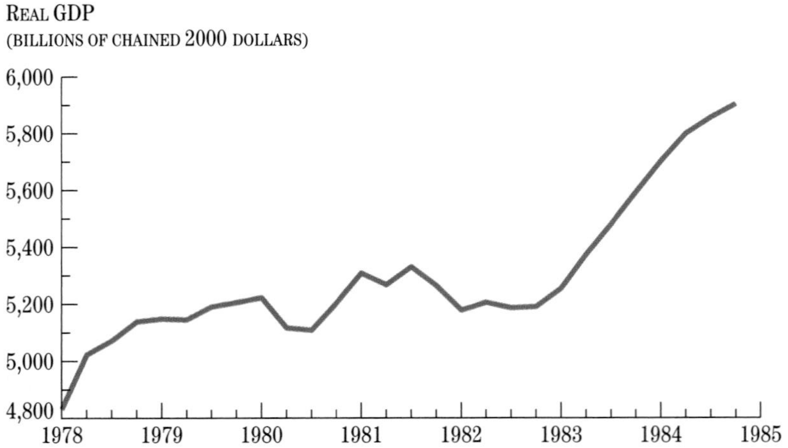

2. What determines potential GDP? What factors could cause the growth rate of potential GDP to slow down? What economic policies can the government use to affect potential GDP?
3. Suppose the U.S. economy is at the trough of a business cycle. What is the relationship between real and potential GDP? Is it likely that real GDP will stay in this position relative to potential GDP for a long period of time (say, 10 years)? Explain briefly.
4. Suppose people start retiring at a later age because of improved medical technology. How will this affect the economy's potential GDP? Why might the government want to encourage later retirement?
5. Using the data from Canada and Britain shown in the table below, plot the unemployment rate on the vertical axis. How do these unemployment rates compare with the U.S. rate shown in Figure 5?

Rate of Unemployment (percent)

Year	*Canada*	*Britain*
1990	7.7	6.9
1991	9.8	8.8
1992	10.6	10.1
1993	10.8	10.5
1994	9.5	9.6
1995	8.6	8.7
1996	8.8	8.1
1997	8.4	7.0
1998	7.7	6.3
1999	7.0	6.0
2000	6.1	5.5

6. Compare Figure 5, showing unemployment, with Figure 8, showing the inflation rate for the same period in the United States. Describe how unemployment and inflation are correlated over the long term and over the short term.
7. Suppose that you had savings deposited in an account at an interest rate of 5 percent and your father told you that he earned 10 percent interest 20 years ago. Which of you was getting the better return? How would your answer change if you were told that the inflation rate in the United States was 12 percent 20 years ago and is 3 percent now?
8. Suppose you have $1,000, which you can put in two different types of accounts at a bank. One account pays interest of 8 percent per year; the other pays interest of 2 percent per year plus the rate of inflation. Calculate the real return you will receive after 1 year if the inflation rate is 5 percent. Which account will you choose if you expect the rate of inflation to be 8 percent? Why?

The Miracle of Compound Growth

Compound growth explains why small differences in the annual economic growth rate make such huge differences in real GDP over time. Here we explain this compounding effect, show how to compute growth rates, and discuss alternative ways to plot growing variables over time.

How Compound Growth Works

Compound growth works just like compound interest on a savings account. Compound interest is defined as the "interest on the interest" you earned in earlier periods. For example, suppose you have a savings account in a bank that pays 6 percent per year in interest. That is, if you put $100 in the account, then after one year you will get $100 times .06, or $6 in interest. If you leave the original $100 plus the $6—that is, $106—in the bank for a second year, then at the end of the second year you will get $106 times .06, or $6.36 in interest. The $.36 is the "interest on the interest," that is, $6 times .06.

At the end of the second year, you have $100 + $6 + $6.36 = $112.36. If you leave that in the bank for a third year, you will get $6.74 in interest, of which $.74 is "interest on the interest" earned in the first two years. Note how the "interest on the interest" rises from $.36 in the second year to $.74 in the third year. Following the same calculations, the "interest on the interest" in the fourth year would be $1.15. After 13 years, the "interest on the interest" is greater than the $6 interest on the original $100! As a result of this compound interest, the size of your account grows rapidly. At the end of 20 years, it is $320.71; after 40 years, your $100 has grown to $1,028.57.

Compound growth applies the idea of compound interest to the economy. Consider, for example, a country in which real GDP is $100 billion and the growth rate is 6 percent per year. After one year, real GDP would increase by $100 billion times .06, or by $6 billion. Real GDP rises from $100 billion to $106 billion. In the second year, real GDP increases by $106 billion times .06, or by $6.36 billion. Real GDP rises from $106 billion to $112.36 billion. Table A.1 shows how, continuing this way, real GDP grows, rounding to the nearest $.1 billion.

TABLE A.1
Example of Compound Growth

	Real GDP (billions)		Real GDP (billions)
Year 0	$100.0	Year 20	$ 320.7
Year 1	$106.0	Year 30	$ 574.3
Year 2	$112.4	Year 40	$1,028.6
Year 3	$119.1	Year 50	$1,842.0
Year 4	$126.2	Year 60	$3,298.8
Year 5	$133.3	Year 70	$5,907.6
Year 10	$179.1		

Thus, in one person's lifetime, real GDP would increase by about 60 times.

Exponential Effects

A convenient way to compute these changes is to multiply the initial level by 1.06 year after year. For example, the level of real GDP after one year is $100 billion times .06 plus $100 billion, or $100 billion times 1.06. After two years, it is $106 billion times 1.06, or $100 billion times $(1.06)^2$. Thus, for n years, we have

$$(\text{Initial level}) \times (1.06)^n = \text{level at end of } n \text{ years}$$

where the initial level could be $100 in a bank, the $100 billion level of real GDP, or anything else. For example, real GDP at the end of 70 years in the table shown earlier is $100 billion times $(1.06)^n$ = $100 billion times 59.076 = $5,907.6 billion, with $n = 70$. Here the growth rate (or the interest rate) is 6 percent. In general, we have:

$$(\text{Initial level}) \times (1 + g)^n = \text{level at end of } n \text{ years}$$

where g is the annual growth rate, stated as a decimal; that is, 6 percent is .06. If you have a hand calculator with a key that does y^x, it is fairly easy to make these calculations, and if you try it you will see the power of compound growth. The term *exponential growth* is sometimes used because the number of years (n) appears as an exponent in the above expression.

When economists refer to average annual growth over time, they include this compounding effect. The growth rate is found by solving for g. That is, the growth rate, stated as a decimal fraction, between some initial level and a level n years later is given by

$$g = \left(\frac{\text{level at end of } n \text{ years}}{\text{initial level}}\right)^{1/n} - 1$$

For example, the average annual growth rate from year 0 to year 20 in the table is

$$g = \left(\frac{320.7}{100}\right)^{1/20} - 1$$
$$= (1.06) - 1$$
$$= .06$$

or 6 percent. Again, if your calculator has a key for y^x, you can make these calculations easily.

To get the annual growth rate for one year, you simply divide the level in the second year by the level in the first year and subtract 1 to get the growth rate.

Rule of 72

You can also find how long it takes something to increase by a certain percentage. For example, to calculate how many years it takes something that grows at rate g to double, you solve $(1 + g)^n = 2$ for n. The answer is approximately $n = .72/g$. In other words, if you divide 72 by the growth rate in percent, you get the number of years it takes to double the amount. This is called the *rule of 72*. If your bank account pays 6 percent interest, it will double in 12 years.

Plotting Growing Variables

You may have noticed that some time-series charts have vertical scales that shrink as the economic variable being plotted gets bigger. Look, for example, at the scale in Figures 1 and 4 for real GDP. This type of scale, which is called a *ratio scale* (or sometimes a proportional scale or logarithmic scale), is used by financial analysts and economists to present variables that grow over time. The purpose of a ratio scale is to make equal percentage changes in the variable have the same vertical distance.

If you plot a variable that grows at a constant rate on a ratio scale, it looks like a straight line, even though it would look as if it were exploding on a standard scale. To show what ratio scales do, real GDP for the past 40 years is plotted in Figure A.1 using a regular scale and a ratio

FIGURE A.1
Comparison of Two Different Scales: Regular versus Ratio

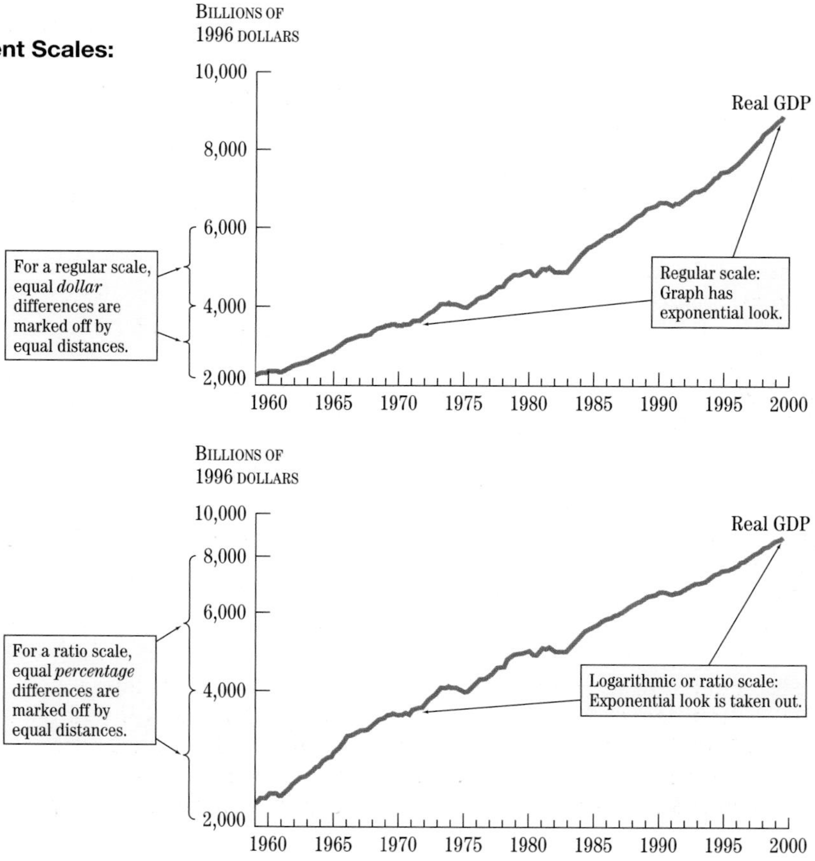

scale. Note how the fluctuations in real GDP in the 1960s look smaller on a regular scale compared with the ratio scale, and how the ratio scale tends to take out the exponential look. This difference is one reason to look carefully at the scales of graphs. (The reason that ratio scales are sometimes called logarithmic scales is that plotting the logarithm of a variable is the same as plotting the variable on a ratio scale.)

KEY POINTS

1. Compound growth is similar to compound interest. Rather than applying the interest rate to the interest from earlier periods, one applies the growth rate to the growth from the previous period.
2. With compound growth, seemingly small differences in growth rates result in huge differences in real GDP.
3. When you see a diagram with the scale shrunk for the higher values, it is a logarithmic or ratio scale.
4. A ratio or logarithmic scale is more useful than a regular scale when a variable is growing over time.

KEY TERM AND DEFINITION

compound growth: applying the growth rate to growth from the previous period; similar to compound interest.

QUESTIONS FOR REVIEW

1. What is the rule of 72?
2. What is a ratio scale?

PROBLEMS

1. Suppose that the annual rate of growth of GDP per capita is 2 percent. How much will real GDP per capita increase in 10 years? How much will it increase in 50 years? Answer the same questions for a growth rate of 1 percent and for a growth rate of 4 percent.
2. According to recent data, China's per capita GDP is growing at about 9 percent a year. How long will it take for China's per capita GDP to double? If China can grow at 9 percent a year for the next 16 years and at 6 percent a year for the following 24 years, how large will China's per capita GDP in 40 years be relative to its per capita GDP today?
3. Plot the data for the example economy in the table in this appendix on a graph at 10-year intervals from year 20 to year 60 on a regular scale. Now create a new graph with a ratio scale by first marking off 300, 600, 1,200, 2,400, and 4,800 at equal distances on the vertical axis. Plot the same data on this graph. Compare the two graphs.

Chapter 6

Measuring the Production, Income, and Spending of Nations

Imagine, if you will, that you were one of a small group of subsistence farmers eking out a living on a small island where the only thing that grew was coconut trees. If you were asked to calculate the production of this economy, all you would have to do was count the number of coconuts that the people living on the island plucked from the trees. But suppose instead that the island also had an abundance of banana plants. Then calculating the production of the economy would require that you count both coconuts and bananas. Understanding whether production had increased over time would be a challenge—would the 500 pounds of bananas and 1,000 coconuts produced this year be considered to be an increase in production compared to last year's crop of 750 pounds of bananas and 750 coconuts? You would have to figure out how to compare bananas to coconuts—perhaps not as impossible a task as comparing apples to oranges, but a challenge nonetheless.

Now imagine, if you will, being asked to calculate the production of the economy of the United States. You would have to add up not just apples and oranges, but millions of other goods. You would also have to think about how to measure the output of doctors, lawyers, teachers, and economists. Some of the goods being produced in the economy would be shipped to other countries. Other goods that people were buying had been shipped to the United States from abroad. Some goods, like bicycle tires, were being used as inputs into the production of other goods, like bicycles. Measuring the production of a nation is indeed a challenge.

In the United States, that challenge has been assigned to the Bureau of Economic Analysis (BEA), an agency of the Department of Commerce. The BEA states its mission as being to promote "a better understanding of the U.S. economy by providing the most timely, relevant, and accurate economic accounts data in an objective and cost-effective manner." Every quarter, the BEA releases the official government statistics on real GDP, the most widely used measure of production in the U.S. economy.

BEA releases are eagerly awaited throughout the economy. Top officials at the White House (including the president) find these data so important that they make sure they get them the night before they are released to the public. Because measuring the economy in a timely and accurate manner is essential for people in financial markets and other lines of business, bond and stock traders in New York, Tokyo, London, and everywhere else keep their eyes glued to their computer terminals when a new government statistic measuring the course of the economy is about to be released. By buying or selling quickly in response to the new information, they can make millions or avoid losing millions.

To economists, measurement of the economy is interesting in its own right, involving clever solutions to intriguing problems. One of the first Nobel Prizes in economics was given to Simon Kuznets for solving some of these measurement problems. As economics students, you cannot help but learn a little about how the economy works when you study how to measure it, just as geology students cannot help but learn a little about earthquakes when they study how the Richter scale measures them. Understanding economic problems, designing possible policy solutions to these problems, and understanding whether the policy solutions did in fact work all require access to reliable data.

The purpose of this chapter is not to train you to go directly to work in the BEA. Instead, the goals are to give you a general understanding of what the measures used by the BEA are, to help you better grasp what the strengths and weaknesses of these measures are, and to make you more familiar with some key macroeconomic relationships that exist in the economy.

MEASURING GDP

To use GDP as a measure of production, we must be precise about *what* is included in production, *where* production takes place, and *when* production takes place.

A Precise Definition of GDP

GDP is a measure of the value of all the newly produced goods and services in a country during some period of time. Let us dissect this definition to determine what is in GDP and what is not, as well as where and when GDP is produced.

- *What?* Both *goods*—such as automobiles and new houses—and *services*—such as bus rides or a college education—are included in GDP. However, only *newly produced* goods and services are included. A 10-year-old baby carriage that is being sold in a garage sale is not in this year's GDP; it was included in GDP 10 years ago, when it was produced.

- *Where?* Only goods and services produced *within the borders* of a country are included in that country's GDP. Goods produced by Americans working in another country are not part of U.S. GDP; they are part of the other country's GDP. Goods and services produced by foreigners working in the United States are part of U.S. GDP.
- *When?* Only goods and services produced *during some specified period* of time are included in GDP. We always need to specify the period during which we are measuring GDP. For example, GDP in 2006 is the production during 2006. GDP for the third quarter of 2006 is the production between July 1 and September 30 of 2006.

Rounded off to the nearest billion, GDP, or total production, was $13,247 billion in the United States in 2006. Rounded off to the nearest trillion, GDP was $13 trillion. That is an average production of about $36 billion worth of goods and services a day for each of the 365 days during the year.

Prices Determine the Importance of Goods and Services in GDP. GDP is a single number, but it measures the production of many different things, from apples to oranges, from car insurance to life insurance, from audio CDs to DVDs. How can we add up such different products? Is a CD more important than a DVD? Does a coconut count more toward GDP than a banana does?

Each good is given a weight when we compute GDP, and that weight is its *price.* If the price of a DVD is greater than that of a CD, then the DVD will count more in GDP. To see this, imagine that production consists entirely of CDs and DVDs. If a DVD costs $15 and a CD costs $10, then producing three DVDs will add $45 to GDP, and producing five CDs will add $50 to GDP. Thus, producing three DVDs plus five CDs adds $95 to GDP, as shown in Table 1.

Although this method of weighting by price might not appeal to you personally—you might like CDs more than DVDs—it is hard to imagine anything more workable. In a market system, prices tend to reflect the cost and value of the goods and services produced. One of the great problems of measuring GDP in centrally planned economies such as the Soviet Union was that the price of goods was set by the government; thus, the weight given each item may have had little to do with either its cost or its value to individuals. Without market prices, measuring GDP in the Soviet Union was difficult.

Intermediate Goods versus Final Goods. When measuring GDP, it is important not to count the same item more than once. Consider bicycle tires.

TABLE 1
Adding Up Unlike Products: CDs and DVDs

5 CDs	$10 per CD	$50 of CD production
+ 3 DVDs	$15 per DVD	+ $45 of DVD production
?		$95 of CD and DVD production
To add up unlike products . . .	*. . . we multiply by their prices to get the dollar value of each . . .*	*. . . and add together the dollar values of each to get the dollar value of the sum.*

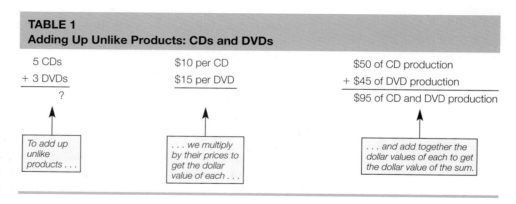

ECONOMICS IN ACTION

Distinguishing Between Stocks and Flows

The economist's distinction between stocks and flows can be illustrated by picturing water flowing into and out of a lake—for example, the Colorado River flowing into and out of Lake Powell behind Glen Canyon Dam. When more water flows in than flows out, the stock of water in Lake Powell rises. Similarly, a positive flow of inventory investment raises the stock of inventory at a firm. And just as the stock of water falls when more water flows out than flows in, negative inventory investment lowers the stock of inventory.

The distinction between stocks and flows is useful in other economic applications as well. The factories in America on December 31, 2006, are a stock. The number of factories built during 2006 is a flow. The funds in your checking account are a stock. The deposit you made last week is a flow.

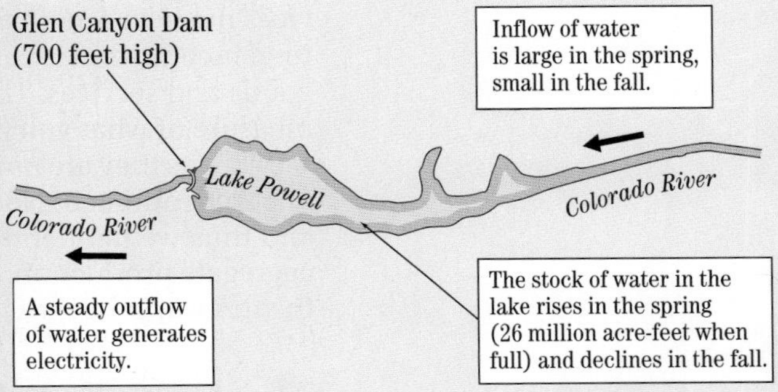
Glen Canyon Dam
(700 feet high)
Inflow of water is large in the spring, small in the fall.
Lake Powell
Colorado River
Colorado River
A steady outflow of water generates electricity.
The stock of water in the lake rises in the spring (26 million acre-feet when full) and declines in the fall.

intermediate good: a good that undergoes further processing before it is sold to consumers.

final good: a new good that undergoes no further processing before it is sold to consumers.

When you buy a $150 bicycle, the tires are considered part of the bicycle. Suppose the tires are worth $20. It would be a mistake to count both the $20 value of the tires and the $150 value of the bicycle, for a total value of $170. That would count the tires twice, which is called *double counting*. When a tire is part of a new bicycle, it is an example of an **intermediate good.** Intermediate goods are part of **final goods,** which by definition are goods that undergo no further processing—in this case, the bicycle. *To avoid double counting, we never count intermediate goods; only final goods are part of the GDP.* If in a few years you buy a new $25 bicycle tire, then the tire will be a final good.

Stocks versus Flows. The distinction between *stocks* and *flows* is one of the most useful concepts in economics, and it is especially important in understanding GDP. GDP is a measure of the flow of new goods and services—it measures the value of all the newly produced goods and services in the economy. GDP is not a measure of the stock of goods and services in the economy—it does not tell us the value of all the goods and services that exist in the economy.

For example, the number of new cars produced in the United States during a given time period is a flow measure, while the number of cars in the United States is a stock measure. Therefore, only the former will count toward GDP. Similarly, U.S. GDP for 2006 will count the value of new houses built in the United States in 2006 (a flow measure), but it will not count the value of all homes in the United States (a stock measure).

The economist's distinction between stocks and flows can be illustrated by picturing water flowing into a bathtub from a tap. The water coming from the tap is a flow measure, while the water that is in the bathtub is a stock measure. GDP in essence is measuring the flow from the tap (the new goods and services added to the economy) and not the water in the tub (all the goods and services that already exist).

Three Ways to Measure GDP. Economists measure GDP in three ways. All three give the same answer, but they refer to conceptually different activities in the economy and provide different ways to think about GDP. All three are reported in the national income and product accounts, the official U.S. government tabulation of GDP put together by economists and statisticians at the Department of Commerce's Bureau of Economic Analysis.

The first way measures the total amount that people *spend* on goods and services made in America. This is the *spending* approach. The second way measures the total income that is earned by all the workers and businesses that produce American goods and services. This is the *income* approach. In this approach, your income is a measure of what you produce. The third way measures the total of all the goods and services as they are *produced,* or as they are shipped out of the factory. This is the *production* approach. Note that each of the approaches considers the whole economy, and thus we frequently refer to them as aggregate spending, aggregate income, and aggregate production, where the word *aggregate* means total. Let us consider each of the three approaches in turn.

The Spending Approach

Typically, total spending in the economy is divided into four components: *consumption, investment, government purchases,* and *net exports,* which equal exports minus imports. Each of the four components corresponds closely to one of four groups into which the economy is divided: consumers, businesses, governments, and foreigners. Before considering each component, look at Table 2, which shows how the $13,247 billion of GDP in the United States in 2006 was divided into the four categories.

consumption: purchases of final goods and services by individuals.

Consumption. The first component, **consumption,** is purchases of final goods and services by individuals. Government statisticians, who collect the data in most countries, survey department stores, discount stores, car dealers, and other sellers to see how much consumers purchase each year ($9,269 billion in

TABLE 2
Components of Spending in 2006 (billions of dollars)

Gross domestic product (GDP)	$13,247
Consumption	9,269
Investment	2,213
Government purchases	2,528
Net exports	−763

Source: U.S. Department of Commerce, Bureau of Economic Analysis.

2006, as given in Table 2). They count anything purchased by consumers as consumption. Consumption does not include spending by business or government. Consumer purchases may be big-ticket items such as a new convertible, an operation to remove a cancerous tumor, a new stereo, a weekend vacation, or college tuition, or smaller-ticket items such as an oil change, a medical checkup, a bus ride, or a driver's education class. Consumption is a whopping 70 percent of GDP in the United States (see Figure 1).

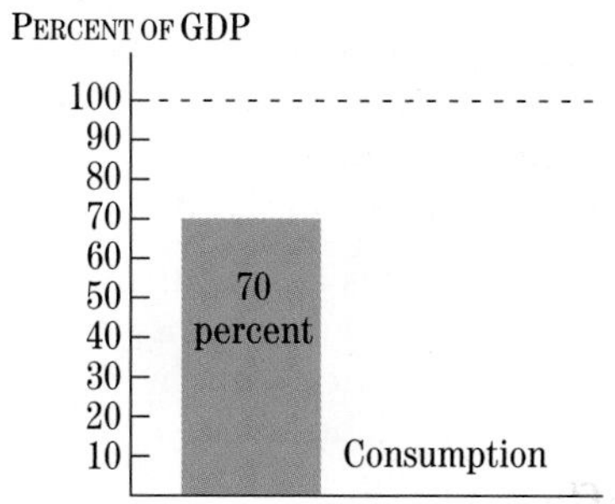

FIGURE 1
Consumption as a Share of GDP
Consumption was 70 percent of GDP in the United States in 2006.

investment: purchases of final goods by firms plus purchases of newly produced residences by households.

■ **Investment.** The second component, **investment,** consists of purchases of final goods by business firms and of newly produced residences by households. When a business such as a pizza delivery firm buys a new car, economists consider that purchase as part of investment rather than as consumption. The firm uses the car to make deliveries, which contributes to its production of delivered pizzas. Included in investment are all the new machines, new factories, and other tools used to produce goods and services. Purchases of intermediate goods that go directly into a manufactured product—such as a tire on a bicycle—are not counted as investment. These items are part of the finished product—the bicycle, in this case—purchased by consumers. We do not want to count such items twice.

The new machines, factories, and other tools that are part of investment in any year are sometimes called *business fixed investment;* this amounted to $1,396 billion in 2006. There are two other items that government statisticians include as part of investment: inventory investment and residential investment.

Inventory investment is defined as the change in *inventories,* which are the goods on store shelves, on showroom floors, or in warehouses that have not yet been sold or assembled into a final form for sale. For example, cars on the lot of a car dealer are part of inventories. When inventory investment is positive, then inventories are rising. When inventory investment is negative, then inventories are falling.

For example, if a car dealer had an inventory of 50 cars on December 31, 2005, got 35 new cars shipped from the factory during 2006, and sold 20 cars to consumers during the year, then the dealer's inventory will be 65 cars on December 31, 2006. The contribution of the car dealer to inventory investment for the year is positive 15 cars because the dealer's inventory rose from 50 cars to 65 cars.

If, instead, the dealer had an inventory of 50 cars on December 31, 2005, got 35 new cars shipped from the factory during 2006, and sold 45 cars to consumers during the year, then the dealer's inventory will be 40 cars on December 31, 2006. The contribution of the car dealer to inventory investment for the year is negative 10 cars because the dealer's inventory fell from 50 cars to 40 cars.

Why is inventory investment included as a spending item when we compute GDP? The reason is that we want an accurate measure of production. Consider the first car example again. If we looked only at consumption, then we would have concluded that only 20 cars were produced in the economy, even though 35 cars were actually produced. We need to add the 15 cars of inventory investment to the 20 cars of consumption to get an accurate measure of production.

What happens when consumers eventually purchase the cars that the dealer has in inventory? Suppose in 2007, consumers buy 25 of the cars that were in the dealer's inventory. For 2007, consumption will rise by 25 cars, while inventory investment will be negative 25 cars, reflecting the fall in the dealer's inventory. Adding 25 cars of consumption to negative 25 cars of inventory investment gives zero cars added to overall

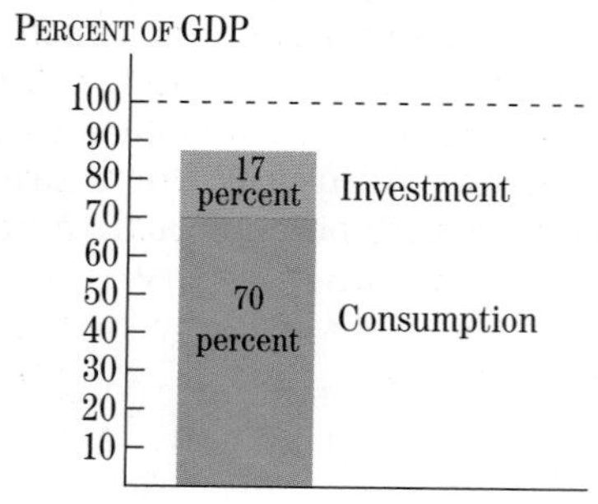

FIGURE 2
Investment and Consumption as a Share of GDP in 2006
Investment is a much smaller share of GDP than is consumption.

GDP in 2007, which is just what we want because none of these cars were produced in 2007; we had already counted them as production for 2006.

In 2006, inventory investment throughout the economy was $50 billion. Some firms subtracted inventories, but others added a greater amount. Inventory investment tends to fluctuate up and down and therefore plays a big role in the business cycle.

The other part of investment that is not business fixed investment is *residential investment*, the purchase of new houses and apartment buildings. About $767 billion worth of housing and apartments were constructed in 2006. Although much of this was purchased by consumers rather than businesses, it is included in investment because it produces services: shelter and, in some cases, a place to relax and enjoy life.

Combining the three parts of investment, we find that investment was $2,213 billion in 2006: $1,396 billion of business fixed investment, $767 billion of residential investment, and $50 billion of inventory investment. Investment was about 17 percent of GDP in 2008 (see Figure 2).

Note the special way the term *investment* is used in this discussion. To an economist, investment means the purchase of new factories, houses, or equipment. In everyday language, however, investment usually refers to an individual's putting away some funds for the future, perhaps in the stock market, such as "I'll invest in the stock market." Be sure to stay aware of this distinction.

government purchases: purchases by federal, state, and local governments of new goods and services.

Government Purchases. The third component of spending, **government purchases,** is spending by federal, state, and local governments on new goods and services. Most U.S. government purchases are for the military. At the state and local levels, education, roads, and police dominate government purchases. Government purchases of goods and services were equal to $2,528 billion in 2006 (see Figure 3).

Not all government outlays are included in government purchases. A government welfare payment or retirement payment to an individual is not a purchase of a good or service; it is a *transfer payment* of income from the government to an individual. Transfer payments do not represent new production of anything, unlike the purchase of a weapon or a new road or a new building. Because GDP measures the production of new goods and services, government outlays on transfer payments like social security, unemployment compensation, and welfare payments are excluded. Only purchases are counted because only these items represent something produced. Government *outlays* are purchases plus transfer payments.

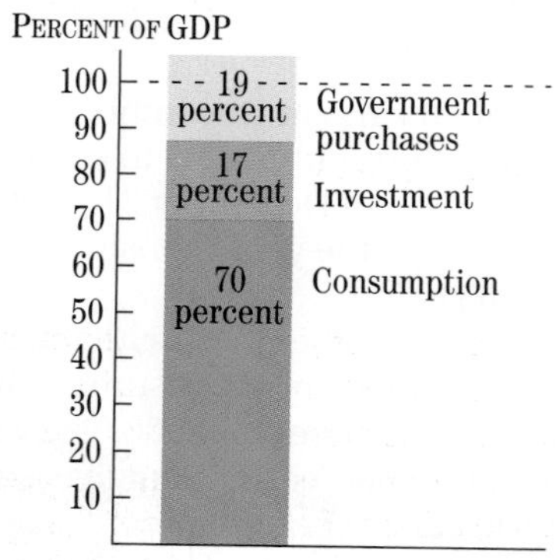

FIGURE 3
Government Purchases, Investment, and Consumption as a Share of GDP in 2006
Government purchases as a share of GDP are greater than investment but less than consumption. When the stacked bar goes above the 100 percent line, there are negative net exports (a trade deficit), as shown here. If the stacked bar stops below the 100 percent line, there is a trade surplus.

Net Exports. The final spending component is **net exports,** the difference between exports and imports. American **exports** are what Americans sell to foreigners, whether pharmaceuticals, computers, grain, or a vacation in Florida. American **imports** are what Americans buy from foreigners, whether cars, plasma TVs, shirts, or a vacation in France. Net exports are defined as exports minus imports. Net exports are a measure of how much more we sell to foreigners than we buy from foreigners. Another term for net exports is the **trade balance.** If net exports are positive, we have a trade surplus. If net exports are negative, we have a trade deficit. By these calculations, the United States had a trade deficit in 2006: $1,466 billion in exports and $2,229 billion in imports. Hence, net exports were a negative $763 billion, and appear in Table 2 as −$763 billion.

net exports: the value of exports minus the value of imports.

exports: the total value of the goods and services that people in one country sell to people in other countries.

imports: the total value of the goods and services that people in one country buy from people in other countries.

trade balance: the value of exports minus the value of imports.

Why are net exports added in when computing GDP by the spending approach? There are two reasons. First, we included foreign goods in consumption and investment spending. For example, an imported Toyota purchased at a car dealer in the United States is included in consumption even though it is not produced in the United States. To measure what is produced in the United States, that Toyota must be deducted. Thus, imports must be subtracted to get a measure of total production in the economy. The second reason is that the exports that Americans sell abroad are produced in the United States, but they are not counted in consumption or investment or government purchases in the United States. Thus, exports need to be added in to get a measure of production. Because, by definition, net exports are exports minus imports, adding net exports to spending is the same as adding in exports and subtracting out imports. Adding net exports to total spending kills two birds with one stone.

In 2006, the United States imported more than it exported, so the sum of consumption plus investment plus government purchases overstated what was produced in America. The sum of these three items exceeds GDP, as shown in Figure 3. In other words, GDP was $763 billion less than the sum of consumption plus investment plus government purchases.

Algebraic Summary. The notion that we can measure production by adding up consumption, investment, government purchases, and net exports is important enough to herald with some algebra.

Let the symbol C stand for consumption, I for investment, G for government spending, and X for net exports. Let Y stand for GDP because we use G for government purchases. We will use these symbols many times again. The idea that production equals spending can then be written as

This is a key equation stating that production equals spending.

$$Y = C + I + G + X$$

This equation states, using algebraic symbols, that production, Y, equals spending: consumption, C, plus investment, I, plus government purchases, G, plus net exports, X (meaning exports minus imports). In 2006 the values of these items (in billions of dollars) were

$$13{,}247 = 9{,}269 + 2{,}213 + 2{,}528 + (-763)$$

This simple algebraic relationship plays a key role in later chapters.

The Income Approach

The income that people earn producing GDP in a country provides another measure of GDP. To see why, first consider a simple example of a single business firm.

Suppose you start a wedding planning business. Your production and sales of wedding planning services in your first year is $50,000; this is the amount you are paid in total by 50 people for the $1,000 service. To produce these services, you pay a catering consultant and a florist consultant $20,000 each, or a total of $40,000, which is your total cost. Your profits are defined as the difference between sales and costs, or $50,000 − $40,000 = $10,000. Now, if you add the total amount of income earned in the production of your wedding planning service—the amount earned by the two consultants plus the profits you earn—you get $20,000 + $20,000 + $10,000. This sum of incomes is exactly equal to $50,000, which is the same as the amount produced. Thus, by adding up the income of the people who produce the output of the firm, you get a measure of the output. The same idea is true for the country as a whole, which consists of many such businesses and workers.

To show how this works, we look at each of the income items in Table 3. We first describe each of these items and then show that when we add the items up, we get GDP.

TABLE 3
Aggregate Income and GDP in 2006 (billions of dollars)

Aggregate income	
Labor income (wages, salaries, fringe benefits)	$7,498
Capital income (profits, interest, rents)	3,218
Depreciation	1,577
Taxes, subsidies, and transfers	995
Net income of foreigners	−30
Statistical discrepancy	−11
Equals GDP	13,247

Source: U.S. Department of Commerce.

labor income: the sum of wages, salaries, and fringe benefits paid to workers.

Labor Income. Economists classify wages, salaries, and fringe benefits paid to workers as **labor income,** or payments to people for their labor. *Wages* refers to payments to workers paid by the hour; *salaries* refers to payments to workers paid by the month or year; and *fringe benefits* refers to retirement, health, and other benefits paid by firms on behalf of workers. As shown in Table 3, labor income was $7,498 billion in 2006.

capital income: the sum of profits, rental payments, and interest payments.

Capital Income. Economists classify profits, rental payments, and interest payments as **capital income.** *Profits* include the profits of large corporations like General Motors or Exxon and also the income of small businesses and farms. The royalties that an independent screenwriter receives from selling a movie script are also part of profits. *Rental payments* are income to persons who own buildings and rent them out. The rents they receive from their tenants are rental payments. *Interest payments* are income received from lending to business firms. Interest payments are included in capital income because they represent part of the income generated by the firms' production. Because many individuals pay interest (on mortgages, car loans, etc.) as well as receive interest (on deposits at a bank, etc.), interest payments are defined as the difference between receipts and payments. Table 3 shows that capital income was $3,218 billion in 2006, much less than labor income. Capital income is about 43 percent of labor income.

depreciation: the decrease in an asset's value over time; for capital, it is the amount by which physical capital wears out over a given period of time.

Depreciation. **Depreciation** is the amount by which factories and machines wear out each year. A remarkably large part of the investment that is part of GDP each year goes to replace worn-out factories and machines. Businesses need to replace depreciated equipment with investment in new equipment just to maintain productive capacity—the number of factories and machines available for use.

The difference between investment, the purchases of final goods by firms, and depreciation is called *net investment,* a measure of how much new investment there is each year after depreciation is subtracted. Net investment was $636 billion ($2,213 billion − $1,577 billion) in 2006. Sometimes the $2,213 billion of investment, including depreciation, is called *gross investment.* The reason for the term *gross* in gross domestic product is that it includes gross investment, not just net investment.

When profits and the other parts of capital income are reported to government statisticians, depreciation has been subtracted out. But depreciation must be included as part of GDP because the new equipment that replaces old equipment must be produced by someone. Thus, when we use the income approach, it is necessary to add in depreciation if we are to have a measure of GDP.

Taxes, Subsidies, and Transfers. When you buy a good, you will often pay a sales tax in addition to the price of the good; sales taxes are collected by businesses and sent directly to the government, either local, state, or federal. For example, the price of gasoline at the pump includes a tax that people who buy gasoline pay as part of the price and that the gasoline station sends to the government. When we tabulate total production by adding up the value of what people spend, we use the prices that businesses charge for a specific good—such as gasoline. That price includes the sales tax that is sent to the government. When we tabulate production by adding up income of consumers and profits of firms, however, the sales tax is not included in firms' profits. Thus, capital income does not include the sales taxes paid by businesses to the government. But those taxes are part of the income generated in producing GDP, the income happens to go to the government. We therefore must add such taxes to capital and labor income. Similarly, there are subsidies from the government to firms that do get included in profits but do not represent income generated in producing GDP. Subsidies need to be subtracted. Similarly, transfer payments, which are payments between parties that do not involve goods or services being exchanged (for example, a charitable contribution to a museum by a corporation), also need to be removed from calculations because they do not represent income generated in producing GDP. Transfers and subsidies are considerably smaller in magnitude than taxes.

Net Income of Foreigners. Foreigners produce part of the GDP in the United States. However, their income is not included in labor income or capital income. For example, the salary of a Canadian hockey player who plays for the Pittsburgh Penguins and keeps his official residence as Canada would not be included in U.S. labor income. But that income represents payment for services produced in the United States and so is part of U.S. GDP. We must add such income payments to foreigners for production in the United States because that production is part of GDP. Moreover, some of the U.S. labor and capital income is earned producing GDP in other countries, and to get a measure of income generated in producing U.S. GDP, we must subtract that out. For example, the salary of a U.S. baseball player who plays for the Toronto Blue Jays and keeps his official residence as the United States represents payment for services produced in Canada and so is not part of U.S. GDP. We must exclude such income payments for production in other countries. To account for both of these effects, we must add *net* income earned by foreigners in the United States—that is, the income earned by foreigners in the United States less what Americans earned abroad—to get GDP. In 2006, Americans earned more abroad ($666 billion) than foreigners earned in the United States ($630 billion); hence, in 2006, *net* income of foreigners was −$30 billion, as shown in Table 3.

Table 3 shows the effects of adding up these five items. The sum is close but not quite equal to GDP. The discrepancy reflects errors made in collecting data on income or spending. This discrepancy has a formal name: the *statistical discrepancy.* In percentage terms the amount is small, less than 1 percent of GDP, considering the different ways the data on income and spending are collected. If we add in the statistical discrepancy, then we have a measure of *aggregate income* that equals GDP. From now on we can use the same symbol (Y) to refer to GDP and to aggregate income, because GDP and aggregate income amount to the same thing.

The circular flow diagram in Figure 4 illustrates the link between aggregate income and aggregate spending. People earn income from producing goods and services, and they spend this income (Y) to buy goods and services (C, I, G, and X).

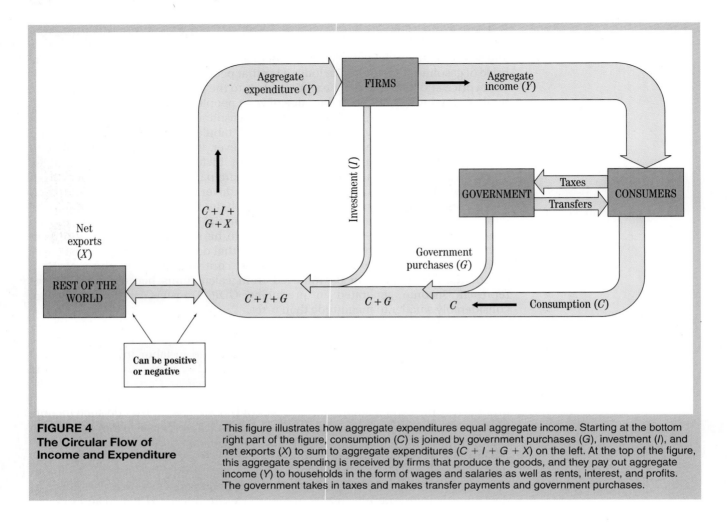

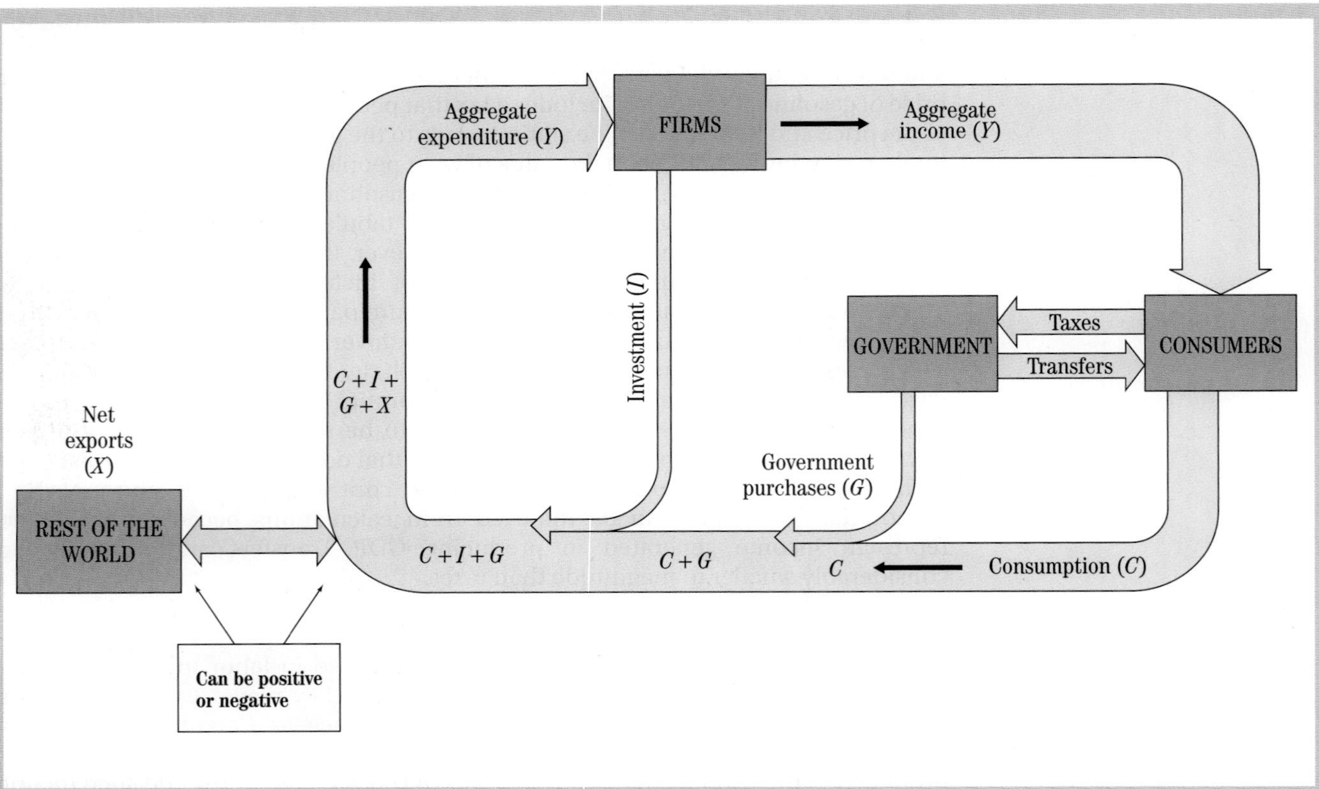

FIGURE 4
The Circular Flow of Income and Expenditure

This figure illustrates how aggregate expenditures equal aggregate income. Starting at the bottom right part of the figure, consumption (C) is joined by government purchases (G), investment (I), and net exports (X) to sum to aggregate expenditures ($C + I + G + X$) on the left. At the top of the figure, this aggregate spending is received by firms that produce the goods, and they pay out aggregate income (Y) to households in the form of wages and salaries as well as rents, interest, and profits. The government takes in taxes and makes transfer payments and government purchases.

The Production Approach

The third measure of GDP adds up the production of each firm or industry in the economy. In order to make this method work, we must avoid the "double counting" problem discussed earlier. For example, if you try to compute GDP by adding new automobiles to new steel to new tires, you will count the steel and the tires that go into producing the new automobiles twice. Thus, when we measure GDP by production, it is necessary to count only the **value added** by each manufacturer. Value added is the value of a firm's production less the value of the intermediate goods used in production. In other words, it is the value the firm adds to the intermediate inputs to get the final output. An automobile manufacturer buys steel, tires, and other inputs and adds value by assembling the car. When we measure GDP by production, we count only the value added at each level of production. Figure 5 shows how adding up the value added for each firm involved in producing a cup of espresso in the economy will automatically avoid double counting and give a measure of the final value of the cup of espresso when it is purchased at a coffeehouse or cafe. The same is true for the economy as a whole.

value added: the value of a firm's production minus the value of the intermediate goods used in production.

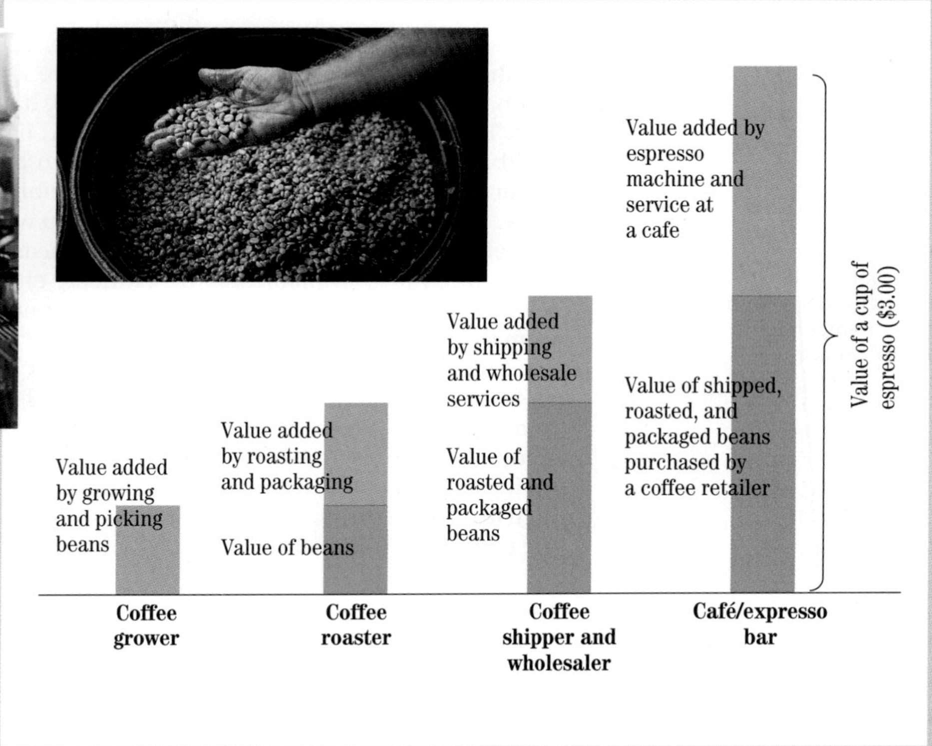

FIGURE 5
Value Added in Coffee: From Beans to Espresso
By adding up the value added at each stage of production, from coffee bean growing to espresso making, we get a measure of the value of a cup of espresso. Double counting is avoided. Using the same procedure for the whole economy permits us to compute GDP by adding up production.

REVIEW

- Gross domestic product (GDP) is a measure of all the goods and services newly produced in the economy during some period of time. GDP is a flow measure—how many new goods and services are being produced in the economy. It is not a stock measure—how many goods and services exist in the economy.
- GDP can be measured in three ways: by adding up all the spending in the economy, by adding up all the income in the economy, and by adding up all the production in the economy. All three give the same answer.
- Spending in the economy can be placed in one of four categories—consumption, investment, government purchases, and net exports.
- The sum of labor income, capital income, depreciation, taxes, subsidies, and transfers, and net income paid to foreigners gives another way to measure GDP.
- GDP can also be measured by adding up production, but with this method we must be careful not to double count. By adding up only the value added by each firm or industry, we automatically prevent double counting. Value added is the difference between a firm's sales and its payments for intermediate inputs to production.

SAVING

total amount of saving: a measure of the amount of resources that a country has for investment, either in its own country or abroad.

Another important macroeconomic measure is the total amount of saving undertaken by an economy. Investment and saving have an important symbiotic relationship. To see why this is, consider what would happen if you decided you wanted to build a factory that makes shoes. In order to build the factory, you would have to either use your own (or a friend or family member's) saving or borrow money from a bank. But the money that a bank lends to you will be some other individual's saving. Therefore the **total amount of saving** is a measure of the amount of resources that the country has available for investment, either in its own country or abroad. Similarly, the total amount of investment depends on how much saving is available from that country and from other countries.

Countries with a high level of saving have a greater ability to undertake investment projects than countries with a low level of saving. It is important to keep in mind, however, that a country with a low level of saving can increase investment substantially if people and firms in other nations are willing to lend to or invest their own savings in that country. The U.S. economy in recent years has been able to sustain a high level of investment even when U.S. saving was low. In this section, we will define the concept of national saving and show how it is calculated.

Individual Saving

For an individual, saving is defined as income less taxes and consumption. If you earn \$25,000 in income during the year and pay taxes of \$5,000 while spending \$18,000 on consumption—food, rent, movies—by definition your saving for the year is \$2,000 (\$25,000 − \$5,000 − \$18,000). But if you instead spend \$23,000 on food, rent, and movies for the year, then your saving is −\$3,000; you will either have to take \$3,000 out of the bank or borrow \$3,000.

National Saving

national saving: aggregate income minus consumption minus government purchases.

For a country, saving is defined in a similar manner: by subtracting from a country's economy what is consumed. We subtract government purchases of goods and services in addition to consumer purchases. **National saving,** the sum of all saving in the economy, is defined as income less consumption and government purchases. That is,

National saving = income − consumption − government purchases

Using the symbol S for national saving and the symbols already introduced for income (Y), consumption (C), and government purchases (G), we define national saving as

Algebraic definition of national saving

$$S = Y - C - G$$

Using the numbers from Table 2, national saving in 2006 was \$1,450 billion (\$13,247 billion − \$9,269 billion − \$2,528 billion).

The major component of national saving is private saving: the sum of all savings by individuals in the economy. Some people save a lot, some do not save at all, and some are *dissaving*—that is, they have negative saving. For example, when people retire, they usually consume a lot more than their income—they are dissaving. When people are middle-aged, their income is usually greater than their consumption—they are saving. Most young people either save very little or, if they are able to borrow, dissave. We define private savings using the symbol T for taxes, as

$$\text{Private saving} = Y - C - T$$

For a country, however, there is also a government, and so we need to include government saving in our calculation of national saving. What do we mean by saving by the government? The difference between the government's receipts from taxes and the government's expenditures, the budget balance, is called government saving. When the balance is positive, there is a budget surplus—the government is saving. When the balance is negative, there is a budget deficit—the government is dissaving. Algebraically, we define government saving as

$$\text{Government saving} = T - G$$

Combining private and government saving, we see that

$$\text{Private saving} + \text{government saving} = (Y - C - T) + (T - G) = (Y - C - G)$$

$$\text{Private saving} + \text{government saving} = \text{national saving}$$

REVIEW

- National saving is an important macroeconomic variable because it is a measure of the resources that a country has available for investment, either in its own economy or abroad.
- A country with a high level of national saving can have a high level of investment if it desires. A country with a low level of national saving can have a high level of investment only if people in other countries are willing to lend their savings to or invest them in the low-saving country.
- National saving is defined as income minus consumption minus government purchases. It can be decomposed into the sum of private saving and government saving.
- Private saving equals income minus consumption minus taxes. Government saving is the difference between government tax receipts and government expenditures, also known as the budget balance.

MEASURING REAL GDP

Economists are also interested in assessing how the economy is changing over time. For example, they might want to know how rapidly the production of goods and services in India has grown over the last decade, and how that increase compares to the change in China's economy. However, the value of goods and services in an economy, as measured by GDP, is determined by both the quantity of goods and services produced and the price of these goods and services. Thus, an increase in the prices of all goods and services will make measured GDP grow, even if there is no increase in the amount of production in the economy.

Suppose, for example, that the prices of all goods in the economy double and that the number of items produced of every good remains the same. Then the dollar value of these items will double even though physical production does not change. A $10,000 car will become a $20,000 car, a $10 CD will become a $20 CD, and so on. Thus, GDP will double as well. Clearly, GDP is not useful for comparing production at different dates when there are increases in all prices. Although the example of doubling all prices is extreme, we do know from Chapter 17 that there is a tendency for prices on the average to rise over time—a tendency that we have called inflation. Thus, when there is inflation, GDP becomes an unreliable measure of the changes in production over time.

real gross domestic product (real GDP): a measure of the value of all the goods and services newly produced in a country during some period of time, adjusted for changes in prices over time. (Ch. 5)

nominal GDP: gross domestic product without any correction for inflation; the same as GDP; the value of all the goods and services newly produced in a country during some period of time, usually a year.

Adjusting GDP for Inflation

Real GDP is a measure of production that corrects for inflation. To emphasize the difference between GDP and real GDP, we will use the term **nominal GDP** to refer to what has previously been defined as GDP.

Calculating Real GDP Growth. To see how real GDP is calculated, consider an example. Suppose that total production consists entirely of the production of audio CDs and DVDs and that we want to compare total production in two different years: 2006 and 2007.

	2006		2007	
	Price	*Quantity*	*Price*	*Quantity*
DVDs	$15	1,000	$20	1,200
CDs	$10	2,000	$15	2,200

Notice that the number of DVDs produced increases by 20 percent and the number of CDs produced increases by 10 percent from 2006 to 2007. Notice also that the price of DVDs is greater than the price of CDs, but both increase between the two years because of inflation. Nominal GDP is equal to the dollar amount spent on CDs plus the dollar amount spent on DVDs which is $35,000 in 2006 and $57,000 in 2007, a substantial 63 percent increase.

$$\text{Nominal GDP in 2006} = \$15 \times 1{,}000 + \$10 \times 2{,}000 = \$35{,}000$$
$$\text{Nominal GDP in 2007} = \$20 \times 1{,}200 + \$15 \times 2{,}200 = \$57{,}000$$

Clearly, nominal GDP is not a good measure of the increase in production: Nominal GDP increases by 63 percent, a much greater increase than the increase in either DVD production (20 percent) or CD production (10 percent). Thus, failing to correct for inflation gives a misleading estimate.

To calculate real GDP, we must use the *same* price for both years and, thereby, adjust for inflation. That is, the number of CDs and DVDs produced in the two years must be evaluated at the same prices. For example, production could be calculated in both years using 2006 prices. That is,

$$\text{Using 2006 prices, production in 2006} = \$15 \times 1{,}000 + \$10 \times 2{,}000 = \$35{,}000$$
$$\text{Using 2006 prices, production in 2007} = \$15 \times 1{,}200 + \$10 \times 2{,}200 = \$40{,}000$$

Keeping prices constant at 2006 levels, we see that the increase in production is from $35,000 in 2006 to $40,000 in 2007, an increase of 14.3 percent.

However, production can also be calculated in both years using 2007 prices. That is,

$$\text{Using 2007 prices, production in 2006} = \$20 \times 1{,}000 + \$15 \times 2{,}000 = \$50{,}000$$
$$\text{Using 2007 prices, production in 2007} = \$20 \times 1{,}200 + \$15 \times 2{,}200 = \$57{,}000$$

Keeping prices constant at 2007 levels, we see that the increase in production is from $50,000 in 2006 to $57,000 in 2007, an increase of 14.0 percent.

Observe that the percentage increase in production varies slightly (14.3 percent versus 14 percent) depending on whether 2006 or 2007 prices are used. Such differences are inevitable, because there is no reason to prefer the prices in one year to those of another year when controlling for inflation. Economists arrive at a single percentage by simply *averaging* the two percentages.[1] In this example, they would conclude that the *increase in real GDP from 2006 to 2007 is 14.15 percent*, the average of 14.3 percent and 14 percent.

This 14.15 percent increase in real GDP is much less than the 63 percent increase in nominal GDP and much closer to the actual increase in the number of CDs and tapes produced. By adjusting for inflation in this way, real GDP gives a better picture of the increase in actual production in the economy.

A Year-to-Year Chain. This example shows how the growth rate of real GDP between the two years 2006 and 2007 is calculated in the case of two goods. The same approach is used for any other two years and more than two goods. To correct for inflation across more than two years, economists simply do a series of these two-year corrections and then "chain" them together. Each year is a link in the chain. For example, if the growth rate from 2005 to 2006 was 12.15 percent, then chaining this together with the 14.15 percent from 2006 to 2007 would imply an average annual growth rate of 13.15 percent for the two years from 2005 to 2007. That is,

Observe that 12.15 percent and 14.15 percent are chained together to get a 13.15 percent average for two years.

2005 2006 2007

12.15 14.15

13.15

By chaining other years together, link by link, the chain can be made as long as we want.

Obtaining the Values of Real GDP. To obtain real GDP in any one year, we start with a *base year* and then use the growth rates to compute GDP in another year. The base year is a year in which real GDP is equal to nominal GDP because GDP is valued using that year's price. Currently, 2000 is the base year for government statistical calculations of GDP in the United States. Thus, real GDP in 2000 and nominal GDP in 2000 are the same: $9,817 billion.

To get real GDP in other years, economists start with the base year and use the real GDP growth rates to find GDP in any other year. Consider 2001. The growth rate of real GDP in 2001—calculated using the methods just described for the entire economy—was .75 percent. Thus, real GDP in 2001 was $9,891 billion, or .75 percent greater than $9,817 billion. The $9,891 billion is 2001 real GDP measured in 2000 dollars. To emphasize that this number is calculated by chaining years together with growth rates, government statisticians say that real GDP is measured in "chained 2000 dollars."

Real GDP versus Nominal GDP over Time. Figure 6 compares real and nominal GDP from 1990 to 2006. Observe that for the 2000 base year, real GDP and nominal GDP are equal. However, by 2005, real GDP had reached about $11.1 trillion, whereas nominal GDP was at $12.5 trillion. Thus, just as in the example, real GDP increased less than nominal GDP. For the years prior to 2000, real GDP is more than nominal GDP because 2000 prices were higher than prices in earlier years. From Figure 6 we can see that nominal GDP would give a very misleading picture of the U.S. economy.

[1] A "geometric" average is used. The geometric average of two numbers is the square root of the product of the two numbers.

ECONOMICS IN THE NEWS

The Monthly Release of GDP Data

Near the end of every month, stories about the latest GDP measurement for the United States appear in most newspapers around the country (and on web pages seen around the world). The stories are a response to the release of GDP data by economic statisticians at the U.S. Department of Commerce, where the national income and product accounts are tabulated.

This story appeared in the *New York Times* on February 1, 2007. The discussion of GDP in this chapter should give you the information you need to understand the article and to judge whether the headline, the reporter's interpretation of the GDP data, and the economists' comments make sense. It reports strong GDP growth for the economy, as reflected in its headline and general tone.

There are several points to keep in mind when reading news stories about GDP.

First, the measures of GDP are reported for each of the four quarters of the year. There is a news story each month because the data are revised twice. In the first month after the end of the quarter, the first estimate of GDP is given. In the second and third months, the estimates are revised as new data about the economy are obtained. Sometimes you have to read carefully to know whether what you are reading is a first-time report or a revision.

Second, the GDP measure for a quarter of a year represents the aggregate production during the quarter, but the amount of production is stated at an *annual rate* to make the magnitude comparable to that of the annual GDP measure.

Third, the GDP measures for each quarter are *seasonally adjusted*. There is always more production in some seasons of the year than in other seasons, and these differences have little to do with where the economy is going. For example, in the fourth quarter (October–December), there is usually more production in anticipation of the holidays. Seasonal adjustments try to take out these fluctuations so that they do not show up in the reported measures of GDP.

You can already see the benefits of taking an economics class. In fact, the 3.5 percent increase is for real GDP, which is the best measure for comparing over time.

Vigorous Consumer Spending Helped Economy Grow 3.5% at the End of 2006

By JEREMY W. PETERS

The economy regained momentum at the end of 2006, pulling out of a midyear slowdown as gas prices fell and Americans reached into their wallets with renewed confidence.

The government said yesterday that its broadest and best-known measure of economic growth, the gross domestic product, advanced at an annual rate of 3.5 percent from October through December. That was noticeably stronger than the 2 percent rate of growth during the third quarter and the 2.6 percent measured in the second quarter.

Spending by consumers—on things like food and visits to the doctor—gave the economy the biggest lift. Spending by the federal government, particularly on the military, also added a significant increase. At the same time, goods and services exported to foreign countries increased, helping shrink the nation's trade deficit.

The swiftness of the expansion in the final months of the year surprised many economists, who were expecting a rate closer to 3 percent. Such strong growth was the latest indication that the economy was showing authentic vigor, despite forecasts of a deeper downturn.

The government also reported yesterday that inflation fell back yesterday on two fronts: in an index of prices that the Federal Reserve watches closely and a separate measure of labor costs.

That seemed to reaffirm the Fed's decision yesterday to hold interest rates steady, though the central bank warned, as it has for many months, that "some inflation risks remain."

The economy's resilience has not been lost on the White House, which has spent the last two days playing up the expansion. President Bush spoke in Manhattan yesterday, noting faster growth in wages and consumer confidence. "The state of our economy is strong," he told an audience at Federal Hall, the site where Congress and the Supreme Court first convened.

The sources of the GDP increase – C, G, and X

But underneath the robust growth numbers, some economists saw signs that the first few months of 2007 might not be as strong as the last few months of 2006. They noted a number of factors that were not likely to repeat, including the spending increase brought about by lower gas prices.

The outlook for the following quarter, and why it may not mirror this particular quarter's good performance

"The boost to consumption in the fourth quarter was all about the fall in oil prices," said Paul Ashworth, senior United States economist with Capital Economics. "That's very much a temporary boost that's now gone."

In addition, businesses cut back investment in equipment and software in the fourth quarter.

Still, the quarter turned out to be much healthier than economists were predicting just two months ago. Many experts thought the slump in the real estate market would have much wider effects on the overall economy. Housing did weigh on overall economic growth. The contraction in residential real estate investment, the sharpest since 1991, subtracted 1.2 percentage points from the overall G.D.P. growth figure in the fourth quarter.

Even though C, G and X were doing well, the I component of GDP was struggling.

Another significant drag was a slowdown at the nation's auto plants, which took another 1.2 percentage points off the G.D.P.

"Housing and autos, when they're down a lot you're supposed to look for a low number—and they were both down a lot," said Robert Barbera, chief economist with ITG.

But consumers helped offset those effects. The drag on spending that many economists said would come as Americans watched their home values falter has not happened. Instead, consumer spending increased at a 4.4 percent annual rate in the fourth quarter, much faster than in the second or third quarters.

For the full year, the gross domestic product grew 3.4 percent, an improvement on 2005, though not quite matching the 3.9 percent rate of 2004.

Some economists expect the effects of the housing slowdown to remain limited. In its statement yesterday, the Fed noted "some tentative signs of stabilization" in housing.

John Ryding, the chief United States economist at Bear Stearns, said that the residual effects from the housing bust "will disappear and vanish over the next couple of quarters," leading to faster growth. "As those factors dissipate, the underlying growth rate picks up," he said.

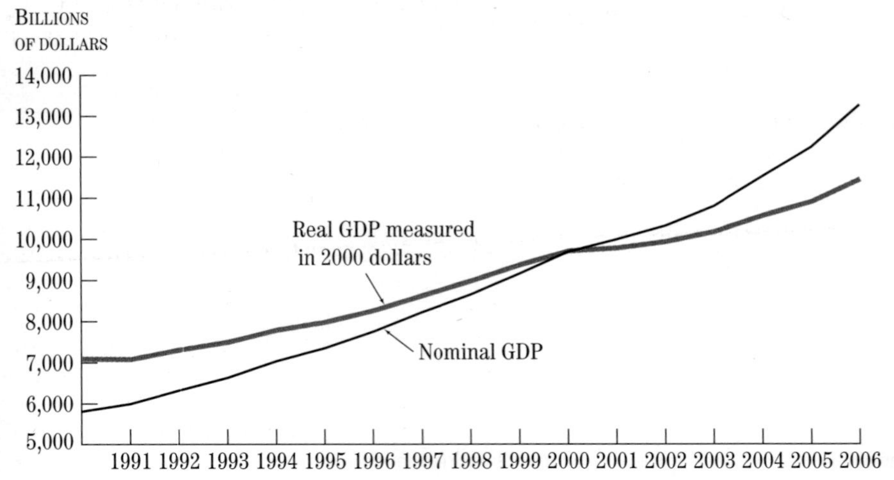

FIGURE 6
Real GDP versus Nominal GDP
Real GDP increases less than nominal GDP because real GDP takes out the effect of rising prices. The chart shows that for the 2000 base year, real GDP and nominal GDP are equal. Nominal GDP is below real GDP in earlier years because prices were generally lower before 2000.

Source: Bureau of Economic Analysis, *National Income and Product Accounts,* Tables 1.1.5 and 1.1.6.

The GDP Deflator

Nominal GDP grows faster than real GDP because of inflation. The greater the difference between nominal GDP growth and real GDP growth, the greater the rate of inflation. If there was deflation, with prices falling, then nominal GDP would increase less than real GDP. Hence, a by-product of computing real GDP is a measure of the rate of inflation.

GDP deflator: nominal GDP divided by real GDP; it measures the level of prices of goods and services included in real GDP relative to a given base year.

price level: the average level of prices in the economy.

More precisely, if we divide nominal GDP by real GDP, we get the **GDP deflator,** a measure of the **price level,** which is the level of all the prices of the items in real GDP. That is,

$$\text{GDP deflator} = \frac{\text{nominal GDP}}{\text{real GDP}}$$

Here the GDP deflator is defined so that its value in the base year, such as 2000, is 1.00. (Sometimes it is scaled to equal 100 in the base year by multiplying by 100.)

The reason for the term *deflator* is that to get real GDP, we can deflate nominal GDP by dividing it by the GDP deflator. That is,

$$\text{Real GDP} = \frac{\text{nominal GDP}}{\text{GDP deflator}}$$

The percentage change in the GDP deflator from one year to the next is a measure of the rate of inflation.

consumer price index (CPI): a price index equal that calculates current price of a fixed market basket of consumer goods and services relative to a base year.

Alternative Inflation Measures

The percentage change in the GDP deflator is not the most widely used measure of inflation. A much more frequently cited measure of inflation is based on the percentage change in the **consumer price index (CPI),** which is the price of a fixed collection—a "market basket"—of consumer goods and services in a given year divided by the price of the same collection in some base year. For example, if the market basket consists of one DVD and two CDs, then the CPI for 2007 compared with the base year 2006 in the previous example would be

$$\frac{\$20 \times 1 + \$15 \times 2}{\$15 \times 1 + \$10 \times 2} = \frac{50}{35} = 1.43$$

The CPI inflation rate is the percent change in the CPI; it measures how fast the prices of the items in the basket increase in price. What are the differences between inflation measured using the CPI and inflation measured using the GDP deflator? The first difference is that the GDP deflator is measuring the price level of all domestically produced goods and services. This includes goods that affect the day-to-day life of consumers, such as the price of milk, the price of orange juice, and the cost of airplane tickets, but it also includes goods that individuals never purchase directly, such as the price of heavy machinery and the price of truck engines. Thus the CPI, as its name suggests, may be a more relevant measure of the price level that consumers care about.

The second difference is that CPI measures the price of a fixed collection of goods and services—the price of the basket—whereas the goods and services that make up GDP, and hence are measured by the GDP deflator, change from year to year. The use of a fixed collection of goods and services in the CPI is one of the reasons economists think the CPI overstates inflation. When the price of goods rises, the quantity demanded should decline; when the price falls, the quantity demanded should rise. Thus, by not allowing the quantities to change when the price changes, the CPI puts too much weight on items with rising prices and too little weight on items with declining prices. The result is an overstatement of inflation; in other words, by assuming that people buy no less of the goods and services that have increased in price and buy no more of the goods and services that have decreased in price, the CPI tends to indicate that prices have gone up by more than they really have. During the 1990s, a group of economists appointed by the U.S. Senate and chaired by Michael Boskin of Stanford University found that the government, by adjusting expenditures according to this overstated CPI, was spending billions of dollars more than it would with a correct CPI. Hence, getting the economic statistics right makes a big difference.

The third difference between the CPI and the GDP deflator is that the CPI market basket can include goods and services that are produced in other countries, whereas the GDP deflator, by definition, will measure the price of domestically produced goods and services. In countries where imported goods lack good domestic substitutes, inflation measured using the CPI may be a better measure of the difficulties that both people and businesses in the economy face.

Figure 7 shows how measures of inflation using the GDP deflator and the CPI compare. The general inflation movements are similar, but the CPI is more volatile. The GDP deflator and the CPI each have strengths and weaknesses relative to the other. So you should think of them as being alternative ways of measuring price levels and inflation rates, rather than thinking of them as being competing measurements.

Yet another measure of inflation is the producer price index (PPI), which measures the prices of raw materials and intermediate goods as well as the prices of final goods sold by producers. Prices of raw materials—oil, wheat, copper—are sometimes watched carefully because they give early warning signs of increases in inflation.

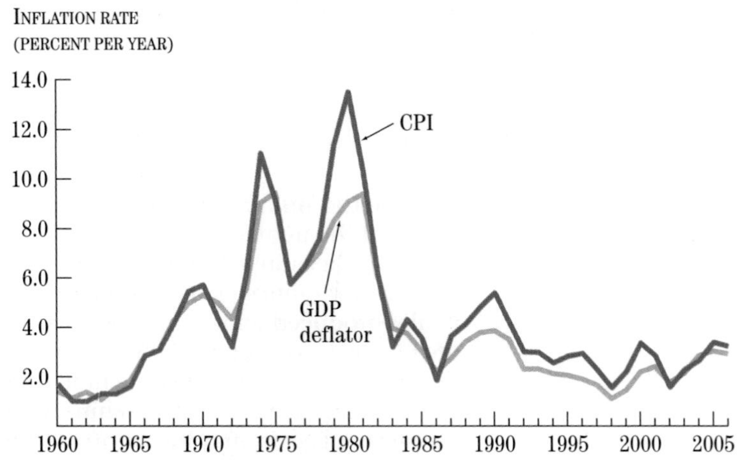

FIGURE 7
Comparison of Measures of Inflation
Measuring inflation with either the CPI or the GDP deflator shows the rise in inflation in the 1960s and 1970s and the lower inflation in the 1980s and 1990s. The CPI is more volatile: It bounces around more. (The inflation rate is based on yearly percent changes in the stated variable.)

REVIEW

- Nominal GDP changes when either the quantity of goods and services changes or the prices of those goods and services change. Therefore the change in nominal GDP is not a good measure of how the physical amount of production in the economy is changing over time.
- Economists use real GDP when they want to compare production over time. Real GDP corrects nominal GDP for inflation by measuring the production of goods and services in the dollars of a given base year, such as 2000.
- The GDP deflator is a measure of the price level in the economy. It is defined as the ratio of nominal GDP to real GDP. The percentage change in the GDP deflator from year to year is a measure of the inflation rate.
- The Consumer Price Index is the most widely used measure of the price level in the economy. It is defined as the price of a representative market basket of goods and services, relative to the price of that basket in a base year. The percentage change in the CPI from year to year is the most widely used measure of the inflation rate.
- There are some important differences between the CPI and the GDP deflator. Each has strengths and weaknesses compared to the other. You should think of them as alternative ways of measuring price levels and inflation rates.

SHORTCOMINGS OF THE GDP MEASURE

Although nominal GDP is the best measure of overall production that we have, it is deficient in several ways. You need to understand what these limitations are, so that you can make informed judgments about what is really happening in the economy. There are three main types of limitations: First, there are revisions to GDP that can change the assessment of the economy; second, some types of production are omitted from GDP; third, the production of goods and services is only part of what affects the quality of life. When you compare two countries, the one with a higher level of GDP is not necessarily better off than the one with a lower level of GDP.

Revisions to GDP

Government statisticians obtain data on GDP from surveys of stores and businesses, and even from income tax data from the Internal Revenue Service. Not all of these data are collected quickly. Data on sales at stores and large firms come in within a month; however, data on exports and imports take several months. Some income tax data are reported only once a year. Information about small firms comes in even more slowly.

For this reason, the statistics on GDP are frequently revised as new data come in. For those who use the GDP data to make decisions, either in business or in government, faulty data on GDP, which are apparent only when the data are revised, can lead to mistakes. Revisions of GDP are inevitable and occur in all countries. These revisions can be quite large in magnitude. For example, in January of 2006, the first estimate for GDP for the fourth quarter of 2005 was given as $12.735 trillion. In March of 2006, the "final revision" of that number was given as $12.766 trillion, a difference of almost $30 billion.

Omissions from GDP

Given the description of how GDP is calculated, you will hardly be surprised to hear that production that does not occur in a formal market is difficult for government statisticians to measure. Examples are work done in the home and illegal commerce. The other principal difficulty in calculating GDP is how to deal with quality improvements in goods. Both of these problems are explained in more detail.

■ **Home Work and Production.** Much of the production that people do at home—making dinner or a sweater, changing the car oil or a baby's diapers, cutting the grass or the kids' hair—is productive activity, but it is not included in GDP because the transactions are not recorded in markets where statisticians measure spending. Such production would be included in GDP if people hired and paid someone else to do any of these things. So if you look after your young siblings after school while your parents are at work, that will typically not count toward GDP, whereas if your parents were to take your siblings to a day-care center and pay for child-care services, that will count toward GDP. Note that some home production is included in GDP. If you run a mail order or telemarketing business out of your home and pay taxes on your income, then this production is likely to be counted in GDP.

■ **Leisure Activity.** Much leisure activity is not included in GDP even though it may be enjoyable. Going to the beach or hiking in the mountains more often and working less might be something you decide to do as your income increases. If people start taking Friday afternoons off, GDP will go down, but the level of well-being may increase. The consumption of leisure is omitted from GDP unless it involves a purchase in the market, such as a ticket to a movie or a ballgame.

■ **The Underground Economy.** A large amount of production is not counted in GDP because it is purposely hidden from the view of the government. Illegal activity—growing marijuana in the California coastal range, selling pharmaceuticals not yet approved by the Food and Drug Administration—is excluded from GDP because no one wants to report this activity to the government. People who get cash payments—perhaps in the form of tips at hotels or restaurants, or babysitting money from a neighbor—may not report this income, perhaps in order to avoid taxes, and thus it is not counted either. If people do not report interest on a loan to a friend or relative, this is also omitted from GDP.

The sum of all the missing items is referred to as the *underground economy.* Estimates of the size of the underground economy are understandably uncertain. They range from about 10 percent of GDP in the United States to about 25 percent in Italy to over 40 percent in Peru.

The underground economy makes GDP a less useful measure of the size of an economy, and we should be aware of it when we use GDP. But the underground economy does not render GDP useless. It is unlikely that the underground economy grows much more or much less rapidly than the rest of the economy. Changes in laws can increase or decrease the incentives to produce outside the legal market economy, but these are unlikely to be large enough to change the estimated growth rates of GDP by much.

■ **Quality Improvements.** Our measure of GDP sometimes misses improvements in the quality of goods and services. For example, a $1,500 notebook computer purchased in 2005 may be of substantially better quality than a $2,000 notebook computer purchased in 2003. So not only has the price of the notebook computer fallen by 25 percent, but in fact the quality-adjusted price has fallen by even more. Government statisticians, especially in developed countries like the United States, have developed sophisticated techniques to measure the quality-adjusted price change of a good accurately. However, these techniques don't always work perfectly, especially when the improvements are in hard-to-measure attributes. So, for example, the government statisticians can look at the amount of memory, the speed of the processor, and the storage capacity of the hard drive to gauge how much the quality of the notebook computer has improved; but they may not be able to gauge as effectively the quality improvements that make a new model car more comfortable and better able to absorb shocks than the old model.

Other Measures of Well-Being

Even if real GDP did include the underground economy and all the improvements in goods and services, it would not serve as the only measure of well-being. There are many other important aspects of the well-being of individuals: a long and healthy life expectancy; a clean environment; a small chance of war, crime, or the death of a child. The production of goods and services in a country can affect these other things, and indeed be affected by them, but it is not a measure of them.

Consider what has happened to some other measures of well-being as real GDP per capita has grown. Life expectancy in the United States has increased from about 69 years in the 1950s to 78 years in 2004. This compares with a life expectancy of only 47 years in the early part of the last century. Infant mortality has also declined, from about 26 infant deaths per 1,000 live births in the mid-1950s to 6.9 in 2000. In the early part of the last century, infant mortality in the United States was 10 deaths for every 100 live births. The fraction of women who die in childbirth has also declined. So by some of these important measures, the quality of life has improved along with real GDP per capita.

But there are still serious problems and room for gains; as death rates from car accidents, heart disease, and stroke have decreased, death rates among young people from AIDS, suicide, and murder have been rising. Also of serious concern is the increasing percentage of children who live in poverty. Thus, the impressive gain in real GDP per capita has been correlated with both gains and losses in other measures of well-being.

Economics in Action

Measuring the Quality of Life Across Nations

"Human development is first and foremost about allowing people to lead a life that they value and enabling them to realize their potential as human beings."

Human Development Report, 2006, published by the United Nations Development Program (UNDP)

By now, you are familiar with the idea that real GDP is not the only measure of a nation's well-being: Other factors, including the health of the country's people, the quality of its environment, peace, and security, are important determinants. Can we come up with an alternative measure of well-being that encompasses a broader range of indicators than just real GDP? How closely would such an indicator track real GDP—in other words, would the richest countries in the world also turn out to be the countries that have the best health, education, environmental, and stability outcomes?

The *Human Development Index (HDI)* calculated by the United Nations is one of the most prominent attempts to measure the overall quality of life by examining a variety of indicators. Every year, the *Human Development Report* focuses on an issue that is critical for the quality of life across all countries (in 2006, the focus was on clean water) and presents several interesting tables of data that can be used to rank and compare countries according to their HDI score. These data are available for everyone to access online. You can find them easily with a simple search.

How is the HDI score calculated? According to the *Human Development Report,* the HDI covers three areas: living a long and healthy life, being educated, and having a decent material standard of living. In each of these areas, an index score (with 1 being the highest value and 0 being the lowest value) is assigned to each country based on data collected on various criteria. The three area indices are then aggregated to come up with the HDI.

While the HDI is a broader measure than GDP, there are a lot of areas that it doesn't cover. The most prominent of these, according to the report, are respect for human rights, inequality, and democracy. Recognizing these limitations, let's take a look at what the rankings look like. The five countries with the highest HDI scores are Norway, Iceland, Australia, Ireland, and Sweden. The five countries with the lowest HDIs are Niger, Sierra Leone, Mali, Burkina Faso, and Guinea Bissau.

An excerpt from the *Human Development Report* for a select group of countries is given below.

	HDI Score	Life Expectancy	Literacy	School Enrollment	Real GDP per Capita
Norway	0.965	79.6	>99%	100%	$38,500
United States	0.948	77.5	>99%	93%	$39,676
Cuba	0.826	77.6	>99%	80%	$5,700
China	0.768	71.9	91%	70%	$5,896
Sri Lanka	0.755	74.3	91%	63%	$4,390
Equatorial Guinea	0.653	42.8	87%	58%	$20,510
India	0.611	63.6	61%	62%	$3,139
Swaziland	0.500	31.3	80%	51%	$5,638
Niger	0.311	44.6	29%	21%	$711

Notice that countries like Norway and the United States have both very high levels of real GDP per capita and high HDI scores. These countries are not just materially rich; they have also been able to use these resources to improve health and education outcomes for their citizens. At the other extreme is Niger—a desperately poor country that suffers from abysmally low levels of education and health, factors that are related to the overall lack of financial resources. The real insights of the HDI do not lie with these extremes, though. The interesting cases are countries like Cuba, China, and Sri Lanka, which have been able to achieve impressive life expectancy and literacy levels despite being substantially poorer than Norway and the United States.

If these are the overachievers, then there are also the underachievers, countries like Swaziland and Equatorial Guinea. Even though the people of Swaziland enjoy almost a third more GDP per capita than the people of

ECONOMICS IN ACTION (continued)

Sri Lanka do, their life expectancy is only 31.3 years. Swaziland is a country that has been hard hit by the AIDS pandemic, and material wealth can do little to improve the lives of its people at this point given the spread of the disease. Another interesting case is Equatorial Guinea, which, despite having a GDP per capita that is three times China's, also suffers from low levels of life expectancy and education. The wealth of Equatorial Guinea comes from oil drilling. Clearly, that wealth has not made its way into the hands of the population at large—Equatorial Guinea seems to be a country where inequality is keeping the quality of life much lower than it needs to be.

You should go and check out the HDI numbers for countries that you have an interest in. Keep in mind, though, that the numbers shown here are for a limited set of criteria. If you were to broaden the criteria to include peace and stability, respect for human rights, and democracy, countries like Sri Lanka, China, and Cuba might not seem to be "overachieving" any more. Nonetheless, the HDI is easily accessible and is a useful reminder of the old adage that money does not always buy happiness. But also keep in mind that as far as countries go, it's a lot easier for a rich country to buy what happiness can be bought than it is for a poor country.

A clean and safe environment is also a factor in the quality of life. But GDP itself does not provide an indication of whether pollution or many of the other measures of the quality of life are improving or getting worse. If a factory produces a lot of output while also putting out a considerable amount of airborne and waterborne pollutants, its production of goods is all that counts toward GDP. There is no mechanism being used to subtract the damage to the environment.

REVIEW

- Real GDP per capita is not without its shortcomings as an indicator of well-being in a society. Certain items are omitted—home production, leisure, the underground economy, and some quality improvements.
- There are other indicators of the quality of life, including vital statistics on mortality and the environment, that can be affected by GDP per capita but that are conceptually distinct and independently useful.

CONCLUSION

In this chapter, we have shown how to measure the size of an economy in terms of its GDP. In the process, we have explained that income, spending, and production in a country are all equal and that GDP can be adjusted to make comparisons over time.

In conclusion, it is important to recall that aggregate income (or production or spending), the subject of our study, tells us much about the quality of life of the people in a country, but it does not tell us everything. As the economist-philosopher John Stuart Mill said in his *Principles of Political Economy,* first published in 1848: "All know that it is one thing to be rich, another to be enlightened, brave or humane . . . those things, indeed, are all indirectly connected, and react upon one another."[2]

[2] John Stuart Mill, *Principles of Political Economy* (New York: Bookseller, 1965), pp. 1–2.

KEY POINTS

1. Gross domestic product (GDP), also known as nominal GDP, is the total production of new goods and services in an economy during a particular period.
2. GDP can be measured in three ways: By adding all spending on new goods and services in the economy, by adding all income earned in the domestic economy, and by adding all the value of goods and services produced in the economy.
3. The spending method of calculating GDP requires adding up expenditures on consumption goods, investment goods (machines, factories, housing, and inventories), government purchases, and net exports (exports − imports).
4. In the income method, GDP is calculated by adding labor income; capital income; depreciation; taxes, subsidies and transfers; and net income of foreigners. Except for a small statistical discrepancy, the income approach gives us the same answer as the spending approach.
5. Value added is used to calculate GDP under the production method. Value added is defined as the difference between the value of the production sold and the cost of inputs to production.
6. Real GDP is a measure of production adjusted for inflation. It is the best overall measure of changes in the production of goods and services over time.
7. The GDP deflator, or the ratio of nominal GDP to real GDP, is a measure of the price level in the economy. The percentage change in the GDP deflator is a measure of inflation.
8. An alternative measure of the price level is the consumer price index (CPI), which is a measure of the price of a basket of representative goods and services in a particular year relative to the price of that basket in a base year. The change in the CPI is an alternative measure of inflation in the economy.
9. National saving is defined as income less consumption less government purchases. Countries that have a high level of national saving have more resources to use for investment in their own economy or abroad. Countries with low levels of national saving need other countries to be willing to lend to or invest their savings in those countries if they are to sustain high levels of investment.
10. GDP is not without its shortcomings. It does not include production in the underground economy or much work done in the home. And it is only one of many measures of well-being.

KEY TERMS

intermediate good
final good
consumption
investment
government purchases
net exports
exports
imports
trade balance
labor income
capital income
value added
total amount of saving
national saving
nominal GDP
GDP deflator
price level
consumer price index (CPI)

QUESTIONS FOR REVIEW

1. Why do we add up total spending in order to compute GDP when GDP is supposed to be a measure of production?
2. Approximately what are the percentages of consumption, investment, government purchases, and net exports in GDP in the United States?
3. What is the significance of value added, and how does one measure it for a single item?
4. Why is the sum of all income equal to GDP?
5. Why is the purchase of a used car not included in GDP? Should it be?
6. Why do we add inventory investment to spending when computing GDP?
7. Why are increases in nominal GDP not a good measure of economic growth?
8. What is national saving?
9. Why does national saving equal the sum of private and government saving?
10. Why is the production of meals in the home not included in GDP? Should it be?

PROBLEMS

1. Determine whether each of the following would be included in GDP, and explain why or why not.
   a. You buy a used CD from a friend.
   b. You purchase a song from an online music provider like iTunes.
   c. You cook a romantic dinner for two on Valentine's Day.
   d. You buy a nice bottle of French wine to serve with dinner.
   e. You take your mom out to brunch on Mother's Day.
   f. The restaurant where you intend to go for brunch purchases strawberries, which it intends to serve at the brunch, from a local vendor.
2. Determine whether each of the following is consumption, investment, or neither. Explain your answer.
   a. A landscaping company buys a new four-wheel-drive vehicle to carry fertilizer and flowers.
   b. A doctor buys a new four-wheel-drive vehicle to use on vacation.
   c. A family puts a new kitchen in their house.
   d. The campus bookstore increases its inventory of textbooks.
   e. Your parents purchase their dream home, newly built to their specification by a local contractor.
   f. Your parents buy a vacation home from a friend who had owned that home for years.
3. A phenomenon of the twentieth century U.S. economy was the replacement of home production by production purchased through markets.
   a. Give an example of a food item that was widely produced by family members in 1900 and that was widely purchased from businesses by 2000.
   b. Give an example of a clothing item that was widely produced by family members in 1900 and that was widely purchased from businesses by 2000.
   c. Give an example of a service that was widely produced by family members in 1900 and that was widely purchased from businesses by 2000.
   d. How does the replacement of home production with production purchased through markets affect real GDP? How does it affect the usefulness of comparisons of real GDP per capita at the end of the twentieth century with the same measure at the beginning of the twentieth century?
   e. The economies of some countries today are more similar to the U.S. economy in 1900 than to the U.S. economy in 2000. How useful are comparisons between real GDP in the United States and in these economies?
4. Recognizing that there may be both positive and negative effects, how will GDP be affected by
   a. The legalization of drugs
   b. A law making the standard workweek 35 hours
   c. The replacement of checks by online banking
   d. A program granting legal status to previously undocumented immigrants working in the United States
5. Suppose there are only the following three goods in the economy.

Year	Good	Price	Quantity
2005	Ice cream cones	$2.50	1,000
	Hot dogs	$1.25	500
	Surfboards	$100.00	10
2006	Ice cream cones	$3.50	800
	Hot dogs	$2.25	400
	Surfboards	$100.00	14

   a. Calculate nominal GDP for 2005 and 2006.
   b. Calculate the percentage change in GDP from 2005 to 2006, first using 2005 prices and then using 2006 prices.
   c. Calculate the percentage change in real GDP from 2005 to 2006, using your answers from part (b).
   d. What is the GDP deflator for 2006 if it equals 1.0 in 2005?
6. Given the information in the following table for three consecutive years in the U.S. economy, calculate the missing data.

Year	Nominal GDP (in billions of U.S. dollars)	Real GDP (in billions of 2000 dollars)	GDP Deflator (2000 = 100)	Inflation (percent change in GDP deflator)	Real GDP per Capita (in 2000 dollars)	Population (in millions)
2000	9,817		100.0	2.2		283.7
2001		9,891		2.4		286.6
2002			104.0		37,450	289.5

7. Look at two scenarios, details of which are provided below, for monthly inventories and sales for a company producing cereal. In both scenarios, the company's sales are the same.
   a. Calculate the inventory investment during each month and the resulting stock of inventory at the beginning of the following month for both scenarios.
   b. Does maintaining constant production lead to greater or lesser fluctuations in the stock of inventory? Explain.

Scenario A

Month	Start-of-the-Month Inventory Stock	Production	Sales	Inventory Investment
Jan.	50	50	45	
Feb.		50	55	
Mar.		50	80	
Apr.		50	50	
May		50	40	

Scenario B

Month	Start-of-the-Month Inventory Stock	Production	Sales	Inventory Investment
Jan.	50	45	45	
Feb.		55	55	
Mar.		80	80	
Apr.		50	50	
May		40	40	

8. Suppose General Motors buys $50 million worth of tires from Goodyear in November of 2006 for use in its Saturn line of cars. Of these tires, $20 million are put into cars that are sold to consumers in December of 2006, and $10 million are put into cars that are produced in December but will not be sold to consumers until February of 2007. The remaining $20 million will be put into cars manufactured and sold in 2007. Describe how each of these tire-related transactions enters into inventory investment calculations in 2006 and 2007.

9. Use the following data for a South Dakota wheat farm.

Revenue	$1,000
Costs	
Wages and salaries	$700
Rent on land	$50
Rental fee for tractor	$100
Seed, fertilizer	$100
Pesticides, irrigation	$50

   a. Calculate the value added by this farm.
   b. Profits are revenue minus costs. Capital income consists of profits, rents, and interest. Show that value added equals capital income plus labor income paid by the farm.
   c. Suppose that, because of flooding in Kansas, wheat prices increase suddenly and revenues rise to $1,100, but the prices of intermediate inputs do not change. What happens to value added and profits in this case?

10. Suppose the data in the following table describe the economic activity in a country for 2006. Given these data, calculate the following:
   a. Inventory investment
   b. Net exports
   c. Gross domestic product
   d. Statistical discrepancy
   e. National saving

   Verify that national saving equals investment plus net exports.

Component of Spending	Value (billions of dollars)
Consumption	$140
Business fixed and residential investment	$27
Inventory stock at the end of 2005	$10
Inventory stock at the end of 2006	$5
Depreciation	$12
Government outlays	$80
Government purchases	$65
Exports	$21
Imports	$17
Labor income	$126
Capital income	$70
Net income of foreigners	$5
Taxes, subsidies, and transfers	$28

Chapter 7

The Spending Allocation Model

In 1994, economists working on the president's Council of Economic Advisers (CEA) predicted that the administration's plan to reduce the share of government purchases in GDP by 1.75 percentage points between 1994 and 1998 would increase the share of investment in GDP by 1 percentage point.[1] Their reasoning was that a reduction in the share of government purchases would lead to lower interest rates in the economy, which in turn would raise investment. The subsequent behavior of the economy confirmed that the president's economic advisers were correct. Between 1994 and 1998, the share of government purchases in real GDP *decreased* from 19 to 17 percent. The impact on investment was even larger than the economists at the CEA had predicted, perhaps because additional factors were also at play, with the share of investment in real GDP *increasing* from 15 to 18 percent over that period.

More recently, Ben Bernanke, the chairman of the Federal Reserve, in his testimony before the U.S. Senate Budget Committee in January of 2007, expressed concerns about the long-run path of budget deficits in the United States. Mr. Bernanke predicted that "if government [deficits] were actually to grow at the pace envisioned . . . the effects on the U.S. economy would be severe. High rates of government borrowing would drain funds away from private capital formation and thus slow the growth of real incomes and living standards over time."

Both the CEA and Mr. Bernanke seem to be predicting that over time, increases in government spending and higher budget deficits would result in less investment and less accumulation of capital in the economy. In this section, we develop an economic model that will help you better understand how lower budget deficits and decreasing the share of government purchases in GDP would result in lower interest rates, and, in turn, how lower interest rates would raise the share of investment in GDP.

[1] *Economic Report of the President*, 1994, p. 83.

The model we develop is called the *spending allocation model* because of its use in determining how GDP is allocated among the major components of spending: consumption, investment, government purchases, and net exports. Because each share of spending must compete for the scarce resources in GDP, an increase in the share of one of the components will lead to a reduction in the share of another component. Our model shows that real interest rates are a key factor that both influences and is influenced by spending. By explaining how real interest rates are determined in the long run, our model helps us predict how much of GDP in the long run goes to each of the four components: consumption, investment, government purchases, and net exports.

The spending allocation model has some very useful applications. You can use it not only to understand the macroeconomic implications of the reduction in government purchases in the early 1990s, but also to understand why the aging of the population of the United States, coupled with the increases in spending that will be required for programs like Medicare and social security, poses a threat to our ability to invest and grow in the decades ahead. As you study the spending allocation model, it is imperative that you keep in mind that this model applies more to the long run than to the short run. Therefore, it is most useful in thinking about economic developments that occur over a period of years instead of months. For example, the Council of Economic Advisors was very careful to note that the positive impact of the reduction in the share of government purchases on the share of investment would take several years to materialize, just as Mr. Bernanke was very careful to talk about implications that were decades into the future instead of implications for the state of the economy in 2007.

THE SPENDING SHARES

We know that GDP is divided into four components: consumption, investment, government purchases, and net exports. Symbolically,

$$Y = C + I + G + X$$

where Y equals GDP, C equals consumption, I equals investment, G equals government purchases, and X equals net exports. This equation is the starting point for determining how large a share of GDP is allocated to each spending component.

Defining the Spending Shares

consumption share: the proportion of GDP that is used for consumption; equals consumption divided by GDP, or C/Y.

We define the spending shares by looking at how GDP is allocated among its various components. The **consumption share** of GDP is the proportion of GDP that is used for consumption. The consumption share of GDP is defined as consumption (C)

investment share: the proportion of GDP that is used for investment; equals investment divided by GDP, or I/Y. Sometimes called investment rate.

net exports share: the proportion of GDP that is equal to net exports; equals net exports divided by GDP, or X/Y.

government purchases share: the proportion of GDP that is used for government purchases; equals government purchases divided by GDP, or G/Y.

divided by GDP, or C/Y. For example, if C = \$6 trillion and Y = \$10 trillion, then the consumption share is $C/Y = .6$, or 60 percent. We can define the other shares of GDP analogously: I/Y is the **investment share,** X/Y is the **net exports share,** and G/Y is the **government purchases share.** Sometimes the investment share is called the *investment rate.*

We can establish a simple relationship between the shares of spending in GDP by taking the equation $Y = C + I + G + X$ and dividing both sides by Y. This simple division gives us a relationship that says that the sum of the shares of spending in GDP must equal 1. Writing that algebraically yields

$$1 = \frac{C}{Y} + \frac{I}{Y} + \frac{G}{Y} + \frac{X}{Y}$$

If we use the shares that existed in 2006 (see Table 2 in Chapter 6), we get

$$1 = \frac{9{,}269}{13{,}247} + \frac{2{,}213}{13{,}247} + \frac{2{,}528}{13{,}247} + \frac{-763}{13{,}247}$$
$$= .6997 + .1670 + .1908 + (-.0575)$$

In other words, consumption accounted for around 70 percent of GDP, investment for 16.7 percent of GDP, government purchases for 19 percent of GDP, and net exports, in deficit at negative \$763 billion, for about negative 5.7 percent of GDP. The negative share for net exports occurs because Americans imported more than they exported in 2006. In this example, the sum of the four shares on the right equals 1, or, in percentage terms, 100 percent. And, of course, this must be true for any year.

Figure 1 shows the four shares of spending in GDP for the last 75 or so years in the United States. A huge temporary fluctuation in the shares of spending in GDP occurred in World War II, when government spending on the military rose sharply.

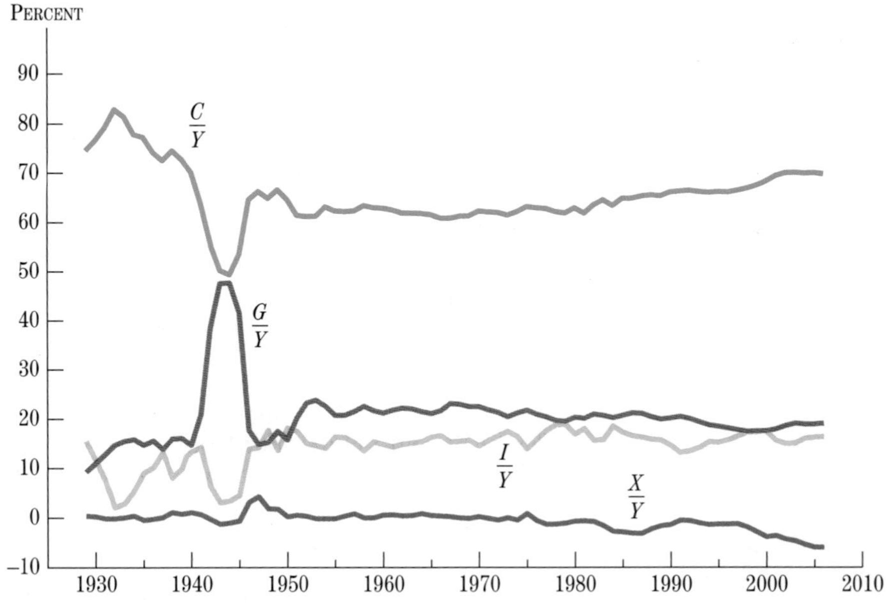

FIGURE 1
History of Spending Shares in GDP
The government purchases share rose sharply during World War II, and all three of the other shares declined. The government purchases share fell in the late 1990s before rising again in recent years.

Government purchases reached almost 50 percent of GDP, and the other three shares declined. Since World War II, the shares have been much steadier, but the movements in government spending as a share of GDP seem to be related to the movements in the investment share of GDP. Between 1990 and 2000, the government purchases share decreased from about 20 percent to 17.5 percent, while the investment share increased from 14.8 percent to 17.7 percent. Between 2000 and 2006, however, the government purchases share increased from 17.5 percent to 19 percent, while the investment share decreased from 17.7 percent to 16.7 percent. The other two shares have shown more sustained patterns: The consumption share has been generally rising during the 25-year period 1981–2006, while the net exports share has been negative for the last 25 years, as the United States has run trade deficits that have gotten progressively larger in recent times (Recall that when net exports are negative, there is a trade deficit.)

If One Share Goes Up, Another Must Go Down

The shares of spending equation demonstrates a simple but important point: A change in one of the shares implies a change in one or more of the other shares. That the shares must sum to 1 means that an increase in any of the shares must entail a reduction in one of the other shares. For example, an increase in the share of spending going to government purchases must result in a decrease in the share going to one or more of the other components of spending. Similarly, a decrease in the government purchases share must result in an increase in some other share, such as the investment share. One cannot have an increase in government purchases as a share of GDP (going from, say, 19 percent to 25 percent) without a decline in the share of either consumption or investment or net exports.

What determines how the shares of GDP are allocated? What is the mechanism through which a change in one share—such as the government share of GDP—brings about a change in one of the other shares? Is it only the investment share that changes in response to a rise in the government share of GDP? Or do the consumption and net exports shares change as well? Which share would change by more as a result of the increase in the government share? To answer these questions, we develop the spending allocation model. At the heart of the spending model lies the real interest rate, which plays an important role in relating changes in one share to changes in another. We begin the derivation of the spending allocation model by taking a closer look at how real interest rates influence the various shares of GDP.

Before beginning this derivation of the spending allocation model, it is important to remember that the spending allocation model relates changes in one spending share to changes in the other spending shares *in the long run.* Recall from Chapter 5 that potential GDP is the economy's long-term trend level of GDP. We will refer to potential GDP as Y^*, to distinguish it from GDP. In the short run, actual GDP can (and does) fluctuate around potential GDP, but in the long run, we know that GDP is equal to potential GDP ($Y = Y^*$).

We will modify the equation that relates the shares to one another to represent a long-run relationship among the values of the spending shares. Since $Y = Y^*$ in the long run, this relationship can easily be written as

$$1 = \frac{C}{Y^*} + \frac{I}{Y^*} + \frac{G}{Y^*} + \frac{X}{Y^*}$$

The intuition is unchanged—an increase in the long-run share of one of the components of GDP implies a decrease in the long-run share of one or more of the other components.

R E V I E W

- GDP is divided into four components: consumption, investment, government purchases, and net exports. Expressing each as a share of GDP is a convenient way to describe how spending is allocated among the components.
- Simple arithmetic tells us that the sum of all the shares of spending in GDP must equal 1. Thus, an increase in the share of GDP going to government purchases, for example, must be accompanied by a reduction in one or more of the other three shares—consumption, investment, or net exports.
- Several interesting patterns emerge when we look at data on these shares for the past 75 years. The government share of GDP rose sharply during World War II, resulting in substantial falls in the other three shares.
- Changes in the government share of GDP seem to be inversely related to changes in the investment share of GDP over the last 25 years. During that period, the consumption share of GDP has been rising, while the net exports share of GDP has remained negative.
- The real interest rate plays a critical role in how changes in one share affect the other shares in the economy over the long run. To develop this relationship further, we redefine the spending shares in terms of potential GDP, because we know that in the long run, GDP will equal potential GDP.

THE EFFECT OF INTEREST RATES ON SPENDING SHARES

In this section, we show that the interest rate affects the three shares of spending by the private sector: consumption, investment, and net exports. Each private-sector spending component competes for a share of GDP along with government purchases, and the interest rate is a key factor in determining how the spending is allocated.

Consumption

In the long run, the value of the consumption share of GDP (C/Y^*) depends on people's decisions to consume, which are like any other choice with scarce resources, as defined in Chapter 1. If people decide to consume a larger fraction of their income, then the consumption share of GDP will increase. Conversely, if people decide to lower the fraction of income that they consume, then the consumption share of GDP will decrease.

Consumption and the Real Interest Rate. Keep in mind that people's decisions to consume more or less of their income today have implications for their consumption decisions tomorrow. Individuals who consume *more* today save *less*, and therefore have less to consume tomorrow. On the other hand, individuals who consume *less* today save *more*, and therefore have more to consume tomorrow. A person's choice between consuming today and consuming tomorrow depends on a relative price, just like any other economic decision. The price of consumption today relative to the price of consumption tomorrow is the real interest rate.

Why is the real interest rate the relative price of current consumption? If the real interest rate is high, then any saving you do today will deliver more funds in the

future, which can then be used for future consumption (a larger home or more college education, for example). Conversely, when the real interest rate is high, increasing current consumption will reduce your saving and result in your passing up opportunities for future consumption.

We can better illustrate this link between the real interest rate and consumption with a numerical example. Suppose you earned enough to buy $1,000 worth of goods, but that you were buying only $900 worth of goods and saving the remainder. If the real interest rate was 2 percent, your saving plus the interest you earned would allow you to consume $102 worth of goods next year. In other words, by consuming $100 less in goods today, you get to consume $102 more in goods tomorrow. But if the real interest rate were 6 percent instead, you would be able to consume $106 worth of goods in a year by consuming $100 less in goods today. The increase in the real interest rate from 2 percent to 6 percent raises the price of consuming $100 worth of goods today by $4 worth of goods in the future.

Even though this may seem like a small amount, keep in mind that small differences in interest rates can add up when you consider saving large sums of money to finance a college education or for retirement. So a higher real interest rate gives people more incentive to consume less and save for the future, whereas a lower real interest rate gives people more incentive to consume today instead of saving for the future. We can therefore conclude that consumption is negatively related to the real interest rate.

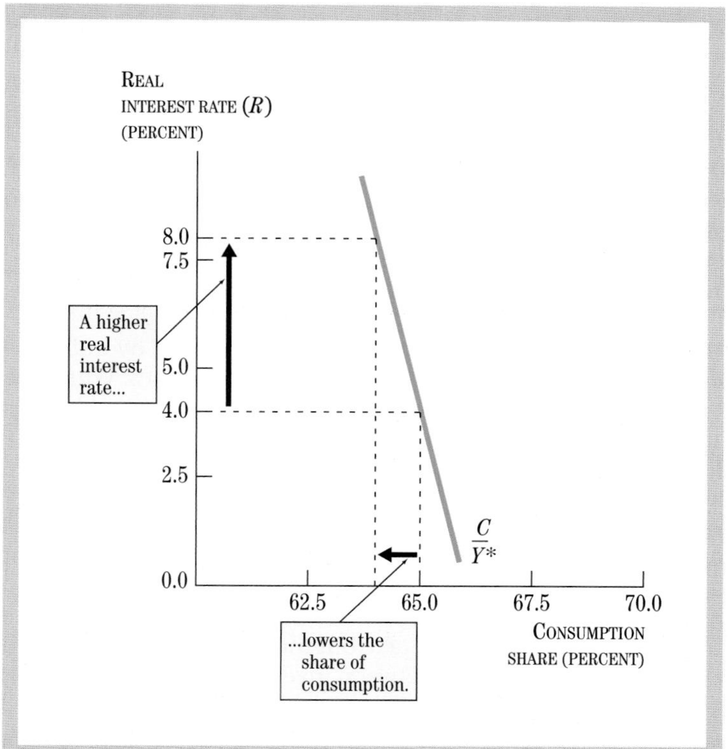

FIGURE 2
The Consumption Share and the Real Interest Rate
A higher real interest rate discourages consumption and encourages saving. Therefore, the share of GDP allocated to consumption will decrease in the long run.

What is true for individuals on average will also be true for the economy as a whole. Figure 2 describes an economy where the consumption share is negatively related to the real interest rate. For this example, when the real interest rate is 4 percent, the share of consumption in GDP will be about 65 percent. If the real interest rate increases to 8 percent, then the share declines to 64 percent. Alternatively, if the real interest rate declines, the consumption share increases.

Movements Along versus Shifts of the Consumption Share Line. Observe that the relationship between the real interest rate and consumption as a share of GDP in Figure 2 looks like a demand curve. Like a demand curve, it is downward-sloping. And like a demand curve, it shows the quantity that consumers are willing to consume at each price, where the price is the real interest rate. A higher price—that is, a higher real interest rate—reduces the amount of goods and services that people will consume, and a lower price—that is, a lower real interest rate—increases the amount that they will consume. As with demand curves, when a change in the price (in this case the real interest rate) leads to a change in the quantity demanded (in this case the consumption share), we see a *movement along* the consumption share line, as shown in Figure 2.

As with a demand curve, it is also important to distinguish such movements along the consumption share line from *shifts of* the consumption share line. The real interest rate is not the only thing that affects consumption as a share of GDP. When a factor other than the real interest rate changes the consumption share of GDP, there is a shift in the consumption share line in Figure 2. For example, an increase in taxes on consumption—such as a national sales tax—would reduce the quantity of goods people would consume relative to their income. In other words, an increase in taxes on consumption would shift the consumption share line in Figure 2 to the left: Less would be consumed relative to GDP at every interest rate. Conversely, a decrease in taxes on consumption would shift the consumption share line in Figure 2 to the right.

Investment

A similar inverse, or negative, relationship exists between investment and the real interest rate. When businesses decide to invest, by buying new machines and equipment or by building a new factory, they need funds for this purpose. Typically, they acquire these funds by borrowing. Higher real interest rates raise the cost of borrowing—the firm would need to produce enough additional output to pay back the loan plus interest, which implies that it would be willing to borrow only if it were confident about the success of the investment project. Another way of stating this is that investment projects that would be undertaken at lower real interest rates may be postponed or canceled when interest rates rise because of the higher costs of borrowing.

Therefore, when real interest rates rise, firms are less likely to spend on investment, fewer purchases of new equipment will be undertaken, and fewer new factories will be built. On the other hand, when real interest rates fall, firms are encouraged to spend more on investment; more equipment will be purchased, and more new factories will be built. Note that this relationship holds even if firms use their own funds to finance their investment projects. Higher real interest rates increase the opportunity cost of using their own funds for investment: Firms are tempted to leave their money in the bank earning the higher interest rate, instead of putting those funds into investment projects.

Recall that investment also includes the purchases of new houses by individuals. Most people need to take out loans (mortgages) to purchase houses. When the real interest rate on mortgages rises, people purchase fewer or smaller houses because they would have to give up too much consumption to repay their mortgage plus interest; when the real interest rate falls, people purchase more or larger houses because they are more easily able to repay their mortgage plus interest. The story would be similar even if individuals used their savings to pay for their new home. A higher real interest rate increases the opportunity cost of taking the money out of the bank account and using it to buy a house.

Combining the behavior of firms that borrow or use their own funds to finance investment projects and that of individuals who take out mortgages or use their own funds to buy houses, the negative relationship between investment as a share of GDP and the interest rate that has been observed in the economy for many years makes sense: A higher real interest rate discourages investment, and a lower real interest rate encourages investment. Figure 3 shows this negative relationship between the interest rate and the investment share. For this example, when the interest rate rises from 4 percent to 8 percent, the investment share decreases from 15 percent to 12 percent. Economists have observed that investment is more sensitive to interest rates than consumption is. Therefore, the line for I/Y^* in Figure 3 is flatter than the line for C/Y^* in Figure 2. As before, when a change in the real interest rate leads to a

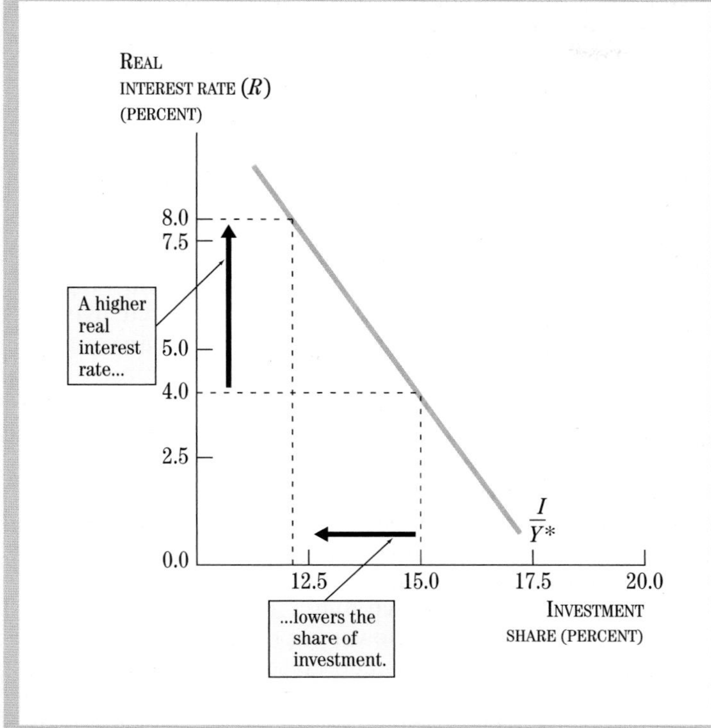

FIGURE 3
The Investment Share and the Real Interest Rate
A higher real interest rate lowers the share of investment. The sensitivity of investment to the interest rate is greater than that of consumption to the interest rate, as shown in Figure 2.

change in the investment share, this is reflected as a *movement along* the consumption share line. An example is shown in Figure 3.

Other factors besides the interest rate also affect investment; when these factors change, the investment share line in Figure 3 will *shift*. For example, an investment tax credit, which lowers a firm's taxes if the firm buys new equipment, would increase the amount that firms would invest at each interest rate. An investment tax credit would shift the investment share line in Figure 3 to the right: The investment that firms are willing to do as a share of GDP at a given interest rate would rise. A change in firms' expectations of the future could also shift the investment share line; if firms feel that new computing or telecommunications equipment will lower their costs in the future, they will purchase the equipment, thereby increasing their investment at a given interest rate; the investment share line will shift to the right. Conversely, pessimism on the part of firms about the benefits of investment could shift the line to the left.

Net Exports

Net exports are also negatively related to the real interest rate. The story behind this relationship is somewhat more involved than that for investment or for consumption. The **exchange rate**—the rate at which one country's currency can be exchanged for another—will play an integral role in this relationship. The story has three parts. First, we need to understand the relationship between the real interest rate and the exchange rate. Then, we need to understand the relationship between the exchange rate and exports and imports. Finally, we will combine these two parts to obtain a relationship between the real interest rate and net exports.

exchange rate: the price of one currency in terms of another in the foreign exchange market. We express the exchange rate as the number of units of foreign currency that can be purchased with one unit of domestic currency.

The Interest Rate and the Exchange Rate. Let us start with the relationship between the interest rate and the *exchange rate*. We will express the exchange rate in terms of the number of units of foreign currency that are needed to purchase one unit of domestic currency, or, in other words, as the price of a unit of domestic currency in terms of foreign currency. Thus, the exchange rates for the dollar for various international currencies will be expressed in the form of euros per dollar, yen per dollar, pounds per dollar, and so on.

A substantial influence on exchange rates is exerted by international investors, who must decide whether to put their funds in assets denominated in dollars—such as an account at a U.S. bank in New York City—or in assets denominated in foreign currencies—such as an account at a Japanese bank in Tokyo. If real interest rates rise in the United States, but not elsewhere, then international investors will put more funds in dollar-denominated assets because they can earn more by doing so. As international investors shift their funds from London, Frankfurt, Tokyo, and other financial centers to New York in order to take advantage of the higher interest rate in the United States, the demand for dollars will rise. This increased demand puts upward pressure on the dollar exchange rate, so that more units of foreign currency

In 2001, this man would have paid around €22,000 in Germany for a jeep that cost $20,000 in the United States. In 2006, the cost to Germans would have gone down to around €15,200 due to the lower exchange rate that year.

will be needed to buy 1 dollar in the foreign exchange market. For example, an increase in the interest rate in the United States might cause the dollar to increase from 100 yen per dollar to 120 yen per dollar. Conversely, a lower interest rate in the United States brings about a lower exchange rate for the dollar. Thus, the interest rate and the exchange rate are positively related.

The Exchange Rate and Net Exports. The next part of the relationship deals with how the exchange rate affects net exports. When the dollar becomes less valuable—i.e., the dollar exchange rate becomes lower—foreign goods imported into the United States become less attractive to U.S. consumers because they are more expensive. For example, at the end of 2006, the dollar exchange rate against the euro was relatively low at .76 euro (€) per dollar compared to the exchange rate five years earlier, at the end of 2001, which was €1.1 per dollar. In 2001, an American consumer could have bought a German-made Audi costing €38,000 for around $34,545 (38,000/1.1). In 2006, when the exchange rate was €.76 per dollar, the Audi would be much more expensive; it would cost $50,000 (38,000/0.76). Thus, a lower exchange rate decreases the quantity demanded of imported goods.

On the other hand, the lower exchange rate makes U.S. exports more attractive to foreign consumers. For example, a $20,000 Jeep Grand Cherokee would have cost a German consumer €22,000 in 2001 but would cost only €15,200 in 2006. Thus, a lower exchange rate increases our exports.

We have shown that a lower exchange rate will raise exports and lower imports. Since net exports is the difference between exports and imports, a lower exchange rate must mean an increase in net exports. Conversely, a higher exchange rate will mean a decrease in net exports.

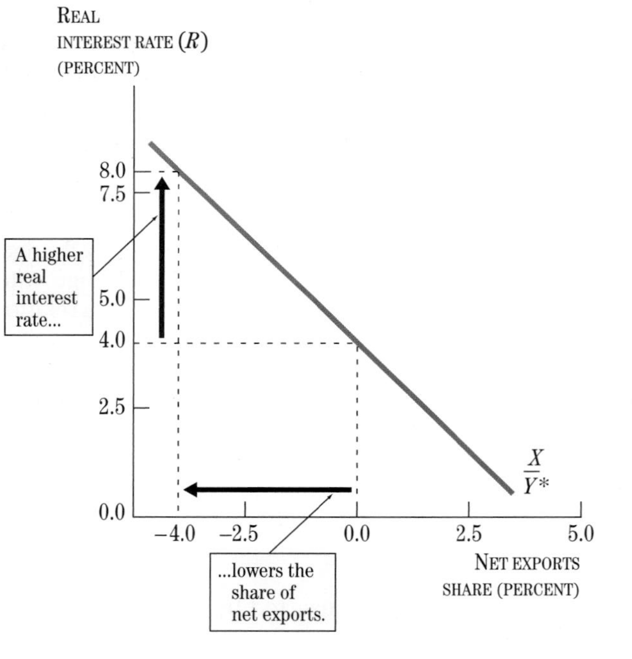

FIGURE 4
The Net Exports Share and the Real Interest Rate
A higher real interest rate lowers the share of net exports because it tends to raise the exchange rate. The higher exchange rate lowers exports and raises imports, thereby lowering net exports. When net exports are negative, there is a trade deficit. When net exports are positive, there is a trade surplus.

Combining the Two Relationships. Finally, we can combine these two relationships—one that relates the real interest rate to the exchange rate, and the other that relates the exchange rate to net exports—to obtain the desired relationship between the real interest rate and net exports:

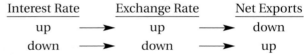

Interest Rate		Exchange Rate		Net Exports
up	→	up	→	down
down	→	down	→	up

If the interest rate goes up, then net exports go down. The link is the exchange rate; the dollar increases in value (the exchange rate rises) as a result of the higher interest rate, which, in turn, makes net exports fall. Of course, all of this works in reverse, too. If the interest rate goes down, then the dollar decreases in value (the exchange rate goes down) and net exports go up.

The relationship between net exports as a share of GDP and the interest rate is shown in Figure 4. Like the consumption share line and the investment share line, the net exports share line is downward-sloping. For this example, when the interest rate goes up from 4 percent to 8 percent, net exports go from zero to about −4 percent of GDP. Remember that when net exports are negative, there is a trade deficit.

Changes in the interest rate lead to movements along the net exports line in Figure 4. Changes in other factors—such as a shift in foreign demand for U.S. products—may cause the line to shift.

Putting the Three Shares Together

We have shown that the consumption, investment, and net exports shares are all negatively related to the interest rate. The three diagrams—Figures 2, 3, and 4—summarize this key idea. Our next task is to determine the interest rate, which will then enable us to determine the particular value of each share.

REVIEW

- Consumption, investment, and net exports are all negatively related to the real interest rate.
- The real interest rate is the price of consumption this year relative to next year. When the real interest rate rises, consumers will be more inclined to forgo current consumption and save so that they can consume more in the future. Accordingly, the share of consumption will rise when the real interest rate rises and fall when the real interest rate falls.
- Changes in the real interest rate affect investment because they change the borrowing costs (and also the opportunity cost of using one's own money) for firms looking to invest in machines and factories and for individuals looking to buy and build homes. Business firms and individuals will spend less on investment when the real interest rate rises. Accordingly, the share of investment will rise when the real interest rate rises and fall when the real interest rate falls.
- Changes in the real interest rate affect net exports through their effects on the exchange rate. A higher real interest rate raises the value of the domestic currency (a higher exchange rate) and thereby discourages exports and encourages imports, while a lower real interest rate results in a fall in the value of the domestic currency (a lower exchange rate), which encourages exports and discourages imports. Accordingly, the share of net exports will rise when the real interest rate rises and fall when the real interest rate falls.
- There is a downward-sloping relationship between the real interest rate and each of these three shares. Changes in the real interest rate are reflected as movements along these curves. Other factors besides the interest rate may also affect consumption, investment, and net exports. When one of these factors changes, the relationship between the interest rate and consumption, investment, or net exports shifts.

DETERMINING THE EQUILIBRIUM INTEREST RATE

Because the interest rate affects each of the three shares (consumption, investment, and net exports), it also affects the *sum* of the three shares. We will refer to the sum of the three shares as the nongovernment share of GDP, or NG/Y, because the fourth component of GDP is the government share. The collective impact is shown by the downward-sloping line in diagram (d) of Figure 5. As before, we are focusing on the shares in the long run, so the diagram shows the sum of consumption, investment, and net exports as a share of potential output (NG/Y^*).

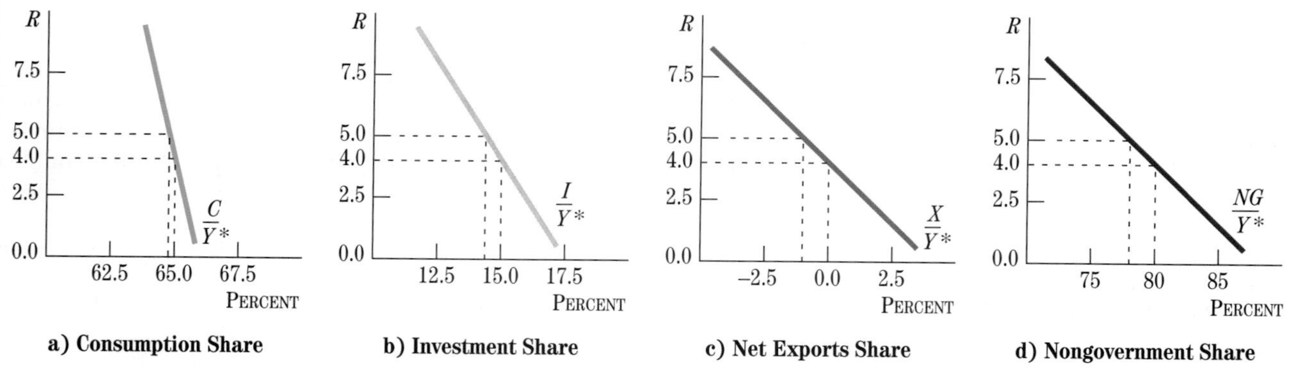

FIGURE 5
Summing Up Consumption, Investment, and Net Exports Shares

Diagrams (a), (b), and (c) are reproductions of Figures 2, 3, and 4. For each interest rate, the three shares are added together to get the sum of shares shown in diagram (d). For example, when the real interest rate is 4 percent, we get 65 percent for consumption share, 15 percent for investment share, and 0 percent for net exports, summing to 80 percent. The sum of the three nongovernment shares is negatively related to the real interest rate (*R*).

The Nongovernment Share of GDP

Note carefully how Figure 5 is put together and how the downward-sloping line in diagram (d) is derived. We have taken the graphs from Figures 2, 3, and 4 and assembled them horizontally in diagrams (a), (b), and (c) of Figure 5. The downward-sloping red line in diagram (d) is the sum of the three downward-sloping lines in diagrams (a), (b), and (c). For example, when the interest rate is 4 percent, the line in diagram (d) shows that the nongovernment share—the sum of investment, consumption, and net exports as a share of GDP—is 80 percent; this is the sum of 65 percent for the consumption share, 15 percent for the investment share, and zero percent for the net exports share. Similarly, the other points in diagram (d) are obtained by adding up the three shares at other interest rate levels. For example, at an interest rate of 5 percent, we see that the sum of the shares of consumption, investment, and net exports is down to about 78 percent.

The Government's Share of GDP and the Share of GDP Available for Nongovernment Use

We have determined that the real interest rate has a negative effect on the consumption, investment, and net exports shares of GDP. What about the impact of real interest rates on government purchases? We will assume that government purchases do not depend on the real interest rate; instead, they are likely to be affected by the decisions made by elected representatives on behalf of the voters who elected them to office. So the share of government purchases (G/Y) will not be affected by fluctuations in interest rates. For example, if the decisions made by elected officials result in a government purchases share that is 22 percent of GDP, then that share will not be affected by changes in the real interest rate. This is shown by the vertical line in diagram (a) of Figure 6.

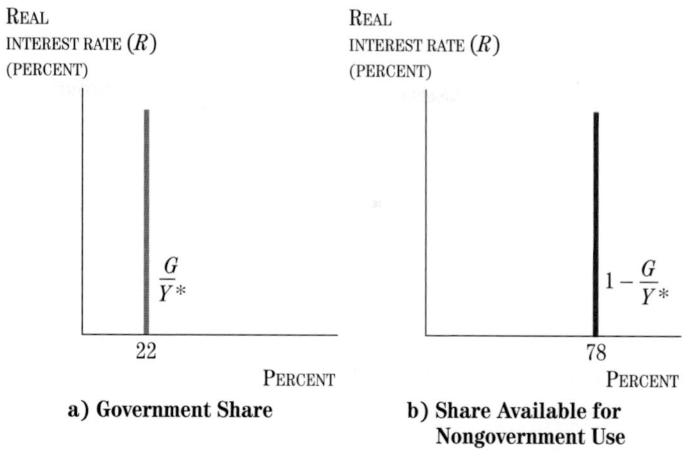

FIGURE 6
Finding the Share Available for Nongovernment Use
If the government share of GDP is known, then the remaining share of GDP is what is available for nongovernment use. In the example given here, a 22 percent share of government purchases means that 78 percent of GDP is available for nongovernment use. Since the share G/Y^* is not dependent on R, the share available for nongovernmental use is also a vertical line, not dependent on R.

The government share determines how much is available for nongovernment use, that is, for either consumption, investment, or net exports. The share available for nongovernment use is easily defined as

$$\text{Share available for nongovernment use} = 1 - \frac{G}{Y}$$

If the government share is not affected by changes in the real interest rate, the share that is available for nongovernment use will also not be affected. For the case shown in diagram (a) of Figure 6, with a share of government purchases of 22 percent, the share available for nongovernment use must equal 78 percent. The share of GDP available for nongovernment use is shown in diagram (b) of Figure 6. As always, we are looking at the long run, so the diagram shows the share of potential output available for nongovernment use.

Finding the Equilibrium Interest Rate

In equilibrium, the nongovernment share of GDP should equal the share of GDP available for nongovernment use. In mathematical terms, we can describe this equilibrium relationship in the long run as

$$\frac{NG}{Y^*} = 1 - \frac{G}{Y^*}$$

What brings this equality about is the real interest rate, which is the key to the spending allocation model. Figure 7 illustrates how the interest rate brings about this equality. Look first at diagram (d). In diagram (d), the share available for nongovernment use ($1 - G/Y^*$) is indicated by the vertical line at 78 percent. The nongovernment share of GDP (NG/Y^*), which is the sum of the consumption, investment, and net export shares, is shown by the downward-sloping line in Figure 7(d). This is the same line we derived in Figure 5(d). The equilibrium is where the nongovernment share equals the share available for nongovernment use. Graphically, this is the intersection of the downward-sloping line and the vertical line. We see in diagram (d) of Figure 7 that the point of intersection for that economy occurs when the interest rate

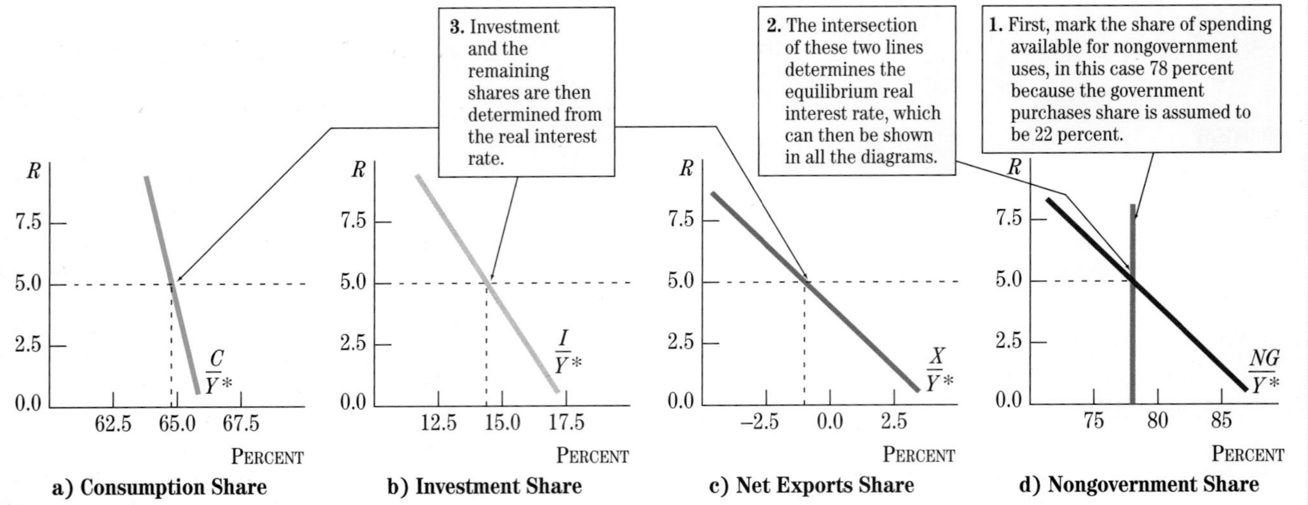
3. Investment and the remaining shares are then determined from the real interest rate.
2. The intersection of these two lines determines the equilibrium real interest rate, which can then be shown in all the diagrams.
1. First, mark the share of spending available for nongovernment uses, in this case 78 percent because the government purchases share is assumed to be 22 percent.
R
7.5
5.0
2.5
0.0
C/Y*
62.5 65.0 67.5
PERCENT
a) Consumption Share
I/Y*
12.5 15.0 17.5
PERCENT
b) Investment Share
X/Y*
−2.5 0.0 2.5
PERCENT
c) Net Exports Share
NG/Y*
75 80 85
PERCENT
d) Nongovernment Share

FIGURE 7
Determining the Equilibrium Real Interest Rate and the Shares of Spending

In this case, government purchases are assumed to be 22 percent of GDP. Mark the implied share available for nongovernment uses, 78 percent, in diagram (d). The equilibrium real interest rate is determined at the intersection of the two lines in diagram (d). Given this real interest rate, we can compute the consumption, investment, and net exports shares of spending in GDP using diagrams (a), (b), and (c).

equilibrium interest rate: the interest rate that equates the sum of the consumption, investment, and net exports shares to the share of GDP available for nongovernment use.

is 5 percent. This is the **equilibrium interest rate,** the interest rate that makes the nongovernment share equal to the share available for nongovernment use.

Once we determine the equilibrium interest rate, we can find the investment, consumption, and net exports shares. Each of these shares depends on the interest rate, as shown in diagrams (a), (b), and (c) of Figure 7. To determine each of the shares, simply draw a line across the three diagrams at the equilibrium interest rate. Then in diagram (a) we find the consumption share, in diagram (b) the investment share, and in diagram (c) the net exports share.

What happens if consumption, investment, or net exports increases? Then the nongovernment share will begin to rise above the share of GDP available after the government takes its share. This rise in spending will be reflected as a rightward shift of the downward-sloping nongovernment share line, which causes the equilibrium interest rate in the economy to increase. Conversely, if consumption, investment, or net exports decreases, then the nongovernment share will begin to fall below the share of GDP available after the government takes its share. This will be reflected as a leftward shift of the downward-sloping nongovernment share line, which causes the equilibrium interest rate in the economy to decrease.

What happens if the share of government purchases increases? Then the share available for nongovernment use will fall, which will be reflected in a leftward shift of the vertical line indicating the share available for nongovernment use. This causes the equilibrium interest rate in the economy to increase. Conversely, if the share of government purchases decreases, then the share available for nongovernment use will rise, which will be reflected in a rightward shift of the vertical line that indicates the share available for nongovernment use. This causes the equilibrium interest rate in the economy to decrease.

The following Economics in Action box traces through this analogy in more detail, including showing you how you can find the impact of a change in one of these shares on the other shares, working through the change in the real interest rate.

ECONOMICS IN ACTION

Using the Spending Allocation Model to Analyze the Long-Run Implications of Shifts in Government Purchases and Consumption

In this case study, you will see how the spending allocation model can be used to predict the effects of actual changes in the economy. We focus on two shifts: a shift in government purchases and a shift in consumption. The goal is to understand how we can use this model to examine what happens to the other components of GDP.

A SHIFT IN THE SHARE OF GOVERNMENT PURCHASES

What happens when the share of government purchases increases or decreases? We know as a matter of arithmetic that some other share must move in a direction opposite to that of the government share.

Suppose that the government share of GDP decreases by 2 percent, as happened in the 1990s as a result of a decrease in defense spending and other budget cuts. The effects of this change are shown in Figure 8. If government purchases as a share of GDP decrease by 2 percent, then we know that the share available for nongovernment use must *increase* by 2 percent. Thus, in diagram (d) of Figure 8, we shift the vertical line marking the available nongovernment share to the right by 2 percentage points. As Figure 8(d) shows, there is now a new intersection of the two lines and a new, lower equilibrium real interest rate. The new real interest rate is 4 percent rather than 5 percent, a decrease of 1 percentage point.

The decrease in the real interest rate is the market mechanism that brings about an increase in the shares of consumption plus investment plus net exports. To see the effect on the consumption, investment, and net exports shares, we draw a horizontal line at a real interest rate of 4 percent, as shown in Figure 8, and read off the implied shares. According to the diagram, the share of consumption increases, the share of investment increases, and the share of net exports increases.

Table 1 allows us to compare the predictions of the model with what really happened when there was a reduction in government purchases in the 1990s. The government purchases share was reduced by 2.2 percent between 1989 and 1997. During that period, all of the

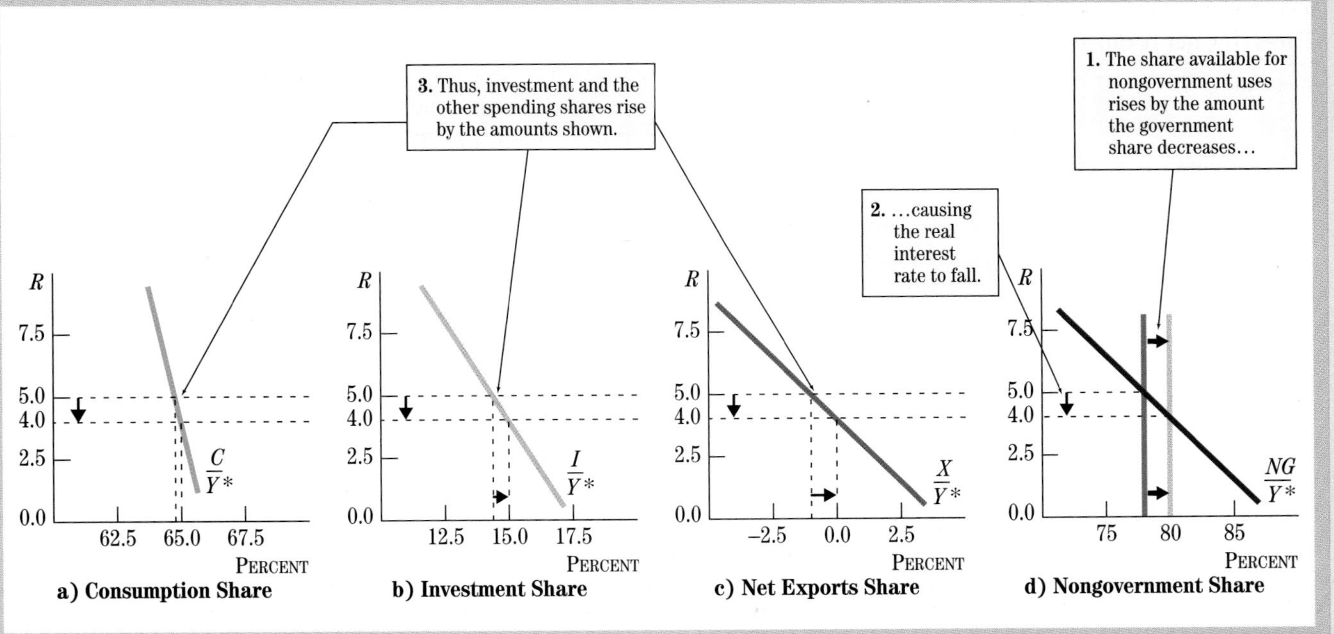

FIGURE 8
A Decrease in the Share of Government Purchases

If the government purchases share of GDP falls, then the share available for nongovernment use must rise by the same amount. This causes a fall in real interest rates, which increases the consumption, investment, and net exports share.

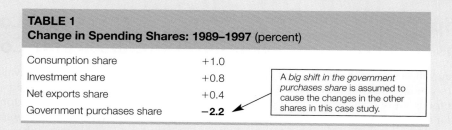

TABLE 1
Change in Spending Shares: 1989–1997 (percent)

Consumption share	+1.0
Investment share	+0.8
Net exports share	+0.4
Government purchases share	**−2.2**

A big shift in the government purchases share is assumed to cause the changes in the other shares in this case study.

other shares increased as a result of the decline in the real interest rate. Although the precise magnitudes may not be exactly the same, the model explains the direction of movement very well.

The same process would work in reverse if we *increased* the share of government purchases. In Figure 8, the real interest rate would have to rise. To find out the effect on the other components of spending, we would draw a horizontal line at a higher real interest rate. That would show us that the shares of investment, net exports, and consumption would fall.

Sometimes a decline in the investment share due to an increase in government purchases is called **crowding out** because investment is "crowded out" by the government purchases. Thus, we have shown that an increase in the share of government purchases causes a crowding out of investment in the long run. However, because the shares of net exports and consumption also fall, the crowding out of investment is not as large as it would otherwise be.

A SHIFT IN CONSUMPTION

The second application of the model involves an increase in the amount that people want to consume. This might occur because of a reduction in sales taxes, which encourages them to consume more relative to their income.

The impact of such a shift in the share of consumption is analyzed in Figure 9. The relationship between the interest rate and the consumption share shifts out in diagram (a); this causes the sum of the investment, consumption, and net exports shares to shift out, as shown by the shift in the line in diagram (d).

The result is an increase in the equilibrium real interest rate and a decline in the share of investment. However, because the share of net exports also declines, the impact on the share of investment is much less than if net exports had

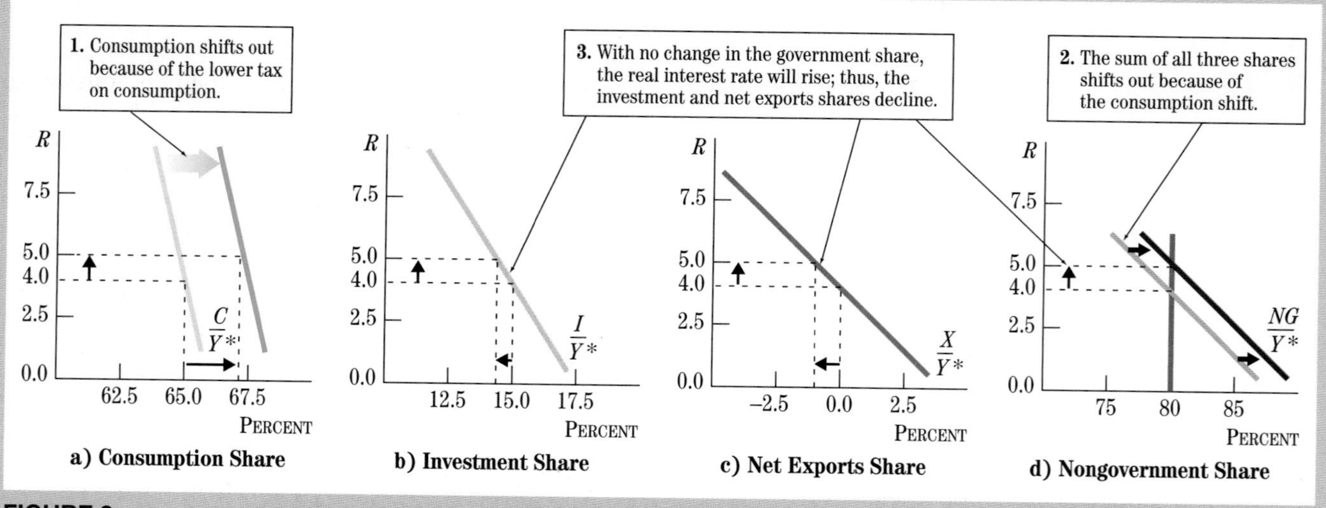

FIGURE 9
A Shift in the Share of Consumption

If the amount of consumption relative to income rises—perhaps because of a tax change that reduces sales taxes—the real interest rate will rise. Both investment and net exports shares decline. The government purchases share is unchanged.

not changed. The ability to engage in international transactions reduces substantially the effect of the increased consumption on capital formation.

The overall prediction of the effects of such a shift is very close to what happened in the United States during the 1980s, as shown in Table 2. As the consumption share rose, the investment share and the net exports share fell. (The government purchases share was nearly unchanged.) According to most estimates, the real interest rate was higher in the 1980s than in the 1970s. Thus, the spending allocation model put forth in this chapter explains the long-term trends in the shares of spending and interest rates under the assumption that there was a shift in the share of consumption.

TABLE 2
Change in Spending Shares: 1979–1989 (percent)

Consumption share	**+3.3**
Investment share	−3.1
Net exports share	−0.5
Government purchases share	+0.3

A big shift in the consumption share is assumed to cause changes in the other shares in this case study.

crowding out: the decline in private investment owing to an increase in government purchases.

The lessons from this case study can also help you understand the statements made by the Council of Economic Advisors and the chairman of the Federal Reserve that were described in the introduction to this chapter.

■ **Analogy with Supply and Demand.** Observe that the intersection of the two lines in diagram (d) of Figure 7 is much like the intersection of a demand curve and a supply curve. The red downward-sloping line—showing how the sum of investment, consumption, and net exports is negatively related to the interest rate—looks just like a demand curve. The blue vertical line—showing the share of GDP available for consumption, investment, and net exports—looks like a vertical supply curve. The intersection of the two curves determines the equilibrium price—in this case, the equilibrium interest rate in the economy as a whole.

■ **The Real Interest Rate in the Long Run.** Having determined the equilibrium interest rate, it is important to mention once more two key features of this model. First, this analysis applies to the *long run*—perhaps three years or more—rather than to short-run economic fluctuations. Moreover, the interest rate in the analysis is the *real* interest rate, which, as defined in Chapter 5, is the nominal interest rate less the expected inflation rate. If the inflation rate is low, there is little difference between the real interest rate and the nominal interest rate; but if inflation is high, there is a big difference, and the real interest rate is a much better measure of the incentives affecting consumers and firms. An interest rate of 50 percent would seem high but would actually be quite low—2 percent in real terms—if people expected inflation to be 48 percent.

REVIEW

- The sum of the consumption, investment, and net exports shares of GDP is called the nongovernment share of GDP. It is negatively related to the interest rate because each of the individual components is negatively related to the interest rate.

- The government share of GDP is assumed to be unaffected by the real interest rate, being determined by the preferences of voters expressed through their elected representatives. The share of GDP available for nongovernment use then can be defined as 1 minus the government share of GDP. This, too, is unaffected by the real interest rate.
- The equilibrium interest rate is determined by the condition that the nongovernment share equals the share available for nongovernment use. Graphically, this is the interest rate at the intersection of the downward-sloping nongovernment share of GDP line and the vertical share of GDP available for nongovernment use line.
- Once we find the equilibrium interest rate, we can then find the shares of consumption, investment, and net exports by looking at the graphs of those relationships.
- We can also use the model to analyze what would happen to the equilibrium interest rate when there is a change in the government share or in one of the three nongovernment shares.
- Once we know the equilibrium interest rate, we can also find out how exactly the other shares in the economy respond to a change in one of the shares. This is helpful in understanding how a change in government purchases affects investment, for example.

THE RELATIONSHIP BETWEEN SAVING AND INVESTMENT

By now you should be able to use the spending allocation model to illustrate how changes in the share of spending in one component of GDP affect the other components. In particular, we were able to use it to show how an increase in the consumption share of GDP or an increase in the government purchases share of GDP leads to a decrease in the investment share of GDP. In this section, we derive a similar relationship between the changes in the shares of GDP that are being *saved* and the share that is being invested. This alternative viewpoint is important to complete your understanding of how one sector of the economy can affect the others. For instance, we will show that the investment share of GDP will decrease when the government's budget deficit as a percentage of GDP rises, all else equal. The rise in the government budget deficit can be caused either by an increase in government spending or by a decrease in tax revenue. The latter effect is much better understood by looking at the economy from the saving side rather than the spending side.

In Chapter 6, we defined national saving (S) as GDP minus consumption minus government purchases, or

$$S = Y - C - G$$

national saving rate: the proportion of GDP that is saved, neither consumed nor spent on government purchases; equals national saving (S) divided by GDP, or S/Y.

The ratio of national saving to GDP, or S/Y, is the **national saving rate.** For example, in 2006, national saving was \$1,450 billion and GDP was \$13,247 billion, so the national saving rate was $\frac{1{,}450}{13{,}247} = .109$ or 11 percent. If we divide each term in the definition of national saving by Y, we can write the national saving rate as 1 minus the shares of consumption and government purchases in GDP. That is,

National saving rate = 1 − consumption share − government purchases share,

or

$$\frac{S}{Y} = 1 - \frac{C}{Y} - \frac{G}{Y}$$

This equation tells us that a change in the economy will affect the national saving rate through its effect on the consumption share and the government purchases share. We will once again express everything in the long run, so the national saving rate in the long run is

$$\frac{S}{Y^*} = 1 - \frac{C}{Y^*} - \frac{G}{Y^*}$$

Note also that the equations tell us that the national saving rate depends on the interest rate. Since the consumption share of GDP is negatively related to the real interest rate and the government share of GDP is unrelated to the real interest rate, you can easily show that the national saving rate is positively related to the real interest rate. When the real interest rate rises, the consumption share of GDP falls, implying that the national saving rate rises. On the other hand, when the real interest rate falls, the consumption share of GDP rises, implying that the national saving rate falls.

Since we know that

$$1 = \frac{C}{Y^*} + \frac{I}{Y^*} + \frac{G}{Y^*} + \frac{X}{Y^*}$$

we can use the above definition of the national saving rate in the long run to write

$$\frac{S}{Y^*} = \frac{I}{Y^*} + \frac{X}{Y^*}$$

or, in other words, the national saving rate equals the investment share plus the net exports share. Both sides of this equation depend on the interest rate, as shown in Figure 10. The upward-sloping line in Figure 10 shows the national saving rate. An increase in the real interest rate causes the saving rate to rise. The downward-sloping line shows the sum of the investment and net exports shares; this sum is negatively related to the real interest rate because both the investment share and the net exports share are negatively related to the real interest rate.

The intersection of the two lines in Figure 10 determines the equilibrium interest rate. The interest rate is exactly the same as that in Figure 7. The only difference is that we are looking at the economy from a government and individual saving perspective rather than from a spending perspective.

Consider the same increase in the consumption share considered in the case study. An upward shift in the consumption share is equivalent to a downward shift in the saving rate. Thus, we shift the interest rate–saving rate relationship to the left in Figure 11, representing a downshift in the national saving rate. As shown in the figure, this leads to a higher interest rate and lower shares for investment and net exports. Hence, the predictions are the same as those of the previous analysis in Figure 9. Similarly, an increase in the government expenditure share is also equivalent to a downward shift in the saving rate. This will also lead to a shift in the interest rate–saving rate relationship to the left in Figure 11, resulting in a higher interest rate and lower shares for investment and net exports.

Obviously, we would not want to derive this alternative way of looking at the economy merely to replicate predictions that we were already able to make. We can

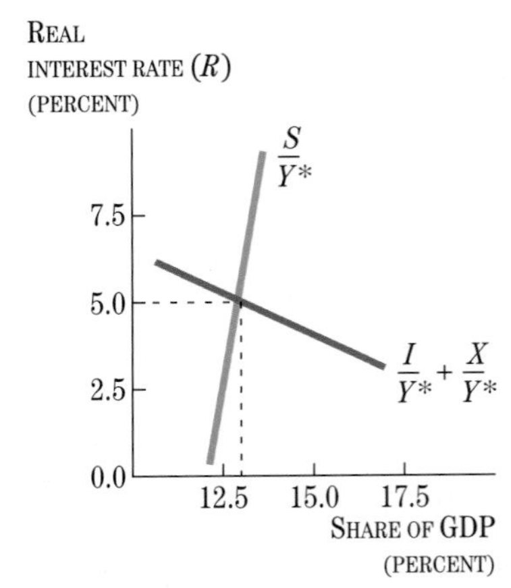

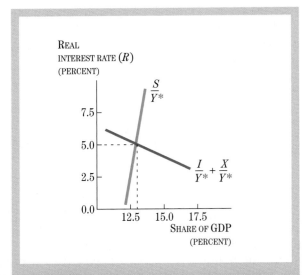

FIGURE 10
Determining the Interest Rate Using the Saving Rate Relationship
The saving rate (green line) depends positively on the real interest rate. The sum (purple line) of the investment share and the net exports share depends negatively on the real interest rate. The equilibrium interest rate is determined at the point where national saving equals investment plus net exports, or the intersection of the two lines.

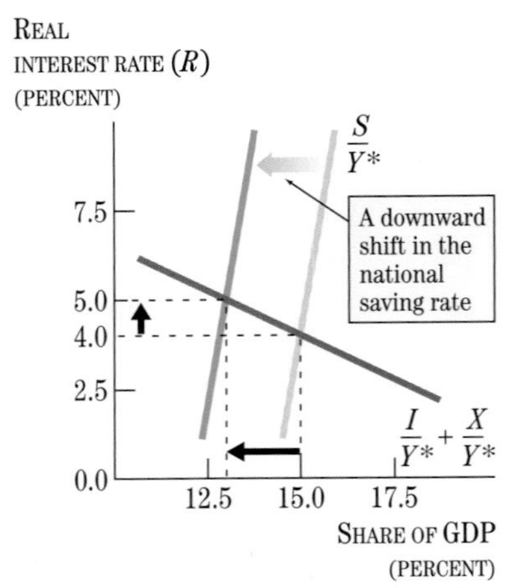

FIGURE 11
The Effect of a Downward Shift in the Saving Rate
The effect is the same as the shift upward in the consumption share illustrated in Figure 9. The lower national saving rate raises real interest rates and lowers the investment share and the net exports share.

make this model adaptable to more situations if we go back to another relationship we derived in Chapter 6, namely, that

$$S = (Y - C - T) + (T - G)$$

where T denotes taxes. This relationship states that national saving is equal to the sum of private and government saving. Therefore, the national saving rate will be the sum of the private saving rate and the government saving rate. The government saving rate is simply the budget balance as a percentage of GDP; when there is a budget deficit, this will be negative. We can express the relationship between saving, investment, and net exports in the economy in more detail then as

$$\text{Private saving rate} + \text{government saving rate} = \frac{I}{Y^*} + \frac{X}{Y^*}$$

This equation has very powerful implications for the economy. If the government budget deficit increases (the government saving rate decreases), then the investment share of GDP will fall, assuming that the private saving rate or the net exports share of GDP does not change. If the economy is to keep its investment share unchanged in the face of rising budget deficits, then either private saving will have to increase to offset the fall in government saving, or the share of net exports will have to decrease. Practically speaking, if the rising demands of an aging society cause budget deficits as a percentage of GDP in the United States to increase (thus reducing the government saving rate), then one or more of the following outcomes will occur:

1. The private saving rate will have to increase, meaning that consumers will most likely have to cut back on spending.

2. The investment rate will decrease, which means less capital accumulation and the likelihood for slower economic growth in the future.
3. The trade balance will worsen, and we will buy more foreign goods while foreigners will buy less of our goods.

REVIEW

- We can apply the concepts used to derive the spending allocation model to examine how changes in saving behavior by consumers and the government affect other sectors of the economy.
- Since national saving is defined as $Y - C - G$, we can show that national saving is equal to the sum of investment and net exports. Expressing this relationship as shares of GDP in the long run, we can show that the national saving rate equals the sum of the investment share and the net exports share of GDP.
- The national saving rate is positively related to the interest rate, whereas the sum of the investment share and the net exports share of GDP is negatively related to the interest rate. The equilibrium real interest rate can be found as the rate that equates the national saving rate and the sum of the investment and net exports shares.
- An increase in the consumption share or the government share is equivalent to a downward shift in the national saving rate. This will result in a higher interest rate and lower the shares of investment and net exports.
- We can disaggregate the national saving rate into the sum of the private saving rate and the government saving rate. This allows us to illustrate that the impact of rising budget deficits will be to create some combination of a lower investment share of GDP, a higher private saving rate, or a worsening of the trade balance.

CONCLUSION

In this chapter, we have developed a model that determines the equilibrium interest rate and explains how the shares of spending are allocated in the whole economy. The model can be used to analyze the impact of a change in government purchases or a shift in consumption or saving behavior.

The model has introduced an important macroeconomic factor to consider when assessing the appropriate size of government. Private investment is affected by the size of government in the economy. Private investment is greater when government purchases are less, even though government spending is needed to provide the roads, education, and legal system that help produce economic growth. What the model shows is that even when government spending does these good things, it reduces the share of GDP available for private investment.

The model also has strong predictions about the appropriate budget policy for the government to follow. In the long run, private investment is affected by the size of government saving in the economy. Private investment is greater when the government saving rate is high. So once the government figures out the appropriate amount of spending to do on the roads, education, and legal system that help produce economic growth, it needs to ensure that it sets the tax rates appropriate for collecting the revenue needed to pay for that expenditure.

ECONOMICS IN THE NEWS

The "Twin Deficits"

In the previous section, you saw that a rising budget deficit would (absent an increase in private saving) lead to a decline in the national saving rate. Furthermore, you saw that a decrease in national saving would lead to either a decline in the investment share or a decline in the net exports share (a worsening trade balance). If the investment share does not fall very much, and budget deficits are large, the economy is likely to experience both budget deficits *and* trade deficits. Economists term this the "twin deficits" scenario. This is an excerpt from a long piece on the twin deficits that appeared a couple of years ago in the *New York Times.* See if you can use the knowledge you gained in this chapter to follow the economic arguments made by the author.

Introduces and defines the twins

If private saving does not rise, then the country will have to look to other countries for help. Otherwise investment will fall.

If foreigners are willing to invest in our economy, then investment can stay stable, but we will end up running large trade deficits.

If we save more and buy fewer goods, that will hurt the Chinese economy because of its dependence on us to buy its exports. So China is happy to lend us money and sell us goods and we seem content to not increase our saving and run trade deficits and budget deficits.

Our Currency, Your Problem

By NIALL FERGUSON

Niall Ferguson is professor of history at Harvard and author of "Colossus: The Price of America's Empire."

Every congressman knows that the United States currently runs large "twin deficits" on its budget and current accounts. Deficit 1, as we well know, is just the difference between federal tax revenues and expenditures. Deficit 2 is generally less well understood: it's the difference between all that Americans earn from foreigners (mainly from exports, services and investments abroad) and all that they pay out to foreigners (for imports, services and loans). When a government runs a deficit, it can tap public savings by selling bonds. But when the economy as a whole is running a deficit—when American households are saving next to nothing of their disposable income—there is no option but to borrow abroad.

There was a time when foreign investors were ready and willing to finance the U.S. current account deficit by buying large pieces of corporate America. But that's not the case today. Perhaps the most amazing economic fact of our time is that between 70 and 80 percent of the American economy's vast and continuing borrowing requirement is being met by foreign (mainly Asian) central banks.

Let's translate that into political terms. In effect, the Bush administration's combination of tax cuts for the Republican "base" and a Global War on Terror is being financed with a multibillion dollar overdraft facility at the People's Bank of China. Without East Asia, your mortgage might well be costing you more. The toys you buy for your kids certainly would.

Why are the Chinese monetary authorities so willing to underwrite American profligacy? Not out of altruism. The principal reason is that if they don't keep on buying dollars and dollar-based securities as fast as the Federal Reserve and the U.S. Treasury can print them, the dollar could slide substantially against the Chinese renminbi, much as it has declined against the euro over the past three years. Knowing the importance of the U.S. market to their export industries, the Chinese authorities dread such a dollar slide. The effect would be to raise the price, and hence reduce the appeal, of Chinese goods to American consumers—and that includes everything from my snowproof hiking boots to the modem on my desk. A fall in exports would almost certainly translate into job losses in China at a time when millions of migrants from the countryside are pouring into the country's manufacturing sector.

So when Treasury Secretary John Snow insists that the United States has a "strong dollar" policy, what he really means is that the People's Republic of China has a "weak renminbi" policy. Sure, this is bad news if you happen to be an American toy manufacturer. But there are three good reasons that the administration is tacitly delighted by the Asian central banks' support. Not only is it keeping the lid on the price of American imports from Asia (a potential source of inflationary pressure). It is also propping up the price of U.S. Treasury bonds; this in turn depresses the yield on those bonds, allowing the federal government to borrow at historically very low rates of interest. Reason No. 3 is that low long-term interest rates keep the Bush recovery jogging along.

A fall in S/Y will shift the saving line and raise real interest rates, but a worsening trade balance will push the X/Y* line down and keep real interest rates low. See if you can show that in Figure 11.*

Sadly, according to a growing number of eminent economists, this arrangement simply cannot last. The dollar pessimists argue that the Asian central banks are already dangerously overexposed both to the dollar and the U.S. bond market. Sooner or later, they have to get out—at which point the dollar could plunge relative to Asian currencies by as much as a third or two-fifths, and U.S. interest rates could leap upward. (When the South Korean central bank recently appeared to indicate that it was shifting out of dollars, there was indeed a brief run on the U.S. currency—until the Koreans hastily issued a denial.)

Are the pessimists right? The U.S. current account deficit is now within sight of 6 percent of G.D.P., and net external debt stands at around 30 percent. The precipitous economic history of Latin America shows that an external-debt burden in excess of 20 percent of G.D.P. is potentially dangerous. . . .

If the United States cannot keep running trade deficits, then further budget deficits would result in a fall in the investment share or require American consumers to sacrifice consumption and increase their saving.

Even the gloomiest pessimists accept that a steep dollar depreciation would inflict more suffering on China and other Asian economies than on the United States. John Snow's counterpart in the Nixon administration once told his European counterparts that "the dollar is our currency, but your problem." Snow could say the same to Asians today. If the dollar fell by a third against the renminbi, according to Nouriel Roubini, an economist at New York University, the People's Bank of China could suffer a capital loss equivalent to 10 percent of China's gross domestic product. For that reason alone, the P.B.O.C. has every reason to carry on printing renminbi in order to buy dollars.

Though neither side wants to admit it, today's Sino-American economic relationship has an imperial character. Empires, remember, traditionally collect "tributes" from subject peoples. That is how their costs—in terms of blood and treasure—can best be justified to the populace back in the imperial capital. Today's "tribute" is effectively paid to the American empire by China and other East Asian economies in the form of underpriced exports and low-interest, high-risk loans.

How long can the Chinese go on financing America's twin deficits? The answer may be a lot longer than the dollar pessimists expect. After all, this form of tribute is much less humiliating than those exacted by the last Anglophone empire, which occupied China's best ports and took over the country's customs system (partly in order to flood the country with Indian opium). There was no obvious upside to that arrangement for the Chinese; the growth rate of per capita G.D.P. was probably negative in that era, compared with 8 or 9 percent a year since 1990.

Meanwhile, the United States may be discovering what the British found in their imperial heyday. If you are a truly powerful empire, you can borrow a lot of money at surprisingly reasonable rates. Today's deficits are in fact dwarfed in relative terms by the amounts the British borrowed to finance their Global War on (French) Terror between 1793 and 1815. Yet British long-term rates in that era averaged just 4.77 percent, and the pound's exchange rate was restored to its prewar level within a few years of peace.

It is only when your power wanes—as the British learned after 1945—that owing a fortune in your own currency becomes a real problem. As opposed, that is, to someone else's problem.

To the extent that consumption and net exports also shrink as government purchases increase, the effect on private investment of an increase in the share of government purchases is smaller. This can also be stated as to the extent that private savings increase and net exports shrink (the trade balance worsens), the effect on private investment of a decrease in the government saving rate is smaller.

Thus, there is a need for balance between government purchases and private investment. The mix will ultimately be determined in the political debate. This chapter provides some economic analysis that is useful in that debate.

KEY POINTS

1. Over the long term, consumption, investment, net exports, and government purchases compete for a share of GDP. The four spending shares must sum to 1.
2. Higher real interest rates raise the price of consumption and lead to a reduction of consumption as a share of GDP.
3. Higher real interest rates also reduce investment by raising the cost of borrowing and by raising the opportunity cost of using one's own funds.
4. Higher real interest rates lower the share of net exports by causing the exchange rate to rise, which reduces exports and raises imports.
5. The combined effect is a downward-sloping relationship between the real interest rate and the nongovernment share of GDP.
6. The government share of GDP is not dependent on the real interest rate. Accordingly, the share of GDP available for nongovernment use, which is 1 minus the government share of GDP, is not dependent on the real interest rate and is shown as a vertical line.
7. The equilibrium interest rate is found by equating the nongovernment share of GDP—the sum of the consumption, investment, and net exports shares—to the share of GDP available for nongovernment use.
8. An increase in the share of government purchases crowds out the investment share of GDP by raising interest rates. The consumption and net exports shares also fall, crowding out the investment less severely. A decrease in the share of government purchases will lead to a lower real interest rate and an increase in all the other shares of spending.
9. The national saving rate is equal to the sum of the investment and net exports shares of GDP. The national saving rate, which equals the sum of private and government saving, is positively related to the real interest rate, while the sum of the investment and net exports shares of GDP is negatively related to the real interest rate.
10. An increase in consumption (a decrease in private saving) or an increase in government purchases (a decrease in government saving) will reduce national saving and shift the national saving curve inward. This will raise the equilibrium real interest rate and lower the investment share of GDP and/or lower the net exports share of GDP (worsen the trade balance).

KEY TERMS

consumption share
investment share
net exports share
government purchases share
exchange rate
equilibrium interest rate
crowding out
national saving rate

QUESTIONS FOR REVIEW

1. Why does an increase in the share of one component of GDP require a decrease in some other share?
2. What is the relationship between the consumption share and the real interest rate?
3. What is the relationship between the investment share and the real interest rate?
4. Explain carefully all the steps that relate the share of net exports to the real interest rate.

5. How do we indicate that the model in this chapter applies much more to the long run than to the short run?
6. Describe the following five relationships: (a) the government share of GDP and the real interest rate, (b) the government share of GDP and the share of GDP available for nongovernment use, (c) the real interest rate and the share of GDP available for nongovernment use, (d) the real interest rate and the nongovernment share of GDP, and (e) the share of GDP available for nongovernment use and the nongovernment share of GDP.
7. What determines the equilibrium interest rate?
8. What is crowding out? Graphically illustrate how it works, using the spending allocation model.
9. Describe the relationships that exist among the following: the national saving rate, the private saving rate, the government saving rate, the net exports share of GDP, and the investment share of GDP.
10. What are the long-term implications of a rise in the government budget deficit as a percentage of GDP (also known as a fall in the government saving rate)?

PROBLEMS

1. Suppose $C = 700$, $I = 200$, $G = 100$, and $X = 0$.
   a. What is GDP? Calculate each component's share of GDP.
   b. Suppose government spending increases to 150, but the other components of GDP do not change. What is government spending's share of GDP now? What is the new nongovernment share?
   c. Suppose that the level of potential GDP (Y^*) is 1,000 and is unaffected by the increase in government spending described above. Without doing any calculations, explain in general terms what happens to C/Y^*, X/Y^*, and I/Y^* after the government spending increase in (b).
   d. Describe the mechanism by which each of these changes happens.
2. Suppose the following equations describe the relationship between the long-run shares of spending in GDP and the interest rate (R), measured in decimal fractions (that is, $R = .05$ means that the interest rate is 5 percent).

$$\frac{C}{Y^*} = .7 - .2(R - .05) \qquad \frac{I}{Y^*} = .2 - .8(R - .05)$$

$$\frac{X}{Y^*} = 0 - .95(R - .05) \qquad \frac{G}{Y^*} = .2$$

   a. Use algebra to determine the values of the interest rate and the long-run shares of spending in GDP.
   b. Do the calculations again for a long-run government share of 17 percent rather than 20 percent (that is, $G/Y^* = .17$).
   c. Suppose that the share of government purchases changes from 20 percent to 17 percent. Describe, in words, the mechanism by which each of the other shares changes.
3. Graph the relationships defined in problem 2 to scale in a four-part diagram like Figure 6. Use the diagram to analyze each of the following situations:
   a. Suppose there is an increase in the foreign demand for U.S. goods that changes the coefficient in the net exports share equation from 0 to .05. What happens to the interest rate and the consumption, investment, net exports, and government purchases shares in the United States in the long run?
   b. Determine how an increase in taxes that reduces the coefficient in the consumption share equation from .7 to .68 would affect the interest rate and the consumption, investment, net exports, and government purchases shares in the long run.
   c. Suppose firms are willing to invest 30 percent rather than 20 percent of GDP at an interest rate of 5 percent. How would this affect the interest rate and the shares of spending in GDP in the long run?
4. Using the diagram provided on the following page, find the equilibrium interest rate when the share of government purchases in the long run is 20 percent. Show what happens to all the variables if there is an increase in investment because of a new tax policy that encourages investment.
5. Describe the long-run impact of a decline in defense spending by 1 percent of GDP on interest rates and on consumption, investment, and net exports as a share of GDP. Consider two different cases:
   a. No other changes in policy accompany the defense cut.
   b. The funds saved from the defense cut are used to increase government expenditures on roads and bridges.

Problem 4

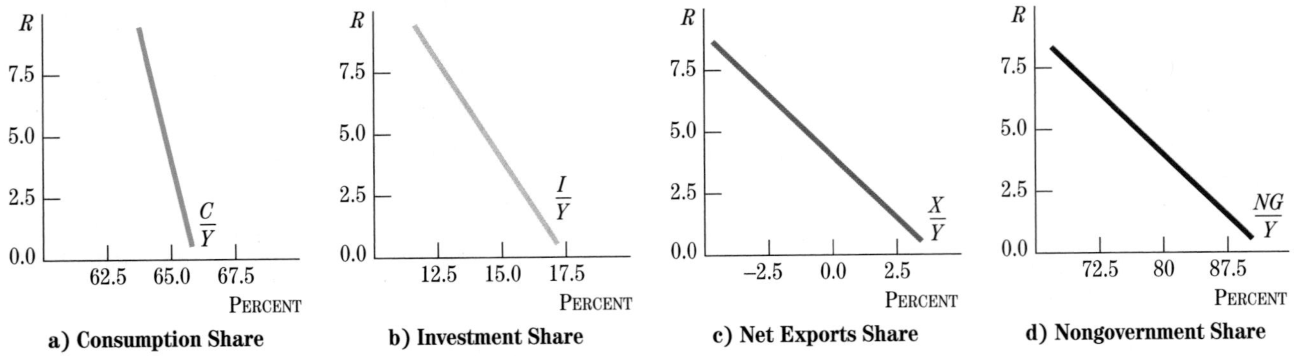

6. Suppose personal income tax rates are cut and government spending is increased. Using a diagram, show what will happen to real interest rates. What will happen to the spending shares of GDP in the long run?
7. Draw two sets of diagrams like Figure 7 to depict two situations. In one set, draw investment and net exports as very sensitive to interest rates—that is, the I/Y and X/Y curves are very flat. In the other set, draw investment and net exports as insensitive to interest rates—that is, the I/Y and X/Y curves are nearly vertical. For the same increase in government's share of GDP, in which set of diagrams will interest rates rise more? Why?
8. If China increases the value of its currency relative to the dollar, what will happen to interest rates in the United States? Explain your answer.
9. Many people believe that the U.S. saving rate is too low. Suppose all private citizens save at a higher rate. Show what happens to investment in this case, using the saving and investment diagram, where the S/Y^* curve shifts. Now show what happens to investment in the same situation using the spending share diagrams.
10. Suppose that the government imposes a consumption tax to discourage consumption and increase saving. Suppose that the impact of the consumption tax is a leftward shift in the C/Y^* line over time. Describe graphically how this affects each of the shares of GDP, using a saving and investment diagram. How would your answer change if the government used the tax money to increase its spending?

Chapter 8

Unemployment and Employment

In early 2007, Jennifer, a 23-year-old college senior, began her final semester of college with a mixture of anticipation and worry. She was excited that in a few short months, she would obtain her degree, (hopefully) move to a new city, and begin work at a job where she could apply the knowledge she had gained from all her years of learning. She was worried because she still had not found a job, even though several of her friends had exciting job opportunities lined up and other friends were headed back to school to pursue graduate degrees. Jennifer had done some research into her prospects of finding a job after graduating from college, and she had learned that in the previous year, the unemployment rate for young women in her age group was 9.6 percent. This was substantially higher than the national unemployment rate of 4.5 percent that she had read about in the newspapers. As most college students do at some point in their lives, Jennifer began to wonder if she would ever find a job.

After thinking some more about her situation, Jennifer began to feel more optimistic. She was interested in working at a nonprofit organization, and many of those organizations had not yet started screening résumés and interviewing applicants. Furthermore, some more research had shown Jennifer that the unemployment rate for college graduates like herself was only 2 percent, much lower than even the national average. Jennifer also realized that she was much better off than her roommate, Anabel, who was an international student from Spain. Anabel had told Jennifer that the overall unemployment rate in Spain was 8.5 percent, and for young female workers it was 20 percent. Jennifer wondered how deep a recession Spain must be in to have unemployment rates that were twice as large as those in the United States. She was surprised when Anabel informed her that the Spanish economy, like the U.S. economy, was doing very well and that an unemployment rate of 8.5 percent in Spain was considered to be low by historical standards.

Unemployment is the macroeconomic variable that affects people most personally. When the economy is booming and unemployment is low, it is easier for individuals to find jobs that are satisfying to them and that also pay well. In contrast, when the economy is in recession and unemployment is high, jobs are harder to find, and people will settle for jobs that do not closely match their skills and don't pay very much money. However, as Jennifer's story illustrates, unemployment rates can, and do, vary among groups of individuals of different gender, age, race, and education. They also vary dramatically across countries, even to the extent that economies that are in recession may have lower unemployment rates than economies that are booming.

Unemployment has painful economic consequences. For those who experience it, there are the obvious hardships of income loss, loss of self-esteem, and an increasing toll on family life. Young people who live in a world of persistent unemployment will fail to acquire job skills that will help them become productive citizens in the future. Beyond these individual and family hardships, there are macroeconomic consequences of unemployment as well. When more workers are unemployed, the production of goods and services is less than it would be if more of those workers were employed. In other words, the economy is underutilizing its productive resources.

It is essential for aspiring macroeconomists to learn more about unemployment and how to reduce it. This chapter will examine the nature and causes of unemployment and teach you how to use a simple model that will help you become more comfortable answering questions such as: Why do unemployment rates differ so much among countries? Is it because of differences in education levels? Is it because of differences in attitudes toward work? Or is it because of differences in the economic policies implemented by the different countries' governments?

UNEMPLOYMENT AND OTHER LABOR MARKET INDICATORS

In this section, we show how unemployment is defined and measured, and we discuss the various causes of unemployment.

How Is Unemployment Measured?

To understand what the data on unemployment mean, one must understand how unemployment is measured. Each month, the U.S. Census Bureau surveys a sample of about 60,000 households in the United States. This survey is called the

Current Population Survey: a monthly survey of a sample of U.S. households done by the U.S. Census Bureau; it measures employment, unemployment, the labor force, and other characteristics of the U.S. population.

unemployed person: an individual who does not have a job and is looking for work.

labor force: all those who are either employed or unemployed.

working-age population: persons over 16 years of age who are not in an institution such as a jail or a hospital.

Current Population Survey. By asking the people in the survey a number of questions, the Census Bureau determines whether each person 16 years of age or over is employed or unemployed.

Who Is Employed and Who Is Unemployed? To be counted as **unemployed,** a person must be looking for work, but not have a job. To be counted as employed, a person must have a job, either a job outside the home—as in the case of a teaching job at a high school or a welding job at a factory—or a *paid* job inside the home—as in the case of a freelance editor or a telemarketer who works for pay at home. A person who has an *unpaid* job at home—for example, caring for children or working on the house—is not counted as employed.

The **labor force** consists of all people 16 years of age and over who are either employed or unemployed. If a person is not counted as either unemployed or employed, then that person is not in the labor force. For example, a person who is working at home without pay and who is not looking for a paid job is considered not in the labor force.

Figure 1 illustrates the definitions of employment, unemployment, and the labor force. Using December 2006 as an example, it shows that out of a **working-age population** of 230.0 million, 145.9 million were employed and 6.8 million were unemployed. The remaining 77.3 million were of working age but were not in the labor force.

The Labor Force and Discouraged Workers. It is difficult to judge who should be counted as being in the labor force and who should not be counted. For example, consider two retired people. One decided to retire at age 65 and is now enjoying retirement in Florida. The other was laid off from a job at age 55 and, after looking for a job for two years, got discouraged and stopped looking, feeling forced into retirement. You may feel that the second person, but not the first, should be counted as unemployed. However, according to the official statistics, neither is unemployed; they are not in the labor force because they are not looking for work. In general, workers, such as the second retired worker, who have left the labor force after not being able to find a job are called *discouraged workers.*

Defining and measuring the labor force is the most difficult part of measuring the amount of unemployment. When a change was made in the way the questions in the Current Population Survey were phrased, it revealed that many women who were working at home without pay were actually looking for a paid job; as a result of the change in the question, these women are now counted as unemployed rather than as out of the labor force.

Part-Time Work. A person is counted as employed in the Current Population Survey if he or she has worked at all during the week of the survey. Thus, part-time workers are counted as employed. The official definition of a *part-time worker* is one who works between 1 and 34 hours per week. About 17 percent of U.S. workers are employed part-time.

There is a big difference between the percentage of men who work part-time and the percentage of women who work part-time. About 25 percent of women work part-time, while only about 11 percent of men do so. Women give personal choice rather than unavailability of full-time jobs as a reason for part-time work more frequently than men do. About a third of employed women who have children under 3 work part time.

Because of part-time work, the average number of hours of work per worker each week is about 34 hours, less than the typical 40 hours a week.

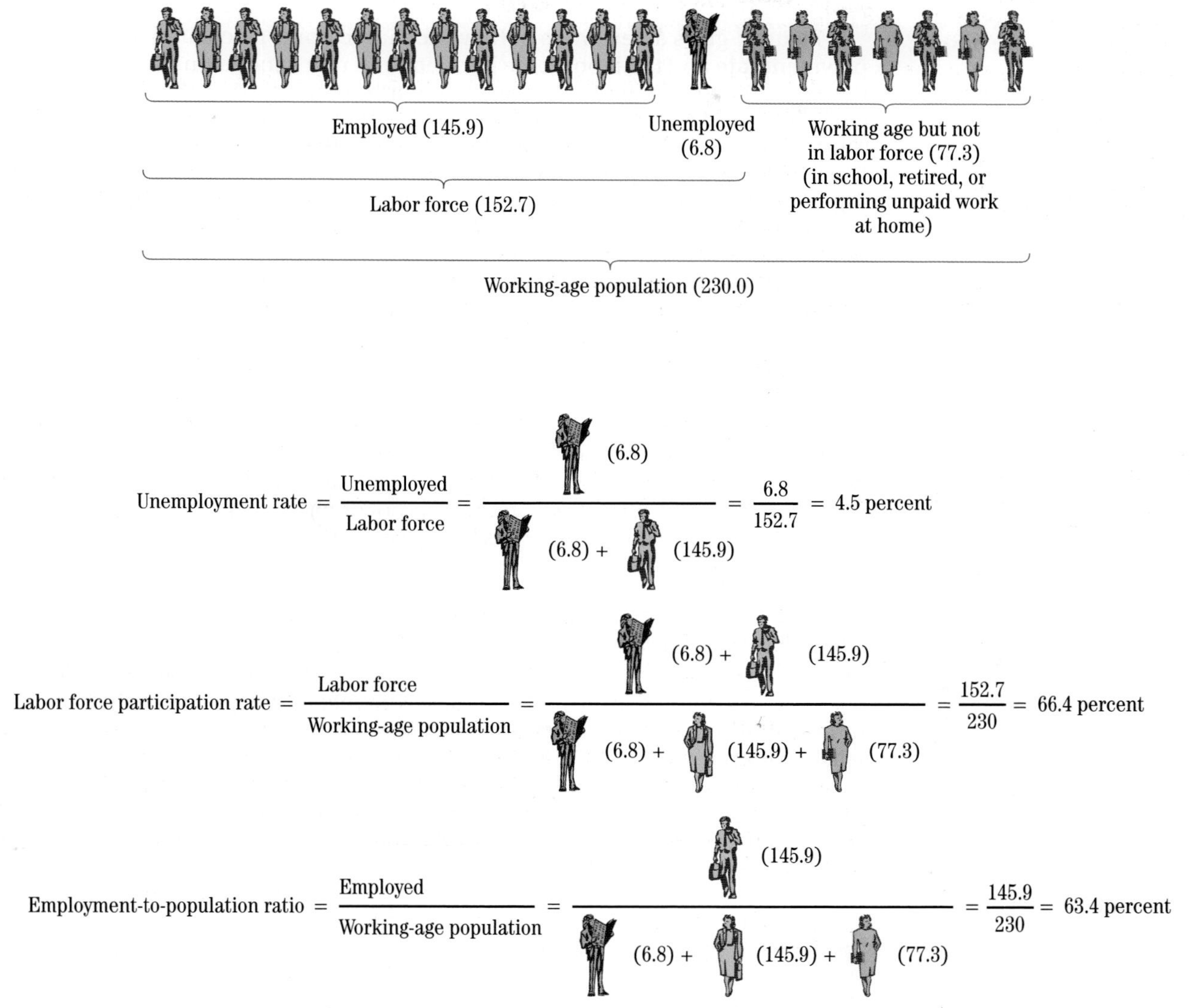

FIGURE 1
How to Find Labor Market Indicators

As shown at the top of this diagram, the working-age (16 years of age and over) population is divided into three groups: employed, unemployed, and not in the labor force. Three key labor market indicators are then computed from these categories. For example, the unemployment rate is the number of people unemployed divided by the number of people in the labor force. (The numbers in parentheses are in millions and are the statistics for December 2006.)

Source: Bureau of Labor Statistics.

unemployment rate: the percentage of the labor force that is unemployed. (Ch. 5)

labor force participation rate: the ratio (usually expressed as a percentage) of people in the labor force to the working-age population.

Comparing Three Key Indicators

Now let us examine the three key indicators of conditions in the labor market. These are

1. The *unemployment rate,* the percentage of the labor force that is unemployed
2. The **labor force participation rate,** the ratio of people in the labor force to the working-age population.

employment-to-population ratio: the ratio (usually expressed as a percentage) of employed workers to the working-age population.

3. The **employment-to-population ratio,** the ratio of employed workers to the working-age population

Figure 1 gives an example of how each indicator is calculated. Both the unemployment rate and the labor force participation rate depend on the labor force, and therefore they have the same measurement difficulties that the labor force does. Only the employment-to-population ratio does not depend on the labor force. The labor force participation rate and the employment-to-population ratio have both had important longer-term upward trends. For example, the employment-to-population ratio has increased in the last 30 years from about 57 percent in 1976 to about 63 percent in 2006. The rising employment-to-population ratio indicates that the U.S. economy has created a lot of jobs over the past three decades. How does one explain this?

The rising percentage of women who are employed is a major factor, as shown in Figure 2. This increase is mainly due to more women entering the labor force, a trend that has been going on since the 1950s. In 1956, about 37 percent of women were in the labor force, but now 59.5 percent of women are. Possible explanations for this trend include reduced discrimination, increased opportunities and pay for women, the favorable experience of many women working for pay during World War II, and the women's movement, which emphasized the attractiveness of paid work outside the home. In recent years, this number has not grown by very much—in fact over the decade from 1996 to 2006, there has been very little change in the labor force participation rate of women.

Aggregate Hours of Labor Input

As we have seen, some people work part-time. Others work full-time; some work overtime. For these reasons, the number of people employed is not a good measure of the labor input to production in the economy. For example, consider two bank tellers who both work half-time; one works 4 hours in the morning, and the other works 4 hours in the afternoon, both 5 days a week. Even though they are two workers, together they work only as much as one full-time bank teller. So to count the labor input of these two part-time tellers as being twice as much as the labor input of one full-time teller would be an obvious mistake. Instead of the number of employed

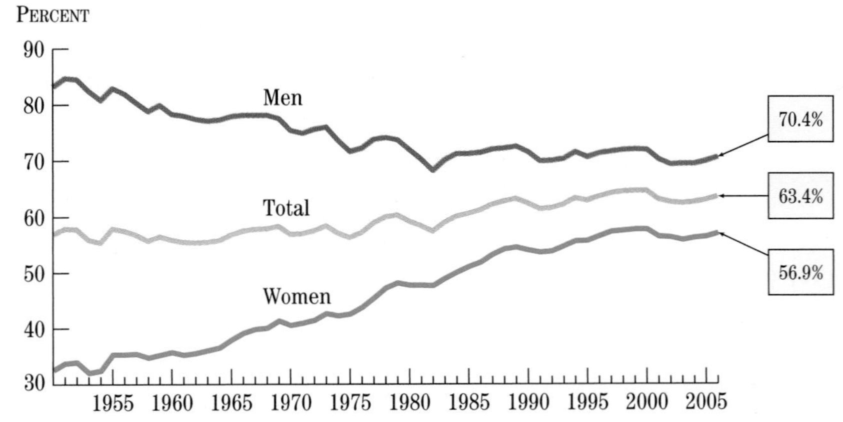

FIGURE 2
Employment-to-Population Ratio for Men, Women, and Everyone

The percentage of working-age women who are employed has increased steadily since the 1950s. The percentage of working-age men who are employed declined until the late 1970s. Since the mid-1990s both have leveled off.

Source: Bureau of Labor Statistics.

people, economists use hours worked to measure labor input. In the example of the bank tellers, the combined labor input of the two part-time tellers is the same as that of the one full-time teller: 40 hours a week.

aggregate hours: the total number of hours worked by all workers in the economy in a given period of time.

Thus, the most comprehensive measure of labor input to the production of real GDP is the total number of hours worked by all workers, or **aggregate hours.** The number of aggregate hours of labor input depends on the number of hours of work for each person and the number of people working.

The growth of aggregate labor hours in the United States is slowing down. It grew by about 2 percent per year in the two decades between 1976 and 1996, but it has increased only by about 1.25 percent a year in the last decade. The main reason for this slowdown is that the growth of the working-age population is slowing down.

Cyclical, Frictional, and Structural Unemployment

The unemployment rate fluctuates over time, sometimes fairly dramatically. Recall from Chapter 5 that the unemployment rate rises when the economy goes into a recession and falls when the economy expands. For example, as shown in Figure 3, when the economy expanded rapidly in the mid- to late 1990s, the unemployment rate was cut in half, falling from a peak of 7.8 percent in mid-1992 to a value of 3.9 percent by the end of 2000. When the U.S. economy went into recession in 2001, the unemployment rate rose back to above 6 percent. As the economy expanded again, the unemployment rate fell back down, reaching 4.5 percent by the end of 2006.

natural unemployment rate: the unemployment rate that exists when there is neither a recession nor a boom and real GDP is equal to potential GDP.

Because the unemployment rate fluctuates so much depending on whether the economy is in a recession or a boom, economists are always interested in understanding what the unemployment rate would have been in the absence of these economic fluctuations. Economists use the term **natural unemployment rate** to refer to the unemployment rate that exists when the economy is not in a recession or a boom

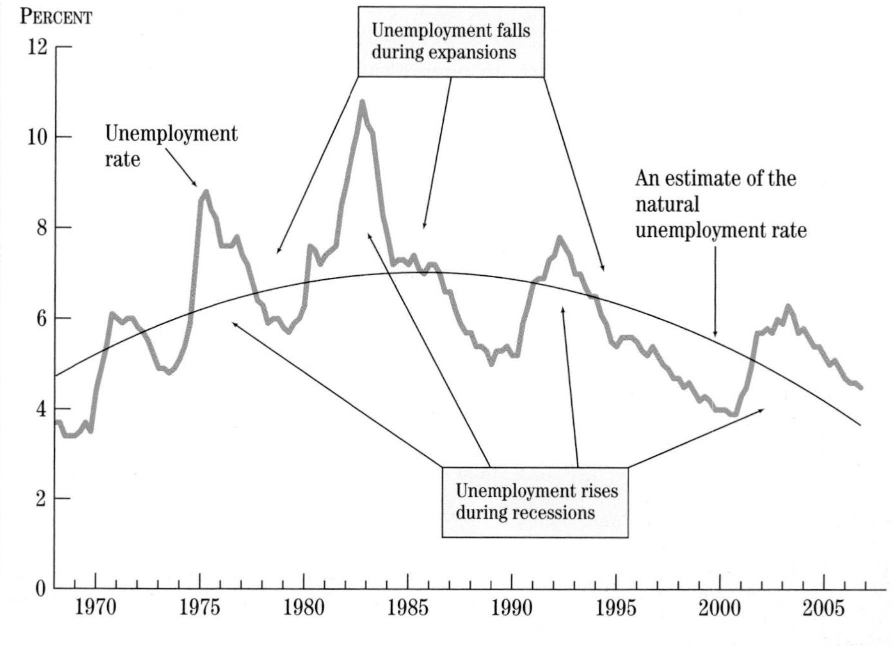

FIGURE 3
The Unemployment Rate
The unemployment rate fluctuates around the natural unemployment rate, rising during recessions and falling when the economy grows rapidly during expansions.
Sources: Bureau of Labor Statistics (unemployment rate); authors' calculation (natural rate).

cyclical unemployment: unemployment due to a recession, when the rate of unemployment is above the natural rate of unemployment.

frictional unemployment: unemployment arising from normal turnover in the labor market, such as when people change occupations or locations, or are new entrants.

structural unemployment: unemployment due to structural problems such as poor skills, longer-term changes in demand, or insufficient work incentives.

and real GDP is equal to potential GDP. The increase in unemployment above the natural rate during recessions is called **cyclical unemployment** because it is related to the short-term cyclical fluctuations in the economy. For example, the increase in the unemployment rate from 2001 to 2002 was cyclical. The natural unemployment rate is caused by a combination of **frictional unemployment** and **structural unemployment.** Frictional unemployment occurs when new workers enter the labor force and must look for work, or when workers change jobs for one reason or another and need some time to find another job. Most frictional unemployment is short-lived. In contrast, some workers are unemployed for a long time, six months or more; they may have trouble finding work because they have insufficient skills or because their skills are no longer in demand as a result of a technological change or a shift in people's tastes toward new products. Such unemployment is called structural unemployment. The amount of frictional unemployment and structural unemployment in the economy is not constant, so the natural unemployment rate changes over time. But such changes are gradual and are not related to short-term economic fluctuations.

An estimate of the natural unemployment rate is shown in Figure 3. The natural rate of unemployment increased in the 1970s. One possible reason for the increase was the influx of young baby-boom workers into the labor force in the 1970s. Young people tend to have higher unemployment rates than older people. The natural unemployment rate declined in the 1990s as the labor force aged. It is important to remember that the natural unemployment rate is not a constant and that economists do not know its value precisely.

When economists use the term *natural unemployment rate,* they do not mean to say that this is "okay" or "just fine." They simply mean that whenever the operation of the overall macroeconomy is close to normal in the sense that real GDP is near potential GDP, the unemployment rate hovers around this natural rate. All else equal, having a low natural rate of unemployment is preferable because it means that in normal times, fewer workers are looking for work but unable to find it.

REVIEW

- Unemployment and employment in the United States are measured by the Current Population Survey.
- An unemployed individual is someone who does not have a job but is looking for work. An employed individual is someone who has a paid job. The labor force consists of all those who are either employed or unemployed.
- Because not all workers work full-time, economists consider the aggregate number of hours worked to be the most comprehensive measure of labor input.
- The unemployment rate is the percentage of the labor force that is unemployed. The unemployment rate in the United States fluctuates cyclically, rising in times of recession and falling in times of expansion.
- The unemployment rate in the absence of cyclical increases or decreases is called the natural rate of unemployment. The natural rate of unemployment is caused by a combination of frictional unemployment (people changing jobs or occupations) and structural unemployment (unemployment caused by poor skills or changes in the types of goods produced in the economy).
- Two other important measures are the labor force participation rate (what fraction of the working-age population is in the labor force) and the employment-to-population ratio (what fraction of the working-age population has a job). Both ratios rose in the period from the 1960s to the 1990s because of more women entering the labor force.

ECONOMICS IN THE NEWS

Unemployment Each Month

Each month—usually on the first Friday—the U.S. Department of Labor releases information about employment and unemployment in the previous month. This summary is excerpted from the news release issued by the Bureau of Labor Statistics on January 5, 2007. You should be able to find the terms discussed in this article in the text.

Note that the unemployment rate for December of 2006 was reported to be 4.5 percent. How does this compare with the unemployment rate in 1996 or in 1986? (See Figure 3.)

Employment Situation Summary: December 2006

http://www.bls.gov/cps/

Nonfarm employment increased by 167,000 in December, and the unemployment rate was unchanged at 4.5 percent, the Bureau of Labor Statistics of the U.S. Department of Labor reported today. Job gains occurred in several service-providing industries, including professional and business services, health care, and food services. Average hourly earnings rose by 8 cents, or 0.5 percent, in December.

Unemployment (Household Survey Data)

The number of unemployed persons (6.8 million) was about unchanged in December, and the unemployment rate held at 4.5 percent. Over the year, these measures declined from 7.3 million and 4.9 percent, respectively. In December, unemployment rates for the major worker groups—adult men (4.0 percent), adult women (3.9 percent), teenagers (15.2 percent), whites (4.0 percent), blacks (8.4 percent), and Hispanics (4.9 percent)—showed little or no change. The unemployment rate for Asians was 2.4 percent not seasonally adjusted.

Total Employment and the Labor Force (Household Survey Data)

In December, both total employment, at 145.9 million, and the employment-population ratio, at 63.4 percent, were little changed. Over the year, total employment grew by 3.1 million and the employment-population ratio rose by 0.6 percentage points. The civilian labor force edged up in December to 152.8 million. The labor force participation rate, at 66.4 percent, was little changed over the month, but the rate was 0.4 percentage point higher than a year earlier.

Persons Not in the Labor Force (Household Survey Data)

About 1.3 million persons (not seasonally adjusted) were marginally attached to the labor force in December, 337,000 fewer than a year earlier. These individuals wanted and were available for work and had looked for a job sometime in the prior 12 months. They were not counted as unemployed because they had not searched for work in the 4 weeks preceding the survey. Among the marginally attached, there were 274,000 discouraged workers in December, down from 451,000 a year earlier. Discouraged workers were not currently looking for work specifically because they believed no jobs were available for them. The other 978,000 persons marginally attached to the labor force in December had not searched for work in the 4 weeks preceding the survey for reasons such as school attendance or family responsibilities.

THE NATURE OF UNEMPLOYMENT

Having examined the aggregate data, let us now look at the circumstances of people who are unemployed. There are many reasons for people to become unemployed, and people's experiences with unemployment vary widely.

Reasons People Are Unemployed

We can divide up the many reasons people become unemployed into four broad categories. People are unemployed because they have either lost their previous job (*job losers*), quit their previous job (*job leavers*), entered the labor force to look for work for the first time (*new entrants*), or re-entered the labor force after being out of it for a while (*re-entrants*). Figure 4 shows how the 4.5 percent unemployment rate in December 2006 was divided into these four categories.

Job Losers. Among the people who lost their jobs in a typical recent year was a vice president of a large bank in Chicago. When the vice president's financial services marketing department was eliminated, she lost her job. After three months of unemployment, which she spent searching for work and waiting for responses to her letters and telephone calls, the former vice president took a freelance job, using her expertise to advise clients on financial planning matters. Within a year, she was making three times her former salary.

The vice president's unemployment experience, although surely trying for her at the time, had a happy ending. In fact, you might say that the labor market worked pretty well. At least judging by her salary, she is more productive in her new job. Although one job was destroyed, another one—a better one, in this case—was created.

This transition from one job to another is part of the dynamism of any free market economy. The economist Joseph Schumpeter called this dynamism *creative destruction*, referring to the loss of whole business firms as well as jobs when new ideas and techniques replace the old. Creative destruction means that something better is created as something else is destroyed. In this case, a better job was created when one job was destroyed. The labor market in the United States is extremely fluid, with a large number of jobs being created and destroyed every month. In December of 2006 alone, 4.9 million workers found jobs while 4.5 million workers lost their jobs.

In an economy with growing employment, more jobs are created than are destroyed. In times of recession, however, when employment is likely to fall, more jobs are destroyed than are created. So the bank manager was "lucky" to have lost her job during a period when finding a comparable job was relatively easy, but many people who lose their jobs are not as "lucky" as the woman in our story.

On average, about half of all unemployed workers are unemployed because they lost their

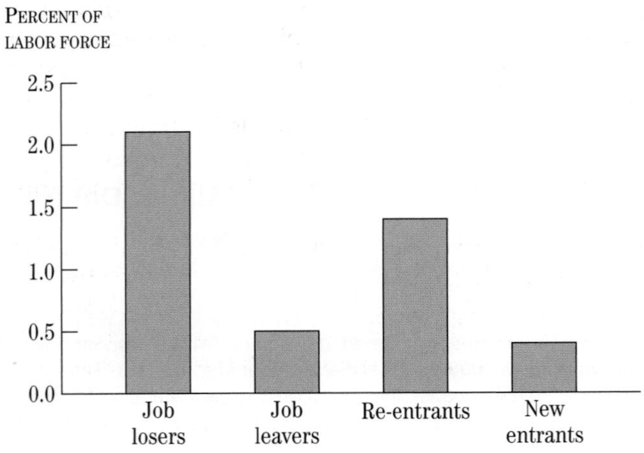

FIGURE 4
Job Losers, Job Leavers, New Entrants, and Re-entrants (December 2006)
A significant part of the unemployment rate consists of people who lost their jobs. The rest consists of people who left their jobs to look for another job or who have just entered or re-entered the labor force.
Source: Bureau of Labor Statistics.

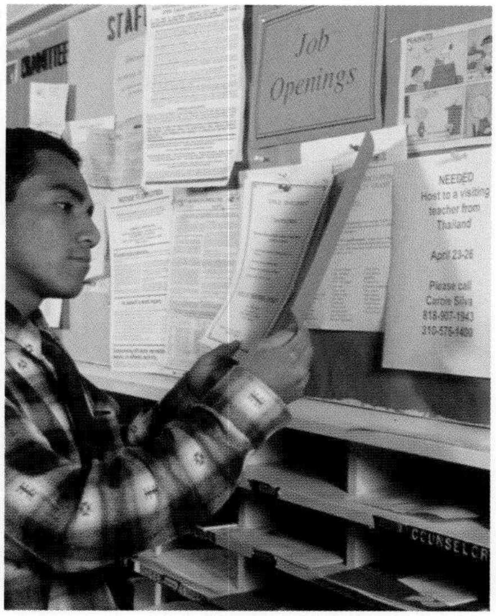

Reasons People Are Unemployed
People are unemployed for different reasons: Some lost their job and are looking for another job (left), others quit their previous job and are still looking for a new job (middle), and still others just entered or re-entered the labor force and are unemployed while looking for work (right).

jobs for one reason or another. People may lose their jobs even when the economy is not in a recession. The economy is always in a state of flux, with some firms going out of business or shrinking and other firms starting up or expanding. Tastes change, new discoveries are made, and competition improves productivity and changes the relative fortunes of firms and workers.

Among the unemployed in recent years were middle-aged computer programmers let go by information-technology firms after several years of employment, flight attendants and pilots laid off by airlines that were cutting back on service because of financial difficulties, and workers in steel plants and auto plants who were no longer needed because of increased use of machinery in the production process. Finding a comparable job was difficult for such workers because most other firms that they could have worked at either were also in financial difficulties and therefore laying off workers instead of hiring them, or were undergoing the same type of structural changes that led to the workers being laid off from their own firms.

The loss of a job not only has disastrous effects on income, but can also have psychological effects. It may mean that a worker's children cannot go to college, or that the worker must sell his or her house. Unemployment compensation provides some relief—perhaps about $200 a week until it runs out. In many cases, though, this is well below what these workers were earning. Until they find a new job, they are obviously part of the millions of unemployed. Some may wait until a comparable job comes along; others may accept a lower-paying job. For example, a laid-off software programmer may take a job as a community college instructor for a much lower salary.

job vacancies: positions that firms are trying to fill, but for which they have yet to find suitable workers.

At the same time that unemployed workers are looking for jobs, there are many firms that have jobs that have not been filled, these are called **job vacancies.** Job vacancies and unemployment exist simultaneously. You might think that these two should not coexist because the unemployed workers should be able to take the unfilled jobs, but unfortunately, that is not always possible. Many job vacancies require different skills from those of unemployed workers, are located in another part of the country, or offer lower wages than these workers' former salaries.

Job Leavers. On average, American workers change jobs every three or four years. Many of these job changes occur when people are young: Young workers are finding out what they are good at or what they enjoy or are rapidly accumulating skills that give them greater opportunities. A small part of unemployment—less than one-fourth—consists of people who quit their previous job to look for another job. While they are looking for work, they are counted as unemployed. There is very little increase in unemployment as a result of quits during recessions. Why? In a recession, when unemployment is high, fewer workers quit their jobs because they fear being unemployed for a long period of time.

New Entrants and Re-entrants. Figure 4 also shows that a large number of the unemployed workers have just entered the work force. If Jennifer, the college student we talked about at the beginning of this chapter, does not have a job lined up before she graduates, then she would be counted as being an unemployed worker for the period of time while she is looking for work. In fact, there is a huge increase in unemployment each June as millions of students enter the labor force for the first time. This is called *seasonal unemployment* because it occurs each graduation "season." In contrast, unemployment is relatively low around the holiday season, when many businesses hire extra employees. Government statisticians smooth out this seasonal unemployment to help them see other trends in unemployment, so newspaper reports on the unemployment rate rarely mention this phenomenon.

Some unemployed workers are re-entering the labor force. For example, a young person may decide to go back to school to improve her skills and then re-enter the labor force afterward. Others might choose to drop out of the labor force for several years to take care of small children at home—a job that is not counted in the unemployment statistics.

Some new entrants and some re-entrants into the labor force find it very difficult to get a job and therefore remain unemployed for long periods of time. In fact, although the hardships of people who lose their jobs are severe, the hardships for many young people, especially for those who dropped out of high school and who seem to be endlessly looking for work, are also severe. Similarly, re-entrants who have been away from the labor market for a long time, perhaps for as long as a couple of decades to raise children, will not find it easy to find work in a labor market that is very different from the one they were last employed in.

The Duration of Unemployment

The hardships associated with unemployment depend on its duration. Figure 5 shows how the unemployment rate divides up according to how long the unemployed workers have been unemployed. A significant fraction of unemployment is very short term. A market economy with millions of people exercising free choice could not possibly function without some very short-term unemployment as people changed jobs or looked for new opportunities.

About one-sixth of unemployed workers are unemployed for more than six months—the truly long-term unemployed. Although the number of short-term unemployed does not vary much over the business cycle, the number of long-term unemployed increases dramatically in recessions.

Unemployment for Different Groups

Regardless of how one interprets the numbers, certain groups of workers experience very long spells of unemployment and suffer great hardships as a result of the

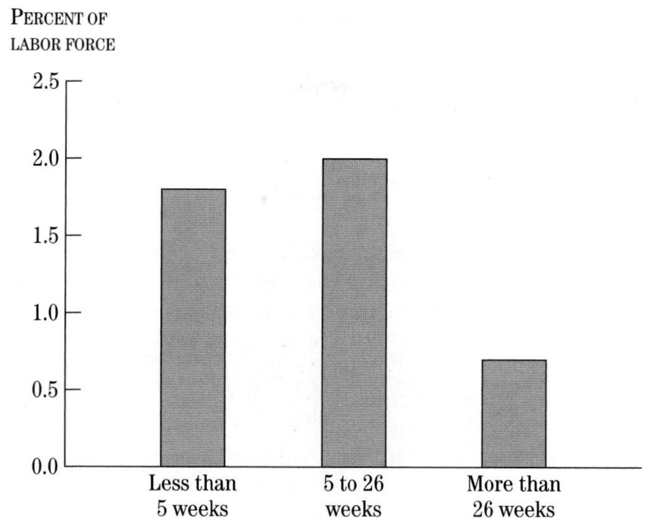

FIGURE 5
Unemployment by Duration (December 2006)
The overall unemployment rate was 4.5 percent in December 2006. About 16 percent of this unemployment was long term—more than 26 weeks.
Source: Bureau of Labor Statistics: Current Employment Survey.

difficulty they have in finding work. Table 1 shows the unemployment rates for several different demographic groups in the United States in three time periods: 1994 and 2004, both periods when the economy had just emerged from recession, and 1999, when the economy was much stronger.

Unemployment is lowest for adult men and women. But unemployment is very high for teenagers. To some extent this is due to more frequent job changes and the period of time required to find work after graduating from school. But many teenagers who are looking for work have dropped out of school and therefore are unskilled and have little or no experience. Their unemployment rates are extremely

TABLE 1
Unemployment Rates for Different Demographic Groups (percent of labor force for each group)

	1994	1999	2004
All persons	5.5	4.0	5.4
All females	5.5	4.1	5.2
All males	5.5	4.0	5.6
All whites	4.8	3.5	4.6
All blacks	9.9	7.8	10.8
All Hispanics	9.3	5.8	6.6
All females, 20 years and older	4.8	3.6	4.7
All males, 20 years and older	4.7	3.3	4.9
All teens, 16–19	17.0	13.4	17.6

Source: Bureau of Labor Statistics.

high, especially those for young minorities. Thus, even when there is good news about the overall unemployment rate, the news may remain bleak for those with low skills and little experience. The overall unemployment rate does not capture the long-term hardships experienced by certain groups.

R E V I E W

- People become unemployed when they lose their job, quit their job, or decide to enter or re-enter the labor force to look for a job.
- Being a new entrant is the least likely reason for a person to be unemployed. Losing a job and looking for work after some time out of the labor force are more likely reasons to be unemployed.
- In a large, dynamic economy like that of the United States, millions of jobs are created and lost during each month. In times of recession, more jobs are lost than are created.
- Many unemployed people are able to find a job fairly quickly. On average, only about one-sixth of unemployed people have been unemployed for six months or more. These workers often lack appropriate skills or were employed in industries that are undergoing fundamental structural changes.
- At the same time that unemployed workers are looking for jobs, firms with job vacancies are looking for workers. Because of skill differences and geographical mismatches, it is not easy to fill vacant jobs with unemployed workers.
- Unemployment rates vary across different groups. Teenagers and minorities in the United States have very high unemployment rates, even in boom years, and are often the first to suffer in times of recession.

MODELING THE LABOR MARKET

Thus far in this chapter, we have introduced key labor market variables, like the unemployment rate and the labor force participation rate; looked at data on both the current values and past trends of these variables, and discussed why people become (and stay) unemployed. In this section, we change our focus from data and definitions to theory, and discuss how to construct a model of the labor market. If we are able to come up with a model that provides a good explanation of the labor market trends we discussed earlier, then we can use this model to identify policy changes, as well as other economic changes, that can help reduce the rate of unemployment in the economy. Lowering the rate of unemployment, especially the natural rate of unemployment, will give individuals the opportunity to earn a living and allow a country to make full use of its labor resources.

Labor Demand and Labor Supply

We begin with the basic supply and demand framework developed in Chapter 3. Figure 6 shows a labor demand curve and a labor supply curve. On the vertical axis is the price of labor (wage), and on the horizontal axis is the quantity of labor

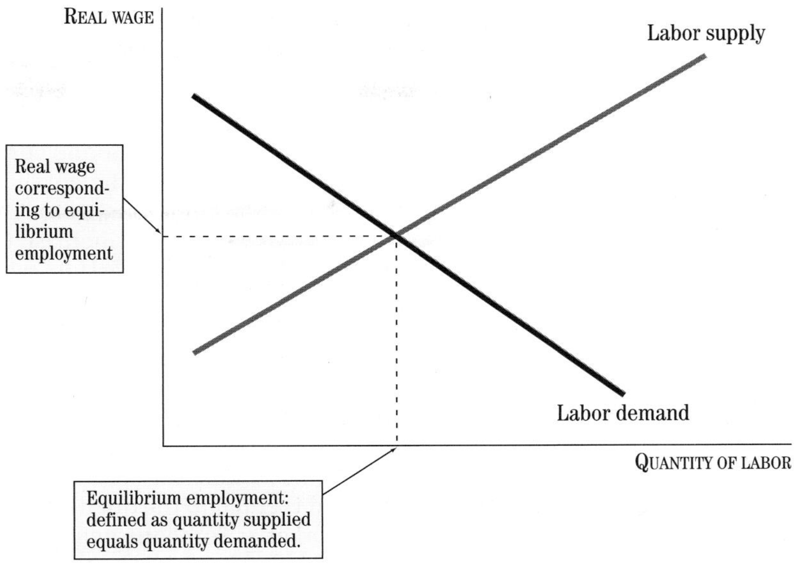

FIGURE 6
Labor Supply, Labor Demand, and Equilibrium Employment
The intersection of the labor supply curve and the labor demand curve determines equilibrium employment and the real wage.

labor demand curve: a downward-sloping relationship showing the quantity of labor firms are willing to hire at each wage.

labor supply curve: upward sloping relationship showing the quantity of labor workers are willing to supply at each wage.

real wage: the wage or price of labor adjusted for inflation; in contrast, the nominal wage has not been adjusted for inflation.

supplied or demanded. In a labor market, the **labor demand curve** describes the behavior of firms, indicating how much labor they would demand at a given wage. The **labor supply curve** describes the behavior of workers, showing how much labor they would supply at a given wage. The *wage*, usually measured in dollars per hour of work, is the price of labor. To explain employment in the whole economy, it is best to think of the wage relative to the average price of goods. In other words, the wage on the vertical axis is the **real wage,** which we define as

$$\text{Real wage} = \frac{\text{wage}}{\text{price level}}$$

Firms consider the wages they must pay their workers in comparison with the price of the products they sell. The workers consider the wage in comparison with the price of the goods they buy. Thus, in the whole economy, it is the real wage that affects the quantity of labor supplied and demanded.

The labor demand curve slopes downward because a lower real wage implies that the wage that the firm has to pay to hire a worker is falling relative to the price of the goods that the firm is selling. This gives firms an incentive to hire more workers and pay existing workers to work more hours—the now familiar result that the quantity demanded of labor rises as the price of labor (the real wage) falls. The labor supply curve slopes upward, because a higher real wage implies that the wage that the worker receives is rising compared to the price of the goods that the worker buys. This gives people more incentive to work and gives those who are working an incentive to work more hours—another familiar result that the quantity supplied of labor rises as the price of labor (the real wage) rises.

As in any market, we would predict that the equilibrium quantity (hours of work) and the equilibrium price (the real wage) should be at the intersection of the labor demand curve and the labor supply curve, as shown in Figure 6.

Explaining Labor Market Trends

Let's see how well we can do using this basic supply and demand framework to analyze labor market behavior. Suppose the economy enters a boom period where firms are facing an increasing demand from consumers for the goods and services they produce. Firms will then be eager to hire more workers to produce the goods and services that their consumers are clamoring for, resulting in an increase in the demand for labor. As the labor demand curve shifts to the right, as shown in Figure 7, both the equilibrium price and the equilibrium quantity of labor will rise. In other words, during an economic expansion, the model predicts that there will be an increase in the real wage and an increase in employment. Suppose instead that the economy had tumbled into a recession, where firms were cutting back on their production and did not need to hire as many workers. Then the demand for labor would shift to the left, and there would be a decrease in the real wage and in employment.

The prediction of the model that wages and employment should rise in expansions and fall in recessions seems intuitive. However, the simple model as depicted in Figure 7 has a glaring weakness. Notice that the economy is at the intersection of the supply curve and the demand curve, no matter whether it is in an expansion or a recession. In other words, the real wage will always adjust so that the quantity of labor demanded is equal to the quantity of labor supplied. Given the definition of an unemployed worker as someone who is looking for work but is unable to find a job, the model implies that unemployment is always zero, no matter what state the economy is in! The simple model, which predicts that the economy will be at the intersection of the supply and demand curves, is inconsistent with the facts. We need to modify the model before we can use it for analysis.

Why Is the Unemployment Rate Always Greater Than Zero?

Economists have developed two different explanations that adapt the standard labor supply and demand analysis to account for unemployment. Though quite different, the explanations are complementary. In fact, it is essential for us to use both simulta-

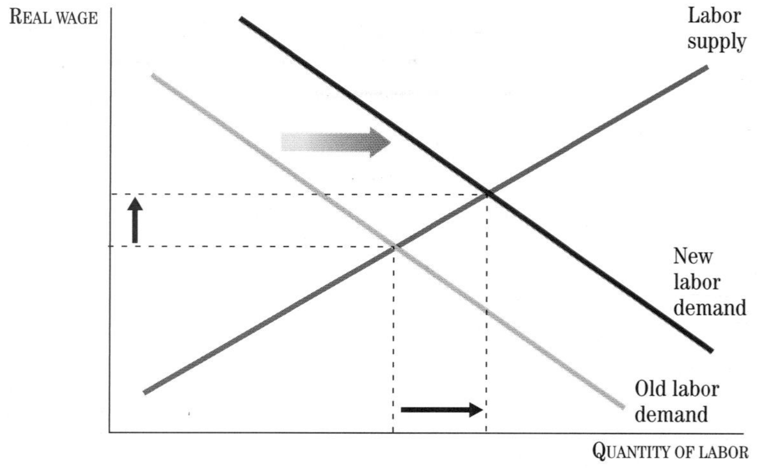

FIGURE 7
Modeling the Labor Market During an Economic Expansion
When the economy enters an expansion period, firms produce more output and thus need more workers. The demand for labor increases, shifting the demand curve to the right. Equilibrium real wages and equilibrium employment rise.

neously if we are to understand unemployment. We will refer to the two explanations as **job rationing** and **job search.**

job rationing: a reason for unemployment in which the quantity of labor supplied is greater than the quantity demanded because the real wage is too high.

job search: a reason for unemployment in which uncertainty in the labor market and workers' limited information requires people to spend time searching for a job.

Job Rationing. The job-rationing story has two parts. One is an assumption that *the wage is higher than what would equate the quantity of labor supplied with the quantity of labor demanded.* There are several reasons why this might be the case, but first consider the consequences for the labor supply and demand diagram. Figure 8 shows the same labor supply and demand curves as Figure 6. However, in Figure 8, the wage is higher than the wage that would equate the quantity of labor supplied with the quantity of labor demanded. At this wage, the number of workers demanded by firms is smaller than the number of workers willing to supply their labor.

The other part of the job-rationing story tells us how to determine the number of workers who are unemployed. This part of the story assumes that the number of workers employed equals the quantity of labor demanded by business firms. When the wage is too high, firms hire a smaller number of workers, and workers supply whatever the firms demand. Figure 8 shows the resulting amount of employment at the given wage as point *A* on the labor demand curve. With employment equal to the number of workers demanded, we see that the number of workers willing to supply their labor is greater than the number of workers employed; the excess supply therefore results in unemployment. In the diagram, the amount of unemployment is measured in the horizontal direction.

This is a situation in which workers would be willing to take a job at the wage that firms are paying, but there are not enough job offers at that wage. In effect, the available jobs are rationed—for example, by a first-come-first-served rule or by seniority. It is as if when enough workers have been hired, the firms close their hiring offices, and the remaining workers stay unemployed. If the wage were lower, then the firms would hire more workers, but the wage is not lower.

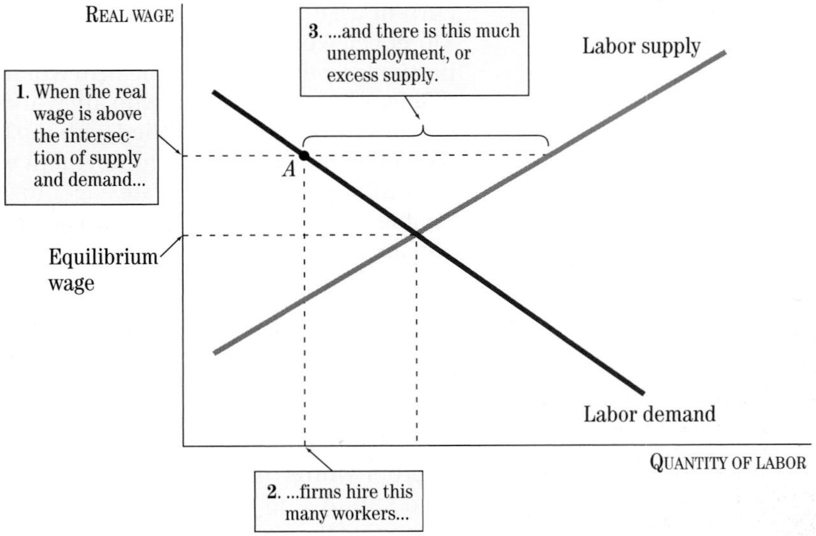

FIGURE 8
Excess Supply of Labor and Unemployment
The supply and demand curves are exactly as in Figure 6, except that the horizontal axis is interpreted as employment here. However, the real wage is too high to bring the quantity supplied into equality with the quantity demanded. The number of workers employed is given by point *A* on the demand curve, where the real wage is above the equilibrium wage. At this higher real wage, the quantity supplied is greater than the quantity demanded—a situation that we can think of as unemployment.

In most markets, a situation of excess supply brings about a reduction in the price—in this case, the wage. Thus, if this explanation of unemployment is to work in practice, there has to be a force at work that prevents the wage from falling. If the theory is to be helpful in explaining unemployment, then the force has to be permanently at work, not just in a recession. Why doesn't the wage fall when there is an excess supply of workers?

There are three explanations why the wage might always be too high to bring the quantity of labor demanded into balance with the quantity of labor supplied.

minimum wage: a wage per hour below which it is illegal to pay workers. (Ch. 4)

1. *Minimum wages.* Most countries have a legal *minimum wage*, or lowest possible wage, that employers can pay their employees. A minimum wage can cause unemployment to be higher than it otherwise would be, as shown on the diagram in Figure 8: Employers would move down and to the right along their labor demand curve and hire more workers if the wage were lower.

   One of the reasons teenage unemployment is high (as shown in Table 1) may be related to the minimum wage. Because many teenagers are unskilled, the wage that firms would be willing to pay them is low. A minimum wage, therefore, may price them out of the market and cause them to be unemployed.

insider: a person who already works for a firm and has some influence over wage and hiring policy.

outsider: someone who is not working for a particular firm, making it difficult for him or her to get a job with that firm even though he or she is willing to work for a lower wage.

2. *Insiders versus outsiders.* Sometimes groups of workers—**insiders,** who have jobs—can prevent the wage from declining. If these workers have developed skills that are unique to the job, or if there is legislation preventing their being fired without significant legal costs, then they have some power to keep wages up. Labor unions may help them keep the wage higher than it would otherwise be. One consequence of the higher wage is to prevent the firm from hiring unemployed workers—the **outsiders**—who would be willing to work at a lower wage. This is a common explanation for the very high unemployment in Europe, and the theory has been developed and applied to Europe by the Swedish economist Assar Lindbeck and the British economist Dennis Snower.

efficiency wage: a wage higher than that which would equate quantity supplied and quantity demanded, set by employers in order to increase worker efficiency—for example, by decreasing shirking by workers.

3. *Efficiency wages.* Firms may choose to pay workers an **efficiency wage**—an extra amount to encourage them to be more efficient. There are many reasons why workers' efficiency or productivity might increase with the wage. Turnover will be lower with a higher wage because workers will have less reason to look for another job: They are unlikely to find a position paying more than their current wage. Lower turnover means lower training costs for employers. Moreover, workers might not shirk as much with a higher wage. This is particularly important to the firm when jobs are difficult to monitor. With efficiency wages, workers who are working are paid more than the wage that equates the quantity supplied with the quantity demanded. When workers are paid efficiency wages, unemployment will be greater than zero. There are unemployed workers who are eager to work at the prevailing wage, but they are unable to obtain those jobs because existing workers value the high-paying jobs and are loath to give them up.

Job Search. We now turn to the second explanation that modifies the standard labor supply and demand analysis. The labor market is constantly in a state of flux, with jobs being created and destroyed and people moving from one job to another. The demand for one type of work falls, and the demand for another type of work increases. Labor supply curves also shift.

In other words, the labor market is never truly in the state of rest conveyed by the fixed supply and demand curves in Figure 6. But how can we change the picture? Imagine labor demand and labor supply curves that constantly bounce around. The demand for labor, the supply of labor, and the wage will be different every period. Figure 6 will be in perpetual motion. Mathematicians use the adjective *stochastic* to describe this constant bouncing around. Economists apply the term *stochastic* to models of the labor market that are in perpetual motion. Rather than a fixed equilibrium of quantity and a fixed wage, there is a *stochastic equilibrium*. This stochastic equilibrium in the labor market is a way to characterize the constant job creation and job destruction that exist in the economy. People enter the work force, move from one job to another, lose their jobs, or drop out of the labor force. Wages change, inducing people to enter or re-enter the market. Figure 9 is a schematic representation of the flows of workers into and out of the labor market.

In a stochastic equilibrium, at any point in time there will be people searching for a job. Many who do so will be unemployed for some time. They lost their job, quit their job, or came back to the job market after an absence from work. One of the reasons they remain unemployed for a while is that they find it to their advantage not to accept the first job that comes along. Rather, they wait for a possibly higher-paying job. While they wait, they are unemployed.

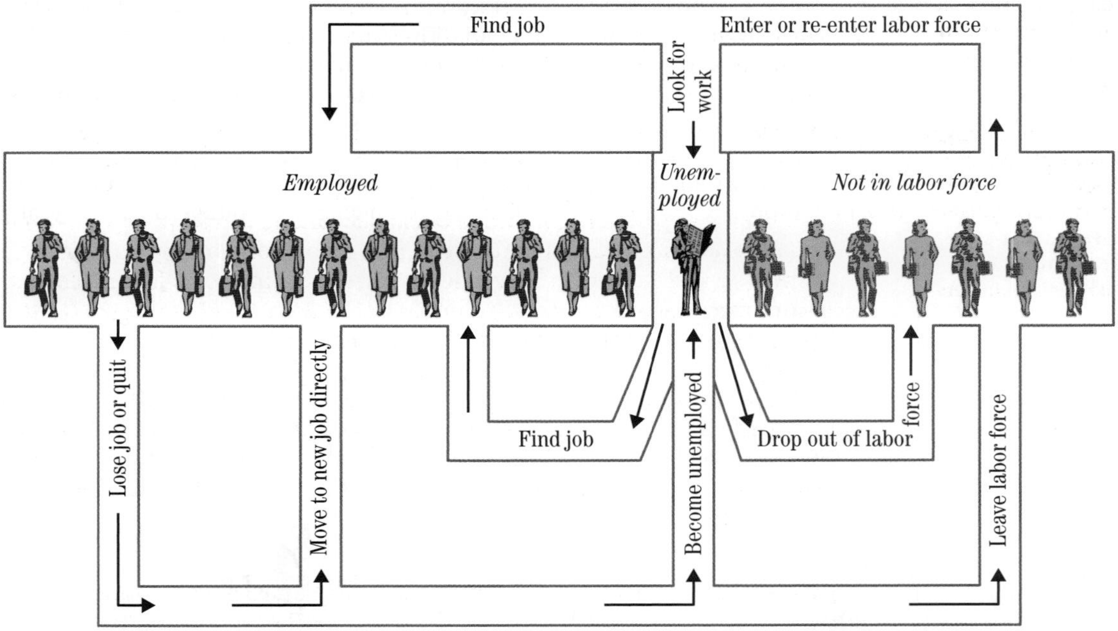

FIGURE 9
Labor Market Flows

The labor market is constantly in a state of flux, as people lose jobs, quit jobs, find jobs, and get into and out of the labor force. Most people pass through the unemployment box for a short period, but among the unemployed, some have not held jobs for a long time.

ECONOMICS IN ACTION

Unemployment Among Young People Around the World

In almost every country, the unemployment rates for teenagers and young adults are generally much higher than those for older workers. Younger workers are less skilled, are inexperienced, have a harder time finding jobs, and tend to change jobs more frequently. Across countries, however, the unemployment rates for young people vary greatly. Figure 10 shows the unemployment rate for young men and women in their early 20s in the United States and two other countries: France and Spain. Observe that unemployment rates are significantly higher in France and Spain than in the United States. In the last 20 years, the United States has had lower unemployment rates for most demographic groups than many countries, though the reverse was true in the 1960s and 1970s.

There is perhaps no more important macroeconomic problem than these high unemployment rates among young people. What factors can explain differences of this magnitude among the countries? We can begin by ruling out cyclical factors such as recessions. The differences in unemployment have persisted for many years through various ups and downs in the overall economy. Hence, the differences must reflect differences in the natural unemployment rate.

Now, let's see whether the supply and demand model, augmented by job rationing and job search, can explain the unemployment differences in Figure 10. According to the model, there are several possible explanations.

DIFFERENCES IN UNEMPLOYMENT COMPENSATION FOR YOUNG ADULTS

The story of job search tells us that a policy of more generous government compensation of unemployed workers leads to higher unemployment rates because unemployed workers can spend more time searching.

In fact, unemployment compensation for young adults is much greater in Spain than it is in the United States—amounting to only 10 percent of the average wage in the United States and as much as 40 percent in Australia and Spain. (Comparable data for France are not available.) Thus, this explanation of unemployment from job search theory appears to fit the facts.

DIFFERENCES IN LIFESTYLES

Suppose that for cultural or religious reasons it is more acceptable in some countries than in others for young adults to live with their parents. Since their basic needs for food and shelter are met, unemployed young people in these countries might have less incentive to take any available job. Therefore, unemployment rates for young adults would tend to be higher.

Figure 11 shows the percentage of young adults living with their parents in the four countries in our case study. Observe from the graph that there is a strong correlation between this percentage and unemployment rates. Spain, which has the highest percentage of 20–24-year-olds living

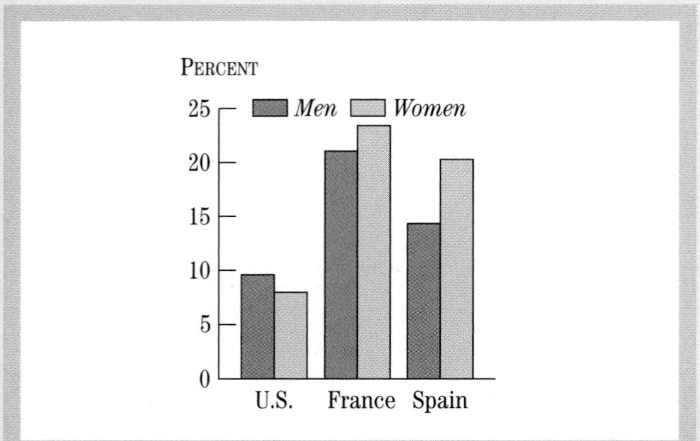

FIGURE 10
Unemployment Rates for Young Adults (ages 20–24)
Large, persistent differences are seen among different countries.

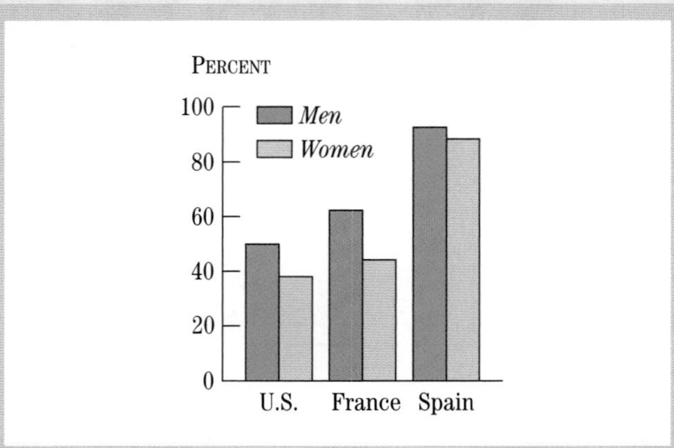

FIGURE 11
Percentage of 20–24-year-olds Still Living with Parents
Observe the close similarity with the unemployment rates for these countries in Figure 10.

with their parents, has some of the highest unemployment rates in the case study. The United States is at the opposite end of the scale: lower unemployment and a lower percentage of young adults living at home. The job-search theory again appears to be consistent with the data, but we need to worry about a reverse effect: It is possible that more young people live with their parents *because* they are unemployed.

DIFFERENCES IN THE MINIMUM WAGE

The supply and demand model predicts that higher minimum-wage laws will raise unemployment for younger people with low skills whose market wage is below the minimum. Minimum wages do differ across countries. Do they explain part of the differences in the unemployment rates for young people?

Figure 12 shows the minimum wage as a percentage of the average wage in each of the four countries in our case study. The United States has a lower minimum wage than France, which suggests that this might be a reason for the lower unemployment rate in the United States.

Note that Spain also has a low minimum wage, even though it has among the highest unemployment rates of the four countries. What could cause this apparent contradiction to the theory? One possibility is that the tradition of young adults living at home is so strong in Spain that it offsets the effect of the low minimum wage. In fact, lifestyle combined with the low minimum wage is a reasonable explanation for Spain's unemployment rates.

DIFFERENCES IN TAXES

Finally, let us consider differences in tax rates on wage income in the different countries. A higher tax rate on wages makes it more expensive for firms to hire workers. Employment declines and unemployment increases. Figure 13 gives the tax rates on wages for the four countries in the case study. The tax rate includes all forms of taxes on wages. Once again, the theory that high taxes on labor can reduce labor demand and increase unemployment appears to be supported when one compares the United States, France, and Spain. France, which has the highest tax rates, has the highest level of unemployment among young workers.

POLICY IMPLICATION AND FORECAST

In sum, the predictions of the labor supply and demand model augmented with job rationing and job search provide a pretty good explanation for the international differences in unemployment rates. According to this analysis, the economic policies that would reduce unemployment among young adults in Europe include allowing a lower minimum wage for young workers, reducing unemployment compensation, and reducing taxes (or even subsidizing employment). None of these policies would be implemented without cost to the workers, the firms that employ them, or the politicians who propose these policies. Therefore, we can predict that differences in unemployment rates in these countries will persist.

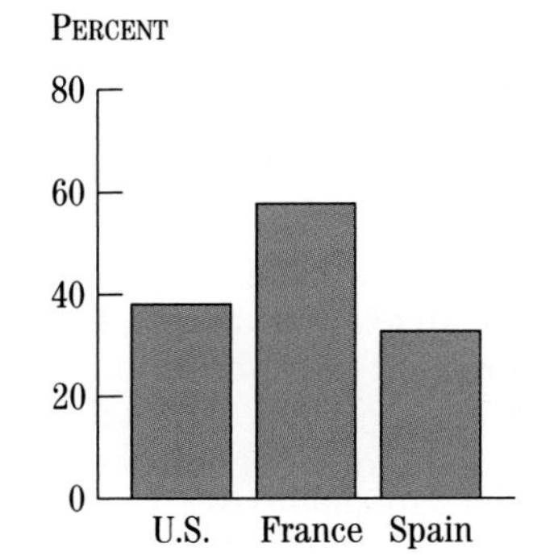

FIGURE 12
Minimum Wage as a Percentage of Average Wage
The minimum is lower in the United States than in France, but lowest in Spain.

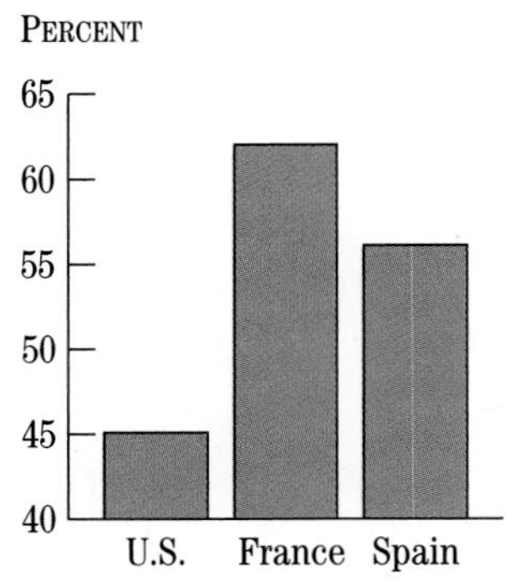

FIGURE 13
Tax Rates on Wages
The United States has a lower tax rate on wage income than the other two countries in the case study.

Policies to Reduce Unemployment. Both the job-rationing model and the job-search model have implications for how public policy can reduce both the rate of unemployment and the natural rate of unemployment. The job-rationing model predicts that high minimum wages, very rigid insider-outsider arrangements, and a greater need to pay efficiency wages can lead to more unemployment. This implies that public policies that reduce minimum wages or encourage more flexible union-employer relationships can help reduce unemployment. Similarly, economic changes and policy changes that make it easier for firms to monitor shirking workers and cheaper to train new workers will enable firms to hire more workers at a reduced efficiency wage. As with any case of rationing, those who are lucky enough to have access to the commodity (in this case, jobs) are better off as a result of the restriction. Policies that remove the constraint and allow the market to reach equilibrium benefit those who are now able to obtain jobs while hurting those who previously had jobs but now earn a lower wage.

The job-search model implies that improved job-placement programs, retraining of unemployed workers, increasing the incentives of unemployed workers to look for work, and decreasing the costs of hiring new workers will all help reduce unemployment. In an economy where unemployment compensation—money paid to workers who have been laid off from their job—is high, workers are likely to spend more time looking for a job or to hold out for a higher-paying job. Reducing unemployment compensation will provide more incentives for workers to look for work and increase the likelihood that they will find a good job match. Here too, you have to consider the tradeoffs before implementing a policy change. Unemployment compensation helps mitigate the hardships associated with unemployment and allows people more time to search. But the more generous unemployment compensation is, the less incentive there is for a worker to actually take a job. If workers choose to continue a perfunctory search for jobs, unemployment will remain high. The challenge is to design an unemployment compensation system that supports workers who lose their jobs without increasing unemployment by a lot.

What about the natural rate of unemployment? If you take a closer look at the labor market flows in Figure 9, you will see that the rate of unemployment that usually prevails in an economy will depend on two things: how great the flows into the group of employed workers are (these flows come from those who were unemployed and those who were already employed), and how great the flows into the group of unemployed workers are (these flows come from both previously employed workers and those who were previously out of the labor force). Economies where the flows into employment are relatively low or the flows into unemployment are relatively high (or both) will have a high natural rate of unemployment. Similarly, economies where the flows into employment are high or the flows into unemployment are low (or both) will have a low natural rate of unemployment.

In the United States, lots of workers lose their jobs in a given month, but many of them are able to find new jobs easily, since there are relatively few restrictions on firms' ability to hire workers. In addition, unemployment compensation in most of the United States typically runs out after 26 weeks; the evidence shows that many people stop searching and take a job just when their unemployment compensation runs out. Furthermore, new entrants to the labor market, like college students, are typically not eligible for unemployment compensation; these young workers are likely to find a job quickly, even if it is a lower-paying position than they would ideally like to have.

In contrast, in an economy like Spain's, workers who lose their jobs may find it difficult to move to another job because stronger unions restrict the quantity of labor demanded by firms or because generous long-term unemployment benefits, available to those without much work experience, discourage unemployed workers and new entrants from intensively searching for work. As a result, the natural rate for unemployment in Spain is likely to be higher than the natural rate in the United States. Furthermore, this can help explain why an American college student would be much more likely to find a job after her graduation from college than her Spanish counterpart would.

REVIEW

- The supply and demand for labor is the starting point for modeling the labor market. The quantity demanded of labor falls as the real wage rises, while the quantity supplied of labor rises. The intersection of the labor supply and demand curves determines the amount of employment and the equilibrium real wage.
- The basic supply and demand framework predicts that employment and wages will rise during economic expansions and fall during recessions. However, since the economy is always at the intersection of the supply and demand curves, the model seems to predict that unemployment is zero—the quantity of labor supplied is always equal to the quantity of labor demanded, and no one is looking for but unable to find work.
- The basic supply and demand theory needs to be modified to account for unemployment. Economists use two approaches, job rationing and job search, to explain why unemployment occurs.
- Job rationing occurs when the wage is too high. Unemployment can be interpreted as the difference between the quantity supplied and the quantity demanded at that high wage. Wages can be too high because of minimum-wage laws, insiders, or efficiency wages.
- Job search is another reason for unemployment. It takes time to find a job, and people have an incentive to wait for a good job.
- Policies that reduce the amount of rationing or lower the cost of search can reduce unemployment.

CONCLUSION

This chapter provided two important lessons about labor markets. The first was an introduction to key concepts such as the unemployment rate and the labor force participation rate. Understanding who the unemployed are, how long they stay unemployed, and how unemployment rates vary across time and across countries is a critical prerequisite for designing policies that can help reduce unemployment.

The second lesson was how to construct a model of the labor market that would replicate the patterns observed in the labor market. That model could then be used to come up with policy recommendations that could help workers obtain jobs and help economies make better use of one of their most important productive resources. We showed that the simple supply and demand model could not realistically describe the labor market, but that augmenting that model to take into account job rationing and job search provides insight into possible policy interventions. Lower minimum wages, less rigid unions, better job training, and less generous unemployment benefits can all help increase the rate at which people who are either unemployed or out of the labor force move into employment, as well as decrease the rate at which employed workers or workers who are out of the labor force move into the ranks of the unemployed. The challenge for policymakers is how to carry out these reforms so as to balance the benefits to currently unemployed workers with the costs to currently employed workers.

KEY POINTS

1. Unemployment and employment data are collected by the Bureau of Labor Statistics and made available in the monthly Current Population Survey.
2. A person is unemployed if he or she is old enough to work and is looking for work, but does not have a job. The unemployment rate is the number of unemployed as a percentage of the labor force, which consists of all the employed and unemployed in the economy.
3. Two other widely used measures of the labor market are the employment-to-population ratio (the number of people employed as a percentage of the working-age population) and the labor force participation rate (the labor force as a percentage of the working-age population). Both of these indicators rose in the United States following the end of World War II as more women entered the work force.
4. Not all workers work full-time; many work part-time, or fewer than 35 hours a week. This is especially common among women with young children. Because of part-time work, economists use aggregate hours worked, rather than aggregate employment, to measure the quantity of labor engaged in production.
5. The unemployment rate tends to rise during recessions and fall during expansion. The unemployment rate when the economy is neither in recession nor in an expansion is called the natural rate of unemployment.
6. People are unemployed for four reasons: They have lost their job, they have quit their job, they have entered the labor force for the first time, or they have re-entered the labor force.
7. The simple labor supply and demand model can predict some aspects of the behavior of labor markets but cannot explain why there is unemployment in the economy.
8. To explain the behavior of unemployment, the simple model needs to be modified to take into account both job rationing, in which the wage is too high to equate supply and demand, and job search, in which unemployed people look for work but are unable to find work if an appropriate job opportunity does not come along.
9. Countries that have low natural rates of unemployment tend to be ones in which it is relatively easy for the unemployed or those out of the labor force to find jobs and/or relatively more unlikely that people who lose their job will be unable to find another job.
10. Economic policies such as exemptions for teenagers from the minimum-wage laws, time limits on unemployment compensation, or the provision of information about job openings to reduce job-search time can reduce the natural unemployment rate.

KEY TERMS

unemployed person
labor force
working-age population
labor force participation rate
employment-to-population ratio
aggregate hours
natural unemployment rate
cyclical unemployment
frictional unemployment
structural unemployment
job vacancies
labor demand curve
labor supply curve
job rationing
job search
insider
outsider
efficiency wage

QUESTIONS FOR REVIEW

1. How do economists define unemployment, and how do they measure how many people are unemployed?
2. How is the working-age population defined?
3. What is the definition of the labor force?
4. What has happened to the employment-to-population ratio for men and women since the 1950s?
5. What is the difference between frictional and structural unemployment?
6. Why isn't the unemployment rate equal to zero?
7. What is the difference between unemployment due to job rationing and unemployment due to job search?
8. What economic policies would reduce the natural rate of unemployment?

PROBLEMS

1. Which of the following people would be unemployed according to official statistics? Which ones would *you* define as unemployed? Why?
   a. A person who is home painting the house while seeking a permanent position as an electrician
   b. A full-time student
   c. A recent graduate who is looking for a job
   d. A parent who decides to stay home taking care of children full-time
   e. A worker who quits his job because he thinks the pay is insufficient
   f. A teenager who gets discouraged looking for work and stops looking
2. The table below contains some information about employment, labor force, and population levels in the United States at the turn of each decade.
   a. Using the data, fill in the table.
   b. Suppose the projection for the working-age population in the year 2020 for the United States is 265 million. If the unemployment rate and the labor force participation rate are the same in 2020 as they were in 2000, how much employment will there be?
   c. Using the same projection of 265 million for the working-age population in 2020, calculate employment with an unemployment rate of 5 percent and a labor force participation rate of 60 percent.
   d. Do the same for a labor force participation rate of 70 percent. Which of these estimates do you think is more realistic? Why?
3. What effect would a decline in part-time employment have on average weekly hours per worker in the United States? If the employment-to-population ratio increases, what will happen to total hours of work in the United States?
4. Job search and advertising are now on the Internet. Using e-mail, job applicants can submit résumés to prospective employers. One popular website of this kind is www.monster.com.
   a. How should this service affect the unemployment rate?
   b. Suppose everybody in the working-age population has access to monster.com. Would you expect unemployment to be eliminated? Explain.

Problem 2

Year	Total Employment (millions)	Unemployment Rate (percent)	Labor Force Participation Rate (percent)	Working-Age Population (millions)
1980		7.2	63.6	168.9
1990		6.3	66.4	190.0
2000		3.9	67.0	213.7

Source: U.S. Department of Labor.

Problem 5

Year	Unemployment Rate (percent)	Labor Force Participation Rate (percent)	Working-Age Population (millions)	Total Employment (millions)	Employment-to-Working-Age-Population Ratio
2000	3.9	67.0	214		
2010	5.0	64.0	240		
2020	5.0	62.0	265		

Source: U.S. Department of Labor.

5. The age distribution of the population changes over time—in the United States, better health care (longer lives) and lower fertility (fewer kids) in recent years mean that there are increasingly larger proportions of people over age 16. At the same time, there is likely to be a decline in the labor force participation rate as baby boomers retire. Using the same method as in the previous problem, calculate total employment and the employment-to-population ratio based on the scenario in the table above.

a. Describe what happens to total employment and the employment-to-population ratio in this scenario.

b. Is it possible that labor force participation would fall so much that total employment would fall? How low would the labor force participation rate have to be in 2020 for total employment to be lower than in 2000?

6. The table below shows the demand for and supply of skilled labor at different hourly wages.

Demand for Labor		Supply of Labor	
Wage/Hour	*Quantity*	*Wage/Hour*	*Quantity*
$12	75	$12	47
14	68	14	54
16	61	16	61
18	54	18	68
20	47	20	75
22	40	22	82

a. Draw the supply and demand curves for labor.

b. What are the wage and quantity of labor at equilibrium?

c. Suppose a law is passed forbidding employers to pay wages less than $20 per hour. What will the new quantity of labor in the market be? Who gains and who loses from this law?

7. Use a supply and demand diagram to show the possible reduction in teenage unemployment from a lower minimum "training" wage for workers under 20 years of age. For what reasons might older unskilled workers complain about such a policy?

8. Use the theories of job rationing and job search to try to explain why the natural rate of unemployment in the United States is below that in France. What can the French government do to try to remedy this situation? Might these remedies be politically unpopular?

9. Why do young workers have higher unemployment rates than older workers? Is there a difference in labor productivity? Why?

10. Why do some firms pay efficiency wages? What would you expect to be true in regions or industries where there is widespread payment of efficiency wages?

Productivity and Economic Growth

For most of human history, there was no economic growth. True, vast quantities of wealth were amassed by kings and queens through conquest and exploitation; coliseums, pyramids, and great walls were constructed by millions of slaves; and great works of art were produced by talented individuals on all continents. But output per hour of work—the productive power of labor that determines the well-being of most people—grew hardly at all for thousands of years. Except for the ruling classes, people lived in extreme poverty.

This situation changed dramatically around the eighteenth century. Figure 1 shows the growth rates of *output per hour of work,* or **productivity,** for different periods during the last three centuries. Observe that there was almost no growth in output per hour of work for most of the 1700s, much as in the thousands of years before. Then, in the late 1700s and early 1800s—the period historians call the Industrial Revolution—economic growth began to pick up, first in Europe and then in the United States. Productivity growth accelerated in the early 1800s and then rose to historically unprecedented levels in the twentieth century. And as productivity rose, people's incomes also rose and poverty declined.

productivity: output per hour of work.

Just as productivity growth raised standards of living and reduced poverty in Europe and the United States in the 200 years since the Industrial Revolution, in the twenty-first century it is spreading around the world to China, India, and many other countries. In fact, differences in productivity growth among countries explain why some countries are poor and some are rich. Simply put, if productivity in a country is high, then that country is rich; if productivity in a country is low, then that country is poor. If you want to reduce the number of poor countries, then you have no choice but to increase productivity in poor countries. The ticket out of poverty is higher productivity.

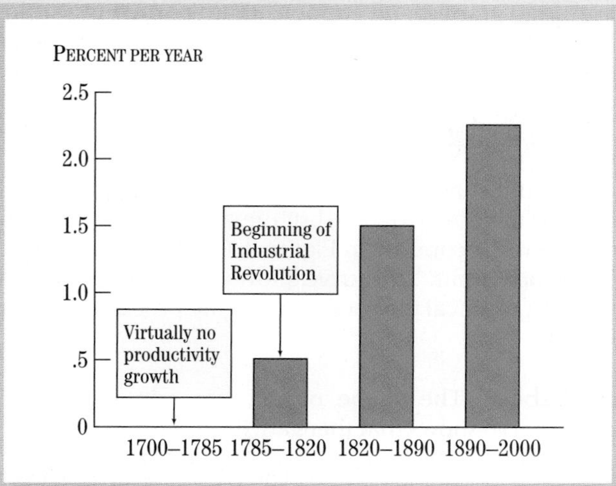

FIGURE 1
Productivity Growth During the Past 300 Years
Productivity is defined as output per hour of work. Productivity *growth* is defined as the percentage increase in productivity from one year to the next. The bars indicate the average productivity growth during the years stated. The data are collected from Europe and the United States.

Why did the growth of real GDP per hour of work begin to increase and then take off in the eighteenth century? Why is productivity growth high in some countries and low in other countries? The purpose of this chapter is to develop a theory of economic growth that helps answer these and many other questions. The theory of economic growth tells us that increases in hours worked can increase the growth of real GDP, but not the growth of real GDP per hour of work. To explain the growth of productivity, we must focus on the two other factors: capital and technology. Capital raises real GDP per hour of work by giving workers more tools and equipment to work with. However, as we will show in this chapter, capital alone is not sufficient to achieve the growth we have seen over the past 200 years. Technology—the knowledge and methods that underlie the production process—has also played a big role.

Understanding the role of capital and technology enables economists to better evaluate the advantages and disadvantages of various economic policies to improve economic growth. For example, should economic policies designed to stimulate economic growth focus more on capital or more on technology? The U.S. economy has benefited from yet another resurgence of productivity growth in the past 10 years. What economic policy will best maintain this high rate of productivity growth?

LABOR AND CAPITAL WITHOUT TECHNOLOGY

To better understand the important role played by technology in driving economic growth, we will begin with a simplified theory in which economic growth depends only on labor and then consider a theory in which it depends on labor and capital.

Labor Alone

Suppose real GDP depends only on labor. That is, the amount of output in the economy can be described by the production function $Y = F(L)$, where Y is real GDP and L is labor input. When labor input increases, real GDP increases.

To understand this production function for the whole economy, it helps to consider the production of a single good. Imagine workers on a one-acre vineyard planting, maintaining, and harvesting grapes, and suppose that the only input that can be varied is labor. With more workers, the vineyard can produce more grapes, but according to the simple story that output depends only on labor, the vineyard cannot increase capital because there is no capital. For example, the vineyard cannot buy wagons or wheelbarrows to haul fertilizer around. The only way the vineyard can increase output is by hiring more workers to haul the fertilizer.

Now, suppose all this is true for the economy as a whole. The firms in the economy can produce more output by hiring more workers, but they cannot increase capital. The situation is shown for the entire economy in Figure 2. On the vertical axis is output. On the horizontal axis is labor input. The curve shows that more labor can produce more output. The curve is a graphical plot of the aggregate production function $Y = F(L)$ for the whole economy.

diminishing returns: a situation in which successive increases in the use of an input, holding other inputs constant, will eventually cause a decline in the additional production derived from one more unit of that input.

Diminishing Returns to Labor. The shape of the curve in Figure 2 is important. The flattening out of the curve shows that there are **diminishing returns** to labor: The greater the number of workers used in producing output, the less the additional output that comes from each additional worker. Why? Consider production of a single good again, such as grapes at the vineyard. Increasing employment at the one-acre vineyard from one to two workers raises production more than increasing employment from 1,001 to 1,002 workers. A second worker could take charge of

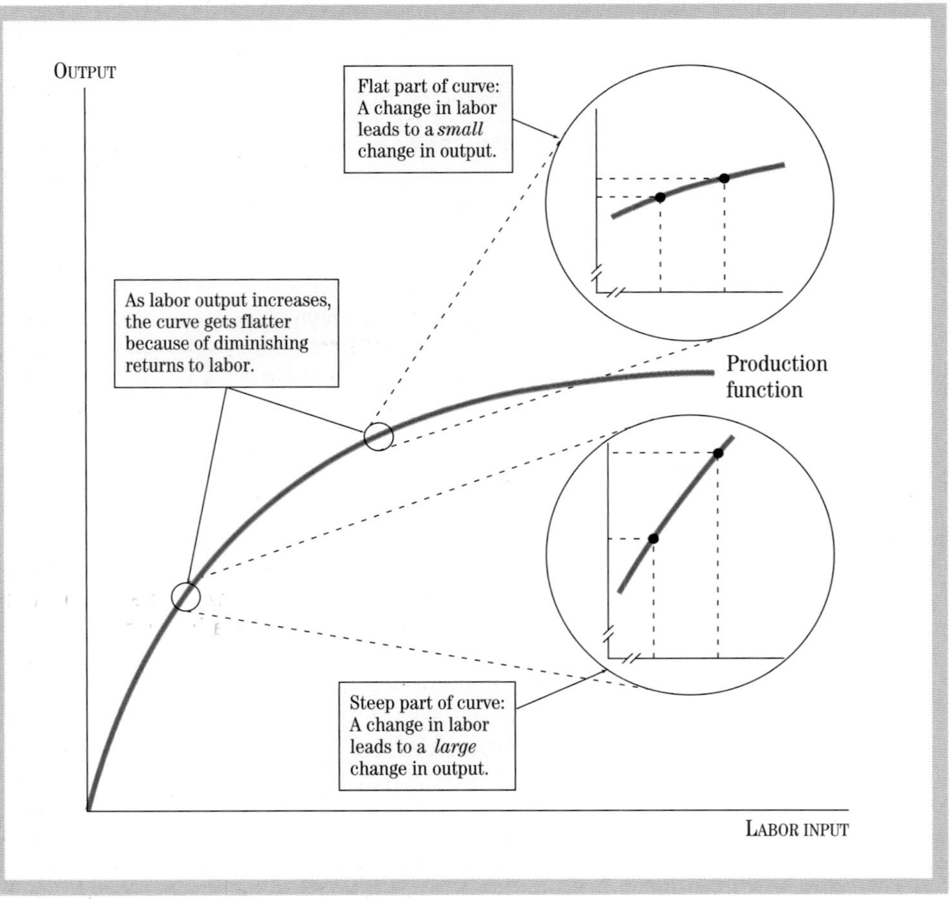
OUTPUT
Flat part of curve: A change in labor leads to a *small* change in output.
As labor output increases, the curve gets flatter because of diminishing returns to labor.
Production function
Steep part of curve: A change in labor leads to a *large* change in output.
LABOR INPUT

FIGURE 2
Only Changes in Labor Can Change Output
The curve shows the production function $Y = F(L)$, where Y is output and L is labor input (hours of work). In this theory, capital and technology are out of the picture. With more labor working on a fixed supply of land, there are diminishing returns, as shown by the curvature of the production function.

irrigation or inspect the vines for insects while the first worker harvested grapes. But with 1,001 workers on the vineyard, the 1,002nd worker could find little to do to raise production. Diminishing returns to labor exist because labor is the only input to production that we are changing. As more workers are employed on the same one-acre plot, the contribution that each additional worker makes goes down. Adding one worker when only one worker is employed can increase production by a large amount. But adding one worker when there are already 1,001 on the one-acre plot cannot add as much. For the same reasons, diminishing returns to labor exist for the whole economy.

Adding Capital

Now let us add capital to the production function. The total amount of capital in the economy increases each year by the amount of net investment during the year. More precisely,

> Recall that net investment is equal to gross investment less depreciation (p. 150). Depreciation is the amount of capital that wears out each year.

$$\begin{array}{c}\text{Capital at the end}\\ \text{of this year}\end{array} = \begin{array}{c}\text{net investment}\\ \text{during this year}\end{array} + \begin{array}{c}\text{capital at the end}\\ \text{of last year}\end{array}$$

For example, if \$10,000 billion is the value of all capital in the economy at the end of last year, then \$100 billion of net investment during this year would raise the capital stock to \$10,100 billion by the end of this year. This is a 1 percent increase in the capital stock.

With capital as an input to production, the production function becomes $Y = F(L, K)$, where K stands for capital. Output can be increased by using more capital, even if the amount of labor is not increased. Consider the vineyard example again. If a wheelbarrow is bought to haul the fertilizer around the vineyard, the vineyard can produce more grapes with the same number of workers. More capital at the vineyard increases output. The same is true for the economy as a whole. By increasing the amount of capital in the economy, more real GDP can be produced with the same number of workers.

Figure 3 illustrates how more capital raises output. The axes are the same as those in Figure 2, and the curve again shows that more output can be produced by more labor. But, in addition, Figure 3 shows that if we add capital to the economy—by investing a certain amount each year—the relationship between output and labor shifts up: More capital provides more output at any level of labor input. To see this, pick a point on the horizontal axis, say, point *A*, to designate a certain amount of labor input. Then draw a vertical line up from this point, such as the dashed line shown. The vertical distance between the curve marked "Less capital" and the curve marked "More capital" shows that additional capital raises production.

Diminishing Returns to Capital. Figure 4 shows that there are *diminishing returns to capital* too. Each additional amount of capital—another wheelbarrow or another hoe—results in a smaller addition to output. Hence, the gaps between the several production functions in Figure 4 get smaller and smaller as more capital is added. As more capital is added, there is less ability to increase output per worker. Compare adding one wheelbarrow to the vineyard without any wheelbarrows with adding one wheelbarrow when there are already fifty wheelbarrows. Clearly, the fifty-first wheelbarrow would increase farm output by only a minuscule amount, certainly much less than the first wheelbarrow. With a one-acre vineyard, there would not even be much room for the fifty-first wheelbarrow!

Diminishing returns to capital also occur for the economy as a whole. Thus, adding more capital per worker cannot raise real GDP per worker above some limit,

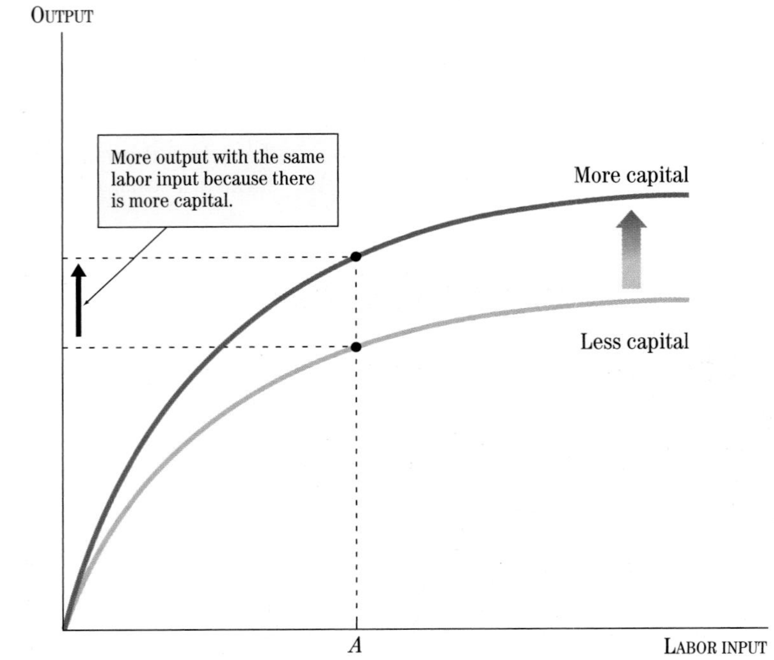

FIGURE 3
Capital Is Also a Factor of Production

The axes are just like those in Figure 2, but now if more capital is added to production, more output can be produced with the same labor input. For example, when labor input is at point *A*, more output can be produced with more capital.

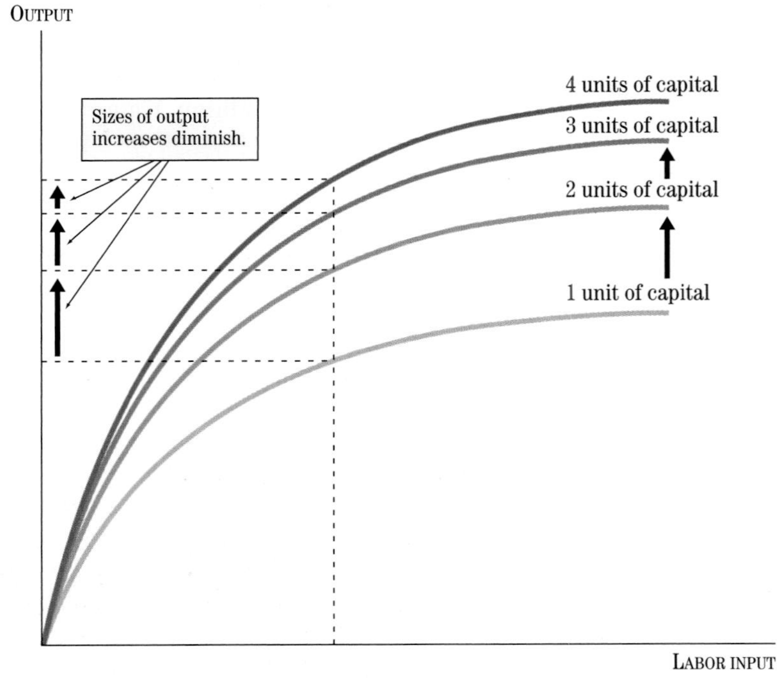

FIGURE 4
Capital Has Diminishing Returns Also

As capital per worker increases, each additional unit of capital produces less output. Thus, there is a limit to how much growth per worker additional capital per worker can bring.

ECONOMICS IN ACTION

The Role of Technology in Economic Growth

In today's highly automated world, the image (left) of women in long skirts packing fruit delicacies into glass jars in the mid- to late 1800s seems quaint beside the image (right) of robotic arms in an assembly line at this modern-day car plant. Yet both represent huge leaps in industrial productivity at different periods of history. Capital and technology played critical roles in the development of each of these increasingly more efficient methods of production.

and even getting close to that limit will require an enormous amount of capital. Eventually, growth in output per hour of work will stop.

Thus, labor and capital alone cannot explain the phenomenal growth in real GDP during the last 200 years.

REVIEW

- Both labor and capital have diminishing returns. A graph of the production function for the economy shows these diminishing returns.
- An economic growth theory with labor and capital alone cannot account for the sustained increase in real GDP per hour of work that began in the late 1700s and continues today.

TECHNOLOGY: THE ENGINE OF GROWTH

We have seen that growth driven by increases in capital and labor, while important, is not sustainable. Diminishing returns imply that the additional output obtained by increasing these inputs becomes smaller and smaller, eventually leading to no further economic growth. In order for output to grow over the very long run, we need not just to *increase* inputs, but also to get more output from *existing* inputs. Technology is what enables us to get more output from a given quantity of inputs.

ECONOMICS IN ACTION

Examples of Changes in Technology That Increased Productivity

Replacing horse-drawn tractors (on the left) with steam-powered tractors (in the center) is an example of a change in technology that increased output per hour of work. Another example is the introduction of computer technology for maintenance scheduling or ordering spare tractor parts on the Internet. What other advances in technology have increased farm output?

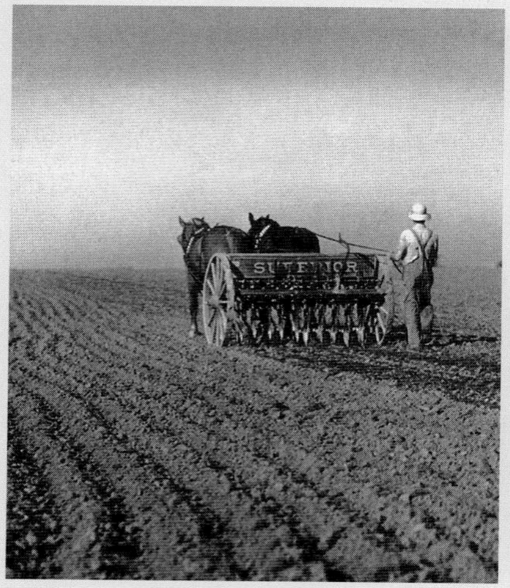

What Is Technology?

technology: anything that raises the amount of output that can be produced with a given amount of labor and capital. (Ch. 5)

Technology is very difficult to define, envision, and measure. A broad definition of *technology* is that it is anything that raises the amount of output that can be produced with a given amount of inputs (labor and capital). In essence, technology is the stock of knowledge or ideas that exist in an economy: the ideas that help produce goods and services such as baby clothes, wine, and television shows; the ideas that help save lives, such as penicillin, vaccines, and heart transplants; and the ideas that help us communicate all over the world, such as cell phones and the Internet.

When we add technology to capital and labor, we have the modern theory of economic growth. The theory can be summarized by the now familiar aggregate production function

$$Y = F(L, K, T)$$

where T stands for technology. Increases in technology will therefore increase output. Such increases in technology are termed *technological progress*. We sometimes use the term **technological change** instead of technological progress.

technological change: improvement in technology over time.

Invention, Innovation, and Diffusion. Technological change occurs when new ideas are developed into new products that increase production, such as the steel plow, the harvester, the combine, the automobile, radar, the telephone, the computer, the airplane, lasers, and fiber-optic cable. Economists distinguish

invention: a discovery of new knowledge.

innovation: application of new knowledge in a way that creates new products or significantly changes old ones.

diffusion: the spreading of an innovation throughout the economy.

between an **invention**, which is the discovery of new knowledge or a new principle, such as electricity, and **innovation**, in which the new knowledge is brought into application with a new product, such as the electric light bulb. Economists also distinguish between the innovation itself and the **diffusion** of the innovation throughout the economy, a process that involves advertising, marketing, and spreading the innovation to new uses, such as the use of the electric lightbulb to create night shifts in factories.

The sewing machine is a good illustration of invention, innovation, and diffusion. By 1847, inventors had built 17 different machines capable of mechanically forming a stitch. But only one of these, Elias Howe's sewing machine, developed into a commercially successful innovation. As Howe tried to sell his invention to consumers, he found out how to modify it to make it more useful and attractive. Soon the invention turned into a popular innovation that was used widely. Wide diffusion of the innovation occurred as others produced household versions of the sewing machine, like the one marketed by the Singer Company. This story also illustrates that innovation and diffusion require the work of an entrepreneur who recognizes the potential of the invention.

Technology depends in part on scientific knowledge, and many people feel that science will become more and more important in driving future technological change. But technology is much more than scientific knowledge. The discovery of DNA did not improve technology until it was applied to genetic engineering. The knowledge of mathematics made the invention and development of computers possible, a technology that has obviously improved productivity.

Organization and Specialization. Technology also includes the way firms are organized. Better organization schemes can mean a smaller bureaucracy and more output per hour of work without the addition of capital. More efficient organization can improve the flow of information within a firm and thereby affect labor productivity. Better incentive programs that encourage workers to communicate their ideas to management, for example, increase productivity.

Henry Ford's idea of the assembly line greatly increased the productivity of workers. The assembly line enabled the car to come to the worker rather than having the worker go to the car. Thus, each worker could specialize in a certain type of activity; through specialization, productivity increased. The assembly line alone is estimated to have reduced the time it took a group of workers to produce a car from 12½ hours to ½ hour. Productivity increased, and so did wages.

New technology can affect how labor and capital are used at a firm. Economists distinguish between *labor-saving* and *capital-saving* technological change. *Labor-saving technological change* means that fewer workers are needed to produce the same amount of output; *capital-saving technological change* means that fewer machines are needed to produce the same amount of output. An example of a labor-saving technological change would be a steam-powered tractor replacing a horse-drawn plow, and later gasoline power replacing steam power, enabling the same worker to plow many more acres. An example of a capital-saving technological change is the night shift. Adding two crews of workers—one working in a steel mill from 4 P.M. to midnight and another working from midnight to 8 A.M.—makes the same steel-making furnaces three times as productive as when the working hours are only from 8 A.M. to 4 P.M.

Specialization of workers at a firm adds to productivity. Adam Smith emphasized the importance of specialization in his *Wealth of Nations;* his term *division of labor* refers to the way a manufacturing task could be divided up among a group of workers, each of whom would specialize in a part of the job.

Because specialization permits workers to repeat the same task many times, their productivity increases, as in the old adage "practice makes perfect." Each time the task is repeated, the worker becomes more proficient—a phenomenon that economists call **learning by doing.** The commonsense principle of learning by doing is that the more one does something, the more one learns about how to do it. For example, as the number of airplanes produced of a particular type—say, a Boeing 777—increases, the workers become more and more skilled at producing that type of airplane. Careful studies of aircraft production have shown that productivity increases by 20 percent for each 100 percent increase in output of a particular type of plane. This relationship between learning and the amount of production is commonly called the "learning curve." Learning is a type of technological progress.

learning by doing: a situation in which workers become more proficient by doing a particular task many times.

Human Capital. Many firms provide training courses for workers to increase their skills and their productivity. *On-the-job training* is a catchall term for any education, training, or skills a worker receives while at work.

Most workers receive much of their education and training before they begin working, whether in grade school, high school, college, or professional schools. Because increases in education and training can raise workers' productivity, such increases are considered another source of technological change.

The education and training of workers, called **human capital** by economists, is similar to physical capital—factories and equipment. In order to accumulate human capital—to become more educated or better trained—people must devote time and resources, much as a firm must devote resources to investment if physical capital is to increase.

human capital: a person's accumulated knowledge and skills.

The decision to invest in human capital is influenced by considerations similar to those that motivate a firm to invest in physical capital: the cost of the investment versus the expected return. For example, investing in a college education may require that one borrow the money for tuition; if the interest rate on the loan rises, then people will be less likely to invest in a college education. Thus, investment in education may be negatively related to the interest rate, much as physical investment is. This is one reason why, in order to encourage more education and thereby increase economic growth and productivity, the U.S. government provides low-interest loans to college students, making an investment in college more attractive. We will return to the government's role in education as part of its broader policy to increase economic growth later in the chapter.

The Production of Technology: The Invention Factory

Technology is sometimes discovered by chance by a lone inventor and sometimes by trial and error by an individual worker. A secretary who experiments with several different filing systems to reduce search time or with different locations for the computer, the printer, the telephone, and the photocopier is engaged in improving technology around the office. Frequently, technological progress is a continuous process in which a small adjustment here and a small adjustment there add up to major improvements over time.

But more and more technological change is the result of huge expenditures of research and development funds by industry and government. Thomas Edison's "invention factory" in Menlo Park, New Jersey, was one of the first examples of a large industrial laboratory devoted to the production of technology. It in turn influenced the development of many other labs, such as the David Sarnoff research lab of RCA. Merck & Co., a drug company, spends nearly $1 billion per year on research and development for the production of new technology.

ECONOMICS IN ACTION

Two Invention Factories: Past and Present

A large amount of technology was produced at Thomas Edison's invention factory (left); still more technology is being produced at the research lab of a modern biotechnology firm like Cetus (right). The amount of new technology can be explained by the laws of supply and demand. For example, a tax credit for expenditures on research will increase the supply of technology. But how is technology different from most other goods? If one person uses more technology, is there just as much available for others to use?

Edison's Menlo Park laboratory had about 25 technicians working in three or four different buildings. In the six years from 1876 to 1882, the laboratory invented the light bulb, the phonograph, the telephone transmitter, and electrical generators. Each of these inventions turned out to be a successful innovation that was diffused widely. For each innovation, a *patent* was granted by the federal government. A patent indicates that the invention is original and gives the inventor the exclusive right to use it until the patent expires. In order to obtain a patent on the rights to an invention, an inventor must apply to the Patent and Trademark Office of the federal government. Patents give inventors an inducement to invent. The number of patents granted is an indicator of how much technological progress is going on. Edison obtained patents at a pace of about 67 a year at his lab.

Edison's invention factory required both labor and capital input, much like factories producing other commodities. The workers in such laboratories are highly skilled, with knowledge obtained through formal schooling or on-the-job training—human capital. A highly trained work force is an important prerequisite to the production of technology.

The supply of technology—the output of Edison's invention factory, for example—depends on the cost of producing the new technology, which must include the great risk that little or nothing will be invented, and the benefits from the new technology: how much Edison can charge for the rights to use his techniques for making light bulbs. Often inventive activity has changed as a result of shifts in the economy that change the costs and benefits. For example, increases in textile workers' wages stimulated the invention of textile machines, because such machines yielded greater profits by enabling the production of more output with fewer workers.

Special Features of Technology

Technology has two special qualities. The first is *nonrivalry*. This means that one person's use of the technology does not reduce the amount that another person can use. If one university uses the same student registration system as another university, that does not reduce the quality of the first university's system. In contrast, most goods are rivals in consumption: If you drink a bottle of Coke, there is one fewer bottle of Coke around for other people to drink.

The second feature of technology is *nonexcludability*. This occurs when the inventor or the owner of the technology cannot exclude other people from using it (see the Economics in Action box on p. 231). For example, the system software for Apple computers shows a series of logos and pull-down menus that can be moved around the screen with a mouse. The idea could easily be adapted for use in other software programs by other companies. In fact, the Windows program of Microsoft has features similar to those of the Apple software, but according to the court that ruled on Apple's complaint that Microsoft was illegally copying, the features were not so similar that Microsoft could not use them. If the court had ruled in favor of Apple, then Apple could have excluded Microsoft from using the Apple features.

As the example of Apple and Microsoft shows, the legal system determines in part the degree of nonexcludability. Trademarks, copyrights, and patents help inventors exclude others from using their inventions without compensation. But it is impossible to exclude others from using much technology.

Thus, technology may *spill over* from one activity to another. If your economics teacher invents a new way to teach economics on a computer, it might spill over to your chemistry teacher, who sees how the technology can be applied to a different subject. Sometimes spillovers occur because research personnel move from one firm to another. Henry Ford knew Thomas Edison and was stimulated to experiment on internal-combustion engines by Edison. Hence, Edison's research spilled over to another industry, but Edison would have found it very difficult to get compensation from Henry Ford even if he had wanted to.

Because inventors cannot be fully compensated for the benefits their ideas provide to others, they may produce too little technology. The private incentives to invent are less than the gain to society from the inventions. If the incentives were higher—say, through government subsidies to research and development—more inventions might be produced. Thus, there is a potential role for government in providing funds for research and development, both in industry and at universities. Before we consider this role, we must examine how to measure technological change in the economy as a whole.

REVIEW

- Technological change has a very broad definition. It is anything that increases production for a given level of labor and capital. Technological change has been an essential ingredient in the increase in the growth of real GDP per hour of work in the last 200 years.
- Technology can be improved by the education and training of workers—investment in human capital. Technology can also be improved through inventions produced in industrial research laboratories, as well as by trial and error. In any case, the level of technology is determined by market forces.
- But technology exhibits nonrivalry in consumption and a high degree of nonexcludability. These are precisely the conditions in which there will be an underproduction of technology.

MEASURING TECHNOLOGY

Both technology and capital cause productivity—real GDP per hour of work—to grow. Is it possible to determine how much productivity growth has been due to technology, as distinct from capital? Surprisingly, the answer is yes. Robert Solow of MIT first showed how to do this and won the Nobel Prize for his innovation. In 1957 he published a paper that contained a simple mathematical formula. It is this formula—called the **growth accounting formula**—that enables economists to estimate the relative contributions of capital and technology.

growth accounting formula: an equation that states that the growth rate of productivity equals capital's share of income times the growth rate of capital per hour of work plus the growth rate of technology.

The Formula

The growth accounting formula is remarkably simple. It can be written as follows:

$$\begin{matrix}\text{Growth rate of}\\ \text{productivity}\end{matrix} = \frac{1}{3}\begin{pmatrix}\text{growth rate of capital}\\ \text{per hour of work}\end{pmatrix} + \begin{matrix}\text{growth rate}\\ \text{of technology}\end{matrix}$$

It is important to know why the growth rate of capital per hour of work is multiplied by a coefficient that is less than 1, or only 1/3 in the formula. The reason is that economists view the production function for the economy as one in which output rises by only 1/3 of the percentage by which capital increases. For example, a vineyard owner can estimate by what percent grape output will rise if the workers have more wheelbarrows to work with. If the number of wheelbarrows at the vineyard is increased by 100 percent and if the 1/3 coefficient applies to the vineyard, then grape production per hour of work will increase by 33 percent. In other words, this is a property of the grape production function. Statistical studies suggest that the 1/3 coefficient seems to apply to the production function for the economy as a whole.

We should not give the impression, however, that economists know the coefficient on capital growth in the growth accounting formula with much precision. There is uncertainty about its size. It could be 1/4 or even 5/12. In any case, the growth accounting formula is a helpful rule of thumb to assist policymakers in deciding what emphasis to place on capital versus technology when developing programs to stimulate economic growth.[1]

Using the Formula

Here is how the formula works. The growth rates of productivity and capital per hour of work are readily determined from available data sources in most countries. Using the formula, we can express the growth rate of technology.

$$\begin{matrix}\text{Growth rate of}\\ \text{technology}\end{matrix} = \begin{matrix}\text{growth rate of}\\ \text{productivity}\end{matrix} - \frac{1}{3}\begin{pmatrix}\text{growth rate of capital}\\ \text{per hour of work}\end{pmatrix}$$

Thus, the growth rate of technology can be determined by subtracting 1/3 times the growth rate of capital per hour of work from the growth rate of real GDP per hour of work.

Consider an example. Suppose the growth rate of real GDP per hour of work is 2 percent per year. Suppose also that the growth rate of capital per hour of work is 3 percent per year. Then the growth rate of technology must be 1 percent per year: $2 - (1/3 \times 3) = 1$. Thus, one-half of the growth of productivity is due to technological change, and one-half to growth of capital per hour of work.

[1] A graphical derivation of the growth accounting formula is found in the appendix to this chapter.

ECONOMICS IN ACTION

Growth Accounting in Practice

Let us consider two practical cases in which the growth accounting formula tells us about the importance of technology for economic growth.

A PRODUCTIVITY GROWTH SLOWDOWN

Table 1 shows productivity growth in the United States for three different periods. It also shows the amount of this productivity growth that is due to the growth of capital and the growth of technology. The table was computed using the growth accounting formula.

If you compare the first two rows of the table, you can see that productivity growth slowed down in the 1970s, from 2.5 percent per year to only 1.2 percent per year. This slowdown was a major concern of policymakers during this period. At first, policymakers were slow to recognize it. When statisticians at the Bureau of Labor Statistics first reported the slowdown in the mid-1970s, many people thought that it was probably temporary and that productivity growth would soon rebound. Instead, productivity continued to grow slowly for nearly 20 years.

What was the reason for the slowdown? The growth accounting formula helps answer the question. According to the formula, both the growth of capital and the growth of technology slowed down. But the slowdown in the growth of technology was larger. Technology growth fell by .8 percentage point from the 1956–1975 period to the 1976–1995 period, while capital growth fell by .5 percentage point. This suggested that a greater focus on policies to stimulate technological change and education would be appropriate.

A PRODUCTIVITY GROWTH REBOUND

After remaining low for nearly a generation, productivity growth finally started to pick up again in the mid-1990s. The last row of Table 1 shows this rebound in productivity growth. In the second half of the 1990s and the first half of the 2000s, productivity growth rose to 2.9 percent—more than it was before the slowdown. Was capital or technology the main reason for the rebound? According to the growth accounting formula, technology growth surged from 1996 to 2006, contributing twice as much as capital.

Check the numbers in the table to make sure the formula was used correctly:

2.5 = 1.1 + 1.4
1.2 = .6 + .6
2.9 = .9 + 2.0

So they check.

TABLE 1
Accounting for the 1970s Productivity Slowdown and the 1990s Productivity Rebound

Period	(1) Productivity Growth	(2) 1/3 Growth Rate of Capital per Hour of Work	(3) Technology Growth
1956–1975	2.5	1.1	1.4
1976–1995	1.2	.6	.6
1996–2006	2.9	.9	2.0

REVIEW

- The growth accounting formula shows explicitly how productivity growth depends on the growth of capital per hour of work and on the growth of technology.
- Using the growth accounting formula along with data on productivity and capital, one can calculate the contribution of technology to economic growth.

TECHNOLOGY POLICY

The growth accounting formula tells us that if economic policy is to help maintain or increase productivity growth, it must provide incentives for, or remove disincentives to, technological progress. What policies might improve technological progress?

Policy to Encourage Investment in Human Capital

One policy is to improve education. A more highly trained work force is more productive. Better-educated workers are more able to make technological improvements. Hence, educational reform (higher standards, incentives for good teaching) and more funding would be ways to increase technological change. Some studies have shown that the U.S. educational system is falling behind other countries, especially in mathematics and science in the K–12 schools; hence, additional support seems warranted in order to increase economic growth.

Policy to Encourage Research and Innovation

Today, the United States and other advanced countries spend huge amounts of money on *research and development (R&D)*. Some of the research supports pure science, but much of it is applied research in engineering and medical technology. About 2.6 percent of U.S. GDP goes to research and development. The government provides much of its R&D funds through research grants and contracts to private firms and universities through the National Science Foundation and the National Institutes of Health and through its own research labs. But private firms are the users of most of the research funds.

The United States spends less on research and development as a share of GDP than other countries, but more in total. Total spending on research is a better measure of the usefulness of the spending than spending as a share of GDP if the benefits spill over to the whole economy.

Increased government support for research and development regardless of industry can be achieved through tax credits. A *tax credit for research* allows firms to deduct a certain fraction of their research expenditures from their taxes in order to reduce their tax bill. This increases the incentive to engage in research and development. Another way to increase the incentive for inventors and innovators is to give them a more certain claim to the property rights from their inventions. The government has a role here in defining and enforcing property rights through patent laws, trademarks, and copyrights.

Technology Embodied in New Capital

Although we have emphasized that capital and technology have two distinct effects on the growth rate of productivity, it is not always possible to separate them in practice. In order to take advantage of a new technology, it may be necessary to invest in new capital. Consider the Thompson Bagel Machine, invented by Dan Thompson, which can automatically roll and shape bagels. Before the machine was invented, bakers rolled and shaped the bagels by hand. According to Dan Thompson, who in 1993 was running the Thompson Bagel Machine Manufacturing Corporation, headquartered in Los Angeles, "You used to have two guys handshaping and boiling and baking who could turn out maybe 120 bagels an hour. With the machine and now the new ovens, I have one baker putting out 400 bagels an hour."[2] That is a productivity increase of over 500 percent! But the new technology is inseparable from the capital. In order to take advantage of the technology, bagel producers have to buy the machine and the new ovens to go with it.

Economists call this *embodied technological change* because it is embodied in the capital. An example of *disembodied technological change* would be the discovery of a new way to forecast the demand for bagels at the shop each morning so that fewer people would be disappointed on popular days and fewer bagels would be wasted on slack days. Taking advantage of this technology might not require any new capital.

[2] *New York Times*, April 25, 1993.

ECONOMICS IN THE NEWS

Productivity Growth

Productivity growth is the focus of this article from the *Washington Post* on January 3, 2007. Note how the author demonstrates the importance of productivity growth, lists the factors that influence it, compares economists' views about whether it is slowing, and gives a stern warning to politicians to take it seriously.

The Big Economic Worry: Productivity Is Slowing

By ROBERT J. SAMUELSON

The start of a new year is a good time to take stock, and there are few better indicators of our long-term economic prospects—and also our prospects for political and social peace—than productivity. . . . The good news is that productivity has been growing strongly; the bad news is that it may be moving to a much slower path. . . . Labor productivity is measured as output per hour worked. Whatever enables people to produce more in a given time (machinery, skills, organization) boosts productivity.

That in turn raises our incomes—or gives us more leisure. It also promotes domestic tranquility by muffling the competition between government and personal spending. Slow productivity growth virtually ensures a collision between the heavy costs of retiring baby boomers—mostly for Social Security and Medicare—and younger workers' living standards. Higher taxes will bite deeply into sluggish incomes. The reason: What seem to be tiny productivity shifts have huge consequences.

Consider: In 2005, the U.S. economy produced $12.5 trillion of goods and services, or gross domestic product (GDP). Per capita income—the average for individuals—was $35,000. If productivity growth averages 2.5 percent a year, the economy reaches $34 trillion in 2035 (in constant 2005 dollars), estimates Moody's Economy.com. Per capita income rises to $73,000. Now, suppose productivity growth averages 1 percent annually. Then GDP in 2035 is only $23 trillion, and per capita income is $48,000. That $13,000 gain ($48,000 minus $35,000) may look large, but it occurs over three decades, and part of workers' gain would be taxed away to pay baby boomers' retirement costs. Typical take-home pay would rise less than 1 percent annually.

Unfortunately, productivity growth seems to be decreasing. In the past year it's been only 1.4 percent. By contrast, it averaged about 3 percent from 2000 to 2005. . . . Some long-term forecasts project that the poor performance will continue. In Moody's Economy.com's outlook, productivity growth averages 1.4 percent a year from 2005 to 2035. The main reason: stunted business investment in new machinery, technologies and buildings, says chief economist Mark Zandi. . . . But Federal Reserve Chairman Ben Bernanke has suggested that the post-1995 trend (2.5 percent or higher) might persist for years. In truth, economists have a dismal record in anticipating and explaining productivity shifts. . . . The great frustration is that something so critical is also so elusive. Productivity ultimately encompasses a society's entire economic culture: its technologies, management, workers' skills and motivation, schools, entrepreneurial spirit, work ethic, ambition and risk-taking, the competitive pressure on companies, government policies, financial markets. Everything counts—and connects with everything else.

Therein lies a caution to the Democratic Congress and the Bush administration. Although government can't easily dictate higher productivity, its policies may perversely favor lower productivity. What's politically expedient today—a dubious tax break, a lazy budget deficit, an expensive regulation—may be economically corrosive tomorrow. Don't ditch the future.

The relationship between capital and technology has implications for technology policies. For example, policies that provide incentives for firms to invest might indirectly improve technology as they encourage investment in new, more productive equipment.

Is Government Intervention Appropriate?

Any time there is a question about whether government should intervene in the economy, such as with the technology policies just discussed, the operation of the private market should be examined carefully. For example, we noted that incentives for technology production may be too low without government intervention. Certainly some of the research a business firm undertakes can be kept secret from others. In such cases, the firm may have sufficient incentive to do the research. But many research results are hard to keep secret. In that case, there is a role for government intervention in subsidizing the research. In general, policies to increase economic growth should be given the test for whether government intervention in the economy is necessary: Is the private market providing the right incentives? If not, can the government do better without a large risk of government failure? If the answers are "no" and "yes," respectively, then government intervention is appropriate.

REVIEW

- Policy proposals to increase productivity growth by providing incentives to increase technology include educational reform, tax credits for research, increased funding for research, moving government support toward areas that have significant spillovers, and improving intellectual property laws to better define the property rights of inventors and extend them globally.
- Many technologies are embodied in new capital. Hence, policies to stimulate capital formation could also increase technology.

CONCLUSION: THE IMPORTANCE OF PRODUCTIVITY GROWTH

There is no concept in economics that is more important to people's economic well-being than productivity growth, and there is wide agreement among economists about this essential principle. For example, William Baumol and his colleagues at New York University wrote in *Productivity and American Leadership:*

> It can be said without exaggeration that in the long run probably nothing is as important for economic welfare as the rate of productivity growth.

Paul Krugman, distinguished economics columnist for the *New York Times*, wrote in his *Age of Diminished Expectations*:

> Compared with the problem of slow productivity growth, all our other long-term economic concerns—foreign competition, the industrial base, lagging technology, deteriorating infrastructure and so on—are minor issues.

And Edward Lazear, chair of the President's Council of Economic Advisers, said:

> Productivity growth is important and it's key, because it means that firms can pay workers higher wages. Indeed, real wage growth over any significant period of time is directly linked to productivity growth. For that reason, we must keep productivity growth strong.

In this chapter, we have defined productivity growth and discussed how capital and technology are its essential determinants. We also pointed out that capital, like labor, is eventually subject to diminishing returns, so that technological progress must be an essential part of productivity growth in the long run.

If economic policymakers want to increase people's income and reduce poverty—whether in the United States or in other countries—they must focus on increasing and maintaining productivity growth. Economists differ about the best way to accomplish this goal; for example, they debate whether policy should focus more on stimulating technology by subsidizing research or on increasing incentives for investment by keeping taxes on investment low. The growth accounting formula helps resolve some of these differences by determining the relative importance of capital and technology. In recent years in the United States, both technology and capital have contributed substantially to productivity growth, suggesting that policy should not focus solely on one determinant at the expense of the other.

KEY POINTS

1. The productivity growth rate—the percentage increase in output per hour of work—determines the economic well-being of people in the long run.
2. Technology, along with labor and capital, determines economic growth. Technological progress explains much of the productivity growth wave that started in the late 1700s and enabled developed countries to get rich.
3. Technology as defined by economists is much broader than "high-tech" products or inventions. Technology includes such things as better organizational structure for a firm and better education for workers as well as innovations like fiber-optic cables.
4. As a commodity, technology has the special features of nonexcludability and nonrivalry.
5. Patent laws attempt to make technology more excludable and thereby increase the incentives to invest.
6. The growth accounting formula is itself a great invention that has enabled economists to better understand the role of technology in the economy.
7. Technology policy has the goal of offsetting disincentives to invest and innovate that exist in the private market.
8. Government support for education and research is a key part of a modern technology policy.

KEY TERMS

productivity
diminishing returns
technological change
invention
innovation
diffusion
learning by doing
growth accounting formula

QUESTIONS FOR REVIEW

1. What is the essential difference between economic growth in the last 200 years and in the 2,000 years before that?
2. Why do capital and labor have diminishing returns?
3. Why are economists so sure that technology played a big role in economic growth during the last 200 years?
4. Why does technology include different ways to organize a business firm?
5. How is technology produced?
6. What is the importance of nonrivalry and nonexcludability for technology?
7. Of what practical use is the growth accounting formula?
8. What is wrong with a growth policy that focuses on capital formation but not on technology?
9. What do patents have to do with economic growth?
10. What is the rationale for government intervention in the production of technology?

PROBLEMS

1. The following table shows how output (shaded) depends on capital and labor.

	Labor				
Capital	*50*	*100*	*150*	*200*	*250*
50	200	324	432	528	618
100	246	400	532	650	760
150	278	452	600	734	858
200	304	492	654	800	936
250	324	526	700	856	1,000

   a. Using the table, draw the production function $Y = F(L)$ when the capital stock (K) is 50. What do you observe about the shape of the production function?
   b. Now draw three similar curves that correspond to a capital stock of 100, 150, and 200. What happens to the production function?
   c. Using the diagrams you drew above, indicate the diminishing returns to labor and to capital.

2. Name one way in which use of the following new technologies has made you more productive:
   a. ATM machines
   b. Cellular telephone
   c. The Internet
   d. Laptop computer

3. Identify each of the following as either a capital-saving or a labor-saving technological change:
   a. A gas station installs gasoline pumps that can be activated by a customer with a credit card.
   b. A university upgrades its phone system to include voicemail.
   c. A university reorganizes its departments in order to cut back on administrative costs.

4. Consider a country in which capital per hour of work from 1950 to 1973 grew by 3 percent per year and output per hour of work grew by about 3 percent per year. Suppose that from 1973 to 1991, capital per hour of work did not grow at all and output per hour of work grew by about 1 percent per year. How much of the slowdown in productivity (output per hour of work) growth was due to technological change? Explain. (Assume that the coefficient on capital in the growth accounting formula is 1/3.)

5. If we estimate the share of capital in income incorrectly, it can affect our estimation of how large technological growth has been. Rework Problem 4 assuming that capital's share is 1/4. Explain intuitively the difference in the importance of technology.

6. According to the spending allocation model in Chapter 7, a decrease in government spending results in, among other things, an increase in investment in the long run. Suppose the capital stock is \$1 trillion and a fall in government spending causes a \$50 billion rise in investment. Determine the effect of the change in government purchases on long-run per capita output growth, using the growth accounting formula. (Assume that the coefficient on capital in the growth accounting formula is 1/3.)

7. **a.** Suppose that a country has no growth in technology, and that capital and labor hours are growing at the same rate. What is the growth rate of real GDP per hour of work? Explain.
   b. Suppose that capital in the country described in part (a) continues to grow at its previous rate and technology growth is still zero, but growth in labor hours falls to half its previous rate. What happens to growth in real GDP per hour of work?

8. Which of the following types of government spending are likely to help economic growth? Why?
   a. Military spending on advertising for recruits
   b. Military spending on laser research
   c. Funding for a nationwide computer network
   d. Subsidies for a national opera company
   e. Extra funding for educational programs

9. Many U.S. companies in the software, music, and movie industries have been asking the Chinese government to better enforce intellectual property rights. Discuss the impact of this enforcement on
   a. Chinese firms
   b. American firms
   c. Chinese consumers

10. Suppose that Lesotho, an extremely poor African country, announces that it will ignore patents held by Western companies on HIV/AIDS-related pharmaceuticals and will instead buy copies of the drugs produced by Indian firms.
   a. Would you support such a decision? Why?
   b. Would your answer change if, instead of Lesotho, it was a richer country like Thailand or Brazil that was threatening to break the patent? Why?

Deriving the Growth Accounting Formula

The growth accounting formula states that

$$\text{Growth rate of productivity} = \frac{1}{3}\left(\begin{array}{c}\text{growth rate}\\ \text{of capital}\\ \text{per hour}\\ \text{of work}\end{array}\right) + \begin{array}{c}\text{growth rate}\\ \text{of technology}\end{array}$$

To derive the formula, we start with the relationship between productivity (Y/L) and capital per hour of work (K/L) shown in Figure A.1. Because of diminishing returns to capital, the line is curved: As capital per hour of work increases, the increased productivity that comes from the additional capital per hour diminishes.

The curve in Figure A.1 is called a **productivity curve;** it can be represented in symbols as $(Y/L) = f(K/L)$, or productivity is a function of capital per hour of work.

An upward shift in the productivity curve due to an increase in technological change is shown in Figure A.2. For example, with capital per hour constant at point A in the figure, more technology leads to more productivity.

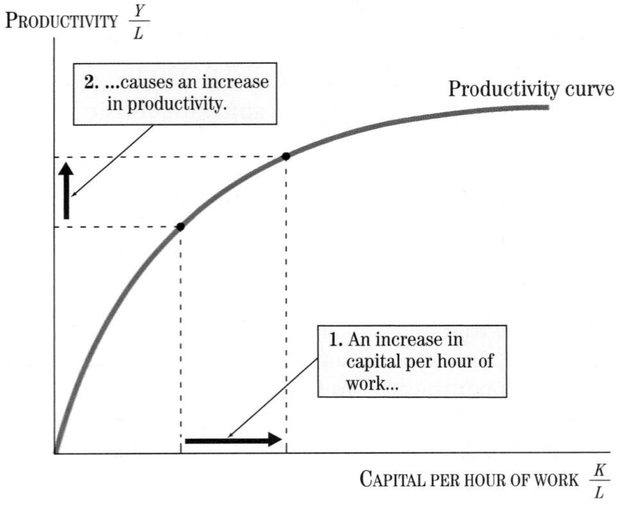

FIGURE A.1
Productivity Curve
Productivity, or output per hour of work, is shown to increase with the amount of capital that workers have, as measured by capital per hour of work. The productivity curve gets flatter as output per hour of work increases because of diminishing returns to capital.

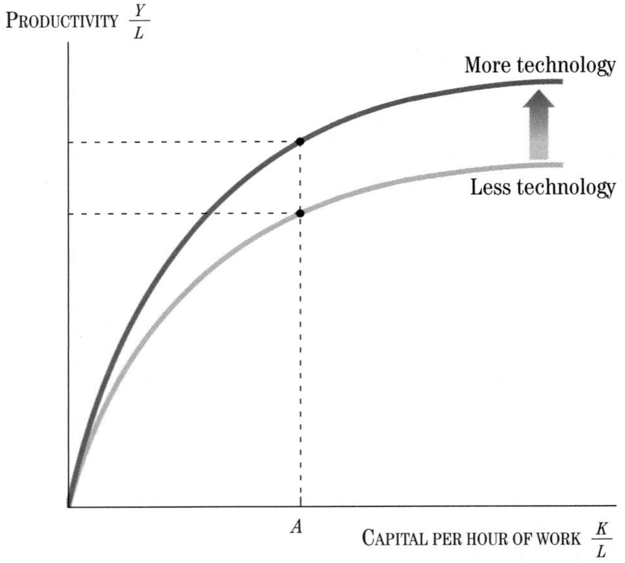

FIGURE A.2
A Shift in the Productivity Curve Due to Technology
An increase in technology permits an increase in productivity even if there is no change in capital per hour of work. For example, if capital per hour of work stays at *A*, productivity increases when the productivity curve shifts up.

Productivity increases in the economy are due to a combination of *movements along* the productivity curve because of more capital per hour and *shifts of* the productivity curve because of technological change. The growth accounting formula is derived by translating the *movements along* and the *shifts of* the curve into two algebraic terms.

In Figure A.3, productivity and capital per hour in two different years (year 1 and year 2) are shown. These could be 2003 and 2004 or any other two years. In this example, the growth rate of productivity is given by the increase in productivity $(C - A)$ divided by the initial level of productivity (A), or $(C - A)/A$. (The definition of the growth rate of a variable is the change divided by the initial level.)

Observe in Figure A.3 how the increase in productivity can be divided into the part due to higher capital per hour

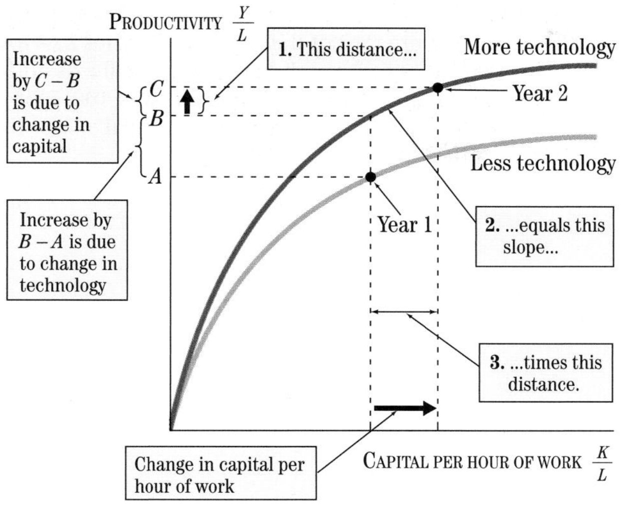

FIGURE A.3
Growth Accounting with Capital per Hour and Technology Increasing
Here a shift in the productivity curve and a movement along the productivity curve due to more capital per hour of work are combined. Productivity increases. The part of the increase due to capital and the part due to technological change are shown in the diagram.

of work $(C - B)$ and the part due to technology $(B - A)$. Thus, we have

$(C - A)/A$		$(C - B)/A$		$(B - A)/A$
Growth rate of productivity	=	term related to capital per hour	+	growth rate of technology

which is already close to the growth accounting formula.

To finish the derivation, we need to examine the first term on the right. How does this term relate to capital per hour of work? The numbered boxes in Figure A.3 show that $C - B$ equals the *change* in capital per hour of work $\Delta(K/L)$ times the *slope* of the productivity curve. (The slope times the change along the horizontal axis gives the changes along the vertical axis.) Let the symbol r be the slope, which measures how much additional capital increases output. Thus, $(C - B)/A$ is given by

$$\frac{\Delta(K/L)r}{(Y/L)} = \frac{\Delta(K/L)\,r\,(K/Y)}{(Y/L)(K/Y)} = \frac{\Delta(K/L)\,r\,(K/Y)}{(K/L)}$$

The expression on the right is obtained by multiplying the numerator and the denominator of the expression on the left by (K/Y). Now the term on the right is simply the growth rate of capital per hour times $r(K/Y)$. The amount of income paid to capital is r times K if capital is paid according to how much additional capital increases output. Aggregate income is given by Y. Thus, the term $r(K/Y)$ is the share of capital income in aggregate income. This share is approximately 1/3. Thus, the expression $(C - B)/A$ is the growth rate of capital per hour of work times 1/3. Thus, the growth accounting formula is derived.

KEY POINTS

1. The productivity curve describes how more capital per hour of work increases productivity, or output per hour of work.
2. The productivity curve shifts up if there is an increase in technology.
3. The growth accounting formula is derived by dividing an increase in productivity into (1) a shift in the productivity curve due to more technology and (2) a movement along the productivity curve due to more capital per worker.

KEY TERM AND DEFINITION

productivity curve: a relationship stating the output per hour of work for each amount of capital per hour of work in the economy.

QUESTIONS FOR REVIEW

1. What is the difference between the productivity curve and the production function?
2. What is the difference between a shift of the productivity curve and a movement along the curve?
3. Why does the share of capital income in total income appear in the growth accounting formula?

PROBLEMS

1. Consider the following relation between productivity and capital per hour for the economy.

Capital per Hour of Work (K/L)	Output per Hour of Work (Y/L)
\$20	\$40
\$40	\$80
\$60	\$110
\$80	\$130
\$100	\$140

   a. Plot the productivity curve.
   b. Suppose that in year 1, $K/L = 40$ and $Y/L = 80$, but in year 2, $K/L = 60$ and $Y/L = 110$. How much has technology contributed to the increase in productivity between the two years?

c. Suppose that between year 2 and year 3, the productivity curve shifts up by $20 at each level of capital per hour of work. If $K/L = 80$ and $Y/L = 150$ in year 3, how many dollars did capital contribute to productivity growth between year 2 and year 3? How much was the contribution as a fraction of the growth rate of capital per worker?

2. Suppose the production function $Y = F(K, L)$ is such that Y equals the square root of the product (K times L). Plot the production function with Y on the vertical axis and L on the horizontal axis for the case where $K = 100$. Plot the productivity curve with Y/L on the vertical axis and K/L on the horizontal axis.

Chapter 10

Money and Inflation

Money provides an essential foundation for the economy, so if you want to understand how the economy works, you have to learn about money. Historians trace the origins of money to the very origins of civilization. As Babylon, Ur, and other ancient cities of Mesopotamia were being built 5,000 years ago, primitive forms of money, such as silver rings or even scraps of silver, were used to buy and sell in the street markets thousands of different goods—mortar, bricks, sandals for workers—that were needed for the construction. The term *shekel*, which meant one-third of an ounce of silver, came into use at that time. Years later, images of kings or goddesses would be impressed on round pieces of silver, giving coins the look they still have today. Without money, it is doubtful that these first large-scale civilizations could have arisen.

If the economy is working smoothly, you hardly notice the importance of money. Of course, you can see money being exchanged at the market—just as the Mesopotamians did—but this is hardly worth a comment. But occasionally the monetary foundation of an economy breaks down, and then you really notice the importance of money. After World War I, the government of Germany printed way too much money, and the price of everything rose by millions of percent, causing havoc in the economy and helping sow the seeds for World War II. In the 1970s, the United States government also created too much money. Though less pronounced than in Germany, inflation rose for more than a decade and the U.S. economy went through one of its roughest periods, with one recession after another. Since the early 1980s, money has been managed much better in the United States; inflation has been low, and economic growth has been far steadier.

Sometimes government control of money completely breaks down. In 2001, 12 different provinces of Argentina started printing their own monies, causing great confusion in the economy. In Iraq (modern Mesopotamia) under Saddam Hussein, the northern provinces used a different money from the southern provinces. After Saddam Hussein fell from power in 2003, a new currency had to be printed and flown into the country to prevent a financial collapse. This was no minor undertaking, as 27 747 planeloads of new currency were shipped into the country—a noticeable reminder of the importance of money.

The purpose of this chapter is to examine the role of money in the economy. After defining money, we show that commercial banks play a key role in providing money in a modern economy. We then examine how central banks—such as the Fed (the Federal Reserve) in the United States or the ECB (European Central Bank) in Europe—can control the supply of money. We also show why *excessive increases in the supply of money cause inflation*—one of the most important principles of macroeconomics.

WHAT IS MONEY?

money: that part of a person's wealth that can be readily used for transactions; money also serves as a store of value and a unit of account.

In a broad sense, money performs three functions in the economy: It can serve as a medium of exchange, a unit of account, and a store of value. More details about the three functions are given below. Economists emphasize the medium of exchange dimension in defining money. They define **money** as the part of a person's wealth that can be readily used for transactions, such as buying a sandwich or a bicycle. This definition differs from the more typical usage, in which the term is used to describe someone's wealth or income—as when we say that "she makes a lot of money" or "he has a lot of money." To an economist, money does not include what a person earns in a year or the total assets that she has, but it does include the portion of that person's wealth—such as the notes and coins in her purse—that can be easily used for transactions.

Three Functions of Money

medium of exchange: something that is generally accepted as a means of payment.

Medium of Exchange. Money serves as a **medium of exchange** in that it is an item that people are willing to accept as payment for what they are selling because they in turn can use it to pay for something else they want. For example, in ancient times, people received coins for their agricultural produce, such as grain, and then used these coins to buy clothing.

The use of coins was a great technological improvement over *barter,* in which goods are exchanged only for other goods. Under a barter system, there is no single medium of exchange. Thus, under a barter system, if you make shoes and want to buy apples, you have to find an apple seller who needs new shoes. The disadvantage of a barter system is that it requires a rare *coincidence of wants* in which the person who wants to consume what you want to sell (shoes, for example) has exactly what you want to consume (apples, for example).

store of value: something that will allow purchasing power to be carried from one period to the next.

■ **Store of Value.** Money also serves as a **store of value** from one period to another. For example, in ancient times, people could sell their produce in September for gold coins and then use the coins to buy staples in January. In other words, they could store their purchasing power from one season to another.

Coins are not the only thing that can serve as a store of value. For example, rice and corn can also be stored from one season to the next; therefore, they can also serve as a store of value. But if you are not a farmer with a large storage bin, coins are much more likely to be used as money.

unit of account: a standard unit in which prices can be quoted and values of goods can be compared.

■ **Unit of Account.** Money also serves a third function: providing a **unit of account.** The prices of goods are usually stated in units of money. For example, prices of shoes or apples in ancient Greece were stated in a certain number of tetradrachmas because people using these coins were familiar with that unit. Originally, units of money were determined by the weight of the metal. The British pound, for example, was originally a pound of silver. That terminology stuck even though, as we will see, modern money is unrelated to silver or any other metal.

To better understand the difference between the unit of account and the medium of exchange, it is helpful to find examples where they are based on different monies. For example, when inflation got very high in Argentina in the early 1990s, the prices of many goods were quoted in U.S. dollars rather than Argentine pesos, but people usually exchanged pesos when they bought or sold goods. Thus, the U.S. dollar was the unit of account, while the medium of exchange was still the peso. But such cases are the exception; the unit of account and the medium of exchange are usually the same money.

Commodity Money

Many items have been used for money throughout history. Salt, cattle, furs, tobacco, shells, and arrowheads have been used as money. Traces of their former use can still be found in our vocabulary. The word *salary* comes from the Latin word for salt, and the word *pecuniary* comes from the Latin word for cattle. In World War II prisoner-of-war camps, cigarettes were used for money. On the island of Yap in the Pacific Ocean, huge stones weighing several tons were used for money.

Throughout history, the most common form of money has been metallic coins, usually made of gold, silver, or bronze. Gold coins were used as early as the seventh century B.C. in Lydia (now western Turkey). The Chinese were issuing bronze coins with a hole in the middle in the fifth century B.C., and in the fourth century the Greeks issued silver coins called tetradrachmas that had the goddess Athena on one side and her sacred animal, the owl, on the other. All these examples of money are commodities and are therefore called *commodity money.* Metals proved to be the most common form of commodity money because they could be divided easily into smaller units, are very durable, and could be carried around.

When gold, silver, and other commodities were used as money, changes in the supply of these commodities would change their price relative to all other goods. An increase in the supply of gold, all else equal, would increase the number of gold coins that people were willing to pay in order to purchase other goods and services. In other words, the price of all other goods in the economy would rise relative to that of gold. Such an increase in the price of all goods in the economy is called inflation, as you may recall from the definitions of key economic concepts given in Chapter 6. Thus, increases in the supply of gold or any other commodity used as money would cause inflation. Whenever there were huge gold discoveries, the price of gold fell and there were increases in inflation in countries that used gold as money. Thus, inflation was determined largely by the supply of precious metals. This relationship between

Stone Money of Yap Island, Micronesia

Silver Coins of Ancient Greece

the supply of money and inflation, which seems so clear in the case of commodity money, has persisted into modern times, even though there are now many other forms of money.

From Coins to Paper Money to Deposits

Although coins and other commodity monies are improvements over barter, there are more efficient forms of money. Starting in the late eighteenth and early nineteenth centuries, *paper money* began to be used widely and supplemented or replaced coins as a form of money. Although there are a few examples of paper money being used earlier, it was at this time that it became generally recognized that paper money was easier to use and could save greatly on the use of precious metals.

Originally, the amount of paper currency was linked by law or convention to the supply of commodities. One reason for this link was the recognition that more money would cause inflation and that limiting the amount of paper money to the amount of some commodity like gold would limit the amount of paper money. Irving Fisher of Yale University, perhaps the most prolific and influential American economist of the early twentieth century, argued for linking paper money to commodities for precisely this reason. Many countries of the world linked their paper money to gold in the nineteenth and early twentieth centuries. They were on a *gold standard,* which meant that the price of gold in terms of paper money was fixed by the government. The government fixed the price by agreeing to buy and sell gold at that price. Today the United States and other countries have severed all links between their money and gold. They are no longer on the gold standard and apparently have no intention of returning. Governments now supply virtually all the coin and paper money—the two together are called **currency.**

currency: money in its physical form: coin and paper money.

Although paper money was much easier to make and to use than coins, it too has been surpassed by a more efficient form of money. Today many people have **checking deposits** at banks or other financial institutions. These are deposits of funds on which an individual can write a check to make payment for goods and

checking deposit: an account at a financial institution on which checks can be written; also called a checkable deposit.

ECONOMICS IN THE NEWS

Counterfeit Money

Counterfeiting is on the rise in the United States and other countries. In response, the U.S. Treasury is redesigning the dollar so that it is more difficult to counterfeit. Recall that money is a reliable medium of exchange only if people are willing to accept it knowing that it can in turn be used to purchase other goods. How does counterfeiting interfere with the role of money as a medium of exchange?

More Counterfeit Money Changed Hands in '06

By BARBARA HAGENBAUGH | USA TODAY

WASHINGTON—The amount of counterfeit money being accepted by consumers and stores in the USA is climbing as crooks are increasingly using inexpensive home computers and printers to produce phony money.

About $62 million entered circulation that was later deemed fake in the 2006 fiscal year, which ended Sept. 30. That represents a more than 10% increase from the prior year and a 69% rise from just three years earlier, according to the latest data from the Secret Service obtained by USA TODAY.

Terry Tilka says he sees fake bills about once a week at Rock Island Brewing, a restaurant/bar he owns in Rock Island, Ill., as well as at a dance club he owns. "It's been worse in the last three or four years than I have ever seen in my 33 years of business," he says.

There has been a noticeable rise in counterfeiting in the past eight months in Pasco County, Fla., says Sgt. Bill Moltzan of the sheriff's office economic crimes unit there.

The crooks are bold. One person who was arrested charged people, including an undercover agent, for a counterfeiting how-to class. One man was arrested after dancers in a strip club realized he was passing out fake bills and called police while the bouncer held the man. A 62-year-old woman known as Grandma was caught this month trying to sell fake money at less than face value.

"Technology is making it easier for the people trying to do this on their own," Moltzan says.

services. The deposits serve as money because people can write checks on them. For example, when a student pays $100 for books with a check, the student's checking deposit at the bank goes down by $100, and the bookstore's checking deposit at the bank goes up by $100. Checking deposits are used in much the same way as when a student pays with a $100 bill, which is then placed in the store's cash register. The student's holding of money goes down by $100, and the store's goes up by $100. Deposits are used by many people as a partial replacement for coin or paper money.

Measures of the Money Supply

money supply: the sum of currency (coin and paper money) and deposits at banks.

Today economists define the **money supply** as the sum of currency (coin and paper money) and deposits at banks. But there are differences of opinion about what types of deposits should be included.

Despite the rise, the amount of fake money in circulation is a fraction of 1% of genuine currency, Secret Service spokesman Eric Zahren says. The fact the money was caught suggests security features that have been added starting in 2003, such as colors and watermarks, make it easier to detect fakes, says Dennis Forgue, head of currency at Harlan J. Berk in Chicago.

The increase in currency caught should be seen "not necessarily as a sign of defeat, but as a sign of success," he says.

But Zahren says the ease of using home computers to make the money has added challenges to catching counterfeiters.

About 54% of the counterfeit currency collected in fiscal 2006 was made using digital technology vs. so-called offset printing, which involves more skill, time and expense. In 1996, only 1% of counterfeits were digitally produced, according to the Secret Service.

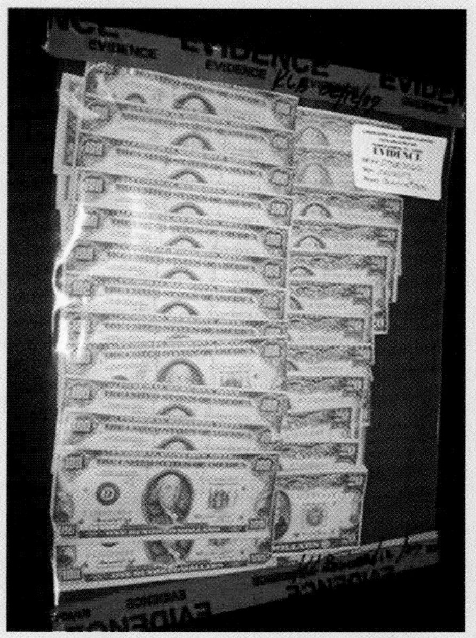

The government has been updating U.S. bills to try to thwart counterfeiters. In 2003, the $20 bill, the most frequently counterfeited currency in the USA, was the first to feature a color other than green. Other features such as a watermark and color-shifting ink also were added. Since then, new $10 bills and $50 bills have entered circulation. This year, a new $5 bill will be introduced.

The narrowest measure of the money supply is called *M1*. The M1 measure consists mainly of currency plus checking deposits (travelers checks are also part of M1 but constitute less than 1 percent of total M1). The items in M1 have a great degree of *liquidity,* which means that they can be quickly and easily used to purchase goods and services.

Many things that people would consider money, however, are not included in M1. For example, if you had no cash but you wanted to buy a birthday gift for a relative, you could withdraw cash from your savings deposit. A *savings deposit* is a deposit that pays interest and from which funds can normally be easily withdrawn at any time. In other words, a savings deposit is also liquid, but not quite as liquid as a checking deposit. Similarly, *time deposits*—which require the depositor to keep the money at the bank for a certain amount of time or else lose interest—are not as liquid as checking deposits, but it is possible to withdraw funds from them. Economists have created a broader measure of the money supply, called *M2,* that includes

TABLE 1
Measures of Money in the United States, February 2007 (billions of dollars)

Currency	751
M1: Currency plus checking deposits	1,359
M2: M1 plus time deposits, savings deposits, and other deposits on which check writing is limited or not allowed	7,112

Source: Federal Reserve Board.

everything that is in M1 plus savings deposits, time deposits, and certain accounts on which check writing is very limited. Still broader concepts of the money supply can be defined, but M1 and M2 are the most important ones. Table 1 shows the total amounts of different definitions of the money supply for the whole U.S. economy in February 2007.

Only about one-half of the M1 definition of the money supply is currency, and only about one-tenth of the M2 definition is currency. There is disagreement among economists as to whether the more narrowly defined M1 or the more broadly defined M2 or something else is the best definition of the money supply. There is probably no best definition for all times and all purposes. For simplicity, in the rest of this chapter we make no distinction between the Ms but simply refer to the money supply, M, as currency plus deposits.

REVIEW

- Commodity money—usually gold, silver, or bronze coins—originally served as the main type of money in most societies. Increases in the supply of these commodities would reduce their price relative to those of all other commodities and thereby cause inflation.
- Later, paper currency and deposits at banks became forms of money.
- There are three roles for money—as a medium of exchange, as a store of value, and as a unit of account.

THE FED, THE BANKS, AND THE LINK FROM RESERVES TO DEPOSITS

We have seen that increases in the supply of commodity money such as gold would increase inflation. So would the excessive printing of paper money (currency) by governments. But in today's world, money consists of both currency and deposits. Nevertheless, it is possible for governments—usually through a central bank—to control the supply of money. In the United States, the central bank is the **Federal Reserve System,** nicknamed the "Fed." To understand how the Fed can control the supply of money, we must first look at how the Fed can control the amount of deposits at banks.

Federal Reserve System (the Fed): the central bank of the United States, which oversees the creation of money in the United States.

bank: a firm that channels funds from savers to investors by accepting deposits and making loans.

A **bank**—such as Bank of America or Citibank—is a firm that channels funds from savers to investors by accepting deposits and making loans. Figure 1 illustrates this function of banks. Banks are a type of *financial intermediary* because they "intermediate" between savers and investors. Other examples of financial intermediaries

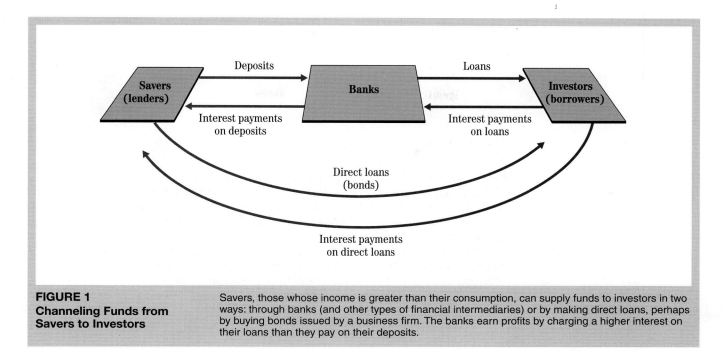

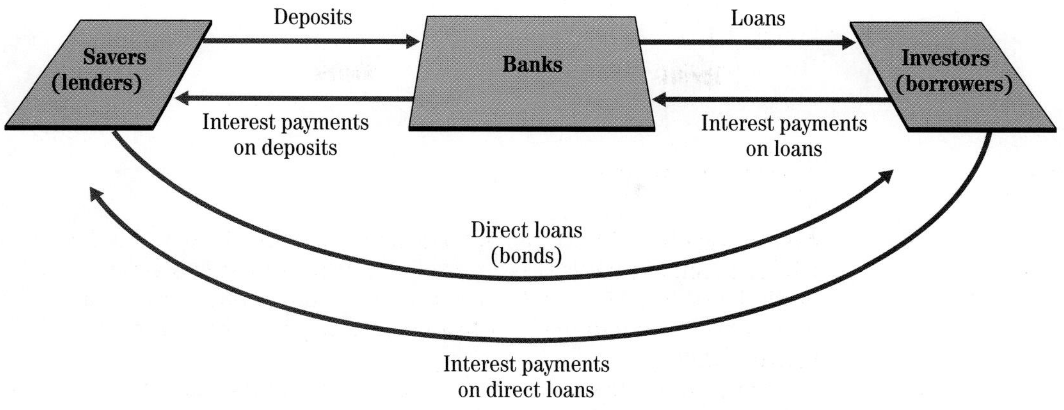

FIGURE 1
Channeling Funds from Savers to Investors

Savers, those whose income is greater than their consumption, can supply funds to investors in two ways: through banks (and other types of financial intermediaries) or by making direct loans, perhaps by buying bonds issued by a business firm. The banks earn profits by charging a higher interest on their loans than they pay on their deposits.

are credit unions and savings and loan institutions. Banks are sometimes called *commercial banks* because many of their loans are to business firms engaged in commerce. Banks accept deposits from people who have funds and who want to earn interest and then lend the funds to other individuals who want to borrow and who are willing to pay interest. A bank earns profits by charging a higher interest rate to the borrowers than it pays to the depositors.

The Fed

The *central bank* of a country serves as a bank to other banks. In other words, commercial banks deposit funds at the central bank, and the central bank in turn makes loans to other commercial banks. We will see that the deposits of the commercial banks at the central bank are very important for controlling the money supply.

The Fed was established as the central bank for the United States in 1913 and now has over 25,000 employees spread all over the country.

Board of Governors. At the core of the Fed is the *Federal Reserve Board,* or Board of Governors, consisting of seven people appointed to nonrenewable fourteen-year terms by the president of the United States and confirmed by the Senate. The Federal Reserve Board is located in Washington, D.C.

One of the governors is appointed by the president as chairman of the board; this appointment also requires Senate confirmation and can be renewed for additional terms. Alan Greenspan was first appointed chairman by President Reagan in 1987 and served until 2006, when Ben Bernanke was appointed by President George W. Bush.

The District Federal Reserve Banks. The Federal Reserve System includes not only the Federal Reserve Board in Washington but also twelve Federal Reserve Banks in different districts around the country (see Figure 2).

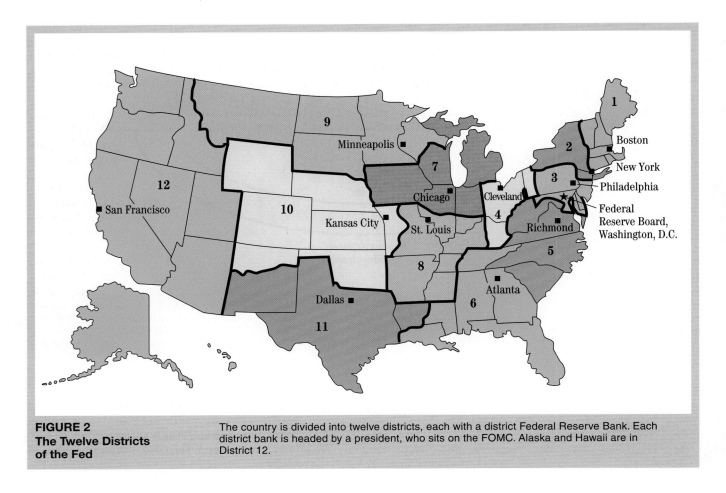

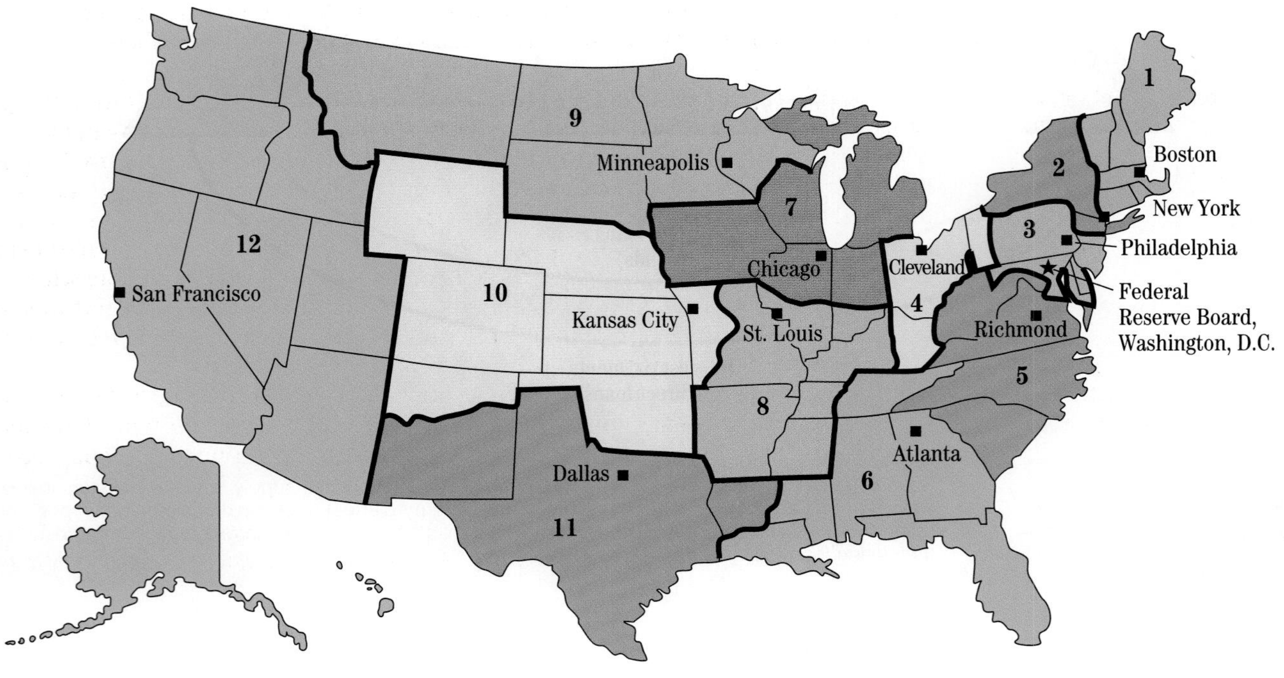

FIGURE 2
The Twelve Districts of the Fed

The country is divided into twelve districts, each with a district Federal Reserve Bank. Each district bank is headed by a president, who sits on the FOMC. Alaska and Hawaii are in District 12.

The term *Fed* refers to the whole Federal Reserve System, including the Board of Governors in Washington and the twelve district banks. Each district bank is headed by a president, who is chosen by commercial bankers and other people in the district and approved by the Board of Governors.

Federal Open Market Committee (FOMC): the committee, consisting of the seven members of the Board of Governors and the twelve presidents of the Fed district banks, that meets about eight times per year and makes decisions about the supply of money; only five of the presidents vote at any one time.

The Federal Open Market Committee (FOMC). The Fed makes decisions about the supply of money through a committee called the **Federal Open Market Committee (FOMC).** The members of the FOMC are the seven governors and the twelve district bank presidents, but only five of the presidents vote at any one time. Thus, there are twelve voting members of the FOMC at any one time. The FOMC meets in Washington about eight times a year to decide how to implement monetary policy. Figure 3 shows the relationship between the FOMC, the Board of Governors, and the district banks.

Even though the chair of the Fed has only one of the twelve votes on the FOMC, the position has considerably more power than this one vote might indicate. The chair also has executive authority over the operations of the whole Federal Reserve, sets the agenda at FOMC meetings, and represents the Fed in testimony before Congress. When journalists in the popular press write about the Fed, they usually talk as if the chair has almost complete power over Fed decisions.

Now that we have described the Fed, let us examine the operation of banks and how they, along with the Fed, create money.

The Banks

A commercial bank accepts deposits from individuals and makes loans to others. To understand how a bank functions, it is necessary to look at its balance sheet, which shows these deposits and loans. Table 2 is an example of a balance sheet for a bank, called BankOne.

asset: something of value owned by a person or a firm.

liability: something of value that a person or a firm owes to someone else.

The different items are divided into *assets* and *liabilities*. An **asset** is something of value owned by a person or a firm. A **liability** is something of value that a person or a firm owes, such as a debt, to someone else. Thus a bank's assets are anything the bank owns and any sum owed to the bank by someone else. A bank's liabilities are anything the bank owes to someone else. People's *deposits* at banks are the main liability of banks, as shown in Table 2. Certain assets, such as the bank's building and furniture, are not shown in this balance sheet because they do not change when the money supply changes. Also, when a bank starts up, the owners must put in some funds, called the bank's capital stock, that can be used in case the bank needs cash in an emergency. This asset is not shown in this balance sheet either.

reserves: deposits that commercial banks hold at the Fed.

Consider each of the assets shown in the balance sheet in Table 2. **Reserves** are deposits that commercial banks hold at the Fed, much as people hold deposits at commercial banks. Remember, the Fed is the bank for the commercial banks. Just as

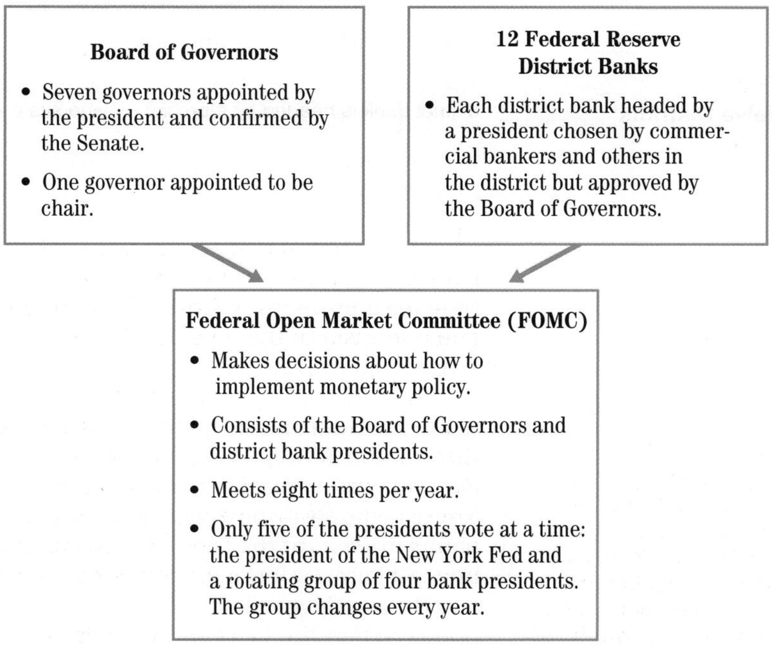

FIGURE 3
The Structure of the Fed
Decisions about monetary policy are made by the FOMC, which consists of the Fed governors and district Fed presidents.

TABLE 2
Balance Sheet of BankOne (millions of dollars)

Assets		Liabilities	
Loans	70	Deposits	100
Bonds	20		
Reserves	10		

This is the initial situation. The ratio of reserves to deposits is .1.

you can hold a deposit at a commercial bank, a commercial bank can hold a deposit at the Fed. Reserves are simply a name for these deposits by commercial banks at the Fed.

required reserve ratio: the fraction of a bank's deposits that it is required to hold at the Fed.

Under U.S. law, a commercial bank is required to hold reserves at the Fed equal to a fraction of the deposits people hold at the commercial bank; this fraction is called the **required reserve ratio.** Banks may in fact choose to hold a greater fraction of their deposits in the form of reserves at the Fed than they are required to. In reality, then, the ratio of reserves to deposits, known as the *reserve ratio,* may differ from the required reserve ratio: It can be larger, but it cannot be smaller. In the following example, we will assume that banks do not exercise this option, so that the reserve ratio is equal to the required reserve ratio. We will also assume that the required reserve ratio is 10 percent, which is very close to what it really is in the United States.

The two other assets of the bank are loans and bonds. *Loans* are made by banks to individuals or firms for a period of time; the banks earn interest on these loans. *Bonds* are promises of a firm or government to pay back a certain amount after a number of years. Bonds are issued by the U.S. government and by large corporations. Banks sometimes buy and hold such bonds, as BankOne has done in Table 2.

The Link Between Reserves and Deposits

Because deposits at banks are a form of money, the Fed must be able to control the total amount of these deposits if it is to control the money supply. The link between the deposits at banks and the reserves at the Fed provides the key mechanism by which the Fed can exert control over the amount of deposits at the commercial banks. To see this, we first look at some examples to show how this link between reserves and deposits works in the whole economy. To make the story simpler for now, we assume that everyone uses deposits rather than currency for their money. (We will take up currency again in the next section.)

A Formula Linking Reserves to Deposits. To see how the Fed can change the amount of deposits in the economy, let us assume that the Fed increases the amount of reserves that banks hold at the Fed. The Fed can cause such an increase in reserves simply by buying something from a bank and paying for it by increasing that bank's reserves at the Fed. The Fed usually buys government bonds when it wants to increase reserves because banks have a lot of bonds.

On any given day, the Fed buys and sells billions of dollars of government bonds. When the Fed buys government bonds, it has to pay for them with something. It pays for them with bank reserves—the deposits banks have with the Fed. For example, if the Fed wants to buy bonds held by Citibank, it says, "We want $10 million worth of bonds, and we will pay for them by increasing Citibank's account with us by $10 million." This is an electronic transaction. Citibank's deposits at the Fed (reserves) have increased by $10 million, and the Fed gets the bonds. It has exchanged bank reserves for the bonds. The buying or selling of bonds by the Federal Reserve is called an **open market operation.**

open market operation: the buying or selling of bonds by the central bank.

So let's assume that the Fed buys \$10 million of government bonds from BankOne and pays for the bonds by increasing BankOne's reserves by \$10 million. Thus reserves rise at banks in the economy. Now, with the reserve ratio the same (in this example equal to .1) for each bank in the economy, there is a formula linking reserves and deposits for the whole economy. It is given by

$$\text{Reserves} = (\text{reserve ratio}) \times \text{deposits}$$

where reserves and deposits refer to the amounts in the whole economy. If we divide both sides of this expression by the reserve ratio, we get

$$\text{Deposits} = \left(\frac{1}{\text{reserve ratio}}\right) \times \text{reserves}$$

Thus, any increase in reserves is multiplied by the inverse of the reserve ratio to get the increase in deposits. For example, if the \$10 million change in reserves is multiplied by $(1/.1) = 10$, we get \$100 million change in deposits.

One could have started the example by assuming that the Fed bought \$10 million in government bonds from some person other than a bank. That person would deposit the check from the Fed in a bank, and in the end, the answer would be exactly the same: A \$10 million increase in reserves leads to a \$100 million increase in deposits.

One could also analyze the effects of a decrease in reserves using the same formula linking reserves and deposits. A decrease in reserves occurs when the Fed sells bonds. For example, a decrease in reserves of \$10 million would lead to a decrease in deposits of \$100 million.

Bank-by-Bank Deposit Expansion. Now let's look at the details of what is going on in the banks. In our example, when the Fed buys bonds, BankOne's holdings of bonds decline by \$10 million, from \$20 million to \$10 million, and BankOne's reserves at the Fed increase by \$10 million, from \$10 million to \$20 million. The balance sheet would then look like Table 3, a change from Table 2. The key point is that there are now \$10 million more reserves in the economy than before the Fed purchased the government bonds from BankOne. The reserves are held by BankOne, but they will not be held for long.

Recall that banks hold reserves equal to a certain fraction of their deposits, a fraction called the reserve ratio, which in this example we are assuming is 10 percent. But now, after the Fed's actions, BankOne has 20 percent of its deposits as reserves, or more than the required 10 percent. Because the reserves do not pay any interest, while loans and bonds do, the bank will have an incentive to reduce its reserves and make more loans or buy more bonds.

Suppose BankOne decreases its reserves by making more loans; with the reserve ratio of .1, the bank can loan \$10 million. Suppose the bank loans \$10 million to UNO, a small oil company, which uses the funds to buy an oil tanker from DOS, a shipbuilding firm. UNO pays DOS with a check from BankOne, and DOS deposits the check in its checking account at its own bank, BankTwo. Now BankTwo must ask

TABLE 3
Balance Sheet of BankOne after Reserves Increase (millions of dollars)

Assets		Liabilities	
Loans	70	Deposits	100
Bonds	10		
Reserves	20		

Note the effect of the Fed's purchase of bonds: Compared with Table 2, bonds are lower and reserves are higher in Table 3. The ratio of reserves to deposits is .2.

TABLE 4
Balance Sheet of BankOne After It Makes Loans

Assets		Liabilities	
Loans	80	Deposits	100
Bonds	10		
Reserves	10		

By making more loans, the bank reduces the ratio of reserves to deposits back to .1.

BankOne for payment; BankOne will make the payment by lowering its reserve account at the Fed and increasing BankTwo's reserve account at the Fed by $10 million. BankOne's balance sheet at the end of these transactions is shown in Table 4.

Hence, after BankOne makes the loan and transfers its reserves to BankTwo, its reserves are back to 10 percent of its deposits. This is the end of the story for BankOne, but not for the economy as a whole because BankTwo now has $10 million more in reserves, and this is going to affect BankTwo's decisions. Let us see how.

Now BankTwo finds itself with $10 million in additional deposits and $10 million in additional reserves at the Fed. (Remember that deposits are a liability to BankTwo and the reserves are an asset; thus, assets and liabilities each have risen by $10 million.) However, BankTwo needs to hold only $1 million in reserves for the additional $10 million in deposits. Thus, BankTwo will want to make more loans until its reserves equal 10 percent of its deposits. It will lend out to other people an amount equal to 90 percent of the $10 million, or $9 million. In Table 5, the increase in deposits, loans, and reserves at BankTwo is shown in the first row. This is the end of the story for BankTwo, but not for the economy as a whole.

The people who get loans from BankTwo will use these loans to pay others. Thus, the funds will probably end up in yet another bank, called BankThree. Then, BankThree will find itself with $9 million in additional deposits and $9 million in additional reserves. BankThree will then lend 90 percent of the $9 million, or

TABLE 5
Deposit Expansion (millions of dollars)

	Deposits	Loans	Reserves
BankTwo	10.00	9.00	1.000
BankThree	9.00	8.10	0.900
BankFour	8.10	7.29	0.810
BankFive	7.29	6.56	0.729
BankSix	6.56	5.90	0.656
BankSeven	5.90	5.31	0.590
BankEight	5.31	4.78	0.531
BankNine	4.78	4.30	0.430
BankTen	4.30	3.87	0.387
.	.	.	.
.	.	.	.
.	.	.	.
Final sum	100.00	90.00	10.000

The numbers in each column get smaller and smaller; if we add up the numbers for all the banks, even those beyond BankTen, we get the sum at the bottom.

$8.1 million, as shown in the second row of Table 5. This process will continue from bank to bank. We begin to see that the initial increase in reserves is leading to a much bigger expansion of deposits. The whole process is shown in Table 5. Each row shows what happens at one of the banks. The sums of the columns show the change for the whole economy. If we sum the columns through the end of the process, we will see that deposits, and thus the money supply, increase by $100 million as a result of the $10 million increase in reserves. The increase in deposits is 10 times the actual increase in reserves—exactly what the formula predicted! In reality, the whole process takes a short period of time (days rather than weeks) because banks adjust their loans and reserves very quickly.

How the Fed Controls the Money Supply: Currency plus Deposits

We have now seen how the Fed can, through an increase in reserves, increase the amount of deposits or, through a decrease in reserves, reduce the amount of deposits. But the money supply includes currency as well as deposits. With currency in the picture, the Fed must keep track of whether people want to hold more currency or less currency compared with deposits.

Although currency and deposits are both part of the money supply, they have different characteristics. For some purposes, people prefer currency to checking deposits, and vice versa. These preferences determine how much currency and checking deposits there are in the economy. If you want to hold more currency in your wallet because you find it is more convenient than a checking deposit, you just go to the bank and reduce your checking deposit and carry around more currency. If you are worried about crime and do not want to have much currency in your wallet, then you go to the bank and deposit a larger amount in your checking account. Thus, people decide on the amount of currency versus deposits in the economy. In Japan, where crime is less prevalent than in many other countries, people use much more currency compared to checking accounts than in other countries. Even Japanese business executives who earn the equivalent of $120,000 a year frequently are paid monthly with the equivalent of $10,000 in cash.

As long as the Fed keeps track of the amount of currency versus deposits that people want to hold, it can control the money supply—the sum of currency plus demands. For example, if it sees the ratio of deposits to currency falling and the money supply falling too, it can increase reserves, thereby increasing deposits and the money supply.

R E V I E W

- Banks serve two important functions: They help channel funds from savers to investors, and their deposits can be used as money.
- Commercial banks hold deposits, called reserves, at the Fed.
- The Fed increases reserves by buying bonds and reduces reserves by selling bonds.
- The deposits at banks expand by a multiple of any increase in reserves. Thus, there is a link between reserves and deposits in the overall economy.
- By keeping track of currency, the Fed can control the total money supply, which is the sum of currency and deposits.

MONEY GROWTH AND INFLATION

Early in this chapter, in the section "Commodity Money," we showed that when gold, silver, or other commodities were the primary form of money, increases in the supply of money would cause inflation. Even though paper currency and deposits are now the main forms of money, the same principle holds today. That is, *all other things being equal,* an increase in the supply of money will cause inflation. In this section we examine this principle by looking at two important episodes of inflation during the twentieth century. Before we do so, we introduce a famous equation that can help us test the principle that an increase in the supply of money eventually causes inflation.

Consider first a simple example. Suppose that all of your transactions are in a video game arcade with food-vending machines and video game machines. You will need money in your pocket to carry out your transactions each day. If you use the vending and video game machines ten times a day, you will need ten times more money in your pocket than if you use the machines once a day. Hence, ten times more transactions means ten times more money. If the prices for vending machine items and minutes on a video game machine double, then you will need twice as much money for each day's activities, assuming that the higher price does not cure your habit. Hence, whether the value of transactions increases because the number of items purchased increases or because the price of each item increases, the amount of money used for transactions will rise.

What is true for you and the machines is true for the whole population and the whole economy. For the whole economy, real GDP is like the number of transactions with the machines, and the GDP deflator (a measure of the average price in the economy) is like the average price of the vending and game machines. Just as the amount of money you use for transactions in the game arcade is related to the number of transactions and the price of each transaction, so too is the supply of money in the economy related to real GDP and the GDP deflator.

The Quantity Equation of Money

quantity equation of money: the equation relating the price level and real GDP to the quantity of money and the velocity of money: The quantity of money times its velocity equals the price level times real GDP.

This relationship between money, real GDP, and the GDP deflator can be summarized by the **quantity equation of money,** which is written

Money supply × velocity = GDP deflator × real GDP

or

$$MV = PY$$

where V is velocity, P is the GDP deflator, and Y is real GDP. For example, if the money supply was $1,000 billion, real GDP was $8,000 billion, and the GDP deflator was 1.1, then a value of 8.8 for velocity would satisfy the quantity equation (1,000 × 8.8 = 1.1 × 8,000).

velocity: a measure of how frequently money is turned over in the economy.

The term **velocity** measures how frequently money is turned over. It is the number of times a dollar is used on average each period to make purchases. To see this, suppose an automatic teller machine (ATM) is installed in the room with the vending machines and video games from the preceding example. Each morning you get cash from the ATM for your morning games, and each day at midday an employee takes the cash from the vending and game machines and restocks the ATM. You then replenish your cash from the ATM to pay for your afternoon use of the games and vending machines; you now need to carry only half as much currency in your pocket as before the ATM was installed, when you had to bring enough cash to last all day. From your perspective, therefore, the velocity of money doubles. Money turns over twice as fast. As this example shows, velocity in the economy depends on technology and, in particular, on how efficient we are at using money.

Now, let's use the quantity equation to show how an increase in the money supply is related to inflation. If you look carefully at the quantity equation of money, you can see that if velocity and real GDP are not affected by a change in money, then an increase in the money supply will increase the GDP deflator (the average level of prices in the economy). A higher percentage increase in money—that is, *higher money growth*—will lead to a higher percentage increase in prices—that is, *higher inflation*. Thus, the quantity equation of money shows that higher rates of money growth lead to higher inflation, just as in the case of commodity money early in the chapter.

A restatement of the quantity equation using growth rates leads to a convenient relationship between money growth, inflation, real GDP growth, and velocity growth. In particular,

$$\text{Money growth} + \text{velocity growth} = \text{inflation} + \text{real GDP growth}$$

For example, if the money supply growth is 5 percent per year, velocity growth is 0 percent per year, and real GDP growth is 3 percent per year, then this equation says that inflation is 2 percent per year. (This growth rate form of the quantity equation follows directly from the quantity equation itself; in general, the rate of growth of a product of two terms is approximately equal to the sum of the growth rates of the two terms. Thus, the growth rate of M times V equals the growth rate of M plus the growth rate of V, and the growth rate of P times Y equals the growth rate of P plus the growth rate of Y.)

The quantity equation tells us that along a long-run economic growth path in which real GDP growth is equal to potential GDP growth, an increase in money growth by a certain number of percentage points will result in the long run in an increase in inflation of the same number of percentage points unless there is a change in velocity growth. Thus, higher money growth will lead to higher inflation in the long run. If velocity growth remains at zero, as in the previous example, and real GDP growth remains at 3 percent per year, then an increase in money growth by 10 percentage points, from 5 to 15 percent, will increase inflation by 10 percentage points, from 2 to 12 percent.

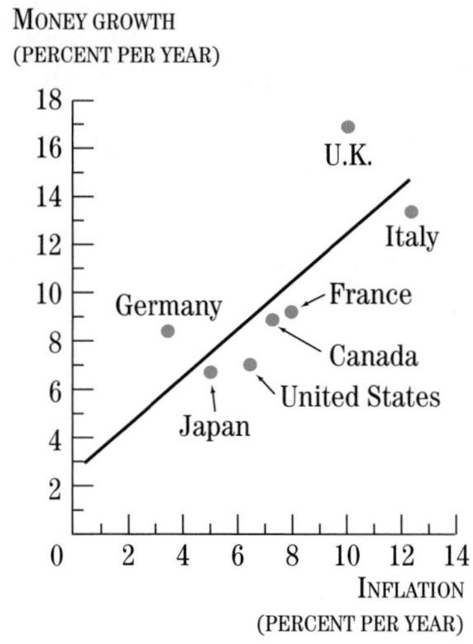

FIGURE 4
The Relation Between Money Growth and Inflation
As the data for these several countries show, higher money growth is associated with higher inflation. The data pertain to the period 1973–1991, when inflation differed greatly among the countries. Inflation and money growth are now lower in all these countries.

Evidence

What evidence do we have that higher money growth leads to more inflation? The quantity equation tells us that we should look for evidence during periods when changes in real GDP and velocity were small compared to changes in money growth and inflation. During such periods, the change in money growth and inflation will be the dominant terms in the quantity equation.

Worldwide Inflation in the 1970s and 1980s. Figure 4 shows such a period: the years from 1973 to 1991, when many economies had big inflations, some much bigger than others. Money growth is plotted on the vertical axis, and inflation on the horizontal axis. In Figure 4, each point represents a country. For countries with higher money growth, inflation was higher. Hence, the quantity equation works well during this period. During the 1990s, inflation has been low in all these countries, so there has not been enough of a difference to test how well the equation works. This period of high inflation is sometimes called the Great Inflation.

ECONOMICS IN ACTION

Hyperinflation and Too Much Money

So much money was printed during the period of German hyperinflation that it became cheaper to burn several million German marks to cook breakfast—as this woman was doing in 1923—than to buy kindling wood with the nearly worthless money. Inflation rose to over 100 percent per week. Shop owners closed their shops at lunchtime to change the prices. Workers were paid twice weekly. People would rush to the stores and buy everything they needed for the next few days. Firms also set up barter systems with their workers, exchanging consumer goods directly for labor.

The hyperinflation was initially caused by the huge increase in money growth. However, once it started, everyone tried to get rid of cash as soon as possible, accelerating the inflationary process. Also, by the time the government received its tax revenue, it was not worth much because prices had risen sharply. So the government had to print even more money. In the last months of hyperinflation, more than 30 paper mills worked at full capacity to deliver paper currency. One hundred fifty printing firms had 2,000 presses running 24 hours a day to print German marks, and they could not keep up with the need for new notes. On November 15, 1923, an economic reform stabilized the inflation rate. By then, the German prices were 100 billion times higher than they had been before the hyperinflation.

100,000,000,000,000 German Mark Reichsbank Note, 1923

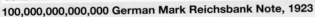

Hyperinflations. Another, more dramatic type of evidence showing that high money growth can cause inflation is hyperinflation. A hyperinflation is simply a period of very high inflation. The inflation in Germany in 1923 is one of the most famous examples of a hyperinflation. The German government had incurred huge expenses during World War I, and huge demands for war reparations from the victors in World War I compounded the problem. Because the government could not raise enough taxes to pay its expenses, it started printing huge amounts of money, which caused the hyperinflation of 1923. Figure 5 shows the *weekly* increase in German prices.

The German hyperinflation of 1923 was not a unique historical episode, and hyperinflation is not necessarily linked to war. Until recently, hyperinflations were common in Latin America. The size of the Latin American inflations is hard to imagine. The inflation rate in Brazil averaged 43.6 percent per year from 1912 to 1996. A Brazilian good that cost one dollar in 1912 would cost a quadrillion dollars

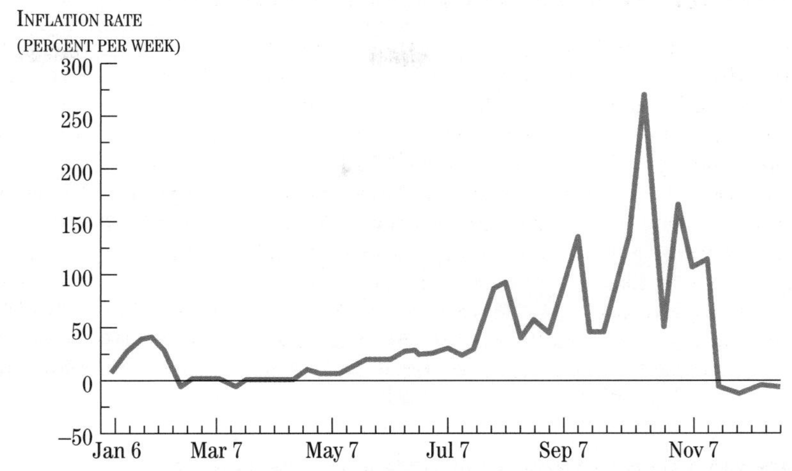

FIGURE 5
German Hyperinflation of 1923
The chart shows the weekly percent change in the price level in Germany in 1923. Inflation rose to truly astronomical levels for several months.

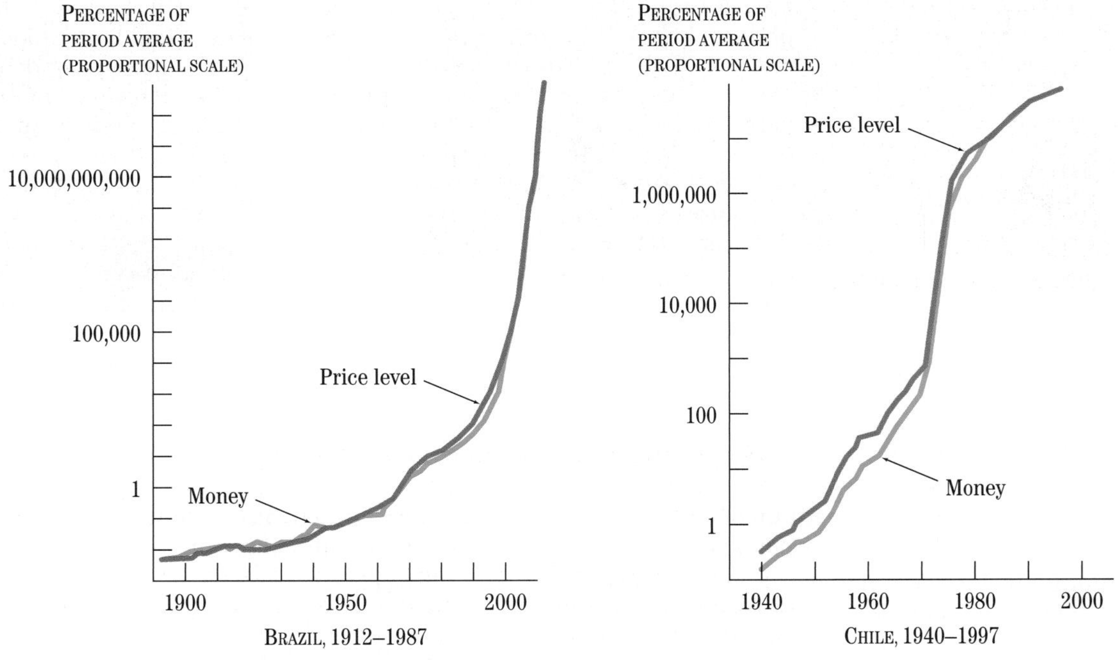

FIGURE 6
Money and Prices in Brazil and Chile During the Twentieth Century
The close relationship between money and the price level is obvious during this period of very high inflation. So far in the twenty-first century, inflation and money growth have been much lower in both countries.
Source: Gerald Dwyer and Rik Hafer, "Are Money Growth and Inflation Still Related?" Federal Reserve Bank of Atlanta, *Review,* Second Quarter 1999.

(1,000 trillion) in the 1990s. Inflation in Chile was also very high—about 90 percent throughout the 1970s.

Figure 6 shows the price level in Brazil and Chile as well as the money supply in both countries. Clearly money and prices are closely related. Fortunately, inflation in Chile has been much lower since the 1990s, and inflation in Brazil has also been declining. Not surprisingly, money growth is much lower now too. Money growth has been the cause of all hyperinflations.

REVIEW

- The quantity equation of money says that the money supply times velocity equals real GDP times the GDP deflator.
- Higher rates of money growth will eventually lead to higher inflation.
- Evidence of the relation between money growth and inflation is found in the 1970s and 1980s in the United States and other large economies, as well as in hyperinflations in Germany in the 1920s and in Brazil, and Chile in the twentieth century.

CONCLUSION

Money has fascinated economists for centuries. The famous quantity equation introduced in this chapter predates Adam Smith and was used by the economist-philosopher David Hume in the eighteenth century. Adam Smith placed money second only to the division of labor in the first chapters of the *Wealth of Nations*.

Although the role of money appears mysterious and has caused some great debates in economics and politics, the ideas presented in this chapter are not controversial. The three functions of money, the deposit expansion process, the technical ability of the central bank to control the money supply, and the fact that money is the cause of inflation in the long run are things many economists now agree on.

Many of the controversies about money pertain to the short-run fluctuations in the economy and revolve around the effects the Fed has on real GDP in the short run. After considering the reasons why real GDP may depart from potential GDP in the short run in Chapters 11 and 12, we will return to the effects the Fed has on short-run fluctuations in the economy.

KEY POINTS

1. Money has three roles: a medium of exchange, a store of value, and a unit of account.
2. Commodity money, ranging from salt to gold coins, has been used in place of barter for many centuries. Now paper money and deposits are also part of money.
3. Commercial banks are financial intermediaries; their deposits are part of the money supply.
4. Commercial banks hold reserves at the central bank.
5. The central bank changes reserves by buying and selling bonds.
6. The central bank can control the money supply by buying and selling bonds.
7. The central bank in the United States is the Federal Reserve System (the Fed).
8. When stated in terms of growth rates, the quantity equation of money describes the relationship between money growth, real GDP growth, and inflation.
9. Higher money growth eventually leads to higher inflation.

KEY TERMS

money
medium of exchange
store of value
unit of account
currency
checking deposit
money supply
Federal Reserve System (the Fed)
bank
Federal Open Market Committee (FOMC)
asset
liability
reserves
required reserve ratio
open market operation
quantity equation of money
velocity

QUESTIONS FOR REVIEW

1. What are the differences between the medium of exchange, store of value, and unit of account roles of money?
2. What are some examples of commodity money?
3. Why is it that currency is a part of money but that an expensive purse to put the currency in is not?
4. What is a bank?
5. What is the Fed, and how is the FOMC organized?
6. What happens to bank reserves when the Fed buys bonds?
7. Why does higher money growth cause inflation?
8. What is the quantity equation of money?

PROBLEMS

1. Which of the following are money and which are not?
   a. A credit card
   b. A debit card
   c. A check in your checkbook
   d. A dollar bill
   e. A necklace containing 8 ounces of gold
2. Cigarettes were a popular form of currency in prisoner of war (POW) camps in World War II, and are still a valuable form of currency in prisons in many countries. Why would cigarettes be likely to serve as currency in such settings?
3. Who are the current members of the Board of Governors of the Federal Reserve? What positions did they hold previously that made them well suited for a position on the board?
4. State whether each of the following statements is true or false. Explain your answers in one or two sentences.
   a. When commodity money is the only type of money, a decrease in the price of the commodity serving as money is inflation.
   b. The same money is always used as both a unit of account and a medium of exchange at any one time in any one country.
   c. The smaller the reserve ratio at banks, the larger the money multiplier.
   d. The Federal Reserve reduces reserves by buying government bonds.
5. Assume that required reserves are 7 percent of deposits and that people hold no currency—all money is held in the form of checking deposits.
   a. Suppose that the Federal Reserve purchases $30,000 worth of government bonds from Ellen (a private citizen), and that Ellen deposits all of the proceeds from the sale into her checking account at Z Bank. Construct a balance sheet, with assets on the left and liabilities on the right, to show how Ellen's deposit creates new assets and liabilities for Z Bank.
   b. How much of this new deposit can Z Bank lend out? Assume that it lends this amount to George, who then deposits the entire amount into his account at Y Bank. Show this on Y Bank's balance sheet.
   c. How much of this new deposit can Y Bank lend out? Suppose Joe takes out a loan for this amount from Y Bank and deposits the money into his account at X Bank. Show this on X Bank's balance sheet.
   d. The process of lending and relending creates money throughout the banking system. As a result of Ellen's deposit, how much money, in the form of deposits, has been created so far? If this process resulting from Ellen's deposit continues forever, how much money will be created?

6. Why are credit cards not included in the money supply even though they can be easily used for transactions? (*Hint:* What do you think happens when you use a credit card to purchase an item at a store?)

7. According to the quantity equation, changes in the money supply will directly lead to changes in the price level if velocity and real GDP are unaffected by the change in the money supply. Will velocity change over time? What factors might lead to changes in velocity? Are those changes related to changes in the money supply?

8. Consider the following table:

Year	Quantity of Money (billions of $)	Velocity	Real GDP (billions of $)	GDP Deflator
2004	$1,375	7.113	$10,703	
2005	$1,373	7.138	$11,049	
2006	$1,366	7.200	$11,415	

   a. Fill in the missing data, using the quantity equation of money.
   b. Why might velocity change in this way?
   c. Calculate the inflation rate for 2005 and for 2006.
   d. If money growth had been 5 percent per year in 2004 and 2005, what would inflation have been, assuming real GDP and velocity as in the table?

Part 3

Economic Fluctuations and Macroeconomic Policy

Chapter 11

The Nature and Causes of Economic Fluctuations

In 2001, the record economic expansion that had begun ten years earlier in the United States ended, and a recession began. A sharp fall in U.S. stock markets, falling consumer confidence, decisions by firms to cut back on investment spending, rapid increases in interest rates by the Federal Reserve in the year 2000, and rising oil prices are all potential explanations for the recession. The recession was worsened by the terrorist attacks of September 11, 2001.

Fortunately, the 2001 recession proved to be short-lived. By 2002 the economy was showing signs of recovery, encouraged by the actions of the government in cutting taxes and the Federal Reserve in lowering interest rates. The recovery gathered steam in 2003 as consumer spending on big-ticket items such as housing increased, with higher investment spending by firms following a few quarters later. By 2004, the economy was growing quite robustly again.

In this chapter, we take a closer look at economic fluctuations of the type that we saw in the early 2000s, as well as other episodes in U.S. history that have had very different features. The goal is to improve our understanding of economic fluctuations, which are defined as departures of the economy from its long-term growth trend. These departures include recessions, which are periods in which GDP declines sharply, moving the economy below its long-term trend. Another type of departure occurs when GDP rises rapidly, moving the economy above its long-term trend. Examples of U.S. recessions include the recession of 2001, the recession of 1990–1991, and the sharp recession that hit the U.S. economy in the early 1980s. Recessions also occur in other countries. For example, a very severe recession devasted the economies of Malaysia, Indonesia, and Korea in the late 1990s.

Studying economic fluctuations is important because recessions bring unemployment and hardship to many people. While the importance of long-run economic growth cannot be overstated, fluctuations around the growth trend affect the livelihood of millions of people. As John Maynard Keynes put it, "Economists set themselves too easy, too useless a task if in tempestuous seasons they can only tell us that when the storm is long past the ocean is flat again." Hence, the study of economic fluctuations is vital to understanding economics.

Economic fluctuations have been common for at least 200 years, but they have changed over time. One notable difference is that recessions have diminished in frequency and moderated in severity in the United States and many other countries, especially over the past 25 years, a phenomenon that many economists call the Great Moderation. A key purpose of studying economic fluctuations is to explain why this Great Moderation has occurred and to determine whether economic policies are responsible for it.

Figure 1 illustrates the nature of economic fluctuations with particular reference to the recession of 2001. As shown in the magnified portion of Figure 1, real GDP was clearly above potential GDP in 1999 and 2000, but in mid-2001, as the recession took hold, real GDP fell below potential GDP. A recovery then started that brought real GDP back to potential GDP by 2004.

Economic fluctuations occur simultaneously with long-term growth, as shown by the longer history in Figure 1. Real GDP has fluctuated around what might otherwise have been a steady upward-moving trend. Although no two economic fluctuations are alike—some are long, some are short; some are deep, some are shallow—they do have common features. Perhaps the most important one is that after a departure of real GDP from potential GDP, the economy eventually returns to a more normal long-run growth path.

"We figure it was HERE when the recession officially began."

In this chapter, we look at the first steps the economy takes as it moves away from potential GDP. In other words, we examine the initial, or short-run, increase or decrease of real GDP above or below potential GDP. We will show that the first steps of real GDP away from potential GDP are caused by changes in aggregate demand. Aggregate demand is the total amount that consumers, businesses, government, and foreigners are willing to spend on all goods and services in the economy. In contrast, the growth of potential GDP is caused by increases in the available supply of inputs to production: labor, capital, and technology.

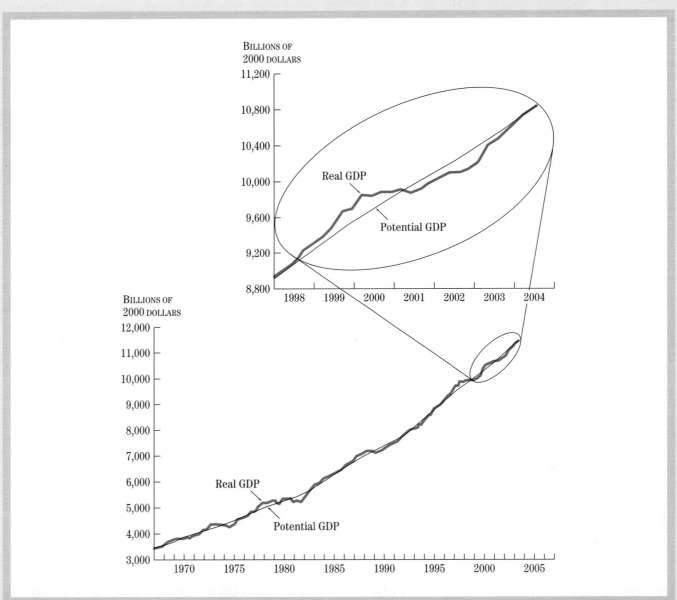

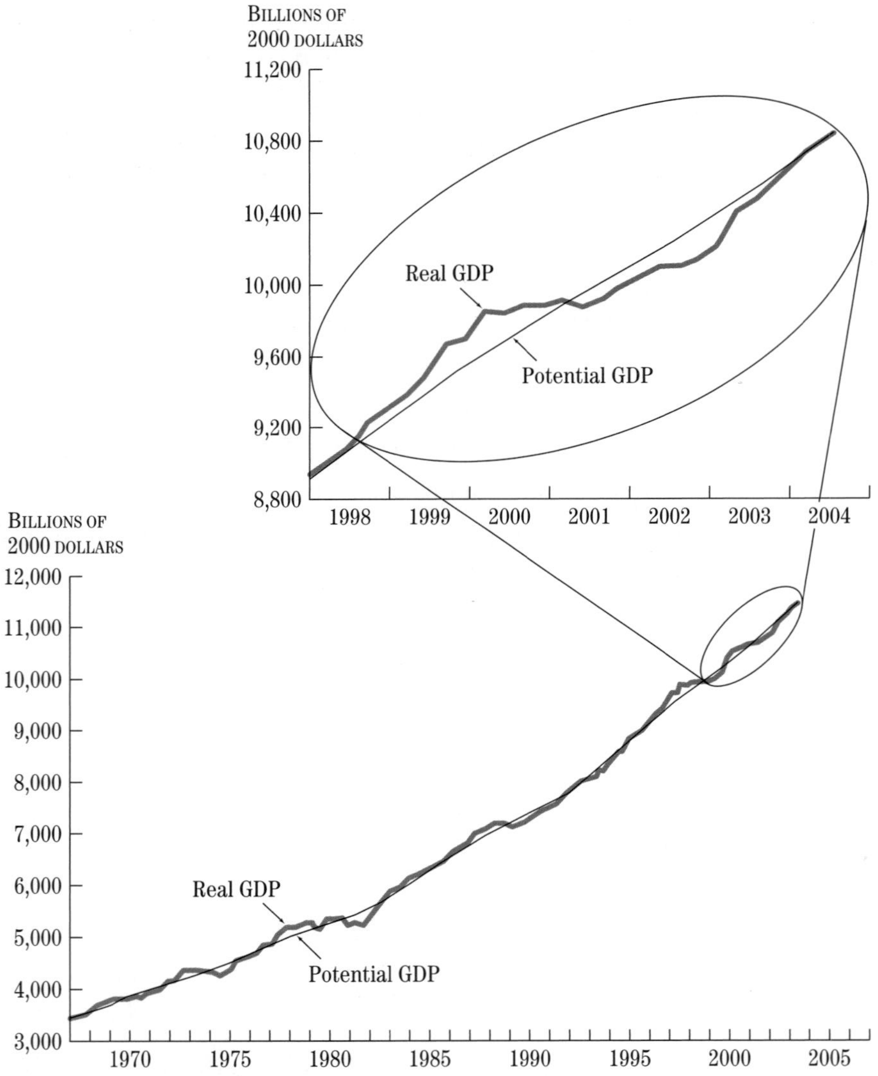

FIGURE 1
Narrowing the Focus on Economic Fluctuations

The magnified economic fluctuations in this figure occurred as real GDP rose above potential GDP in the late 1990s and then fell below potential GDP as the economy went into a recession in 2001. By 2004, the economy had recovered and real GDP was again back to potential GDP.

CHANGES IN AGGREGATE DEMAND LEAD TO CHANGES IN PRODUCTION

Figure 2 illustrates the essential idea used to explain economic fluctuations: that increases or decreases in real GDP to levels above or below potential GDP occur largely because of increases or decreases in aggregate demand in the economy. Changes in aggregate demand occur when consumers, business firms, government, or foreigners expand or cut back their spending. Potential GDP in three years is represented by points *a, b,* and c in Figure 2. These three values of potential GDP are part of the longer-term steady increase in potential GDP over time due to increases in the supply of labor and capital and improvements in technology. Potential GDP represents what firms would want to produce in "normal times," when the economy is not in a recession. In normal times, real GDP is equal to potential GDP. Years 1 and 2 in Figure 2 are assumed to be normal years. However, year 3 is not a normal year. Point *d* in the left panel of the figure shows a recession because real GDP has declined from point *b*. Real GDP is below potential GDP at point *d*. Firms produce less and lay off workers. Unemployment rises. Eventually—this part of the story comes in later

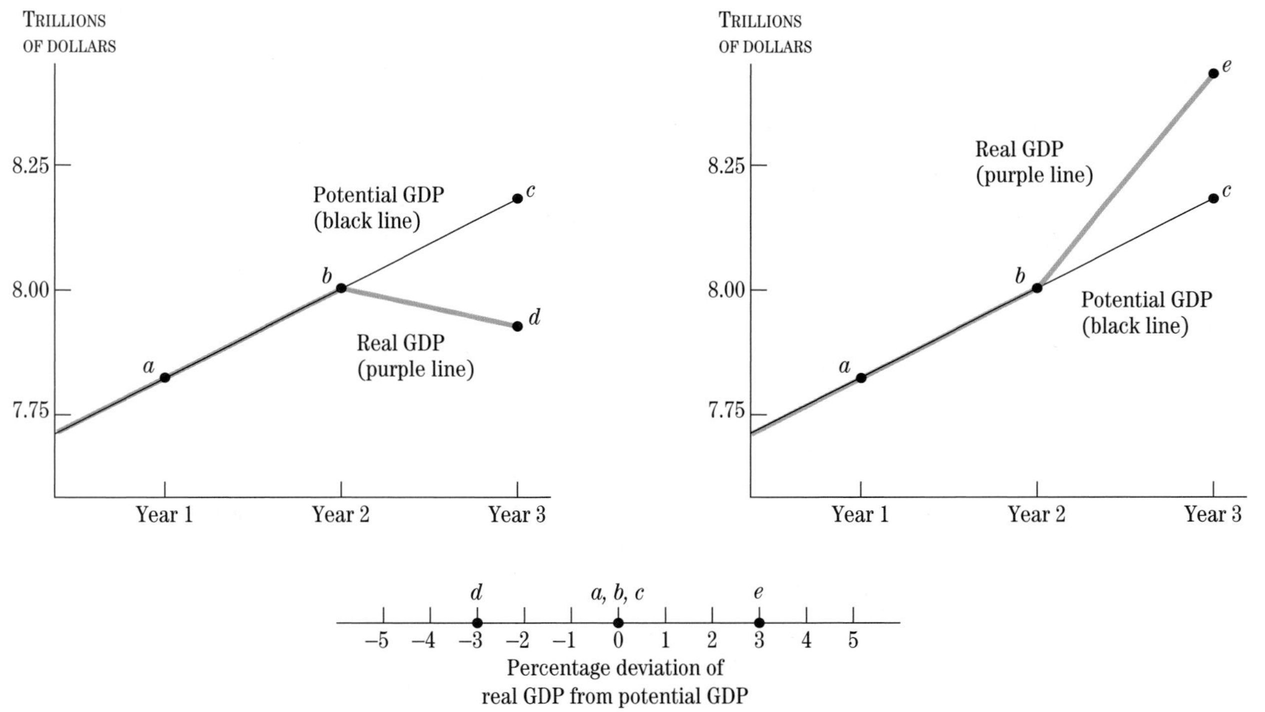

FIGURE 2
The First Step of an Economic Fluctuation

Potential GDP is shown by the black upward-sloping line in both diagrams. Points *a, b,* and *c* represent three different levels of potential GDP in three years. A downward departure of real GDP (shown in purple) from potential GDP is illustrated by point *d* on the left. Since real GDP falls, this is a recession. An upward departure of real GDP from potential GDP is illustrated by point *e* on the right. The departures are explained by changes in aggregate demand. The line at the bottom shows the percent deviation of real GDP from potential GDP.

chapters—if demand stays low, firms begin to cut their prices, and real GDP moves back toward potential GDP. Thus, in recessions, changes in aggregate demand cause fluctuations in real GDP.

Point *e* in the right panel represents another departure of real GDP from potential GDP. In this case, real GDP rises above potential GDP. Firms produce more in response to the increase in aggregate demand; they employ more workers, and unemployment declines. Eventually—again, this part of the story comes in later chapters—if demand for their product stays high, firms raise their prices, and real GDP goes back down toward potential GDP.

potential GDP: the economy's long-term growth trend for real GDP, determined by the available supply of capital, labor, and technology. Real GDP fluctuates above and below potential GDP. (Ch. 5)

Economists frequently measure the departures of real GDP from *potential GDP* in percentages rather than in dollar amounts. For example, if potential GDP is \$8.0 trillion and real GDP is \$8.4 trillion, then the percentage departure of real GDP from potential GDP is 5 percent: $(8.4 - 8.0)/8.0 = .05$. If real GDP were \$7.6 trillion and potential GDP remained at \$8.0 trillion, then the percentage departure would be -5 percent: $(7.6 - 8.0)/8.0 = -.05$. Percentages make it easier to compare economic fluctuations in different countries that have different sizes of real GDP. At the bottom of the two panels in Figure 2 is a horizontal line representing the size of the fluctuations in real GDP around potential GDP in percentage terms for year 1, year 2, and year 3. Points *d* and *e* in Figure 2 represent the first steps of an economic fluctuation.

Production and Demand at Individual Firms

Why do firms produce more—bringing real GDP above *potential GDP*—when the demand for their products rises? Why do firms produce less—bringing real GDP below potential GDP—when the demand for their products falls? These questions have probably occupied more of economists' time than any other question in macroeconomics. Although more work still needs to be done, substantial improvements in economists' understanding of the issues have been made in the last 20 years.

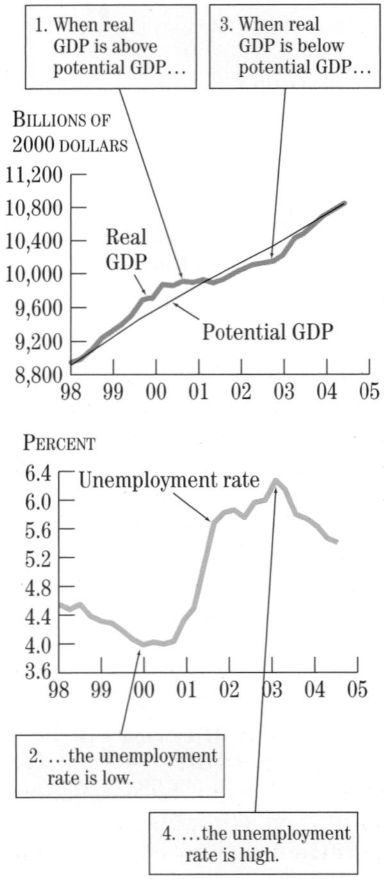

The Unemployment Rate and the Deviations of Real GDP from Potential GDP. First consider some simple facts about how firms operate. In normal times, when real GDP is equal to potential GDP, most firms operate with some excess capacity so that they can expand production without major bottlenecks. Small retail service businesses from taxi companies to dry cleaners can usually increase production when customer demand increases. Another taxi is added to a busy route and one of the drivers is asked to work overtime. One of the dry cleaning employees who has been working part time is happy to work full time. The same is true for large manufacturing firms. When asked what percent of capacity their production is in normal times, manufacturing firms typically answer about 80 percent. Thus, firms normally have room to expand production: Capacity utilization sometimes goes up to 90 percent or higher. If firms need more labor in order to expand production, they can ask workers to work overtime, call workers back from previous layoffs, or hire additional workers. *The unemployment rate drops below the natural unemployment rate when real GDP rises above potential GDP.*

In recessions, when demand declines, these same firms clearly have the capability to reduce production, and they do. In recessions, capacity utilization goes down to 70 percent or lower. Firms ask workers to stop working overtime, they move some workers to part time, or they lay off some workers. Some firms institute hiring freezes to make sure the personnel office does not keep hiring workers. *The unemployment rate rises above the natural unemployment rate when real GDP falls below potential GDP.* For example, the unemployment rate rose to more than 7 percent when the 1990–1991 recession brought real GDP below potential GDP. The relationship between the unemployment rate and the movements of real GDP relative to potential GDP is illustrated in the margin at left.

ECONOMICS IN ACTION

Real-Life Examples of How Firms Respond to Demand

Consider a typical service firm at the start of the 1990–1991 recession. Mayflower, the moving company named after the ship that moved the Pilgrims, found the demand for its moving and storage services growing rapidly in the boom of the late 1980s. The company expanded production by moving more households and, as a result, increased its employment from 6,800 workers in 1987 to 11,400 in 1989. In 1990, as the recession took hold, demand for Mayflower's services began to fall. The company reduced production—moved fewer households—and employment fell from 11,400 in 1989 to 10,900 in 1990, a decline of about 5 percent.

Consider the example of a construction firm at about the same time. As is typical in recessions, construction was hit hard in the 1990–1991 recession. Trammell Crow, the real estate construction company based in Dallas, Texas, found the demand for its construction services falling off dramatically in 1990. Hence, the firm produced fewer of these services. It built fewer shopping malls and convention centers. Total square feet under construction by Trammell Crow fell from 44 million in 1989 to 27 million in 1990. Employment at Trammell Crow also fell from the year 1989 to 1990. Employment had expanded rapidly during the 1988–1989 boom. Thus, Trammell Crow is another example showing how fluctuations in demand cause a change in production.

Production Decisions by Actual Firms
Individual firms—Mayflower moving services being just one example—raise production during booms when the demand for their goods or services rises, and lower production during recessions when the demand for their goods or services declines. These decisions by individual firms lead to fluctuations of real GDP above or below potential GDP.

Could Economic Fluctuations Also Be Due to Changes in Potential GDP?

Recall from Chapter 5 that *potential GDP* depends on the economy's *aggregate supply,* which is determined by the available *capital, labor,* and *technology*. A drought or a flood would reduce aggregate supply.

real business cycle theory: a theory of macroeconomics that stresses that shifts in potential GDP are a primary cause of fluctuations in real GDP; the shifts in potential GDP are usually assumed to be caused by changes in technology.

Our discussion thus far of the production decisions of individual firms has shown why it is natural to identify fluctuations in real GDP with fluctuations in aggregate demand. To be sure, economic fluctuations also occur because of changes in potential GDP. For example, when agriculture was a much larger fraction of real GDP, droughts and floods had more noticeable effects on real GDP. Although agriculture is currently a very small fraction of total production, the possibility that increases or decreases in potential GDP may still play a large role in economic fluctuations is a topic currently being examined by economists. Economic theories that emphasize changes in potential GDP as a source of economic fluctuations are called **real business cycle theories.** Most frequently, changes in technology are assumed to be the reason for changes in potential GDP in real business cycle theories.

The factors that underlie potential GDP growth—population, capital, technological know-how—tend to evolve relatively smoothly. Population growth, for example, is much steadier than real GDP growth. We do not have a drop in the population every few years and a sudden spurt the next year. Slowdowns in population growth occur gradually over time as birthrates and death rates change. Similarly, although

ECONOMICS IN THE NEWS

Assessing the Macroeconomic Impact of a Terrorist Attack

In the aftermath of the terrorist attacks of September 11, 2001, economists were called upon to analyze the potential effects on the U.S. economy. At the time, there were fears that the attacks could drive the economy into a longer recession, although many economists speculated that the effect would not be as long-lasting as had been feared. This article, published almost a year after the attacks, summarized the impact of the tragedy on the economy. It concluded that while certain sectors, such as the airline industry, were still feeling the impacts of the attacks, most sectors of the economy had recovered. The question for policymakers now is whether the economy would recover so quickly from a more serious terrorist attack, such as a nuclear or chemical attack.

September 11 was one of the many negative factors affecting the economy in 2001/2002.

A Year After Sept. 11, Attacks' Economic Impact Lingers, but Effect Is Disparate

By ADAM GELLER, AP Business Writer—September 11, 2002

NEW YORK—A year ago, planted in front of televisions, numbed by endless images of the World Trade Center's destruction, consumers froze—and briefly forgot to consume. Investors stopped investing, and dumped stock. Travelers stopped traveling, at least by plane. Scores of companies slashed thousands of jobs, and economists warned that the combined effects could snowball.

But a year after terrorists attacked the trade center, the Pentagon—and by extension, the economy—the impact has not proven to be nearly as deep or as lasting as was feared. The economic consequences of Sept. 11 still linger, certainly. But the toll has proved disparate, inflicting the heaviest damage on sectors such as travel and tourism while leaving others unscathed. And it turns out events before and after have played a far larger role in shaping the economy than the attacks.

"I would say the impact has been less than we had initially thought in terms of economic contraction," said Gus Faucher, a senior economist with Economy.com, a research firm in West Chester, Pa. "It's a contributing factor to the weak economy, but it's not the primary factor."

Sizing up the impact of the attacks is complicated because the economy was already in a recession before last September. In the months since, it has been buffeted by other crises, including the collapse of Enron and a host of other corporate scandals, severe problems in the telecommunications industry, and the drop-off in the stock market. "Economically, the

individual factories or machines may be lost in a hurricane or flood, such losses do not happen in such a massive way across the whole country that they would show up as a recession or a boom in the whole economy. Thus, the amount of capital changes slowly over time. Even technological change does not seem capable of explaining most fluctuations. It is true that some inventions and innovations raise productivity substantially in certain sectors of the economy over short periods of time. The impact on the whole economy is more spread out and gradual, however. Moreover, people do not suddenly forget how to use a technology. There do not seem to be sudden decreases in technological know-how. For these reasons, potential GDP usually tends to grow relatively smoothly over time, compared to the fluctuations in aggregate demand.

stock market setback may have had more of an impact than the terrorist attacks because it shaved some $7 trillion from our wealth," said Sung Won Sohn, an economist with Wells Fargo and Co.

Some of the expectations that shaped economic forecasts immediately after the attacks, particularly fears of a long war in Afghanistan with heavy American casualties, did not come to pass, said Ross DeVol, director of regional studies for the Millken Institute in Santa Barbara, Calif. The think tank early this year estimated the attacks would result in the elimination of 1.6 million jobs nationwide. But DeVol says now the number will probably be 1.2 million or less, most concentrated in industries like air travel and tourism, or in New York City.

The uneven impact means that assessments of the damage vary by vantage point. "The attacks certainly accelerated the action," said Terry Mercer, a technical illustrator for Boeing Corp., who's been unable to find work since the aerospace giant eliminated his job and 5,000 others from its Wichita, Kan., operations. "But everybody's feeling was that it (some cuts) was going to be coming anyway. We didn't have a lot of work even before the attacks."

The landscape looks very different to home builder Bob Simmons of McLean, Va., who said he was prepared for the worst last fall—but never had time to stop and wait for it. "For me, it's almost like a recap of last August except we have about 10 percent more sales," said Simmons, who builds homes in the suburbs of Washington, D.C.

Even in bad times, some sectors continue to flourish.

Economists say the healthy housing market shows how a variety of factors helped mitigate the damage of Sept. 11. Consumers, told one of the best things they could for their nation was to shop, did just that. Record low interest rates kept families buying homes, and refinancing mortgages put cash in their pockets for other purchases. Detroit's zero-percent financing for new cars late last year captured consumers' attention. Government spending pumped additional money into the economy. "Who knows what the psychology was, but (the attack) was not as big a blow as we were expecting," said Economy.com's Faucher. "People still went out to dinner, they still went out to the mall to buy things and things just held up better than expected."

REVIEW

- Economic fluctuations are largely a result of fluctuations in aggregate demand.
- When aggregate demand decreases, firms produce less; real GDP falls below potential GDP. Unemployment rises. When aggregate demand increases, firms first produce more; real GDP rises above potential GDP. Firms also hire more workers, and the unemployment rate falls.
- Short-run fluctuations in potential GDP also occur, but in reality most of the larger fluctuations in real GDP seem to be due to fluctuations of real GDP around a more steadily growing potential GDP.

FORECASTING REAL GDP

To illustrate how we use the idea that changes in aggregate demand lead to short-run fluctuations in real GDP, we will focus on an important macroeconomic task: short-term economic forecasting of real GDP about one year ahead. To *forecast* real GDP, economic forecasters divide aggregate demand into its four key components: consumption, investment, government purchases, and net exports. Remember that real GDP can be measured by adding together the four types of spending: what people *consume,* what firms *invest,* what *governments purchase,* and what *foreigners purchase* net of what they sell in the United States. In symbols, we have

$$Y = C + I + G + X$$

In other words, real GDP (Y) is the sum of consumption (C), investment (I), government purchases (G), and net exports (X).

A Forecast for Next Year

Suppose that it is December 2007 and a forecast of real GDP (Y) is being prepared for the year 2008. Using the preceding equation, a reasonable way to proceed would be to forecast consumption for the next year, then forecast investment, then forecast government purchases, and, finally, forecast net exports. When forecasting each item, the forecaster would consider a range of issues: Consumer confidence might affect consumption; business confidence might be a factor in investment; the electoral prospects of the political party controlling Congress might be a factor in government purchases; and developments in foreign countries might affect the forecast for net exports. In any case, adding these four spending items together would give a forecast for real GDP for the year 2008. For example, one economist may forecast that $C = \$8{,}000$ billion, $I = \$1{,}500$ billion, $X = -\$500$ billion, and $G = \$2{,}000$ billion. Then that economist's forecast for real GDP is $11,000 billion. Forecasts are typically expressed as growth rates of real GDP from one year to the next. If real GDP in 2007 is $10,800, then the forecast would be for 1.9 percent growth for the year 2008.

Impact of a Change in Government Purchases

The preceding forecast is prepared by making one's best assumption about what is likely for government purchases and the other three components of spending. Another type of forecast—called a *conditional forecast*—describes what real GDP will be under alternative assumptions about the components of spending. For example, in the year 2007, the congress or the president of the United States might want an estimate of the effect of a proposal to change government purchases on the economy in 2008. A conditional forecast would be a forecast of real GDP conditional on this change in government purchases.

Suppose the proposal is to cut federal government purchases by $100 billion in real terms in one year. What is the effect of such a change in government purchases on aggregate demand in the short run? If the government demands $100 billion less, then firms will produce $100 billion less. A forecast conditional on a $100 billion spending cut would be $100 billion less for real GDP, or $10,900 billion. Again, we just add up $8,000 billion, $1,500 billion, −$500 billion, and now $1,900 billion. Real GDP growth for the year is now forecast to be about 1.0 percent, conditional on the policy proposal.

The forecast is based on the equation $Y = C + I + G + X$ and the idea that changes in aggregate demand cause real GDP fluctuations. Although simple, it is specific and substantive. According to this method of forecasting, changes in aggregate

ECONOMICS IN ACTION

The Professional Forecasters

Short-term forecasting of real GDP—usually one year ahead—has become a major industry employing thousands of economists, statisticians, and computer programmers. Each month the *Blue Chip Economic Indicators* tabulates the forecasts of the top forecasting firms, such as Econoclast, Macroeconomic Advisors, and UCLA Business Forecasting. The average of all these forecasters is called the Blue Chip Consensus. If a government forecast differs much from this forecast, it is frequently criticized.

Consider, for example, the forecast for real GDP growth in the United States in 2004, as the economy was recovering from the 2001 recession. The consensus forecast—the average of the economists surveyed in January 2004 by the Blue Chip Service—was that U.S. GDP growth would be 4.6 percent.

What did growth turn out to be in 2004? It turned out to be 4.4 percent. The forecasters were almost exactly right in their prediction! This isn't always the case, though. In 2001, when the economy was hit by unforeseeable negative shocks, the actual growth rate turned out to be 1.2 percent, whereas the prediction had been for a growth rate of 3.4 percent.

Sometimes economists put probabilities on their forecasts. For example, in March 2007, Alan Greenspan, the former chairman of the Fed, said that there was a one-third probability of a recession before the end of the year.

demand are responsible for most of the short-run ups and downs in the economy. It is this explanation that most economic forecasters use when they forecast real GDP for one year ahead.

REVIEW

- The four components of spending can be added to make a forecast for real GDP. Making such a forecast is an important application of macroeconomics.
- Forecasts may be conditional on a particular event, such as a change in government purchases or a change in taxes.

THE RESPONSE OF CONSUMPTION TO INCOME

In the forecasting example, we assumed that none of the other components—consumption, investment, or net exports—change in response to the decline in government purchases. For example, consumption (C) was unchanged at $8,000 billion when we altered G in our conditional forecast. But these components of spending are likely to change. Thus, something important is missing from the procedure [illegible]ction

[illegible]	Income
[illegible]	1,000
2,600	2,000
3,200	3,000
3,800	4,000
4,400	5,000
5,000	6,000
5,600	7,000
6,200	8,000
6,800	9,000
7,400	10,000
8,000	11,000
8,600	12,000
9,200	13,000
9,800	14,000

for forecasting real GDP. To improve the forecast, we must describe how the other components of aggregate demand—consumption, investment, and net exports—might change in response to other developments in the economy. We will eventually consider the response of consumption, investment, and net exports to many factors, including interest rates, exchange rates, and income. However, bringing all these factors into consideration at once is complicated, and we must start with a simplifying assumption. Here the *simplifying assumption* is that consumption is the only component of expenditures that responds to income, and that income is the only influence on consumption. Consumption is a good place to begin because it is by far the largest component of real GDP. Before we finish developing a complete theory of economic fluctuations, we will consider the other components and the other influences. Let us begin by examining why consumption may be affected by income.

The Consumption Function

consumption function: the positive relationship between consumption and income.

The **consumption function** describes how consumption depends on income. The notion of a consumption function originated with John Maynard Keynes, who wrote about it during the 1930s. Research on the consumption function has been intense ever since. For each individual, the consumption function says that the more income one has, the more one consumes. For the national economy as a whole, it says that the more income Americans have, the more Americans consume. For the world economy as a whole, it says that the more income there is in the world, the more the people in the world consume. Table 1 gives a simple example of how consumption depends on income in the U.S. economy.

As you can see from the table, as income increases from \$1,000 billion to \$2,000 billion, consumption increases as well, from \$2,000 billion to \$2,600 billion, and as income increases from \$3,000 billion to \$4,000 billion, consumption increases from \$3,200 billion to \$3,800 billion. More income means more consumption, but the consumption function also tells us *how much* consumption increases when income increases. Each change in income of \$1,000 billion causes an increase in consumption of \$600 billion. The changes in consumption are smaller than the changes in income. Notice that, in this example, at very low levels of income, consumption is greater than income. If consumption were greater than income for a particular individual, that individual would have to borrow. At higher levels of income, when consumption is less than income, the individual would be able to save.

The consumption function is supposed to describe the behavior of individuals because the economy is made up of individuals. Consequently, it summarizes the behavior of all people in the economy with respect to consumption. The simple consumption function is not meant to be the complete explanation of consumption. Recall that it is based on a simplifying assumption.

marginal propensity to consume (MPC): the slope of the consumption function, showing the change in consumption that is due to a given change in income.

The Marginal Propensity to Consume. A concept related to the consumption function is the **marginal propensity to consume,** or **MPC** for short. The marginal propensity to consume measures how much consumption changes for a given change in income. The term *marginal* refers to the additional amount of consumption that is due to a change in income. The term *propensity* refers to the inclination to consume. By definition,

$$\text{Marginal Propensity to Consume (MPC)} = \frac{\text{change in consumption}}{\text{change in income}}$$

What is the MPC for the consumption function in Table 1? Observe that the change in consumption from row to row is 600. The change in income from row to

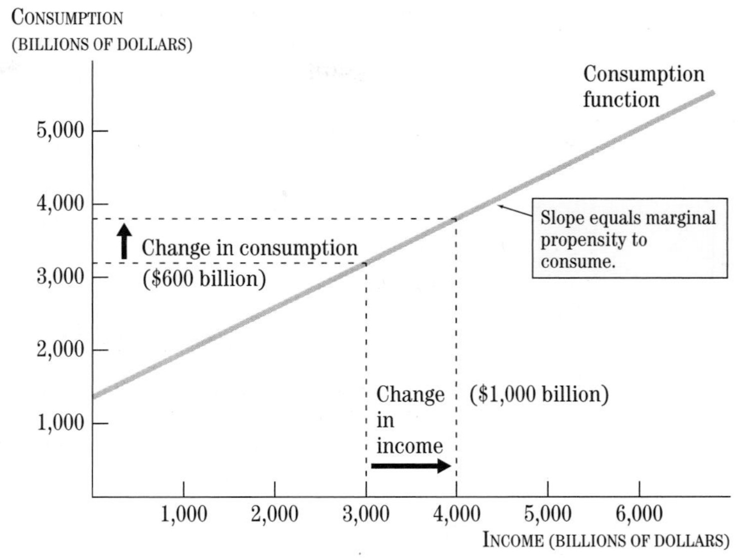

FIGURE 3
The Consumption Function
For the economy as a whole, more income leads to more consumption, as shown by the example of an upward-sloping consumption function in the figure. This represents the sum of all the individuals in the economy, many of whom consume more when their income rises. The graph is based on the numbers in Table 1.

row is 1,000; thus the MPC = 600/1,000 = .6. Although this is only a simple example, it turns out that the MPC for the U.S. economy is around that magnitude.

Figure 3 graphs the consumption function by putting income on the horizontal axis and consumption on the vertical axis. We get the upward-sloping line by plotting the pairs of observations on consumption and income in Table 1 and connecting them with a line. This line, which demonstrates that consumption rises with income, is the consumption function. Its slope is equal to the MPC. For this example, the MPC = .6. The graph shows that at low levels of income, consumption is greater than income, but at high levels of income, consumption is less than income.

Which Measure of Income? The consumption function is a straight-line relationship between consumption and income. Income in the relationship is sometimes measured by *aggregate income* (*Y*), which is also equal to real GDP, and sometimes by disposable income. *Disposable income* is the income that households receive in wages, dividends, and interest payments plus transfers they may get from the government minus any taxes they pay to the government. Disposable income is the preferred measure of income when one is interested in household consumption because this is what households have available to spend. But the consumption function for the whole economy for aggregate income and that for disposable income look similar because aggregate income and disposable income fluctuate and grow together. In the United States and most other countries, taxes and transfers are nearly proportional to aggregate income.

For the rest of this chapter, we will use aggregate income, or real GDP, as the measure of income in the consumption function. We put real GDP, or income (we drop the word *aggregate* in *aggregate income*), on the horizontal axis of the consumption function diagram, because real GDP and income are always equal. Figure 4

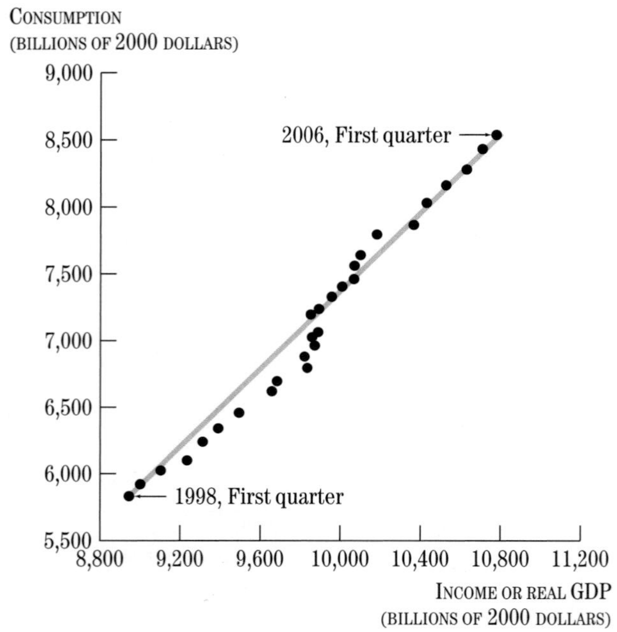

FIGURE 4
Consumption versus Aggregate Income
The graph shows the close relationship between consumption and aggregate income, or real GDP, in the U.S. economy. The points fall close to the straight line drawn in the diagram.

shows the actual relationship between consumption and income, or real GDP. Note, however, that when we consider an explicit change in taxes, we must take into account the difference between disposable income and income.

What about Interest Rates and Other Influences on Consumption?

Other factors besides income affect consumption. For example, you may recall from Chapter 7 that people's consumption is affected by the interest rate. Also, people's wealth—including their savings in a bank and their house—may affect their consumption. A person with a large amount of savings in a bank might consume a considerable amount even if the person's income in any one year is very low. Why have we not brought the interest rate or wealth into the picture here?

The answer is simple. To keep the analysis manageable at the start, we are putting the interest rate and other influences aside. We eventually return to consider the effects of interest rates and other factors on consumption. But during economic fluctuations, the effects of changes in income on consumption are most important, and we focus on these now.

REVIEW

- The consumption function describes the response of consumption to changes in income. The elementary consumption function ignores the effects of interest rates and wealth on consumption.
- The marginal propensity to consume (MPC) tells us *how much* consumption changes in response to a change in income.
- For the economy as a whole, the consumption function can be expressed in terms of aggregate income or disposable income. Aggregate income is always equal to real GDP.

FINDING REAL GDP WHEN CONSUMPTION AND INCOME MOVE TOGETHER

Now let us use the consumption function to get a better prediction of what happens to real GDP in the short run when government purchases change. In other words, we want to improve the conditional forecast of real GDP when there is a change in government purchases by taking the consumption function into account. Again, as in the earlier example of forecasting, let us assume that government spending will decline by $100 billion next year. Our goal is to find out what happens to real GDP in the short run.

Economics in Action

Making *Time*'s Top 100

John Maynard Keynes was chosen by *Time* magazine as one of the 100 most influential people in the twentieth century. Keynes was the inventor of the marginal propensity to consume and of the broader idea emphasized in this chapter that a decline in aggregate demand could bring the economy below its potential.

Keynes was always active in bringing economics into practice. He gained notoriety in his thirties for a best-selling book called *The Economic Consequences of the Peace,* written in only two months during the summer of 1919. Keynes was an economic adviser to the British government, and he accompanied the prime minister to the Versailles peace conference in 1919 at the end of World War I. At that peace conference, the victors demanded heavy reparations from Germany, harming the German economy and thereby helping Hitler in his rise to power. In his 1919 book, Keynes predicted serious harm from the stiff reparations and ridiculed the heads of government at the conference, including his own prime minister, David Lloyd George, and the American president, Woodrow Wilson.

Keynes's most influential book, however, was *The General Theory of Employment, Interest and Money.* He wrote it in the midst of the Great Depression, providing an explanation for a worldwide tragedy that prevailing economic theory—with its microeconomic emphasis—hardly addressed. Much of the *General Theory* is difficult to read unless you are an economist, because as Keynes put it, his book is chiefly addressed to "my fellow economists." But Keynes's well-developed writing skills emerge in some of the less technical passages, especially those on speculation and expectations in financial markets. Keynes's ideas, such as the marginal propensity to consume and the importance of aggregate demand, spread rapidly and had a lasting influence: Referring to these ideas as the "Keynesian revolution" is no exaggeration.

Keynes appeared on the cover of *Time* magazine in 1965, when the influence of his economics was at its peak in Washington. However, in the 1970s, when inflation was rising and economic growth was slowing, Keynes's theory was criticized because it did not deal with inflation and with long-run economic growth. Moreover, by emphasizing aggregate demand so much, Keynes's theory suggested to some policymakers that increases in government spending could increase real GDP almost without limit, regardless of supply constraints.

Keynes's *Tract on Monetary Reform,* written in 1923, focused more on inflation than did the *General Theory.* His earlier writings suggest that if he had lived longer, he might have explained the high inflation of the 1970s as effectively as he explained the Great Depression of the 1930s.

John Maynard Keynes, 1883–1946

Born: Cambridge, England, 1883
Education: Cambridge University, graduated 1906
Jobs: India Office, London, 1906–1909
Cambridge University, 1909–1915
British Treasury, 1915–1919
Cambridge University, 1919–1946
Major Publications: *The Economic Consequences of the Peace,* 1919; *A Tract on Monetary Reform,* 1923; *A Treatise on Money,* 1930; *The General Theory of Employment, Interest and Money,* 1936

Our first attempt at forecasting said that a reduction in government spending is going to reduce real GDP. But now we see that something else must happen, because consumption depends on income, and real GDP is equal to income. A reduction in government spending will reduce income. The consumption function tells us that a reduction in income must reduce consumption, which further reduces GDP.

Here is the chain of logic in brief:

1. A cut in government spending reduces real GDP.
2. Real GDP = income; thus income is reduced.
3. Consumption depends on income; thus consumption is reduced.
4. A reduction in consumption further reduces real GDP.

In sum, consumption will decline when we reduce government spending.

For example, when the government reduces defense spending, the firms that produce the defense goods find demand falling and produce less. Some of the defense workers are going to either work fewer hours a week or be laid off. Therefore, they will receive a reduced income or no income at all. In addition, the profits at the defense firms will decline; thus, the income of the owners of the firms will decline. With less income, the workers and the owners will spend less; that is, their consumption will decline. This is the connection between government spending and consumption that we are concerned about: The change in government purchases reduces defense workers' income, which results in less consumption.

Consider a specific case study. This type of logic was applied by economists to estimate the impact of closing Fort Ord, the military base near Monterey Bay in California, on the Monterey economy. When the estimates were made, the base employed 3,000 civilians and 14,000 military personnel. Payroll was $558 million. Thus, closing the base would reduce incomes by as much as $558 million as these workers were laid off or retired. Although some workers might quickly find jobs elsewhere, there would be a decline in income that would result in a reduction in consumption by those workers. Using an MPC of .6, consumption would decline by $335 million (.6 times 558) if income was reduced by $558 million. This would tend to throw others in the Monterey area out of work as spending in retail and service stores declined. This would further reduce consumption, and so on. Although this case study refers to a small region of the entire country, the same logic applies to the economy as a whole.

The 45-Degree Line

We can use a convenient graph to calculate how much income and consumption change in the whole economy and thereby find out what happens to real GDP. In Figure 5 there is a line that shows graphically that income in the economy is equal to spending. In Figure 5, income is on the horizontal axis and spending is on the vertical axis. All the points where spending equals income are on the upward-sloping line in Figure 5. The line has a slope of 1, or an angle of 45 degrees with the horizontal axis, because the distances from any point on the line to the horizontal axis and the vertical axis are equal. Along that line—which is called the **45-degree line**—spending and income are equal.

45-degree line: the line showing that expenditure equals aggregate income.

The Expenditure Line

expenditure line: the relation between the sum of the four components of spending $(C + I + G + X)$ and aggregate income.

Figure 6 shows another relationship called the **expenditure line.** As in Figure 5, income, or real GDP, is on the horizontal axis, and spending is on the vertical axis. The top line in Figure 6 is the expenditure line. It is called the expenditure line because it shows how expenditure, or spending, depends on income. The four components that make up the expenditure line are consumption, investment, government purchases, and net exports. However, the expenditure line shows how these four components depend on income. It is this dependency of spending on income that is the defining characteristic of the expenditure line. Here is how the expenditure line is derived.

The consumption function is shown as the lowest line in Figure 6. It is simply the consumption function from Figure 3, which says that the higher income is, the more

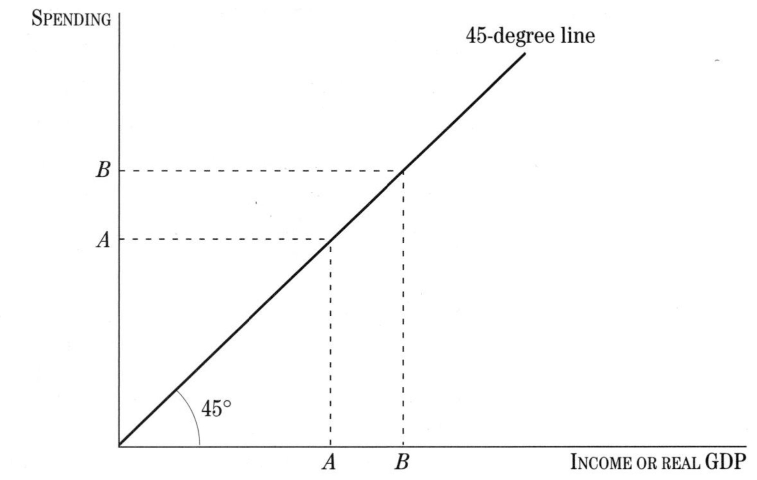

FIGURE 5
The 45-Degree Line
This simple line is a graphical representation of the income equals spending identity. The pairs of points on the 45-degree line have the same level of spending and income. For example, the level of spending at A is the same dollar amount as the level of income at A. Moreover, because income equals real GDP, we can put either income or real GDP on the horizontal axis.

people want to consume. The next line above the consumption function in Figure 6 is parallel to the consumption function. This line represents the addition of investment to consumption at each level of income. It says that investment is so many billions of dollars in the U.S. economy, and the distance between the lines is this amount of investment. For example, if investment equals $800 billion, the distance between the consumption function and this next line is $800 billion.

The reason the line is parallel to the consumption line is that we are starting our explanation by saying that investment does not depend on income. This simplifying assumption means that investment is a constant number, and the distance between the lines is the same regardless of income. We just add the same amount at each point.

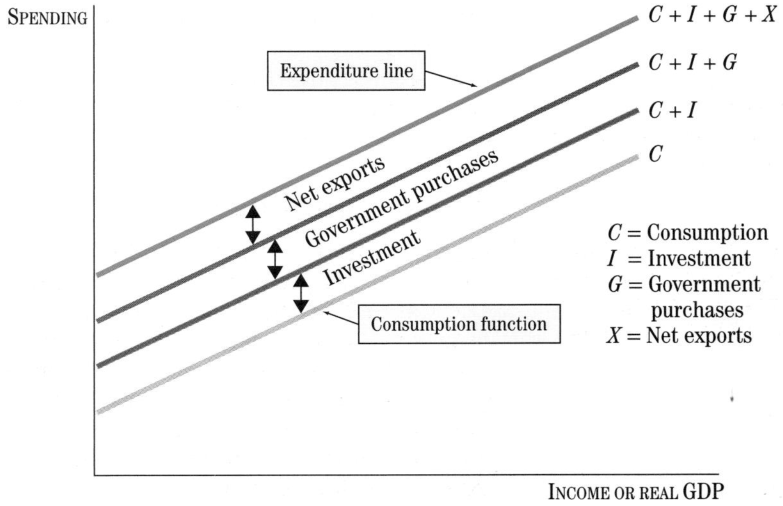

FIGURE 6
The Expenditure Line
By adding investment (*I*), government purchases (*G*), and net exports (*X*) to the consumption function, we build the expenditure line.

The next line in Figure 6 adds in a constant level of government purchases. This line is also parallel to the other lines because the increase at every level of income is the same. The distance between the lines represents a fixed level of government purchases, say, $2,000 billion, at every level of income.

Finally, to get the top line in Figure 6, we add in net exports. For simplicity, we assume that net exports do not depend on income, an assumption that we will change soon. Thus, the top line is parallel to all the other lines. The top line is the sum of $C + I + G + X$. It is the expenditure line. The most important thing to remember about the expenditure line is that it shows how the sum of the four components depends on income.

Before we can use the expenditure line, we must know what determines its slope and what causes it to shift.

The Slope of the Expenditure Line. Observe in Figure 6 that the expenditure line is parallel to the consumption function. Therefore, the slope of the expenditure line is the same as the slope of the consumption function. We already know that the slope of the consumption function is the MPC. Hence, the slope of the expenditure line is also equal to the MPC.

Because the MPC is less than 1, the aggregate expenditure line is flatter (the slope is smaller) than the 45-degree line, which has a slope of exactly 1. This fact will soon be used to find real GDP.

Shifts in the Expenditure Line. The expenditure line can shift for several reasons. Consider first what happens to the expenditure line if government purchases fall because of a cut in defense spending. As shown in Figure 7, the expenditure line shifts downward in a parallel fashion. The expenditure line is simply the sum $C + I + G + X$. Because G is less at all income levels, the line shifts down. The expenditure line is lowered because the distance between the consumption function and the other lines declines (see Figure 6). The reverse of this, an increase in government purchases, will cause the expenditure line to shift up.

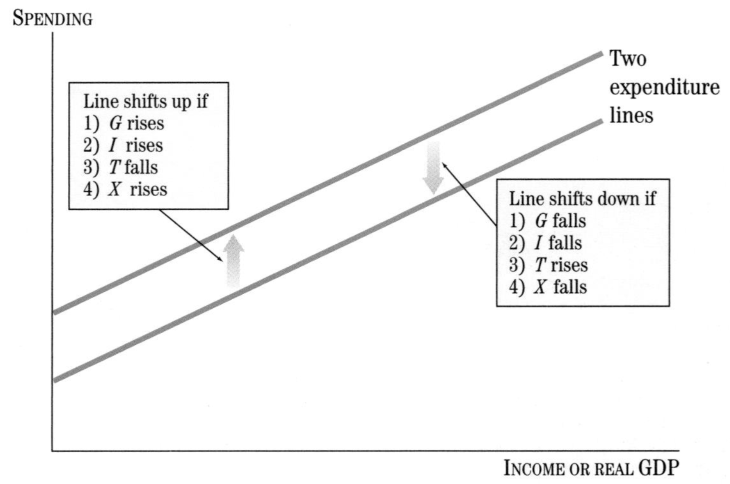

FIGURE 7
Shifts in the Expenditure Line
The expenditure line shifts down if (1) government purchases (G) fall, (2) investment (I) falls, (3) taxes (T) increase, or (4) net exports (X) fall. The expenditure line shifts up if (1) government purchases rise, (2) investment rises, (3) taxes are cut, or (4) net exports rise.

What happens to the expenditure line if investment falls? Investment, remember, is the gap between the first and second lines in Figure 6. If investment declines (as might happen if businesses become pessimistic about the future and invest less), then the expenditure line shifts downward. With less investment, the gap between the lines shrinks. The reverse of this, an increase in investment, will cause the expenditure line to shift up, as shown in Figure 7.

A change in net exports, perhaps because of a change in the demand for U.S. exports to other countries, will also shift the expenditure line. A downward shift in net exports lowers the expenditure line, and an upward shift in net exports raises the expenditure line.

Finally, the expenditure line can also be shifted by changes in taxes. At any given level of income, an increase in taxes means that people have less to spend, and this will cause people to consume less. Hence, the expenditure line shifts down when taxes rise. The reverse of this, a cut in taxes, causes the expenditure line to shift up. We will use the symbol T to refer to taxes. For example, if $T = \$1{,}500$ billion, then people pay and the government receives $1,500 billion in taxes.

Determining Real GDP Through Spending Balance

Having derived the expenditure line and the 45-degree line, we can combine the two to find real GDP. Figure 8 shows the expenditure line and the 45-degree line combined in one diagram. Observe that the two lines intersect. They must intersect because they have different slopes. Real GDP is found at the point of intersection of these two lines. Why?

Income and spending are always equal, and the 45-degree line is drawn to represent this equality. Therefore, at any point on the 45-degree line, income equals spending. Moreover, income and spending must be on the expenditure line, because only at points on that line do people consume according to the consumption function.

spending balance: the level of income or real GDP at which the 45-degree line and the expenditure line cross; also called equilibrium income.

If both relationships hold—that is, income and spending are the same (we are on the 45-degree line) and people's consumption is described by the consumption function (we are on the expenditure line)—then logically we must be at the intersection of these two lines. We call that point of intersection **spending balance.** The level of

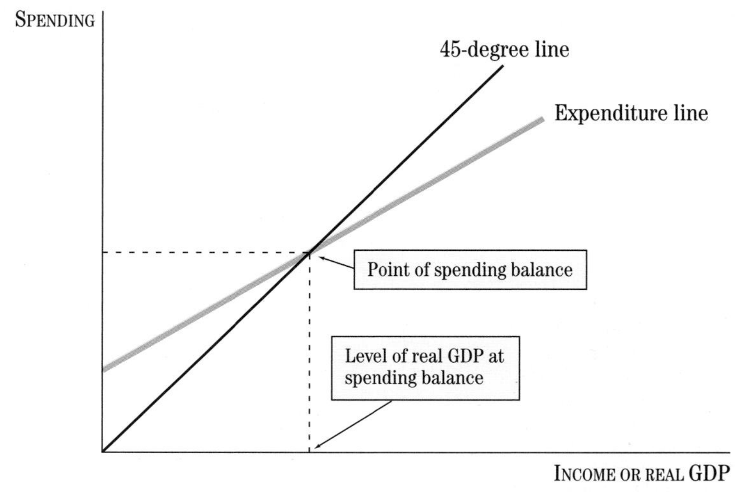

FIGURE 8
Spending Balance
Spending balance occurs when two relations are satisfied simultaneously: (1) income equals spending, and (2) spending equals consumption, which is a function of income, plus investment plus government purchases plus net exports. Only one level of income gives spending balance. That level of income is determined by the intersection of the 45-degree line and the expenditure line.

income determined by that point is just the right level to cause people to purchase an amount of consumption that—when added to investment, government purchases, and net exports—gives exactly the same level of income. We would not have spending balance at either a higher or a lower level of income. The diagram in Figure 8 showing that the 45-degree line and the expenditure line cross is sometimes called the "Keynesian Cross" after John Maynard Keynes.

Table 2 provides an alternative way to determine spending balance. It uses a numerical tabulation of the consumption function rather than graphs. Total expenditure is obtained by adding the four columns on the right of Table 2. Consumption is shown to depend on income according to the same consumption function as in Table 1. Observe that there is only one row where income equals total expenditure. That row is where spending balance occurs. The row is shaded and corresponds to the point of intersection of the 45-degree line and the expenditure line in Figure 8.

Because the point of spending balance is at the intersection of two lines, we can think of it as an equilibrium, much as the intersection of a demand curve and a supply curve for wheat is an equilibrium. Because real GDP is not necessarily equal to potential GDP at this intersection, however, there is a sense in which the equilibrium is temporary; eventually real GDP will move back to potential GDP, as we will show in later chapters.

The point of spending balance is also an equilibrium in the sense that economic forces cause real GDP to be at that intersection. To see this, consider Table 2. As we noted, the shaded row corresponds to the intersection of the 45-degree line and the expenditure line: Income or real GDP equals expenditure. Suppose that income or real GDP were less than expenditure, as in one of the rows above the shaded row in Table 2. This would not be an equilibrium because firms would not be producing enough goods and services (real GDP) to satisfy people's expenditure on goods and services. Firms would increase their production, and real GDP would rise until it equaled expenditure. Similarly, if real GDP were greater than expenditure, as in one of the rows below the shaded row in Table 2, firms would be producing more than people would be buying. Hence, firms would reduce their production, and real GDP would fall until it equaled expenditure.

A Better Forecast of Real GDP

Now let us return to forecasting real GDP using these new tools. Recall the example of making a forecast of real GDP for the year 2008 (from the vantage point of December

TABLE 2
A Numerical Example of Spending Balance (billions of dollars)

Income or Real GDP	Total Expenditure	Consumption	Investment	Government Purchases	Net Exports
6,000	8,000	5,000	1,500	2,000	−500
7,000	8,600	5,600	1,500	2,000	−500
8,000	9,200	6,200	1,500	2,000	−500
9,000	9,800	6,800	1,500	2,000	−500
10,000	10,400	7,400	1,500	2,000	−500
11,000	11,000	8,000	1,500	2,000	−500
12,000	11,600	8,600	1,500	2,000	−500
13,000	12,200	9,200	1,500	2,000	−500
14,000	12,800	9,800	1,500	2,000	−500

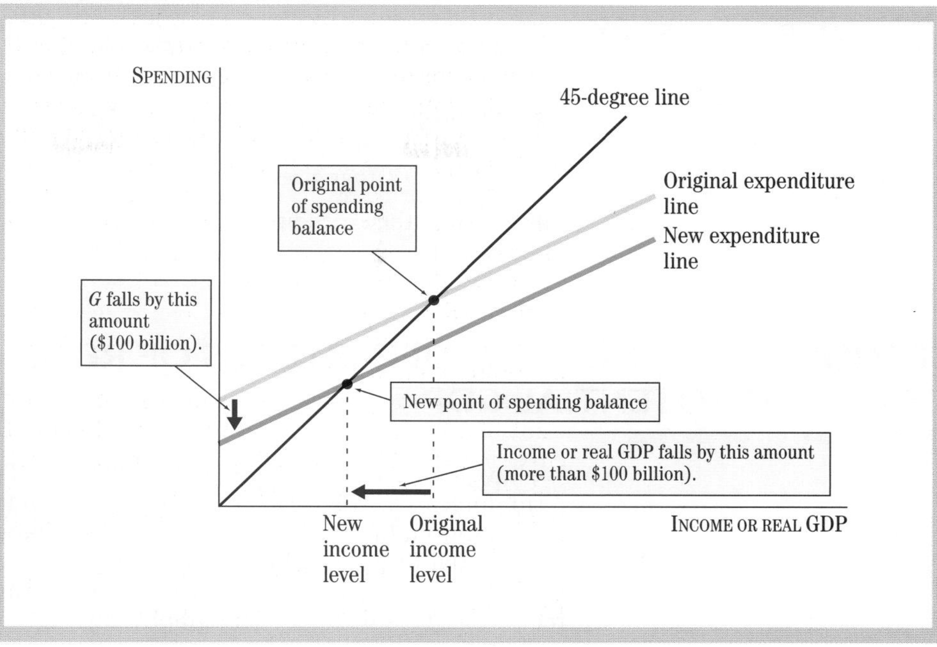

FIGURE 9
From One Point of Spending Balance to Another
The expenditure line shifts down because of a decline in government purchases. This shifts down the forecast for real GDP. A forecast of real GDP conditional on the decline in government purchases would therefore be lower.

2007), conditional on a proposed decline in government purchases of $100 billion. Our new tools will enable us to take into account the effect of this decline on consumption, which we ignored in the simple forecast.

Figure 9 shows two expenditure lines. The top expenditure line is without the change in government purchases. In this case, G = $2,000 billion, C = $8,000 billion, I = $1,500 billion, and X = −$500 billion, yielding income, or real GDP, of $11,000 billion. For the conditional forecast, we assume that G is cut by $100 billion, to $1,900 billion. In Figure 9, that causes the expenditure line to shift down to the "new" line. Observe that the expenditure line shifts down by $100 billion—a parallel shift. This new expenditure line cuts the 45-degree line at a lower point.

Logic tells us that the economy will now operate at a different point of spending balance, where the expenditure line and the 45-degree line now intersect. Thus we move from one intersection to a new intersection as a result of the decline in the expenditure line. The new point of spending balance is at a lower level of GDP.

We now have a prediction that real GDP will fall if government spending declines. Observe in Figure 9 that the decline in real GDP is larger than the $100 billion decline in government purchases and, therefore, larger than the $100 billion decline in real GDP in the simple forecast. The reason is that in addition to the decrease in government purchases, consumption has fallen because income has declined. The initial $100 billion is *multiplied* to create a larger than $100 billion change in real GDP because of the induced change in consumption. This multiplier phenomenon, which makes the change in real GDP larger than the change in government purchases, is called the *Keynesian multiplier* and applies to increases as well as to decreases in government purchases. In Figure 9, the multiplier looks quite large; the horizontal arrow is at least twice as large as the vertical arrow. It is certainly large enough to influence the government's decision to reduce government purchases. The example and the application illustrate that it is not just for fun that we have derived the expenditure line. It is an essential tool of the practicing macroeconomist.

REVIEW

- Spending balance occurs when the identity $Y = C + I + G + X$ and the consumption function relating C to Y hold simultaneously.
- Spending balance can be shown on a graph with the 45-degree line and the expenditure line. The intersection of the two lines determines a level of income, or real GDP, that gives spending balance.
- A shift in the expenditure line brings about a new level of spending balance.

SPENDING BALANCE AND DEPARTURES OF REAL GDP FROM POTENTIAL GDP

We have shown how to compute a level of real GDP for the purpose of making short-term forecasts. This level of real GDP is determined by aggregate demand—consumption, investment, government purchases, and net exports. It is not necessarily equal to potential GDP, which depends on the supply of labor, capital, and technology. Thus, we can have real GDP departing from potential GDP, as it does in recessions. Let's now show this graphically.

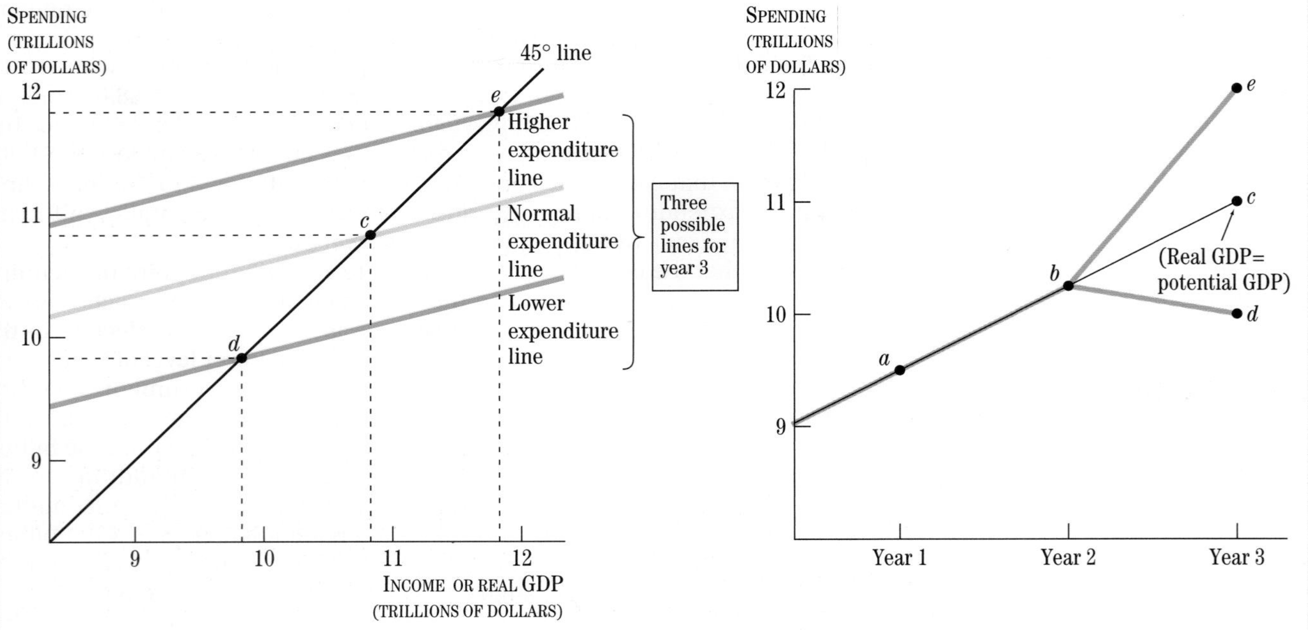

FIGURE 10
Spending Balance and Departures of Real GDP from Potential GDP

This figure shows how the levels of real GDP found through spending balance can explain the first steps of a recession or boom. The left panel shows spending balance for three expenditure curves; one (*c*) gives real GDP equal to potential GDP, a second (*e*) gives real GDP above potential GDP, and a third (*d*) gives real GDP below potential GDP. As shown in the right panel, two of these entail departures of real GDP from potential GDP.

Stepping Away from Potential GDP

Figure 10 illustrates how the departures of real GDP from potential GDP can be explained by shifts in the expenditure line. The left panel of the figure shows three different expenditure lines. Each line corresponds to a different level of government purchases or a different level of net exports or investment. The right panel of Figure 10—which is much like Figure 2—shows real GDP and potential GDP during a three-year period. There is a close connection between the left and right panels of Figure 10. The vertical axes are identical, and the points *c, d,* and *e* represent the same level of spending in both panels.

Observe how the three expenditure lines intersect the 45-degree line at three different levels of real GDP. Let us suppose that the middle expenditure line intersects the 45-degree line at a level of real GDP that is the same as potential GDP in year 3. This is point *c*. The lower expenditure line represents a recession; real GDP at the intersection of this expenditure line and the 45-degree line (point *d*) is at a level below potential GDP and also below the level of real GDP in year 2. Thus, real GDP would decline from year 2 to year 3 with this expenditure line. On the other hand, the higher expenditure line corresponds to the case in which real GDP is above potential GDP in year 3.

By referring to these values of real GDP as the *first* steps, we are emphasizing that they are not the end of the story. We will see that there are forces in the economy that tend to bring real GDP back toward potential GDP. This calculation of real GDP gives only the short-run impact of changes in government spending, investment, net exports, or taxes.

REVIEW

- Shifts in the expenditure line can explain the departures of real GDP from potential GDP.
- When the expenditure line shifts down, real GDP declines, and, if it was previously equal to potential GDP, it will fall below potential GDP. Upward shifts in the expenditure line will bring real GDP above potential GDP.
- The expenditure line can shift for many reasons. Changes in taxes, government purchases, investment, and net exports will cause the expenditure line to shift.

CONCLUSION

With this chapter, we have begun to develop a theory of economic fluctuations. We have shown how economists explain departures of real GDP from potential GDP, using the idea that these fluctuations are due to changes in aggregate demand. A recession occurs when aggregate demand falls, bringing real GDP below potential GDP. We used this explanation to make short-term forecasts of real GDP. The expenditure line—showing how the demand for consumption, investment, and net exports depends on income—and the 45-degree line are key parts of the forecasting process. However, our analysis thus far has made several simplifying assumptions. For example, we assumed that the only thing people's consumption decisions respond to is a change in income.

In the next chapter, we show that consumption as well as investment and net exports responds to interest rates and inflation. The responses to interest rates and inflation will explain why real GDP returns to potential GDP in the long run.

KEY POINTS

1. Economic fluctuations are temporary deviations of real GDP from potential GDP.
2. Employment and unemployment fluctuate with real GDP. Unemployment increases in recessions and decreases in booms.
3. The fluctuations in real GDP and potential GDP are mainly due to fluctuations in aggregate demand.
4. The idea that fluctuations in real GDP are mainly due to aggregate demand is used to find real GDP when making a short-term forecast.
5. Real GDP can be predicted on the basis of forecasts of consumption, investment, net exports, and government purchases. But these items depend on income and, thus, on the forecast of real GDP itself.
6. The consumption function describes how consumption responds to income.
7. The expenditure line is built up from the consumption function.
8. The 45-degree line tells us that expenditures equal income.
9. Combining the expenditure line and the 45-degree line in a diagram enables us to determine the level of income, or real GDP.
10. The level of real GDP that gives spending balance changes when government spending changes. Real GDP will decline in the short run when government purchases are cut.

KEY TERMS

real business cycle theory
consumption function
marginal propensity to consume (MPC)
45-degree line
expenditure line
spending balance

QUESTIONS FOR REVIEW

1. Why do theories of economic fluctuations focus on aggregate demand rather than potential GDP as the main source of short-run economic fluctuations?
2. Why do theories of economic growth focus on potential GDP (with its three determinants) rather than aggregate demand as the main source of economic growth?
3. Why does the unemployment rate rise when real GDP falls below potential GDP?
4. What is the normal rate of capacity utilization in manufacturing firms? What is the significance of this normal rate for explaining economic fluctuations?
5. What accounting identity does the 45-degree line represent?
6. Why does the expenditure line have a slope less than 1?
7. Why do economic forecasters have to take into account the consumption function?
8. Why is real GDP given by the intersection of the 45-degree line and the expenditure line?

PROBLEMS

1. In the early part of 2001, the U.S. economy was hit by a sudden plunge in stock markets, accompanied by a slowdown in consumer and investor spending. Explain why these events would move real GDP below potential GDP.
2. Recall that aggregate demand is made up of consumption, investment, government purchases, and net exports. How did the terrorist attacks on September 11, 2001, affect the components of aggregate demand in the three-month period that immediately followed?

3. Suppose the information in the following table described the economic situation in the United States at the end of 2006.

Year	Real GDP (billions of 2000 dollars)	Potential GDP (billions of 2000 dollars)
2004	10,703	10,703
2005	11,049	10,971
2006	11,415	11,245
2007 (pessimistic forecast)	11,655	11,525
2007 (optimistic forecast)	11,723	11,525

   a. Graph real GDP over time, placing the year on the horizontal axis. Calculate the growth rate of real GDP between 2004 and 2005, and between 2005 and 2006.
   b. The optimistic forecast for the year 2007 is based on the possibility that businesses are optimistic about the economy. What will the growth rate of real GDP be if the optimistic forecast turns out to be true?
   c. The pessimistic forecast is based on the possibility that businesses will be pessimistic about the economy. What will the growth rate of real GDP be if this forecast is correct?
   d. What is the deviation (in terms of dollars and as a percentage) of real GDP from potential GDP in 2007 if the optimistic forecast is correct? What is the deviation (in terms of dollars and as a percentage) from potential GDP in 2007 if the pessimistic forecast is correct?

4. When a war begins, what happens to the relationship between GDP and potential GDP? Does your answer depend on the size of the war or its duration?

5. Sketch a diagram with a 45-degree line and an expenditure line that describes macroeconomic spending balance. What factors determine how steep the expenditure line is? Show on the diagram that, when there is an increase in government purchases, U.S. income increases by more than the upward shift in government purchases.

6. Suppose government purchases will increase by $100 billion, and a forecasting firm predicts that real GDP will rise in the short run by $100 billion as a result. Would you say that that forecast is accurate? Why? If you were running a business and you subscribed to that forecasting service, what questions would you ask about the forecast?

7. Suppose that business executives are very optimistic, and they raise their investment spending. What happens to the expenditure line? How will this affect real GDP? Sketch a diagram to demonstrate your answer.

8. Suppose that American goods suddenly become unpopular in Europe. What happens to net exports? How will this shift the expenditure line? What happens to real GDP? Demonstrate this in a diagram.

9. The following table shows the relationship between income and consumption in an economy.

Income (Y) (in billions of dollars)	Consumption (C) (in billions of dollars)
0	5
10	11
20	17
30	23
40	29
50	35
60	41
70	47
80	53
90	59
100	65

Assume that investment (I) is $5 billion, government purchases (G) are $4 billion, and net exports (X) are $2 billion.
   a. What is the numerical value of the marginal propensity to consume?
   b. Construct a table that is analogous to Table 2 for this economy. What is the level of income at the point of spending balance?
   c. For this level of income, calculate national saving. Is national saving equal to investment plus net exports?
   d. Sketch a diagram with a 45-degree line and an expenditure curve that describes the preceding relationships. Show graphically what happens to income when the government lowers taxes.

10. In 2005, the Department of Defense announced its Base Realignment and Closure (BRAC) plan outlining which military bases were going to be shut down. This plan immediately caused great concern among the congressional representatives in whose districts the bases designated for closure were located. Suppose that a military base that employs 10,000 people was closed down. Describe the different sectors of the local economy that would be affected by the shutdown.

Deriving the Formula for the Keynesian Multiplier and the Forward-Looking Consumption Model

The Keynesian Multiplier

Here we derive a formula for the **Keynesian multiplier,** which gives the *short-run* impact on real GDP of things such as cuts in military purchases or a new federal program for construction of roads and bridges. We show how the multiplier depends on the marginal propensity to consume and on the marginal propensity to import.

A Graphical Review

Figure A.1 is a diagram like the one derived in Chapter 11, with income or real GDP on the horizontal axis and spending on the vertical axis. The 45-degree line equates spending and income. There are two expenditure lines in Figure A.1. The "new" expenditure line is $100 billion higher than the "old" expenditure line, representing an upward shift due to an increase in government purchases, for example. Both expenditure lines show that expenditure in the economy—the sum of consumption plus investment plus government purchases plus net exports, or $C + I + G + X$—rises with income. We assume that the marginal propensity to consume (MPC) is equal to .6. Thus, the slope of both expenditure lines is .6.

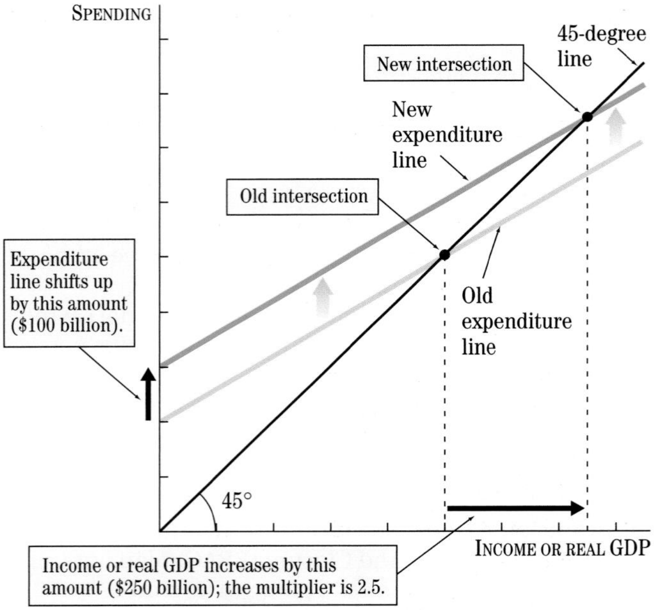

FIGURE A.1
Graphical Calculation of the Multiplier
An upward shift in the expenditure line raises real GDP in the short run by a multiple of the shift in the expenditure line. The multiplier can be found graphically. It is the ratio of the length of the black horizontal arrow to the length of the black vertical arrow.

Note that the "new" expenditure line intersects the 45-degree line at a different point from the "old" expenditure line. At this new intersection, the level of income, or real GDP, is higher than at the old intersection. On the horizontal axis, the black arrow pointing to the right shows this shift to a higher level of real GDP. Look carefully at the diagram to note the *size* of the change in real GDP along the horizontal axis and compare it with the change in the expenditure line. Observe that the horizontal change is *larger* than the vertical change. This is due to the multiplier. In fact, the term *multiplier* is used because the change in real GDP is a multiple of the shift in the aggregate expenditure line.

The multiplier is the ratio of the change in real GDP to the shift in the expenditure line, regardless of the reason for the shift in the expenditure line (whether it is due to a change in government purchases, a change in taxes, a change in investment, or a change in foreign demand). Thus, the multiplier is equal to the ratio of the length of the arrow along the horizontal axis to the length of the arrow along the vertical axis in Figure A.1. You can find the multiplier by measuring these lengths. If you do so, you will find that for the expenditure line with a slope of .6 in Figure A.1, the multiplier is 2.5.

The multiplier applies to anything that shifts the expenditure line. For example, an increase in government purchases of $100 billion would shift the expenditure line up by $100 billion. This would increase real GDP by $250 billion if the multiplier for government purchases is 2.5.

The Algebraic Derivation

We now want to derive a formula for the multiplier using algebra. Let us focus first on the case where the MPC is .6. To be specific, let us suppose that the particular reason for a change in the aggregate expenditure line is an increase in government purchases. Then the multiplier is the ratio of the change in real GDP to the change in government purchases.

The identity that income or real GDP (Y) equals consumption (C) plus investment (I) plus government purchases (G) plus net exports (X) can be written algebraically as

$$Y = C + I + G + X$$

To find the multiplier, we want to determine the impact of a *change* in government purchases on real GDP. That is, we want to find the change in Y that occurs when G changes. Any change in Y must come either directly from a change in G or indirectly from a change in C, I, or X, according to the preceding identity. Denote the change in any of these items by the Greek letter Δ. Then we can write the identity in terms of changes:

$$\Delta Y = \Delta C + \Delta I + \Delta G + \Delta X$$

That is, the *change* in real GDP is equal to the *change* in consumption plus the *change* in investment plus the *change* in government purchases plus the *change* in net exports. Now consider each of the four terms on the right.

The change in government purchases (ΔG) equals \$100 billion. For convenience, to make things simple, we continue to assume that there is no change in investment or in net exports. In other words, we assume that neither responds to changes in income. Expressed in symbols, $\Delta I = 0$ and $\Delta X = 0$.

But we cannot assume that $\Delta C = 0$. The *consumption function* tells us that consumption changes when income changes. The consumption function we use for the algebraic calculation has an MPC of .6. Using algebra, we write $\Delta C = .6\Delta Y$. That is, the change in consumption equals .6 times the change in income; for example, if the change in income ΔY = \$10 billion, then the change in consumption ΔC = \$6 billion if the MPC is .6.

Now let us take our ingredients:

1. $\Delta Y = \Delta C + \Delta I + \Delta G + \Delta X$.
2. The changes in investment and net exports are zero ($\Delta I = \Delta X = 0$).
3. The change in consumption is .6 times the change in income ($\Delta C = .6\Delta Y$).

Replacing ΔI with zero and ΔX with zero removes ΔI and ΔX from the right-hand side of the identity. Replacing ΔC with $.6\Delta Y$ in the same identity results in

$$\Delta Y = .6\Delta Y + \Delta G$$

Note that the term ΔY appears on both sides of this equation. Gathering terms in ΔY on the left-hand side of the equation gives

$$(1 - .6)\Delta Y = \Delta G$$

Dividing both sides by ΔG and by $(1 - .6)$ results in

$$\begin{aligned}\Delta Y/\Delta G &= 1/(1 - .6)\\ &= 1/.4\\ &= 2.5\end{aligned}$$

Thus, the change in income, or real GDP, that occurs when government purchases change, according to this calculation, is 2.5 times the change in government purchases. That is, $\Delta Y = 2.5\Delta G$. The number 2.5 is the multiplier. The algebraic calculation agrees with the graphical calculation.

You can perform this same calculation for *any value* of the marginal propensity to consume (MPC), not just .6. To see this, note that the change in consumption equals the MPC times the change in income, where the MPC is any number. Using the same approach as in the case of MPC = .6, we obtain a *formula for the multiplier*, which is

$$\frac{\Delta Y}{\Delta G} = \frac{1}{(1 - \text{MPC})}$$

The derivation of this formula is summarized in Table A.1.

TABLE A.1
Derivation of a Formula for the Keynesian Multiplier

Start with the identity

$$Y = C + I + G + X$$

and convert it to change form:

$$\Delta Y = \Delta C + \Delta I + \Delta G + \Delta X$$

Substitute $\Delta I = 0$, $\Delta X = 0$, and

$$\Delta C = \text{MPC} \times \Delta Y$$

into the change form of the identity to get

$$\Delta Y = \text{MPC} \times \Delta Y + \Delta G$$

Gather terms involving ΔY to get

$$(1 - \text{MPC}) \times \Delta Y = \Delta G$$

Divide both sides by ΔG and by $1 - \text{MPC}$ to get

$$\frac{\Delta Y}{\Delta G} = \frac{1}{1 - \text{MPC}}$$

Following the Multiplier Through the Economy To get a more complete understanding of the formula for the multiplier, it is useful to examine what happens as a change in government purchases winds its way through the economy.

Assume that the government increases its military purchases, perhaps to build a new missile defense system. In this example, the government increases purchases of electronic and aerospace equipment at defense firms. The immediate impact of the change in government purchases is an increase in the production of this equipment. With an increase in demand, defense firms produce more, and real GDP rises. The initial increase in real GDP from an increase in government purchases of $100 billion is that same $100 billion. If the government is purchasing more equipment, the production of equipment increases. We call this initial increase in real GDP the *first-round* effect, which includes only the initial change in government purchases.

The first round is not the end of the story. A further increase in real GDP occurs when the workers employed in making the equipment start working more hours and new workers are hired. As a result, the workers' income rises, and the profits made by the manufacturers increase. With both wage income and profit income rising, income in the economy as a whole rises by $100 billion. According to the consumption function, people will consume more. How much more? The consumption function tells us that .6 times the change in income, or $60 billion, will be the additional increase in consumption by the workers and owners of the defense firms. Real GDP rises by $60 billion, the increased production of the goods the workers and owners consume. This $60 billion increase in real GDP is the *second-round* effect. It is hard for anyone to know what the workers in the defense industry or the owners of the defense firms will start purchasing; presumably it will be an array of goods: clothes, movies, and restaurant meals. But with an MPC of .6, we do know that they will purchase $60 billion more of these goods. The increase in production spreads throughout the economy. After this second round, real GDP has increased by $160 billion, the sum of $100 billion on the first round and $60 billion on the second round. This is shown in the first and second rows of Table A.2.

The story continues. The workers who make the clothes and other goods and services for which there is $60 billion more in spending also have an increase in their income. Either they are no longer unemployed or they work more hours. Similarly, the profits of the owners of those firms increase. As a result, they consume more. How much more? According to the consumption function, .6 times the increase in their income. The increase in income outside of defense production was $60 billion, so the increase in consumption must now be .6 times that, or a $36 billion increase. This increase is the *third-round* effect. As the increase permeates the economy, it is impossible to say what particular goods will increase in production, but we know that total production continues to increase. After three rounds, real GDP has increased by $196 billion, as shown in the third row of Table A.2.

TABLE A.2
A Numerical Illustration of the Multiplier at Work
(billions of dollars)

Round	Change in Real GDP	Cumulative Change in Real GDP
First round	100.000	100.000
Second round	60.000	160.000
Third round	36.000	196.000
Fourth round	21.600	217.600
Fifth round	12.960	230.560
.	.	.
.	.	.
.	.	.
After an infinite number of rounds	0.000	250.000

The increase does not stop there. Another $36 billion more in consumption means that there is $36 billion more in income for people somewhere in the economy. This increases consumption further, by .6 times the $36 billion, or $21.6 billion. According to the column on the right of Table A.2, the cumulative effect on real GDP is now up to $217.6 billion after four rounds. Observe that each new entry in the first column is added to the previous total to get the cumulative effect on real GDP.

The story is now getting repetitive. We multiply .6 times $21.6 billion to get $12.96 billion. The total effect on real GDP is now $230.56 billion at the fifth round. In fact, we are already almost at $250 billion. If we kept on going for more and more rounds, we would get closer and closer to the $250 billion amount obtained from the graphs and the formula for the multiplier.

What If Net Exports Depend on Income? Thus far, we have made the simplifying assumption that net exports do not respond to income. When net exports do respond to income, the formula for the multiplier is a bit different. We now incorporate this response into our analysis.

We first need to consider how net exports respond to income. Recall that net exports are exports minus imports. To examine the effect of income on net exports, we look first at exports and then at imports.

Exports are goods and services that we sell to other countries—aircraft, pharmaceuticals, telephones. Do U.S. exports depend on income in the United States? No, not much. If Americans earn a little more or a little less, the demand for U.S. exports is not going to increase or decrease. What is likely to make the demand for U.S. exports increase or decrease is a change in income abroad—changes in income in Japan, Europe, or Latin America will affect demand for U.S. exports. U.S. exports will not be affected even if the United States has a recession. Of course, if Japan or Europe has a recession, that is another story. In any case, we conclude that U.S. exports are unresponsive to the changes in U.S. income.

Imports are goods and services that people in the United States purchase from abroad—automobiles, sweaters, vacations. Does the amount purchased of these goods and services change when our incomes change? Yes, because imports are part of consumption. Just as we argued that consumption responds to income, so must imports respond to income. Higher income will lead to higher consumption of both goods purchased in the United States and goods purchased abroad. That reasoning leads us to hypothesize that imports are positively related to income. The hypothesis turns out to be accurate when we look at observations on income and imports.

The **marginal propensity to import (MPI)** is the amount that imports change when income changes. Suppose the MPI is .2. The MPI is smaller than the MPC because most of the goods we consume when income rises are not imported.

If exports are unrelated to income and imports are positively related to income, then net exports—exports less imports—must be negatively related to income.

Algebraically, we have

$$\Delta X = -\text{MPI} \times \Delta Y$$

Using this expression for ΔX, we can now follow the same algebraic steps we followed earlier to derive a formula for the multiplier. The multiplier now depends on the MPI along with the MPC. The derivation is summarized in Table A.3. The formula for the multiplier is

$$\frac{\Delta Y}{} = \frac{1}{1 - \text{MPC} + \text{MPI}}$$

For example, if MPC = .6 and MPI = .2, the multiplier is 1.7.

TABLE A.3
Derivation of a Formula for the Keynesian Multiplier with Both the MPC and the MPI

Start with

$$\Delta Y = \Delta C + \Delta I + \Delta G + \Delta X$$

Assume that

$$\Delta I = 0$$

and that

$$\Delta C = \text{MPC} \times \Delta Y$$

and that

$$\Delta X = -\text{MPI} \times \Delta Y$$

Putting the above expressions together, we get

$$\Delta Y = (\text{MPC} \times \Delta Y) + \Delta G - (\text{MPI} \times \Delta Y)$$

and solving for the change in Y, we get

$$\frac{\Delta Y}{\Delta G} = \frac{1}{1 - \text{MPC} + \text{MPI}}$$

The Forward-Looking Consumption Model

Although the consumption function introduced in Chapter 11 gives a good prediction of people's behavior in many situations, it sometimes works very poorly. For example, the marginal propensity to consume (MPC) turned out to be very small when taxes were cut in 1975; people saved almost the entire increase in disposable income that resulted from the tax cut. However, the MPC turned out to be very large for the tax cuts in 1982, only seven years later; people saved very little of the increase in disposable income in that case. The forward-looking consumption model was designed to explain such changes in the MPC.

The **forward-looking consumption model** assumes that people anticipate their future income when making consumption decisions. The forward-looking consumption model was developed independently and in different ways by two Nobel Prize–winning economists, Milton Friedman and Franco Modigliani. Friedman's version is called the **permanent income model,** and Modigliani's version is called the **life-cycle model.** Both models improved on the idea that consumption depends only on current income.

Forward-Looking People

The forward-looking model starts with the idea that people attempt to look ahead to the future. They do not simply consider their current income. For example, if a young medical doctor decides to take a year off from a high-paying suburban medical practice to do community service at little or no pay, that doctor's income will fall below the poverty line for a year. But the doctor is unlikely to cut consumption to a fraction of the poverty level of income. Even if the doctor were young enough to have little savings, borrowing would be a way to keep consumption high and even buy an occasional luxury item. The doctor is basing consumption decisions on expected income for several years in the future—making an assessment of a more permanent income, or a life-cycle income—not just for one year.

There are many other examples. Farmers in poor rural areas of Asia try to save something in good years so that they will be able to maintain their consumption in bad years. They try not to consume a fixed fraction of their income. In many cases, the saving is in storable farm goods like rice.

As these examples indicate, instead of allowing their consumption to vary with their income, which may be quite erratic, most people engage in **consumption smoothing** from year to year. Once people estimate their future income prospects, they try to maintain their consumption around the same level from year to year. If their income temporarily falls, they do not cut their consumption by much; *the marginal propensity to consume (MPC) is very small—maybe about .05—in the case of a temporary change in income.* But if they find out that their income will increase permanently, they will increase their consumption a lot; *the MPC is very large—maybe .95—in the case of a permanent change in income.* For example, if a new fertilizer doubles the rice yield of a rice farmer's land permanently, we can expect that the farmer's consumption of other goods will about double because of higher permanent income.

The difference between the forward-looking consumption model and the simple consumption function where consumption depends only on current income is illustrated in Figure A.2. In the right panel of Figure A.2, income is expected to follow a typical life-cycle pattern: lower when young, higher when middle-aged, and very low when retired. However, consumption does not follow these ups and downs; it is flat. The left panel shows the opposite extreme: the standard consumption function with a fixed MPC. In this case, people consume a lot when they are middle-aged but consume very little when they are young or old.

Occasionally, some people are prevented from completely smoothing their income because they have a **liquidity constraint;** that is, they cannot get a loan, and so they cannot consume more than their income. Such liquidity constraints do not appear to be important enough in the economy as a whole to negate the forward-looking model completely. Of course, not all people try to smooth their income; some people like to go on binges, spending everything, even if the binge is followed by a long lull.

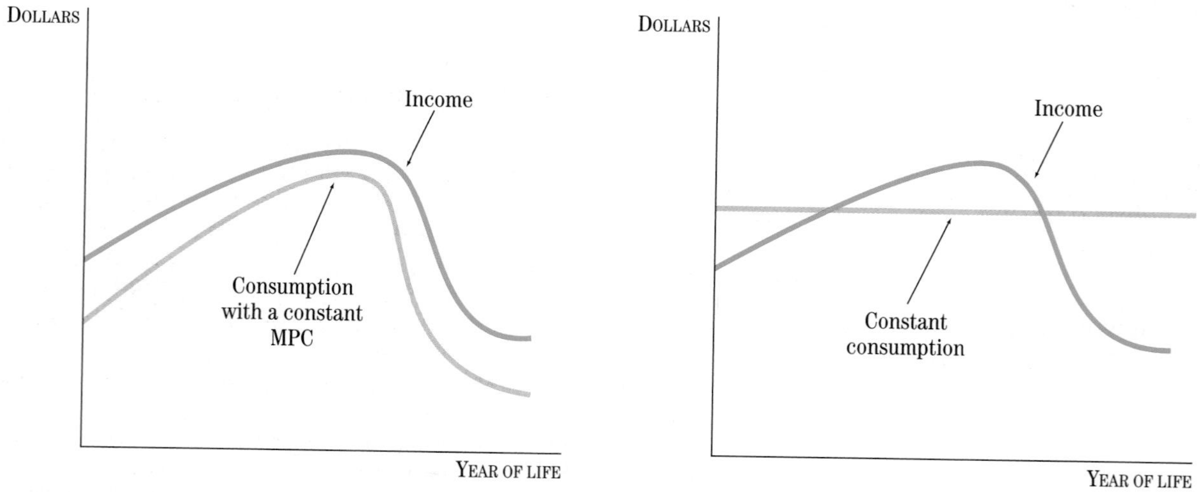

FIGURE A.2
Two Extreme Forms of Consumption Behavior
The right panel shows the future outlook of a young person or family described by the forward-looking model of consumption. The left panel shows the outlook of a young family with a constant MPC. The path of income is the same in both cases.

Tests and Applications of the Forward-Looking Model

Observations on consumption and income for the economy as a whole indicate that the forward-looking model significantly improves our understanding of observed changes in the MPC. For example, economists have demonstrated that the measured MPC for the economy as a whole is lower for the temporary changes in income that occur during recessions and booms than for the more permanent increases in income that occur as potential GDP grows over time. Studies of thousands of individual families over time show that the individual MPC for temporary changes in income is about one-third of the MPC for permanent changes in income.

Permanent versus Temporary Tax Cuts The forward-looking model is also the most promising explanation for the low MPC during the tax cut of 1975. That tax cut was explicitly temporary—a one-time tax rebate, good for only one year. In contrast, the tax cut in the early 1980s was explicitly permanent and was expected to apply for many years into the future. The MPC was large in this case.

With a permanent tax cut, the MPC is high, so there is a big impact on real GDP. For a temporary tax cut, the MPC is low, so there is only a small impact on GDP. In estimating the effects of various tax proposals on the economy, economic forecasters try to take these changes in the MPC into account.

Anticipating Future Tax Cuts or Increases The forward-looking model changes our estimate of the impact of changes in taxes that are expected to occur in the future. For example, if people are certain of tax cuts in the future, they may begin to increase their consumption right away, before the tax decreases. In this case, the MPC is technically huge, because consumption increases with little or no observed change in current income. Conversely, people may reduce their consumption in anticipation of a tax increase.

It is difficult to know how large these effects are because we do not observe people's expectations of the future. Estimates based on the assumption that people forecast the future no better and no worse than economic forecasters—this is the *rational expectations assumption*—suggest that the effects are large and significant.

In situations where the expectations effects are obvious, we do see an impact. For example, in December 1992, after the 1992 presidential election, when a tax increase became more likely, there was evidence that many people who could do so shifted their reported income for tax purposes from 1993 to 1992. But whether people held back their consumption in anticipation of future tax increases is difficult to say. In any case, because people's behavior is affected by their expectations of the future, attempts to estimate the impact of a policy proposal like a change in taxes need to take these expectations into account.

KEY POINTS

1. The multiplier can be found with graphs and with algebra. The algebraic approach results in a convenient formula.
2. The formula for the multiplier is 1/(1 − MPC) when net exports do not depend on income.
3. If net exports are negatively related to income, then the formula for the multiplier is 1/(1 − MPC + MPI).
4. The forward-looking consumption model explains why the MPC is low in some cases and high in others. It helps economists deal with the uncertainty in the multiplier.
5. The forward-looking consumption model also implies that anticipated changes in taxes affect consumption and are a further reason for uncertainty about the MPC. Although such effects have been observed, it is difficult to estimate their size in advance.
6. The rational expectations assumption, which suggests that people forecast the future no better and no worse than economic forecasters, is one basis for making such estimates. With this assumption, the effects of anticipated tax changes on consumption are quite high.

KEY TERMS AND DEFINITIONS

Keynesian multiplier: the ratio of the change in real GDP to the shift in the expenditure line; the formula is 1/(1 − MPC), where MPC is the marginal propensity to consume.

marginal propensity to import (MPI): the change in imports because of a given change in income.

forward-looking consumption model: a model that explains consumer behavior by assuming that people anticipate future income when deciding on consumption spending today.

permanent income model: a type of forward-looking consumption model that assumes that people distinguish between temporary changes in their income and permanent changes in their income; the permanent changes have a larger effect on consumption.

life-cycle model: a type of forward-looking consumption model that assumes that people base their consumption decisions on their expected lifetime income rather than on their current income.

consumption smoothing: the idea that although their incomes fluctuate, people try to stabilize consumption spending from year to year.

liquidity constraint: the situation in which people cannot borrow to smooth their consumption spending when their income is low.

QUESTIONS FOR REVIEW

1. Why is the size of the multiplier positively related to the MPC?
2. Why is the size of the multiplier negatively related to the marginal propensity to import?
3. How does the forward-looking consumption model differ from the consumption function with a fixed MPC?
4. Why is the MPC for a temporary tax cut less than the MPC for a permanent tax cut? Are there examples that prove the point?
5. What is consumption smoothing?
6. Why do changes in future taxes that are anticipated in advance affect consumption?

PROBLEMS

1. Are the following statements true or false? Show using algebra.
   a. The multiplier is greater than 1 and rises if the marginal propensity to consume rises.
   b. The multiplier for an economy in which net exports respond to income is smaller than the multiplier for an economy in which net exports do not respond to income.
2. The following table shows real GDP and imports (in billions of dollars) for an economy.

Real GDP or Income	Imports
2,000	400
3,000	500
4,000	600
5,000	700
6,000	800
7,000	900

   Suppose that exports are equal to $700 billion.
   a. Construct a graph showing how imports depend on income.
   b. Construct a graph showing how net exports depend on income.
   c. If the level of real GDP that occurs at spending balance is $6,000 billion, will there be a trade surplus or a trade deficit? What type of policy regarding government purchases would bring the trade deficit or trade surplus closer to zero?
   d. If the marginal propensity to consume is .6, what is the size of the multiplier?
3. **a.** Suppose Joe spends every additional dollar of income that he receives. What is Joe's marginal propensity to consume? What does his consumption function look like?
   b. Suppose that Jane spends half of each additional dollar of income that she receives. What is Jane's marginal propensity to consume? What does her consumption function look like?
   c. What differences in Joe's and Jane's incomes or jobs might explain the differences in their MPCs?
4. Suppose Uncle George sent you a check for $500 tomorrow because he is proud of your excellent grades and feels that you are a credit to the family. What would you do with the largest part of the money? Would you spend it, would you save it, or would you pay down your credit card debt (technically a form of saving)? Why? If Uncle George said that he would send you $500 every month while you are in college, would you allocate the funds among spending, saving, and debt reduction any differently? Why or why not?
5. Each month, a certain fraction of employees' pay is withheld and sent to the government as part of what is owed for personal income taxes. If the taxes owed for the year are less than the amount withheld, then a refund is sent early in the following year. If the taxes owed for the year exceed the amount withheld, then additional taxes must be paid by April 15. In 1992, the amount of income tax *withheld* was lowered by about $10 billion to increase consumption and real GDP and thereby speed recovery from the 1990–1991 recession. However, the amount of taxes owed was not changed. Discuss why the impact of this change would be smaller than that of an actual cut in taxes of $10 billion during that year.

Chapter 12

The Economic Fluctuations Model

Now that we have seen the forces that can end an expansion and start a recession, it is time to examine the fascinating dynamic process through which recession ends and a new expansion begins. Can government actions cut the length of a recession or speed up the expansion? In 2003, for example, there was a great national debate about whether additional tax cuts were needed to speed up the recovery from the 2001 U.S. recession. In the end, taxes were cut, but the legislation passed the Congress by only a very narrow margin—one vote in the Senate.

In order to address important policy questions like these, we need a model of economic fluctuations—a simplified description of how the economy adjusts over time when it moves away from potential GDP, as in a recession.

The purpose of this chapter is to present, in graphical form, an economic fluctuations model. Economic fluctuations models are used to make decisions about monetary policy at the Fed and at other central banks all over the world. Private business analysts use the ideas to track the economy and predict central bank decisions.

This model is much newer than the supply and demand model, which has been around for over 100 years. It combines Keynes's idea, developed 50 years ago, that aggregate demand causes the departure of real GDP from potential GDP with newer ideas, developed in the 1980s and 1990s, about how expectations and inflation adjust over time.

Though newer, the economic fluctuations model is analogous to the supply and demand model (Chapter 3). Just as we presented the supply and demand model in a graph consisting of three elements:

- A *demand curve*
- A *supply curve*
- An *equilibrium* at the intersection of the two curves

we present the economic fluctuations model in a graph consisting of three elements:

- An *aggregate demand* (*AD*) *curve*
- An *inflation adjustment* (*IA*) *line*
- An *equilibrium* at the intersection of the curve and the line

We use the economic fluctuations model to explain fluctuations in real GDP and inflation in much the same way that we used supply and demand curves to explain quantity and price in the peanut or other microeconomic markets. In the microeconomic supply and demand model, the intersection of the *demand curve* and the *supply curve* gives us a prediction of price and quantity. In the economic fluctuations model, the intersection of the *aggregate demand* (AD) *curve* and the *inflation adjustment* (IA) *line* gives us a prediction of real GDP and inflation.

We will start our construction of the economic fluctuations model by deriving the aggregate demand curve and then the inflation adjustment line. We will then show how their intersection determines real GDP and inflation.

THE AGGREGATE DEMAND CURVE

aggregate demand (*AD*) curve: a line showing a negative relationship between inflation and the aggregate quantity of goods and services demanded at that inflation rate.

The **aggregate demand (*AD*) curve** is a relationship between two economic variables: real GDP and the inflation rate. Real GDP is usually measured as the percentage deviation from potential GDP, and the inflation rate is usually measured as the annual percentage change in the overall price level from year to year. Figure 1 shows an aggregate demand curve for the United States. Observe that inflation is measured on the vertical

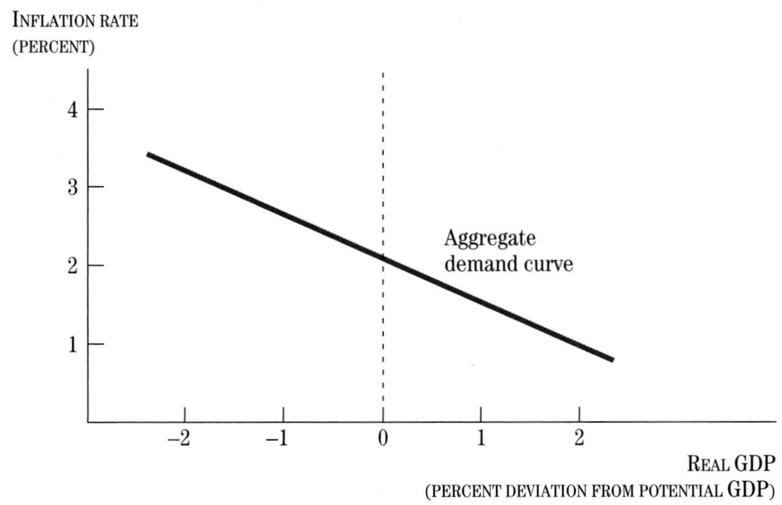

FIGURE 1
The Aggregate Demand Curve
The aggregate demand curve shows that higher inflation and real GDP are negatively related.

axis, that real GDP is measured on the horizontal axis, and that we have drawn a vertical dashed line to mark the point where real GDP equals potential GDP. The aggregate demand curve shows different combinations of real GDP and inflation. It is downward-sloping from left to right because real GDP is negatively related to inflation along the curve. The term *aggregate demand* is used because we interpret the movements of real GDP away from potential GDP as being due to fluctuations in the sum (aggregate) of the demand for consumption, investment, net exports, and government purchases.

Why does the aggregate demand curve slope downward? We will answer this question and derive the curve in three stages. First, we show that there is a negative relationship between the real interest rate and real GDP. Second, we show that there is a positive relationship between inflation and the real interest rate. Third, we show that these two relationships imply that there is a negative relationship between real GDP and inflation, and that that relationship is the aggregate demand curve. The following schematic chart shows how the three stages fit together.

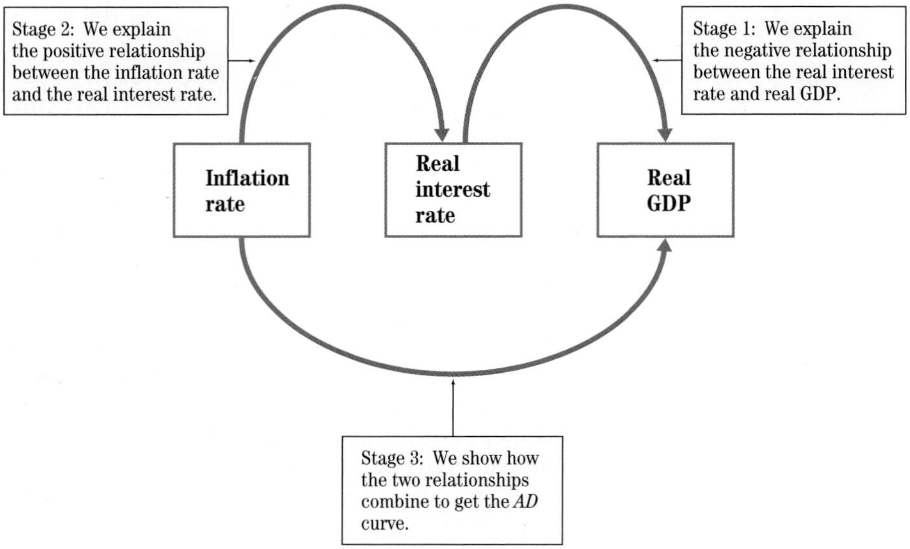

Interest Rates and Real GDP

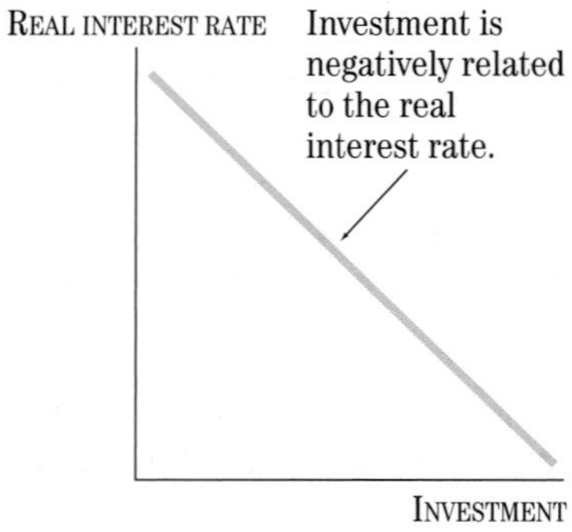

Consumption, investment, and net exports are each negatively related to the interest rate. Combining these components helps provide an explanation of the negative relationship between real GDP and the interest rate. Keep in mind that the real interest rate is a better measure of the effects of interest rates on investment, consumption, and net exports because it corrects for inflation. Recall from Chapter 5 that the real interest rate equals the stated, or nominal, interest rate minus the inflation rate. The negative effect of the real interest rate on consumption, investment, and net exports is no different from that discussed in Chapter 7. If you have already studied that chapter, the next few pages will serve as review.

Investment. Investment is the component of expenditure that is probably most sensitive to the real interest rate. Recall that part of investment is the purchase of new equipment or a new factory by a business firm. Many firms must borrow funds to pay for such investments. Higher real interest rates make such borrowing more costly. The additional profits the firm might expect to earn from purchasing a photocopier or a truck are more likely to be lower than the interest costs on the loan if the real interest rate is high. Hence, businesses that are thinking about buying a new machine and need to borrow funds will be less inclined to purchase such an investment good if real interest rates are higher, and so higher real interest rates reduce investment spending by businesses. Also, remember that part of investment is the purchase of new houses. Most people need to take out a mortgage in order to buy a house. Like any loan, the mortgage has an interest rate, and higher interest rates make mortgages more costly. Hence, with higher real interest rates, fewer people take out mortgages and buy new houses. Spending for new housing declines.

The same reasoning works to show why lower real interest rates will increase investment spending: Lower real interest rates reduce the cost of borrowing and make investment more attractive to firms and households.

To summarize, both business investment and housing investment decline when the real interest rate rises, and they increase when the real interest rate falls. At any time there are some firms or households deciding whether to buy a new machine or a new house, and they are going to be less inclined to buy such things when the interest rate is higher.

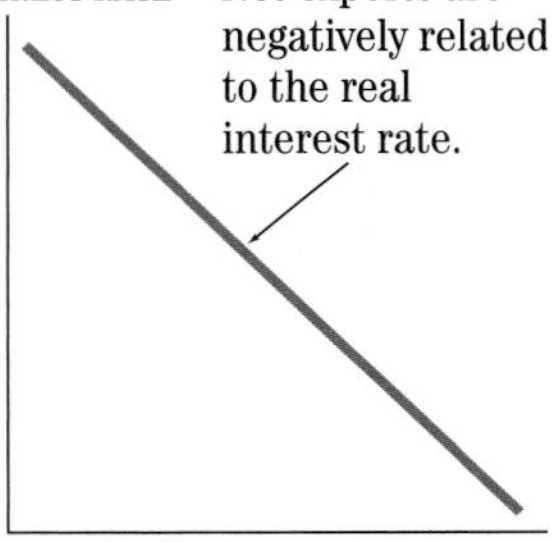
REAL INTEREST RATE
Net exports are negatively related to the real interest rate.
NET EXPORTS

Net Exports. The negative relationship between net exports and the real interest rate requires a somewhat more involved explanation than the relationship between the real interest rate and investment. The relationship exists because higher real interest rates in the United States tend to lead to a higher dollar exchange rate and, in turn, a higher exchange rate reduces net exports.

A higher real interest rate in the United States compared with other countries increases the demand for U.S. dollar bank accounts and other assets that pay interest. That increased demand bids up the price of dollars; hence, the exchange rate—the price of dollars—rises. Now, with a higher exchange rate, net exports will be lower because U.S.-produced exports become more expensive to foreigners, who must pay a higher price for dollars, and imported foreign goods become cheaper for Americans, who can get more foreign goods for higher-priced dollars. With exports falling and imports rising, net exports—exports less imports—must fall. In sum, higher real interest rates reduce net exports.

The same reasoning works for lower real interest rates as well. If the real interest rate falls in the United States, then U.S. dollar bank accounts are less attractive compared with bank accounts in other currencies, such as those of Germany or Japan. This bids down the price of dollars, and the exchange rate falls. Now, with a lower exchange rate, net exports will be higher because U.S.-produced exports are less expensive to foreigners and imported foreign goods are more expensive for Americans. With exports rising and imports falling, net exports must rise. Thus, lower real interest rates increase net exports.

To summarize, there is a negative relationship between the interest rate and the net exports that works through the exchange rate, as shown below.

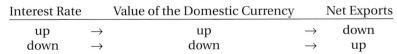

Interest Rate		Value of the Domestic Currency		Net Exports
up	→	up	→	down
down	→	down	→	up

If the interest rate goes up, then the value of the domestic currency goes up, causing net exports to go down. If the interest rate goes down, then the value of the domestic currency goes down, causing net exports to go up.

Consumption. We have shown that two of the components of expenditure—investment and net exports—are sensitive to the real interest rate. What about consumption?

Although consumption is probably less sensitive to the real interest rate than the other components, there is some evidence that higher real interest rates encourage people to save a larger fraction of their income. Higher real interest rates encourage people to save because they earn more on their savings. Because more saving means less consumption, this implies that consumption is negatively related to the interest rate. However, most economists feel that the effect of interest rates on consumption is much less than on investment and net exports.

The Overall Effect. To summarize the discussion thus far, investment, net exports, and consumption are all negatively related to the real interest rate. The overall effect of a change in real interest rates on real GDP can now be assessed.

Figure 2 shows the 45-degree line and two different expenditure lines corresponding to two different interest rates. Higher interest rates shift the expenditure line down because a higher interest rate lowers investment, net exports, and consumption, which are all part of expenditure.

Observe how the downward shift of the expenditure line leads to a new point of spending balance. The intersection of the expenditure line with the 45-degree line occurs at a lower level of real GDP. Note that real GDP is lower not only because the higher real interest rate lowers investment, net exports, and consumption, but also because a decline in income will lower consumption further. Real GDP declines by the amount shown on the horizontal axis, which is larger than the downward shift in the expenditure line. *Thus, an increase in the real interest rate lowers real GDP.*

What about a decline in the real interest rate? A lower real interest rate will raise the expenditure line. In that case, when the expenditure line shifts up, the point of spending balance at the intersection with the 45-degree line will be at a higher level of real GDP. *Thus, a decrease in the real interest rate raises real GDP.*

In sum, we have shown that there is a negative relationship between the real interest rate and real GDP.

Finished with Stage 1: Real GDP is negatively related to the real interest rate.

Why?

- Consumption (C) is negatively related to the *real interest rate.*
- Investment (I) is negatively related to the *real interest rate.*
- Net exports (X) are negatively related to the *real interest rate.*

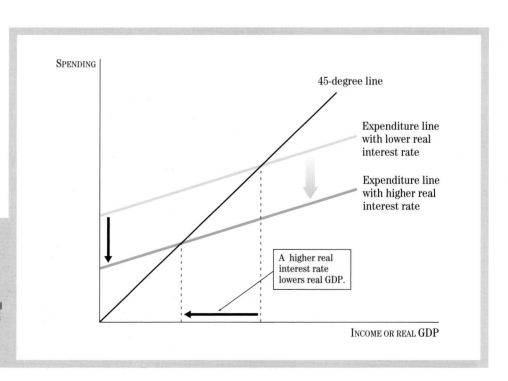

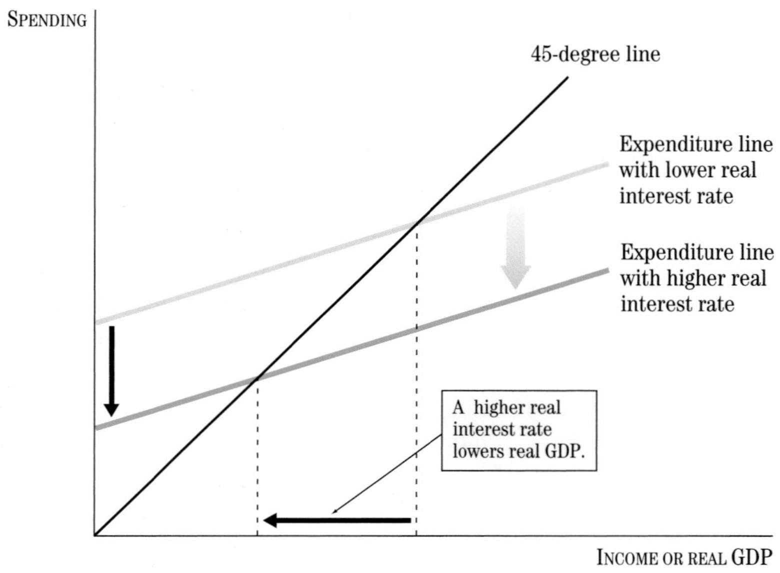

FIGURE 2
The Interest Rate, Spending Balance, and Real GDP
A higher real interest rate shifts the expenditure line down because consumption, investment, and net exports depend negatively on the real interest rate. Thus, real GDP declines with a higher real interest rate. Conversely, a lower real interest rate raises real GDP.

Interest Rates and Inflation

Now that we have seen why interest rates affect real GDP, let us proceed to the second stage in our analysis. We want to show why a rise in inflation will increase the real interest rate and thereby lower real GDP, or why a decline in inflation will decrease the real interest rate and thereby raise real GDP.

Central Bank Interest Rate Policy. The easiest way to see why the real interest rate rises when the inflation rate increases is to examine the behavior of the Fed. The Fed and central banks in other countries typically follow policies in which they respond to an increase in the inflation rate by raising the nominal interest rate. By far the most widely followed and analyzed decision by the Fed is its nominal interest rate decision.

Why do central banks raise the nominal interest rate when they think the inflation rate is rising? The inflation rate is ultimately the responsibility of the Fed, and the goal of controlling inflation requires that the central bank raise the nominal interest rate so that the real interest rate rises when the inflation rate rises. If the central bank raises the real interest rate successfully, then the higher real interest rate will reduce investment, consumption, and net exports. The reduced demand will then reduce inflationary pressures and bring inflation back down again.

The goal of controlling inflation also requires that the central bank lower the real interest rate when inflation falls. Suppose that the inflation rate starts to fall. If the central bank lowers the nominal interest rate so that the real interest rate falls, then the lower real interest rate will increase investment, consumption, and net exports. The increase in demand will put upward pressure on inflation.

Table 1 illustrates these actions of the Fed using a hypothetical example. For each inflation rate, a nominal interest rate decision by the Fed is shown. For example, when inflation is 2 percent, the nominal interest rate decision is 4 percent. When inflation rises to 4 percent, the nominal interest rate decision by the Fed is 7 percent. Thus, when inflation rises, the central bank raises the nominal interest rate, and when inflation falls, the central bank lowers the nominal interest rate.

TABLE 1
A Numerical Example of Central Bank Interest Rate Policy

(a) Inflation Rate	(b) Nominal Interest Rate Decision (made by the central bank)	Resulting Real Interest Rate (b) − (a)
0.0	1.0	1.0
1.0	2.5	1.5
2.0	4.0	2.0
3.0	5.5	2.5
4.0	7.0	3.0
5.0	8.5	3.5
6.0	10.0	4.0
7.0	11.5	4.5
8.0	13.0	5.0

Note that the nominal interest rate rises more than inflation rises in Table 1. The reason is that for an increase in the nominal interest rate to reduce demand, the real interest rate must rise because investment, consumption, and net exports depend negatively on the real interest rate, as described in the previous section. The nominal interest rate has to rise by more than the inflation rate in order for the real interest rate to rise and demand to decline. If, instead, the nominal interest rate rose by less than the increase in the inflation rate, then the real interest rate would not rise; rather, it would fall. The behavior of the central bank illustrated in the third column of Table 1 is called a **monetary policy rule** because it describes the systematic response of the real interest rate to inflation as decided by the central bank.

monetary policy rule: a description of how much the interest rate or other instruments of monetary policy respond to inflation or other measures of the state of the economy.

How the Fed Changes the Interest Rate. Keep in mind that the central bank does not set interest rates by decree or by direct control. Governments sometimes do control the price of goods; for example, some city governments control the rents on apartments. The central bank does not apply such controls to the interest rate. Rather, it enters the market in which short-term interest rates are determined by the usual forces of supply and demand. In the United States, the short-term interest rate the Fed focuses on is the interest rate on overnight loans between banks. This is called the **federal funds rate,** and the overnight loan market is called the federal funds market because reserves at the Fed are what are loaned or borrowed in this market. When the Fed wants to lower this interest rate, it supplies more reserves to this market. When it wants to raise the interest rate, it reduces reserves. Recall from Chapter 10 that the Fed can change the amount of reserves in the banking system through *open market operations*—that is, by buying and selling government bonds. If the Fed wants to increase reserves and thereby lower the federal funds rate, it buys government bonds. If the Fed wants to decrease reserves and thereby increase the federal funds rate, it sells government bonds.

federal funds rate: the interest rate on overnight loans between banks that the Federal Reserve influences by changing the supply of funds (bank reserves) in the market.

Actions the Fed takes: To reduce the federal funds rate, the Fed increases the supply of reserves by buying bonds. To raise the federal funds rate, the Fed decreases the supply of reserves by selling bonds. The buying and selling of bonds are called *open market operations.*

A Graph of the Response of the Interest Rate to Inflation. Figure 3 represents the monetary policy rule graphically, using the information in Table 1. When the inflation rate rises, the nominal interest rate rises along the green upward-sloping line. When the inflation rate declines, the nominal interest rate declines. The nominal interest rate must rise by more than the inflation rate if the *real* interest rate is to rise when inflation rises; this requires that the slope of the monetary policy rule in Figure 3 be greater than 1. For example, if the slope is 1.5, then when the inflation

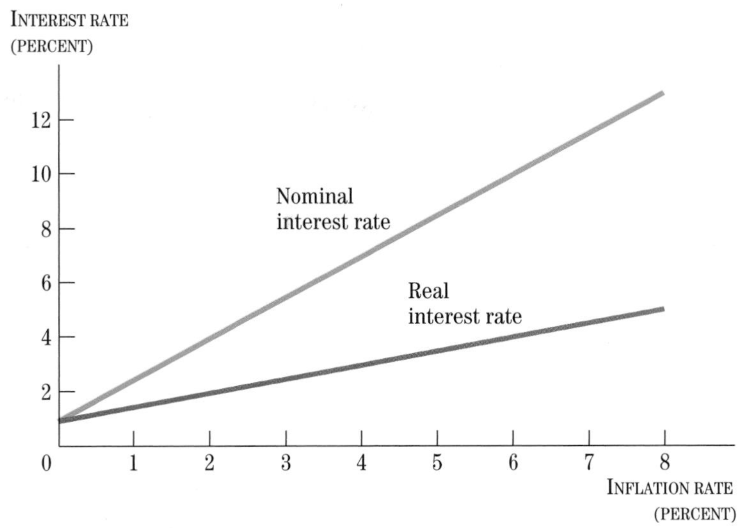

FIGURE 3
A Monetary Policy Rule
The monetary policy rule shows that the Fed raises the real interest rate when inflation rises and lowers the real interest rate when inflation falls. In order to accomplish this, the Fed has to move the nominal interest rate by more than 1 percentage point when there is a 1 percentage point change in the rate of inflation.

rate increases by 1 percentage point, the interest rate rises by 1.5 percentage points, as in Table 1. In other words, the nominal interest rate rises by 0.5 percentage point *more* than the inflation rate rises, causing the *real* interest rate to rise by 0.5 percentage point. The resulting real interest rate decision of the Fed is indicated by the purple line: The real interest rate changes by 0.5 percentage point when the inflation rate changes by 1 percentage point. The real interest rate policy rule is shown in Figure 4.

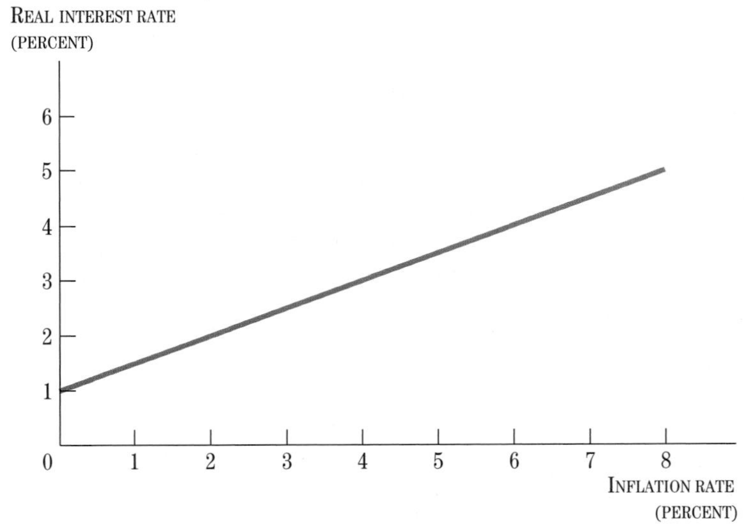

FIGURE 4
The Real Interest Rate Is Positively Related to Inflation
From now on, the monetary policy rule of the Fed will be presented as a relationship between the inflation rate and the real interest rate. When inflation rises, the Fed raises the real interest rate (through a more than proportional increase in the nominal interest rate), whereas when inflation falls, the Fed lowers the real interest rate (by decreasing the nominal rate in a more than proportional manner).

target inflation rate: the central bank's goal for the average rate of inflation over the long run.

Finished with Stage 2: The interest rate is positively related to inflation.

The Fed and other central banks tend to

- Raise the real interest rate when inflation rises.
- Lower the real interest rate when inflation falls.

This is the *behavioral description* of the people at the Fed, much as a demand curve is a behavioral description of consumers. This response is called a *monetary policy rule.*

Most central banks have a **target inflation rate,** the inflation rate that the central bank tries to maintain on average over the long run. Because of various shocks to the economy, the central bank cannot control the inflation rate perfectly; sometimes the inflation rate will rise above the target inflation rate, and sometimes the inflation rate will fall below the target inflation rate. By reacting to these movements in inflation according to a monetary policy rule—that is, by increasing the interest rate when inflation rises and cutting the interest rate when inflation falls—the central bank will cause the actual inflation rate to move back toward the target inflation rate over time. Some central banks, such as the Bank of England and the Reserve Bank of New Zealand, have explicit inflation targets. Other central banks, like the Fed, have implicit inflation targets that are not explicitly announced, but that can be assessed by observing central bank decisions over time. The target inflation rate for many central banks is about 2 percent. For the economy described in Figure 3, at the target inflation rate of 2 percent, the central bank sets real interest rates at 2 percent by choosing a nominal rate of 4 percent.

A Good Simplifying Assumption. The behavior of the central bank described in this section provides the easiest explanation of the response of interest rates to inflation, but it is not the only possible explanation. Economists have found that the general upward-sloping relationship in Figure 4, which we call the monetary policy rule, is common to many different types of monetary policies, including policies in which the central bank focuses on money growth. Although the position and shape of the monetary policy rule will differ for these different types of policies, the overall response of interest rates to inflation will be similar. Our reason for using this particular derivation is that it is the easiest to explain and describes the actual behavior of the Fed and other central banks.

Derivation of the Aggregate Demand Curve

Thus far, we have shown that the level of real GDP is negatively related to the real interest rate and that the real interest rate is positively related to the inflation rate through the central bank's policy rule. We now combine these two concepts to derive the aggregate demand curve—the inverse relationship between the inflation rate and real GDP.

The chain of reasoning that brings about the aggregate demand curve can be explained by considering what would happen if the inflation rate rose. First, the interest rate would rise because the Fed would raise the real interest rate in response to the higher inflation rate. Next, the higher real interest rate would mean less investment spending, a decline in net exports, and a decline in consumption. Lower investment spending would occur because investment would be made more costly by the high real interest rate. American goods would become more expensive, and foreign goods would become cheaper. Thus, net exports—exports minus imports—would decline.

The opposite chain of events would occur if there were a fall in inflation. First, the Fed would lower the real interest rate according to the monetary policy rule. The lower real interest rate, in turn, would cause investment, net exports, and consumption to rise. Hence, real GDP would rise.

In sum, we see that when the inflation rate rises, real GDP decreases, and when the inflation rate falls, real GDP increases. In other words, there is a negative relationship between inflation and real GDP. When we graph this relationship in a diagram with real GDP on the horizontal axis and inflation on the vertical axis, we get a

ECONOMICS IN THE NEWS

The Fed Raises and Then Lowers the Interest Rate

These two press statements from the Fed's Federal Open Market Committee (FOMC) show how changes in the Fed's target interest rate are determined by changes in the inflation rate, much as assumed by the monetary policy rule in Figure 3.

In the first statement, the Fed explains why it increased the interest rate: there was concern that "pressure on resources" could "foster inflationary imbalances." In the second, which was issued the following year, the Fed explains why it cut interest rates: there was recognition that "inflation pressures remain contained."

The Fed issues such statements right after every FOMC meeting, whether the interest rate is changed or not. Economists and financial analysts study the wording of the statements carefully, trying to ascertain what the Fed's next move might be.

For immediate release: May 16, 2000

The Federal Open Market Committee voted today to raise its target for the federal funds rate by 50 basis points to 6-1/2 percent. In a related action, the Board of Governors approved a 50 basis point increase in the discount rate to 6 percent.

Increases in demand have remained in excess of even the rapid pace of productivity-driven gains in potential supply, exerting continued pressure on resources. The Committee is concerned that this disparity in the growth of demand and potential supply will continue, which could foster inflationary imbalances that would undermine the economy's outstanding performance.

Against the background of its long-term goals of price stability and sustainable economic growth and of the information already available, the Committee believes the risks are weighted mainly toward conditions that may generate heightened inflation pressures in the foreseeable future.

In taking the discount rate action, the Federal Reserve Board approved requests submitted by the Boards of Directors of the Federal Reserve Banks of Boston, Cleveland, Richmond, and San Francisco. The discount rate is the rate charged depository institutions when they borrow short-term adjustment credit from their district Federal Reserve Banks.

For immediate release: January 3, 2001

The Federal Open Market Committee decided today to lower its target for the federal funds rate by 50 basis points to 6 percent.

These actions were taken in light of further weakening of sales and production, and in the context of lower consumer confidence, tight conditions in some segments of financial markets, and high energy prices sapping household and business purchasing power. Moreover, inflation pressures remain contained. Nonetheless, to date there is little evidence to suggest that longer-term advances in technology and associated gains in productivity are abating.

The Committee continues to believe that, against the background of its long-run goals of price stability and sustainable economic growth and of the information currently available, the risks are weighted mainly toward conditions that may generate economic weakness in the foreseeable future.

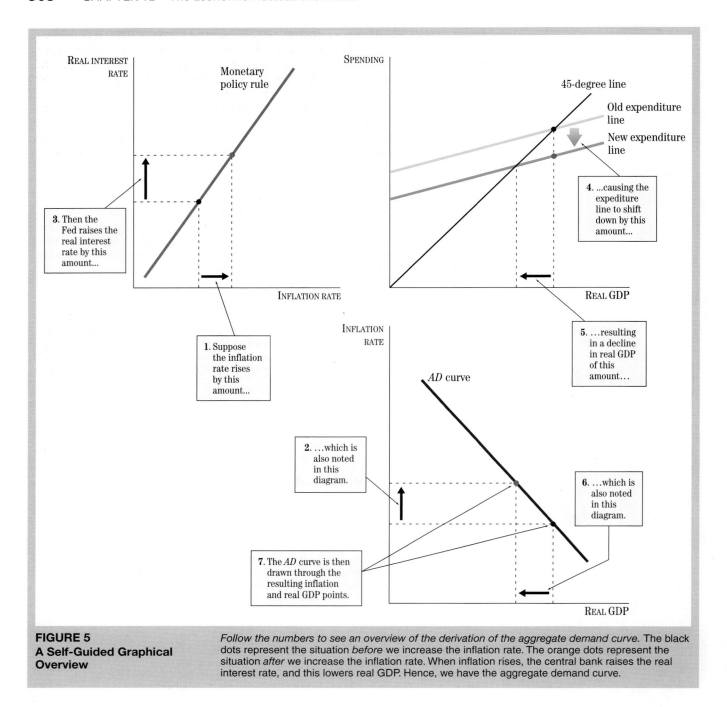

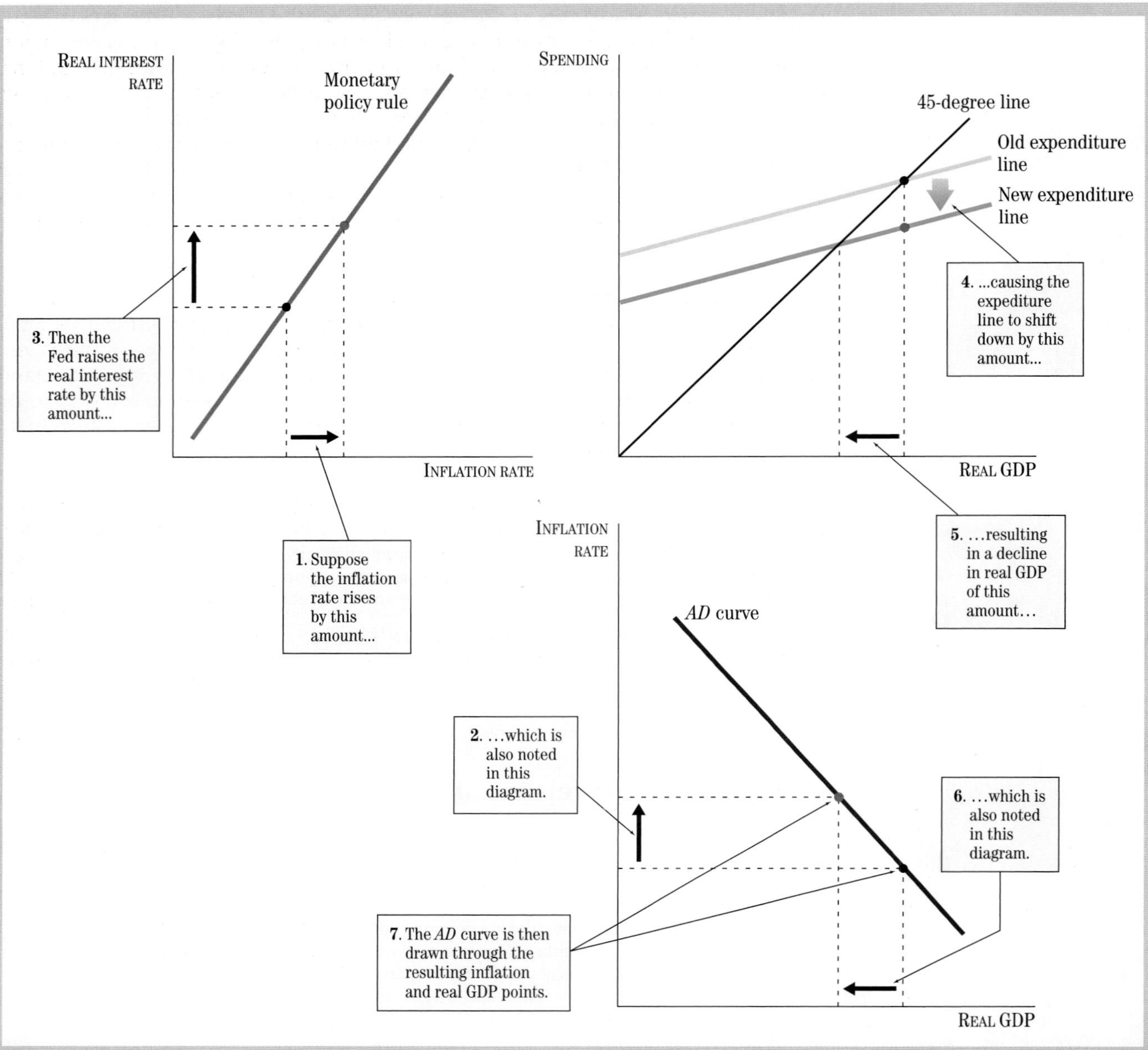

FIGURE 5
A Self-Guided Graphical Overview

Follow the numbers to see an overview of the derivation of the aggregate demand curve. The black dots represent the situation *before* we increase the inflation rate. The orange dots represent the situation *after* we increase the inflation rate. When inflation rises, the central bank raises the real interest rate, and this lowers real GDP. Hence, we have the aggregate demand curve.

downward-sloping curve like the one shown in Figure 1; this curve is the aggregate demand curve, which we have thus derived.

If you would like to go over the derivation again, seeing all the paragraphs together on the same page, a self-guided graphical overview is provided in Figure 5. If you read the explanatory boxes in numerical order, you will trace through the chain of events following an increase in inflation, including the Fed's real interest rate increase according to its policy rule and the decline in real GDP.

Movements Along the Aggregate Demand Curve. Thus far, we have explained why the aggregate demand curve has a negative slope—that is, why higher inflation means a lower real GDP. A change in real GDP due to a change in inflation is thus a *movement along* the aggregate demand curve. Recall that in microeconomics, a similar movement along the demand curve occurs when a *change in the price* leads to a *change in quantity demanded.* When inflation rises, causing the Fed to raise the interest rate, and real GDP declines, there is a movement up and to the left along the aggregate demand curve. When inflation declines and the Fed lowers the interest rate, causing GDP to rise, there is a movement down and to the right along the aggregate demand curve.

Shifts of the Aggregate Demand Curve. Now, the inflation rate is not the only thing that affects aggregate demand. Changes in government purchases, shifts in monetary policy, shifts in foreign demand for U.S. exports, changes in taxes, and changes in consumer confidence, among other things, affect aggregate demand. When any of these factors changes aggregate demand, we say there is a *shift* in the aggregate demand curve. Let us briefly consider some of those sources of shifts in the aggregate demand curve.

Government Purchases Imagine that government purchases rise. We know from our analysis of spending balance in Chapter 11 that an increase in government purchases will increase real GDP in the short run. This increase in real GDP occurs at any inflation rate: at 2 percent, at 4 percent, or at any other level. Now, if real GDP increases at a given inflation rate, the aggregate demand curve will shift to the right. This is shown in Figure 6. The new aggregate demand curve will be parallel to the original aggregate demand curve because no matter what the inflation rate is in the

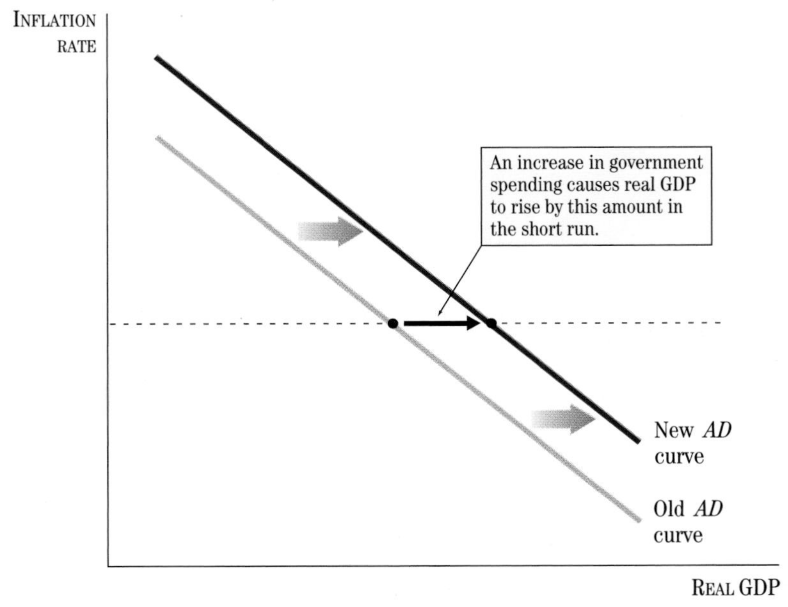

FIGURE 6
How Government Purchases Shift the Aggregate Demand Curve
An increase in government purchases shifts the *AD* curve to the right. Real GDP rises by the same amount at every level of inflation.

economy, the shift in government purchases is going to have the same effect on real GDP. The same reasoning implies that a decline in government spending shifts the aggregate demand curve to the left.

Changes in the Target Inflation Rate Suppose the Fed has an inflation target of 2 percent. Consider what happens when the Fed shifts its policy objectives. Suppose, for instance, that a new Fed chair becomes convinced that inflation should be higher, say, 3 percent. In order to get inflation to rise, the Fed will immediately try to increase spending by lowering the real interest rate: The *AD* curve will shift to the right, as shown in Figure 7. In contrast, suppose that the new Fed chair wants to lower inflation, say, to 1 percent. In order to get inflation to fall, the Fed will immediately try to lower spending by raising the real interest rate: The *AD* curve will shift to the left.

Other Changes Many other changes in the economy (other than a change in the inflation rate, which is a movement along the *AD* curve) will shift the *AD* curve. We considered many such possibilities in Chapter 11; their effects on the aggregate demand curve are listed in Figure 8. For example, an increase in the foreign demand for U.S. products will increase net exports, raise real GDP, and shift the aggregate demand curve to the right. A drop in consumer confidence that reduces the amount of consumption at every level of income will shift the aggregate demand curve to the left. Finally, an increase in taxes shifts the aggregate demand curve to the left, while a decrease in taxes shifts the aggregate demand curve to the right.

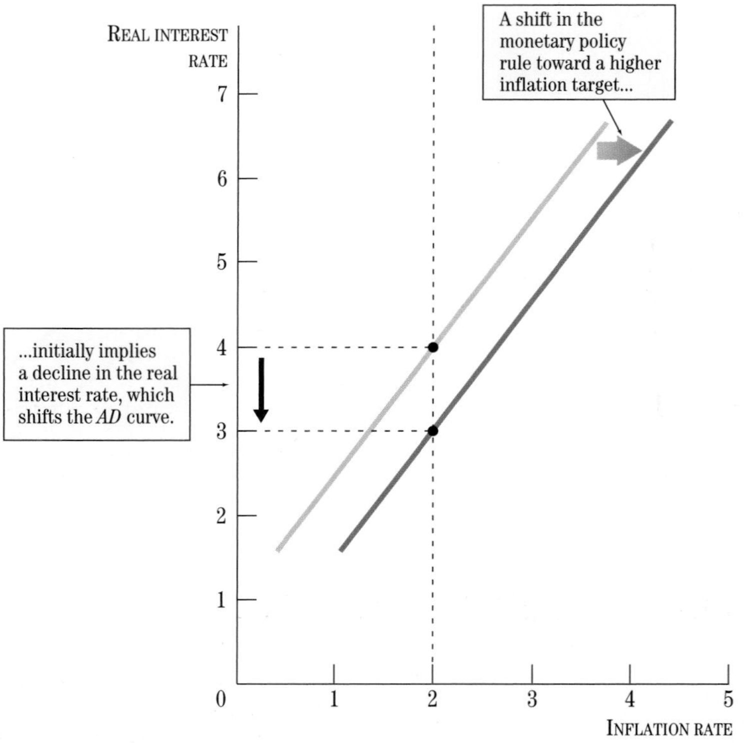

FIGURE 7
A Shift in the Monetary Policy Rule
A shift in the policy rule to higher inflation implies a decline in the real interest rate. The lower real interest rate increases real GDP in the short run. As a result, at a given inflation rate, the *AD* curve shifts to the right.

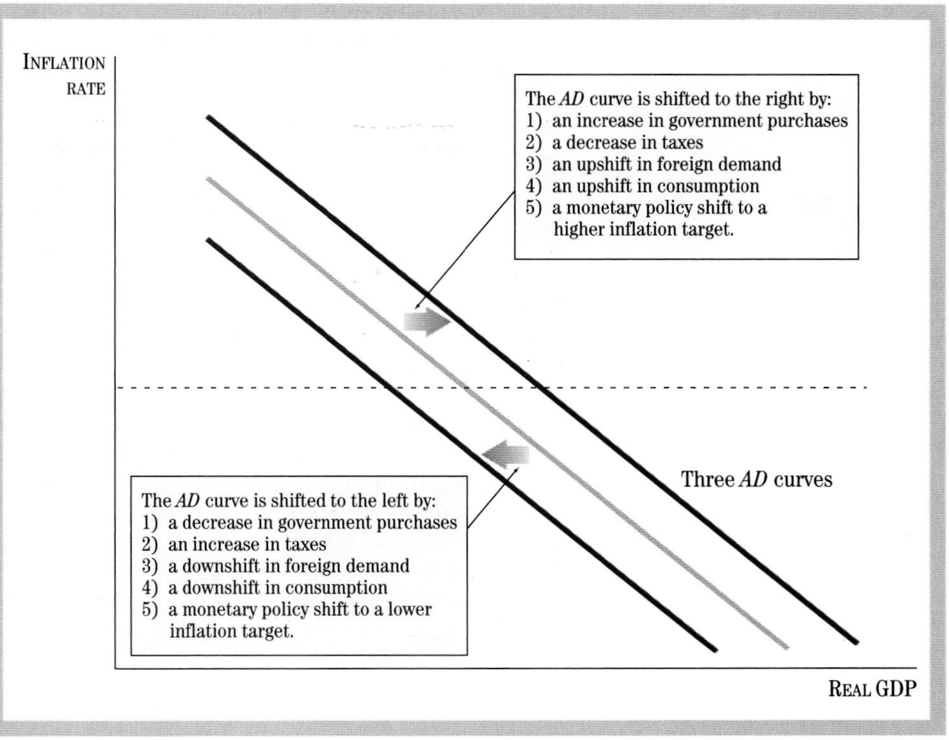

INFLATION RATE
The AD curve is shifted to the right by:
1) an increase in government purchases
2) a decrease in taxes
3) an upshift in foreign demand
4) an upshift in consumption
5) a monetary policy shift to a higher inflation target.
Three AD curves
The AD curve is shifted to the left by:
1) a decrease in government purchases
2) an increase in taxes
3) a downshift in foreign demand
4) a downshift in consumption
5) a monetary policy shift to a lower inflation target.
REAL GDP

FIGURE 8
A List of Possible Shifts in the Aggregate Demand Curve
Many things shift the *AD* curve. An increase in government purchases shifts the *AD* curve to the right. A change in the monetary policy rule toward a higher inflation target shifts the *AD* curve to the right. A decline in government purchases and a change in the monetary policy rule toward a lower inflation target shift the curve to the left.

REVIEW

- The aggregate demand curve is an inverse relationship between inflation and real GDP.
- Investment, net exports, and consumption are negatively related to the real interest rate. Hence, real GDP falls when the real interest rate rises, and vice versa.
- When inflation increases, the central bank raises the real interest rate, and this lowers real GDP. Conversely, when inflation falls, the central bank lowers the real interest rate, and this raises real GDP. It does so by moving nominal interest rates by more than 1 percentage point when inflation changes by 1 percentage point. These are movements along the aggregate demand curve.
- The aggregate demand curve shifts to the right when the central bank changes its monetary policy rule toward more inflation and shifts to the left when the central bank changes its policy rule toward less inflation.
- Higher government purchases shift the aggregate demand curve to the right. Lower government purchases shift the aggregate demand curve to the left.

THE INFLATION ADJUSTMENT LINE

Having derived the aggregate demand curve and studied its properties, let us now look at the inflation adjustment line, the second element of the economic fluctuations model. The **inflation adjustment (*IA*) line** is a flat line showing the level of inflation in the economy at any point in time. Figure 9 shows an example of the inflation adjustment line in a diagram with inflation on the vertical axis and real GDP on

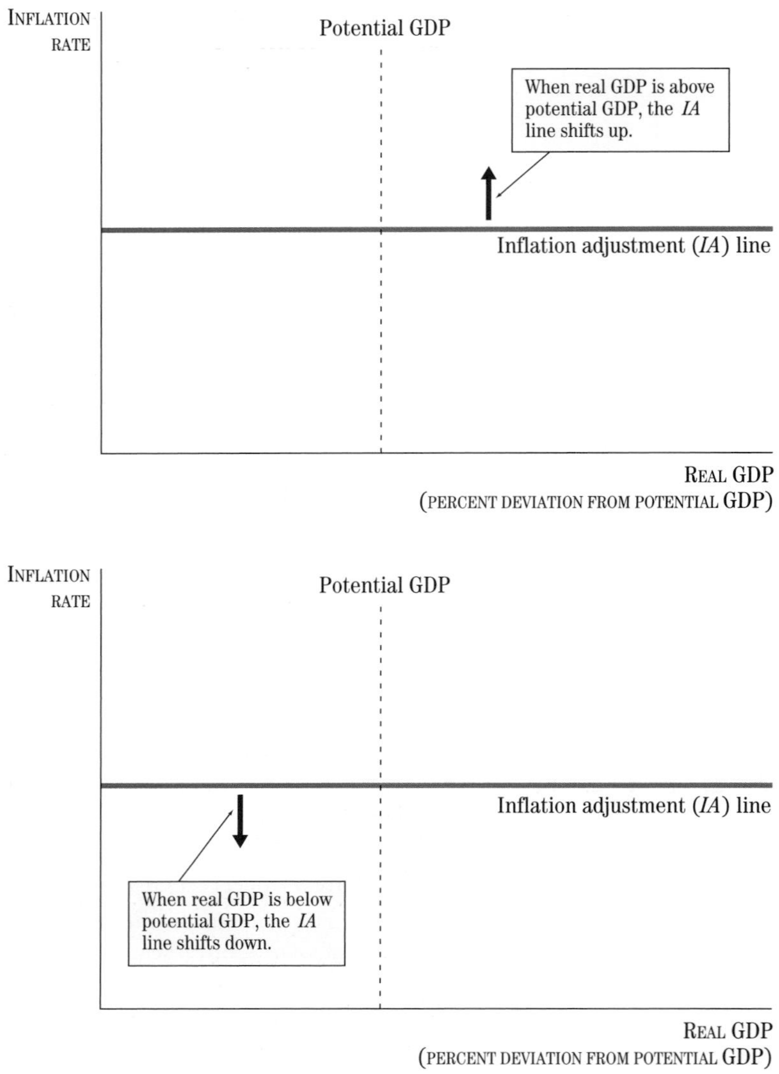

FIGURE 9
Inflation Adjustment and Changes in Inflation
In the top panel, real GDP is above potential GDP and inflation is rising; the inflation adjustment line shifts up. In the bottom panel, real GDP is below potential GDP and inflation is falling; thus, the inflation adjustment line shifts down.

the horizontal axis. For example, if the line touches 4 percent on the vertical axis, it tells us that inflation is 4 percent.

inflation adjustment (*IA*) line: a flat line showing the level of inflation in the economy at a given point in time. It shifts up when real GDP is greater than potential GDP, and it shifts down when real GDP is less than potential GDP; it also shifts when expectations of inflation or raw materials prices change.

The inflation adjustment line describes the economic behavior of firms and workers setting prices and wages in the economy. There are several important features about the slope and position of the inflation adjustment line.

The Inflation Adjustment Line Is Flat

That the inflation adjustment line is flat indicates that firms and workers adjust their prices and wages in such a way that the inflation rate remains steady in the short run as real GDP changes. Only over time does inflation change significantly and the line move. In the short run, inflation stays at 4 percent, or wherever the line happens to be when real GDP changes.

In interpreting the inflation adjustment line, it is helpful to remember that it is part of a *model* of the overall economy and is thus an approximation of reality. In fact, inflation does not remain *perfectly* steady, and the inflation adjustment line can have a small upward slope. But it is a good approximation to assume that the inflation adjustment line is flat.

There are two reasons why inflation does not change very much in the short run even if real GDP and the demand for firms' products changes: (1) expectations of continuing inflation and (2) staggered wage and price setting at different firms throughout the economy.

Expectations of Continuing Inflation. Expectations about the price and wage decisions of other firms throughout the economy influence a firm's price and wage decisions. For example, if the overall inflation rate in the economy has been hovering around 4 percent year after year, then a firm can expect that its competitors' prices will probably increase by about 4 percent per year, unless circumstances change. To keep prices near those of the competition, this firm will need to increase its price by about 4 percent each year. Thus, the inflation rate stays steady at 4 percent per year.

Wage adjustments are also influenced by expectations. If firms and workers expect that workers at other firms will be getting large wage increases, then meeting the competition will require similar large wage increases. A smaller wage increase would reduce the wage of the firm's workers relative to that received by other workers. Many firms base their wage decisions on the wages paid by other firms. If they see the wages at other firms rising, they will be more willing to increase wages.

Firms and workers also look to expectations of inflation when deciding on wage increases. In an economy with 4 percent inflation, wages will have to increase by 4 percent for workers just to keep up with the cost of living. Lower wage increases would result in a decline in workers' real wages.

Staggered Price and Wage Setting. Not all wages and prices are changed at the same time throughout the economy. Rather, price setting and wage setting are staggered over months and even years. For example, autoworkers might negotiate three-year wage contracts in 1996, 1999, 2002, and so on. Dockworkers might negotiate three-year contracts in 1997, 2000, 2003, and so on. Bus companies and train companies do not adjust their prices at the same time, even though they may be competing for the same riders. On any given day, we can be sure that there is a wage or price adjustment somewhere in the economy, but the vast majority of wages and prices do not change.

Staggered price and wage setting slows down the adjustment of prices in the economy. When considering what wage increases are likely in the next year, firms and workers know about the most recent wage increases. For example, an agreement made by another firm to increase wages by 4 percent per year for three years into the future will affect the expectations of wages paid to competing workers in the future. This wage agreement will not change unless the firm is on the edge of bankruptcy, and perhaps not even then. Hence, workers and firms deciding on wage increases will tend to match the wage increases recently made at other firms. Thus, price and wage decisions made today are directly influenced by price and wage decisions made yesterday.

As with many things in life, when today's decisions are influenced by yesterday's decisions, inertia sets in. The staggering of the decisions makes it difficult to break the inertia. Unless there is a reason to make a change—such as a persistent decline in demand or a change in expectations of inflation—the price increases or wage increases continue from year to year. The flat inflation adjustment line describes this inertia.

The Inflation Adjustment Line Shifts Gradually When Real GDP Departs from Potential GDP

The following is a shorthand summary of inflation adjustment in the economy as a whole:

If real GDP = potential GDP, then the inflation rate does not change (*IA* line does not shift).

If real GDP > potential GDP, then the inflation rate increases (*IA* line shifts up).

If real GDP < potential GDP, then the inflation rate decreases (*IA* line shifts down).

The inflation adjustment line does not always stay put; rather, it may shift up or down from year to year. If real GDP stays above potential GDP, then inflation starts to rise. Firms see that the demand for their products is remaining high, and they begin adjusting their prices. If the inflation rate is 4 percent, then the firms will have to raise their prices by more than 4 percent if they want their relative prices to increase. Hence, inflation starts to rise. The inflation adjustment line is shifted upward to illustrate this rise in inflation; it will keep shifting upward as long as real GDP is above potential GDP.

However, if real GDP is below potential GDP, then firms will see that the demand for their products is falling off, and they will adjust their prices. If inflation is 4 percent, the firms will raise their prices by less than 4 percent—perhaps by 2 percent—if they want the relative price of their goods to fall. Hence, inflation will fall. The inflation adjustment line is shifted down to illustrate this fall in inflation. Figure 9 shows the direction of these shifts.

If real GDP stays at potential GDP, neither to the left nor to the right of the vertical potential GDP line in Figure 9, then inflation remains unchanged. This steady inflation is represented by an unmoving inflation adjustment line year after year.

Changes in Expectations or Commodity Prices Shift the Inflation Adjustment Line

Even if real GDP is at potential GDP, some special events in the economy can cause the inflation adjustment line to shift up or down. One important example is *shifts in expectations* of inflation. If firms and workers expect inflation to rise, they are likely to raise wages and prices by a large amount to keep pace with the expected inflation. Thus, an increase in expectations of inflation will cause the inflation adjustment line to shift up to a higher inflation rate. And a decrease in expectations of inflation will cause the inflation adjustment line to shift down.

Another example is a change in commodity prices that affects firms' costs of production. For example, we will examine the effects on inflation of an oil price increase in Chapter 13. By raising firms' costs, such an oil price increase would lead firms to charge higher prices, and the inflation adjustment line would rise, at least temporarily.

Does the Inflation Adjustment Line Fit the Facts?

Are these assumptions about the inflation adjustment line accurate? Does inflation rise when real GDP is above potential GDP and fall when real GDP is below potential GDP? While there are exceptions, the answer is generally yes. Look back at Figure 8 on Chapter 5 for evidence.

One of the biggest declines in inflation occurred in the recession of 1982, when real GDP was far below potential GDP. Inflation also fell during the recessions of 1990–1991 and 2001 when real GDP fell below potential GDP. In 1998 and 1999, real GDP rose above potential GDP, but inflation did not immediately start to rise. This led some commentators to think that the inflation adjustment relationship was changing, but by late 1999 and 2000, inflation rose as predicted by the theory.

REVIEW

- The inflation adjustment (*IA*) line, the second element of the economic fluctuations model, is a flat line showing the level of inflation in the economy at any point in time. The inflation adjustment line describes the economic behavior of firms and workers setting prices and wages in the economy.
- Firms do not change their prices instantaneously when the demand for their product changes. Thus, when aggregate demand changes and real GDP departs from potential GDP, the inflation rate does not immediately change; the inflation adjustment line does not shift in response to such changes in the short run.
- Staggered wage and price setting tends to slow down the adjustment of inflation in the economy as a whole.
- Over time, inflation does respond to departures of real GDP from potential GDP. This response can be described by upward and downward shifts in the inflation adjustment line over time.

COMBINING THE AGGREGATE DEMAND CURVE AND THE INFLATION ADJUSTMENT LINE

We have now derived two relationships—the aggregate demand curve and the inflation adjustment line—that describe real GDP and inflation in the economy as a whole. The two relationships can be combined to make predictions about real GDP and inflation.

Along the aggregate demand curve in Figure 1, real GDP and inflation are negatively related. This curve describes the behavior of firms and consumers as they respond to a higher real interest rate caused by the Fed's response to higher inflation. They respond by lowering consumption, investment, and net exports. This line presents a range of possible values of real GDP and inflation.

The inflation adjustment line in Figure 9, on the other hand, tells us what the inflation rate is at any point in time. Thus, we can use the inflation adjustment line to determine exactly what inflation rate applies to the aggregate demand curve. For example, if the inflation adjustment line tells us that the inflation rate for 2007 is 3 percent, then we can go right to the aggregate demand curve to determine what the level of real GDP will be at that 3 percent inflation rate. The inflation adjustment line tells us the current location of inflation—and therefore real GDP—on the aggregate demand curve.

Figure 10 illustrates the determination of real GDP and inflation graphically. It combines the aggregate demand curve from Figure 1 with the inflation adjustment line from Figure 9. At any point in time, the inflation adjustment line is given, as shown in Figure 10. The inflation adjustment line intersects the aggregate demand curve at a single point. It is at this point of intersection that inflation and real GDP are determined. The intersection gives an *equilibrium* level of real GDP and inflation. At that point, we can look down to the horizontal axis of the diagram to determine the level of real GDP corresponding to that level of inflation. For example, the point of intersection in the left panel of Figure 10 might be when inflation is 5 percent and real GDP is 2 percent below potential GDP. The point of intersection in the right panel is at a lower inflation rate when real GDP is above potential GDP. The point of intersection in the middle panel of Figure 10 has real GDP equal to potential GDP.

As Figure 10 makes clear, the intersection of the inflation adjustment line and the aggregate demand curve may give values of real GDP that are either above or

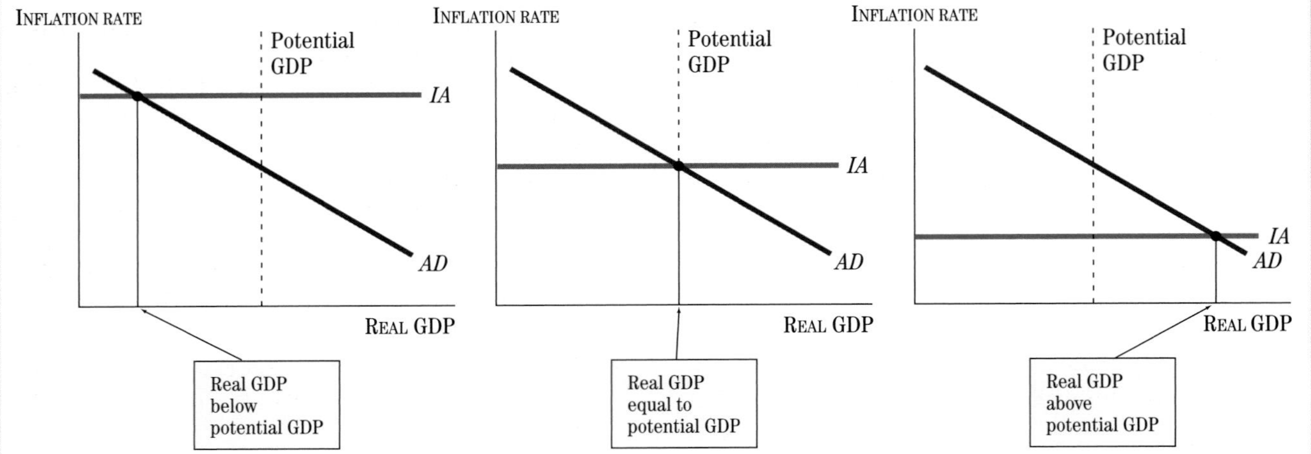

FIGURE 10
Determining Real GDP and Inflation

Real GDP is determined at the intersection of the *AD* curve and the *IA* line. All three panels have the same *AD* curve and the same vertical line marking potential GDP. Three different levels of the *IA* line give three different levels of real GDP: less than, equal to, and greater than potential GDP.

below potential GDP. But if real GDP is not equal to potential GDP, then the economy has not fully recovered from a recession, as on the left of Figure 10, or returned to potential GDP after being above it, as on the right. To describe dynamic movements of inflation and real GDP, we must consider how the inflation adjustment line and the aggregate demand curve shift over time. That is the subject of Chapter 13.

REVIEW

- In any year, the inflation adjustment line tells what the inflation rate is. Using the aggregate demand curve, we can then make a prediction about what real GDP is.
- The intersection of the aggregate demand curve and the inflation adjustment line gives a pair of observations on real GDP and inflation at any point in time.

CONCLUSION

With the essential elements of the economic fluctuations model—the aggregate demand curve, the inflation adjustment line, and their intersection—put together, we are now ready to use the model to explain the fluctuations of real GDP and inflation. In reviewing the model, it is useful to consider the scissors analogy mentioned in our discussion of the supply and demand model in Chapter 3.

The aggregate demand curve is like one blade of the scissors. The inflation adjustment line is the other blade. Either blade alone is insufficient to explain economic fluctuations. Either blade alone is an incomplete story. But when the two blades of the scissors are put together to form a pair of scissors, they become a practical tool to explain the ups and downs in the economy. And compared to the complexity and vastness of the whole economy with millions of firms and consumers, this particular pair of scissors is amazingly simple.

KEY POINTS

1. Investment, net exports, and consumption depend negatively on the real interest rate. Hence, real GDP, which includes investment, net exports, and consumption, depends negatively on the real interest rate.
2. Central banks' actions to adjust the nominal interest rate to maintain low inflation result in a relationship between the real interest rate and inflation. When inflation rises, the real interest rate rises. When inflation falls, the real interest rate falls.
3. The combined behavior of (1) the real interest rate response to inflation and (2) the private sector adjusting spending in response to the interest rate generates an inverse relationship between real GDP and inflation—the aggregate demand curve.
4. Movements along the aggregate demand curve occur when inflation rises, causing the real interest rate to rise and real GDP to fall. Such movements along the curve also occur when inflation falls, the interest rate declines, and real GDP rises.
5. The aggregate demand curve shifts for many reasons, including a change in government purchases and a change in monetary policy toward a higher inflation target.
6. When adjusting prices, firms respond slowly to changes in demand and take into account expectations of inflation. So do workers when wages are being adjusted. As a result, inflation tends to increase when real GDP is above potential GDP and tends to decrease when real GDP is below potential GDP.
7. The staggering of price and wage decisions tends to slow the adjustment of prices in the economy as a whole.
8. When combined with the aggregate demand curve, the inflation adjustment line provides us with a way to determine real GDP and inflation.

KEY TERMS

aggregate demand (*AD*) curve
monetary policy rule
federal funds rate
target inflation rate
inflation adjustment (*IA*) line

QUESTIONS FOR REVIEW

1. Why are investment, net exports, and consumption inversely related to the real interest rate?
2. Why is real GDP inversely related to the real interest rate in the short run?
3. Why does the real interest rate rise when inflation begins to rise?
4. Why is real GDP inversely related to inflation in the short run? What is this relationship called?
5. What are examples of movements along the aggregate demand curve?
6. Why does a change in government purchases shift the aggregate demand curve to the right or left?
7. Why does a shift in monetary policy shift the aggregate demand curve to the right or left?
8. Why does inflation increase when real GDP is above potential GDP?
9. What is the significance of expectations of inflation for inflation adjustment?
10. Why does staggered price setting slow down price adjustment in the economy?

PROBLEMS

1. Compare and contrast the graphs used in the microeconomic supply and demand model with those used in the economic fluctuations model.
2. Which of the following statements are true, and which are false? Explain your answers in one or two sentences.
   a. An increase in the U.S. real interest rate will cause the dollar exchange rate to decline.
   b. The central bank typically raises the real interest rate when inflation rises.
   c. A higher real interest rate leads to greater net exports because the higher interest rate raises the value of the dollar.

3. Suppose the Fed is considering two different policy rules, shown in the following table. Graph the policy rules.

Inflation	Policy Rule 1 Interest Rate	Policy Rule 2 Interest Rate
0	1	3
2	3	5
4	5	7
6	7	9
8	9	11

If the Fed is currently following policy rule 1 and then shifts to policy rule 2, which way will the aggregate demand curve shift? What reasons might the Fed have for changing its policy?

4. Suppose you have the following information on the Fed's and the European Central Bank's (ECB) policy rules:

Fed real interest rate = .5(inflation rate − 2)

ECB real interest rate = .2(inflation rate − 2) + 1

   a. Graph these policy rules. If the inflation rate is 2 percent in both countries, what will be the real interest rate in each country?
   b. Some argue that Europe has a much lower tolerance for inflation than the United States. Can you tell—either from the diagram or from the equations—whether this is true?

5. The table below gives a numerical example of an aggregate demand curve.
   a. Sketch the curve in a graph.
   b. What is the average rate of inflation in the long run?
   c. Suppose that the central bank shifts policy so that the average rate of inflation in the long run is 2 percentage points higher than in (b). Sketch a new aggregate demand curve corresponding to the higher inflation rate.

Real GDP (percent deviation from potential GDP)	Inflation (percent per year)
3.0	1.0
2.0	1.5
1.0	2.0
0.0	3.0
−1.0	4.0
−2.0	6.0
−3.0	9.0

6. State which of the following changes cause a shift in the aggregate demand curve and which ones are a movement along it. Also provide the direction of the change.
   a. A cut in government purchases
   b. A crash in the U.S. stock market
   c. A shift to a lower inflation target in the monetary policy rule
   d. Being thrifty becoming fashionable
   e. An increase in the European interest rate

7. The following table gives an example of an inflation adjustment line in the year 2006.

Real GDP (percent deviation from potential GDP)	Inflation (percent per year)
3.0	2.0
2.0	2.0
1.0	2.0
0.0	2.0
−1.0	2.0
−2.0	2.0
−3.0	2.0

   a. Sketch the line in a graph.
   b. If real GDP is above potential GDP in the year 2006, will the inflation adjustment line shift up or down in the year 2006? Explain.
   c. In the same graph as part (a), sketch in the aggregate demand curve given in Problem 5. Find the equilibrium level of real GDP and inflation in the year 2006.
   d. Show what happens to the inflation adjustment line if there is a sudden increase in inflation expectations.

8. Suppose that a decline in unionization reduces the amount of wage contracts that are being signed and also brings about a reduction in the length of the typical wage contract that is signed. What would the impact on the *IA* curve for that economy be? Explain.

9. Give three examples of goods and services that you buy whose prices change only periodically and therefore contribute to staggered pricing in the economy.

10. Suppose potential GDP is $5,000 billion. Use the data on the next page to graph the aggregate demand curve.

Inflation (percent)	Real GDP (billions of dollars)
5	4,800
4	4,900
3	5,000
2	5,100
1	5,200

a. Suppose the current inflation rate is 2 percent. Draw the inflation adjustment line. What is the current value of real GDP?

b. In the long run, what will the inflation rate be if there is no change in economic policy? Explain how this adjustment takes place.

Chapter 13

Using the Economic Fluctuations Model

Because the economic fluctuations model provides a very good description of recessions, expansions, and other vital developments in a modern dynamic economy, it is one of the most useful models in economics. Economists at the Federal Reserve Board use such a model to forecast inflation and GDP—essential ingredients in the Fed's decision-making. Business economists use such a model to analyze interest rates and exchange rates—key factors for business and private investment decisions. Economists at the President's Council of Economic Advisers or at the Congressional Budget Office in Washington use such a model to determine whether a tax cut is needed to stimulate the economy, or the impact of a new spending program. Indeed, economists all over the world use such a model to study events in their own countries.

The purpose of this chapter is to show how to use this model. We use the model to determine the path the economy takes after a shift in aggregate demand, whether that shift is due to a big change in government purchases, a shift in monetary policy, or some other factor. We trace the path of real GDP from the time of its initial departure from potential GDP—as in a recession—to its recovery. We explain why a recovery occurs and how long it takes to occur. We then look at the effect of price shocks on the economy, and examine a case study that demonstrates how well the model works in practice in explaining the most recent recession experienced by the United States.

Keeping in mind that there is a similarity between *using* the supply and demand model and *using* the economic fluctuations model will help you learn the material in this chapter.

CHANGES IN GOVERNMENT PURCHASES

We first use the economic fluctuations model to examine the forces leading to a return of real GDP to potential GDP. To do so, we focus on a particular example, a change in government purchases. In Chapter 11, we showed how a change in government purchases could push real GDP away from potential GDP in the short run. Now let's see the complete story.

Real GDP and Inflation over Time

Suppose the government cuts military purchases permanently. We want to examine the effects of this decrease in government purchases on the economy in the short run (about one year), the medium run (two to three years), and the long run (four to five years and beyond). The three lengths of time given in the parentheses are approximations; in reality, the times will not be exactly these lengths, but somewhat longer or shorter. We use the term *short run* to refer to the initial departure of real GDP from potential GDP, *medium run* to refer to the recovery period, and *long run* to refer to when real GDP is nearly back to potential GDP.

Figure 1 shows the aggregate demand curve and the inflation adjustment line on the same diagram. The intersection of the aggregate demand curve and the inflation adjustment line determines a level of inflation and real GDP. Let us assume

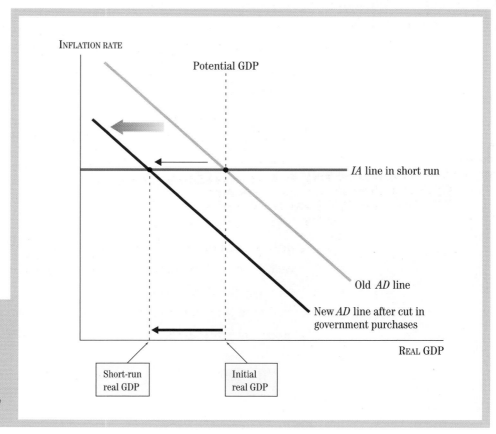

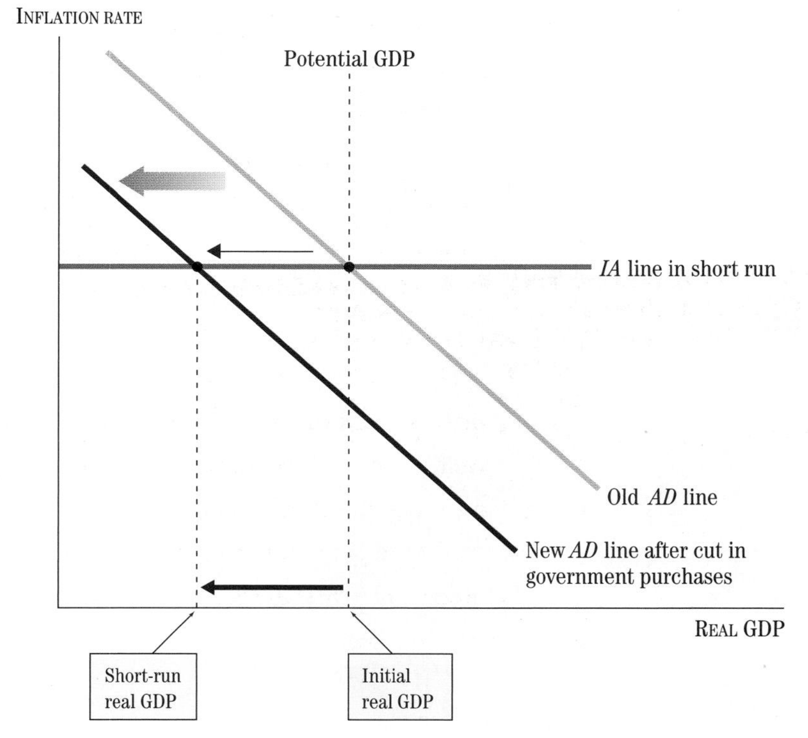

FIGURE 1
Short-Run Effects of a Reduction in Government Purchases
In the short run, the *IA* line does not move. Thus, in the short run, real GDP declines by the amount of the shift in the *AD* curve, as noted on the horizontal axis.

that we began with real GDP equal to potential GDP. Thus, the initial intersection of the aggregate demand curve and the inflation adjustment line occurs at a level of real GDP equal to potential GDP.

Now, recall from Chapter 12 that a change in government purchases shifts the aggregate demand curve; in particular, a decline in government purchases shifts the aggregate demand curve to the left. Because the inflation adjustment line is flat, and because it does not move in the short run, a change in government purchases—shown by the shift from the "old" to the "new" aggregate demand curve in Figure 1—leads to a change in real GDP of the same amount as the shift in the aggregate demand curve. This is the short-run effect. The decrease in government purchases initially moves the aggregate demand curve to the left, and real GDP falls to the point indicated by the intersection of the inflation adjustment line and the new aggregate demand curve. At the new intersection, real GDP is below potential GDP.

As real GDP falls below potential GDP, employment falls because the decline in demand forces firms to cut back on production and lay off workers. The model predicts that unemployment rises, just as it does during actual declines in real GDP.

Now consider what happens over time. The tendency for inflation to adjust over time is represented by upward or downward shifts of the inflation adjustment line. Only in the short run does the inflation adjustment line stay put. What is likely to happen over time when real GDP is below potential GDP? Inflation should begin to decline, because firms will increase their prices by smaller amounts. We represent a decline in inflation by shifting the inflation adjustment line down, as shown in Figure 2. The initial impact of the change in government spending took us to a point we label *SR*, for short run, in Figure 2. At that point, real GDP is lower than potential GDP. Hence, inflation will fall and the inflation adjustment line shifts down, as shown in the diagram. There is now a new point of intersection; we label that point *MR*, for medium run.

Note that real GDP has started to recover. At the point labeled *MR* in the diagram, real GDP is still below potential GDP, but it is higher than at the low (*SR*) point in the downturn. The reason real GDP starts to rise is that the lower inflation rate causes the central bank to lower the real interest rate. The lower real interest rate increases investment spending and causes net exports to rise. As a result, real GDP rises, and as it does, firms start to call back workers who were laid off. As more workers are employed, unemployment begins to fall.

Because real GDP is still below potential GDP, there is still a tendency for inflation to fall. Thus, the inflation adjustment line continues to shift downward until real GDP returns to potential GDP. Figure 2 shows a third intersection at the point marked *LR*, for long run, where production has increased all the way back to potential GDP. At this point, real GDP has reached long-run equilibrium in the sense that real GDP equals potential GDP. With real GDP equal to potential GDP, the inflation adjustment line stops shifting down. Inflation is at a new lower level than before the decline in government purchases, but at the final point of intersection in the diagram, it is no longer falling. Thus, real GDP remains equal to potential GDP.

Note how successive downward shifts of the inflation adjustment line with intersections along the aggregate demand curve trace out values for real GDP and inflation as the economy first goes into recession and then recovers. In the short run, a decline in production comes about because of the decrease in government spending; that decline is followed by successive years of reversal as the economy recovers and real GDP returns to potential GDP. This behavior is shown in the sketch in the lower part of Figure 2. Thus, we have achieved one of the major goals of this chapter: showing how real GDP returns to potential GDP after an initial departure due to a shift in aggregate demand. In the case where the shift in aggregate demand is large enough to cause real GDP to decline, as in a recession, we have shown how recessions end and recoveries take the economy back to normal.

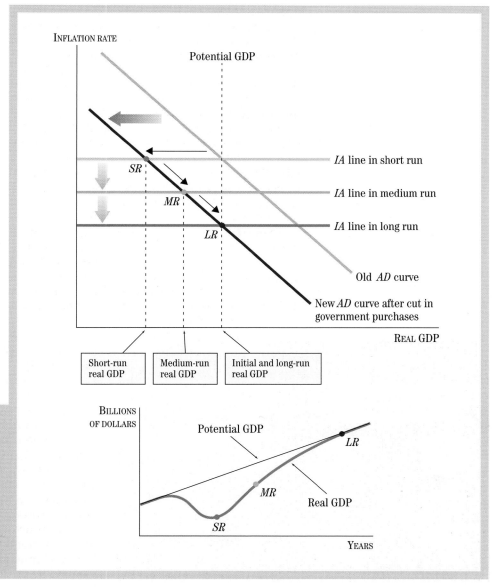

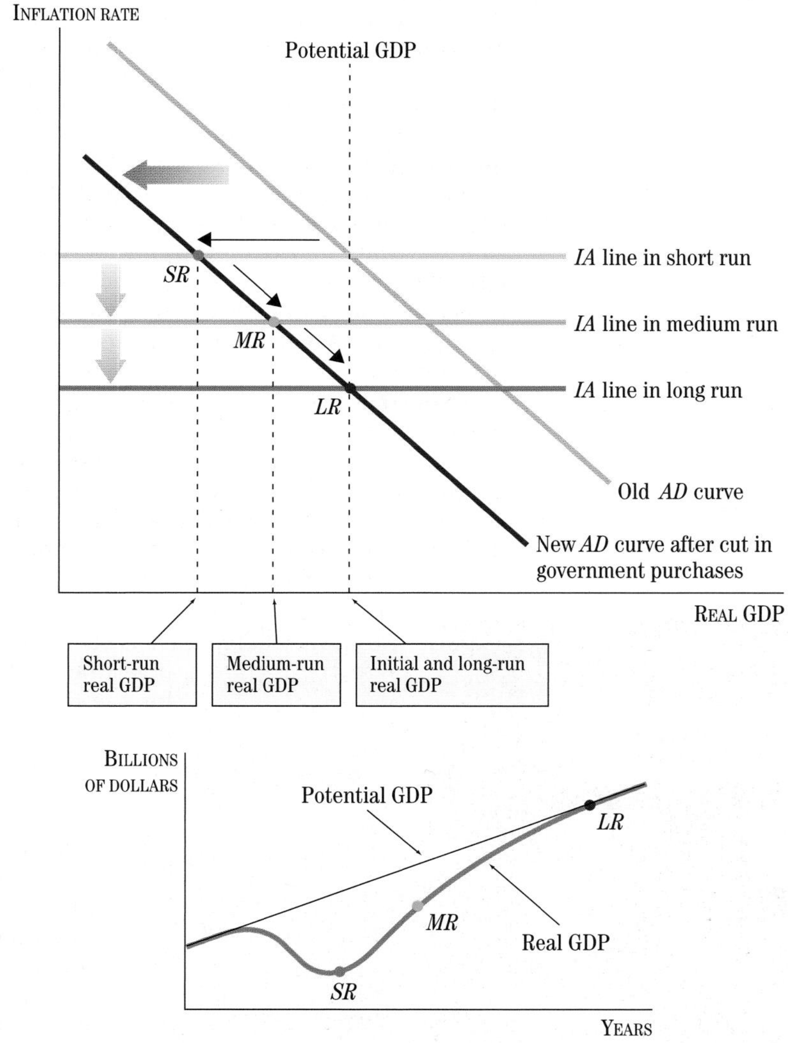

FIGURE 2
Dynamic Adjustment After a Reduction in Government Purchases
Initially, the reduction in government purchases shifts the *AD* curve to the left. This reduces real GDP to the point labeled *SR*, or the short run. Then the *IA* line begins to shift down because real GDP is less than potential GDP. The *IA* line keeps shifting down until real GDP is back to potential GDP.

Details on the Components of Spending

It is possible to give a more detailed description of what happens to consumption, net exports, and investment during this temporary departure from, and return to, potential GDP.

Let's focus first on the short run and then on the long run. Figure 3 summarizes how each component of real GDP changes in the short run and the long run. The arrows in the table indicate what happens compared with what would have happened in the absence of the change in government purchases. The path of the economy in the absence of the hypothetical change is called the *baseline.* The term *baseline* is commonly used in public policy discussions to refer to what would happen if a contemplated policy action were not taken; the arrows in the table tell whether a variable is up or down relative to the baseline. In this case, the *baseline* for real GDP is potential GDP. Thus, a downward-pointing arrow in the real GDP column means that real GDP is below potential GDP; the sideways arrows indicate that real GDP is equal to the baseline or potential GDP; an upward-pointing arrow would mean that real GDP is above potential GDP.

Short Run. The decline in government spending gets things started, lowering aggregate demand and the level of real GDP. With lower real GDP, income is down, and so people consume less, as explained by the consumption function in Chapter 11. In the short run, investment does not change because interest rates have not yet changed. However, net exports rise because the lower level of income in the United States means that people will import less from abroad. Recall that *net exports is defined as exports minus imports.* Thus, if imports fall, then net exports must rise.

These short-run effects are shown in the first row in the table. Real GDP and consumption are down *relative to the baseline.* Net exports are up *relative to the baseline.*

Long Run. Now consider the long run, approximately four to five years. By this time, real GDP has returned to potential GDP. Government spending is still lower than it was originally because we have assumed that this is a permanent decline in military spending. Because real GDP is equal to potential GDP, aggregate income in the economy—which equals real GDP—is back to normal. Because income is back to normal, the effects of income on consumption and net exports are just what they would have been in the absence of the change in government purchases.

What about interest rates and their effect on consumption, investment, and net exports? We know that real GDP is back to potential GDP, so the sum of consumption, investment, and net exports must be higher to make up for the decrease in government purchases. Thus, the real interest rate must remain lower, because investment, consumption, and net exports depend negatively on the real interest rate. With a lower real interest rate, more real GDP will go to investment, net exports, and consumption to make up for the decline in the amount of real GDP going to the government. The diagram in Figure 3 shows that consumption, investment, and net exports are higher in the long run. We would expect the consumption effects to be small, however, because consumption is not very sensitive to interest rates. Most of the long-run impact of the decline in government purchases is to raise investment and net exports.

	Y	*C*	*I*	*X*	*G*
SR	↓	↓	↔	↑	↓
LR	↔	↑	↑	↑	↓

FIGURE 3
More Detailed Analysis of a Reduction in Government Purchases
The arrows in the diagram keep track of the changes in the major variables relative to the baseline.

To summarize, a decrease in government purchases has negative effects on the economy in the short run.

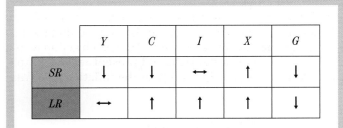

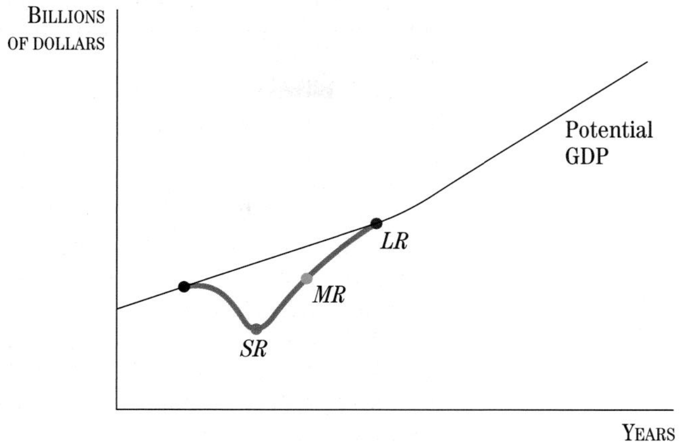

FIGURE 4
Increase in the Long-Term Growth After a Recession Caused by a Decrease in Government Purchases
The higher investment share of real GDP that results from the decline in government purchases leads to more capital and a higher growth of potential GDP. After the recession, real GDP will grow along, or fluctuate around, this higher growth path.

Real GDP declines. Workers are laid off. Unemployment rises. In the long run, the economy is back to potential GDP, and consumption, investment, and net exports have gone up. Workers are called back, and unemployment declines to where it was before the recession. In the long run, the decrease in government purchases permits greater private investment and more net exports. The increase in investment benefits long-run economic growth, as we know from Chapter 7; hence, the path of potential GDP over time has risen, and now real GDP is growing more quickly, as shown in Figure 4.

Observe also that the rate of inflation is lower in the long run than it was before the temporary decline in real GDP. Inflation declined during the period when real GDP was lower than potential GDP, and it did not increase again. This lower inflation rate means that the Fed has implicitly allowed the *target* rate of inflation—the average level of inflation over the long run—to drift down. If the Fed had wanted to keep the target rate of inflation from falling, it would have had to lower interest rates before the inflation rate started to fall. This decline in the interest rate would have pushed the aggregate demand curve back to the right and thereby kept the inflation rate from falling. Such a cut in the interest rate by the Fed would be appropriate if it knew that the reduction in government spending was permanent and would therefore lower the real interest rate in the long run.

A good example occurred in the mid-1990s when government purchases were cut in an effort to reduce the federal budget deficit. Economists argued that the Fed should cut interest rates by an extra amount. They recognized that such action would cause the aggregate demand curve to shift to the right and prevent real GDP from declining in the short run while at the same time keeping the inflation rate from falling in the long run.

The Return to Potential GDP After an Increase in Government Spending

What if real GDP rises above potential GDP? Surprisingly, the adjustment of real GDP back to potential GDP can be explained using the same theory. For example, suppose an increase in real GDP above potential GDP is caused by an increase in government purchases for new highway construction. Starting from potential GDP, the aggregate demand curve would shift to the right. Real GDP would increase above potential GDP in the short run.

With real GDP above potential GDP, however, firms start to raise their prices more rapidly; inflation begins to rise. We would represent that as an upward shift in the inflation adjustment line. In the medium run, real GDP would still be above potential GDP, and inflation would continue to rise. Eventually, real GDP would go back to potential GDP. Thus, we predict that real GDP goes back to potential GDP. However, in this case, because government purchases have risen, the new long-run equilibrium will have a higher interest rate, and the sum of consumption, investment, and net exports will be lower.

REVIEW

- Using the inflation adjustment line and the aggregate demand curve, we can now explain both the initial steps of real GDP away from potential GDP and the return to potential GDP.
- In the short run, a decline in government purchases shifts the aggregate demand curve to the left and causes real GDP to fall below potential GDP.
- In the medium run, when the interest rate starts to fall, real GDP begins to increase again. Investment and net exports start to rise and partly offset the decline in government purchases.
- In the long run, real GDP returns to potential GDP. Interest rates are lower, and consumption plus investment plus net exports has risen.

CHANGES IN MONETARY POLICY

A large change in government spending is, of course, not the only thing that can temporarily push real GDP away from potential GDP. Changes in taxes, consumer confidence, or foreign demand can also cause recessions. But a particularly important factor is a change in monetary policy.

Consider, for example, a change in monetary policy that aims to lower the rate of inflation. Suppose that the inflation rate is too high, say 10 percent, as it was in the late 1970s, and the Fed decides to reduce the inflation rate to 3 percent. In effect, the central bank changes the target inflation rate from 10 percent to 3 percent. A reduction in the inflation rate is called **disinflation. Deflation** means declining prices, or a negative inflation rate, which is different from a declining inflation rate. The aim of the policy in this example is disinflation, not deflation.

disinflation: a reduction in the inflation rate.

deflation: a decrease in the overall price level, or a negative inflation rate.

Figure 5 shows the short-run, medium-run, and long-run impact of such a shift in monetary policy. Recall from Chapter 12 (see Figures 7 and 8 in that chapter) that a change in monetary policy will shift the aggregate demand curve. A change in monetary policy toward higher inflation will shift the *AD* curve to the right, and a change in monetary policy toward lower inflation will shift the *AD* curve to the left. In this case, we are examining a change in monetary policy that aims to lower the inflation rate, so the change shifts the aggregate demand curve to the left. This occurs because the Fed raises interest rates to curtail demand and thereby lower inflationary pressures.

One effect of the increase in the interest rate is to lower investment. In addition, the higher interest rate causes the dollar to appreciate, and this tends to reduce net exports. Since inflation is slow to adjust, we do not move the inflation adjustment

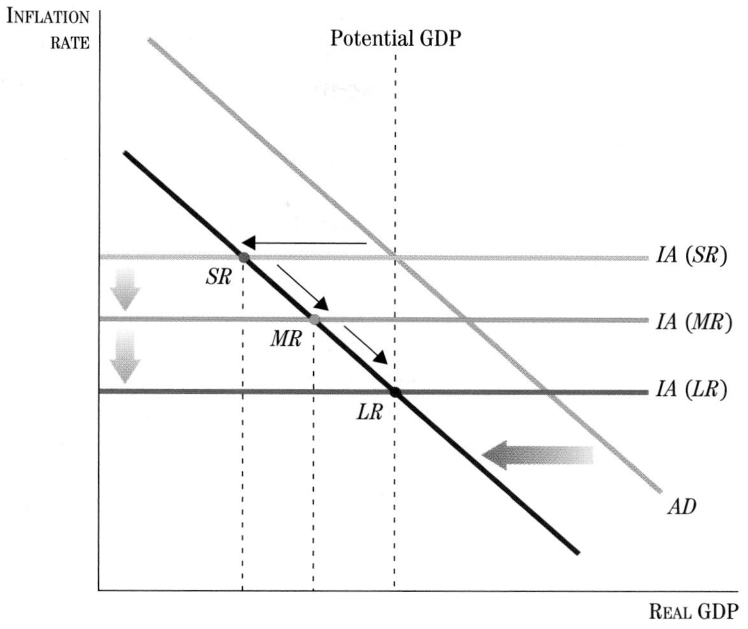

FIGURE 5
Disinflation: A Transition to Lower Inflation
The figure shows how a change in monetary policy to a lower target for inflation affects real GDP over time. In the end, inflation is lower and real GDP is back to potential GDP.

line yet. Thus, inflation remains at 10 percent in the short run. At this time, things seem very grim. The short-run effect of the change to a new monetary policy is to cause real GDP to fall below potential GDP. If the disinflation is large enough, this might mean a decline in real GDP, or a recession. If the disinflation is very small and gradual, then the decline in real GDP could result in a *temporary growth slowdown.* In a temporary growth slowdown, real GDP growth does not turn negative, as it does in a recession.

In any case, with real GDP below potential GDP, inflation will begin to decline. We show this in the diagram in Figure 5 by moving the inflation adjustment line down. The lower inflation adjustment line, labeled *MR* for medium run, intersects the aggregate demand curve at a higher level of real GDP. Thus, the economy has begun to recover. The recovery starts because as inflation comes down, the Fed begins to lower the interest rate. As the interest rate declines, investment and net exports begin to rise again, and we move back along the aggregate demand curve.

However, at this medium-run situation, real GDP is still below potential GDP, so the inflation rate continues to decline. We show this in the diagram by shifting the inflation adjustment line down again. To make a long story short, we show the inflation adjustment line shifting all the way down to where it intersects the aggregate demand curve at potential GDP. Thus, in the long-run equilibrium, the economy has fully recovered, and the inflation rate is at its new lower target. The long-run equilibrium has consumption, investment, and net exports back to normal.

The overall dynamic impacts of this change in monetary policy are very important. The initial impact of a monetary policy change is on real GDP. It is only later that the change shows up in inflation. Thus, there is a long lag in the effect of monetary policy on inflation.

Lower inflation is likely to make potential GDP grow faster, perhaps because there is less uncertainty and productivity rises faster. If this is so, the return of real GDP to potential GDP will mean that real GDP is higher, and the long-run benefits of the disinflation to people in the economy may be great over the years. But such changes in the growth of real GDP will appear small in the span of years during which a disinflation takes place and will not change the basic story that a reduction in the rate of inflation, unless it is very gradual, usually results in a recession.

The Volcker Disinflation

The scenario we just described is very similar to the disinflation in the United States in the early 1980s under Paul Volcker, the head of the Fed from 1979 to 1987. First, interest rates skyrocketed as the disinflation began. The federal funds rate went over 20 percent. By any measure, real GDP fell well below potential GDP in the early 1980s. Workers were laid off, the unemployment rate rose to 10.8 percent, investment declined, and net exports fell. Eventually, pricing decisions began to adjust and inflation began to come down. As inflation came down, the Fed began to lower the interest rate. The economy eventually recovered: In 1982, the recovery was under way, and by 1985, the economy had returned to near its potential. The good news was that inflation was down from over 10 percent to about 4 percent.

Reinflation and the Great Inflation

reinflation: an increase in the inflation rate caused by a change in monetary policy.

The opposite of disinflation might be called **reinflation,** an increase in the inflation rate caused by a shift in monetary policy. This could be analyzed with our theory simply by reversing the preceding process, starting with a change in monetary policy to a higher inflation rate target. This would cause the aggregate demand curve to shift right. Real GDP would rise above potential GDP, and unemployment would decline. But eventually inflation would rise and real GDP would return to potential.

Although it would be unusual for central bankers to explicitly admit they were raising the target inflation rate, there could be political pressures that would lead to less concern about inflation. In such a case, there would be an implicit rise in the target for inflation.

Reinflation is one way to interpret the Great Inflation in the United States and other countries in the 1970s. In the late 1960s and 1970s, the Fed and other central banks around the world let the inflation rate increase. There were other things going on at that time, including a quadrupling of oil prices, but without the inflationary monetary policy, the decade-long inflation would not have been sustained for so long.

REVIEW

- Disinflation is a reduction in inflation. It occurs when the central bank shifts monetary policy in the direction of a lower inflation target.
- According to the theory of economic fluctuations, disinflation has either a temporary slowing of real GDP growth or a recession as a by-product. A higher interest rate at the start of a disinflation lowers investment spending and net exports. This causes real GDP to fall below potential GDP. Eventually the economy recovers. Inflation comes down, and so does the interest rate.
- The large disinflation in the early 1980s in the United States was accompanied by a recession, as predicted by the theory.

ECONOMICS IN ACTION

Explaining the Recovery from the Great Depression

The Great Depression was the biggest economic downturn in American history. There is simply no parallel either before or since. As shown in the figure, from 1929 to 1933, real GDP declined 35 percent. Between 1933 and 1937, real GDP rose 33 percent; it then declined 5 percent in a recession in 1938. Real GDP increased by a spectacular 49 percent between 1938 and 1942. By 1942, real GDP had caught up with potential GDP, as estimated in the figure.

There is still much disagreement among economists about what caused the Great Depression—that is, what caused the initial departure of real GDP from potential GDP. In their monetary history of the United States, Milton Friedman and Anna Schwartz argue that it was caused by an error in monetary policy that produced a massive leftward shift in the aggregate demand curve. Unfortunately, it took several years of continually declining real GDP, declining inflation, and even deflation before the errors in monetary policy were corrected.

Another explanation is that there was a downward shift in consumption and investment spending that lowered total expenditures. Peter Temin of MIT has argued that such a spending shift was a cause of the Great Depression.

But whatever the initial cause, there seems to be more consensus that monetary policy was eventually responsible for the recovery from the Great Depression. Interest rates (in real terms) fell precipitously in 1933 and remained low or negative throughout most of the second half of the 1930s. These low interest rates led to an increase in investment and net exports. Christina Romer of the University of California at Berkeley estimates that without the monetary response, "the U.S. economy in 1942 would have been 50 percent below its pre-Depression trend path, rather than back to its normal level." Could the recovery from the Great Depression have been associated with an increase in government purchases or a reduction in taxes? Evidently not. Romer shows that government purchases and tax policy were basically unchanged until 1941, when government spending increased sharply during World War II. By that time, the economy had already made up most of the Depression decline in real GDP relative to potential GDP.

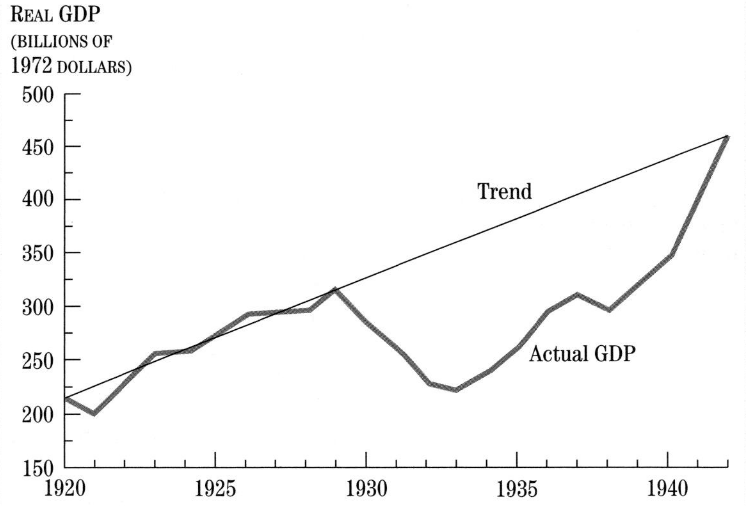

Actual and Trend Real GDP

PRICE SHOCKS

demand shock: a shift in one of the components of aggregate demand that leads to a shift in the aggregate demand curve.

price shock: a change in the price of a key commodity such as oil, usually because of a shortage, that causes a shift in the inflation adjustment line; also sometimes called a supply shock.

Shifts in the aggregate demand curve are called **demand shocks.** The change in government purchases and the shift in monetary policy described in the previous two sections of this chapter are examples of demand shocks. However, shifts in the aggregate demand curve are not the only things that can push real GDP away from potential GDP. In particular, the inflation adjustment line can shift.

What Is a Price Shock?

Shifts in the inflation adjustment line are called **price shocks.** A price shock usually occurs when a temporary shortage of a key commodity, or group of commodities, drives up prices by such a large amount that it has a noticeable effect on the rate of inflation. Oil price shocks have been common in the last 25 years. For example, oil prices rose sharply in 1974, in 1979, in 1990, in 2000, and again in 2005. After such shocks, there have usually been declines in real GDP and increases in unemployment. Hence, such shocks appear to move real GDP significantly, though temporarily, away from potential GDP.

Price shocks are sometimes called *supply shocks* in an attempt to distinguish them from demand shocks due to changes in government spending or monetary policy. However, a shift in potential GDP—rather than a shift in the inflation adjustment line—is more appropriately called a supply shock. Shifts in potential GDP—such as a sudden spurt in productivity growth due to new inventions—can, of course, cause real GDP to fluctuate. Recall that *real business cycle theory* places great emphasis on shifts in potential GDP. Although a price shock might be accompanied by a shift in potential GDP, it need not be. Here we are looking at departures of real GDP from potential GDP and thus focusing on price shocks.

real business cycle theory: a theory of macroeconomics that stresses that shifts in potential GDP are a primary cause of fluctuations in real GDP; the shifts in potential GDP are usually assumed to be caused by changes in technology. (Ch. 11)

The Effect of Price Shocks

How does our theory of economic fluctuations allow us to predict the effect of price shocks? The impact of a price shock can be illustrated graphically, as shown in Figure 6. In the case of a large increase in oil prices, for example, the inflation adjustment line will shift up to a higher level of inflation. Why? Because a large increase in oil prices will at first lead to an increase in the price of everything that uses oil in production: heating homes, gasoline, airplane fuel, airfares, plastic toys, and many other

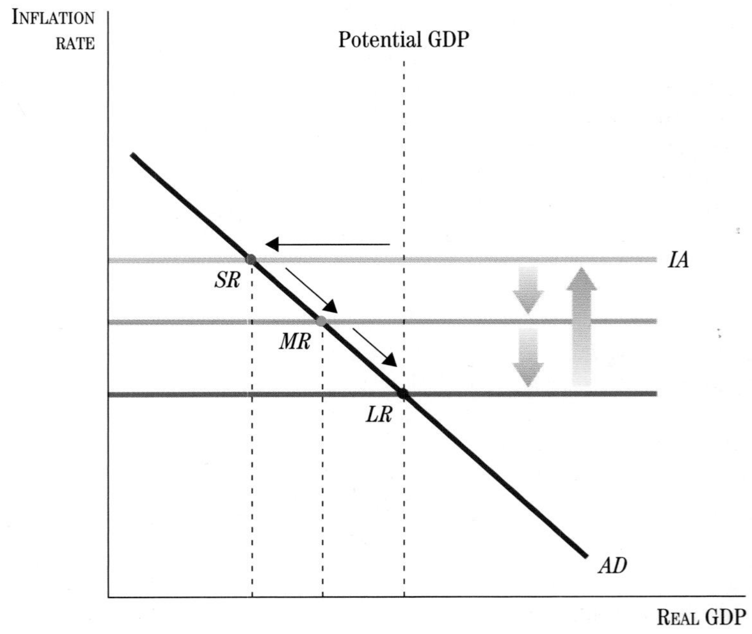

FIGURE 6
A Price Shock
Initially, inflation and the *IA* line rise because of a shock to oil or agricultural prices. This causes real GDP to fall. With real GDP below potential GDP, inflation begins to decline. As inflation declines, real GDP returns to potential GDP.

ECONOMICS IN ACTION

The 2001 Recession and Recovery

Let's see how the economic fluctuations model can explain the recession of 2001 and the recovery from that recession.

The behavior of real GDP in the years around the 2001 recession is shown graphically in Figure 1 in Chapter 11. The graph of real GDP shows real GDP fluctuating around potential GDP. There is a period when real GDP was above potential GDP and a period when real GDP was below potential GDP.

The best explanation of these economic fluctuations is achieved by combining a rightward shift of the *AD* curve with a subsequent leftward shift of the *AD* curve. To see how this works, look at the *AD-IA* diagram to the right. It shows a shift in the *AD* curve to the right. This shift first causes real GDP to rise above potential GDP, and then leads to rising inflation as the *IA* line shifts up gradually. Three intersections of the *AD* curve and the *IA* curve, labeled SR_1, MR_1, and LR_1, show this movement.

The figure then shows a shift in the *AD* curve to the left. This shift causes a recession, with real GDP falling below potential GDP, and leads to a reduction in inflation as the *IA* line shifts down gradually over time. Three intersections of the *IA* line and the *AD* curve during this period are labeled SR_2, MR_2, and MR_2. In sum, the movements in real GDP and inflation are represented by patching together two shifts of the *AD* curve.

The time-series sketches in the lower part of the figure show the movement in real GDP that is traced out by the combination of these shifts. If you compare these fluctuations in real GDP with what actually happened, shown in Figure 1 in Chapter 11, you will see a close resemblance. The model seems to explain the actual data very well.

WHY DID THE *AD* CURVE SHIFT OUT?

One reason was the rapid rise in the stock market, particularly in technology stocks. The rising stock market led to both higher consumption, as stock-owning households spent some of their new-found wealth, and higher investment, as firms rushed to put out new products or to upgrade their technology infrastructure to take advantage of the Internet.

WHY DID THE *AD* CURVE SHIFT IN?

The Federal Reserve, concerned about higher inflation down the road, made a preemptive strike by raising interest rates, leading to a further slowdown in investment by firms. Once the stock market started to fall, consumer confidence soon followed. These cutbacks in spending moved the *AD* curve to the left and moved the economy into recession.

Eventually, the fall in inflation resulted in the Fed's lowering interest rates and moving the economy back toward potential, just as the model predicted. In the year 2001, the Fed lowered interest rates on eleven separate occasions!

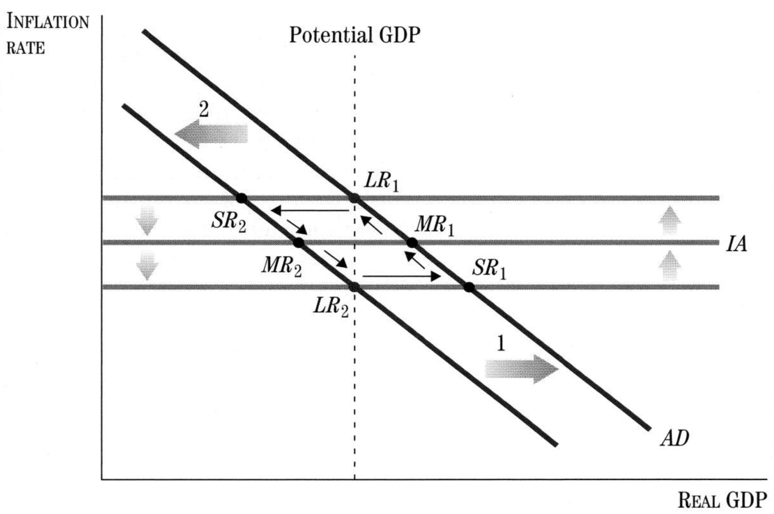

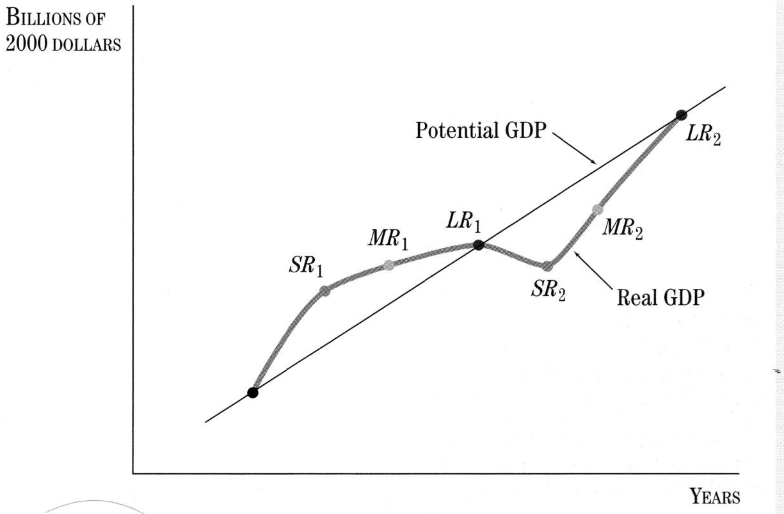

things. The overall inflation rate is affected. When the inflation rate rises, the inflation adjustment line must shift up.

The immediate impact of the shock is to lower real GDP, as the intersection of the inflation adjustment line with the aggregate demand curve moves to the left. The reason this occurs is that the higher inflation rate causes the central bank to raise interest rates, reducing investment spending and net exports.

With real GDP below potential GDP, however, the reduction in spending will put pressure on firms to adjust their prices. The lower price increases bring about a lower rate of inflation. Thus, in the period following the rise of inflation, we begin to see a reversal. Inflation starts to decline. As inflation falls, interest rates begin to decline, and the economy starts to recover again. The rate of inflation will return to where it was before the price shock.

Temporary Shifts in the Inflation Adjustment Line. In this analysis of the price shock, the central bank raises interest rates, and the resulting decline in real GDP exerts a countervailing force to reduce inflation. It is possible for some price shocks to have only a temporary effect on inflation. Such a temporary effect can be shown graphically as a rise followed by a quick fall in the inflation adjustment line. In such a situation—where the price shock would be expected to automatically reverse itself—it would be wise for the central bank to delay raising the interest rate. Then if the price shock has only a temporary effect on inflation, the decline in real GDP can be avoided. In reality, whenever there is a price shock, there is a great debate about whether it will have a temporary or a permanent effect on inflation. The debate is rarely settled until after the fact.

Price shocks can also occur when commodity prices fall. In this case there would be a *downward* shift in the inflation adjustment line—just the opposite of the case of an increase in commodity prices—and this would cause real GDP to rise as the Fed lowered interest rates. For example, in 1986 there was a decline in oil prices. This resulted in a temporary decrease in inflation and a rise in real GDP—exactly what would be predicted by the theory of economic fluctuations.

stagflation: the situation in which high inflation and high unemployment occur simultaneously.

Stagflation. An important difference between price shocks and demand shocks is that in the case of a price shock, output declines while inflation rises. With demand shocks, inflation and output are positively related over the period of recession and recovery. The situation in which inflation is up and real GDP is down is called **stagflation.** As we have shown, price shocks can lead to stagflation.

REVIEW

- A price shock is a large change in the price of some key commodity like oil. Such shocks can push real GDP below potential GDP.
- In the aftermath of a price shock, the interest rate rises. Eventually, with real GDP below potential GDP, inflation begins to come down, and the economy recovers.

CONCLUSION

Using a diagram with the aggregate demand curve and the inflation adjustment line, we can explain not only the first steps toward recessions but also the recovery of the economy. The model works well in explaining actual economic fluctuations and is thus useful for analyzing macroeconomic policy, as we do in Chapters 14 and 15.

That the model implies that real GDP returns toward potential GDP in the long run is an attractive feature of the model because, in reality, all recessions have ended. Real GDP appears to fluctuate around potential GDP rather than getting stuck forever in a recession. The tendency for real GDP to return toward potential GDP allows us to use the theory of long-run growth when discussing long-run trends in the economy. As the economy fluctuates, potential GDP gradually increases over time.

KEY POINTS

1. Using the economic fluctuations model is much like using the supply and demand model in microeconomics. You need to understand whether a particular change in the economy is reflected in a shift of the aggregate demand curve or the inflation adjustment line, as well as the direction in which the respective curves shift.
2. An increase in government purchases temporarily causes real GDP to rise, but eventually real GDP returns to potential GDP.
3. A decline in government purchases temporarily reduces real GDP, but over time the economy recovers.
4. Shifts in monetary policy, including explicit attempts to disinflate or reinflate, cause real GDP to depart from potential GDP temporarily. But eventually real GDP returns to potential GDP and only the inflation rate is changed.
5. Price shocks can cause recessions. A price shock that raises the inflation rate will cause the interest rate to rise and real GDP to fall.
6. If the Fed sets interest rates according to a monetary policy rule, then it will raise interest rates following a rise in inflation, and eventually inflation will come back down.
7. If a price shock is clearly temporary, then the Fed should not change the interest rate.
8. Shifts of the aggregate demand curve and the inflation adjustment line trace out actual observations fairly closely. Thus, the economic fluctuations model works well, but, like most models in economics and elsewhere, it is not perfect.

KEY TERMS

disinflation
deflation
reinflation
demand shock
price shock
stagflation

QUESTIONS FOR REVIEW

1. What causes the economy to recover after a recession?
2. What is the difference between the long-run and short-run effects of a change in government spending?
3. What is disinflation, and how does the central bank bring it about?
4. What is reinflation, and what impact does it have on real GDP in the short run and the long run?
5. What is a price shock, and why have price shocks frequently been followed by increases in unemployment?
6. What is the difference between a price shock and a supply shock?
7. Why do monetary policy errors lead to economic fluctuations?
8. In what way is the economic fluctuations model discussed in this chapter consistent with real-world observations?

PROBLEMS

1. Using the aggregate demand curve and the inflation adjustment line, describe what would happen to real GDP and inflation in the short run, in the medium run, and in the long run if there were a permanent increase in government spending. Assume that the economy was initially at potential output prior to the increase. Be sure to provide an economic explanation for your results.
2. Consider an economy that is at potential output. Using the aggregate demand curve and the inflation adjustment line, describe what would happen to real GDP and inflation in the short run, in the medium run, and in the long run if there was a cut in government spending on defense. Be sure to provide an economic explanation for your results.
3. For each of the scenarios in Problems 1 and 2, describe what would happen to consumption, investment, and net exports in the short run and in the long run.
4. Suppose there was an increase in government spending that had the long-run effects that you described in Problem 1. If the central bank wants to return to the original inflation rate that existed before the increase, how can it achieve its objective? Describe the proposed change in policy and its short-run, medium-run, and long-run effects on real GDP and inflation.
5. Suppose there is a sharp increase in gasoline prices when the time comes for you to graduate. Use the economic fluctuations model to explain why you might have difficulty in finding a job in the six months after you graduate.
6. The economy begins at potential GDP with an inflation rate of 2 percent. Suppose there is a price shock that pushes inflation up to 6 percent in the short run, but the effect on inflation is viewed as temporary by the Fed. It expects the inflation adjustment line to shift back down to 2 percent the next year, and in fact the inflation adjustment line does shift back down.
   - **a.** If the Fed follows its usual policy rule, where will real GDP be in the short run? How does the economy adjust back to potential?
   - **b.** Now suppose that since the Fed is sure that this inflationary shock is only temporary, it decides not to follow its typical policy rule, but instead maintains the interest rate at its previous level. What happens to real GDP? Why? What will the long-run adjustment be in this case? Do you agree with the Fed's handling of the situation?
7. Suppose that there are two countries that are very similar except that one has a central bank with a higher target inflation rate. The two countries have identical potential GDP and are both at their long-run equilibrium. Explain this situation by using two diagrams with an aggregate demand curve and an inflation adjustment line. Explain how these different equilibrium levels of inflation are possible.
8. If U.S. productivity increases, what will happen to potential GDP? What will happen to the inflation rate?
9. Would an increase in government spending lead to a higher rate of inflation in the long run? Show that the answer depends on where the economy was, relative to potential GDP, prior to the increase.
10. China's economy has seen dramatic increases in investment, consumer spending, government expenditure on infrastructure, and exports to the United States and to Europe. However, inflation in China has remained fairly moderate. Explain why this may be the case using the aggregate demand curve and the inflation adjustment line.

Chapter 14

Fiscal Policy

Over the last decade, the budgetary situation of the federal government has resembled a roller coaster ride, moving from deficit to surplus to deficit again. In 1997, the U.S. government ran a budget deficit for the *twenty-eighth* year in a row. Further deficits were projected for 1998, 1999, 2000, and beyond. The political debate centered around how to trim spending and raise revenue to lower the budget deficit.

Then, seemingly overnight, there was a radical change. A budget surplus appeared in 1998. More surpluses appeared in 1999, and by 2000, forecasts called for budget surpluses as far as the eye could see. Tax revenues increased because incomes rose rapidly. The political debate changed accordingly, focusing on how to best distribute the surplus among domestic spending, tax cuts, and paying down the federal debt.

Just as the tax cuts were being passed by Congress, the budgetary situation took another turn, this time for the worse. The arrival of the U.S. recession in 2001 and the higher government expenditures on homeland security and on the military for the wars in Afghanistan and Iraq sent the budget into deficit mode again. As the economy recovered, the deficits came down, but the retirement of the baby boom generation and the aging of the population mean growing deficits in the future.

An understanding of the U.S. budget and the factors that caused the deficit to come and go and come again is vital if we are to understand fiscal policy—spending and taxation decisions taken by the government. In this section, we will show how countercyclical fiscal policies (such as tax cuts and spending increases in recessions) can help move the economy to potential output and minimize economic fluctuations. Expansionary fiscal policy may have played a significant role in cushioning the economy during the most recent recession, and therefore, fiscal policy remains a useful tool that policymakers have at their disposal.

We will begin this chapter by reviewing the U.S. budget, the deficit, and the debt. We will then move on to a discussion of the effectiveness and scope of fiscal policy in minimizing economic fluctuations.

THE GOVERNMENT BUDGET

federal budget: a summary of the federal government's proposals for spending, taxes, and the deficit.

The **federal budget** is the major summary document describing fiscal policy in the United States. The budget includes not only the estimates of the surplus or deficit that get so much attention, but also proposals for taxes and spending. Let's look at how the federal budget in the United States is put together.

Setting the Annual Budget

In the United States, the president submits a new budget to Congress each year for the following fiscal year. The fiscal year runs from October to October. For example, *The Budget of the United States: Fiscal Year 2009* applies to spending and taxes from October 1, 2008, through September 30, 2009. It was submitted to Congress by the president in early 2008. The president typically devotes part of the State of the Union address to describing the budget and fiscal policy. Also at the start of each year, the *Economic Report of the President* is released, providing the economic forecasts underlying the budget, prepared by the Council of Economic Advisers (CEA). The Congressional Budget Office (CBO) makes its own economic forecasts.

In putting together the federal budget, the president proposes specific spending programs that fit into an overall philosophy of what government should be doing. However, in any one year, most of the spending in the budget is determined by ongoing programs, which the president usually can do little to change. For example, payments of social security benefits to retired people are a large item in the budget, but the amount of spending on social security depends on how many eligible people there are. As more people retire, spending automatically goes up unless the social security law is changed. Thus, in reality, the president can change only a small part of the budget each year.

balanced budget: a budget in which tax revenues equal spending.

budget surplus: the amount by which tax revenues exceed government spending.

budget deficit: the amount by which government spending exceeds tax revenues.

A Balanced Budget versus a Deficit or Surplus. Taxes to pay for the spending programs are also included in the budget. As part of the budget, the president may propose an increase or a decrease in taxes. *Tax revenues* are the total dollar amount the government receives from taxpayers each year. When tax revenues are exactly equal to spending, there is a **balanced budget.** When tax revenues are greater than spending, there is a **budget surplus.** When spending is greater than tax revenues, there is a **budget deficit,** and the government must borrow to pay the difference.

Note the difference between **tax rate** and **tax revenues.** For the income tax, if the average tax rate is 20 percent and income is $3,000 billion, then tax revenues are $600 billion.

Budget Deficit	Budget Balance	Budget Surplus
Tax revenues < spending	Tax revenues = spending	Tax revenues > spending

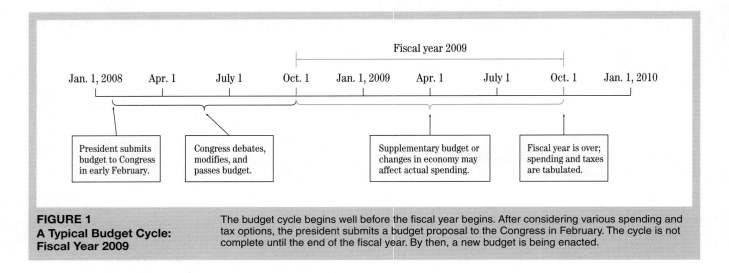

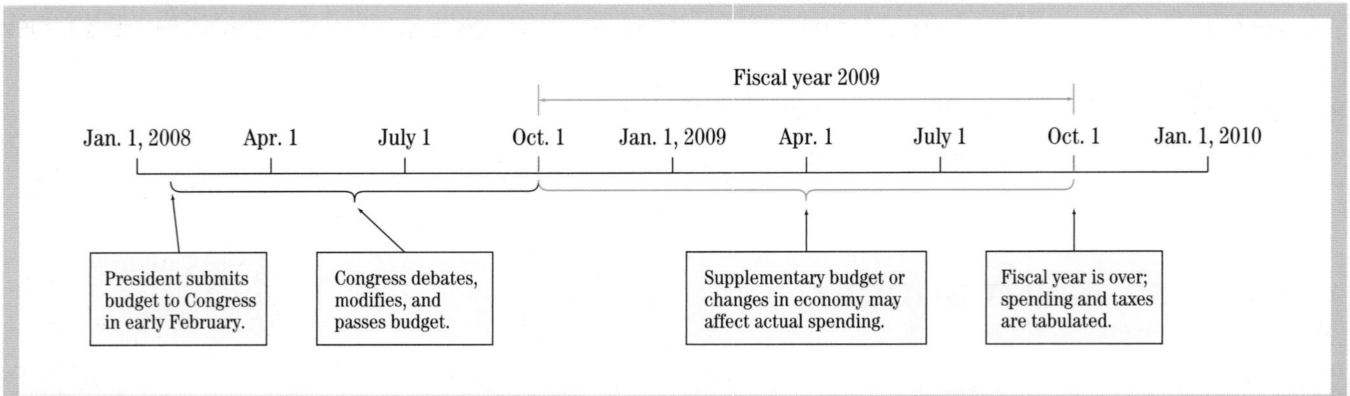

FIGURE 1
A Typical Budget Cycle: Fiscal Year 2009

The budget cycle begins well before the fiscal year begins. After considering various spending and tax options, the president submits a budget proposal to the Congress in February. The cycle is not complete until the end of the fiscal year. By then, a new budget is being enacted.

The Proposed Budget versus the Actual Budget. Keep in mind that the budget the president submits is only a *proposal.* The actual amounts of tax revenues and spending during the fiscal year are quite different from what is proposed. There are two main reasons for this difference.

First, Congress usually modifies the president's budget, adding some programs and deleting others. Congress deliberates on the specific items in the president's budget proposal for months before the fiscal year actually starts. After the president's budget has been debated and modified, it is passed by Congress. Only when the president signs the legislation is the budget enacted into law. Because of this congressional modification, the enacted budget is always different from the proposed budget. Figure 1 shows the fiscal year 2009 budget moving from a proposal in early 2008 to enactment in late 2009 to completion at the beginning of October 2009. The same *budget cycle* occurs every year, but it does not always progress smoothly. In many years the president and Congress do not settle on a budget until well into the fiscal year.

Second, because of changes in the economy and other unanticipated events such as wars and natural disasters, the actual amounts of spending and taxes will be different from what is enacted. After the fiscal year has begun and the budget has been enacted, various *supplementals* are proposed and passed. A supplemental is a change in a spending program or a change in the tax law that affects the budget in the current fiscal year.

TABLE 1
FY 2008 Federal Tax Revenues and Expenditures (billions of dollars)

Tax revenues	2,663	
Personal income		1,247
Corporate income		315
Payroll		927
Other		174
Expenditures	2,902	
Social security		613
Medicare and Medicaid		765
Defense		583
Interest		261
Other		680
Deficit	239	

Source: Economic Report of the President, 2007, Table B-80.

A Look at the Federal Budget

Table 1 contains a summary of the federal budget for fiscal year 2008. The full budget, which is over 2,000 pages long, provides much more detail.

The Deficit. Table 1 shows more expenditures than tax revenues, so there is a deficit. Budget deficits have been common in the United States for many years. For every year from 1970 to 1997, there was a deficit. From 1998 to 2001, there were four consecutive years of surplus. This run of surpluses ended in 2002 with another string of deficits. Deficits are projected to increase in the future unless there is a change in government programs.

Economics in Action

How Should Social Security Be Reformed?

Social security is a pay-as-you-go system: The payroll taxes paid by employers and employees are used to fund social security benefit payments to eligible retirees, disabled workers, survivors of deceased workers, and dependents of beneficiaries.

Individuals can begin to collect full retirement benefits when they are between 65 and 67 years of age. However, because the number of retirees is rising relative to the number of workers who pay the payroll tax, benefits are rising much faster than taxes. To avoid a ballooning deficit, social security will have to be reformed.

Social security has been famously described as the "third rail of American politics," and a heated political debate is taking place about how to reform it. A CNN/*USA Today*/Gallup poll on May 1, 2005, found that more than 81 percent of the respondents believed that substantial changes to social security were needed, but there seemed to be significant disagreement on what changes should be made.

Two rival reform plans illustrate the disagreement. One has been proposed by Martin Feldstein of Harvard University, and the other by Peter Diamond of MIT and Peter Orszag, director of the Congressional Budget Office.

Martin Feldstein presents a bold social security reform plan that combines the existing system with new individual investment accounts. (Such personal accounts were also part of President George W. Bush's proposal.) A portion of individual payroll taxes would be diverted to these investment accounts, while the remainder would be used to fund the traditional social security system. At retirement, the worker would collect a traditional social security benefit, in addition to being able to draw income from the assets accumulated in the individual account. Feldstein calculates a real rate of return on the investment accounts that is substantially higher than the implicit rate of return from social security. If this higher return is realized, individual benefits could rise without increasing taxes. But that is a big if.

Diamond and Orszag have proposed a plan that makes "modest adjustments" to the present system. Their plan is more akin to replacing the tires than to buying a new car. They argue that a combination of modest benefit reductions and tax increases are needed.

They lay out the implications of their plans for people in various age groups. Workers who are older than 55 will see no changes in benefits. Workers in younger cohorts will see larger changes, with the youngest workers seeing the largest fall in benefits (9 percent for a 25-year-old). The payroll tax will rise from 12.4 percent today to 13.2 percent in 2035 and 15.4 percent in 2078. Their plan does not allow for individual investment accounts. One of their major concerns here is that the success of individual investment accounts depends on the ability of individuals to make smart investment decisions, taking risk into account. As a result, returns might be less than hoped for.

1. In what areas do you think the Feldstein plan is stronger or weaker than the Diamond/Orszag plan?
2. Diamond and Orszag are concerned about the risks associated with individual investment accounts, particularly if there is a crash in the financial markets. Under the Feldstein plan, should the government promise to help out individuals if such a crash should occur?

Taxes and Spending. The tax revenues of $2,663 billion include *personal income taxes* paid by individuals on their total income, *corporate income taxes* paid by businesses on their profits, and *payroll taxes,* a percentage of wages paid by workers and their employers that supports government programs such as social security. Payroll taxes provide a large amount of revenues, nearly as much as personal income tax revenues.

On the expenditure side of the budget, one must distinguish between *purchases* of goods and services (such as defense), *transfer payments* (such as social security and Medicare and Medicaid), and *interest payments.* Only purchases are included in the symbol G that we have been using in the text. Purchases represent *new* production, whether of computers, federal courthouses, or food for military troops.

Interest payments are what the federal government pays every year on its debt. The government pays interest on its borrowings just like anyone else. Total interest payments equal the interest rate multiplied by the amount of government debt outstanding. For example, if the interest rate on government debt is 5 percent and total outstanding debt held by the public is $5,000 billion, then interest payments would be $250 billion (.05 × $5,000).

A very large part of the budget—nearly 50 percent—consists of social security, Medicare, and Medicaid. Social security and Medicare provide income and health care for the elderly, and Medicaid provides health care for people and families with very low incomes. As Figure 2 shows, under current law in the United States, these three entitlement programs are projected to grow very rapidly because of the increase in the elderly population as the baby boomers retire and then live longer, and because of increased spending on health care. If Congress and the president do not change the law to either reduce the growth of spending or increase tax revenue, then the federal deficit will grow to be as much as 20 percent of GDP, which would be a disaster for the economy. Because of the growing debt needed to finance the deficit, interest payments on the debt would absorb an enormous share of GDP, causing interest rates to rise and reducing private investment and economic growth. For this reason, fiscal policy experts have been urging that the laws be changed as soon as

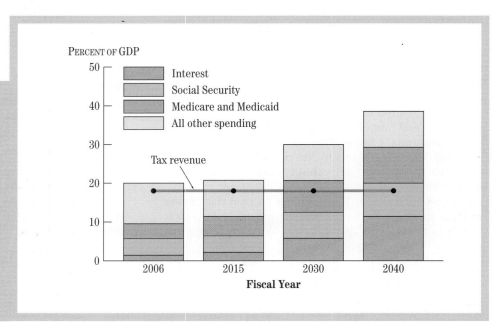

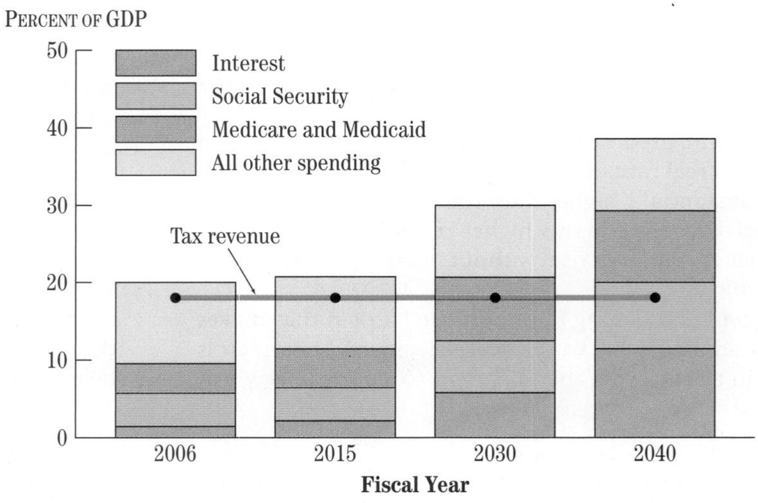

FIGURE 2
Wake-Up Call: Federal Revenue and Expenditure Projections

Social security, Medicare, and Medicaid are projected to increase rapidly in the future unless Congress and the president change the law. In the projection shown here, tax revenues grow as mandated by current tax law or at about the same rate as GDP. This means they stay at about 20 percent of GDP. Because spending growth is much more rapid, a huge, unsustainable budget deficit is the inevitable result.

Source: Government Accounting Office, Controller General's Wake-Up Call Tour, March 2007.

possible to avoid this fiscal catastrophe. So far nothing has been done because of political disagreements about how to address the problem. See the box on page 339.

The Federal Debt

federal debt: the total amount of outstanding loans owed by the federal government.

The **federal debt** is the total amount of outstanding loans that the federal government owes. If the government runs a surplus, the debt comes down by the amount of the surplus. If there is a deficit, the debt goes up by the amount of the deficit.

Consider an example involving thousands of dollars rather than trillions of dollars. Think of a student, Sam, who graduates from college with a $14,000 outstanding loan. In other words, he has a debt of $14,000. Suppose that the first year he works, his income is $30,000, but he spends $35,000. Sam's deficit for that year is $5,000, and his debt rises to $19,000. Assume that in his second year of work, he has income of $35,000 and spends $38,000; his deficit is $3,000, and his debt rises to $22,000. Each year his debt rises by the amount of his deficit. In the third year, Sam earns $40,000 and spends $33,000; he has a surplus of $7,000. This would reduce his debt to $15,000.

The laws of accounting that we apply to Sam also apply to Uncle Sam. A federal government deficit of $239 billion means that the outstanding government debt increases by $239 billion. Figure 3 shows the debt, deficit, and surpluses in the United States since 1955. Observe how the debt started to decline in 1998 when surpluses began, and started to increase again once the surpluses ended in 2002.

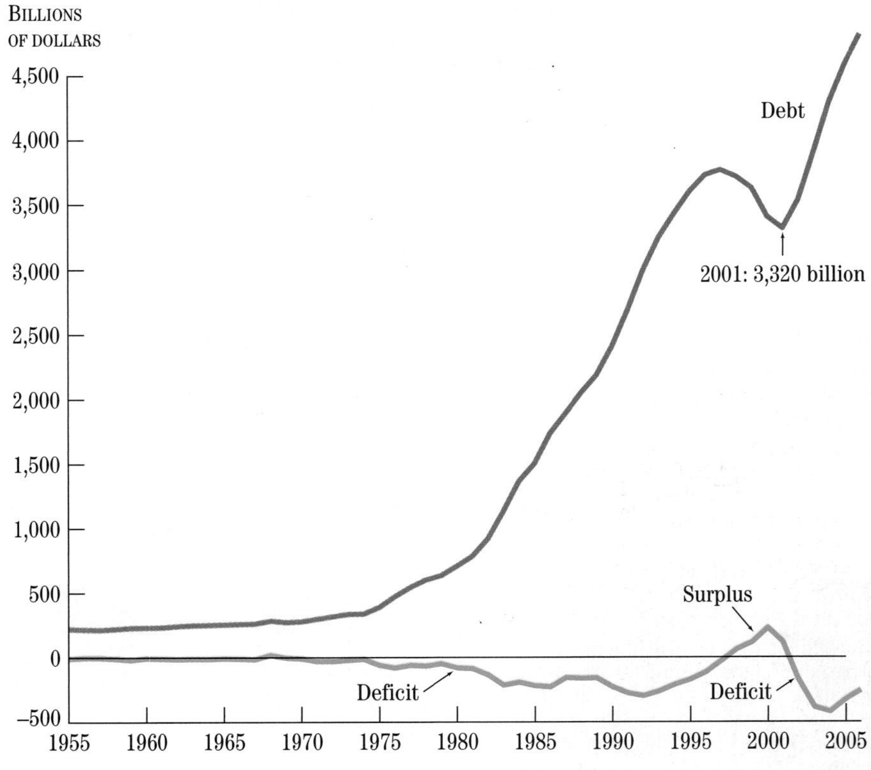

FIGURE 3
The Rise and Fall of Government Debt
When there is a deficit, the debt increases. When there is a surplus, the debt falls. The debt in 1950 was largely due to deficits during World War II.

debt to GDP ratio: the total amount of outstanding loans the federal government owes divided by nominal GDP.

The Debt to GDP Ratio. When looking at the debt and the deficit over time, it is important to consider the size of the economy. For example, a $3 trillion debt may not be much of a problem for an economy with a GDP of $10 trillion but could be overwhelming for an economy with a GDP of $1 trillion. An easy way to compare the debt to the size of the economy is to measure the debt as a percentage of GDP—the **debt to GDP ratio.** It is appropriate to consider the ratio of debt to nominal GDP rather than real GDP because the debt is stated in current dollars, just as nominal GDP is.

Figure 4 shows the behavior of the debt as a percentage of GDP in the United States since 1950. Note that the debt was a very high percentage of GDP at the end of World War II because the U.S. government had borrowed large amounts to finance its military expenditures during the war. The debt to GDP ratio rose in the 1980s and then leveled off and fell in the 1990s, but it began to increase again when deficits returned. The deficit was about 37 percent of GDP in each of the years 2004 to 2006. The debt to GDP ratio is a good overall gauge of how a government is doing in managing its fiscal affairs.

State and Local Government Budgets

Much of the government spending and taxation in the United States occurs outside of the federal government, in state and local governments. Although fiscal policy usually refers to the plans of the federal government, it is the combined action of federal, state, and local governments that has an impact on the overall economy. For example, in the 1990–1991 recession, many states cut back on spending and raised taxes; both actions would tend to reduce real GDP in the short run, just as reduced spending and higher taxes at the federal level would. Taken as a whole, state and local governments are a large force in the economy. In 2004 state and local government expenditures were about two-thirds of federal government expenditures.

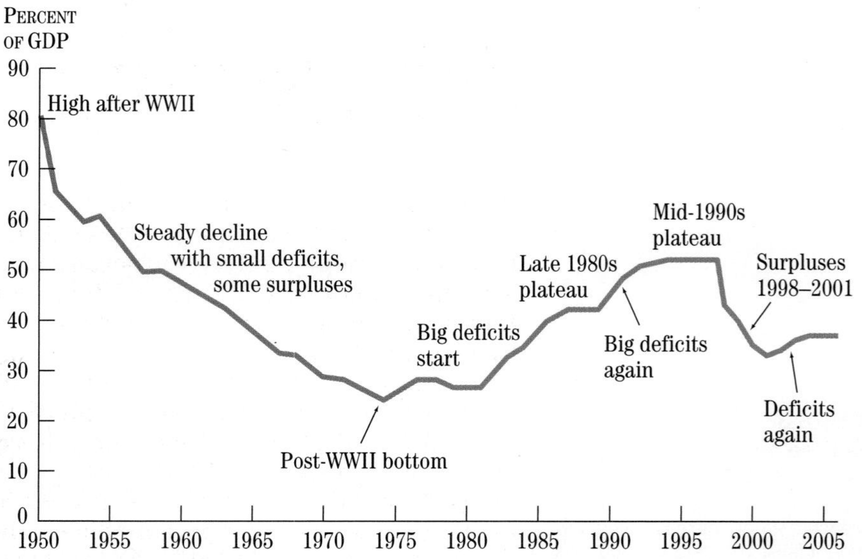

FIGURE 4
Debt as a Percentage of GDP
Relative to the size of GDP, the debt declined during the years after World War II. After rising for 20 years, the debt fell as a percentage of GDP in the late 1990s before rising again when deficits returned.

Most of the state and local government expenditures are for public schools, local police, fire services, and roads. Observe that state and local government *purchases* of goods and services are larger than federal government purchases, especially when national defense is excluded.

Like the federal government, the state and local governments have, on average, been running deficits after a few years of surpluses in the late 1990s.

REVIEW

- In the United States, the president submits a budget to Congress giving proposals for spending, for taxes, and for the deficit or surplus. The actual budget is different from the proposed budget because of congressional modifications and unforeseen events like unusually fast or slow economic growth.
- A budget surplus occurs when spending is less than tax revenues. Deficits occur when spending exceeds revenues.
- When a government or individual runs a deficit, the debt increases. Surpluses reduce the debt.
- It is appropriate to consider the debt in relation to the size of the economy by measuring it as a percentage of GDP.
- Federal government expenditures are larger than state or local government expenditures, but state and local government purchases are larger than federal government purchases.

COUNTERCYCLICAL FISCAL POLICY

Government spending and taxes are called the *instruments* of fiscal policy. They are the variables that affect the economy. Now let's see how changes in the instruments of fiscal policy affect the size of economic fluctuations.

Impacts of the Instruments of Fiscal Policy

We first consider a change in government purchases and then go on to consider a change in taxes.

Changes in Government Purchases. We know that if there is a change in government purchases, real GDP will initially change. If real GDP equaled potential GDP at the time of the change in government purchases, then real GDP would move away from potential GDP. Hence, a first lesson about fiscal policy is "do no harm." Erratic changes in government purchases can lead to fluctuations of real GDP away from potential GDP.

But suppose real GDP was already away from potential GDP. Then the change in government purchases could move real GDP closer to potential GDP. This is shown in Figure 5. In the top panel, real GDP starts out below potential GDP. An increase in government purchases shifts the aggregate demand curve to the right and moves real GDP back toward potential GDP. In the bottom panel, real GDP is above potential GDP, and a decrease in government purchases shifts the aggregate demand curve to the left, bringing real GDP back toward potential GDP. The important point is that a change in government purchases shifts the aggregate demand curve from wherever it happens to be at the time of the change.

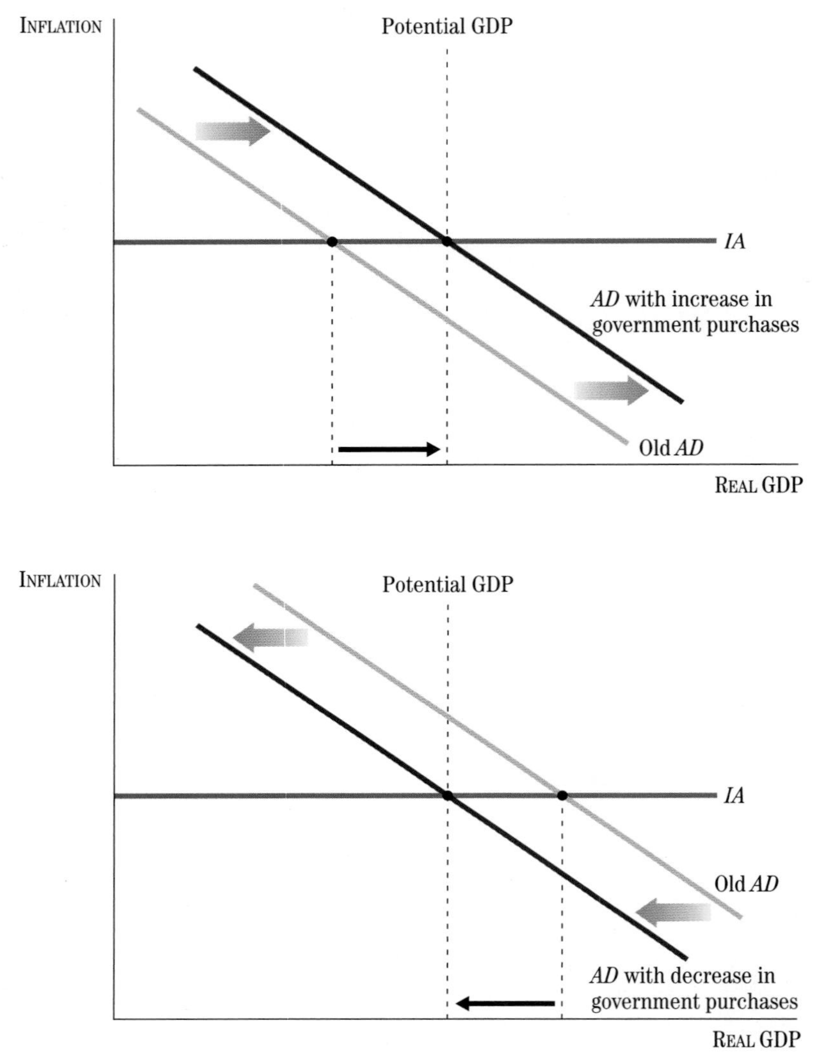

FIGURE 5
Effect of a Change in Government Purchases
If real GDP is below potential GDP, as in the top panel, an increase in government purchases, which shifts the *AD* curve to the right, will move real GDP toward potential GDP. If real GDP is above potential GDP, as in the bottom panel, a decrease in government purchases will move real GDP toward potential GDP. These are short-run effects.

Now, these effects of government purchases are short term. Eventually, prices will adjust; consumption, investment, and net exports will change; and real GDP will return to potential GDP. Nevertheless, as we will see, the short-run impacts of government purchases provide fiscal policy with the potential power to reduce the size of economic fluctuations.

A decrease in government purchases on roads and bridges is one example of a leftward shift in the aggregate demand curve. An increase in government purchases for defense works in the opposite direction. Because the changes in government spending affect investment, in the long run they may affect potential GDP. But for now, we focus on how they can move the economy closer to potential GDP.

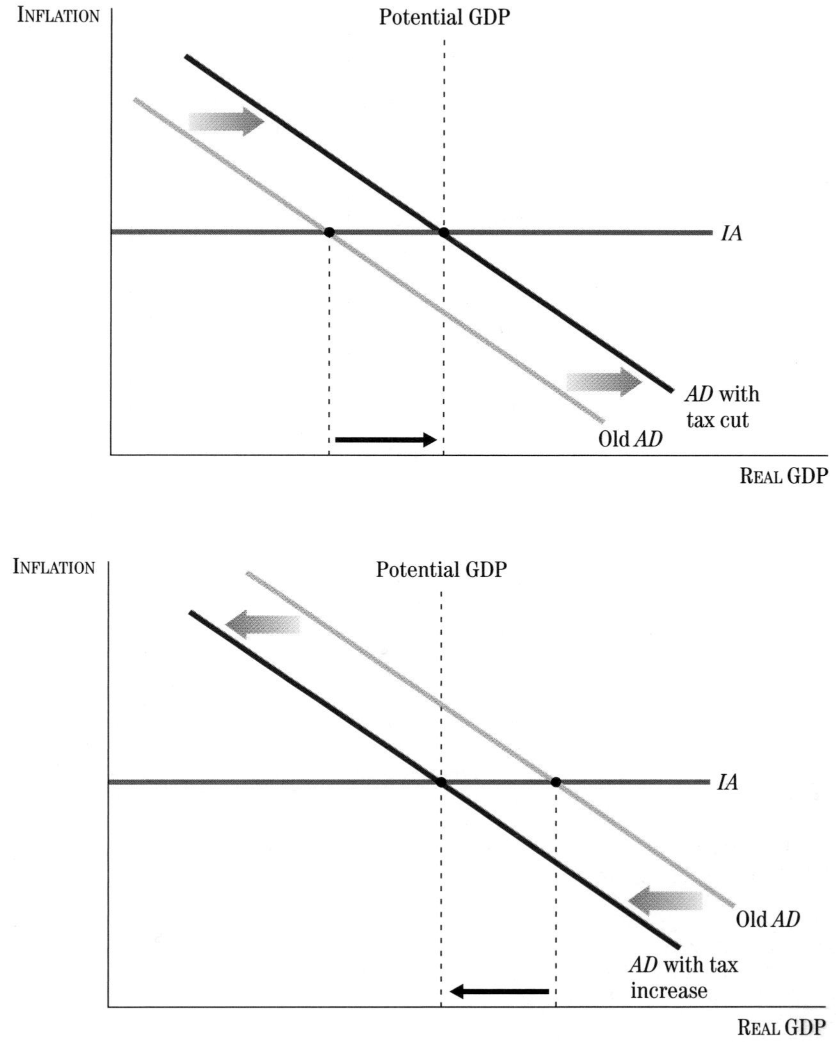

FIGURE 6
Effects of a Change in Taxes
A decrease in taxes shifts the *AD* curve to the right and can move real GDP toward potential GDP, as in the top panel. An increase in taxes moves real GDP toward potential in the lower panel.

Changes in Taxes. A change in taxes also affects real GDP in the short run. At any given level of real GDP, people will consume less if there is a tax increase because they have less income to spend after taxes. They will consume more if there is a tax cut. In either case, the aggregate demand curve will shift. The top panel of Figure 6 shows how a tax cut will shift the aggregate demand curve to the right and push real GDP closer to potential GDP if it is below potential GDP. The bottom panel shows a tax increase reducing real GDP from a position above potential GDP. Again, these are short-term effects. Eventually prices will adjust and real GDP will return to potential GDP.

Both increases and decreases in taxes can also affect potential GDP. For example, if an increase in tax rates causes some people to work less, then the labor supply will not be as large and potential GDP will be lower. But here our focus is on the departures of real GDP from potential GDP.

Countercyclical Fiscal Policy

countercyclical policy: a policy designed to offset the fluctuations in the business cycle.

Because government spending and taxes affect real GDP in the short run, fiscal policy can, in principle, offset the impact of shocks that push real GDP away from potential GDP. Such use of fiscal policy is called **countercyclical policy,** because the cyclical movements in the economy are being "countered," or offset, by changes in government spending or taxes. Recessions can be countered by cuts in taxes or increases in spending.

Figure 7 shows what such a policy would ideally do. A possible recession in the year 2009 is shown, perhaps caused by a drop in foreign demand for U.S. products. Without any change in government purchases or taxes, the economy would eventually recover, as shown in the figure. But suppose that the government quickly cuts taxes or starts a road-building program. The hope is that this will raise real GDP, as shown in the figure, and hasten the return to potential GDP.

How would this work when prices are adjusting and the inflation rate is changing as well? Figure 8 provides the analysis. The recession is seen to be caused by the leftward shift in the aggregate demand curve. But the cut in taxes or increase in spending shifts the aggregate demand curve in the opposite direction. The aggregate demand curve shifts back to the right. If these countercyclical measures are timely enough and neither too small nor too large—both big ifs—then the recession may be small and short-lived. The example shows real GDP falling only slightly below potential GDP.

Figure 9 shows a less ideal case. Here government purchases are increased, but the response is too late. The increase occurs the year after the recession, during the recovery; the excessive growth in aggregate demand could cause inflation to increase.

Disagreements about the usefulness of fiscal policy boil down to an assessment of whether Figure 7 or Figure 9 is more likely. Let's first consider some examples.

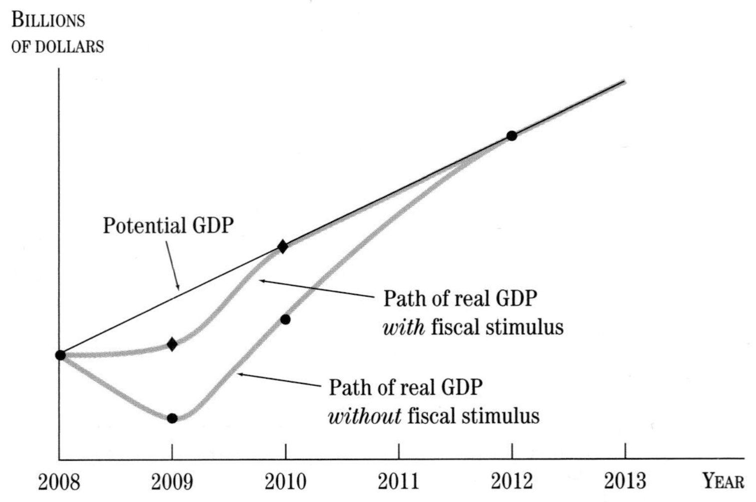

FIGURE 7
Effect of a Well-Timed Countercyclical Fiscal Policy
The figure shows a likely path of recovery from a recession caused by a decline in demand for U.S. products. A well-timed cut in taxes or increase in government purchases can reduce the size of the recession and bring real GDP back to potential GDP more quickly. The size of the economic fluctuation is smaller. The analysis is shown in Figure 8.

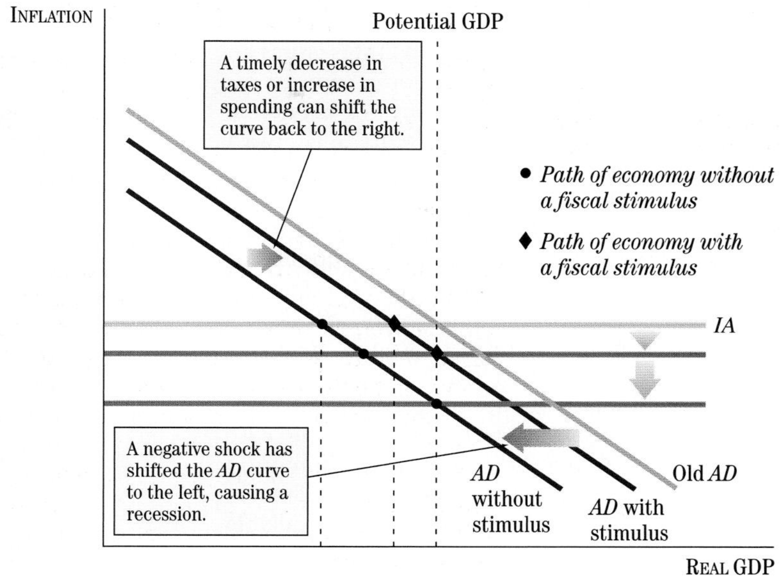

FIGURE 8
Analysis of a Well-Timed Countercyclical Fiscal Policy
A decline in demand—perhaps through a decrease in exports—shifts the *AD* curve to the left. Without a countercyclical fiscal policy, real GDP recovers back to potential GDP, but a timely cut in taxes or increase in government purchases can offset the drop in demand and bring real GDP back to potential GDP more quickly.

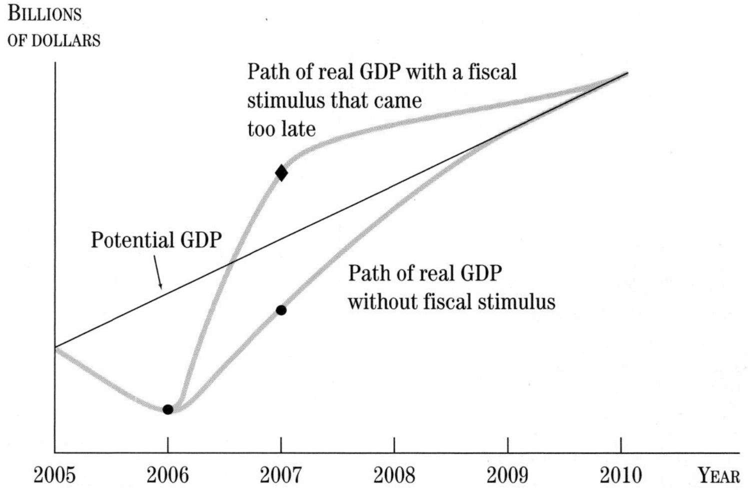

FIGURE 9
Effect of a Poorly-Timed Fiscal Policy
Here, in contrast to Figure 7, the fiscal stimulus comes too late, when the economy is already recovering, possibly leading to an increase in inflation.

Economics in Action

The *Economic Report of the President*

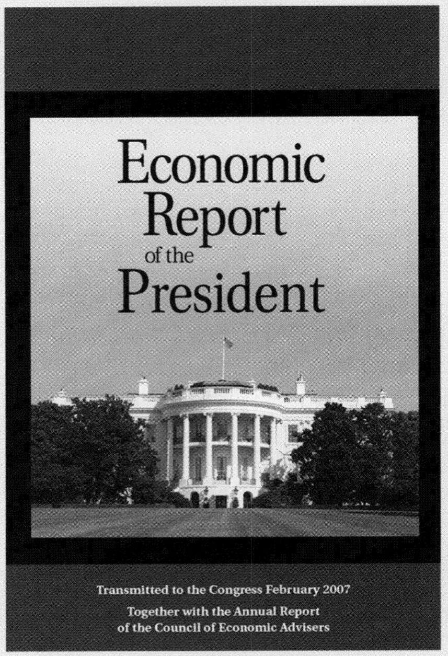

Economic
Report
of the
President
Transmitted to the Congress February 2007
Together with the Annual Report
of the Council of Economic Advisers

Early each year, the president of the United States issues an economic report, which contains the economic forecast for the year prepared by the president's Council of Economic Advisers (CEA). Most economic reports are filled with interesting economic facts and applications to the pressing fiscal policy issues of the day.

President John Kennedy's 1963 *Economic Report* made the case for his tax cuts, arguing that "it is appropriate to reduce significantly the highest income tax rates at the same time that a more comprehensive tax base is provided." Nearly 20 years later, President Ronald Reagan's 1982 *Economic Report* argued that the lower tax rates he advocated would stimulate economic growth. President Bill Clinton's 1994 *Economic Report* presented the case for "shifting federal spending priorities from consumption to investment," a key fiscal policy principle of his administration. These and the latest economic reports are available online at fraser.stlouis.org and are worth surfing through.

The *Economic Report of the President* always attracts news attention and sometimes generates huge controversy. For example, the 2004 *Economic Report* explained, as part of an argument in favor of international trade, why distinguishing between a manufacturing job and a service job is difficult, saying that making a hamburger—a service job—was really a lot like manufacturing. The innocent comparison generated a tidal wave of ridicule because it sounded like the president's advisers were belittling the decline in manufacturing jobs in the United States. A CBS News report was headlined "Building Blue-Collar . . . Burgers? Bush Report: Fast Food Work a Form of Manufacturing?" It said

> "The annual economic report—most of which consists of charts and statistics—has been the focus of unusual scrutiny this year, perhaps reflecting the presidential campaign and concern about the lack of job creation despite an ongoing recovery. . . . 'When a good or service is produced at lower cost in another country, it makes sense to import it rather than to produce it domestically. This allows the United States to devote its resources to more productive purposes,' the report read. The statement, which reflects standard economic theory about the efficiencies of trade, was denounced by Democrats and Republicans alike. 'These people, what planet do they live on?' asked Democratic presidential candidate and North Carolina Sen. John Edwards. Even Republican House Speaker Dennis Hastert wrote to the White House protesting the claim."

Not surprisingly all the reports since the 2004 *Economic Report* have been given extra scrutiny by the White House to prevent such embarrassing outbreaks, but they continue to be a valuable resource where you can see economics being used in action.

discretionary fiscal policy: changes in tax or spending policy requiring legislative or administrative action by the president or Congress.

Discretionary Changes in the Instruments of Fiscal Policy. **Discretionary fiscal policy** refers to specific changes in laws or administrative procedures, such as a change in an existing program to speed up spending, the creation of a new program (such as a new welfare program), or a change in the tax system (such as lower tax rates). These changes in the law are discretionary changes because they require action on the part of the Congress or the president.

One of the most significant post–World War II discretionary fiscal policy actions was the tax cut proposed by President John F. Kennedy in 1963 and enacted after his death when Lyndon Johnson was president. The early 1960s were a period when real GDP was below potential GDP, and this large discretionary tax cut was a factor in speeding the economic recovery. This cut in taxes also probably stimulated the growth of potential GDP and was therefore good for the long run.

Another example was the 1968 temporary income tax surcharge that raised tax rates by 10 percent. It was passed during the Vietnam War, when real GDP was above potential GDP, perhaps because the aim was to bring real GDP back toward potential GDP.

Another large discretionary fiscal policy action was the Reagan tax cut of the early 1980s, which lowered personal income tax rates by 25 percent. This tax cut helped the economy recover from the 1981–1982 recession. Like the Kennedy tax cut, this tax cut also probably raised the growth rate of potential GDP.

A more recent example of a discretionary fiscal policy was the Economic Growth and Tax Relief Reconciliation Act of 2001, enacted by Congress in June 2001. Among the sweeping changes in tax law introduced by this plan were lower income tax rates, more generous tax exemptions for married couples, and more generous tax exemptions for children. The first part of the plan was a $300 ($600 for couples) rebate check that the government mailed out to eligible taxpayers in the summer of 2001. The tax cut was helpful in raising spending during the recession, although the extent to which it helped is the source of some debate among economists, since many of the provisions were to be phased in over the next ten years instead of being effective immediately.

Automatic Changes in the Instruments of Fiscal Policy. Discretionary actions by the government are not the only way in which taxes and spending can be changed. In fact, many of the very large changes in taxes and spending are automatic. Income tax revenues expand when people are making more and fall when people are making less. Thus, tax revenues respond automatically to the economy. Tax payments rise when the economy is in a boom and more people are working. Tax revenues fall when the economy is in a slump and unemployment rises.

These changes in tax revenues are even larger with a progressive income tax. With a *progressive tax* system, individual tax payments *rise* as a proportion of income as income increases. With a progressive tax, a person earning $100,000 per year pays proportionately more in taxes than a person earning $20,000 per year. Because of this progressive tax system, as people earn more, they pay a higher tax rate, and when they earn less, they pay a lower tax rate.

Parts of government spending also change automatically. Unemployment compensation, through which the government makes payments to individuals who are unemployed, rises during a recession. When unemployment rises, so do payments to unemployed workers. Social security payments also increase in a recession because people may retire earlier if job prospects are bad. Welfare payments rise in a recession because people who are unemployed for a long period of time may qualify for welfare. As poverty rates rise in recessions, welfare payments increase.

automatic stabilizers: automatic tax and spending changes that occur over the course of the business cycle that tend to stabilize the fluctuations in real GDP.

These automatic tax and spending changes are called **automatic stabilizers** because they tend to stabilize the fluctuations of real GDP. How significant are these automatic stabilizers? Consider the 2001 recession. Real GDP in 1999 and 2000 was above potential GDP. But by late 2001 and 2002, real GDP was dropping below potential GDP. As this happened, government spending went up and taxes went down.

The magnitude of these effects was quite large. The difference between proposed and actual taxes and spending in the 2002 budget provides an estimate of the effect of the recession on taxes and spending. Tax revenue was $336 billion less than had been proposed before the recession. Thus, taxes were automatically reduced by this amount. However, spending was $50 billion more than had been proposed before the recession. Thus, spending rose by $50 billion in response to the recession. The combined effect of a $336 billion reduction in taxes and a $50 billion increase in spending was vital in keeping the recovery going. Since tax receipts went down in the recession and transfer payments went up, people's consumption was at a higher level than it would otherwise have been. These automatic changes in tax revenues and government spending tended to stabilize the economy and probably made the recession less severe than it would otherwise have been. These changes did not completely offset other factors, however, because there still was a recession.

The Discretion versus Rules Debate for Fiscal Policy

For many years economists have debated the usefulness of discretionary and automatic fiscal policy. Automatic fiscal policy is an example of a fiscal policy rule describing how the instruments of fiscal policy respond to the state of the economy. Thus, the debate is sometimes called the "discretion versus rules" debate.

The case for discretionary fiscal policy was made by President Kennedy's Council of Economic Advisers, which included Walter Heller and Nobel Prize–winning economist James Tobin. Proponents of discretionary fiscal policy argue that the automatic stabilizers will not be large enough or well-timed enough to bring the economy out of a recession quickly. Critics of discretionary policy, such as Milton Friedman, another Nobel Prize winner, emphasize that the effect of policy is uncertain and that there are long lags in the impact of policy. By the time spending increases and taxes are cut, a recession could be over; if so, the policy would only lead to an overshooting of potential GDP and an increase in inflation. Three types of lags are particularly problematic for discretionary fiscal policy: a *recognition lag,* the time between the need for the policy and the recognition of the need; an *implementation lag,* the time between the recognition of the need for the policy and its implementation; and an *impact lag,* the time between the implementation of the policy and its impact on real GDP.

Although lags and uncertainty continue to contribute to the discretion versus rules debate, other issues have also become central. Many economists feel that policy rules are desirable because of their stability and reliability. A fiscal policy rule emphasizing the automatic stabilizers might make government plans to reduce the deficit more believable. Countercyclical fiscal policy raises the deficit or reduces the surplus during recessions. With discretionary policy, there is no guarantee that the surplus will return or increase after the recession. With an automatic policy rule, there is an expectation that the deficit will decline after the recession is over.

REVIEW

- Countercyclical fiscal policy is undertaken by governments to reduce economic fluctuations. The aim is to keep real GDP closer to potential GDP.
- Two types of countercyclical fiscal policy are (1) discretionary policy, such as the 1964 Kennedy-Johnson tax cut, the 1981 Reagan tax cut, and the 2001, Bush tax cuts, and (2) automatic stabilizers, such as changes in unemployment payments, social security payments, and tax revenues due to changes in people's incomes.

THE STRUCTURAL VERSUS THE CYCLICAL SURPLUS

structural surplus: the level of the government budget surplus under the scenario where real GDP is equal to potential GDP; also called the full-employment surplus.

We noted earlier that taxes and spending change automatically in recessions and recoveries. These automatic changes affect the budget, so in order to analyze the budget, it is important to try to separate out these automatic effects. The *structural,* or *full-employment, surplus* was designed for this purpose. The **structural surplus** is what the surplus would be if real GDP equaled potential GDP.

Figure 10 introduces a graph to help explain the structural surplus. On the horizontal axis is real GDP. On the vertical axis is the budget surplus: tax revenues less expenditures. The budget is balanced when the surplus is zero, which is marked by a horizontal line in the diagram. The region below zero represents a situation in which taxes are less than spending and the government has a deficit. The region above zero is a situation in which the government budget has a surplus. On the horizontal axis, *A, B,* and *C* represent three different levels of real GDP.

The upward-sloping line in Figure 10 indicates that as real GDP rises, the budget surplus gets larger. Why? The automatic stabilizers are the reason. When real GDP rises, tax revenues rise and spending on transfer programs falls. Because the surplus is the difference between tax revenues and spending, the surplus gets larger. Conversely,

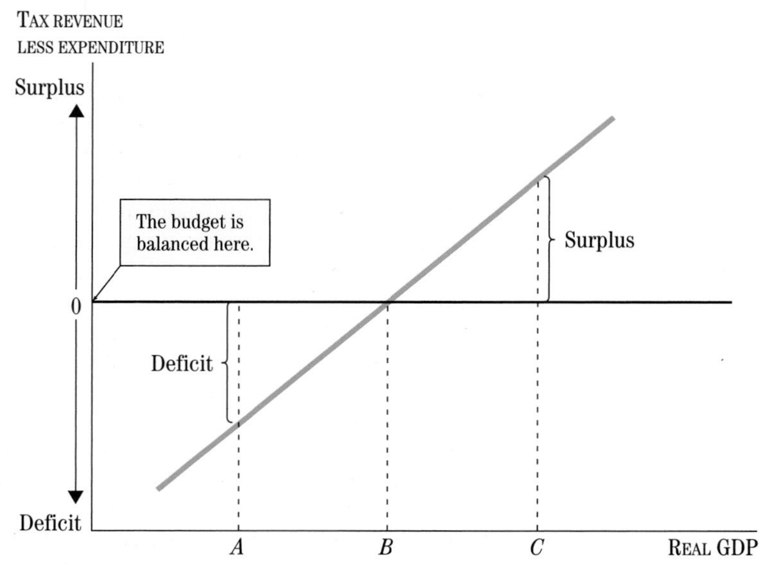

FIGURE 10
The Effect of Real GDP on the Budget
When real GDP falls, the budget moves toward deficit because spending rises and tax receipts fall. When real GDP is at point *A*, there is a deficit; at point *B*, the budget is balanced; and at point *C*, there is a budget surplus.

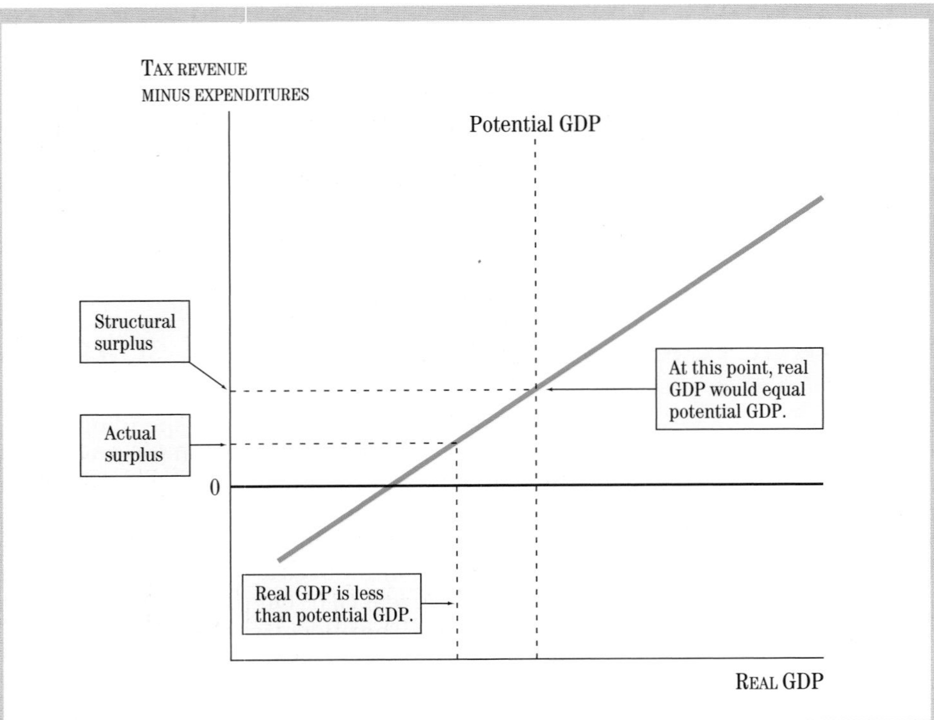

FIGURE 11
The Structural Surplus versus the Actual Surplus in a Recession Year
The surplus that would occur when real GDP is equal to potential GDP is called the structural surplus, as shown in the figure. The actual surplus falls below the structural surplus when real GDP falls below potential GDP. If there is a big recession, there could be an actual deficit even though there is a structural surplus.

when real GDP falls, tax receipts decline and spending on transfer programs increases, so the surplus falls. The upward-sloping line in Figure 10 pertains to a particular set of government programs and tax laws. A change in these programs or laws would *shift* the line. For example, a decrease in tax rates would shift the line down.

Figure 11, a similar diagram, shows potential GDP and real GDP in a year when real GDP is below potential GDP. Imagine raising real GDP up to potential GDP. We would predict that the surplus would go up, because tax receipts would rise as the economy grew and transfer payments would go down since there would be fewer people unemployed, fewer people retiring, and fewer people on welfare. As we move to the right in the diagram, the surplus gets larger. The structural surplus occurs when real GDP equals potential GDP.

The structural surplus provides a way to separate out cyclical changes in the budget caused by cyclical changes in the economy.

REVIEW

- Because tax revenues and spending fluctuate as the economy fluctuates, the surplus, or deficit, is cyclical. Deficits frequently arise or get bigger in recessions.
- The structural surplus adjusts the actual surplus for these cyclical changes in the economy.

CONCLUSION

Because the government is such a large player in the economy, its fiscal actions (spending, taxing, and borrowing) exert a powerful influence on real GDP and employment. Such actions can cause real GDP to depart from potential GDP and can alter the long-term growth rate of potential GDP.

A first principle of fiscal policy, therefore, is that government not take actions that would harm the economy. Avoiding erratic changes in fiscal policy and making sure that taxes are not increased during recessions are part of this first principle.

A second principle is that fiscal policy can be used to help smooth the fluctuations in the economy. Tax cuts and spending increases during recessions can help offset the declines in demand that cause recessions. Conversely, tax increases and spending cuts during booms can help offset the forces leading to inflation in the economy.

There is debate among economists about whether the government is capable of taking discretionary actions that will have these effects. Policy lags and uncertainty make discretionary fiscal policy difficult. There is little disagreement, however, about the importance of automatic stabilizers, under which tax and spending actions occur automatically without legislation. Automatic stabilizers cause the deficit to rise in recessions and fall during better times.

Another part of government policy that has powerful effects on the economy is monetary policy. We take up monetary policy in Chapter 15.

KEY POINTS

1. Fiscal policy consists of the government's plans for spending and taxes.
2. The government's budget is the primary document of fiscal policy. It gives the priorities for spending and taxes. In the United States, the president must submit a budget proposal to Congress.
3. The United States had large federal budget deficits from 1970 to 1997, surpluses from 1998 to 2001, and deficits since then.
4. Because Congress modifies the proposals and because of unanticipated events, the actual budget differs considerably from the proposed budget.
5. Changes in spending and taxes can move real GDP away from potential GDP in the short run. But in the long run, real GDP returns to potential GDP.
6. Discretionary changes in taxes and spending can be used to keep real GDP near potential GDP.
7. Lags and uncertainty make discretionary fiscal policy difficult.
8. Automatic stabilizers are an important part of fiscal policy. Tax revenues automatically decline in recessions. Transfer payments move in the reverse direction.

KEY TERMS

federal budget
balanced budget
budget surplus
budget deficit
federal debt
debt to GDP ratio
countercyclical policy
discretionary fiscal policy
automatic stabilizers
structural surplus

QUESTIONS FOR REVIEW

1. Why are actual expenditures and revenues always different from the president's proposals?
2. How is the government's debt affected by the government's budget surplus?
3. Why would a tax cut in a recession reduce the size of the recession?
4. Why might a proposal to cut taxes in a recession do little to mitigate the recession?
5. What is meant by the discretion versus rules debate?
6. What are automatic stabilizers, and how do they help mitigate economic fluctuations?
7. What is the difference between the structural surplus and the actual surplus?
8. What would happen to the actual surplus in a recession?

PROBLEMS

1. Suppose you have the following data on projected and actual figures for the U.S. budget for 2006 (in billions of dollars).

	Projected Budget	Actual Budget
Taxes	2,286	2,407
Expenditures	2,709	2,655

   a. What was the projected budget surplus or deficit? What was the actual budget surplus or deficit? Why might this happen?
   b. If the government debt was $4,592 billion at the end of 2005, what was the debt at the end of 2006?
   c. If real GDP was $12,300 billion in 2005, what is the debt to GDP ratio? How does this compare to the debt to GDP ratio around 1990?

2. Examine the hypothetical budget data, shown below, for calendar years 2005–2008 (in billions of dollars).

Year	Budget Surplus	Government Debt as of January 1	GDP
2005	−150	1,000	4,000
2006	−100	1,150	4,200
2007	100		4,800
2008	200		5,400

   a. Fill in the missing values in the table.
   b. What is the percentage change in debt and GDP from 2005 to 2006?
   c. Calculate the debt to GDP ratio for each year. How does this ratio change over time? Why?

3. Suppose you are in charge of deciding the appropriate fiscal policy for an economy where real GDP is less than potential GDP. One of your economic advisers recommends a reduction in government spending. Using an *AD-IA* diagram, indicate the short-run, medium-run, and long-run effects of this plan. Did you receive good advice from your economic adviser?
4. Suppose the economy is currently $100 billion above potential GDP, and the government wants to pursue discretionary fiscal policy to cool off the economy. Show this situation using an *AD-IA* diagram.
5. Suppose Congress is considering a balanced budget amendment to the Constitution that requires that the budget be balanced every fiscal year. Explain how this law could make the economy more unstable.
6. Do you think that a zero national debt would be best for the country? Why or why not? Do you think that a zero level of debt would best for you? Why or why not?
7. Suppose you get a summer job working in Congress and a recession begins while you are there. Write a memo to your boss, who is a member of Congress, on the pros and cons of a big highway- and bridge-building program to combat the recession.
8. Will projects such as Senator Ted Stevens of Alaska's proposed "bridge to nowhere," a $300 million bridge that would connect two remote Alaskan communities, help the national economy avoid a recession? How would you reconcile this with your answer to Problem 7?

9. Suppose that real GDP has just fallen below potential GDP in a recession and the Council of Economic Advisers is trying to forecast the recovery from the recession. They are uncertain about whether Congress will pass the president's proposed tax cut right away or will delay it a year. Trace out two possible scenarios with an *AD-IA* diagram that describes the impact of the uncertainty.

10. Suppose the government surplus is 3 percent of real GDP, but economists say that the structural surplus is 2 percent. Is real GDP currently above or below potential GDP? Why? Draw the diagram showing this situation.

Chapter 15

Monetary Policy

The conversation took place in the early 1980s in a bar in Washington, D.C. At the time, the Fed was raising interest rates to double-digit levels in order to reduce the inflation rate—a difficult process that was later called the "Volcker Disinflation." Several economists were there, most notably James Tobin, the Nobel Prize–winning monetary economist from Yale University, and Paul Volcker, the chairman of the Federal Reserve Board. They were all relaxing, trying to let their hair down after a daylong economics conference. Professor Tobin was complaining about how the high interest rates were causing the economy to sink, and it was he who asked the key question: "Paul, why don't you just lower the interest rate?" Somewhat surprised that someone would ask such a sensitive question, Volcker shot back, "I do not set the interest rate. I set the money supply, and the market then sets the interest rate."

This barroom conversation of nearly 20 years ago says much about how monetary policy has changed over the years. First, we now know that the sky-high interest rates during the Volcker Disinflation worked in the sense that inflation did come down and has stayed down since then—a big difference from the Great Inflation of the 1970s. Second, the Fed has become much more transparent about its actions. Rather than being vague or evasive about its interest rate decisions, it candidly admits to setting the interest rate, and it announces its decision after each meeting, explaining why it made the decision in a written statement. Third, under the leadership of Volcker's successors—Alan Greenspan and Ben Bernanke—the Fed acts more aggressively and quickly than in the years before Volcker to head off inflation before it rises. Correspondingly, it also lowers interest rates more aggressively if a recession begins. In sum, there has been a revolution in the conduct of monetary policy, and textbooks such as this one have had to be revised to take this revolution into account. When the first edition of this text was being written in the early 1990s, the Federal

Reserve still did not publicly announce its interest rate decisions. It let the people in the markets go figure it out.

The purpose of this chapter is to explain how modern monetary policy works. We will first explain why central banks that are independent may bring about better economic performance than those without independence from the government. We will then examine the complex decisions faced by the independent monetary policymaker, and also consider some policy tools that such policymakers have at their disposal. Finally, we will look at how governments sometimes choose to restrict their monetary policymakers' freedom by choosing to tie the value of their currency to another country's currency.

WHY ARE CENTRAL BANKS INDEPENDENT?

The most important feature of a central bank, whether it is the Fed, the Bank of Japan, or the European Central Bank, is the degree of independence from the government that the law gives it.

Fed officials are appointed to long terms that may span several different presidents; the four-year term of the chair of the Fed does not necessarily coincide with the term of any president. For example, Paul Volcker served through most of the Reagan years, even though he was appointed by President Carter. Alan Greenspan, originally appointed by President Reagan, served throughout the eight years of the Clinton presidency. Therefore, like Supreme Court justices in the United States, Fed officials develop an independence from governmental influence.

central bank independence: a description of the legal authority of central banks to make decisions on monetary policy with little interference by the government in power.

What is the rationale for **central bank independence?** The main rationale, as explained below, is that an independent central bank can prevent the government in

William McChesney Martin 1951–1969 | **Arthur Burns 1969–1978** | **G. William Miller 1978–1979** | **Paul Volcker 1979–1987** | **Alan Greenspan 1987–2006** | **Ben Bernanke 2006–**

Fifty-five Years of Fed Chairs
There have been six chairs of the Federal Reserve Board during the past 55 years. Inflation was low during most of Martin's term but rose in the late 1960s and even more in the 1970s under Burns and Miller. Inflation fell dramatically under Volcker and remained low under Greenspan. Bernanke began his term with inflation pressures rising.

power from using monetary policy in ways that appear beneficial in the short run but that can harm the economy in the long run.

The "Gain Then Pain" Scenario

We showed in Chapter 13 that a shift in monetary policy toward a higher inflation target will temporarily raise real GDP above potential GDP, but that only inflation will be higher in the long run. Such a change in monetary policy would first entail a reduction in interest rates and would shift the aggregate demand (*AD*) curve to the right, as shown in Figure 1. Real GDP would rise along with investment, consumption, and net exports; unemployment would fall. In the short run, there would be no effect on inflation because of the slowness of firms to change their price decisions. The economic gain from the reduction in unemployment without an increase in inflation might help in a reelection campaign, or it might enable the government to push legislation for new programs through the political system. The economic pain—higher inflation in the long run, also shown in Figure 1—would not be seen until after the election or after the legislation is passed.

Thus, there is a natural tendency toward higher inflation in the political system. If the government in power had complete control over the decisions of the central bank, it could take actions to make the economy look good in the short run for political purposes and not worry that the economy might look bad in the long run. Removing the central bank from the direct control of the government reduces this politically induced bias toward higher inflation because it is then more difficult for the government to get the central bank to take such actions.

The Phillips Curve. Observe that during the period of time when the *IA* line is shifting up in the gain then pain scenario, real GDP is above potential GDP, and the inflation rate is higher than at the start of the scenario. For example, there is higher inflation and higher real GDP at the point labeled *MR* in Figure 1 than at the starting

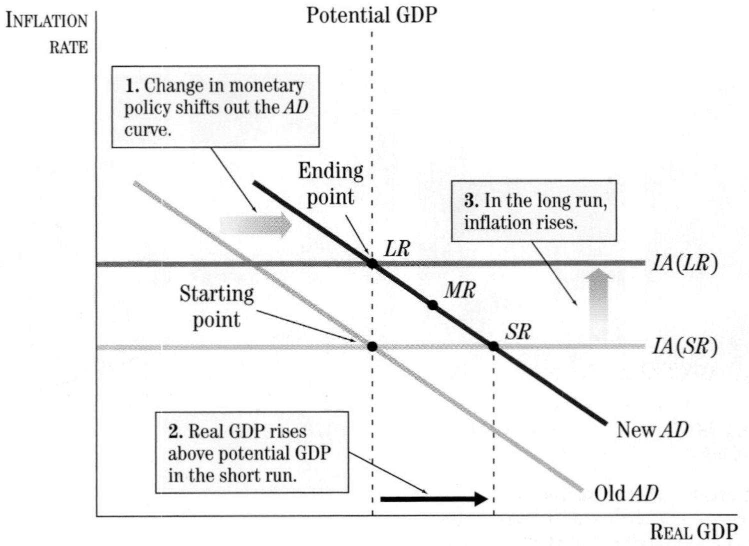

FIGURE 1
The "Gain Then Pain" Scenario
The Fed can temporarily stimulate the economy in the short run—real GDP rises above potential GDP. But soon inflation starts to rise. In the long run, the inflation rate is higher and real GDP is back to potential GDP.

point. And during this period, the unemployment rate is lower because the unemployment rate falls when real GDP rises. In sum, during the period of time between the initial shift of the *AD* curve and the end of the scenario, the unemployment rate is *down* and the inflation rate is *up*. Thus, there is a negative correlation between unemployment and inflation.

In fact, a negative correlation between unemployment and inflation has been observed for many years in the real world, because of such shifts in the *AD* curve. This negative correlation between inflation and unemployment is called the *Phillips curve,* after A. W. Phillips, the economist who first showed that such correlations existed in British data from 1861 to 1957. A replica of the original Phillips curve is shown in Figure 2.

The Phillips curve was used in the 1960s and 1970s to justify a monetary policy that included higher inflation. People argued that higher inflation would lead to lower unemployment. In other words, they argued that there was a long-run tradeoff between inflation and unemployment.

How did they use the Phillips curve to support this view? Look at the Phillips curve in Figure 2. You might think that a monetary policy that aimed for higher inflation could lead to a lower unemployment rate in the long run. That is what the curve seems to suggest. But the theory in the *AD-IA* diagram and, in particular, the gain then pain scenario shows that there is no such tradeoff in the long run. If monetary policy raised inflation, eventually real GDP would return to potential GDP, the unemployment rate would return to the natural rate, and we would be left with only higher inflation, not lower unemployment.

It has become a basic principle of modern macroeconomics—implied by the *AD-IA* diagram—that there is no long-run tradeoff between inflation and unemployment. The facts are consistent with the principle: In the 1950s and early 1960s, inflation was low; in the late 1960s and 1970s, inflation was high; and in the 1980s and 1990s, inflation was low again. But the average unemployment rate in all these periods was roughly the same, around 5 or 6 percent. Furthermore, the lower unemployment rate in the late 1990s did not result in much higher inflation. Any tendency for unemployment and inflation to be negatively correlated will disappear in the long run. This does not mean that there will be no short-run gain from a higher-inflation monetary policy. It does mean that there will be long-run pain.

Check your thinking about the implications of the gain then pain scenario for the relationship between unemployment and inflation.

In the short run, between the start and end of the scenario:

Inflation ↑
Real GDP > potential GDP
Unemployment rate < natural rate

So there is a negative correlation between inflation and unemployment, a Phillips curve.

In the long run:

Inflation ↑
Real GDP = potential GDP
Unemployment rate = natural rate

So there is no long-run tradeoff between inflation and unemployment.

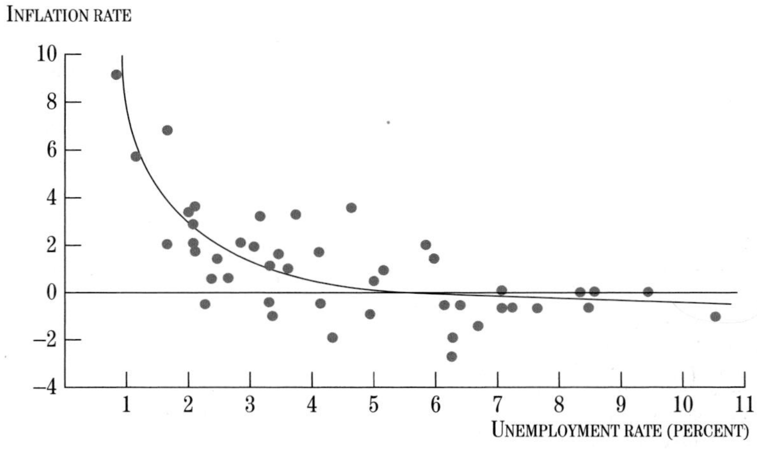

FIGURE 2
The Original Phillips Curve

A. W. Phillips first published this graph. Each point represents one year. The negatively sloped curve drawn through the scatter of points had enormous influence and led some to argue, mistakenly, that there was a long-run tradeoff between inflation and unemployment.

political business cycle: a business cycle caused by politicians' use of economic policy to overstimulate the economy just before an election.

The Political Business Cycle. The **political business cycle** is the tendency of governments to use economic policy to cause real GDP to rise and unemployment to fall just before an election and then let the economy slow down right after the election. Many economic and political studies have shown that an incumbent's chances of being reelected are increased greatly if the economy is doing well. After the election, inflation may rise and cause a bust, but that would be long before the next election.

Research in the 1970s by William Nordhaus of Yale University uncovered some evidence of a political business cycle in the United States. For example, the strong economy before the 1972 election may have been due to a monetary policy change that pushed real GDP above potential GDP. On the other hand, the U.S. economy was in a recession just before the 1980 and 1992 elections—the exact opposite of a political business cycle. Thus, the evidence for a political business cycle in the United States is no longer strong. In any case, political business cycles are harmful to the economy. Preventing political business cycles is another reason for having a central bank that has some independence from the politicians that are in power.

Time Inconsistency. The temptation to use monetary policy for short-run gain despite the long-run pain is difficult for governments to resist. Even governments whose sole aim is to improve the well-being of the average citizen will say that they want low inflation but then stimulate the economy in order to lower unemployment, even though they are fully aware of the inflationary consequences down the road.

time inconsistency: the situation in which policymakers have the incentive to announce one economic policy but then change that policy after citizens have acted on the initial, stated policy.

This situation is known as **time inconsistency** because governments say they want low inflation but are later inconsistent by following policies that lead to higher inflation. They act like a teacher who tells the class that there will be an exam to get the students to study, but then, on the day of the exam, announces that the exam is canceled. The students are happy to miss the exam, and the teacher does not have to grade it. Everyone appears better off in the short run.

However, just as the teacher who cancels the exam will lose credibility with future classes, a central bank that tries the inconsistent policy will lose credibility. People will assume that the central bank will actually raise inflation even if it says it is aiming for low inflation.

Potential Disadvantages of Central Bank Independence

Central bank independence is no guarantee against monetary policy mistakes, however, and it could even lead to more mistakes. In principle, an independent central bank could cause more inflation than a central bank under the control of the government. For example, those in charge of the central bank could—after they are appointed—succumb to arguments that high inflation is not so harmful after all. Or, at the other extreme, those in charge of the central bank thus become so focused on inflation that they are blinded to the effects of monetary policy on real GDP and employment and thus either cause a recession or make an existing recession deeper or longer. Therefore, a disadvantage of central bank independence is that it can be taken too far.

Whether independent or not, central banks need to be held *accountable* for their actions. If those in charge of the central bank do not perform their job well, it is appropriate that they not be reappointed. When the central bank of New Zealand was given greater independence in the 1980s, its accountability was formalized very explicitly: If the head of the central bank does not achieve low inflation goals agreed to in advance, the head is fired. But the central bank has independence in determining how to achieve these goals.

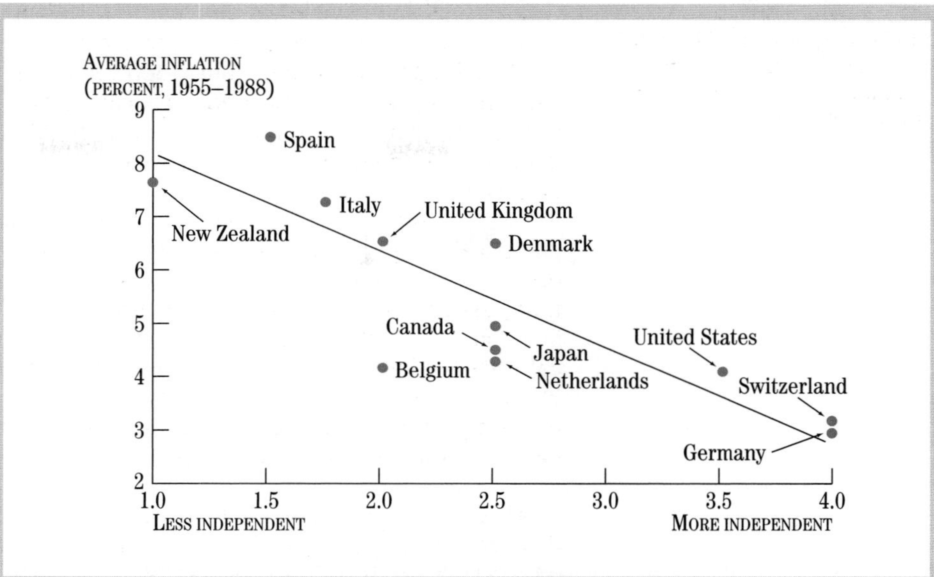

FIGURE 3
Central Bank Independence and Inflation
The scatter plot shows that the more independent a central bank is, the lower the average inflation rate. The independence of the central bank is calculated by studying the laws of each country, including the length of the term of office of the head of the central bank (a longer term means more independence) and restrictions on the central bank lending to the government.

Is there any evidence that independence has led to better inflation performance without any increase in the severity or frequency of recessions? If you look at Figure 3, you will see that central banks that have more independence have had lower inflation. This lower inflation has not been associated with more or longer recessions. Note that the graph shows New Zealand *before* the central bank was given more independence; since then, it has moved down and to the right, toward lower inflation.

REVIEW

- The gain then pain scenario shows that a central bank can lower unemployment below the natural unemployment rate in the short run, but by doing so it will raise inflation in the long run.
- The Phillips curve is a negative correlation between inflation and unemployment. However, there is no long-run tradeoff between inflation and unemployment.
- Central bank independence insulates the central bank from short-run political pressures to overstimulate the economy, which would ultimately raise inflation.
- Countries with more independent central banks have tended to have lower inflation than countries with less independent central banks.

ECONOMICS IN THE NEWS

Anatomy of a Hump

This article from *The Economist* magazine summarizes the latest economic research on the dramatic changes in monetary policy which led to the rise and fall of inflation—a graph of which looks a lot like a camel's hump.

What Caused the Great Inflation? And What Might Bring It Back?

From *The Economist*—March 8, 2007

If you were to draw the path of inflation in the typical big, rich economy over the past half century, your picture would look much like a dromedary's back: a low flat line in the 1960s; a knobbly hump of high and volatile price rises in the 1970s; dramatic disinflation in the 1980s; and low, stable inflation rates since. Japan and Germany, which were quicker to quell inflation, are well-known exceptions. But for the rest, the shape and timing of the Great Inflation bulge look remarkably similar.

This is a bulge that today's central bankers are anxious not to repeat. So it is no surprise that several governors from America's Federal Reserve are attending a conference on March 9th to discuss a new report on the Great Inflation, written by a weighty group of macroeconomists from academia and Wall Street. ("Understanding the Evolving Inflation Process" by Stephen Cecchetti, Peter Hooper, Bruce Kasman, Kermit Schoenholtz and Mark Watson.)

Most scholars agree on a basic explanation of the hump, placing both blame and credit squarely on central bankers. Consumer prices accelerated in the late 1960s because monetary policy was too loose. German and Japanese central bankers realised this earlier than others and tightened policy accordingly. Eventually others followed suit, and general disinflation began in the early 1980s. Since then inflation has stayed under control because central bankers are credibly committed to price stability and far better at their job.

Beyond that broad tale lie several debates about important details. Economists differ on how much non-monetary phenomena, such as closer trade integration, affect the inflation process. They also offer competing explanations for why central bankers botched things so badly a generation ago. One possibility is that they simply got the numbers wrong, consistently over-estimating their economies' speed limits. Others blame theoretical misjudgments, particularly the belief that higher inflation could buy a lasting drop in unemployment. A third approach emphasises political pressure. Inflation got out of hand because central banks were under the thumb of politicians who preferred rising prices to higher joblessness.

In this latest report the authors subject such controversies to painstaking cross-country forensics. They show that price stability across the G7 countries has been far more closely correlated than economic stability. Almost everywhere, inflation took off between 1969 and 1970. And every country, except Germany and Japan, failed to tame it until the mid-1980s. Output, however, was less tightly synchronised. Although recessions in many countries have become less wrenching in recent decades, output volatility began to ease in the mid-1980s in America, but not until the early 1990s in Britain, Canada and France.

What to make of these differences? The Great Inflation, because it was felt simultaneously across countries, must have had a common cause. This cannot have been the 1970s oil shocks, because consumer prices started accelerating long before the price of crude did. Easy money is the only remaining suspect. And although the Great Disinflation was also simultaneous across many countries, GDP growth settled down at very different times. This implies that better monetary policy cannot take full credit for today's less painful recessions.

The statistical magnifying glass also casts doubt on some favourite alibis for monetary misrule. Bad data, for example, do not get central bankers off the hook: revisions to statistics on trend growth and unemployment were not big enough to excuse the scale of inflation. Instead, monetary policy was simply too loose. The authors show that the central bankers of the 1970s failed to adhere to the modern "Taylor rule," a formula that links the appropriate level of short-term interest rates to the deviation of output from its trend and inflation from its target. Of course John Taylor, a Stanford economist, did not formalise his rule until 1993. But even without this guide, central banks should not have flunked the basic tenets of sound money.

Hawks v Camels

Neither the Taylor rule, inflation targets, nor any other bits of the modern central bankers' toolkit were necessary to end high inflation. But the scholars think these tools have helped to keep inflation down, which, in turn, has spawned a virtuous circle. When inflation is low and stable, a temporary uptick in consumer prices has far less impact on long-term price trends. The economists' model implies that less than 1% of a temporary price surge is translated into a permanent rise in inflation today, compared with 60% three decades ago.

That may give today's policymakers more leeway than their predecessors enjoyed. But since this wiggle-room is the legacy of low inflation volatility, it cannot be taken for granted. Were central bankers to lose their guard, inflation could soon resurge.

More worrying, the economists pour cold water on many a policymaker's favourite gauge of his own performance, namely the public's expectations of future inflation. Central bankers often cite low inflation expectations as evidence that monetary policy is appropriate. That may be a mistake. This paper argues that expectations were a good guide to future price pressure only when inflation was high. But now, if anything, inflation expectations are a backward-looking indicator, lagging measures of actual inflation.

All told, this statistical sleuthing suggests today's central bankers have little room for complacency. Inflation remains low and stable because policymakers are vigilant, not because any deep, structural changes insulate the modern economy from price pressure. If central bankers relax, higher, more volatile inflation could easily return. Rudyard Kipling's camel, remember, got its hump for being "most 'scrutiatingly idle."

RUNNING MONETARY POLICY

The previous section showed the inflationary harm caused by a monetary policy that intentionally pushes the aggregate demand curve to the right and raises real GDP above potential GDP. But even independent central bankers who have no intention of pursuing such an inflationary policy must still worry about shocks or unintentional shifts in the aggregate demand curve that would push real GDP away from potential GDP.

In fact, when the inflation rate is at the target inflation rate, monetary policy is a constant struggle to manage aggregate demand so as to keep real GDP near potential GDP, and thereby prevent inflation from veering away from its target. In this section, we illustrate this struggle, focusing on the operation of monetary policy in the United States.

Aggregate Demand: Just Right, Too Hot, or Too Cold?

First consider Figure 4, which illustrates the problem monetary policy faces in trying to keep real GDP near to potential GDP. There are three graphs in Figure 4, each illustrating a different situation.

The Goldilocks Economy: Just Right. In the middle graph, the aggregate demand curve intersects the inflation adjustment line at the point where real GDP equals potential GDP and the inflation rate is equal to the target inflation rate.

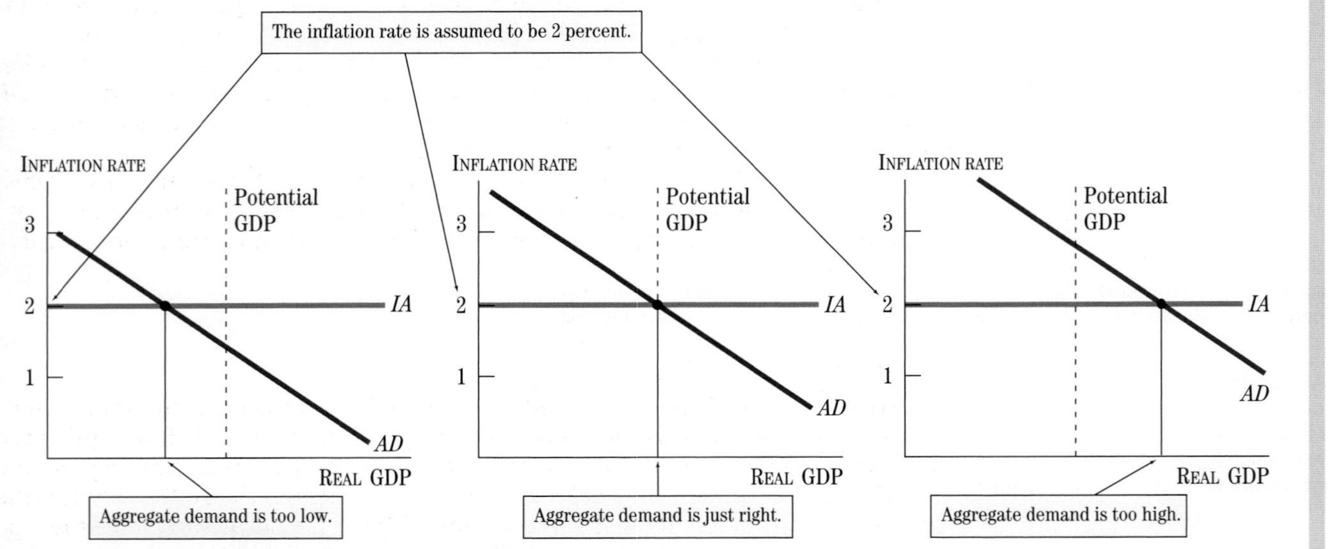

FIGURE 4
Aligning the Aggregate Demand Curve

The aggregate demand curve is lined up correctly when real GDP equals potential GDP and the inflation rate is on target, as in the graph in the middle. Otherwise, aggregate demand is too high, and the Fed must raise the interest rate; or aggregate demand is too low, and the Fed must lower the interest rate.

Because real GDP is equal to potential GDP, there is no tendency for inflation to rise or to fall. Thus, this graph represents an ideal point: The inflation rate is equal to the target inflation rate, and real GDP is equal to potential GDP. The aggregate demand curve is in the correct place, because it intersects the inflation adjustment line at the point where real GDP equals potential GDP *and* where the inflation rate equals the target inflation rate. Financial market analysts refer to this situation as a "Goldilocks economy": not too hot, not too cold, just right.

A Misalignment: Aggregate Demand Is Too High. In contrast to the middle panel in Figure 4, the other two panels represent misalignments of real GDP and potential GDP. In the right-hand panel, aggregate demand has increased too much—perhaps because of an expansionary shift in consumption, investment, or net exports. At this position, there are inflationary forces in place that will soon cause the inflation adjustment line to rise. Unlike the short-run position in Figure 1 (the gain then pain scenario, where the central bank has intentionally shifted monetary policy), the situation in the right-hand panel of Figure 4 is unintentional. The task of monetary policy is to try to prevent such misalignments, and to correct them once they occur.

How would the central bank correct this type of misalignment? It would raise the real interest rate above the level it would choose in the middle graph. The higher real interest rate would reduce aggregate demand and bring the *AD* curve back to a point where it intersected the inflation adjustment line at potential GDP. Financial market analysts would say that the Fed was trying to "cool off the economy" by raising the interest rate in this way.

Another Type of Misalignment: Aggregate Demand Is Too Low. The left panel of Figure 4 represents the opposite, but no less undesirable, type of misalignment of real GDP and potential GDP. In this case, aggregate demand has gotten too low—perhaps because of a contractionary shift in consumption, investment, or net exports. With real GDP less than potential GDP, the inflation adjustment line will soon fall below the target inflation rate. Moreover, with real GDP below potential GDP, unemployment has increased. Monetary policy should try to prevent or correct this type of misalignment, too.

To correct such a misalignment, the central bank would lower the real interest rate below the level it would choose in the middle graph. The lower real interest rate would increase consumption, investment, and net exports and bring the *AD* curve back to the right.

Monetary Policy in 2006

In early 2006, the Fed was concerned that real GDP was growing faster than potential GDP. The situation was like the one in the "Aggregate Demand Is Too High" graph of Figure 4. Inflation had begun to increase, and with real GDP rising above potential GDP, the Fed was concerned that inflation would rise further. The Fed's analysis is the same as that contained in the *AD-IA* diagram, which is not surprising, since the type of model used by the economists at the Fed is essentially the same as the one in that diagram.

Why had the aggregate demand curve shifted? One factor was the U.S. housing market. With home prices having risen rapidly in 2004 and 2005, people were feeling wealthier, and they had raised their consumption purchases, shifting up aggregate demand.

Because of this shift in the aggregate demand curve, the Fed felt that it would have to raise the nominal interest rate to raise the real interest rate and rein in aggregate demand to bring real GDP back into equality with potential GDP. In early 2006, the Fed raised the federal funds rate to 5.25 percent from 4.5 percent. The Federal Open Market committee then decided that 5.25 percent was enough for the time being, and it issued a statement explaining its decision. It then held the interest rate at 5.25 percent, and indeed the economy slowed as the aggregate demand curve shifted back.

The Inherent Uncertainty in Monetary Policy

This example also illustrates that, in practice, it is not easy for the Fed to keep real GDP near potential GDP by varying the interest rate. Although the Fed increased interest rates to rein in aggregate demand, there was concern that real GDP would not respond as quickly as in the past. At the time, it appeared that investment and consumption might be more responsive than the Fed thought they would be to the increase in the interest rate.

In general, there is a great deal of uncertainty about how long it takes for a change in the interest rate to affect aggregate demand. Other things affect aggregate demand too, and some of those things might work in the opposite direction to the change in interest rates.

Moreover, potential GDP is very difficult to estimate. Recall that potential GDP is determined by the underlying supply of labor, capital, and technological change. In many situations, central banks do not know for sure whether real GDP is or is not equal to potential GDP. Uncertainty about potential GDP is particularly high during periods when technology seems to be changing rapidly and the path of potential GDP is changing, as it was in 2006.

Increased Transparency and Predictability

Observe that in order to bring real GDP into alignment with potential GDP in this case study, the Fed reacted to the *gap*, or the *difference*, between real GDP and potential GDP. That is, it raised the real interest rate when real GDP rose above potential GDP. Similarly, if real GDP were to fall below potential GDP, as shown in the top left graph of Figure 4, the Fed would lower the real interest rate.

This type of interest rate reaction to the gap between real GDP and potential GDP is typical of the Fed and many other central banks. Just as responding promptly and by enough to an increase in inflation represents a good policy, so does moving the aggregate demand curve in a way that brings real GDP back into equality with potential GDP.

Central banks have endeavored to be more transparent and predictable in their responses to inflation and real GDP. Some have formally announced a target for inflation; others, such as the Fed, have been more informal about their inflation target. The increased predictability can be described using the concept of a monetary policy rule, as we discussed in Chapter 12. In fact, it is possible to combine the reaction to inflation and the reaction to the gap into one monetary policy rule, and thereby obtain a more accurate description of central bank behavior. Remember that a monetary policy rule is a description of a central bank's behavior in the same sense that a microeconomic demand curve is a description of a person's consumption behavior. Just as a person's purchase decisions may depend on two variables, (1) price and (2) income, so too the central bank's real interest rate decisions may depend on two variables, (1) the inflation rate and (2) the gap between real GDP and potential GDP.

TABLE 1
Real Interest Rate Reaction to Inflation and to the Gap Between Real GDP and Potential GDP (Compare with Table 1 in Chapter 12 on page 304.)

		Percent Gap Between Real GDP and Potential GDP		
		−2	*0*	*2*
Inflation Rate (percent)	0	0	1	2
	2	1	2	3
	4	2	3	4
	6	3	4	5
	8	4	5	6

(The entries in the shaded area show the real interest rate for each inflation rate and gap between real GDP and potential GDP.)

Table 1 shows a numerical example of this type of policy rule. On the left is the inflation rate. On the top is the gap between real GDP and potential GDP. The entries in the shaded part of the table show the real interest rate. For example, the blue entry shows that when inflation is 2 percent and real GDP is equal to potential GDP (the percent gap between real GDP and potential GDP is zero), the real interest rate is 2 percent. When inflation rises to 4 percent, the real interest rate rises to 3 percent. Each column of Table 1 tells the same story: When inflation rises, the central bank raises the real interest rate. Note that in order to raise the real interest rate, the nominal interest rate has to rise by more than inflation rises.

Now observe in Table 1 that the central bank's response also depends on what happens to real GDP. When real GDP rises above potential GDP—and the gap increases—the central bank raises the real interest rate. And when real GDP falls below potential GDP, the central bank lowers the real interest rate.

The monetary policy rule in Table 1 is a more accurate description of monetary policy than the rule in Chapter 12 Table 1 because central banks do react to the gap between real GDP and potential GDP, as the discussion of Fed policy makes clear. Hence, financial market analysts use monetary policy rules like this one to predict interest rate changes in many different countries. The policy rule in Table 1 above is called the Taylor rule after John B. Taylor of Stanford University.

REVIEW

- Monetary policy is a constant struggle to keep aggregate demand from getting too high or too low. The Fed carries out this policy by trying to keep the aggregate demand curve in a position where real GDP is equal to potential GDP and the inflation rate is equal to the target inflation rate.
- The Fed and other central banks increase the real interest rate when real GDP grows above potential GDP and lower the real interest rate when real GDP falls below potential GDP.
- In early 2006, the Fed increased the real interest rate because it thought real GDP was greater than potential GDP.
- The response of the real interest rate to the gap between real GDP and potential GDP can be combined with the response to inflation in order to get a monetary policy rule that accurately describes central bank behavior.

MONEY AND OTHER INSTRUMENTS OF MONETARY POLICY

Look back for a quick review: Chapter 10, page 254, defines open market operations and shows how the Fed uses them to make changes in the supply of bank reserves. Chapter 12, page 304, shows how the Fed increases or decreases the federal funds rate through such changes in the supply of bank reserves.

So far, we have focused entirely on the Fed's decisions about the interest rate, and in particular about the overnight interest rate called the federal funds rate. Recall from Chapter 12 that the Fed changes the overnight interest rate by increasing or decreasing the supply of bank reserves in the overnight market where the federal funds rate is determined. Recall that the federal funds rate is the interest rate on overnight loans of reserves between banks. The Fed changes the supply of bank reserves by *open market operations,* which, as defined in Chapter 10, are purchases or sales of bonds by the Fed. Purchases of bonds increase the supply of bank reserves and thus lower the overnight interest rate. Sales of bonds decrease the supply of bank reserves and thus raise the overnight interest rate.

The overnight interest rate is now the main instrument of monetary policy at central banks around the world, but it is not the only instrument. The money supply, the discount rate, and reserve requirements are other potential instruments of policy. In this section we examine how the changes in the interest rate have important implications for the amount of money that the Fed supplies. We also define the discount rate and show how it and reserve requirements fit into monetary policy decisions.

Money Demand, the Interest Rate, and the Money Supply

money demand: a relationship between the nominal interest rate and the quantity of money that people are willing to hold at any given nominal interest rate.

The quantity of money in the economy is closely related to the interest rate decisions of the central bank. To show this, we first look at the demand for money and show that it depends on the nominal interest rate.

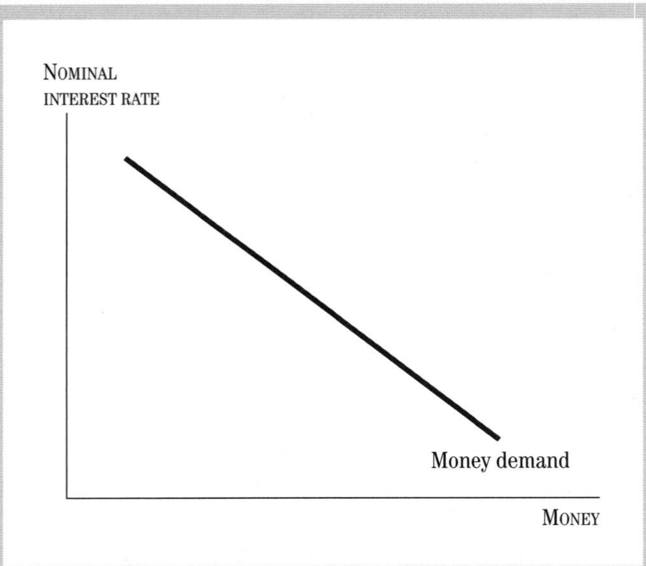

FIGURE 5
The Demand for Money
The interest rate is the opportunity cost of holding money. A higher interest rate on Treasury bills or other interest-bearing assets raises the opportunity cost of holding money and lowers the quantity of money demanded.

Money Demand. **Money demand** is defined as a relationship between the interest rate and the quantity of money people are willing to hold at any given interest rate. As shown in Figure 5, the amount of money demanded is negatively related to the nominal interest rate. One reason people hold money is to carry out transactions: to buy and sell goods and services. People will hold less money if the nominal interest rate is high. That is, a higher interest rate reduces the amount of money people want to carry around in their wallets or hold in their checking accounts. Conversely, a lower nominal interest rate will increase the amount of money people want to hold. Why is money demand negatively related to the nominal interest rate?

Money (currency plus checking deposits) is only part of the wealth of most individuals. People also hold some of their wealth in financial assets that pay interest. For example, some people have time deposits at banks. Others hold securities, such as Treasury bills. If you bought 3-month Treasury bills in January 2006, they paid 4.9 percent interest. Holding money is different from holding time deposits or Treasury bills because currency does not pay interest and checking deposits pay low, or no, interest. If you hold all your money in the form of cash in your wallet, clearly you do not earn any interest. Thus, an individual's decision to hold money is best viewed as an alternative to holding some other financial asset, such as a Treasury bill. If you hold money, you get little or no interest; if you hold one of the alternatives, you earn interest.

The interest rate on the vertical axis in Figure 5 is the average nominal interest rate on these other interest-bearing assets that people hold as alternatives to money. Now, if the interest rate on these alternatives rises, people want to put more funds in the alternatives and hold less as money. If they hold the funds as currency, they get no interest on the funds. If they hold the funds in a checking account, they may get a small amount of interest, but certainly less than they would get from other financial assets. There is a lower quantity of money demanded at higher interest rates because putting the funds in interest-bearing assets becomes more attractive compared to keeping the funds in a wallet.

The interest rate on the alternatives to holding money is the *opportunity cost* of holding money. When the opportunity cost increases, people hold less money. When the opportunity cost decreases, people hold more money.

Figure 5 represents money demand in the economy as a whole. The curve is obtained by adding up the money demanded by all the individuals in the economy at each interest rate. The money held by businesses—in cash registers or in checking accounts—should also be added in.

The Interest Rate and the Quantity of Money. Using the money demand curve, it is possible to find the quantity of money in the economy that will be associated with any given nominal interest rate decision by the Fed. First, note that there is a very close correlation between the federal funds rate set by the Fed and interest rates on Treasury bills and other interest-bearing assets that people can hold as an alternative to holding money. This close correlation is shown in Figure 6. Thus, when the Fed changes the federal funds rate, other interest rates tend to change in the same direction.

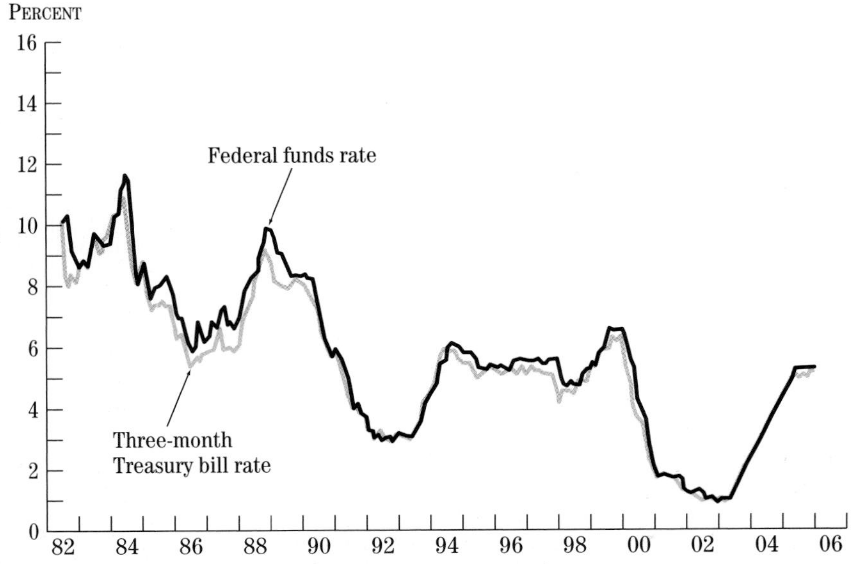

FIGURE 6
Short-Term Interest Rates
The federal funds rate is the interest rate the Fed sets. Other short-term interest rates, such as the three-month Treasury bill rate, move up and down with the federal funds rate. Note the double-digit interest rates back during the Volcker Disinflation.

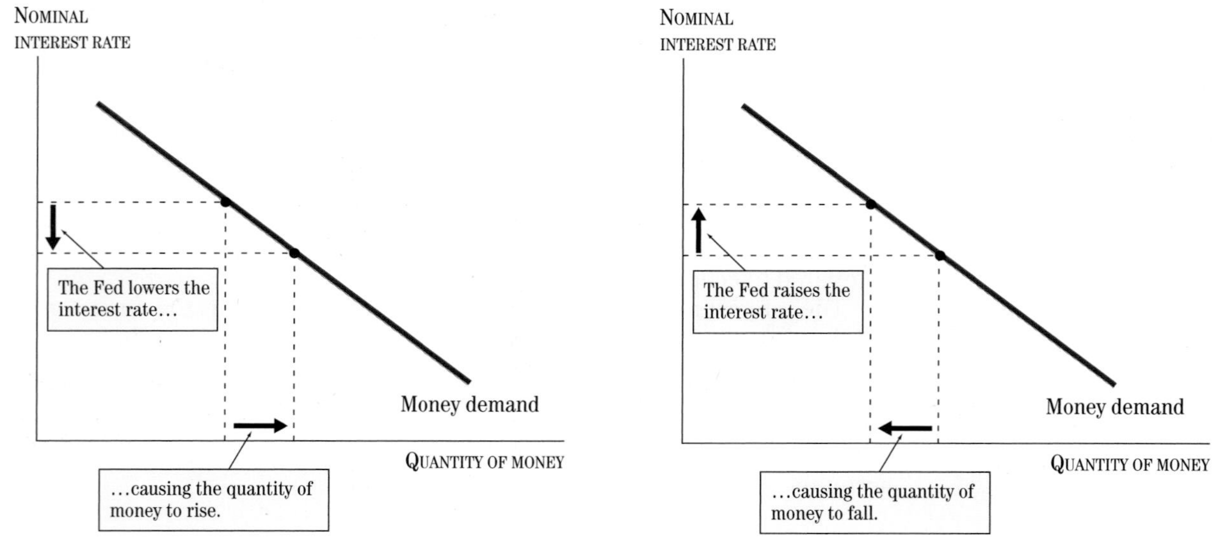

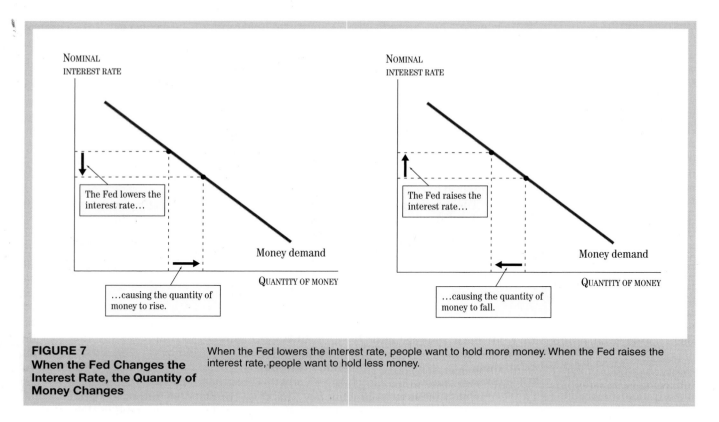

FIGURE 7
When the Fed Changes the Interest Rate, the Quantity of Money Changes

When the Fed lowers the interest rate, people want to hold more money. When the Fed raises the interest rate, people want to hold less money.

Now, for any given interest rate, one can use the money demand curve to find the quantity of money in the economy. This is illustrated in Figure 7. If the Fed lowers the federal funds rate, then the lower interest rate increases the quantity of money demanded and, as shown in the left panel, the quantity of money in the economy rises. Or, if the Fed raises the interest rate, the quantity of money in the economy decreases, as shown in the graph on the right of Figure 7.

What About Focusing on the Money Supply? One question you might ask about Figure 7 is, "Where is the money supply?" Recall from Chapter 10 that the Fed controls the quantity of money supplied in the economy. Does the quantity of money supplied equal the quantity of money demanded? Yes, of course it does. The demand and supply of money is no different from any other demand and supply model. As monetary policy now works in the United States and most other countries, the central bank automatically adjusts the money supply so that it intersects the money demand curve at the nominal interest rate chosen by the central bank. For example, as the interest rate falls in the left graph of Figure 7, the money supply is automatically increased so that the intersection of money demand and money supply moves as shown. Figure 8 shows how the money supply shifts in both cases shown in Figure 7.

Such movements in the money supply occur as the Fed makes open market purchases or sales to change the interest rate. When the Fed decides to lower the interest rate, for example, it must increase reserves. And we know from Chapter 10 that when the Fed increases reserves, the money supply increases. Thus, the increase in the money supply in the left graph of Figure 8 is exactly what the analysis in Chapter 10 tells us will happen when the central bank increases reserves. Whether you focus on the interest rate or the money supply, the story is the same.

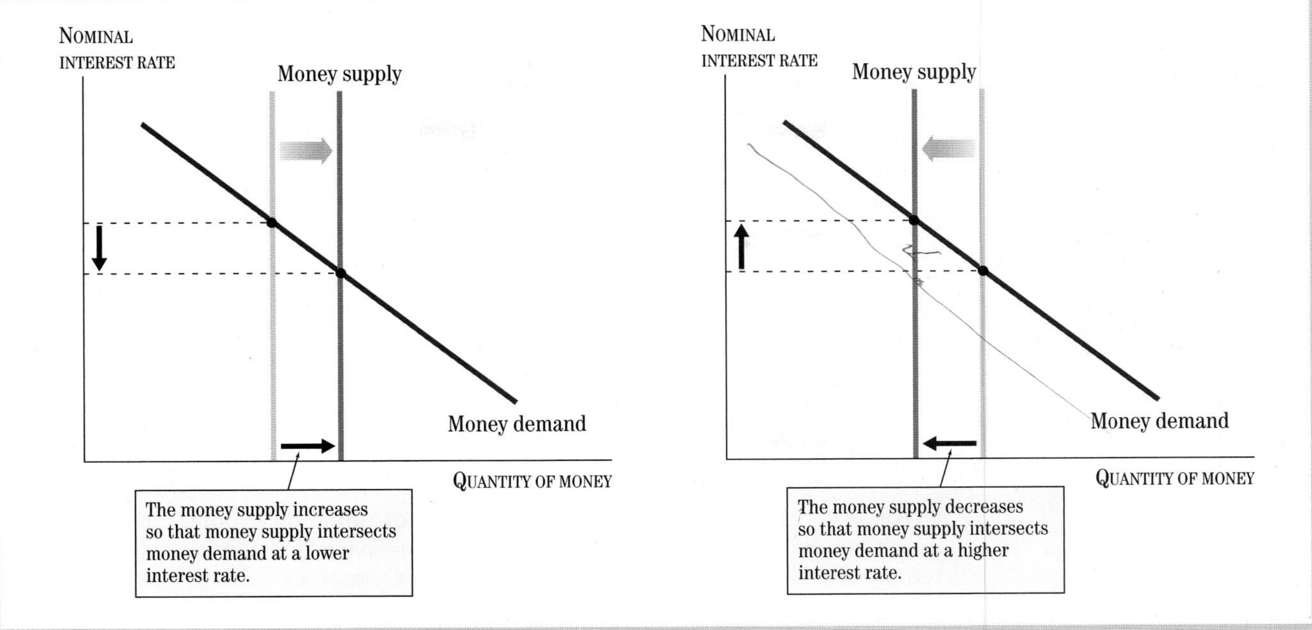
NOMINAL INTEREST RATE
Money supply
Money demand
QUANTITY OF MONEY
The money supply increases so that money supply intersects money demand at a lower interest rate.
NOMINAL INTEREST RATE
Money supply
Money demand
QUANTITY OF MONEY
The money supply decreases so that money supply intersects money demand at a higher interest rate.

FIGURE 8
Money Supply Changes Implied by Interest Rate Changes

When the Fed decides to lower or raise the interest rate, the money supply must change.

Then why doesn't the Fed simply focus on the money supply? Because the money demand curve tends to shift around a lot; if the Fed simply kept the money supply constant, there would be fluctuations in the interest rate as money demand shifted back and forth. These fluctuations in the interest rate would cause fluctuations in real GDP—perhaps large enough to cause a recession—and thus would not be good policy.

Some economists, such as Milton Friedman, have argued that the Fed should simply hold the growth of the money supply constant, a policy that is called a *constant money growth rule.* However, central banks now feel that money demand shifts around too much for a constant money growth rule to work well. Nevertheless, an inflationary monetary policy—such as the gain then pain scenario—would mean that there would be an increase in money growth. Money growth would increase as the Fed lowered the interest rate. As we saw in Chapter 10, throughout history higher money growth has been associated with higher inflation.

Those who object to the constant money growth rule do not object to keeping inflation low. They feel that a constant money growth rule will lead to more and larger fluctuations in real GDP and inflation than other policies would. That is why they recommend that the Fed and other central banks focus more on interest rates.

Two Other Instruments of Monetary Policy

In addition to the federal funds rate and the money supply, two other instruments are sometimes used in conducting monetary policy.

discount rate: the interest rate that the Fed charges commercial banks when they borrow from the Fed.

The Discount Rate. The **discount rate** is the rate the Fed charges commercial banks when they borrow from the Fed. To understand why commercial banks borrow from the Fed, we must consider another role of central banks: the role of *lender of last* *resort.* During recessions and depressions in the nineteenth and early twentieth centuries, there were frequently "runs" on banks, in which people scrambled to withdraw their deposits for fear that the bank was going under. Rumors caused runs even on sound banks. By agreeing to lend to banks if they experience a run, the Fed can bolster confidence in the bank. The mere existence of a central bank that is willing to lend reduces the chances of runs by raising confidence. That is why the Fed stands ready to make loans to banks.

However, if the discount rate fell much below the federal funds rate, then banks would save on interest costs by borrowing from the Fed rather than borrowing in the federal funds market. Thus, the Fed must make sure that the discount rate does not depart too much from the federal funds rate. When the Fed changes the federal funds rate, it frequently changes the discount rate as well so that the two rates stay near each other. The federal funds rate is the main focus of monetary decisions. The discount rate is usually adjusted when the federal funds rate changes. In August 2007, the Fed lowered the discount rate in response to the financial market turmoil related to sub-prime mortgages. This action came before the Fed made a decision to cut the federal funds rate.

Reserve Requirements. Another tool of monetary policy is the reserve requirement. If the Fed decreases the required reserve ratio—that is, decreases reserve requirements—then the banks will demand fewer reserves and the federal funds rate will fall.

In practice, however, the Fed very rarely changes reserve requirements, and when it does so, its aim is not to change the federal funds rate, because open market operations are sufficient to achieve any desired change in that rate. Sometimes the Fed changes reserve requirements in order to affect the profits of banks. For example, in 1990, the Fed lowered reserve requirements in order to raise banks' profits and thereby reduce the chance that some banks would become insolvent during the 1990–1991 recession. Banks do not receive interest on reserves; thus, lower reserve requirements mean that they can make more profits by making more interest-earning loans.

In 1990, when the Fed lowered reserve requirements, it used open market sales to reduce the supply of reserves. This action exactly offset the effect of the reserve requirement change on the interest rate.

REVIEW

- The Fed affects the short-term nominal interest rate by changing reserves through open market operations.
- Money demand depends negatively on the nominal interest rate.
- When the Fed changes the interest rate, the quantity of money changes.
- Changes in the quantity of money supplied automatically match these changes. Changes in reserves mean changes in the money supply.
- The Fed also has two other instruments: the discount rate and reserve requirements. But the main instrument of monetary policy is the federal funds rate.

THE EXCHANGE RATE AND MONETARY POLICY

The exchange rate is another important economic variable that is influenced by monetary policy. When the Fed increases the interest rate, the dollar tends to appreciate in value. The reason is that the higher U.S. interest rate makes dollar assets

Quick review: The *exchange rate* is the rate at which one country's currency is exchanged for another country's currency. For example, one U.S. dollar could be exchanged for 10.80 Mexican pesos on December 31, 2006. An *appreciation* of the dollar—say, from 11 to 12 pesos—means that it can be exchanged for more pesos.

flexible exchange rate policy: a policy in which exchange rates are determined in foreign exchange markets and governments do not agree to fix them.

fixed exchange rate policy: a policy in which a country maintains a fixed value of its currency in terms of other currencies.

more attractive, and this bids up the price of dollars. Conversely, when the Fed lowers the interest rate, the dollar depreciates.

These changes in the exchange rate affect net exports. For example, an appreciation of the dollar makes imported goods more attractive to Americans and makes U.S. exports less attractive to foreigners. Thus, imports rise and exports fall, causing net exports (exports minus imports) to decline. The decline in net exports in turn causes real GDP to decline. Such changes in exchange rates are an essential part of the impact of monetary policy in the economic fluctuations model explained in Chapters 12 and 13 because the United States follows a **flexible exchange rate policy,** allowing the exchange rate to fluctuate in this way.

But what if the Fed did not want the exchange rate to change? Or what if the U.S. government and another country, such as Japan, agreed to fix the exchange rate? Such a policy is called a **fixed exchange rate policy.** How would that affect monetary policy?

Such questions are not simply hypothetical. Throughout history, governments have decided from time to time to adopt fixed exchange rate policies. The United States and most developed countries were part of a fixed exchange rate system—called the Bretton Woods system—from the end of World War II until the early 1970s. Most recently, twelve countries in Europe have permanently fixed their exchange rates by forming a monetary union with a single currency, the euro. Until recently, Argentina fixed its exchange rate to the U.S. dollar. Other countries, like Ecuador, have adopted the U.S. dollar as their currency, and some people have suggested that the other countries in the Western Hemisphere join with the United States in a permanently fixed exchange rate system, with countries in Asia joining a fixed exchange rate system with Japan. There would then be three large fixed exchange rate systems in the world—centered around the dollar, the euro, and the yen. Some have even imagined a whole world with fixed exchange rates—with the dollar, the yen, and the

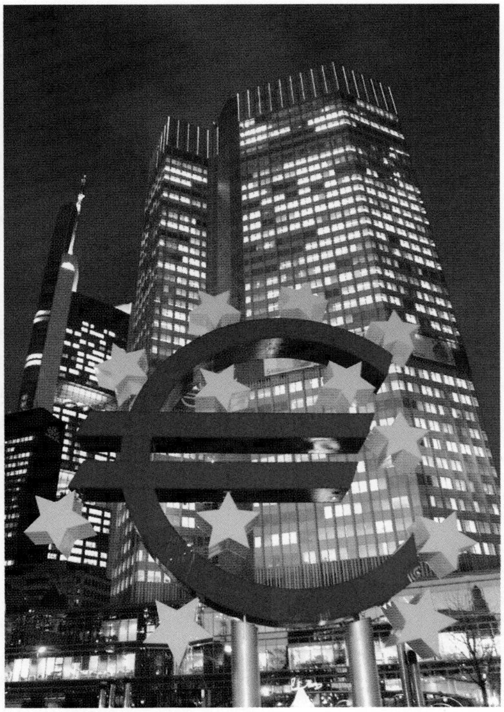

A Single European Currency and a Single Central Bank
The euro is the single currency used in the European Monetary Union. On January 1, 2002, euro notes and coins came into circulation in twelve European countries, replacing the national currencies of each of the countries, including Germany, where the European Central Bank (shown at right) is located. The seven banknote denominations have a common design in all the countries, while the eight coin denominations have different national designs on one side and a common European design on the other. Ten new member states joined the European Union in May 2004, and they are expected to introduce the euro in their countries as soon as they have met the conditions set out by the Treaty on European Union.

euro all fixed together. Thus, it is important to look at the implications of a fixed exchange rate for monetary policy, as we do in this section, not only to understand what is happening in different countries today, but also to understand proposals that would affect the United States and the whole world in the future.

The Effects of a Fixed Exchange Rate System on Monetary Policy

Suppose the United States decided to set up or join a fixed exchange rate system with Japan. Suppose also that after the United States joins the system, inflation starts to rise in the United States, and monetary policymakers want to raise the interest rate. Such an increase in the interest rate will tend to raise the value of the dollar relative to the Japanese currency. But if the dollar were fixed in value, as it would be with a fixed exchange rate policy, such a rise in the dollar would not be possible. Hence, if exchange rates were fixed, the Fed could not raise the interest rate in the United States relative to the interest rate in Japan. The fixed exchange rate would impose a serious restriction on U.S. monetary policy because interest rates in the United States could not be changed.

In general, if two countries have a fixed exchange rate and people are free to move funds back and forth between the two countries, then the interest rates in the two countries must move together. If, in the example of the United States and Japan, the Fed wanted to raise interest rates, then the Bank of Japan would have to raise interest rates by the same amount. But that might not be in the best interests of Japan, especially if the Japanese economy was in a recession. Like the two steering wheels of a driver's training car, which move in tandem, interest rates in any two countries with a fixed exchange rate must move together.

The connection between interest rates in different countries is very visible to people in smaller countries that fix their currencies to the dollar, as Argentina painfully found out in 2001 and 2002. In 1991, Argentina chose to fix the value of the peso to the dollar, thus forcing its central bank to give up an independent monetary policy. When interest rates in the United States fell in the mid-1990s, this was beneficial to Argentina, as its interest rates fell as well. However, when U.S. rates rose very rapidly in the year 2000 as the Fed battled inflation, Argentina was forced to raise its interest rates as well, pushing the weakened economy into a recession that lasted almost four years.

Ever since the twelve countries in the European Monetary Union permanently fixed their exchange rates with each other, there has effectively been only one overnight interest rate in Europe. The central banks of Germany, France, Italy, Spain, and other countries in the European Monetary Union have had to band together into a new European Central Bank. The overnight interest rates in France, Germany, Italy, and the other countries move together, so there is really only one interest rate to decide about. With the European Monetary Union, there cannot be separate monetary policies in Germany and in France. They have only one monetary policy. If real GDP fell below potential GDP in France and remained equal to potential GDP in all the other countries, then a reduction in the interest rate by the European Central Bank, which would be right for France, would be wrong for Europe as a whole, so it probably would not occur. In such a circumstance it might be necessary to use countercyclical *fiscal* policy in France—spending increases or tax cuts, as described in the previous chapter—because monetary policy would not be changed.

A real-life example of the effect of fixed exchange rates on monetary policy arose in Britain in 1992. At that time, interest rates were rising in Germany because the German inflation rate was rising. But policymakers in Britain, which was facing hard economic times, did not want British interest rates to rise. The British faced a decision: Either they could raise their interest rates to keep them near Germany's, or they could let their interest rates fall below Germany's. In the latter case, their exchange rate would depreciate. For much of 1991 and 1992, the British kept their exchange rate stable, and that required a rise in British interest rates. But by the end of 1992, increasingly poor economic conditions in Britain forced the British to give up the fixed exchange rate. Then interest rates in Britain could fall.

Interventions in the Exchange Market

Why wasn't it possible for the British government to go into the exchange market and buy and sell foreign exchange and thereby prevent these changes in the exchange rate? For example, if the British government purchases British pounds, this increases the demand for pounds and thereby raises the pound exchange rate. Thus, if the high interest rates in Germany were reducing the value of the British pound, why couldn't the British government buy pounds to offset these pressures? Such buying and selling of foreign currency by governments is called **exchange market intervention.** Such intervention does occur, and it can affect the exchange rate for short periods of time. However, the world currency markets are so huge and fast-moving that even governments do not have the funds to affect the exchange rate for long by buying and selling foreign exchange.

exchange market intervention: purchases and sales of foreign currency by a government in exchange markets with the intention to affect the exchange rate.

If there is a substantial interest rate advantage in favor of one currency, funds will flow into that currency, driving up its value; exchange market intervention by governments cannot do much about this. Empirical studies have shown that exchange market intervention—if it is not matched by a change in interest rates by the central bank—can have only small effects on the exchange rate.

Another possibility is to prevent funds from flowing between the countries. If there were a law restricting the flow of funds into and out of a country, then that country could have both a fixed exchange rate and a separate interest rate policy. Such controls on the flow of capital were discussed intensely after the collapse of fixed exchange rates in Asia in 1997, and Malaysia did institute some restrictions on financial capital flows. However, such restrictions have disadvantages. They are difficult to enforce, and they can reduce the amount of foreign capital a country needs for development.

Why Fixed Exchange Rates?

If fixed exchange rates lead to the loss of a separate monetary policy, then why do countries form fixed exchange rate systems? One reason to adopt a fixed exchange rate is that exchange rate volatility can interfere with trade. This is certainly one of the reasons the European countries set up the European Monetary Union. Firms may not develop long-term relationships and contacts with other countries if they are worried about big changes in the exchange rate.

Another, perhaps more important, reason is that some countries have had a history of very poor monetary policies. For example, Italy had very high inflation before it decided to join with the other countries of Europe in a monetary union. And Argentina had many years of hyperinflation before it fixed its exchange rate with the United States and gave up having its own monetary policy.

The goal of fixing the exchange rate in these cases is to adopt the good monetary policy of a country whose central bank has a history of good policy: the Fed in the case of Argentina, and the central banks of Germany and France in the case of Italy. In these cases, the benefits of a fixed exchange rate system may outweigh the loss of a separate monetary policy. However, the evidence is mixed. In the case of Italy, the policy seems to have worked: Inflation has been in single digits for many years.

However, in Argentina, where the policy seemed to work well initially in bringing inflation down, restricting the hand of monetary policymakers seemed to make it very tough for the country to recover from its recession of the late 1990s.

REVIEW

- Interest rates must move together in countries with fixed exchange rates and with a free flow of funds between the countries.
- With a fixed exchange rate, there can be no separate monetary policy for each country.
- By permanently fixing exchange rates, a country can adopt the monetary policy of another country.

CONCLUSION

Monetary policymaking is a powerful, but difficult, job. Central bankers like to say that the job is like driving a car by looking only through the rear-view mirror. They have to take actions that greatly affect the economy without knowing where the economy is going, only where it has been.

In this chapter, we have seen exactly why the job is difficult. It is difficult to resist political pressure to raise inflation for short-term benefits at the expense of long-term costs. And it is difficult to keep aggregate demand in line with potential GDP in a world where potential GDP is hard to estimate and policy effects on aggregate demand are uncertain.

We have also learned that while monetary policy has a powerful effect, it cannot do everything. It cannot lower unemployment permanently, and trying to do so will only raise inflation. And a country cannot have both a fixed exchange rate and the ability to adjust interest rates to control inflation and prevent recessions.

All these ideas are useful for understanding the frequent headlines and news stories about the Fed. And they help take some of the mystique out of what many people feel is the most mysterious institution in the world.

KEY POINTS

1. Central bank independence is a way to avoid political business cycles and the temptation to raise inflation for short-term gain.
2. The gain then pain scenario illustrates that a monetary policy shift to high inflation has short-run benefits but long-run costs.
3. An important task of monetary policy is to manage aggregate demand so that real GDP equals potential GDP.
4. In early 2000, the Fed raised the real interest rate to reduce aggregate demand. In 2001 and 2002, it lowered the real interest rate to increase aggregate demand in the midst of a recession.
5. A good monetary policy rule is responsive to real GDP as well as to inflation.
6. The demand for money is negatively related to the interest rate.
7. The Fed changes the quantity of money when it changes the interest rate.
8. Reserve requirements are rarely changed. The Fed can also increase the money supply by lowering the discount rate. This is typically, but not always, done in conjunction with lowering the federal funds rate.
9. Fixed exchange rates restrict monetary policy.

KEY TERMS

central bank independence
political business cycle
time inconsistency
money demand
discount rate
flexible exchange rate policy
fixed exchange rate policy
exchange market intervention

QUESTIONS FOR REVIEW

1. What are the advantages and disadvantages of central bank independence?
2. What is an example of a political business cycle?
3. Why would the Fed raise real interest rates if real GDP were above potential GDP?
4. Why is it important that real GDP be close to potential GDP?
5. What is the Phillips curve?
6. Why is the demand for money inversely related to the interest rate?
7. What is the opportunity cost of holding money?
8. Why is there a loss of monetary policy independence with fixed exchange rates?
9. Why would a country adopt a fixed exchange rate policy?

PROBLEMS

1. Why is an independent central bank more likely to put emphasis on price stability rather than on keeping unemployment low, compared to a central bank that is not independent?
2. The original Federal Reserve Act of 1913 allowed the secretary of the Treasury to be a member of the Federal Reserve Board, but a later amendment prohibited this. How would allowing the secretary of the Treasury to be a member affect the conduct of monetary policy?
3. What is the discount rate? How does it differ from the federal funds rate? Describe how the Fed affects each of these interest rates.
4. Banks can borrow from each other on the federal funds market or borrow from the Fed. Banks borrow far more on the federal funds market than from the Fed. You can borrow from your friends or from your parents. Who are you more likely to borrow from? Why do you think banks prefer to borrow from each other?
5. During the early 1990s in Japan, there was deflation and real GDP was below potential GDP. Draw a diagram showing the situation in Japan. Suppose the Japanese central bank decided that it had to reinflate and set a target inflation rate of 2 percent. How would it accomplish this? Show the short-run, medium-run, and long-run effects.
6. Using the aggregate demand curve and the inflation adjustment line, show what the Fed should do if real GDP is below potential GDP and the current inflation rate is equal to the target inflation rate, which is the ideal inflation rate from the Fed's perspective.
7. The Taylor Rule states that the central bank should set the short-term nominal interest rate (i) based on the inflation gap [the difference between inflation (π) and desired inflation (π^*)] and the output gap [the percentage difference between real GDP (Y) and potential GDP (Y^*)]. An example of a Taylor Rule would be the formula

$$i - \pi = 1.5 + .5\,(\pi - \pi^*) + .5\left(\frac{Y - Y^*}{Y^*}\right)$$

The term on the left-hand side is the real interest rate. Consider the following table:

	Base Scenario	Scenario B	Scenario C
Inflation rate (π), %	2.0	4.0	2.0
Target inflation rate (π^*), %	2.0	2.0	2.0
Output gap, %	0.0	0.0	2.0
Real interest rate			
Nominal interest rate			

a. Fill in the real and nominal interests rates chosen by the policymaker in the base scenario.

b. How does scenario B differ from the base scenario in terms of the inflation and output gaps? Calculate the real interest rate. Has the real interest rate moved in the direction that would move the inflation rate toward its target?

c. How does scenario C differ from the base scenario in terms of the inflation and output gaps? Calculate the real interest rate. Has the real interest rate moved in the direction that would move output toward the potential level?

d. Suppose a new chair of the central bank is appointed and she switches to a new policy rule of the form given below. Recalculate the real and nominal interest rates for the three scenarios. What has been the effect of the change in weights?

$$i - \pi = 1.5 + .75\,(\pi - \pi^*) + .25\left(\frac{Y - Y^*}{Y^*}\right)$$

8. Suppose there are two countries, identical except for the fact that the central bank of one country lets interest rates rise sharply when real GDP rises above potential GDP and the other does not. Draw the aggregate demand curve for each country. What are the benefits and drawbacks of each country's policy?

9. Sweden and the United Kingdom chose not to join the European Monetary Union (EMU). Explain what a decision to join the EMU would imply for the monetary policymaking abilities of the central banks of these two countries.

10. Explain why restricting flows of funds into or out of a country can give that country's central bank the ability to conduct monetary policy even with a fixed exchange rate. What are some of the disadvantages of such a restriction?

Financial Markets

Most noneconomists do not think of the field of economics as being particularly glamorous or exciting. For them, the exception to this rule seems to be financial markets. People always seem to want to know more about what is likely to happen next in the stock market, and about what stocks they should buy or sell. An economist who is able to speak authoritatively on such topics is much more likely to be in demand at a cocktail party than one whose interests lie in other areas of economic research. You too will soon encounter this feeling. The next time you have a gathering of your extended family, tell people that you intend to major in economics, then see what topics people want to engage you in conversation about. It is very likely that financial markets will be high on the list.

So what is it about financial markets that attracts so much interest and attention? One obvious answer is that financial markets touch the lives of more people than any other market except the labor market. Parents saving for their children's college education, a young couple saving up money for a down payment on a home, a middle-aged worker saving for retirement, or an elderly retiree trying to make sure she has enough money to cover her living and medical needs—all of these people know that their lives depend a great deal on what the returns in financial markets turn out to be. Another reason is that financial markets are very volatile by nature—they rise or fall considerably over short periods of time. Volatility leads to a great deal of interest among people in understanding how to either profit off of or better protect themselves from the fluctuations.

In this chapter, we will study financial markets such as the stock market and the bond market, where companies access financial capital by issuing stocks and bonds, respectively. We will pay particular attention to how the volatility of these markets affects the demand for financial capital. According to the *Wall Street Journal,* "If a 25-year-old earning $30,000 invests 10% a year and realizes an annual return of 6%, he or she will accumulate about $1.1 million by age 65." Essentially, if you can put $10 a day into an investment account that pays a reasonable rate of return, your chances of becoming a millionaire are very high. But even though one can do very well over the long term by investing in stocks and other assets, stock prices do not always rise. In fact, stock prices did not rise much at all in the 1970s, and they fell sharply in the 1930s. Recently, there was a 30 percent decrease in the Dow Jones stock index in less than six months in 2002, and a more than 70 percent decrease in the Nasdaq stock index in less than three years. Stock prices are volatile, and thus stocks can be very risky. Therefore, we will also develop some new tools to handle risk and uncertainty.

THE DISTINCTION BETWEEN PHYSICAL CAPITAL AND FINANCIAL CAPITAL

Some basic terminology about physical and financial capital is useful in studying financial markets. *Physical capital* refers to all the machines, factories, oil tankers, office buildings, and other physical resources used in the production of goods or services. In previous chapters on the behavior of firms, we simply used the term *capital* when we were referring to physical capital because we were not contrasting it with financial capital. Firms combine physical capital with labor inputs to produce goods and services. They obtain physical capital by either building it, buying it, or renting it. For example, McDonald's might hire a construction firm to build a new facility near a highway. A local school district may purchase several hundred computers for use in classrooms. A real estate developer may rent a construction crane for a year to help move building materials onto the site of a large apartment building project.

An important characteristic of physical capital is that it provides productive services for a number of years. Residential housing—single-family homes, apartments, and trailers—is also a form of physical capital. It provides productive services in the form of living space that people can enjoy year after year. Government-owned roads, schools, and military equipment are also physical capital. It is useful to think of government capital as helping to produce services, whether transportation services, educational services, or national security.

Another important characteristic of physical capital is that it does not remain in new condition permanently. The gradual decline in the productive usefulness of capital is called *depreciation*. Trucks, trailers, roads, machines, and even buildings wear out and must eventually be either replaced or refurbished.

depreciation: the decrease in an asset's value over time; for capital, it is the amount by which physical capital wears out over a given period of time. (Ch. 6)

In order to purchase, rent, or build capital, a firm needs to obtain funds. These funds are an example of *financial capital*. Firms can obtain financial capital in two different ways: by issuing debt (borrowing) or by issuing equity (selling an ownership stake in the firm).

When a firm wants to borrow money, it can take out a bank loan. When it does so, it agrees to pay back the amount it borrowed plus interest at a future date. The amount of interest is determined by the *interest rate*. If the amount borrowed is $10,000 and is due in one year and the interest rate is 10 percent per year, then the borrower pays the lender $11,000 at the end of the year. The $11,000 includes the *principal* on the loan ($10,000) plus the *interest payment* ($1,000 = .1 times $10,000).

Larger firms can issue *corporate bonds*. A bond is an agreement by the issuer to make a specified number of payments in the future in exchange for a sum of money today. Both loans and bonds are a type of contract called a **debt contract,** in which the lender agrees to provide funds today in exchange for a promise that the borrower will pay back the funds with interest at a future date.

debt contract: a contract in which a lender agrees to provide funds today in exchange for a promise from the borrower, who will repay that amount plus interest at some point in the future.

Firms are not the only entities that take out debt contracts. Most people who buy a house get a *mortgage*, which is a loan of funds to purchase real estate. In addition, many people get loans from banks to buy cars and consumer appliances. The biggest single issuer of bonds in the United States is the federal government. The federal government borrows funds by selling *government bonds*. State and local governments also issue bonds to finance physical capital investments like building a new public school, fixing a highway, or building a tunnel.

Firms also obtain financial capital by issuing *stock*, or shares of ownership in the firm. Shares of ownership are a type of contract called an **equity contract.** The purchaser of an equity contract acquires an ownership share in the firm that is typically proportional to the size of the equity contract. In contrast to a debt contract, where the payments by the firm (the interest payments) do not depend on the firm's profits, in an equity contract, the payments by the firm do depend on the firm's profits. Firms that make lots of profits will pay out more in *dividends* to their shareholders. Shareholders can also benefit if the firm increases in value because their shares are worth more when they are sold.

equity contract: shares of ownership in a firm; payments to the owners of the shares depend on the firm's profits.

Once bonds or stocks have been issued, they can be exchanged or traded. There are highly organized financial markets for trading stocks and bonds. The government and corporate bond markets are located in New York City, London, Tokyo, and other large financial centers. The stock markets include the New York Stock Exchange, the Nasdaq, several regional stock exchanges in the United States, and many stock exchanges in other countries.

Having defined some key terms, we now proceed to discuss the different types of financial markets.

REVIEW

- Physical capital and financial capital are distinct but closely related. Physical capital refers to the machines, buildings, and physical resources needed to produce output. To expand their physical capital, firms need to raise funds in some way. These funds are known as financial capital.
- Firms can buy, build, or rent physical capital. They can acquire financial capital by means of debt contracts or equity contracts.
- Debt contracts, such as bonds or loans, allow borrowers access to a sum of money today in exchange for a promise to repay that sum of money plus interest in the future. Equity contracts allow firms to obtain money today in exchange for handing over an ownership stake in the firm.
- The bonds or stocks that firms issue can be traded. Organized markets for trading bonds and stocks are found in all the world's financial centers.

MARKETS FOR FINANCIAL CAPITAL

As we discussed earlier, firms that want to acquire physical capital need to obtain financial capital. Firms can obtain financial capital by issuing stocks and bonds. Stocks and bonds are traded on financial markets. Their prices are determined by the

return: the income received from the ownership of an asset; for a stock, the return is the dividend plus the capital gain.

capital gain: the increase in the value of an asset through an increase in its price.

capital loss: the decrease in the value of an asset through a decrease in its price.

dividend yield: the dividend stated as a percentage of the price of the stock.

rate of return: the return on an asset stated as a percentage of the price of the asset.

actions of buyers and sellers, like prices in any other market. Understanding what drives the equilibrium prices of stocks and bonds is important for determining firms' ability to acquire financial capital. The ease of acquiring financial capital will in turn help determine how much physical capital firms can acquire and how much output they can produce.

Stock Prices and Rates of Return

Prices of the stocks of most large firms can be found in daily newspapers. Investors are interested in buying those stocks whose prices are likely to rise and that are more likely to pay back their profits to shareholders in the form of dividends. We can define the annual **return** from holding a stock as the *dividend* plus the *capital gain* during the year. The **capital gain** during the year is the increase in the price of the stock during the year. A **capital loss** is a negative capital gain: a decrease in the price. When comparing dividends across companies, we typically look at the **dividend yield,** the dividend stated as a percentage of the price. Similarly, in comparing returns across companies, we typically look at the **rate of return,** the return stated as a percentage of the price of the stock.

> **Check the result.**
> The dividend was $.32. The closing price was $41.36. Dividing .32 by 41.36 gives .008, or 0.8 percent.

A simple example can illustrate these terms. For example, the dividend for Hewlett-Packard in 2006 was $.32 per year. At its year-end stock price of $41.36, the dividend yield was 0.8 percent. In 2006, the price of Hewlett-Packard stock rose from $29.28 to $41.36, a capital gain of $12.08. Combined with the dividend, the total return was $12.40, a rate of return of 42.3 percent. In this example, the capital gain is a much bigger portion of the rate of return than the dividend; this is a defining characteristic of "growth stocks," of which Hewlett-Packard is an example.

earnings: the accounting profits of a firm.

price-earnings ratio: the price of a stock divided by its annual earnings per share.

You can also figure out which firms are the most profitable, and hence more likely to generate a high rate of return for their shareholders, by looking at the firms' accounting profits, also known as **earnings.** Firms pay out some of their profits as dividends; the rest of the profits are retained and invested in physical capital or research. Stock tables also list the **price-earnings ratio:** the price of the stock divided by the annual earnings per share. The price-earnings ratio for Hewlett-Packard in 2006 was 17.1. With the price of the stock at $41.36, this means that earnings for the year were $2.4187 per share ($41.36/$2.4187 = 17.1). A firm's earnings ultimately influence the return on the firm's stock, so the price-earnings ratio is closely watched.

Bond Prices and Rates of Return

Bond prices for both corporate and government bonds can also be found in the financial pages of the newspaper. The "Economics in Action" box in this chapter shows you how to read the prices of different types of bonds.

coupon: the fixed amount that a borrower agrees to pay to the bondholder each year.

maturity date: the date when the principal on a loan is to be paid back.

face value: the principal that will be paid back when a bond matures.

There are four key characteristics of a bond: *coupon, maturity date, face value,* and *yield*. The **coupon** is the fixed amount that the borrower agrees to pay the bondholder each year. The **maturity date** is the time when the coupon payments end and the principal is paid back. The **face value** is the amount of principal that will be paid back when the bond matures. The bond boldfaced in the box has a maturity date of February 2037 and a coupon equal to 4.75 percent of the face value of the bond. That is, 4.75 percent, or $47.50, a year on a bond with a face value of $1,000, will be paid until 2037, and in February 2037, the $1,000 face value will be paid back. (The coupon is called a "rate" because it is measured as a percentage of the face value.)

Once bonds have been issued by the government, they can be sold or bought in the bond market. In the bond market, there are bond traders who make a living buying and selling bonds. The bond traders will *bid* a certain price at which they will buy,

ECONOMICS IN ACTION

Understanding Stock and Bond Price Listings in Newspapers

Newspaper stock tables, such as this one from the *Financial Times* (March 1, 2007), summarize information about firms and the stocks that they issue. The table here is part of a much bigger table in which all the stocks traded on the New York Stock Exchange are listed in alphabetical order. Other tables provide information about stocks traded on other stock exchanges, such as the Nasdaq or the London Stock Exchange, in exactly the same way.

To understand how to read this table, focus on one company, such as the computer firm Hewlett-Packard, which was started in a garage by David Packard and William Hewlett in the 1930s. The information in the table pertains to a single day, February 28, 2007 (which was why the data were reported on March 1, the following day). According to the table, the price of Hewlett-Packard stock decreased by 45 cents to 38.93 on that day. Key terms introduced in this chapter—such as dividend yield and price-earnings ratio—are highlighted. To check your understanding, see if you can find out each of the critical pieces of information for one of the other firms in the table, such as Hershey, the maker of Hershey's Kisses.

52 weeks Hi	Lo	Stock	Yld %	PE	Vol 1000s	Close	Net Chg
21.84	19.26	HealthMgmt	1.2	26.3	18476	19.87	−.09
47.69	37.35	Heinz	3.1	25.1	1406	45.67	−.20
57.00	49.34	Hershey	2.0	22.6	1146	52.99	+.11
56.02	38.50	Hess Cp	0.8	8.7	2378	53.19	+.14
43.53	**29.79**	**Hew.-Pack**	**0.8**	**17.1**	**10833**	**38.93**	**−.45**
37.53	23.00	HiltonHotl	0.5	25.4	2900	34.90	−.40
43.81	33.13	HomeDep	2.3	14.2	10254	39.45	−.15

High and low for previous year		Stock name	Dividend as a percent of price	Price-earnings ratio	Number of shares traded (in 1000s)	Closing price	Change in price from previous day
52 weeks Hi	Lo	Stock	Yld %	PE	Vol 1000s	Close	Net Chg
43.53	29.79	Hew.-Pack	0.8	17.1	10833	38.93	−.45

and they will *ask* a certain price at which they will sell. The bid price is slightly lower than the ask price, which enables the bond traders to earn a profit by buying at a price that is slightly lower than the price at which they sell.

yield: the annual rate of return on a bond if the bond were held to maturity.

The **yield,** or yield to maturity, is defined as the annual rate of return on the bond if the bond were bought at the current price and held to maturity. When people refer to the current interest rate on bonds, they are referring to the yield on the bond. Observe that the yield on the boldfaced bond maturing in February 2037 was 4.68 percent on March 1, 2007, slightly below the 4.75 percent coupon rate.

Why are bond yields different from the coupon rate? There is an inverse, or negative, relationship between the yield and the price. Why is there an inverse relationship? This is because the payments of the bond are fixed—the borrower (bond issuer) agrees to pay back the lender (bondholder) the principal on the maturity date and make coupon payments in the interim—regardless of what the buyer paid for the bond.

The *Financial Times* also reports the prices of bonds, which, once they have been issued by a firm or by a government, are actively traded in bond markets. The table below reports information on government-issued bonds from the United Kingdom and the United States. Focus on the highlighted bond; it has a coupon rate of 4.75 percent and matures in February 2037. Thus, in February 2007, there were 30 years left to maturity on this newly issued bond. Sometimes bond price tables report the price that is *bid* for bonds by bond traders and the price that is *asked* for bonds by the traders. Only the bid price is given in this table, but the bid and ask are very close to each other. (There is enough of a difference to give the traders some profit; note that the price asked by the trader is always greater than the price bid.)

Notice that the reported yield is different from the coupon rate for all the bonds listed. Also notice that this difference is especially pronounced for some of the U.K. bonds.

Mar 1	Redemption date	Coupon	Bid price	Bid yield	Day chg yield	Wk chg yield	Month chg yield	Year chg yield
UK	12/07	7.25	101.3200	5.45	−0.01	−0.07	−0.16	+1.07
	03/12	5.00	99.7300	5.06	−0.09	−0.19	−0.30	+0.78
	08/17	8.75	132.7290	4.75	−0.05	−0.19	−0.25	+0.58
	03/36	4.25	100.1500	4.24	−0.01	−0.15	−0.17	+0.40
US	02/09	4.75	100.2344	4.63	−0.01	−0.24	−0.33	−0.08
	02/12	4.63	100.5391	4.50	−0.01	−0.23	−0.34	−0.13
	02/17	4.63	100.5313	4.56	—	−0.17	−0.28	−0.03
	02/37	**4.75**	**101.1406**	**4.68**	**+0.01**	**−0.15**	**−0.25**	**+0.12**

Source: Reuters.

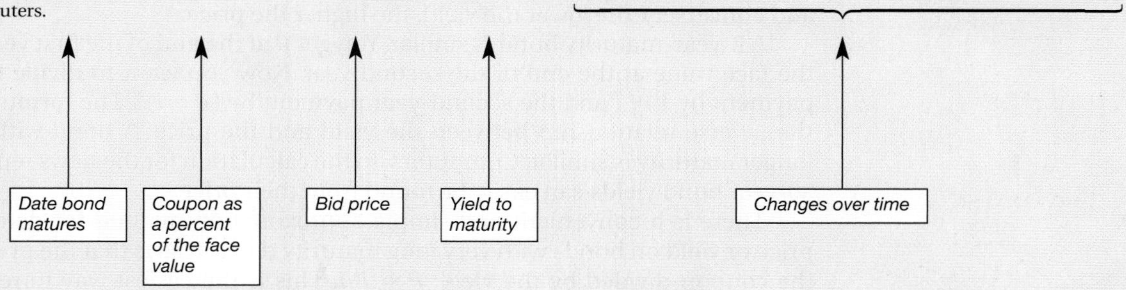

Here is a typical quote on bond yields:
"The price of the 30-year Treasury bond rose less than 1/8 point, or less than $1.25 for a bond with $1,000 face value, to 84 4/32. Its yield, which moves in the opposite direction of its price, dropped to 7.60% from 7.61% on Thursday."

The higher the price you pay today to get this fixed stream of interest and principal payments in the future, the lower the rate of return (yield) you earn. So unlike the coupon rate, which stays fixed, the yield will fluctuate with price. Furthermore, as the price rises, the yield will fall, and vice versa.

Why do bond yields fluctuate? Consider a simple example. Suppose you just bought a 1-year bond for $100 that says that the government will pay 5 percent of the face value, or $5, plus $100 at the end of the 1-year period. Now suppose that just after you bought the bond, interest rates on bank deposits suddenly jumped to 10 percent. Your bond says that you earn 5 percent per year, so if you hold it for the entire year, your rate of return is less than you could get on a bank deposit. Suddenly the bond looks much less attractive. You would probably want to sell it, but everyone else knows the bond is less attractive, also. You would not be able to get $100 for the bond. The price would decline until the rate of return on the bond was close to the interest rate at the bank. For example, if the price fell to $95.45, then the payment of $105 at the end of the year would result in a 10 percent rate of return [that is, .10 = (105 − 95.45)/95.45]. In other words, the yield on the bond would rise until it reached a value closer to 10 percent than to 5 percent.

If you look at the U.K. government bonds in the box, you will notice a bond maturing in 2017 with a coupon rate of 8.75 percent and a yield of 4.75. This bond must have been issued at a time when market interest rates were closer to 8.75 percent. As interest rates in the United Kingdom fell, people found that holding the bond was a more attractive proposition than keeping money in the bank, so they bid up the price of the bond, driving down the yield until it approached the new market interest rates in the United Kingdom. This implies that periods of falling interest rates are good for bondholders and bond issuers because the prices of their bonds rise, while periods of rising interest rates are bad for both bondholders and bond issuers.

Based on these considerations, there is a formula that gives the relationship between the price and the yield for bonds of any maturity. Let P be the price of the bond. Let R be the coupon. Let F be the face value. Let i be the yield. The formula relating to the price and the yield in the case of a 1-year bond is indicated in the first row of Table 1.

For a 1-year bond, a coupon payment of R is paid at the end of 1 year together with the face value of the bond. The price P is what you would be willing to pay *now, in the present,* for these future payments. It is the *present discounted value* of the coupon payment plus the face value at the end of the year. By looking at the formula in the first row of Table 1, you can see the negative relationship between the price (P) of the bond and the yield (i) on the bond. The higher the yield, the lower the price; and conversely, the lower the yield, the higher the price.

A 2-year-maturity bond is similar. You get R at the end of the first year and R plus the face value at the end of the second year. Now you want to divide the first-year payment by $1 + i$ and the second-year payment by $(1 + i)^2$. The formula still shows the inverse relationship between the yield and the price. A bond with a 3-year or longer maturity is similar. Computers do the calculation for the news reports, so even 30-year bond yields can easily be found from their price.

There is a convenient and simple approximation method for determining the price or yield on bonds with very long maturity dates. It says that the price is equal to the coupon divided by the yield: $P = R/i$. This is the easiest way to remember the inverse relationship between the price and the yield. It is a close approximation for long-term bonds like the 30-year bond.

TABLE 1
Bond Price Formula

One-year maturity:	$P = \frac{R}{1+i} + \frac{F}{1+i}$
Two-year maturity:	$P = \frac{R}{1+i} + \frac{R}{(1+i)^2} + \frac{F}{(1+i)^2}$
Three-year maturity:	$P = \frac{R}{1+i} + \frac{R}{(1+i)^2} + \frac{R}{(1+i)^3} + \frac{F}{(1+i)^3}$
For very long term:	$P = \frac{R}{i}$

P = price of bond
R = coupon
F = face value
i = yield

REVIEW

- Firms that want to purchase physical capital need financial capital to do so. They obtain financial capital by issuing stocks and bonds. Stocks and bonds are traded on financial markets.
- The return from holding stock is the dividend plus the change in the price. The rate of return is equal to the return measured as a percentage of the price of the stock.
- The return from holding bonds to maturity is the yield of the bond. Bond yields and bond prices move in opposite directions.
- Periods of falling interest rates are good for bondholders and bond issuers because the prices of bonds rise, while periods of rising interest rates are bad for both bondholders and bond issuers.

THE TRADEOFF BETWEEN RISK AND RETURN

One of the hallmarks of financial markets is volatility. The prices of individual stocks and bonds rise and fall over time. Over the long run, stock prices show a positive trend, but there are periods of significant decline from time to time, and the prices of individual stocks traded in the financial markets are very volatile. Similarly, even though you can always earn a rate of return equivalent to the yield by holding a bond issued by the U.S. government to maturity, in the interim the price of the bond will vary.

In the example discussed earlier, the price of a share of Hewlett-Packard increased by over 42 percent in 2006, but in 2000, the price fell by over 80 percent. For individual stocks, a change in price of 5 or 10 percent in one day is not uncommon. Because of such variability, buying stocks is a risky activity. The price of bonds can also change by a large amount. For example, from mid-1996 to mid-1997, the price of government bonds rose by nearly 20 percent, but from mid-1993 to mid-1994, the price of government bonds *fell* by nearly 20 percent! Thus, government bonds are also a risky investment.

In this section we show that the riskiness of stocks and bonds affects the decision of people to trade in financial markets. To do so, we first examine how individuals behave when they face risk.

Behavior Under Uncertainty

Most people do not like uncertainty. They are *risk averse* in most of their activities. Given a choice between two jobs that pay the same wage, most people will be averse to choosing the riskier job where there is a good chance of being laid off. Similarly, given a choice between two investments that pay the same return, people will choose the less risky one.

Let us examine this idea of risk aversion further. To be more precise, suppose that Melissa has a choice between the two alternatives shown in Table 2. She must decide what to do with her life savings of $10,000 for the next year. At the end of the year, she plans to buy a house, and she will need some money for a down payment. She can put her $10,000 in a bank account, where the interest rate is 5 percent, or she can buy $10,000 worth of a stock that pays a dividend of 5 percent and will incur either a capital gain or a capital loss. In the bank, the value of her savings is safe, but if she buys the stock, there is a 50 percent chance that the price of the stock will fall

TABLE 2
Two Options: Different Risks, Same Expected Return

Low-Risk Option	High-Risk Option
A bank deposit with	*A corporate stock with either*
5 percent interest (return = $500)	a. A 5 percent dividend and a 30 percent price decline ($500 − $3,000 = −$2,500)
	b. A 5 percent dividend and a 30 percent price increase ($500 + $3,000 = $3,500)

by 30 percent and a 50 percent chance that the price of the stock will rise by 30 percent. In other words, the risky stock will leave Melissa with the possibility of a return of −$2,500 (a loss) or a return of $3,500 (a gain). The bank account leaves her with a guaranteed $500 return.

expected return: the return on an uncertain investment calculated by weighting the gains or losses by the probability that they will occur.

Both the options in Table 2 have the same **expected return.** The expected return on an investment weights the different gains or losses according to how probable they are. In the case of the safe bank account, there is a 100 percent chance that the return is $500, so the expected return is $500. In the case of the stock, the expected return would be −$2,500 times the probability of this loss (1/2) plus $3,500 times the probability of this gain (also 1/2). Thus, the expected return is $500 (−2,500/2 + 3,500/2 = −1,250 + 1,750 = 500), the same as the return on the bank account.

The expected return is one way to measure how attractive an investment is. The word *expected* may appear misleading, since in the risky option $500 is not "expected" in the everyday use of the word. You do not expect $500; you expect either a loss of $2,500 or a gain of $3,500. If the term is confusing, think of the expected return as the average return that Melissa would get if she could take the second option year after year for many years. The losses of $2,500 and gains of $3,500 would average out to $500 per year after many years. (The term *expected return* has been carried over by economists and investment analysts from probability and statistics, where the term *expected value* is used to describe the mean, or the average, of a random variable.)

Given that the expected returns are the same, if Melissa is a risk-averse person (i.e., if she would dread a capital loss more than she would cherish a capital gain of a similar magnitude), she will choose the less risky of these two options. Although it is clear that Melissa would choose the less risky of the two options in Table 2, perhaps there is some compensation that Melissa would accept to offset her risk aversion. Although most people are averse to risk, they are willing to take on some risk if they are compensated for it. In the case of a risky financial investment, the compensation for higher risk could take the form of a higher expected return.

How could we make Melissa's expected return higher in the risky investment? Suppose Melissa had the choice between the same safe option as in Table 2 and a high-risk stock that paid a dividend of 20 percent. This new choice is shown in Table 3; the difference is that the risky stock now offers a dividend of 20 percent, much greater than the 5 percent in the first example and much greater than the 5 percent on the bank account. With the greater chance of a higher return on the stock, Melissa might be willing to buy the stock. Even in the worst situation, she loses just $1,000, which may still leave her with enough for the down payment on her new house. The expected return for the high-risk option is now $2,000, much greater than the $500 for the bank account (−1,000/2 + 5,000/2 = −500 + 2,500 = 2,000).

In other words, Melissa would probably be willing to take on the risky investment. And if the 20 percent dividend in the example is not enough for her, some higher

TABLE 3
Two Options: Different Risks, Different Expected Returns

Low-Risk Option	High-Risk Option
A bank deposit with	*A corporate stock with either*
5 percent interest (return = $500)	a. A 20 percent dividend and a 30 percent price decline ($2,000 − $3,000 = −$1,000)
	b. A 20 percent dividend and a 30 percent price increase ($2,000 + $3,000 = $5,000)

Playing It Safe?
Most people are risk-averse when it come to large sums, but many are risk lovers when the stakes are low or when they can limit their potential losses—such as at casinos where people can choose to gamble a set amount or combine gambling with entertainment.

dividend (25 percent? 30 percent?) would be. This example illustrates the general point that risk-averse people are willing to take risks if they are paid for it.

Before we develop the implication of our analysis of individual behavior under uncertainty, we should pause to ask about the possibility that some people might be risk lovers rather than risk avoiders. The billions of dollars that are bet in state lotteries in the United States and in private gambling casinos in Las Vegas, Atlantic City, and Monte Carlo indicate that some people enjoy risk. However, with few exceptions, most of the gambling on lotteries, slot machines, and even roulette wheels represents a small portion of the income or wealth of the gambler. Thus, you might be willing to spend $.50 or even $5 on lottery tickets or a slot machine for the chance of winning big, even if the odds are against you. Many people get enjoyment out of such wagers; but if the stakes are large compared to one's income or wealth, then few people want to play. For small sums, some people are risk lovers, but for large sums, virtually everybody becomes a risk avoider to some degree or another.

Risk and Rates of Return in Theory

What are the implications of our conclusion that investors will be willing to take risks if they are compensated with a higher return on the stock or bond? In the stock market, the prices of individual stocks are determined by the bidding of buyers and sellers. Suppose a stock, AOK, had a price that gave it the same expected rate of return as a bank account. Now AOK, being a common stock, clearly has more risk than a bank account because its price can change. Hence, no risk-averse investor will want to buy AOK. Just as Melissa will prefer to put her funds in a bank account in the example in Table 2 rather than into the risky option, investors will put their funds in a bank rather than buy AOK. People who own shares of AOK will sell and put their funds into a bank. With everybody wanting to sell AOK and no one wanting to buy it, the price of AOK will start to fall.

Now, the price and the expected rate of return are inversely related—recall that for a stock, the rate of return is the return divided by the price. Thus, if the price falls and the dividend does not change, the rate of return will rise. This fall in the price will drive up the expected rate of return on AOK. As the expected rate of return increases, it will eventually reach a point where it is high enough to compensate risk-averse investors. In other words, when the expected rate of return rises far enough above the bank account

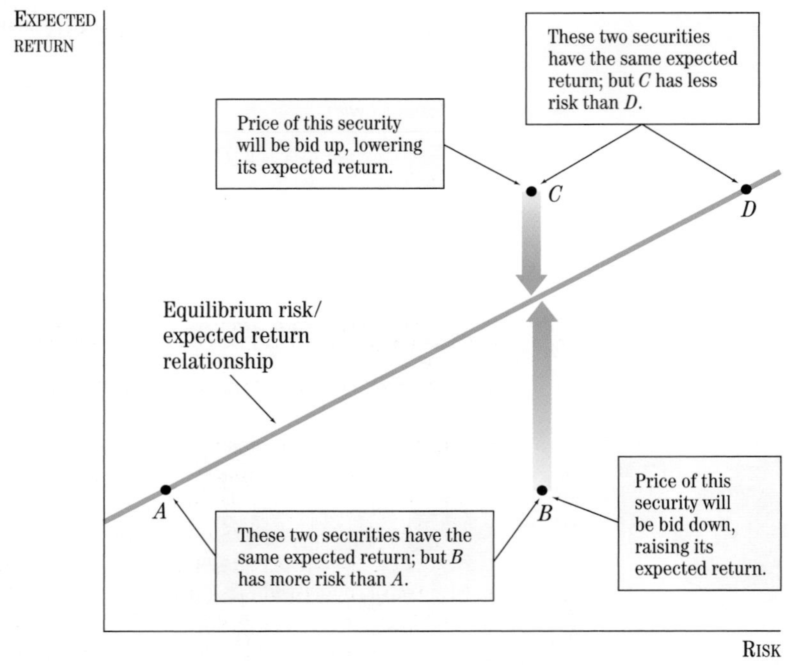

FIGURE 1
The Equilibrium Relationship Between Return and Risk
More risky securities tend to have higher returns on average over the long term. For example, bank deposits are low risk and have a low expected return. Corporate stocks are higher risk—their price fluctuates—but on average over the long term have a higher return. The higher return is like a compensating wage differential in the labor market. It compensates those who take on more risk.

rate to compensate people for the risk, the price fall will stop. We will have an equilibrium where the expected rate of return on the stock is higher than the interest rate on the safe bank account. The higher rate of return will be associated with the higher risk.

Now some stocks are more risky than others. For example, the risk on the stocks of small firms tends to be higher than the risk on the stocks of larger firms, because small firms tend to be those that are just starting up. Not having yet proved themselves, small firms have a higher risk. People like Melissa will sell the more risky stocks of smaller companies until the expected rate of return on those stocks is high enough compared with the less risky stocks of larger companies.

In equilibrium, we therefore expect to see a positive relationship between risk and the expected rate of return on securities. Securities with higher risks will have higher returns than securities with lower risks. Figure 1 shows the resulting **equilibrium risk-return relationship.**

equilibrium risk-return relationship: the positive relationship between the risk and the expected rate of return on an asset, derived from the fact that, on average, risk-averse investors who take on more risk must be compensated with a higher return.

There is probably no more important lesson about capital markets than this relationship. Individual investors should know it well. It says that to get a higher rate of return *on average over the long run,* you have to accept a higher risk. Again, the market forces at work are the same as the ones that led to the compensating wage differentials in the labor market. In the labor market, the higher wage in some jobs is the price that workers accept to take on the greater risk, or, more generally, the less pleasant aspects of the job.

Risk and Return in Reality

How well does this theoretical relationship work in reality? Very well. A tremendous amount of data over long periods of time on the financial markets support it. Table 4 presents data on the average return over 75 years for the four important types of securities we have mentioned in the theoretical discussion. The most risky of the four—the stocks of small firms—has the highest rate of return. Next highest in risk

TABLE 4
Average Rates of Return for Different Risks, 1926–2001

	Average Rate of Return per Year (percent)	Risk (average size of price fluctuations)
U.S. Treasury bills	3.8	3.2
Long-term corporate bonds	5.8	8.6
Large-company stocks	10.7	20.2
Small-company stocks	12.5	33.2

Note: These rates of return are not adjusted for inflation. The average rate of inflation was about 3 percent, which can be subtracted from each of the average returns to get the real return. The risk is the "standard deviation," a measure of volatility commonly used in probability and statistics.

Source: Data from Ibbotson Associates, *Stocks, Bonds, Bills and Inflation,* 2004 yearbook, Table 6–7.

are the common stocks of large firms. The least risky—short-term Treasury bills that are as safe as bank deposits—has the smallest rate of return. Long-term bonds, where price changes can be large, have a rate of return greater than that of Treasury bills. Although the relative risks of these four types of securities may seem obvious, a measure of the differences in the sizes of their price volatility is shown in the second column and confirms the intuitive risk rankings.

In general, Table 4 is a striking confirmation of this fundamental result of financial markets that higher expected rates of return are associated with higher risk.

Diversification Reduces Risk

The familiar saying "Don't put all your eggs in one basket" is particularly relevant to stock markets. Rather than a basket of eggs, you have a portfolio of stocks. A *portfolio* is a collection of stocks. Putting your funds into a portfolio of two or more stocks, whose prices do not always move in the same direction, rather than one stock is called **portfolio diversification.** The risks from holding a single stock can be reduced significantly by putting half your funds in one stock and half in another. If one stock falls in price, the other stock may fall less, may not fall at all, or may even rise.

portfolio diversification: spreading the collection of assets owned in order to limit exposure to risk.

Holding two stocks in equal amounts is the most elementary form of diversification. With thousands of stocks to choose from, however, diversification is not limited to two. Figure 2 shows how sharply risk declines with diversification. By holding 10 different stocks rather than 1, you can reduce your risk to about 30 percent of what it would be with 1 stock. If you hold some international stocks, whose behavior will be even more different from that of any one U.S. stock, you can reduce the risk even further. Mutual fund companies provide a way for an investor with only limited funds to diversify by holding 500 or even 5,000 stocks along with other investors. Some mutual funds—called *index funds*—consist of all the stocks in an index like the Standard & Poor's (S&P) 500 Index, a weighted average of the stocks of 500 major companies.

Efficient Market Theory

The shares of firms' stock on the market can be traded quickly at any time of day. For most large and medium-sized companies, some people are always willing to buy and sell. If people hear that Intel has made a discovery that is expected to raise its profits, they rush to buy Intel stock. If people suddenly learn about a decline in a company's profits or about losses, then people rush to sell that company's stock. This rush to buy and sell changes prices instantaneously, so that the price adjusts rapidly to good news or bad news. The rapid adjustment means that there are rarely any unexploited profit opportunities for regular investors without inside information or a special

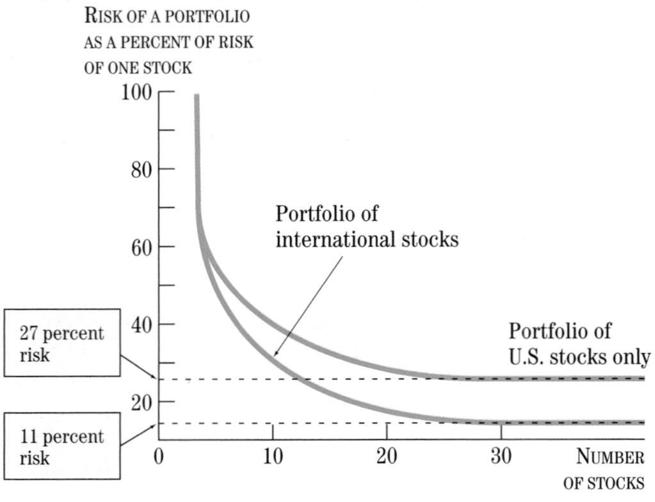

FIGURE 2
Risk Declines Sharply with Diversification
By holding more than one stock, the risk can be reduced. By holding 10 U.S. securities, the risk is reduced to 30 percent of the risk of holding 1 security. Diversifying internationally permits one to reduce risk further. (The risk is measured by the standard deviation.)

efficient market hypothesis: the idea that markets adjust rapidly enough to eliminate profit opportunities immediately.

ability to anticipate news, whether good or bad. The **efficient market hypothesis** states that there is an elimination of profit opportunities in financial markets as stock prices adjust quickly to new information. Rates of return greater than those due to the price of risk disappear soon after any good news about a stock appears.

Many tests over the years have found the efficient market hypothesis to be a close approximation of security price determination. It has led to the growth in popularity of index funds, where investors do not pay advisers to tell them when to buy and sell stock. They simply invest in a fund that includes a large number of stocks.

CORPORATE GOVERNANCE PROBLEMS

When corporations issue stock to buy physical capital or start up operations, a separation between the owners of the corporation—the stockholders—and the managers of the corporation is created. This separation leads to incentive problems—the manager might not act in the interest of the shareholder. Here we show how these problems can be analyzed with a theory called *asymmetric information theory.*

Consider a start-up firm. When an entrepreneur at a start-up firm obtains financial capital by issuing stock, a special relationship is formed. Those who supplied the financial capital by buying the stock relationship is formed. Those who supplied the financial capital by buying the stock become owners or at least part owners of the company. If the entrepreneur does well and the company is a success, they reap large returns.

Asymmetric Information: Moral Hazard and Adverse Selection

asymmetric information: different levels of information available to different people in an economic interaction or exchange.

Shareholders of a firm have less information than the managers about how the firm is doing even though the shareholders put a considerable amount of funds in the firm. These differences in information, called **asymmetric information,** can cause several problems. First, the manager might not act in the interest of the owners. Taking unnecessary business trips on the company's aircraft to exotic areas or not working hard to find the right employees is harmful to the shareholders' interests.

moral hazard: in insurance markets, a situation in which a person buys insurance against some risk and subsequently takes actions that increase the risk; analogous situations arise when there is asymmetric information in other markets.

Such actions are against the interest of the shareholders. They are called **moral hazards,** a term borrowed from research on the insurance industry, where asymmetric information is also a problem. Moral hazards in insurance occur when people are less careful about trying to prevent fires after they get fire insurance. In the case of the firm, the manager may be less careful about the firm after the shareholders' or investors' funds have been obtained.

adverse selection: in insurance markets, a situation in which the people who choose to buy insurance will be the riskiest group in the population; analogous situations apply in other markets.

Another problem is that those entrepreneurs who have more risky projects would seek equity financing—where dividend payments to shareholders would be optional—rather than debt financing, where interest payments are required. This is called **adverse selection,** another term borrowed from insurance. In insurance, adverse selection occurs when people who are unhealthy select health insurance while healthy people do not. In this case, managers who have more risky projects elect equity financing more than those who have less risky projects. This makes potential shareholders or investors less willing to supply funds to equity markets. Finding ways to write contracts between principals—the owners or shareholders and agents (the managers)—to reduce the problems of moral hazard or adverse selection requires paying attention to incentives.

Incentives to Overcome Adverse Selection and Moral Hazard Problems

Severe adverse selection and moral hazard problems can prevent the formation of business relationships between principals and agents. For example, people may be unwilling to buy stock in a firm because they believe that managers may use that money for their own benefit rather than for the company's interests. One of the more egregious cases of recent times was the indictment of Dennis Kozlowski, who was sentenced to 8 to 25 years in prison for misappropriating hundreds of millions of dollars. Similarly, investors may worry that firms that are interested in obtaining equity financing from the public precisely because they have been able to borrow from other lenders.

profit sharing: programs in which managers and employees receive a share of profits earned by the firm.

A Shareholder Meeting: Principals, Agents, Asymmetric Information
Theories of corporate governance view a firm's shareholders (shown in the crowd) as the *principals* and the managers (shown on the stage) as the agents. Management incentive plans such as profit sharing are seen as ways of fostering good management performance when the principals have little information about what the *agents* actually do—a situation called *asymmetric information.*

One way in which problems of moral hazard and adverse selection can be limited is through the use of **profit sharing** agreements, whereby managers and employees are given a share of the profits earned by the firm. That way the agents of the firms have a financial stake in the firm's success, and hence have their interests aligned with the principals—agents gain when the principal gains and the agent loses when the principal loses. In recent years many U.S. airlines have implemented profit sharing plans for their employees.

Another way to overcome the problems caused by moral hazard and adverse selection is to join with a group of investors and take over a company so that the problematic management team can be replaced. The mere threat of such a takeover can be an incentive for management to act in shareholder's interest rather than their own. Perhaps the most well-known takeover case in recent time was the purchase of RJR Nabisco for over $30 billion by KKR, a firm specializing in takeovers. In the last few years, there has been a rise to prominence of *private equity* firms like the Blackstone Group, which specialize in buying

ECONOMICS IN THE NEWS

Corporate Greed

Dennis Kozlowski, the former CEO of Tyco International, became the symbolic figure of corporate managers wasting, and in Kozlowski's case defrauding, shareholder money. The article points out other high profile cases and discusses the impact that the Kozlowski case might have on other corporate executives, with designs on stealing shareholder funds. It's important to realize that criminal charges cannot be brought for bad business decisions, so that most problems related to moral hazard will not be solved via the legal system.

Some of the more lavish uses of shareholder funds

Other examples of corporate executives who were convicted of stealing corporate funds and committing financial fraud

The punishment meted out to Kozlowski and Swartz indicates the severity of their crimes.

Ex-Tyco Officers Sentenced

Pair Get Up to 25 Years in Prison, Must Pay Almost $240 Million

By BEN WHITE | Washington Post Staff Writer

NEW YORK, Sept. 19— A state judge on Monday sentenced former Tyco International Ltd. executives L. Dennis Kozlowski and Mark H. Swartz to 8 1/3 to 25 years in prison for looting the company of hundreds of millions of dollars to pay for lavish parties, luxurious homes and extravagances such as a $6,000 shower curtain.

In a case that came to symbolize corporate greed, state Supreme Court Judge Michael J. Obus also ordered Kozlowski and Swartz to pay nearly $240 million in fines and restitution. Kozlowski and Swartz were immediately taken into custody and led from a packed courtroom in handcuffs as family members of both men sobbed. The men are likely to serve at least part of their sentences in one of New York's 16 maximum-security state prisons.

The sentences for Kozlowski and Swartz follow lengthy terms meted out to other white-collar defendants convicted in a wave of criminal cases that followed the collapse of the Internet bubble and multibillion-dollar frauds at companies such as WorldCom Inc. and Enron Corp.

Former WorldCom chairman Bernard J. Ebbers, 64, was sentenced to 25 years in prison for orchestrating an $11 billion accounting fraud at his company. Because of Ebbers's age, that could amount to a life sentence. John J. Rigas, the 80-year-old founder of Adelphia Communications Corp., received 15 years in prison for stealing millions from the cable company for personal extravagances, hiding more than $2.3 billion in debt and lying to investors. Rigas's son and former Adelphia chief financial officer Timothy J. Rigas was given 20 years in prison for his role in the scheme.

Prosecutors and many shareholder groups say long sentences are necessary to deter future abuses and restore investor confidence. But some defense lawyers question the extent to which a few high-profile cases will deter bad behavior at smaller public companies that present less tempting targets for prosecutors. "Officers and directors of major corporations, multinational corporations, clearly get the message," said defense attorney Jacob S. Frenkel. "The question is whether the message has been conveyed thoroughly to officers and directors at small and mid-size companies."

Kozlowski and Swartz will be able to cut one-sixth off of their 8 1/3 -year minimum sentence if they behave well and take part in prison programs, said Linda Foglia, a spokeswoman for the state Department of Correctional Services. That would reduce the point at which they can be paroled to six years and 11 months. Inmates are eligible to apply for work release two years before their first possible parole date, and parole officials will decide how much of the 8 1/3 to 25 years the former executives must serve. Several legal experts said it was unlikely either man would serve more than 10 years in total.

There is no parole in the federal system, under which many other white-collar defendants have been tried and sentenced. Though their sentences may be cut shorter than other executives', the time Kozlowski and Swartz spend behind bars may be in a harsher environment. Obus did not specify where the two former executives will serve their terms. He said that decision would be made by state corrections officials. But he said he did not view either man as a security risk, indicating he would not object if they are sent to a lower-security facility.

Former prosecutor David Gourevitch, however, said there were no facilities in the state system comparable to federal minimum-security prisons such as the one where entrepreneur Martha Stewart spent her five-month sentence. "In the federal system, outside of maximum-security places, generally people are physically safe. I don't think anybody would say that about New York state prison," Gourevitch said. "And from a state perspective, this is one of the longest sentences in a corporate fraud case that I can recall."

Foglia said that in most cases, defendants sentenced to more than six years are sent to maximum-security prisons. She said it would be several weeks before the state decides where to send Kozlowski and Swartz. In the meantime, they will stay at a holding facility known as the Tombs in Lower Manhattan and then be sent to Rikers Island, the temporary jail for New York City inmates before they are sent to state prisons.

In June, a jury found former Tyco chief executive Kozlowski, 58, and former chief financial officer Swartz, 45, guilty of criminal counts of grand larceny, conspiracy, securities fraud and eight of nine counts of falsifying business records.

Obus imposed the same prison sentence on both men. He ordered Kozlowski to pay a $70 million fine and Swartz to pay a $35 million fine. He ordered both men to repay Tyco a combined $134.4 million in restitution of illegal bonuses and other illicit payments.

Kozlowski and Swartz each made brief statements in court Monday, asking Obus to be lenient. Lawyers for each also pleaded with the court to recognize the former executives' charitable works and the scores of letters sent on their behalf by friends and family.

Prosecutors, by contrast, asked Obus to send a message that corporate theft will be treated the same as grand larceny committed with a handgun. They asked for the maximum term of 15 to 30 years for both men.

In imposing the sentence, Obus said, "The heart of this case is basic larceny" and described the charges as "extremely serious." He expressed befuddlement at Kozlowski's and Swartz's plights, at one point asking, "how the defendants, with all they had going for them, managed to get themselves into this disastrous position."

Attorneys for Kozlowski and Swartz said they would seek to have their clients released on bail pending appeal of their convictions. At the sentencing hearing on Monday, state prosecutors said the Securities and Exchange Commission staff had recommended that the agency bring an accounting fraud case against Tyco. Tyco has said it expects to settle the SEC suit and has set aside $50 million for that purpose. The SEC often simultaneously files and settles accounting cases.

shares of a public company and taking it private, so that they can replace the existing management with managers who presumably can improve the firm's performance.

However, such takeovers have also been criticized. Some say that the threat of being bought out by a hostile takeover firm or a private equity firm leads management to adopt a more short-sighted attitude toward the operation of the company's affairs than is ideal. Companies also expend considerable resources constructing "takeover defenses," which attempt to make it more difficult for outsiders to use a hostile takeover to take control of the firm.

REVIEW

- Financial markets are very volatile; both stock prices and bond prices tend to rise and fall over time. The riskiness of bonds and stocks affects the willingness of people to buy and sell these financial assets, and hence affects their return.
- We can calculate the expected return of a risky asset by weighting the possible gains and losses by the probability that these gains or losses will occur. Given the choice between a risky asset and a safe asset that have the same expected return, an individual who is risk averse will always choose the safe asset.
- Risk-averse investors will hold risky assets only if they are compensated in the form of a higher expected return. Thus, when buyers and sellers trade stocks or bonds in the market, a relationship between return and risk emerges: Higher risk is associated with higher returns.
- Investors can reduce risk by diversifying their portfolio, that is, by holding many different stocks. Mutual funds and index funds offer diversification opportunities even to investors who have very little money to put into the stock market.
- Earning stock returns in excess of those justified by the greater level of associated risk is difficult. The efficient market hypothesis predicts that stock prices adjust quickly to eliminate such lucrative return opportunities.

CONCLUSION

In this chapter we have seen how to employ some basic economic tools to analyze capital markets. In reviewing the lessons learned, it is helpful to see how they may apply to you personally.

First, by diversifying a portfolio of stocks, you can reduce risk substantially. Conversely, by holding an undiversified portfolio, you are needlessly incurring risk.

Second, be aware of the efficient market hypothesis that profit opportunity disappears quickly in financial markets. Instead of buying and selling securities frequently, investors may be better off investing in a mutual fund—like an index fund.

Third, if you do try to pick your own portfolio rather than use a mutual fund, concentrate on areas you are familiar with. If you go into a medical career, you may know more than even the best investors about the promise of a new medical device or drug.

Fourth, over the short run, holding corporate stocks is more risky than putting your funds in a bank account, but over the long term, the higher rate of return on stocks outweighs the risks for most people. However, if you need money in the short term—to pay next year's tuition, for example—stocks may not be worth the risk.

KEY POINTS

1. Physical capital refers to the physical resources used to produce goods and services.
2. Firms raise money for investing in physical capital by issuing stocks and bonds. Once issued, the stocks and bonds trade on financial markets.
3. The rate of return on stocks is equal to the dividend plus the change in the price as a percentage of the price. The rate of return on bonds held to maturity is the yield of the bond.
4. The rate of return on stocks tends to rise when firms have higher earnings, which are either paid out in the form of dividends or reinvested in the company. The rate of return on bonds tends to rise in periods when market interest rates are falling.
5. Stock markets and bond markets tend to be extremely volatile. To understand how the riskiness of these assets affects their return, we need to understand how investors behave.
6. Risk-averse investors will buy more risky stocks or bonds only if the expected rate of return is higher.
7. In market equilibrium, there is a positive relationship between risk and rate of return. If you want to get a higher rate of return, you have to accept higher risk.
8. Diversification helps reduce risk. Even individuals with limited resources can diversify their portfolios by investing in mutual funds.

KEY TERMS

depreciation
debt contract
equity contract
return
capital gain
capital loss
dividend yield
rate of return
earnings
price-earnings ratio
coupon
maturity date
face value
yield
expected return
equilibrium risk-return relationship
portfolio diversification
efficient market hypothesis
asymmetric information
moral hazard
adverse selection
profit sharing

QUESTIONS FOR REVIEW

1. What is the difference between physical capital and financial capital?
2. What is the difference between a stock and a bond?
3. What determines the rate of return on stocks?
4. What determines the rate of return on bonds?
5. What does it mean for an individual to be risk-averse?
6. How do the actions of risk-averse individuals influence the relationship between risk and return in financial markets?
7. What is diversification? How does it affect risk?
8. What do economists mean when they say that financial markets are efficient?

PROBLEMS

1. Which of the following are physical capital, and which are financial capital?
   a. A Toyota Camry at Avis Car Rental
   b. A loan you take out to start a newspaper business
   c. New desktop publishing equipment
   d. A bond issued by the U.S. government
   e. A pizza oven at Pizza Hut
2. The U.S. government issues a 1-year bond with a face value of $1,000 and a zero coupon. If the yield is 10 percent, what will the market price of the bond be? Now suppose you observe that the bond price falls by 5 percent. What happens to its yield?
3. Suppose a 2-year bond has a 5 percent coupon and $1,000 face value, and the current market interest rate is 5 percent. What is the price of the bond? Now suppose that you believe that the interest rate will remain at 5 percent this year, but will fall to 3 percent next year. How much are you willing to pay for the 2-year bond today? Why?

4. Consider the following possibilities for your stock market investment portfolio:

	Good Market	Bad Market	Disastrous Market
Probability	.50	.30	.20
Rate of return	.25	.10	−.25

a. What is the expected return of your stock market investment portfolio?
b. Would you choose this expected return or take a safe return of 7 percent from a savings deposit in your bank? Why?
c. Suppose your teacher chooses the safe return from the bank. Is your teacher risk averse? How can you tell?

5. You are considering the purchase of stocks of two firms: a biotechnology corporation and a supermarket chain. Because of the uncertainty in the biotechnology industry, you estimate that there is a 50-50 chance of your either earning an 80 percent return on your investment or losing 80 percent of your investment within a year. The food industry is more stable, so you estimate that you have a 50-50 chance of either earning 10 percent or losing 10 percent. Which stock would you buy if you were a risk-averse individual? Why? What do you think other investors (most of whom are risk averse) would do? What would be the effect of these actions on the relative prices of the two stocks?

6. Graph the data on risk and expected return (in percent) for the following securities.

Asset	Expected Rate of Return	Risk
Bank deposit	3	0
U.S. Treasury bills	4	3
Goodcorp bonds	9	10
ABC stock	11	24
XYZ stock	13	24
Riskyco stock	16	39

Draw an equilibrium risk-return line through the points. Which two assets should have changes in their prices in the near future? In which direction will their prices change?

7. Suppose a study indicated that stock prices were usually lower during the Christmas season than during the rest of the year. What would be the likely reaction of the market?

8. Suppose you have $10,000 and must choose between investing in your own human capital or investing in physical or financial capital. What factors will enter into your decision-making process? How much risk will be involved with each investment? What would you do? Why?

Present Discounted Value

A dollar in the future is worth less than a dollar today. This principle underlies all economic decisions involving actions over time. Whether you put some dollars under the mattress to be spent next summer, borrow money from a friend or family member to be paid back next year, or are a sophisticated investor in stocks, bonds, or real estate, that same principle is essential to making good decisions. Here we explain why the principle is essential and derive a formula for determining exactly *how much* less a dollar in the future is worth than a dollar today. The formula is called the *present discounted value formula.*

Discounting the Future

First let's answer the question, why is the value of a dollar in the future less than the value of a dollar today? The simplest answer is that a dollar can earn interest over time. Suppose a person you trust completely to pay off a debt gives you an IOU promising to pay you $100 in one year; how much is that IOU worth to you today? How much would you be willing to pay for the IOU today? It would be less than $100, because you could put an amount less than $100 in a bank and get $100 at the end of a year. The exact amount depends on the interest rate. If the interest rate is 10 percent, the $100 should be worth $90.91 because, if you put $90.91 in a bank earning 10 percent per year, at the end of the year you will have exactly $100. That is, $90.91 plus interest payments of $9.09 ($90.91 times .1 rounded to the nearest penny) equals $100.

The process of translating a future payment into a value in the present is called **discounting.** The value in the present of a future payment is called the **present discounted value.** The interest rate used to do the discounting is called the **discount rate.** In the preceding example, a future payment of $100 has a present discounted value of $90.91, and the discount rate is 10 percent. If the discount rate were 20 percent, the present discounted value would be $83.33 (because if you put $83.33 in a bank for a year at a 20 percent interest rate, you would have, rounding to the nearest penny, $100 at the end of the year). The term *discount* is used because the value in the present is *less* than the future payment; in other words, the payment is "discounted," much as a $100 bicycle on sale might be "discounted" to $83.33.

Finding the Present Discounted Value

The previous examples suggest that there is a formula for calculating present value, and indeed there is. Let

the present discounted value be PDV
the discount rate be i
the future payment be F

The symbol i is measured as a decimal, but we speak of the discount rate in percentage terms; thus we would say "the discount rate is 10 percent" and write "$i = .1$."

Now, the present discounted value PDV is the amount for which, if you put it in a bank today at an interest rate i, you would get an amount in the future equal to the future payment F. For example, if the future date is one year from now, then if you put the amount PDV in a bank for one year, you would get PDV times $(1 + i)$ at the end of the year. Thus, the PDV should be such that

$$PDV \times (1 + i) = F$$

Now divide both sides by $(1 + i)$; you get

$$PDV = \frac{F}{1 + i}$$

which is the formula for the present discounted value in the case of a payment made one year in the future. That is,

$$\text{Present discounted value} = \frac{\text{payment in one year}}{(1 + \text{the discount rate})}$$

For example, if the payment in one year is $100 and the discount rate $i = .1$, then the present discounted value is $90.91 [$100/(1 + .1)], just as we reasoned previously.

To obtain the formula for the case where the payment is made more than one year in the future, we must recognize that the amount in the present can be put in a bank and earn interest at the discount rate for more than one year. For example, if the interest rate is 10 percent, we could get \$100 at the end of 2 years by investing \$82.64 today. That is, putting \$82.64 in the bank would give \$82.64 times (1.1) at the end of one year; keeping all this in the bank for another year would give \$82.64 times (1.1) times (1.1), or \$82.64 times 1.21, or \$100.00, again rounding off. Thus, in the case of a future payment in 2 years, we would have

$$PDV = \frac{F}{(1+i)^2}$$

Analogous reasoning implies that the present discounted value of a payment made N years in the future would be

$$PDV = \frac{F}{(1+i)^N}$$

For example, the present discounted value of a \$100 payment to be made 20 years in the future is \$14.86 if the discount rate is 10 percent. In other words, if you put \$14.86 in the bank today at an interest rate of 10 percent, you would have about \$100 at the end of 20 years. What is the present discounted value of a \$100 payment to be made 100 years in the future? The above formula tells us that the *PDV* is only \$.00726, less than a penny! All of these examples indicate that the higher the discount rate or the further in the future the payment is to be received, the lower the present discounted value of a future payment.

In many cases, we need to find the present discounted value of a *series* of payments made in several different years. We can do this by combining the previous formulas. The present discounted value of payments F_1 made in 1 year and F_2 made in 2 years would be

$$PDV = \frac{F_1}{(1+i)} + \frac{F_2}{(1+i)^2}$$

For example, the present discounted value of \$100 paid in one year and \$100 paid in 2 years would be \$90.91 plus \$82.64, or \$173.55. In general, the present discounted value of a series of future payments $F_1, F_2, \ldots, F_N$ over N years is

$$PDV = \frac{F_1}{(1+i)} + \frac{F_2}{(1+i)^2} + \cdots + \frac{F_N}{(1+i)^N}$$

KEY POINTS

1. A dollar to be paid in the future is worth less than a dollar today.
2. The present discounted value of a future payment is the amount you would have to put in a bank today to get that same payment in the future.
3. The higher the discount rate, the lower the present discounted value of a future payment.

KEY TERMS AND DEFINITIONS

discounting: the process of translating a future payment into a value in the present.

present discounted value: the value in the present of future payments.

discount rate: an interest rate used to discount a future payment when computing present discounted value.

QUESTIONS FOR REVIEW

1. Why is the present discounted value of a future payment of \$1 less than \$1?
2. What is the relationship between the discount rate and the interest rate?
3. What happens to the present discounted value of a future payment as the payment date stretches into the future?
4. Why is discounting important for decisions involving actions at different dates?

PROBLEMS

1. Find the present discounted value of
   a. \$100 to be paid at the end of 3 years.
   b. \$1,000 to be paid at the end of 1 year plus \$1,000 to be paid at the end of 2 years.
   c. \$10 to be paid at the end of 1 year, \$10 at the end of 2 years, and \$100 at the end of 3 years.
2. Suppose you win \$1,000,000 in a lottery and your winnings are scheduled to be paid as follows: \$300,000 at the end of 1 year, \$300,000 at the end of 2 years, and \$400,000 at the end of 3 years. If the interest rate is 10 percent, what is the present discounted value of your winnings?
3. You are considering two job offers. You expect to work for the employer for five years. For simplicity, we assume that you will be paid at the end of each year. The two offers are summarized in the following table.

Year	Offer 1	Offer 2
1	\$30,000	\$40,000
2	\$33,000	\$30,000
3	\$36,000	\$33,000
4	\$39,000	\$36,000
5	\$42,000	\$39,000

The primary difference between the two offers is a signing bonus of \$10,000 paid under Offer 2. The annual salary paid in years 2 through 5 is higher under Offer 1 than under Offer 2. If the interest rate is 5 percent, which is the better offer? If the interest rate is 10 percent, which is better?

Part 4

Trade and Global Markets

Chapter 17

Economic Growth and Globalization

Half a million foreign students are now studying in colleges and universities in the United States. Maybe you know some of these students. Maybe you *are* one of these students. There are also about half a million foreign students studying in Germany, France, Japan, and other countries. Many of those foreign students are Americans. Studying abroad is one of the ways in which technical knowledge is spread around the world. It is part of the globalization process. Thanks to improvements in telecommunications, including the Internet, the ability to spread information and interact with people in other countries is increasing rapidly.

This highly visible diffusion of information raises some fundamental questions about economic theory, especially about economic growth theory. While economic growth theory tells us how technology and capital have provided people with the means to raise their productivity, there is something disquieting about the theory when we look around the world. As we compare living standards, it is clear that people in some countries are much better off than people in other countries. Why has the theory applied so unevenly to different countries around the world, with some growing rapidly and others being stuck in poverty and not growing at all? Why hasn't the spread of technological information allowed poor countries to grow faster? Will acceleration of globalization change all this?

In this chapter, we look for answers to these crucial questions about the uneven patterns of economic growth in different countries. We begin our quest for the answers by looking at economic growth performance in different parts of the world.

CATCHING UP OR NOT?

If technological advances can spread easily, as seems reasonable with modern communications, then poorer regions with low productivity and low income per capita will tend to catch up to richer regions by growing more rapidly. Why? If the spread of new technology is not difficult, then regions with lower productivity can adopt the more advanced technology of other regions to raise their productivity. Recall from the *growth accounting formula* that an increase in the growth of technology leads to an increase in productivity growth.

growth accounting formula: Productivity growth rate = $\frac{1}{3}\begin{pmatrix}\text{growth rate of capital}\\ \text{per hour of work}\end{pmatrix}$ + (growth rate of technology) (Ch. 9)

Investment in new capital would also tend to cause poor regions to catch up to the rich. Consider a relatively poor region in which both capital per worker and output per worker are low. Imagine several hundred workers constructing a road with only a little capital—perhaps only a few picks and shovels, not even a jackhammer. With such low levels of capital, the returns to increasing the amount of capital would be very high. The addition of a few trucks and some earthmoving equipment to the construction project would bring huge returns in higher output. Regions with relatively low levels of capital per worker would therefore attract a greater amount of investment, and capital would grow rapidly. The growth accounting formula tells us that productivity grows rapidly when capital per worker grows rapidly. Thus, productivity would grow rapidly in poorer regions where capital per worker is low.

A rich region where the capital per worker is high, however, would gain relatively little from additional capital. Such a region would attract little investment, and the growth rate of capital would be lower; therefore, the growth of productivity would also be lower.

In summary, economic growth theory predicts that regions with low productivity will grow relatively more rapidly than regions with high productivity. Regions with low productivity will tend to catch up to the more advanced regions by adopting existing technology and attracting capital.

Figure 1 illustrates this catch-up phenomenon. It shows the level of productivity on the horizontal axis and the growth rate of productivity on the vertical axis. The downward-sloping line is the **catch-up line.** A country or region on the upper left-hand part of the line is poor—with low productivity and, therefore, low income per capita—but growing rapidly. A country on the lower right-hand part of the line is rich—with high productivity and, therefore, high income per capita—but its growth is relatively less rapid. That the catch-up line exists and is downward-sloping is a prediction of growth theory.

catch-up line: the downward-sloping relation between the level of productivity and the growth of productivity predicted by growth theory.

Catch-up Within the United States

Let us first see how the catch-up line works when the regions are the states within the United States. Figure 2 presents the data on real income per capita and the growth rate of real income per capita for each of the states. Because productivity and real income per capita move closely together, we can examine the accuracy of the catch-up line using the real income per capita data. (Again, the adjective *real* means that the income data are adjusted for inflation.) Real income per capita in 1880 is on the horizontal axis, and the growth rate of real income per capita from 1880 to 1980 is on the vertical axis. Each point on the scatter diagram represents a state, and a few of the states are labeled. If you pick a state (observe Nevada, for example, down and to the right), you can read its growth rate by looking over to the left scale, and you can read its 1880 income per capita level by looking down to the horizontal scale.

The diagram clearly shows a tendency for states with low real income per capita in 1880 to have had high growth rates since then. The state observations fall

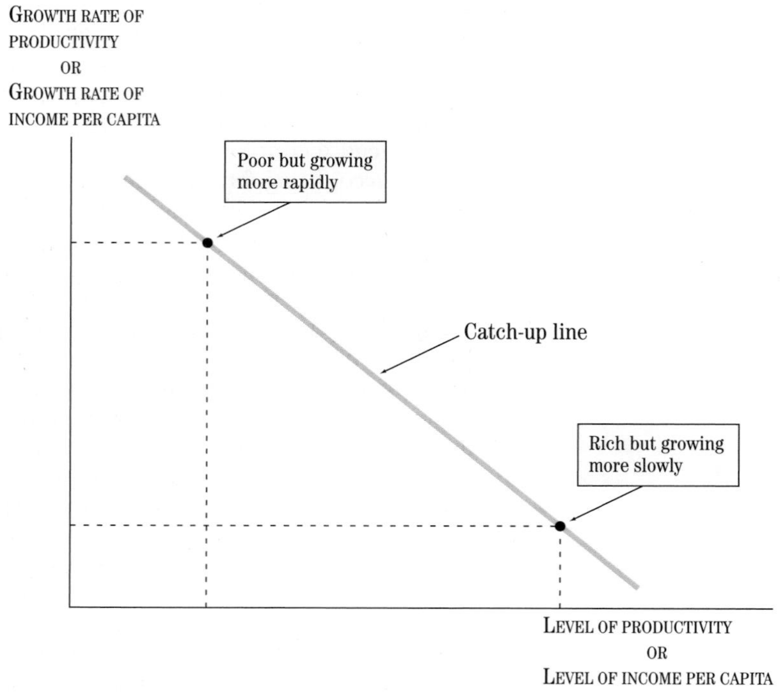

FIGURE 1
The Catch-up Line
Growth theory with spreading technology and diminishing returns to capital and labor predicts that regions with lower productivity will have higher growth rates of productivity. The catch-up line illustrates this prediction. Because productivity is so closely related to income per capita, the catch-up line can also describe a relationship between income per capita and the growth rate of income per capita.

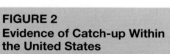

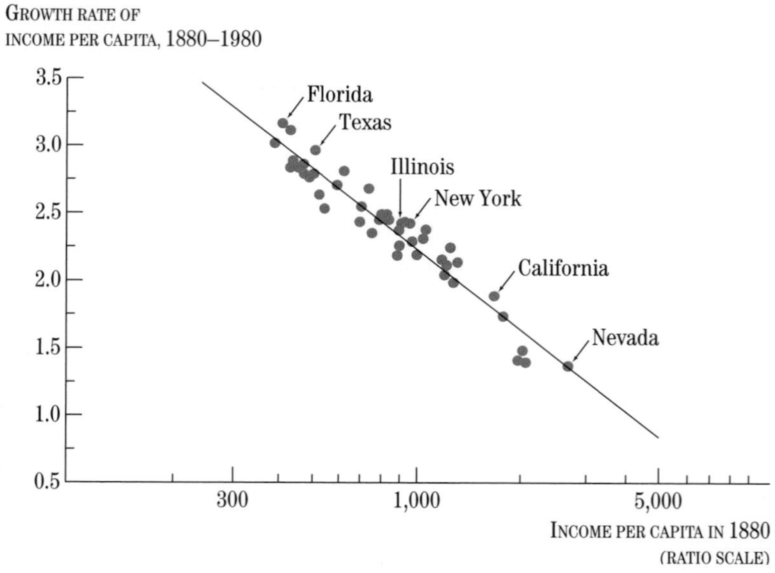

FIGURE 2
Evidence of Catch-up Within the United States
In the United States, those states that had low real income per capita in 1880 grew relatively rapidly compared to states that had high income per capita. The poor states tended to catch up to the richer states. A catch-up line is drawn through the dots.

remarkably near a catch-up line. Southern states like Florida and Texas are in the high-growth group. On the other hand, in states that had a relatively high income per capita in 1880, income per capita grew relatively slowly. This group includes California and Nevada.

Thus, the theory of growth works quite well in explaining the relative differences in growth rates in the states of the United States. There is a tendency for relatively poor regions to grow more rapidly than relatively rich regions.

Catch-up in the Advanced Countries

What if we apply the same thinking to different countries? After all, communication is now global. Figure 3 is another scatter diagram with growth rate and income per capita combinations. It is like Figure 2 except that it plots real GDP per capita in 1960 against growth in real GDP per capita from 1960 to 2000 for several advanced countries.

Observe in Figure 3 that the richer countries, such as the United States, grew less rapidly. In contrast, relatively less rich countries, such as Japan, Ireland, and Spain, grew more rapidly. Canada and France are somewhere in between. These countries tend to display the catch-up behavior predicted by growth theory. Apparently, technological advances are spreading and capital-labor ratios are rising more rapidly in countries where they are low and returns to capital are high. So far, our look at the evidence confirms the predictions of growth theory.

Catch-up in the Whole World

However, so far we have not looked beyond the most advanced countries. Figure 4 shows a broader group of countries that includes not only the more advanced countries in Figure 3 but also countries that are still developing. It is apparent that there is little tendency for this larger group of countries to fall along a catch-up line.

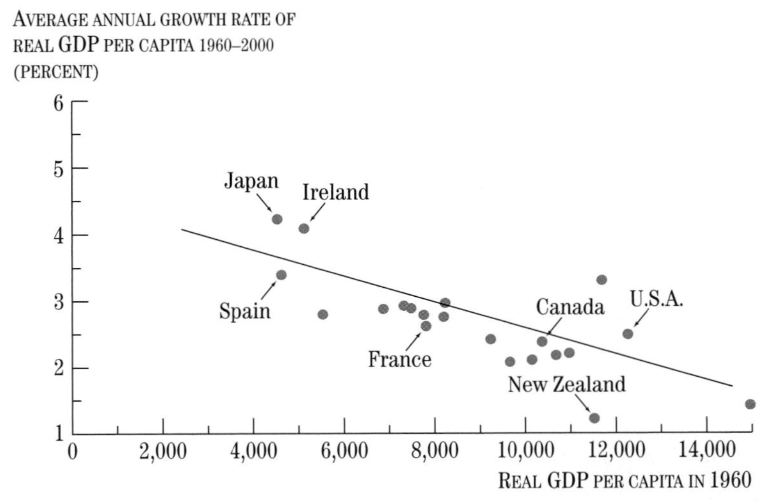

FIGURE 3
Evidence of Catch-up in More Advanced Countries, 1960–2000
For the advanced countries shown in the diagram, GDP per capita growth has been more rapid for those that started from a lower level of GDP per capita. Thus, there has been catching up, as shown by the catch-up line drawn through the points.

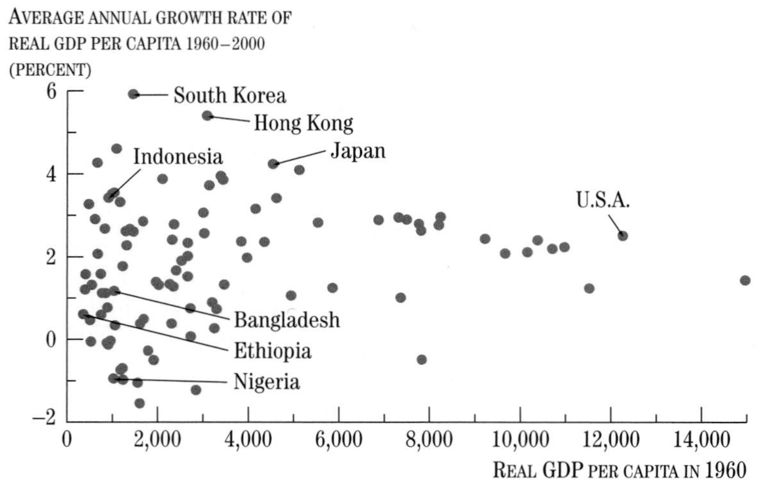

FIGURE 4
Lack of Catch-up for Developing Countries, 1960–2000
Unlike the states in the United States or the advanced countries, there has been little tendency for poor countries to grow more rapidly than rich countries. The gap between rich and poor has not closed.

The countries with very low growth rates, such as Bangladesh and Ethiopia, are also the countries with very low GDP per capita. On the other hand, many countries with higher growth rates had a much higher GDP per capita. Japan and Hong Kong had higher growth rates than Nigeria and Ethiopia even though their GDP per capita was above that of these countries.

Comparing countries like Indonesia and South Korea with countries like Bangladesh and Nigeria is striking. South Korea and Indonesia had about the same real GDP per capita as Nigeria and Bangladesh in 1960, but South Korea and Indonesia surged ahead with a more rapid growth rate over the next 30 years, leaving Bangladesh and Nigeria behind. And this is not the exception. Contrary to the predictions of economic growth theory, which says that technological advances should spread and capital per hour of work should rise from low levels, Figure 4 shows little tendency for relatively poor countries to grow relatively rapidly. It appears that something has been preventing either the spread and the adoption of new technology or the increase in investment needed to raise capital-labor ratios. We examine possible explanations as this chapter proceeds.

REVIEW

- Economic growth theory predicts that poorer regions will tend to catch up to richer ones. The flow of technology around the world and investment in new capital will bring this about.
- Data for the states in the United States and for the more advanced countries show that such catch-up exists and is quite strong.
- However, there has been little evidence of catch-up in the world as a whole. Many of the poor countries have fallen even further behind the developed countries, while other poor countries, in particular those in East Asia, have grown very rapidly.

ECONOMIC DEVELOPMENT

As well as raising questions about economic growth theory, the lack of catch-up evidenced in Figure 4 presents a disturbing situation. There are huge disparities in world income distribution, and billions of people in low-income countries lack the necessities that those in high-income countries frequently take for granted.

Billions Still in Poverty

The richest countries in the world, with more than $10,000 income per capita, account for about 850 million people. The United States, with 300 million people, is among the richest, along with Japan and most of Western Europe. Another 650 million people live in countries that have an income per capita between $5,000 and $10,000. But the vast majority of the world's people—about 70 percent—live in countries with an income per capita of less than $5,000 per year. This is below the poverty level in advanced countries. Income per capita in Argentina, Venezuela, and Malaysia is only about one-third that in the United States. In China and Peru, income per capita is only one-eighth that in the United States. Income per capita for Ethiopia is a mere 2 percent of that in the United States.

Today there are more than 3 billion people—half the human race—who live on less than 2 U.S. dollars per day. Every year some 3 million people die for lack of immunization, 1 million die from malaria, 3 million die from water-related diseases, and 2 million die from exposure to stove smoke inside their own homes. In addition, HIV/AIDS has ravaged the populations of developing nations, particularly in Africa, killing 3 million people in 2003 alone. More than 1 billion people don't have safe water to drink, 2 billion have no electricity, and 2 billion lack adequate sanitation.

Low income per capita is a serious economic problem, but the implications go well beyond economics. Large differences in income per capita and vast amounts of poverty can lead to war, revolution, or regional conflicts. Will these differences persist? Or is the lack of catch-up that has left so many behind a thing of the past?

Geographical Patterns

Figure 5 shows the location of the relatively rich and the relatively poor countries around the world. Notice that the higher-income countries tend to be in the northern part of the world. Exceptions to this rule are Australia and New Zealand, with relatively high income per capita. Aside from these exceptions, income disparity appears to have a geographical pattern—the North is relatively rich and the South relatively poor. Often people use the term *North-South problem* to describe world income disparities.

But whether it is North versus South or not, there do appear to be large contiguous regions where many rich or many poor countries are located together. The original increase in economic growth that occurred at the time of the Industrial Revolution started in northwestern Europe—England, France, and Germany. It then spread to America, which industrialized rapidly in the nineteenth and twentieth centuries. It also spread to Japan during the late-nineteenth-century Meiji Restoration, one of the main purposes of which was to import Western technology into the Japanese economy.

Terminology of Economic Development

economic development: the process of growth by which countries raise incomes per capita and become industrialized; also refers to the branch of economics that studies this process.

Economic development is the branch of economics that endeavors to explain why poor countries do not develop faster and to find policies to help them develop faster. Economists who specialize in economic development frequently are experts on the

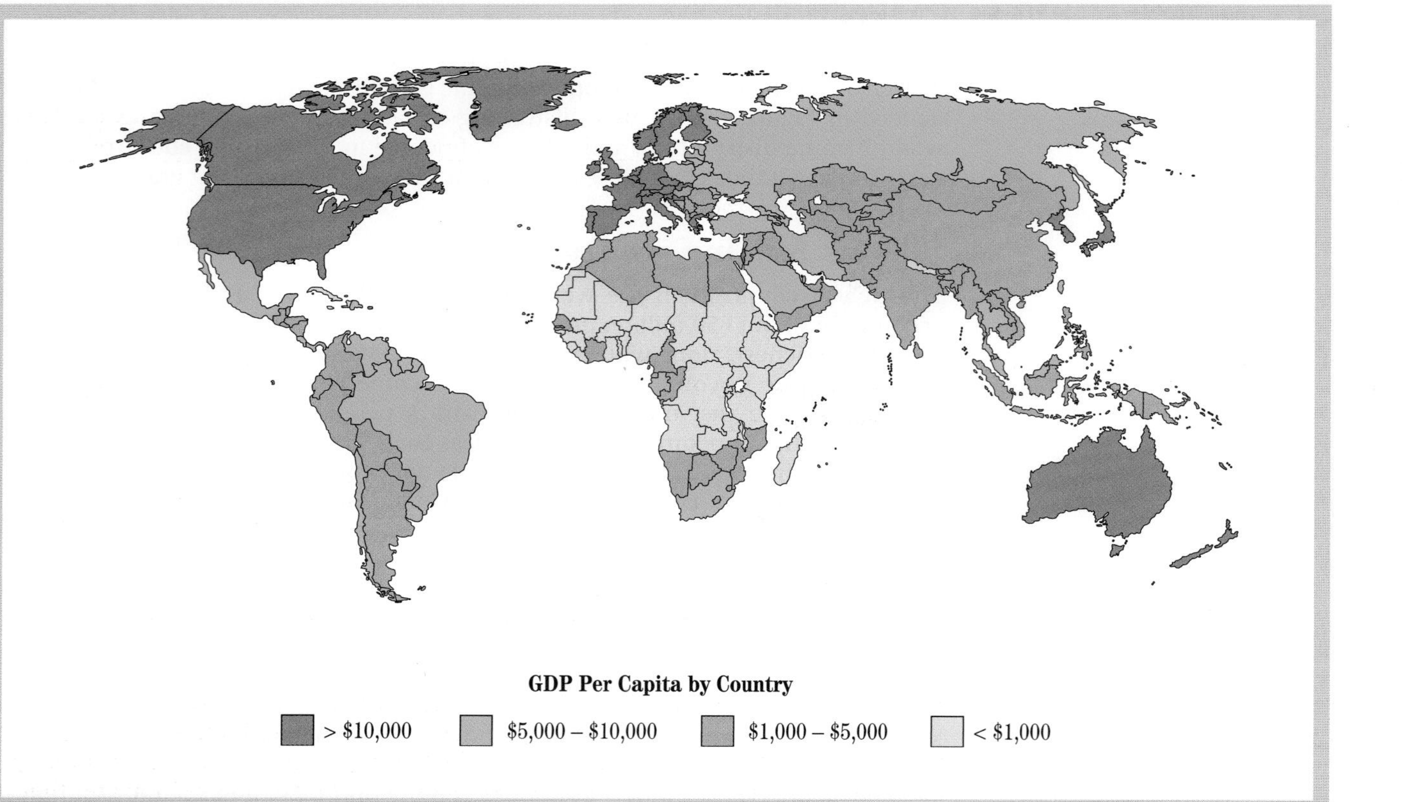

FIGURE 5
Rich and Poor Countries Around the World

The highest-income regions tend to be located in North America, Europe, Japan, Australia, and the Middle East.

developing country: a country that is poor by world standards in terms of real GDP per capita.

problems experienced by particular countries—such as a poor educational system, political repression, droughts, or poor distribution of food. The term **developing country** describes those countries that are relatively poor. In contrast, the term *industrialized country* or *advanced economy* describes relatively well-off countries. Sometimes the term *less-developed country (LDC)* is used rather than *developing country*. There are also terms to distinguish between different developing countries. For example, *emerging market countries* such as Chile and Malaysia are relatively poor countries that are growing rapidly.

Table 1 shows the shares of world GDP produced by advanced economies and developing countries. Thus, this table looks at aggregate income (which equals GDP) rather than at income per capita. Over 50 percent of world GDP comes from industrialized countries.

Most striking is the more than 27 percent share of world GDP in Asia outside of Japan. This large share is due to the emerging market countries and to China. China's GDP is already almost twice as large as Japan's. Although income per capita is less, China is a major force in the world economy.

Economic development economists working at universities, the World Bank, the International Monetary Fund, the United Nations, and of course in the developing countries themselves focus their research on reasons why poor countries have grown

TABLE 1
Shares of World GDP Produced by Different Countries

	Number of Countries	Percent of World GDP
Advanced Economies	**29**	**52.3**
Major industrialized countries	7	41.1
United States		20.1
Japan		6.4
Germany		4.1
France		3.0
Italy		2.7
United Kingdom		3.0
Canada		1.8
Other advanced economies	22	11.2
Developing Countries	**145**	**47.7**
Africa	48	3.3
Asia	23	27.1
Middle East	13	2.8
Western Hemisphere	33	7.4
Central and Eastern Europe	15	3.3
Russia	1	2.6
Transcaucas and Central Asia	13	1.2

Source: From *World Economic Outlook*, September 2006, p. 182. Reprinted by permission of International Monetary Fund.

so slowly. We now proceed to examine these reasons; in doing so, we will touch on some of the central issues of economic development. Our examination will consider the two key determinants of increasing productivity—improvements in technology and higher capital per worker. We consider technology in the next section and then go on to consider capital in the following section.

REVIEW

- The slow productivity growth in poor countries has resulted in extreme income inequality around the world. The growth miracle has spread to parts of the world, but productivity in many developing countries of the world has remained low.
- With a few exceptions, most of the rich countries are in the northern regions of the globe and most of the poor countries are in the southern regions, giving rise to the term *North-South problem*.
- About 70 percent of the world's population lives in countries with less than $5,000 income per capita.

SPREADING AND USING TECHNOLOGY

There are two important facts to remember about economic growth. First, a large and persistent increase in economic growth began during the Industrial Revolution about 200 years ago, and this increase in economic growth raised income per capita in some countries to levels experienced only by royalty throughout most of human history. Second, economic growth did not spread throughout much of the world, leaving people in many countries hardly better off than their ancestors. Could these two facts be linked? Could they have the same explanation? A number of ideas have been put forth to explain the increase in economic growth in the late 1700s, and some of these may help explain why growth has not accelerated in many developing countries.

Empowering Entrepreneurs

Some economists and historians have pointed to developments in science as the explanation of the rapid increase in economic growth in Europe in the 1700s. But if that is the explanation, why did the Industrial Revolution not begin in China or in the Islamic nations, where scientific knowledge was far more advanced than in Europe? Others note the importance of natural resources, but these were available in many other countries where there was no Industrial Revolution; also, growth in Japan has been high since the mid-nineteenth century, yet Japan has almost no natural resources. Still others have focused on exploitation, slavery, colonialism, and imperialism, but these evils existed long before the Industrial Revolution.

What, then, is the reason for this increase in economic growth that we associate with the Industrial Revolution? Historians of capitalist development from Karl Marx onward have stressed that in the 1700s, for the first time in human history, entrepreneurs were gaining the freedom to start business enterprises. Economic historian Angus Maddison shows in an influential book, *Phases of Capitalist Development,* that the Dutch were the first to lead in productivity, with the British and then the United States soon catching up. He also shows that in the 1700s, many Dutch farmers owned their land, the feudal nobility was small and weak, and the potential power was in the hands of entrepreneurs. Hence there was greater freedom to produce and sell manufactured and agricultural products. By the late 1700s and early 1800s, similar conditions existed in the United Kingdom and the United States. Firms could ship their products to market and hire workers without political restrictions.

Moreover, these firms were able to earn as much as they could by selling whatever they wanted at whatever price the market determined. They began to invent and develop products that were most beneficial to individuals. The business enterprises could keep the profits. Profits were no longer confiscated by nobles or kings. Individual property rights—including the right to earn and keep profits—were being established and recognized in the courts.

This knitting cooperative in Ecuador opens up a market for women who traditionally knitted at home for their families. The freedom to start businesses and to produce and sell manufactured products without restriction is a critical piece of the economic growth puzzle for many developing countries.

Karl Marx—although known more for his critique of capitalism—saw earlier than others that the unleashing of business enterprises and entrepreneurs was the key to economic growth. He credited the business and entrepreneurial class—what he called the bourgeois class—with the creation of more wealth than had previously been created in all of history.

In sum, the sudden increase in technology and productivity may have occurred when it did because of the increased freedom that entrepreneurs had to start businesses, to invent and apply new ideas, and to develop products for the mass of humanity where the large markets existed.

Remaining Problems in Developing Countries

If true, the idea that the economic growth surge in the late 1700s and 1800s was caused by the removal of restrictions on business enterprises may have lessons for economic development. In many developing countries, there are restrictions on entrepreneurial activity and weak enforcement of individual property rights.

Regulation and Legal Rights. Good examples of these restrictions have been documented in the research of economist Hernando de Soto on the economy of Peru. De Soto showed that there is a tremendous amount of regulation in the developing countries. This regulation has been so costly that a huge informal economy has emerged. The **informal economy** consists of large numbers of illegal businesses that can avoid the regulations. Remarkably, de Soto found that 61 percent of employment in Peru was in the informal, unregulated, illegal sector of the economy. In the city of Lima, around 33 percent of the houses were built by this informal sector. About 71,000 illegal vendors dominated retail trade, and 93 percent of urban transportation was in the informal sector.

informal economy: the portion of an economy characterized by illegal, unregulated businesses.

This large informal sector exists because the costs of setting up a legal business are high. It takes 32 months—filling out forms, waiting for approval, getting permission from several agencies—for a person to start a retail business. It takes 6 years and 11 months to start a housing construction firm. Hence, it is essentially impossible for someone to try to start a small business in the legal sector. Therefore, the informal sector grows.

Why does it matter if the informal sector is large? How does this impede development? Precisely because the sector is informal, it lacks basic legal rights such as the enforcement of the laws of property rights and contracts. These laws cannot be enforced in a sector that is outside the law. Bringing new inventions to market requires the security of private property so that the inventor can capture the benefits from taking the risks. Without this, the earnings from the innovation might be taken away by the government or by firms that copy the idea illegally. For example, if a business in the informal sector finds that another firm has reneged on a contract to deliver a product, that business has no right to use the courts to enforce the contract because the business itself is illegal.

The explanation given earlier for why the Industrial Revolution occurred in Western countries seems to point to this as a reason. In Europe in the 1700s, a new freedom for businesses to operate in the emerging market economy led to new products and technology. Laws to prevent theft or fraud gave people more certainty about reaping the returns from their entrepreneurship.

Lack of Human Capital. In order for existing technology to be adopted—whether in the form of innovative organizational structures of firms or as new products—it is necessary to have well-trained and highly skilled workers. For example, it is hard to make use of sophisticated computers to increase productivity when there are few skilled computer programmers.

Recall that human capital refers to the education and training of workers. Low investment in human capital is a serious obstacle to increasing productivity because it hampers the ability of countries that are behind to use new technology.

In fact, economists have found that differences in human capital in different countries can explain why some countries have been more successful at catching up than others. The developing countries that have been catching up most rapidly—in particular the newly industrialized countries like South Korea, Hong Kong, Taiwan, and Singapore—have strong educational systems in grade school and high school. This demonstrates the enormous importance of human capital for raising productivity.

ECONOMICS IN ACTION

The Millennium Challenge Corporation

The Millenium Challenge Corporation (MCC) is a new foreign aid program through which the United States gives assistance to very poor countries. It was established by an act of Congress in 2003, and its stated mission is to reduce poverty by promoting economic growth. In designing the MCC, the administration and Congress took account of the basic principles of economic development that have emerged from economic research in recent years. They are exactly the ones described in this chapter. Hence the MCC is an excellent example of economics in action.

The basic idea is to give more aid to countries that are following pro-growth policies. How do you determine which countries those are? Numerical indicators are used. Countries that rank high on the indicators get assistance from the MCC. Countries that rank low do not. The MCC uses 16 indicators. They include indicators of:

- *Open trade policy.* The numerical measure of openness is taken from the Heritage Foundation's Index of Economic Freedom. The index is based on average tariff rates and other barriers to trade. Open economies—those with low trade barriers—tend to grow faster than more closed economies.
- *Days to start a business.* This index comes from the World Bank. The shorter the time it takes to start a business, the more entrepreneurs are empowered. Bureaucratic barriers to business formation hinder entrepreneurship.
- *Regulatory quality rating.* The World Bank also measures the burden on business arising from licensing requirements and bureaucratic corruption. Excessive regulations and their arbitrary application deter investment and raise the cost of doing business, thereby reducing economic growth.
- *Rule of law.* This index comes from Freedom House. It attempts to measure the effectiveness and predictability of the judiciary and the enforceability of contracts.
- *Civil liberties.* This is another Freedom House indicator. It evaluates freedom of expression, association and organizational rights, rule of law and human rights, and personal autonomy and economic rights.

Of course, none of these indicators is a perfect measure of actual policies, but overall they provide an excellent measure of the kinds of economic policies that promote economic growth. In fact, if you rank countries on these criteria, you will find that they correlate highly with the level of development.

Countries that have ranked relatively high on the list and have been awarded MCC grants thus far include Ghana, Madagascar, Georgia, and Honduras. It will take a while before a full evaluation of the effectiveness of this program can be made, but the preliminary results indicate that at the least it is encouraging better economic policies. If it works well, then more of this new type of foreign aid should follow.

REVIEW

- The removal of restrictions on private enterprise and enforcement of individual property rights may have been the key factors unleashing the growth of productivity at the time of the Industrial Revolution. Similar restrictions in developing countries may have tended to stifle development in recent years.
- An educated work force is needed to adopt technology. Better-educated and more highly skilled workers—those with human capital—can also use available capital more efficiently.

INCREASING CAPITAL PER WORKER

In addition to obstacles to the spread and adoption of new technology, there are obstacles to the increase in capital per worker that can prevent poor countries from catching up.

Population Growth

In order for the capital-to-labor ratio to increase, it is necessary to invest in new capital. However, the amount of investment in new capital must be larger than the increase in labor, or capital will increase by less than labor and the ratio of capital to labor—the factor influencing productivity—will fall. Thus, high population growth raises the amount of investment needed in order to increase, or even maintain, the level of capital per worker. High population growth rates can, therefore, slow down the increase in capital per worker.

Population growth rates have declined substantially in locations where income per capita has risen to high levels, such as Europe, Japan, and the United States. Economic analysis of the determinants of population indicates that the high income per capita and resulting greater life expectancy may be the reason for the decline in population growth. When countries reach a level of income per capita where people can survive into their old age without the support of many children, or where there is a greater chance of children reaching working age, people choose to have fewer children. Hence, higher income per capita in developing countries would probably reduce population growth in these countries.

National Saving

Capital accumulation requires investment, which requires saving. From our national income accounting equation, $Y = C + I + G + X$, we get the equation $Y - C - G = I + X$, which states that national saving is equal to the sum of investment plus net exports. Recall that national saving is the sum of private saving and government saving. In some developing countries where income per capita is barely above subsistence levels, the level of private saving—people's income less their consumption—is low. Government saving—tax receipts less expenditures—is also often low, perhaps because there is little income to tax and because governments have trouble controlling expenditures. Saving rates in Africa are low compared with the higher saving rates in advanced economies and in Asia.

> National saving
> = investment + net exports
> $S = I + X$

For a poor country, it is natural for national saving to be less than investment and thus for imports to be greater than exports (net exports less than zero). In other words, a poor country naturally looks to investment from abroad as a source of capital formation for economic growth.

Foreign Investment from the Advanced Economies

foreign direct investment: investment by a foreign entity in at least a 10 percent direct ownership share in a firm.

Investment from abroad can come in the form of **foreign direct investment,** such as when the U.S. firm Gap Inc. opens a store in Mexico. Technically, when a foreign firm invests in more than 10 percent of the ownership of a business in another country, that investment is defined as direct investment.

Foreign investment also occurs when foreigners buy smaller percentages (less than 10 percent) of firms in developing economies. For example, foreign investment in Mexico takes place when a German buys newly offered common stock in a Mexican firm. In that case, the foreign investment from abroad is defined as **portfolio investment,** that is, less than 10 percent of ownership in a company.

portfolio investment: investment by a foreign entity in less than a 10 percent ownership share in a firm.

Another way investment can flow in from abroad is through borrowing. Firms in developing economies or their governments can borrow from commercial banks, such as Bank of America, Mizuho, or Crédit Lyonnais. Sometimes the governments of developing economies obtain loans directly from the governments of industrialized economies. Borrowing from government-sponsored international financial institutions, such as the International Monetary Fund (IMF) and the World Bank, can also occur.

Activists such as U2 star Bono have been effective proponents of efforts to improve the effectiveness of foreign aid. By working with the governments of the United States, the United Kingdom, and others, they have helped improve and increase foreign aid through such programs as the Millennium Challenge Corporation and 100 percent debt cancellation of World Bank loans to the poorest countries.

World Bank: an international agency, established after World War II, designed to promote the economic development of poorer countries through lending channeled from industrialized countries.

International Monetary Fund (IMF): an international agency, established after World War II, designed to help countries with balance of payments problems and to ensure the smooth functioning of the international monetary system.

The **World Bank** and the **International Monetary Fund (IMF)** were established after World War II as part of a major reform of the international monetary system. Both institutions make loans to the developing countries. They serve as intermediaries, channeling funds from the industrialized countries to the developing countries.

Many of the World Bank's loans are for specific projects—such as building a $100 million dam for irrigation in Brazil and a $153 million highway in Poland. Although these project loans have been helpful, they are much smaller in total than private investment in these countries.

In recent years, the IMF has tried to use its loans to encourage countries to implement difficult economic reforms. Frequently, it tries to induce countries to make these reforms by making the loans conditional on the reforms; this is the idea of *conditionality*. Under conditionality, the IMF gives loans to countries only if the countries undertake economic reform—such as eliminating price controls or privatizing firms. This conditionality is viewed as a way to encourage reforms that are difficult to put into effect because of the various vested interests in each country.

However, the IMF has been heavily criticized in recent years for going too far with its conditions and actually giving bad economic advice to developing countries. For example, during the financial crisis in East Asia in 1997 and 1998, the IMF insisted that the countries in crisis implement politically controvercsial reforms before it would agree to make loans to deal with the crisis.

REVIEW

- High rates of population growth and low national saving rates are two of the obstacles to raising capital per worker in developing economies.
- The International Monetary Fund makes loans to developing countries. The loans are frequently conditional on an economic reform program, a practice that came under heavy criticism in the Asian financial crisis of the 1990s.
- The World Bank makes loans mainly for specific projects.

ECONOMICS IN ACTION

Is There a Global Saving Glut?

In March 2005, Ben Bernanke, new chairman of the Federal Reserve, remarked that "over the past decade a combination of diverse forces has created a significant increase in the global supply of saving—a global saving glut," and that this increase in saving helped to explain "the relatively low level of long-term real interest rates in the world today." However, a recent article in the *Economist* magazine showed that world saving rates had in fact decreased slightly, from about 23 percent of world GDP in the 1990s to about 22 percent of world GDP in 2004. If world saving had decreased, why was Bernanke talking about a "saving glut," and why had world interest rates fallen over the last decade?

We can utilize the saving-investment diagram introduced in Chapter 7, and shown here, to illustrate the mechanism that Bernanke was discussing in his lecture. The world interest rate is measured on the vertical axis, and world saving or investment as a share of world GDP is shown on the horizontal axis. Recall that along the saving curve, the saving rate rises as the interest rate rises because a higher interest rate gives people a greater incentive to save. Recall also that along the investment curve, the investment rate declines as the interest rate rises because a higher interest rate discourages businesses from investing in plants and equipment. (We can conveniently ignore net exports in the analysis because for the whole world, net exports must be zero.) The world investment rate must equal the world saving rate; hence, the equilibrium interest rate is found at the intersection of the two curves.

How would you use this diagram to explain the fact that both the world saving rate fell and the world interest rate fell? We know that the world saving curve shifted left, so the only possibility is that the world investment curve must have shifted left even further. This caused the equilibrium real interest rate to decline even though saving was declining. So Bernanke's discussion of a "saving glut" was simply a statement that the countries of the world were saving more than they wanted to invest, not necessarily that they were saving more than they had been doing before. In order to restore equilibrium between world saving and world investment, the world interest rate fell, driving investment higher and reducing saving until the two became equal again.

Why was global investment so low? The *Economist* suggests that a series of events in the late 1990s and early 2000s, including the financial crisis in East Asia and the collapse of the dot-com bubble in the United States in 2000, may have reduced the desire to invest in virtually all economies other than China and India. Similarly, increases in saving in countries like Japan and Germany may have led to the imbalance between saving and investment that resulted in world interest rates falling to restore equilibrium.

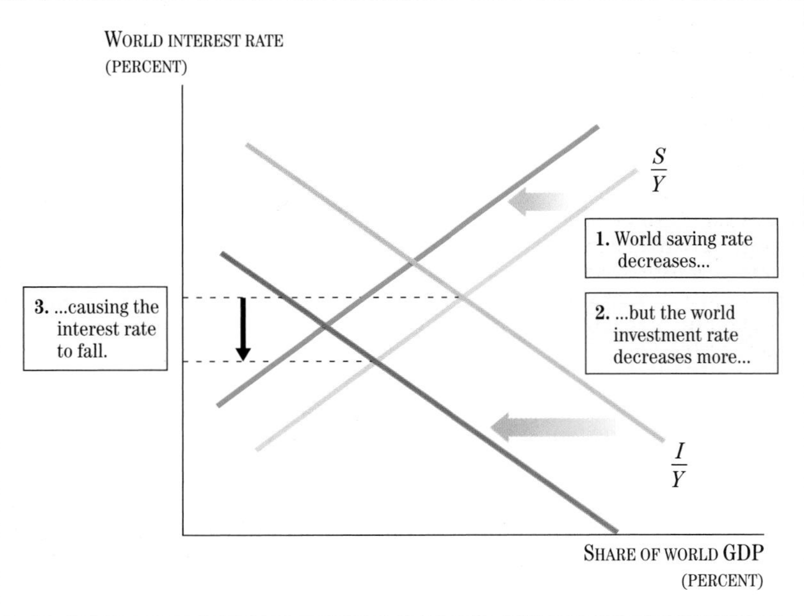

CONCLUSION

In this chapter, we have shown how productivity has increased in many countries because of higher capital per worker and technological change. In some cases there has been a convergence of productivity, with the poorer countries moving closer to the richer countries. However, for many developing countries, productivity has not been catching up, and income per capita remains very low. Many countries in Africa are still in extreme poverty.

Among the possible explanations for the lack of catch-up are obstacles to the spread of technology, such as government restrictions on entrepreneurs and a shortage of human capital, and obstacles to higher capital per worker, such as low saving rates and low foreign investment. The removal of similar obstacles in Western Europe in the eighteenth century may have been the cause of the Industrial Revolution. Their removal today may result in another great growth wave in the developing economies.

In fact, there are already signs of the removal of such obstacles to economic growth. Hence, in the absence of retrenchments or setbacks from terrorism, military conflicts, or increased protectionism due to an antiglobalization movement, we may see higher productivity growth in the poorer countries in the future than we have seen in the past. If so, the economic landscape of the world will be transformed.

Suppose, for example, that real GDP in the industrialized countries grows at a 2.5 percent pace for the next 50 years. Suppose that real GDP in all the other countries of the world grows at 5 percent per year. With these growth rates, the countries that we now classify as developing would produce 75 percent of world GDP in the year 2050, and the countries we now classify as industrialized would produce 25 percent—a complete about-face from the current situation. This, of course, is an example, not a forecast, but it hints at some of the amazing possible effects of globalization on the future.

KEY POINTS

1. Economic growth theory pinpoints capital accumulation and technological change as the two key ingredients of productivity growth. In a world without obstacles to the spread of technology or to investment in new capital, growth theory predicts that poor regions will catch up to rich regions.
2. Catch-up has occurred in the states of the United States and among the industrialized countries but is distressingly absent from developing countries.
3. Low incomes and poverty have persisted for the vast majority of the world's population while other countries have become richer.
4. Insufficient capital accumulation in the poor countries, due to high population growth, low saving rates, or insufficient capital flows from the advanced countries, is part of the problem.
5. Higher population growth means that more investment is required in order to raise capital per worker.
6. Some countries may have poor growth performance because of restrictions on markets and a lack of property rights. The lifting of those restrictions in Europe in the 1700s was a cause of the economic growth associated with the Industrial Revolution.
7. The removal of such restrictions may be a key to increased productivity and economic development.
8. Low investment in human capital is another reason for low productivity growth.
9. In many countries today, especially in Latin America and Asia, there is a great potential for higher economic growth, as the market system is being encouraged and restrictions on entrepreneurs are being removed.
10. Another great growth wave would change the economic landscape of the whole world.

KEY TERMS

catch-up line
economic development
developing country
informal economy
foreign direct investment
portfolio investment
World Bank
International Monetary Fund (IMF)

QUESTIONS FOR REVIEW

1. Why does economic growth theory predict that productivity and real income per capita will grow relatively more rapidly in poor countries?
2. In what way does the catch-up line describe more rapid growth in poor countries?
3. Why is catch-up observed among the industrialized economies but not for the whole world?
4. Why is the identity that investment plus net exports equals saving important for understanding the flow of capital around the world?
5. What is the difference between foreign direct investment and portfolio investment?
6. Why is human capital important for the spread of technology?
7. What do government restrictions on entrepreneurs have to do with economic growth?
8. What harm does an informal economy cause?
9. What role do international organizations like the IMF and the World Bank play in promoting economic growth and economic development?
10. What is the significance of conditionality for IMF loans?

PROBLEMS

1. Plot on a scatter diagram the data for the Asian countries that appear below. Does there appear to be a catch-up line in the scatter diagram?

Country	Per Capita Real GDP in 1960 (2000 U.S. dollars)	Average Annual Rate of Growth from 1960 to 2000 (%)
Thailand	1,051	4.6
Pakistan	526	2.9
Philippines	1,581	1.3
China	746	4.3
Malaysia	1,918	3.9
Indonesia	403	3.4

2. The rule of 72 gives the approximate doubling time of a variable if you know its rate of growth. For example, if the population of a country is 200 million and the rate of growth of its population is 2 percent per year, then it will take approximately 36 years for the country's population to reach 400 million. Assume that per capita income in 2006 is $40,000 in the United States and $5,000 in China. If the per capita growth rate in China is 9 percent a year, how long will it take for China to reach a per capita income level that is equivalent to the United States's 2006 per capita income level?
3. Which of the following will increase the likelihood of poor countries catching up to rich countries, and which will decrease the likelihood? Explain.
   - **a.** Industrial countries do not allow their technology to be bought or leased by firms in developing countries.
   - **b.** Worldwide saving rates shift up.
   - **c.** The legal system in developing countries is improved to protect property rights.
   - **d.** Governments in developing countries make use of their international aid to buy armaments from developed countries.
   - **e.** Investment in human capital increases in the developing countries.
4. The states of the United States have moved toward one another in real income per capita over the past 100 years, but the countries of the world have not. What differences are there between state borders and country borders that might explain this problem?
5. Figure 2 shows that California and Nevada had very high levels of per capita income in 1880. What was the source of their high income? Identify some countries in the world that currently have relatively high per capita income for a similar reason.
6. Figure 5 identifies the countries with the highest GDP per capita in the world. What characteristics of the labor forces in these countries provide part of the explanation for their higher incomes?
7. Suppose a developing country does not allow foreign investment to flow into the country and, at the same time, has a very low saving rate. Use the fact that saving equals investment plus net exports and the growth accounting formula to explain why this country will have difficulty catching up with the industrialized countries. What can the country do to improve its productivity if it does not allow capital in from outside the country?
8. Most developing countries have low saving rates and governments that run budget deficits. What will be required for such countries to have large increases in their capital stocks? What will happen if industrialized countries' saving rates decline as well? How does this affect the developing countries' prospects for catching up?

Chapter 18

The Gains from International Trade

Bangalore, an Indian city of about 6 million people, has undergone a remarkable economic transformation in recent times. Bangalore is now one of the leading cities in the production of computer software; according to India's National Association of Software and Service Companies, the value of software produced in Bangalore has increased 750-fold in the last 15 years. The rapid increase in jobs in the software and information technology industry has brought prosperity to an increasing number of workers in Bangalore. An article that appeared in *USA Today* on March 22, 2004, describes the transformation of the lives of Bangalore's software workers, who earn a salary doing work outsourced by U.S. companies and then spend their earnings on IBM computers, Hyundai cars, Domino's Pizza, and Stairmasters (to work off the pizza!).

Similar stories can be told about U.S. trade with many countries in the world. Every day, people in countries like China, Germany, Korea, Japan, and Sri Lanka buy American products: Caterpillar tractors, Motorola cellular phones, Microsoft software, Boeing 747s, and Merck pharmaceuticals. At the same time, Americans drive cars made in Germany and Japan, listen to CDs and MP3s on electronic equipment made in China and Malaysia, play tennis wearing Nike shoes made in Korea, or go swimming in Ocean Pacific swimsuits made in Sri Lanka.

These stories about firms selling their products around the world and people consuming goods made in other countries illustrate reasons why people benefit from international trade. First, international trade allows firms such as Merck access to a very large world market, enabling them to invest heavily in research and reduce costs by concentrating production. Second, international trade allows different countries to specialize in what they are relatively efficient at producing, such as pharmaceuticals in the United States or electronic equipment in Malaysia.

gains from trade: improvements in income, production, or satisfaction owing to the exchange of goods or services. (Ch. 1)

This chapter explores the reasons for these *gains from trade* and develops two models that can be used to measure the actual size of these gains. We begin, however, with a brief look at recent trends in international trade.

RECENT TRENDS IN INTERNATIONAL TRADE

international trade: the exchange of goods and services between people or firms in different nations. (Ch. 1)

tariff: a tax on imports.

quota: a governmental limit on the quantity of a good that may be imported or sold.

commerce clause: the clause in the U.S. Constitution that prohibits restraint of trade between states.

International trade is trade between people or firms in different countries. Trade between people in Detroit and Ottawa, Canada, is international trade, whereas trade between Detroit and Chicago is trade within a country. Thus, international trade is just another kind of economic interaction; it is subject to the same basic economic principles as trade between people in the same country.

International trade differs from trade in domestic markets, however, because national governments frequently place restrictions, such as **tariffs** or **quotas,** on trade between countries that they do not place on trade within countries. For example, the Texas legislature cannot limit or put a tariff on the import of Florida oranges into Texas. The **commerce clause** of the U.S. Constitution forbids such restraint of trade between states. But the United States can restrict the import of oranges from Brazil. Similarly, Japan can restrict the import of rice from the United States, and Australia can restrict the import of Japanese automobiles.

International trade has grown much faster than trade within countries in recent years. Figure 1 shows the exports for all countries in the world as a percentage of the world GDP. International trade has doubled as a proportion of the world GDP during the last 30 or so years. Why has international trade grown so rapidly? What economic or technological forces have led to this increase in globalization?

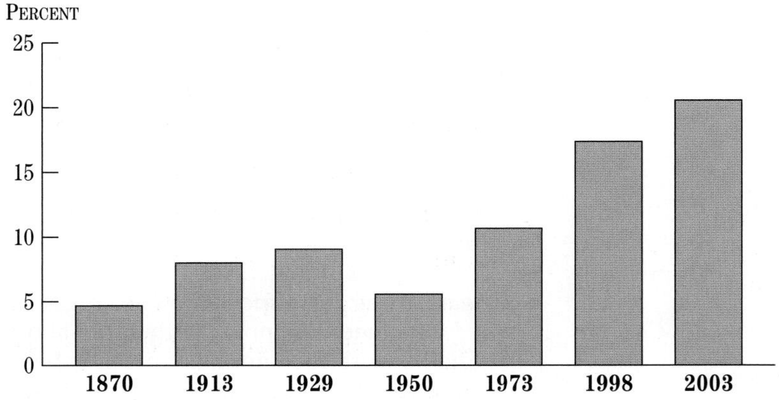

FIGURE 1
World Exports as a Share of GDP

The faster growth of exports compared to GDP is probably due to the reduction in trade restrictions and the lower cost of transportation, both characteristics of greater globalization.

Source: Angus Maddison, *The World Economy: A Millenial Perspective,* (OECD, 2001), Table F-5.

One reason is that the cost of transportation and communication has been reduced dramatically. The cost of air travel fell to 9.5 cents per mile in 2000 from 87 cents per mile in 1930, while the cost of a three-minute phone call from New York to London fell to $.24 in 2002 from $315 in 1930 (adjusting the 1930 prices for general inflation). E-mail and the Internet, unheard of in 1930, reduce costs even further.

However, the most important reason that trade has expanded so rapidly is that government restrictions on trade between countries have come down. Western European countries are integrating into a single market. Canada, Mexico, and the United States have agreed to integrate their economies into a free trade area, where the term *free* indicates the elimination of restrictions on trade. Previously closed economies have opened themselves to world trade through major political and economic reforms. The formerly closed economies in Eastern Europe, Russia, and, especially, China have joined the world trading system. Export-oriented countries in Asia are growing rapidly, and governments in South America such as Argentina and Chile are opening their economies to competition and foreign trade.

These countries are making these changes in an effort to help people. But how do people gain from international trade? Let's now consider that question.

REVIEW

- The basic principles of economics apply to international trade between people in different countries.
- There is a greater tendency for governments to interfere with trade between countries than with trade within their own country.
- International trade has grown rapidly in recent years because of reduced transportation and communication costs and, especially, lower government barriers to trade.

COMPARATIVE ADVANTAGE

comparative advantage: a situation in which a person or country can produce one good at a lower opportunity cost than another person or country. (Ch. 1)

According to the theory of *comparative advantage,* a country can improve the income of its citizens by allowing them to trade with people in other countries, even if the people of the country are less efficient at producing all items.

Getting a Gut Feeling for Comparative Advantage

First, consider a parable that conveys the essence of comparative advantage. Rose is a highly skilled computer programmer who writes computer-assisted drawing programs. Rose owns a small firm that sells her programs to architects. She has hired an experienced salesman, Sam, to contact the architects and sell her software. Thus, Rose specializes in programming, and Sam specializes in sales.

absolute advantage: a situation in which a person or country is more efficient at producing a good in comparison with another person or country.

You need to know a little more about Rose. Rose is a friendly, outgoing person, and because she knows her product better than Sam does, she is better than Sam at sales. We say that Rose has an **absolute advantage** over Sam in both programming and sales because she is better at both jobs. But it still makes sense for Rose to hire Sam because her efficiency at programming compared to Sam's is greater than her efficiency at sales compared to Sam's. We say that Rose has a *comparative advantage* over Sam in programming rather than in sales. If Rose sold her programs, then she would have to sacrifice her programming time, and her profits would fall. Thus, even though Rose is better at both programming and sales, she hires Sam to do the selling so that she can program full time.

All this seems sensible. However, there is one additional part of the terminology that may at first seem confusing but is important. We said that Rose has the comparative advantage in programming, not in sales. But who does have the comparative advantage in sales? Sam does. Even though Sam is less efficient at both sales and programming, we say that he has a comparative advantage in sales because, compared with Rose, he does relatively better at sales than he does at programming. A person cannot have a comparative advantage in both of only two activities.

opportunity cost: the value of the next-best forgone alternative that was not chosen because something else was chosen. (Ch. 1)

Opportunity Cost, Relative Efficiency, and Comparative Advantage. The idea of comparative advantage can also be explained in terms of *opportunity cost*. The opportunity cost of Rose or Sam spending more time selling is that she or he can produce fewer programs. Similarly, the opportunity cost of Rose or Sam spending more time writing programs is that she or he can make fewer sales.

Observe that, in the example, Sam has a lower opportunity cost of spending his time selling than Rose does; thus, it makes sense for Sam to do the selling rather than Rose. In contrast, Rose has a lower opportunity cost of spending her time writing computer programs than Sam does; thus, it makes sense for Rose to write computer programs rather than Sam.

Opportunity costs give us a way to define comparative advantage. A person with a lower opportunity cost of producing a good than another person has a comparative advantage in that good. Thus, Rose has a comparative advantage in computer programming, and Sam has a comparative advantage in sales.

Comparative advantage can also be explained in terms of relative efficiency. A person who is relatively more efficient at producing good X than good Y compared to another person has a comparative advantage in good X. Thus, again, we see that Rose has a comparative advantage in computer programming because she is relatively more efficient at producing computer programs than at making sales compared to Sam.

From People to Countries. Why is this story about Rose and Sam a parable? Because we can think of Rose and Sam as two countries that differ in efficiency at producing one product versus another. In the parable, Rose has a comparative advantage over Sam in programming, and Sam has a comparative advantage over Rose in sales. In general, *country A has a comparative advantage over country B in the production of a good if the opportunity cost of producing the good in country A is less than in country B*, or, alternatively but equivalently stated, *if country A can produce the good relatively more efficiently than other goods compared to country B*. Thus, if you understand the Rose and Sam story, you should have no problem understanding comparative advantage in two countries, which we now examine in more detail.

Productivity in Two Countries

Consider the following two goods: (1) vaccines and (2) TV sets. Different skills are required for the production of vaccines and TV sets. Vaccine production requires knowledge of chemistry and biology, and the marketing of products where doctors make most of the choices. Producing TV sets requires knowledge of electrical engineering and microcircuitry, and the marketing of goods where consumers make most of the choices.

ECONOMICS IN THE NEWS

The Economic Impact of Outsourcing

Perhaps no trend in international trade has attracted as much recent attention as the increase in global outsourcing, whereby a U.S.-based company uses a foreign company to perform a portion of the work involved in producing a good or a service. This article, which appeared in the *New York Times* on June 19, 2005, discusses why some of the fears associated with outsourcing may be a little misplaced.

True or False: Outsourcing Is a Crisis

By EDUARDO PORTER

June 19, 2005, Late Edition Final

If you read only the headlines, the future of globalization may seem scary, indeed. American jobs have already been heading abroad. And as telecommunications and more powerful computers enable companies to take even more jobs overseas, the service sector, which accounts for about 85 percent of the United States work force, will be increasingly vulnerable to competition from the cheap labor pools of the developing world.

So the question looms: Is America on the verge of losing oodles of white-collar jobs? Probably not. The threat of global outsourcing is easily overstated. The debate over the global competition for jobs is awash in dire projections. All those legal assistants in New York and Washington, for example, could be replaced with smart young graduates from Hyderabad. Office support occupations—jobs like data entry assistant, file clerk and the entire payroll department—could also be carried out in remote locations. "We are really at the beginning stages of this, and it is accelerating rapidly," said Ron Hira, assistant professor of public policy at the Rochester Institute of Technology.

Describes what outsourcing is

In a study published this year, two economists at the Organization for Economic Cooperation and Development in Brussels estimated that 20 percent of the developed world's employment could be "potentially affected" by global outsourcing. That could include all American librarians, statisticians, chemical engineers and air traffic controllers, the study said. What does "potentially affected" mean? Even if offshoring didn't drain away all these jobs, global competition for employment—including workers in developing countries who earn so little by comparison—could severely dent the livelihoods of American workers. "It isn't going to hurt in terms of jobs," said William J. Baumol, an economics professor at New York University who has studied the costs of globalization. "It is going to hurt in terms of wages."

Identifies occupations most likely to be affected

But even if millions of tasks can be done by cheaper labor on the other side of the planet, businesses won't rush to move every job they can to wherever the cost is lowest. The labor market isn't quite that global, and it's unlikely to be anytime soon. In a new set of reports, the McKinsey Global Institute, a research group known for its unabashedly favorable view of globalization, argued that 160 million service jobs—about 10 percent of total worldwide employment—could be moved to remote sites because these job functions

Potential number of jobs affected

don't require customer contact, local knowledge or complex interactions with the rest of a business.

Yet after surveying dozens of companies in eight sectors, from pharmaceutical companies to insurers, it concluded that only a small fraction of these jobs would actually be sent away. The report estimates that by 2008, multinational companies in the entire developed world will have located only 4.1 million service jobs in low-wage countries, up from about 1.5 million in 2003. The figure is equivalent to only 1 percent of the total number of service jobs in developed countries.

The number of jobs that may actually be outsourced

Some sectors, like retail and health care, are likely to put very few jobs in poor countries. McKinsey estimated that less than 0.07 percent of health care jobs in 2008 would be outsourced to low-wage countries. But even designers of packaged software, whose work can easily be done abroad, will outsource only 18 percent of their jobs, the report said.

Moving tasks to faraway sites isn't simple. According to McKinsey's study, many business processes are difficult to separate into discrete chunks that can be sent away. Many insurance companies use information technology systems that have been cobbled together over time and would be difficult to manage remotely. Managers can be unwilling or unprepared to work overseas. And sometimes the tasks that can be sent offshore are too small to make the move worthwhile.

Limitations on outsourcing

To top it off, there aren't that many suitable cheap workers available. Human-resources managers interviewed for the McKinsey study said that for reasons ranging from poor language skills to second-rate education systems, only about 13 percent of the young, college-educated professionals in the big developing countries are suitable to work for multinationals. And competition from local companies reduces this pool.

Sure, there are a billion Indians, but only a tiny percentage of the Indian work force have the appropriate qualifications. "Only a fraction have English as a medium of instruction, and only a fraction of those speak English that you or I can understand," said Jagdish N. Bhagwati, a professor of economics at Columbia University.

Of course, many of these obstacles can be overcome with time. The pool of adequate workers in poorer countries will grow, and companies will eventually iron out many of the logistical complications.

But that is likely to take a while. "The rate at which companies are willing and able is much slower than you would realize," said Diana Farrell, director of the McKinsey Global Institute. "We see this as being evolutionary, continuous but measured change."

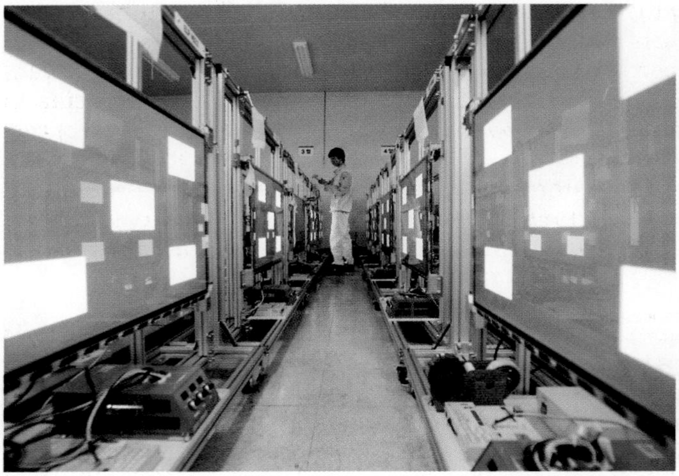

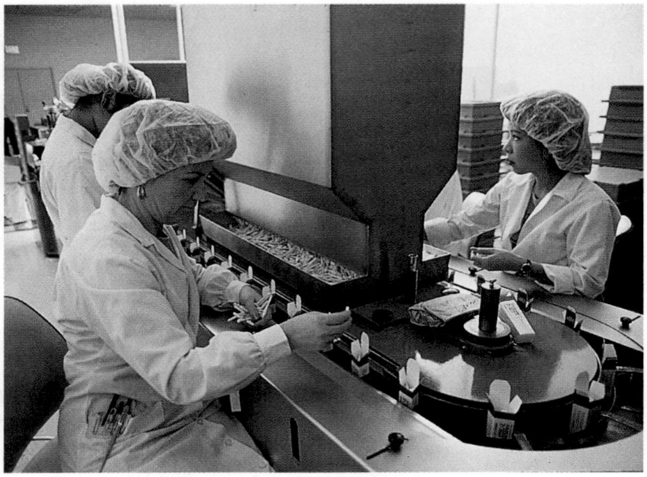

Electronics versus Pharmaceuticals
In the example used in this chapter, Korea has a comparative advantage in an electronic good (TV sets), and the United States has a comparative advantage in a pharmaceutical (vaccines). Thus, with trade, the electronic good will be produced in Korea, as shown in the left-hand photo, and the pharmaceutical good will be produced in the United States, as shown in the right-hand photo.

Table 1 provides an example of productivity differences in the production of vaccines and TV sets in two different countries, the United States and Korea. Productivity is measured by the amount of each good that can be produced by a worker per day of work. To be specific, let us suppose that the vaccines are measured in vials, that the TVs are measured in numbers of TV sets, and that labor is the only factor of production in making vaccines and TV sets. The theory of comparative advantage does not depend on any of these assumptions, but they make the exposition much easier.

According to Table 1, in the United States it takes a worker one day of work to produce 6 vials of vaccine or 3 TV sets. In Korea, one worker can produce 1 vial of vaccine or 2 TV sets. Thus, the United States is more productive than Korea in producing both vaccines and TV sets. We say that a country has an *absolute advantage* over another country in the production of a good if it is more efficient at producing that good. In this example, the United States has an absolute advantage in both vaccine and TV set production.

However, the United States has a comparative advantage over Korea in the production of vaccines rather than TV sets. To see this, note that a worker in the United States can produce 6 times as many vials of vaccine as a worker in Korea but only 1.5 times as many TV sets. In other words, the United States is relatively more efficient in vaccines than in TV sets compared with Korea. Korea, being able to produce TV sets

TABLE 1
Example of Productivity in the United States and Korea

	Output per Day of Work	
	Vials of Vaccine	*Number of TV Sets*
United States	6	3
Korea	1	2

relatively more efficiently than vaccines compared to the United States, has a comparative advantage in TV sets.

Observe also how opportunity costs determine who has the comparative advantage. To produce 3 more TV sets, the United States must sacrifice 6 vials of vaccine; in other words, *in the United States, the opportunity cost of 1 more TV set is 2 vials of vaccine*. In Korea, to produce 2 more TV sets, the Koreans must sacrifice 1 vial of vaccine; in other words, *in Korea, the opportunity cost of 1 more TV set is only 1/2 vial of vaccine*. Thus, we see that the opportunity cost of producing TV sets in Korea is lower than in the United States. By examining opportunity costs, we again see that Korea has a comparative advantage in TV sets.

An American Worker's View. Because labor productivity in both goods is higher in the United States than in Korea, wages are higher in the United States than in Korea in the example. Now think about the situation from the point of view of American workers who are paid more than Korean workers. They might wonder how they can compete with Korea. The Korean workers' wages seem very low compared to theirs. It doesn't seem fair. But as we will see, comparative advantage implies that American workers can gain from trade with the Koreans.

A Korean Worker's View. It is useful to think about Table 1 from the perspective of a Korean worker as well as that of a U.S. worker. From the Korean perspective, it might be noted that Korean workers are less productive in both goods. Korean workers might wonder how they can ever compete with the United States, which looks like a productive powerhouse. Again, it doesn't seem fair. As we will see, however, the Koreans can also gain from trade with the Americans.

Finding the Relative Price

Another example of relative prices may be helpful:
Price of U2 concert = $45
Price of U2 T-shirt = $15
Relative price = 3 T-shirts per concert

To measure how much the Koreans and Americans can gain from trade, we need to consider the *relative price* of vaccines and TVs in Korea and the United States. The relative price determines how much vaccine can be traded for TVs and, therefore, how much each country can gain from trade. For example, suppose the price of a TV set is $200 and the price of a vial of vaccine is $100. Then 2 vials of vaccine cost the same as 1 TV set; we say the relative price is 2 vials of vaccine per TV set. The next few paragraphs show how to determine the relative price from data on the costs of production.

Relative Price Without Trade. First, let us find the relative price with no trade between the countries. The relative price of two goods should depend on the relative costs of production. A good for which the cost of producing an additional quantity is relatively low will have a relatively low price.

Consider the United States. In this example, a day of work can produce either 6 vials of vaccine or 3 TV sets. With labor as the only factor of production, 6 vials of vaccine cost the same to produce as 3 TV sets; that is, 2 vials of vaccine cost the same to produce as 1 TV set. Therefore, the relative price should be 2 vials of vaccine per TV set.

Now consider Korea. Electronic goods should have a relatively low price in Korea because they are relatively cheap to produce. A day of work can produce either 1 vial of vaccine or 2 TV sets; thus 1 vial of vaccine costs the same to produce as 2 TV sets in Korea. Therefore, the relative price is 1/2 vial of vaccine per TV set.

Relative Price with Trade. Now consider what happens when the two countries trade without government restrictions. If transportation costs are negligible and markets are competitive, then the price of a good must be the same in the United States and Korea. Why? Because any difference in price would quickly be eliminated by trade; if the price of TV sets is much less in Korea than in the United States, then traders will buy TV sets in Korea and sell them in the United States and make a profit; by doing so, however, they reduce the supply of TV sets in Korea and increase the supply in the United States. This will drive up the price in Korea and drive down the price in the United States until the price of TV sets in the two countries is the same. Thus, with trade, the price of vaccines and the price of TV sets will converge to the same levels in both countries. The relative price will therefore converge to the same value in both countries.

If the relative price is going to be the same in both countries, then we know the price must be somewhere between the prices in the two countries before trade. That is, the price must be between 2 vials of vaccine per TV set (the U.S. relative price) and 1/2 vial of vaccine per TV set (the Korean relative price). We do not know exactly where the price will fall between 1/2 and 2. It depends on the *demand* for vaccines and TV sets in Korea and the United States. *Let us assume that the relative price is 1 vial of vaccine per TV set after trade,* which is between 1/2 and 2 and is a nice, easy number for making computations. The calculation of the price with trade is summarized in Table 2.

Measuring the Gains from Trade

How large are the *gains from trade* due to comparative advantage? First, consider some examples.

One Country's Gain. Suppose that 10 American workers move out of electronics production and begin producing pharmaceuticals. We know from Table 1 that these 10 American workers can produce 60 vials of vaccine per day. Formerly, the 10 American workers were producing 30 TV sets per day. But their 60 vials of vaccine can be traded for TV sets produced in Korea. With the relative price of 1 vial per TV set, Americans will be able to exchange these 60 vials of vaccine for 60 TV sets. Thus, Americans gain 30 more TV sets by moving 10 more workers into vaccine production. This gain from trade is summarized in Table 3.

The Other Country's Gain. The same thing can happen in Korea. A Korean manufacturer can now hire 30 workers who were formerly working in vaccine production to produce TV sets. Vaccine production declines by 30 vials, but TV production increases by 60 TV sets. These 60 TV sets can be traded with Americans for 60 vials of vaccine. The reduction in the production of vaccine of 30 vials results in

TABLE 2
The Relative Price (The relative price—vials of vaccine per TV set—must be the same in both countries with trade.)

	United States	Korea
Relative price before trade:	2 vials of vaccine per TV set	1/2 vial of vaccine per TV set
Relative price range after trade:	Between 1/2 and 2	Between 1/2 and 2
Relative price assumption:	1	1

TABLE 3
Changing Production and Gaining from Trade in the United States and Korea

	United States (10 workers)		
	Change in Production	*Amount Traded*	*Net Gain from Trade*
Vaccines	Up 60 vials	Export 60 vials	0
TV sets	Down 30 sets	Import 60 sets	30 sets
	Korea (30 workers)		
	Change in Production	*Amount Traded*	*Net Gain from Trade*
Vaccines	Down 30 vials	Import 60 vials	30 vials
TV sets	Up 60 sets	Export 60 sets	0

an import of vaccine of 60 vials; thus, the gain from trade is 30 vials of vaccine. The Koreans, by moving workers out of vaccine production and into TV set production, are getting more vaccine. This gain from trade for Korea is summarized in Table 3. Observe that the exports of TV sets from Korea equal the imports of TV sets to the United States.

Just Like a New Discovery. International trade is like the discovery of a new idea or technique that makes workers more productive. It is as if workers in the United States figured out how to produce more TV sets with the same amount of effort. Their trick is that they actually produce vaccines, which are then traded for the TV sets. Like any other new technique, international trade improves the well-being of Americans. International trade also improves the well-being of the Koreans; it is as if they discovered a new technique, too.

A Graphical Measure of the Gains from Trade

The gains from trade due to comparative advantage can also be found graphically with production possibilities curves, as shown in Figure 2. There are two graphs in the figure—one for the United States and the other for Korea. In both graphs, the horizontal axis has the number of TV sets and the vertical axis has the number of vials of vaccine produced.

Production Possibilities Curves Without Trade. The solid lines in the two graphs show the production possibilities curves for vaccines and TV sets in the United States and in Korea before trade. To derive them, we assume, for illustrative purposes, that there are 10,000 workers in the United States and 30,000 workers in Korea who can make either vaccines or TV sets.

If all the available workers in the United States produce vaccines, then total production will be 60,000 vials of vaccine ($6 \times 10{,}000$) and zero TV sets. Alternatively, if 5,000 workers produce vaccines in the United States and 5,000 workers produce TV sets, then total production will be 30,000 vials of vaccine ($6 \times 5{,}000$) and 15,000 TV sets ($3 \times 5{,}000$). The solid line in the graph on the left of Figure 2 shows these possibilities and all other possibilities for producing vaccines and TV sets. It is the production possibilities curve without trade.

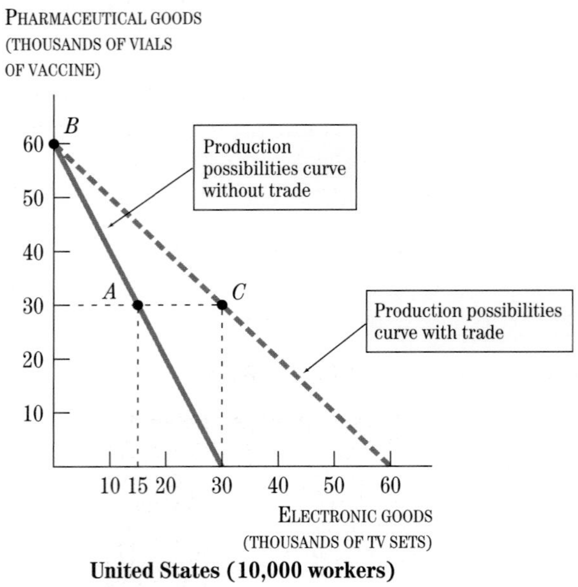

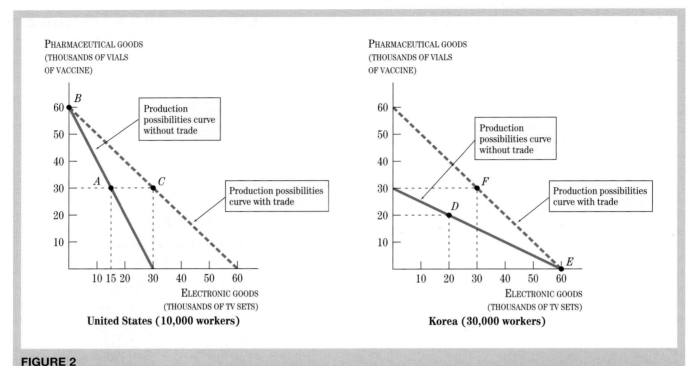

FIGURE 2
Comparative Advantage
On the left, Americans are better off with trade because the production possibilities curve shifts out with trade; thus, with trade, Americans reach a point like *C* rather than *A*. The gains from trade due to comparative advantage are equal to the distance between the two production possibilities curves—one with trade and the other without trade. On the right, Koreans are also better off because their production possibilities curve also shifts out; thus, Koreans can reach point *F*, which is better than point *D*. To reach this outcome, Americans specialize in producing at point *B* and Koreans specialize in producing at point *E*.

Korea's production possibilities curve without trade is shown by the solid line in the graph on the right of Figure 2. For example, if all 30,000 Korean workers produce TV sets, a total of 60,000 TV sets can be produced (2 × 30,000). This and other possibilities are on the curve.

The slopes of the two production possibilities curves without trade in Figure 2 show how many vials of vaccine can be transformed into TV sets in Korea and the United States. The production possibilities curve for the United States is steeper than that for Korea because an increase in production of 1 TV set reduces vaccine production by 2 vials in the United States but by only 1/2 vial in Korea. The slope of the production possibilities curve is the opportunity cost; the opportunity cost of producing TV sets in the United States is higher than it is in Korea.

Production Possibilities Curves with Trade. The dashed lines in the two graphs in Figure 2 show the different combinations of vaccine and TV sets available in Korea and the United States when there is trade between the two countries at a relative price of 1 vial of vaccine for 1 TV set. These dashed lines are labeled "production possibilities curve with trade" to contrast them with the "production possibilities curve without trade" label on the solid line. The diagram shows that the production possibilities curves with trade are shifted out compared with the curves without trade.

ECONOMICS IN ACTION

Doing Politics and Economics

David Ricardo was a man of action. He went to work as a stockbroker at age 14 and eventually accumulated a vast fortune, including a beautiful country estate. He then became one of the most influential economists of all time. He also ran for and won a seat in the British Parliament from which to argue his economic position.

As an economist, Ricardo continued the tradition of Adam Smith. In fact, he got interested in economics after reading Smith's *Wealth of Nations* during a vacation. But Ricardo greatly extended and improved on Smith's theories and made them more precise. Along with Smith and Thomas Robert Malthus—who was Ricardo's close friend but frequent intellectual opponent—Ricardo is considered by historians to be in the classical school, which argued for laissez-faire, free trade, and competitive markets in eighteenth- and nineteenth-century Britain.

Ricardo grappled with three of the most important policy issues in economics: inflation, taxes, and international trade. But Ricardo's most famous contribution is to international trade—in particular, his theory of comparative advantage. Ricardo used this theory when he was in Parliament to argue for repeal of the restrictions on agricultural imports known as the corn laws.

Ricardo's theory of comparative advantage is a good example of how he improved on the work of Adam Smith.

Smith used commonsense analogies to illustrate the gains from trade; one of his examples was "The tailor does not attempt to make his own shoes, but buys them from the shoemaker." As with this tailor and shoemaker example, Smith focused on cases in which one person had an absolute advantage in one good and the other person had an absolute advantage in the other good. But Ricardo showed how there were gains from trade even if one person was better at producing both goods. Here is how Ricardo put it way back in 1817:

Two men can both make shoes and hats, and one is superior to the other in both employments; but in making hats, he can only exceed his competitor by one-fifth or 20 per cent., and in making shoes he can excel him by one-third or 33 per cent.;—will it not be for the interest of both that the superior man should employ himself exclusively in making shoes, and the inferior man in making hats?

DAVID RICARDO, 1772–1823

Born: London, 1772

Education: Never attended college

Jobs:
Stockbroker, 1786–1815
Member of Parliament, 1819–1823

Major Publications:
The High Price of Bullion, 1810
On the Principles of Political Economy and Taxation, 1817
A Plan for a National Bank, 1824

To see how the production possibilities curve with trade is derived, consider how the United States could move from point *A* to point *C* in Figure 2. At point *A*, without trade, Americans produce and consume 15,000 TV sets and 30,000 vials of vaccine by having 5,000 workers in each industry. Now suppose all U.S. workers move out of TV set production into vaccine production, shifting U.S. production to zero TV sets and 60,000 vials of vaccine, as shown by point *B*. Then by trading some of the vaccine, Americans can obtain TV sets. As they trade more vaccine away, they move down the production possibilities curve with trade: 1 less vial of vaccine means 1 more TV set along the curve. If they move to point *C* in the diagram, they have traded 30,000 vials of vaccine for 30,000 TV sets. Americans now have 30,000 TV sets and are left with 30,000 vials of vaccine. By producing more vaccine, the Americans get to purchase more TV sets. The distance from point *A* (before trade) to point *C* (after trade) in Figure 2 is the gain from trade: 15,000 more TV sets.

It would be possible, of course, to choose any other point on the production possibilities curve with trade. If Americans prefer more TV sets and fewer vials of vaccine, they can move down along that dashed line, trading more of their vaccine for more TV sets. In general, the production possibilities curve *with* trade is further out than the production possibilities curve *without* trade, indicating the gain from trade.

Observe that the slope of the production possibilities curve with trade is given by the relative price: the number of vials of vaccine that can be obtained for a TV set. When the relative price is 1 vial per TV set, the slope is -1 because 1 less vial gives 1 more TV set. If the relative price were 1/2 vial per TV set, then the production possibilities curve with trade would be flatter.

The gains to Korea from trade are illustrated in the right-hand graph of Figure 2. For example, at point *D*, without trade, Koreans produce 20,000 TV sets with 10,000 workers and, with the remaining 20,000 workers, produce 20,000 vials of vaccine. With trade, they shift all production into TV sets, as at point *E* on the right graph. Then they trade the TV sets for vaccine. Such trade allows more consumption of vaccine in Korea. At point *F* in the right diagram, the Koreans could consume 30,000 vials of vaccine and 30,000 TV sets, which is 10,000 more of each than before trade at point *D*. As in the case of the United States, the production possibilities curve shifts out with trade, and the size of the shift represents the gain from trade.

This example of Americans and Koreans consuming more than they were before trade illustrates the *principle of comparative advantage: By specializing in producing products in which they have a comparative advantage, countries can increase the amount of goods available for consumption.* Trade increases the amount of production in the world; it shifts out the production possibilities curves.

Increasing Opportunity Costs: Incomplete Specialization. One of the special assumptions in the example we have used in Table 2 and Figure 2 to illustrate the theory of comparative advantage is that opportunity costs are constant rather than increasing. It is because of this assumption that the production possibilities curves without trade in Figure 2 are straight lines rather than the bowed-out lines that we studied in Chapter 1. With increasing opportunity costs, the curves would be bowed out.

The straight-line production possibilities curves are the reason for *complete* specialization, with Korea producing no vaccines and the United States producing no TV sets. If there were increasing opportunity costs, as in the more typical example of the production possibilities curve, then complete specialization would not occur. Why? With increasing opportunity costs, as more and more workers are moved into the production of vaccine in the United States, the opportunity cost of producing more vaccine will rise. And as workers are moved out of vaccine production in Korea, the opportunity cost of vaccine production in Korea will fall. At some point, the U.S. opportunity cost of vaccine production may rise to equal Korea's, at which point further specialization in vaccine production would cease in the United States. Thus, with increasing opportunity costs and bowed-out production possibilities curves, there will most likely be incomplete specialization. But the principle of comparative advantage is not changed by increasing opportunity costs. By specializing to some degree in the goods they have a comparative advantage in, countries can increase world production. There are still substantial gains from trade, whether between Rose and Sam or between America and Korea.

REVIEW

- Comparative advantage shows that a country can gain from trade even if it is more efficient at producing every product than another country. A country has a comparative advantage in a product if it is relatively more efficient at producing that product than the other country.
- The theory of comparative advantage predicts that there are gains from trade from increasing production of the good a country has a comparative advantage in and reducing production of the other good. By exporting the good it has a comparative advantage in, a country can increase consumption of both goods.
- Comparative advantage is like a new technology in which the country effectively produces more by having some goods produced in another country.

REASONS FOR COMPARATIVE ADVANTAGE

What determines a country's comparative advantage? There are some obvious answers. For example, Central America has a comparative advantage over North America in producing tropical fruit because of weather conditions: Bananas will not grow in Kansas or Nebraska outside of greenhouses.

In most cases, however, comparative advantage does not result from differences in climate and natural resources. More frequently, comparative advantage is due to decisions by individuals, by firms, or by the government in a given country. For example, a comparative advantage of the United States in pharmaceuticals might be due to investment in research and in physical and human capital in the areas of chemistry and biology. An enormous amount of research goes into developing technological know-how to produce pharmaceutical products.

In Korea, on the other hand, there may be less capital available for such huge expenditures on research in the pharmaceutical area. A Korean comparative advantage in electronic goods might be due to a large, well-trained work force that is well suited to electronics and small-scale assembly. For example, the excellent math and technical training in Korean high schools may provide a large labor force for the electronics industry.

Comparative advantages can change over time. In fact, the United States did have a comparative advantage in TV sets in the 1950s and early 1960s, before the countries of East Asia developed skills and knowledge in these areas. A country may have a comparative advantage in a good it has recently developed, but then the technology spreads to other countries, which develop a comparative advantage, and the first country goes on to something else.

Perhaps the United States's comparative advantage in pharmaceuticals will go to other countries in the future, and the United States will develop a comparative advantage in other, yet unforeseen areas. The term *dynamic* comparative advantage describes changes in comparative advantage over time because of investment in physical and human capital and in technology.

Labor versus Capital Resources

To illustrate the importance of capital for comparative advantage, imagine a world in which all comparative advantage can be explained through differences between countries in the amount of physical capital that workers have to work with. It is such a world that is described by the Heckscher-Ohlin model, named after the two Swedish economists, Eli Heckscher and Bertil Ohlin, who developed it. Ohlin won a Nobel Prize for his work in international economics. The Heckscher-Ohlin model provides a particular explanation for comparative advantage.

capital abundant: a higher level of capital per worker in one country relative to another.

labor abundant: a lower level of capital per worker in one country relative to another.

capital intensive: production that uses a relatively high level of capital per worker.

labor intensive: production that uses a relatively low level of capital per worker.

Here is how comparative advantage develops in such a model. Suppose America has a higher level of capital per worker than Korea. In other words, America is **capital abundant** compared to Korea, and—what amounts to the same thing—Korea is **labor abundant** compared to America. Pharmaceutical production uses more capital per worker than electronics production; in other words, pharmaceutical production is relatively **capital intensive,** while electronics production is relatively **labor intensive.** Hence, it makes sense that the United States has a comparative advantage in pharmaceuticals: The United States is relatively capital abundant, and pharmaceuticals are relatively capital intensive. On the other hand, Korea has a comparative advantage in electronics because Korea is relatively labor abundant, and electronics are relatively labor intensive. Thus, the Heckscher-Ohlin model predicts that if a country has a relative abundance of a factor (labor or capital), it will have a comparative advantage in those goods that require a greater amount of that factor.

The Effect of Trade on Wages

An important implication of the Heckscher-Ohlin model is that trade will tend to bring factor prices (the price of labor and the price of capital) in different countries into equality. In other words, if the comparative advantage between Korea and the United States was due only to differences in relative capital and labor abundance, then trade would tend to increase real wages in Korea and lower real wages in the United States.

factor-price equalization: the equalization of the price of labor and the price of capital across countries when they are engaging in free trade.

More generally, trade tends to increase demand for the factor that is relatively abundant in a country and decrease demand for the factor that is relatively scarce. This raises the price of the relatively abundant factor and lowers the price of the relatively scarce factor. Suppose the United States is more capital abundant than Korea and has a comparative advantage in pharmaceuticals, which are more capital intensive than electronics. Then with trade, the price of capital will rise relative to the price of labor in the United States. The intuition behind this prediction—which is called **factor-price equalization**—is that demand for labor (the relatively scarce factor) shifts down with trade as the United States increases production of pharmaceuticals and reduces its production of electronic goods. On the other hand, the demand for capital (the relatively abundant factor) shifts up with trade. Although there is no immigration, it is as if foreign workers competed with workers in the labor-scarce country and bid down the wage.

Because technology also influences wages and productivity, it has been hard to detect such movements in wages due to factor-price equalization. Wages of workers in the developed world with high productivity due to high levels of technology remain well above wages of workers in the less-developed world with low productivity due to low levels of technology.

In other words, changes in technology can offset the effects of factor-price equalization on wages. If trade raises technological know-how sufficiently, then no one has to suffer from greater trade. In our example of comparative advantage, American workers are paid more than Korean workers both before and after trade; that is because their overall level of productivity is higher. Workers with higher productivity will be paid more than workers with lower productivity even in countries that trade.

Factor-price equalization can explain another phenomenon: growing wage disparity in the United States during the past 25 years, in which the wages of high-skilled workers have risen relative to the wages of less-skilled workers. The United States is relatively abundant in high-skilled workers, and developing countries are relatively abundant in low-skilled workers. Thus, high-skilled workers' wages should rise and low-skilled workers' wages should fall in the United States, according to factor-price equalization. In this application of factor-price equalization, the two factors are high-skilled workers and low-skilled workers.

In the next section, we show that there are gains in efficiency and lower cost from trade that can benefit all workers.

REVIEW

- Comparative advantage changes over time and depends on the actions of individuals in a country. Thus, comparative advantage is a dynamic concept.
- International trade will tend to equalize wages in different countries. Technological differences, however, can keep wages high in high-productivity countries.

GAINS FROM EXPANDED MARKETS

In the introduction to this chapter, we mentioned the gains from trade that come from larger-sized markets. Having discussed the principle of comparative advantage, we now examine this other source of the gains from trade.

An Example of Gains from Trade Through Expanded Markets

Let us start with a simple example. Consider two countries that are similar in resources, capital, and skilled labor, such as the United States and Germany. Suppose there is a market in Germany and the United States for two medical diagnostic products—magnetic resonance imaging (MRI) machines and ultrasound scanners. Suppose the technology for producing each type of diagnostic device is the same in each country. We assume that the technology is identical because we want to show that trade will take place without differences between the countries.

Figure 3 illustrates the situation. Without trade, Germany and the United States each produce 1,000 MRIs and 1,000 ultrasound scanners. This amount of production meets the demand in the two separate markets. The cost per unit of producing each MRI machine is \$300,000, while the cost per unit of producing each ultrasound scanner is \$200,000. Again, these costs are the same in each country.

Effects of a Larger Market. Now suppose that the two countries trade. Observe in Figure 3—and this is very important—that the *cost per unit* of producing MRIs and ultrasound scanners *declines as more are produced*. Trade increases the size of the market for each product. In this example, the market is twice as large with trade as without it: 2,000 MRIs rather than 1,000 and 2,000 ultrasound scanners rather than 1,000. The production of MRIs in the United States can expand, and the production of ultrasound scanners in the United States can contract. Similarly, the production of ultrasound scanners in Germany can expand, and the production of MRIs in Germany can contract. With the United States specializing in production of MRIs, the cost per unit of MRIs declines to \$150,000. Similarly, the cost per unit of ultrasound scanners declines to \$150,000. The United States exports MRIs to Germany so that the number of MRIs in Germany can be the same as without trade,

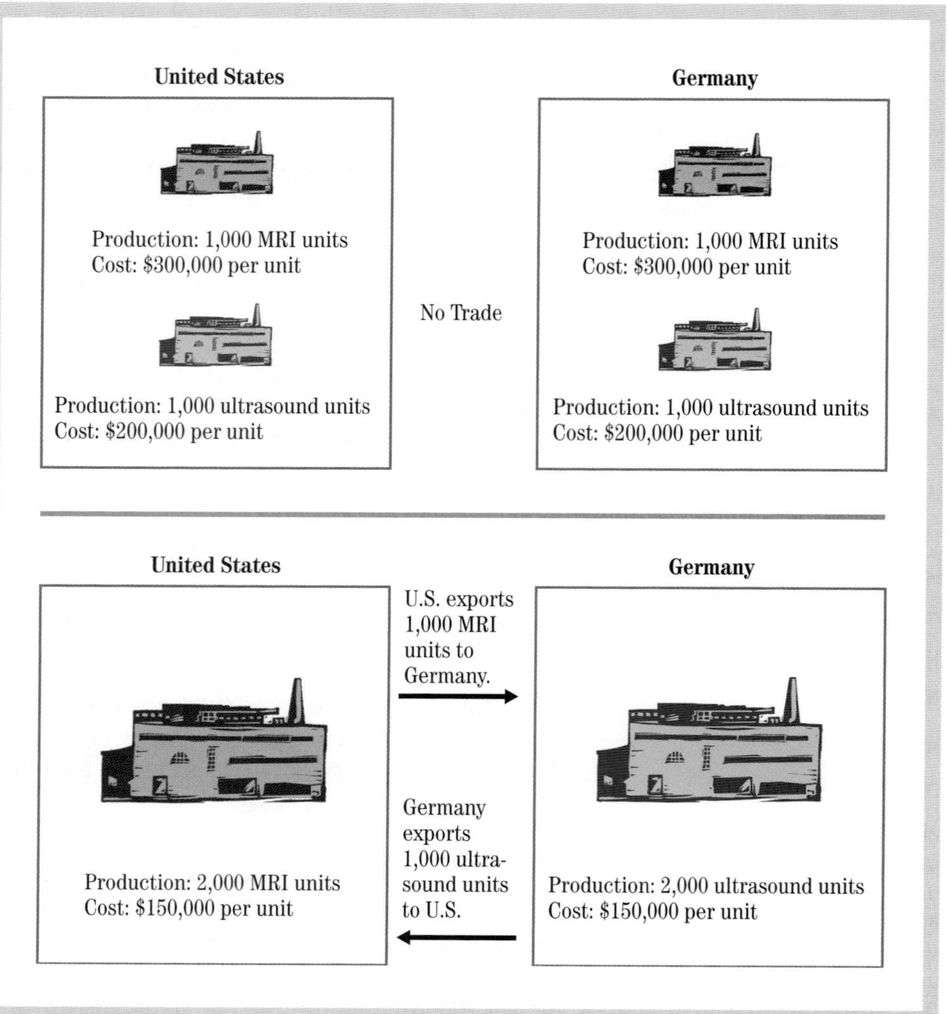

FIGURE 3
Gains from Global Markets
In this example, the technology for producing magnetic resonance imaging (MRI) machines and ultrasound scanners is assumed to be the same in the United States and Germany. In the top panel, with no trade between the United States and Germany, the quantity produced in each country is low and the cost per unit is high. With trade, the U.S. firm increases its production of MRIs and exports to Germany; the German firm increases its production of ultrasound scanners and exports to the United States. As a result, cost per unit comes down significantly.

and Germany exports ultrasound scanners to the United States. The gain from trade is the reduction in cost per unit. This gain from trade has occurred without any differences in the efficiency of production between the two countries.

Note that we could have set up the example differently. We could have had Germany specializing in MRIs and the United States specializing in ultrasound scanner production. Then the United States would have exported ultrasound scanners, and Germany would have exported MRIs. But the gains from trade would have been exactly the same. Unlike the comparative advantage motive for trade, the expanded markets motive alone cannot predict what the direction of trade will be.

Intraindustry Trade versus Interindustry Trade. MRIs and ultrasound scanners are similar products; they are considered to be in the same industry, the medical diagnostic equipment industry. Thus, the trade between Germany and the United States in MRIs and ultrasound scanners is called **intraindustry trade,** which means trade in goods in the same industry.

intraindustry trade: trade between countries in goods from the same or similar industries.

interindustry trade: trade between countries in goods from different industries.

In contrast, the trade that took place in the example of comparative advantage was **interindustry trade,** because vaccines and TV sets are in different industries. In that example, exports of vaccines from the United States greatly exceed imports of vaccines, producing a U.S. industry trade surplus in vaccines. Imports of TV sets into the United States are much greater than exports of TV sets, producing a U.S. industry trade deficit in TV sets.

These examples convey an important message about international trade: Trade due to comparative advantage tends to be interindustry, and trade due to expanded markets tends to be intraindustry. In reality, a huge amount of international trade is intraindustry trade. This indicates that creating larger markets is an important motive for trade.

Measuring the Gains from Expanded Markets

The medical equipment example illustrates how larger markets can reduce costs. To fully describe the gains from trade resulting from larger markets, we need to consider a model.

A Relationship Between Cost per Unit and the Number of Firms. Let us examine the idea that *as the number of firms in a market of a given size increases, the cost per unit at each firm increases.* The two graphs in Figure 4 are useful for this purpose. In each graph, the downward-sloping line shows how cost per unit (or average total cost) at a firm decreases as the quantity produced at that firm increases. Cost per unit measured in dollars is on the vertical axis, and the quantity produced and sold is on the horizontal axis. Observe that cost per unit declines through the whole range shown in the graph. Cost per unit declines because the larger quantity of production allows a firm to achieve a greater division of labor and more specialization.

Focus first on the graph on the left. The total size of the market (determined by the number of customers in the market) is shown by the bracket on the horizontal axis. We assume that the firms in the market have equal shares of the market. For example, if there are 4 firms in the market, then each firm will produce 1/4 of the market. Suppose that there are 4 firms; then, according to Figure 4, the cost per unit at each firm will be $30. This is the cost per unit for the quantity labeled by the box "1 of 4," which means that this is the quantity produced by each 1 of the 4 firms.

Now, suppose that there are 3 firms in the market and each firm produces 1/3 of the market. The cost per unit at each firm will be $25, as shown by the box labeled "1 of 3" in Figure 4. Cost per unit at each firm is lower with 3 firms than with 4 firms in the market because each firm is producing more—that is, 1/3 of the market is more than 1/4 of the market. Continuing in this way, we see that with 2 firms in the market, the cost per unit is $20. And with 1 firm in the market, the cost per unit is $10. In sum, as we decreased the number of firms in the market, each firm produced more and cost per unit decreased. If the number of firms in the market increased, then cost per unit at each firm would increase.

The Effect of the Size of the Market. Now compare the graph on the left of Figure 4 with the graph on the right. The important difference is that the graph on the right represents a larger market than the graph on the left. The bracket in the right-hand graph is bigger to show the larger market.

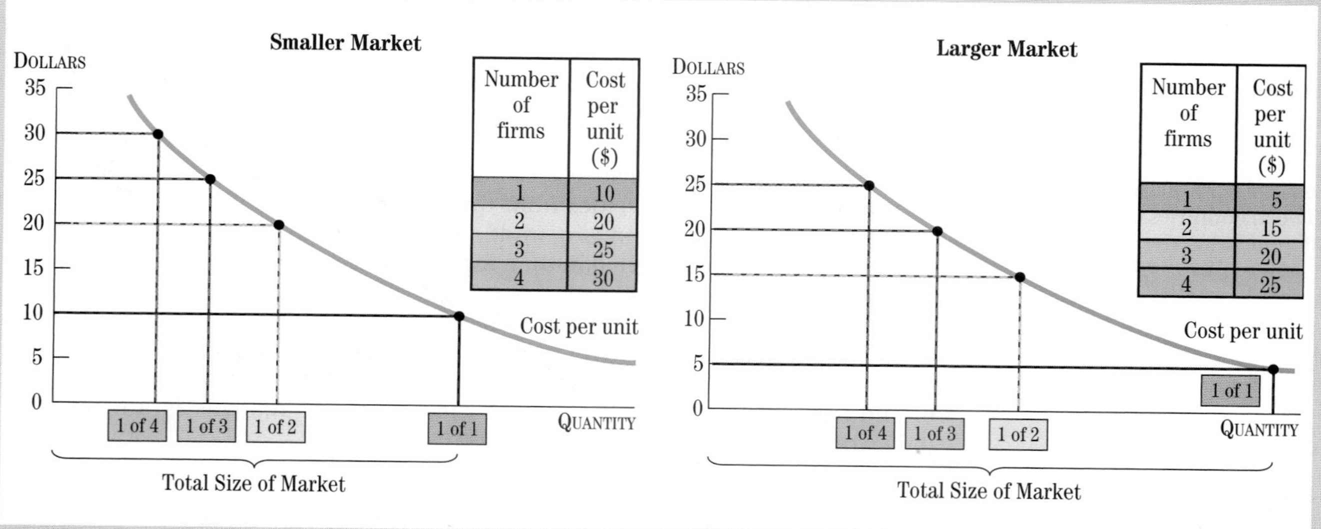

FIGURE 4
Cost per Unit: The Number of Firms and Market Size
(1) The market on the right is larger than the market on the left. Hence, cost per unit is lower on the right with the larger market.
(2) Regardless of the size of the market, cost per unit declines as the number of firms declines.

By comparing the graph on the left in Figure 4 (smaller market) with that on the right (larger market), we see that an increase in the size of the market reduces cost per unit at each firm, holding the number of firms in the industry constant. For example, when there is 1 firm in the market, cost per unit is $5 for the larger market compared with $10 for the smaller market. Or with 4 firms, cost per unit is $25 for the larger market compared with $30 for the smaller market. Compare the little tables in Figure 4. As the market increases in size, each firm produces at a lower cost per unit.

Figure 5 summarizes the information in Figure 4. It shows the positive relationship between the number of firms in the market, shown on the horizontal axis, and the cost per unit at each firm. As the figure indicates, more firms mean a higher cost per unit at each firm. (Be careful to note that the horizontal axis in Figure 5 is the *number* of firms in a given *market*, not the quantity produced by a given firm.) When the size of the market increases, the relationship between the number of firms in the market and the cost per unit shifts down, as shown in Figure 5. In other words, as the market increases in size, cost per unit declines at each firm if the number of firms does not change.

A Relationship Between the Price and the Number of Firms. A general feature of most markets is that as the number of firms in the market increases, the price at each firm declines. More firms make the market more competitive. Thus, there is a relationship between the price and the number of firms, as shown in Figure 6. As in Figure 5, the number of firms is on the horizontal axis. The curve in Figure 6 is downward-sloping because a greater number of firms means a lower price.

Equilibrium Price and Number of Firms. In the long run, as firms either enter or exit an industry, price will tend to equal cost per unit. If the price for each unit were greater than the cost per unit, then there would be a profit opportunity for

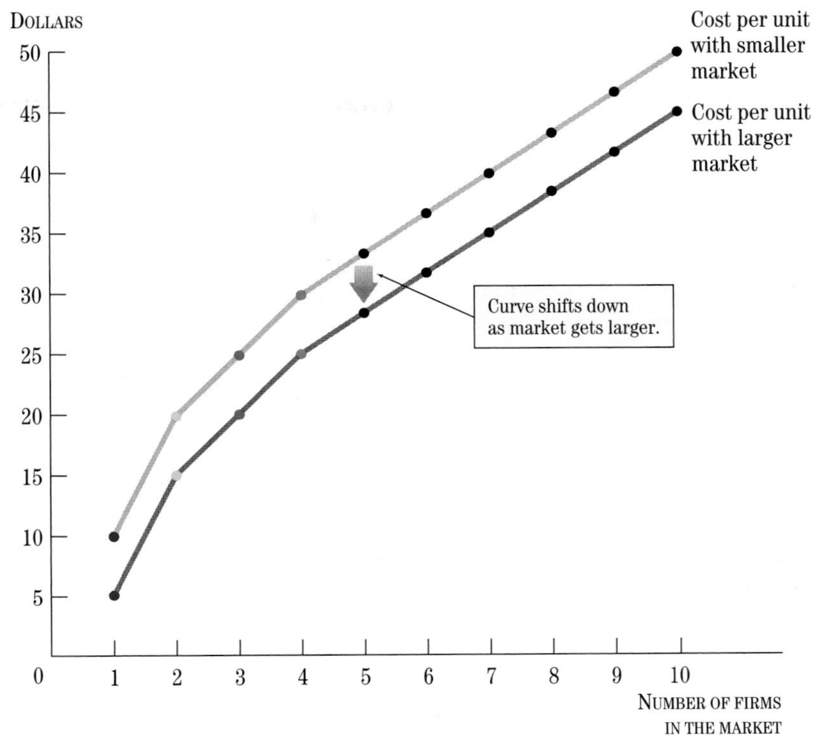

FIGURE 5
The Relationship Between Cost per Unit and the Number of Firms
The first four points on each curve are plotted from the two tables in Figure 4 for 1 to 4 firms; the other points can be similarly obtained. Each curve shows how cost per unit at each firm rises as the number of firms increases in a market of a given size. The curve shifts down when the size of the market increases.

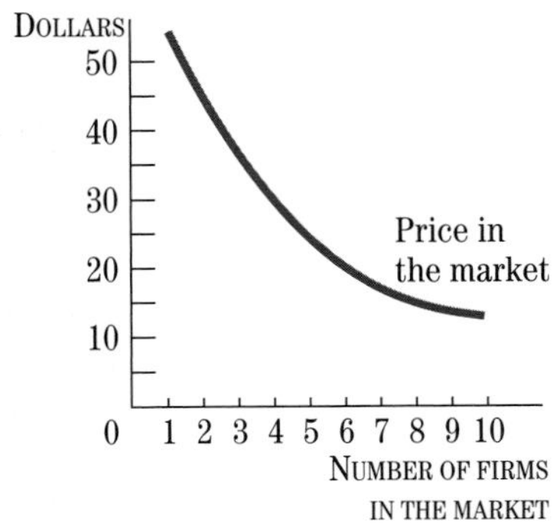

FIGURE 6
The Relationship Between the Price and the Number of Firms
As the number of firms increases, the market price declines. This curve summarizes this relationship.

new firms, and the number of firms in the industry would rise. If the price were less than the cost per unit, then firms would exit the industry. Only when price equals cost per unit is there a long-run equilibrium. Because price equals cost per unit, the curves in Figure 5 and 6 can be combined to determine the price and the number of firms in long-run equilibrium. As shown in Figure 7, there is a long-run equilibrium in the industry when the downward-sloping line for Figure 6 intersects the upward-sloping line (for the smaller market) from Figure 5. At this point, price equals cost per unit.

Corresponding to this long-run equilibrium is an equilibrium number of firms. More firms would lower the price below cost per unit, causing firms to leave the industry; fewer firms would raise the price above cost per unit, attracting new firms to the industry. Figure 7 shows how the possibility of entry and exit results in a long-run equilibrium with price equal to cost per unit.

Increasing the Size of the Market. Now let us see how the industry equilibrium changes when the size of the market increases due to international trade. In Figure 8, we show how an increase in the size of the market, due perhaps to the creation of a free trade area, reduces the price and increases the number of firms.

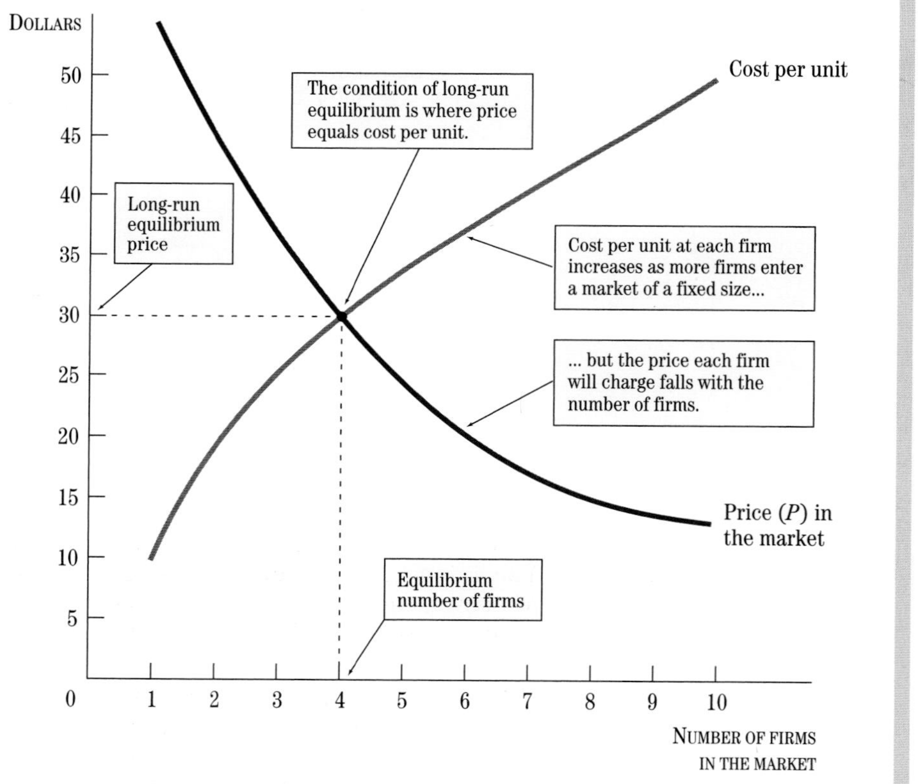

FIGURE 7
Long-Run Equilibrium Number of Firms and Cost per Unit
A condition for long-run equilibrium is that price equals cost per unit. In this diagram, this condition is shown at the intersection of the two curves.

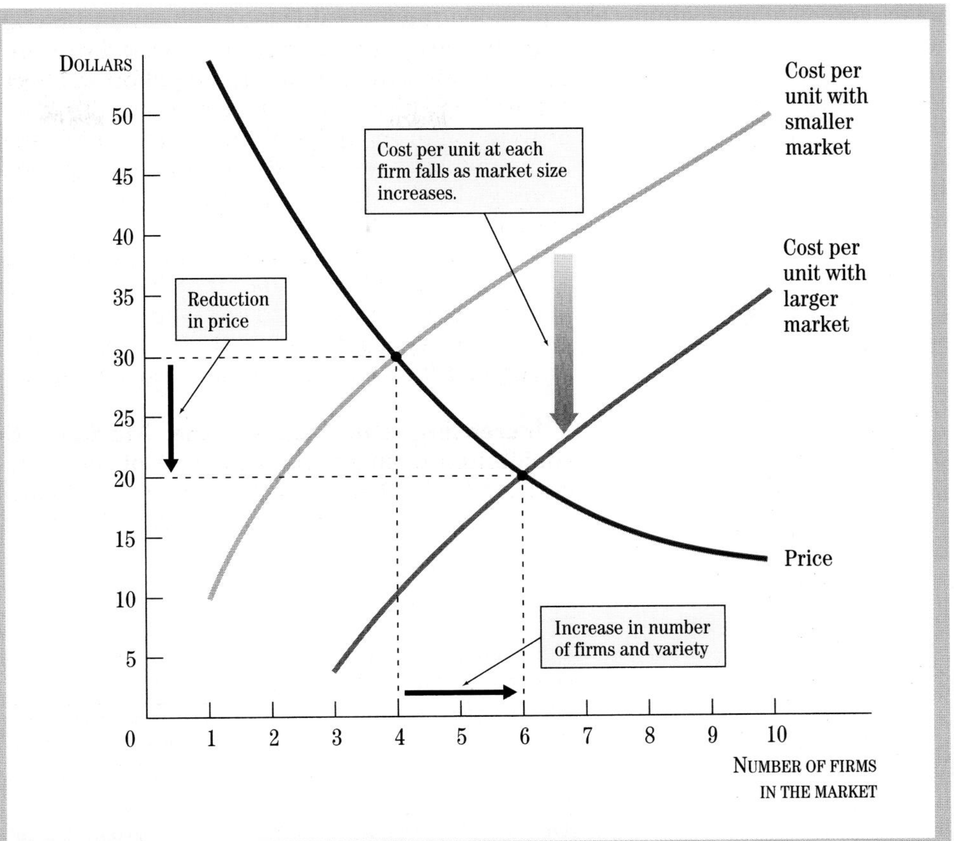

FIGURE 8
Gains from Trade Due to Larger Markets
When trade occurs, the market increases from the size of the market in one country to the combined size of the market in two or more countries. This larger market shifts the upward-sloping line down because cost per unit for each firm is lower when the market is bigger. In the long-run equilibrium at the intersection of the two new curves, the price is lower and there are more firms. With more firms, there is more variety. Lower price and more variety are the gains from trade.

The curve showing the cost per unit of each firm shifts down and out as the market expands; that is, for each number of firms, the cost per unit declines for each firm. This brings about a new intersection and a long-run equilibrium at a lower price. Moreover, the increase in the number of firms suggests that there will be more product variety, which is another part of the gains from trade.

The North American Automobile Market. The gains from trade due to larger markets arise in many real-world examples. Trade in cars between Canada and the United States now occurs even though neither country has an obvious comparative advantage. Before 1964, trade in cars between Canada and the United States was restricted. Canadian factories thus had to limit their production to the Canadian market. This kept cost per unit high. When free trade in cars was permitted, the production in Canadian factories increased, and the Canadian factories began to export cars to the United States. With more cars produced, cost per unit declined.

REVIEW

- Lowering cost per unit through the division of labor requires large markets. International trade creates large markets.
- A graphical model can be used to explain the gains from international trade; the model shows that a larger market reduces prices.

CONCLUSION

In this chapter, we have focused on the economic gains to the citizens of a country from international trade. We have mentioned two reasons for such gains: comparative advantage and larger markets that reduce cost per unit. Both reasons apply to trade within a country as well as to international trade. Most of the chapter was spent showing how to measure the gains due to comparative advantage and larger markets.

In concluding this chapter, it is important to point out that the benefits of international trade go well beyond economic gains.

International trade sometimes puts competitive pressure on governments to deliver better policies. Within the United States, competition between states can make regulatory and tax policies more efficient. Similarly, competition can make regulatory policies in countries more efficient.

International trade can also improve international relations. Trade enables Americans to learn more about Southeast Asians or Europeans or Latin Americans. This improves understanding and reduces the possibilities for international conflict. Developing international trade with Russia and the other countries of the former Soviet Union might even reduce the possibility of another cold war or new international conflict in the future. If many people have an economic stake in a relationship, they will not like a military action that threatens that relationship.

KEY POINTS

1. The principles of economics can be used to analyze international trade just as they can be used to analyze trade within a country.
2. International trade is different from within-country trade because national governments can place restrictions on the trade of goods and services between countries and on immigration.
3. According to the principle of comparative advantage, countries that specialize in producing goods that they have a comparative advantage in can increase world production and raise consumption in their own country.
4. The gains from trade due to comparative advantage can be shown graphically by shifting out the production possibilities curve.
5. The relative price of two goods with trade is between the relative prices in the two countries without trade.
6. Comparative advantage is a dynamic concept. If people in one country improve their skills or develop low-cost production methods through research, they will alter the comparative advantage.
7. If differences in the relative abundance of capital and labor are the reason for differences in comparative advantage, then international trade will tend to equalize real wages.
8. Lower cost per unit in larger markets is another key reason for gains in trade.
9. When the size of the market increases, the price declines, there are more firms, and there is greater variety of products.

KEY TERMS

tariff
quota
commerce clause
absolute advantage
capital abundant
labor abundant
capital intensive
labor intensive
factor-price equalization

QUESTIONS FOR REVIEW

1. Why has international trade grown so rapidly in recent years?
2. What is the difference between absolute advantage and comparative advantage?
3. If the relative price of two goods is 4 in one country and 6 in another country before trade, in what range will the relative price be after trade?
4. What is the difference between the production possibilities curve before trade and after trade?
5. In what sense is comparative advantage a dynamic concept?
6. Why does trade take place even if one country does not have an absolute advantage over another?
7. What is the difference between capital abundant and capital intensive?
8. Why might costs per unit decline when the market increases in size?
9. What is the difference between interindustry trade and intraindustry trade?

PROBLEMS

1. Suppose France has 250 units of labor and Belgium has 100 units of labor. In France, 1 unit of labor can produce 1 box of chocolates or 3 bottles of wine. In Belgium, 1 unit of labor can produce 2 boxes of chocolates or 4 bottles of wine.
   a. Draw the production possibilities curve for each country.
   b. Which country has an absolute advantage in wine production? In chocolate production?
   c. Which country has a comparative advantage in wine production? In chocolate production?
2. Bill and Hillary are two very smart lawyers who also have an active interest in public policy. Bill can write a law paper in 3 months or a policy paper in 1 month. Hillary can write a law paper or a policy paper in 1 month. Bill and Hillary like each other a lot and would like to get married. However, since the marriage of two lawyers is often fraught with difficulty, they decide that one of them should write law papers while the other writes policy papers.
   a. Draw a production possibilities curve for Bill and one for Hillary.
   b. Who has an absolute advantage in writing law papers? In writing policy papers?
   c. Who has a comparative advantage in writing law papers? In writing policy papers?
   d. Explain how to reconcile your answers to (b) and (c).
3. Suppose that the United States has 200 million units of labor and Mexico has 100 million units, and that the production of wheat and strawberries per unit of labor in the United States and Mexico is as follows:

	Wheat	Strawberries
Mexico	1 bushel	3 pints
United States	2 bushels	3 pints

   a. What is the shape of the production possibilities curves for each country? What does this shape imply about the nature of the tradeoff between wheat and strawberries? Is this a realistic assumption? Explain.
   b. Which country has a comparative advantage in wheat production? Why?
   c. With free trade between the United States and Mexico, is it possible that 1 bushel of wheat will trade for 1 pint of strawberries? Why or why not?
   d. Suppose the free trade price is 1 bushel of wheat for 2 pints of strawberries. Draw a diagram indicating the production possibilities curve with and without trade.
4. Suppose there are two goods, wheat and clothing, and two countries, the United States and Brazil, in the world. The production of wheat and clothing requires only labor. In the United States, it takes 1

unit of labor to produce 4 bushels of wheat and 1 unit of labor to produce 2 items of clothing. In Brazil, it takes 1 unit of labor to produce 1 bushel of wheat and 1 unit of labor to produce 1 item of clothing. Suppose the United States has 100 units of labor and Brazil has 120.

a. Draw the production possibilities curve for each country without trade. Which country has the absolute advantage in each good? Indicate each country's comparative advantage.

b. In what range will the world trading price ratio lie when these countries open up to free trade? Will both countries be better off? Why? Show this on your diagram.

5. "Developing countries should exploit their own comparative advantage and quit trying to invest in physical and human capital to develop high-tech industries." Comment.

6. Suppose you found that exports from the United States to China were mainly goods, such as airplanes, that require much capital compared to labor, and that exports from China to the United States were mainly goods, such as toys, that require much labor compared to capital. Are these patterns consistent with comparative advantage?

7. "Comparative advantage suggests that high-skilled workers in developed economies and low-skilled workers in developing countries will be more supportive of free trade than low-skilled workers in developed economies and high-skilled workers in developing countries will be." Comment.

8. Comparative advantage explains interindustry trade in different goods between countries. How do economists explain intraindustry trade, that is, trade in the same industry between countries? Why might people in the United States want to buy German cars, and Germans want to buy cars from the United States?

9. Suppose that each firm in an industry has the total costs shown below.

Quantity of Output	Total Costs (dollars)
1	50
2	54
3	60
4	68
5	80
6	90
7	105
8	112

a. Suppose that the quantity demanded in the market is fixed at 4. Calculate the average total cost for each firm when there are 1, 2, and 4 firms in the industry. Draw a diagram indicating the relationship between average total cost and number of firms.

b. Suppose the quantity demanded in the market expands because of an opening of trade and is now fixed at 8. Draw a diagram similar to the one in part (a) indicating the relationship between average total cost and the number of firms. Why does the opening of trade cause this shift in the curve?

10. The following relationship between price, cost per unit, and the number of firms describes an industry in an economy.

Number of Firms	Cost per Unit ($)	Price ($)
1	10	90
2	20	80
3	30	70
4	40	60
5	50	50
6	60	46
7	70	43
8	80	40
9	90	38
10	100	36

a. Graph (1) the relationship between cost per unit and number of firms and (2) the relationship between price and number of firms. Why does one slope up and the other slope down?

b. Find the long-run equilibrium price and number of firms.

c. Now suppose the country opens its borders to trade with other countries; as a result, the relationship between cost per unit and the number of firms becomes as follows:

Number of Firms	Cost per Unit ($)
1	5
2	10
3	15
4	20
5	25
6	30
7	35
8	40
9	45
10	50

Find the long-run equilibrium price and number of firms.

d. What are the gains from expanding the market through the reduction in trade barriers?

Chapter 19

International Trade Policy

In a democracy, there is a big difference between having an economic idea and implementing the idea in practice. Even if you have the greatest economic idea in the world, you have to spread the word, convince people, debate those in opposition, and even compromise if the idea is to be voted on favorably, signed into law, or serve as the basis for an international agreement.

We started this book with the central idea of economics—that people make purposeful choices with scarce resources and interact with other people when they make these choices. We have now seen that this central idea spawns many other powerful ideas—from the opportunity costs facing Tiger Woods to comparative advantage in international trade between countries.

Indeed, there is no better illustration of the difference between ideas and their implementation than the difference between the international trade *theory* of the previous chapter and international trade *policy*, which we take up now. From David Ricardo working in the British parliament to repeal protectionist trade laws 150 years ago to the present-day economists testifying in Congress in favor of a new trade agreement, the goal is the same: to achieve the economic gains from trade in practice in a democracy. It is not easy, but it is fascinating to watch or to participate in, and it is a fitting capstone to a book about economics.

We begin by examining the economic impact of the trade barriers that currently exist, reviewing the political history of past trade barriers in the United States, and considering the political-economic arguments given in favor of trade barriers. We discuss some of the arguments made by those protesting free trade agreements. We then go on to evaluate alternative political mechanisms in terms of their effectiveness in reducing trade barriers.

TARIFFS AND QUOTAS

Governments use many methods to restrict international trade. Policies that restrict trade are called *protectionist policies* because the restrictions usually protect industries from foreign imports.

Examining the economic impact of trade restrictions helps you understand why some industries lobby for protectionist policies. As you delve into the economic analysis, think about whether a protectionist policy would help or hurt you. If the United States restricts trade in clothing, how would this restriction affect U.S. clothing producers, foreign clothing producers, U.S. retailers that sell clothing, and U.S. consumers who buy clothing? How would the restriction affect U.S. employment in clothing production and the price of clothing? We'll see that there are winners and losers as a result of trade restrictions, but that the gains for the winners will be smaller than the losses of the losers. That is, the losses from trade restrictions outweigh the gains, creating deadweight loss.

As you learn the impact of a new trade restriction, check your understanding by considering the removal of an existing trade restriction. Again, there will be winners and losers as a result of removing trade restrictions, but the gains for the winners will be larger than the losses of the losers. Removing trade restrictions therefore eliminates deadweight loss.

Tariffs

ad valorem tariff: a tax on imports evaluated as a percentage of the value of the import.

specific tariff: a tax on imports that is proportional to the number of units or items imported.

The oldest and most common method by which a government restricts trade is the *tariff*, a tax on goods imported into a country. The higher the tariff, the more trade is restricted. An **ad valorem tariff** is a tax equal to a certain percentage of the value of the good. For example, a 15 percent tariff on the value of goods imported is an ad valorem tariff. If $100,000 worth of goods are imported, the tariff revenue is $15,000. A **specific tariff** is a tax on the quantity sold, such as 50 cents for each kilogram of zinc.

The economic effects of a tariff are illustrated in Figure 1. We consider a particular good—automobiles, for example—that is exported from one country (Japan, for example) and imported by another country (the United States, for example). An

Seattle, 1999
The goal of the WTO is to reduce trade barriers. But not everyone agrees with the goal, as the protest against the WTO meeting in Seattle reminds us. Though large antitrade protests have been less common in recent years, protectionist or isolationist sentiments continue to build as people worry about competition from China and other developing countries.

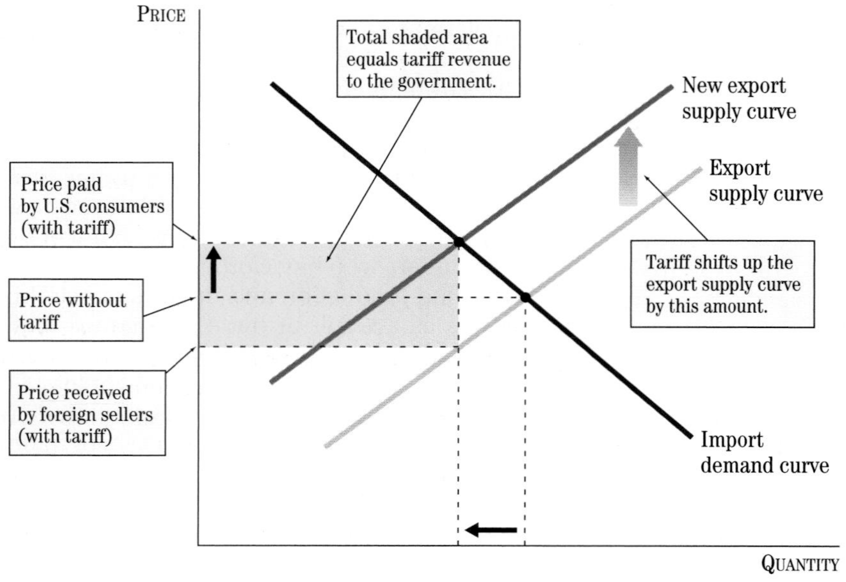

FIGURE 1
The Effects of a Tariff
A tariff shifts the export supply curve up by the amount of the tariff. Thus, the price paid for imports by consumers rises and the quantity imported declines. The price increase (upward-pointing black arrow) is less than the tariff (upward-pointing blue arrow). The revenue to the government is shown by the shaded area; it is the tariff times the amount imported.

import demand curve and an *export supply curve* are shown in Figure 1. The *import demand curve* gives the quantity of imported goods that will be demanded at each price. It shows that a higher price for imported goods will reduce the quantity of the goods demanded. A higher price for Nissans and Toyotas, for example, will lead to a smaller quantity of Nissans and Toyotas demanded by Americans. Like the standard demand curve, the import demand curve is downward-sloping.

The *export supply curve* gives the quantity of exports that foreign firms are willing to sell at each price. In the case of Nissans and Toyotas, the export supply curve gives the quantity of Nissans and Toyotas that Japanese producers are willing to sell in the United States. The supply curve is upward-sloping, just like any other supply curve, because foreign producers are willing to supply more cars when the price is higher.

In equilibrium, for any single type of good, the quantity of exports supplied must equal the quantity of imports demanded. Thus, the intersection of the export supply curve and the import demand curve gives the amount imported into the country and the price.

When the government imposes a tariff, the supply curve shifts up, as shown in Figure 1. The tariff increases the marginal cost of supplying cars to the United States. The amount of the tariff in dollars is the amount by which the supply curve shifts up; it is given by the length of the blue arrow in Figure 1.

The tariff changes the intersection of the export supply curve and the import demand curve. At the new equilibrium, a lower quantity is imported at a higher price. The price paid for cars by consumers rises, but the increase in the price is less than the tariff. In Figure 1, the upward-pointing black arrow shows the price increase. The blue arrow, which shows the tariff increase, is longer than the black arrow along the vertical axis. The size of the price increase depends on the slopes of the demand curve and the supply curve.

Economics in Action

From Steel to Shrimp: The Same Old Tariff Story

Consider the case for and against a tariff to protect two different industries—steel and shrimp. In 2002, an increasing amount of steel in the United States was being imported, and steel prices were low. Many U.S. steel-producing companies were in debt, and in the past five years, 30 steelmakers had sought bankruptcy protection. To avoid additional bankruptcies and loss of jobs, the steel industry lobbied for protection from imported steel. In March 2002, President Bush imposed tariffs on steel imports. The tariffs were as high as 30 percent and were to last three years.

We would predict that a tariff on steel would increase the price of steel in the United States, increasing the profits of steelmakers and hurting steel consumers. As predicted, steel prices increased, steelmakers profited, and the steel-consuming industry was hurt by the higher prices. Some manufacturers claimed that the tariffs jeopardized more jobs in the steel-consuming industry than they saved in the steel-producing industry. Steelmakers in the rest of the world filed complaints with the World Trade Organization. The WTO ruled that the U.S. tariffs on steel were illegal. In December 2003, President Bush reversed this protectionist policy, removing the tariffs on steel. If you were determining trade policy, how would you view the tradeoff between U.S. steel jobs and the effects of the higher price of steel on the U.S. manufacturing industry?

Between 2000 and 2004, shrimp imports in the United States increased 70 percent. This increase in the supply of shrimp caused the price of shrimp to tumble. U.S. shrimp fishermen lobbied for tariffs on imported shrimp, claiming that foreign shrimp was being dumped on the U.S. market at prices below production costs. In July 2004, the United States proposed tariffs on shrimp imported from some countries.

U.S. consumers benefit from the increase in shrimp imports and the tumble in shrimp prices. Foreign shrimp producers profit from their sale of shrimp in the United States. U.S. shrimp producers are requesting protection from these low shrimp prices. With tariffs we would expect profits for U.S. shrimp producers to increase, imports to fall, the price of shrimp to increase, and foreign producers' profits to fall. If you were determining trade policy, how would you view this tradeoff between the health of the U.S. shrimp-producing industry and the price of shrimp for U.S. consumers? Does your answer to these questions about tradeoffs depend on whether the protected industry is steel or shrimp?

The price received by suppliers equals the price paid by consumers less the tariff that must be paid to the government. Observe that the price received by the sellers declines as a result of the tariff.

The amount of revenue that the government collects is given by the quantity imported times the tariff, which is indicated by the shaded rectangle in Figure 1. For example, if the tariff is $1,000 per car and 1 million cars are imported, the revenue is $1 billion. Tariff revenues are called *duties* and are collected by customs.

The tariff also has an effect on U.S. car producers. Because the tariff reduces imports from abroad and raises their price, the demand for cars produced by import-competing companies in the United States—General Motors or Ford—increases. This increase in demand will raise the price of U.S. cars. Thus, consumers pay more for both imported cars and domestically produced cars.

Quotas

Another method of government restriction of international trade is the *quota*. A quota sets a limit, a maximum, on the amount of a given good that can be imported. The United States has quotas on the import of ice cream, sugar, cotton, peanuts, and other commodities. Foreigners can supply only a limited amount of these goods to the United States.

The economic effect of a quota is illustrated in Figure 2. The export supply curve and the import demand curve are identical to those in Figure 1. The quota, the maximum that foreign firms can export to the United States, is indicated in Figure 2 by the solid purple vertical line labeled "quota." Exporters cannot supply more goods than the quota, and, therefore, American consumers cannot buy more than this amount. We have chosen the quota amount to equal the quantity imported with the tariff in Figure 1. This shows that if it wants to, the government can achieve the same effects on the quantity imported using either a quota or a tariff. Moreover, the price increase in Figure 2, represented by the black arrow along the vertical axis, is the same as the price increase in Figure 1. Viewed from the domestic market, therefore, a quota and a tariff are equivalent. If the quota is set to allow in the same quantity of imports as the tariff, then the price increase will be the same. Consumers will pay more for imports in both cases, and the demand for domestically produced goods that are substitutes for imports will increase. The price of domestically produced cars will also increase if there is a quota on foreign cars.

Then what is the difference in the effects of a tariff and a quota? Unlike the situation with a tariff, no revenue goes to the government with a quota. The difference between the price that the foreign suppliers get and the higher price that the consumers pay goes to the holders of the quota—the ones who are allowed to import into the country. Frequently foreign countries hold the quotas. The revenue the quota holders get is indicated by the shaded rectangle in Figure 2. It is equal to the quantity imported times the difference between the price paid by the consumers and the price received by the producers. The size of that rectangle is identical to the size of the rectangle showing the revenue paid to the government in the case of the tariff in Figure 1.

On January 1, 2005, the 1973 Multi-Fiber Agreement, a set of quotas on textiles and apparel, expired. This system of global quotas restricting imports added an estimated 20 percent to the cost of clothing, while benefiting companies in places like the Philippines that specialized in supplying clothing under this quota system. The lifting of the quotas created widespread fears among U.S. and European Union clothing manufacturers about the flood of cheap Chinese apparel into these markets.

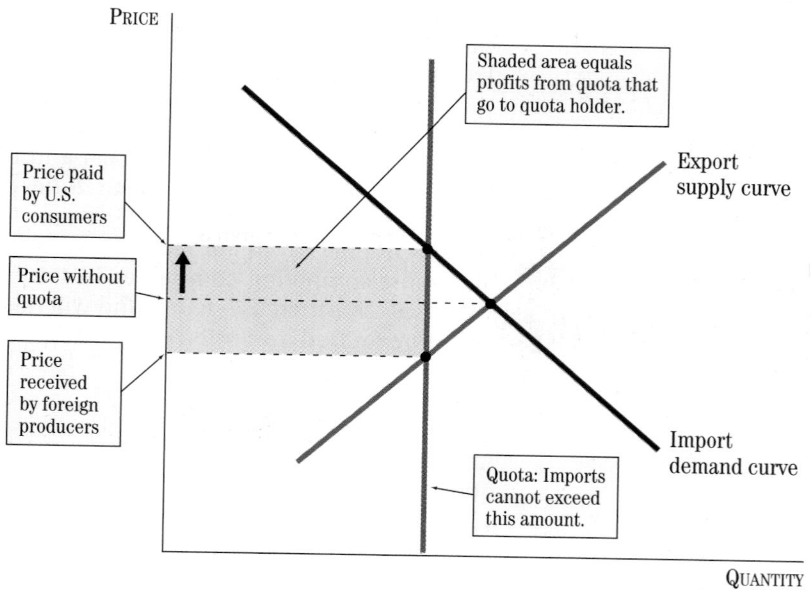

FIGURE 2
The Effects of a Quota
A quota can be set to allow the same quantity of imports as a tariff. The quota in this figure and the tariff in Figure 1 allow the same quantity of imports into the country. The price increase is the same for the quota and the tariff. But, in the case of a quota, the revenue goes to quota holders, not to the U.S. government.

ECONOMICS IN THE NEWS

The End of the Multi-Fiber Agreement

This news story from the Associated Press discusses the economic impact of the termination of the Multi-Fiber Agreement (MFA) on the economy of Sri Lanka. In this particular case, the cost to Sri Lanka is the loss of the quota rents that the country had earned under the Multi-Fiber agreement. The winners will be the lower-cost producers in countries like Mexico, who will no longer be shut out of the U.S. market, as well as consumers in the U.S. market.

Sri Lanka's Revenue from Garment Exports to America Set to Drop 20 Percent as Trade Agreement Expires

November 15, 2004—*Associated Press*
Colombo, Sri Lanka

The expiration of the MFA by the end of 2004

SRI LANKA's revenue from garment and textile exports to the United States, its biggest customer, is expected to fall about 20 percent next year following the expiration of a preferential trade agreement, an industry official said Monday. The United States has purchased an annual average of about US$2.5 billion (€1.9 billion) garments and textiles from Sri Lanka since the two countries signed the Multi-Fiber Agreement in 1974. But the agreement is set to expire next month.

Benefits to U.S. consumers

Tuli Cooray, who heads a committee of Sri Lankan business and government officials advising the industry, said American buyers will probably switch to lower cost manufacturers in China, Mexico and elsewhere in South Asia. As a result, he said Sri Lanka's shipments of garments and textiles to the United States will likely fall about 20 percent to about US$2 billion (€1.5 billion), in 2005.

Impact on Sri Lanka

Cooray said most small and medium garment manufacturers may need to downsize to stay in business, but added that the industry will bounce back by focussing on markets closer to home, such as India and Japan. "We don't envisage any serious shocks," Cooray told Dow Jones Newswires. "We have already initiated talks with Indian partners amid efforts to obtain a piece of that market," he said.

Overseas shipments of textiles and garments comprise 50 percent of Sri Lanka's total export earnings, and the United States has been the largest buyer of garments from Sri Lanka.

A coalition of U.S. producers claimed that 650,000 jobs were at risk. Since then, the European Union and the United States have both struggled to find a solution that will work for China and for domestic manufacturers, retailers, and consumers.

Since the expiration of the quotas, exports from China have surged, adding to downward pressure on prices of clothing in the United States. In contrast, exports from countries like the Philippines and Sri Lanka, that previously had quotas, have suffered. The surge in exports from China has caused U.S. clothing producers to lobby for new quotas though U.S. clothing retailers are opposed to them. If you were determining trade policy, how would you view this tradeoff between U.S. clothing prices and U.S. clothing production?

The Costs of Trade Restrictions

Trade barriers such as tariffs and quotas distort prices and reduce the quantity consumed, benefiting domestic producers at the expense of domestic consumers and foreign producers. For example, the United States imposes quotas on sugar to increase the price of domestic sugar beets and sugar cane. Producers receive $1 billion a year in additional surplus as a result of higher prices, but U.S. consumers lose $1.9 billion, for a net loss of $.9 billion to the United States.

The Multi-Fiber Agreement, which ended in January 2005, was another trade restriction that had substantial implications for U.S. consumers. The estimated loss to U.S. consumers was $24 billion a year, and the cost to the U.S. economy was around $10 billion a year.

REVIEW

- The most common ways for government to restrict foreign trade are tariffs and quotas. Each has the same effect on price and quantity.
- With a tariff, the revenue from the tariff goes to the government. With a quota, that revenue goes to quota holders.
- Trade restrictions alter the allocation of resources in the economy and are significant sources of deadweight loss.

THE HISTORY OF TRADE RESTRICTIONS

revenue tariff: an import tax whose main purpose is to provide revenue to the government.

As stated earlier, tariffs are the oldest form of trade restriction. Throughout history, governments have used tariffs to raise revenue. **Revenue tariffs,** whose main purpose is raising revenue, were by far the most significant source of federal revenue in the United States before the income tax was made constitutional by the Sixteenth Amendment to the U.S. Constitution in 1913 (see Figure 3). Revenue tariffs are still common in less-developed countries because they are easy for the government to collect as the goods come through a port or one of a few checkpoints.

U.S. Tariffs

Tariffs are a big part of U.S. history. Even before the United States was a country, a tariff on tea imported into the colonies led to the Boston Tea Party. One of the first acts of the U.S. Congress placed tariffs on imports. Figure 4 summarizes the history of tariffs in the United States since the early 1800s.

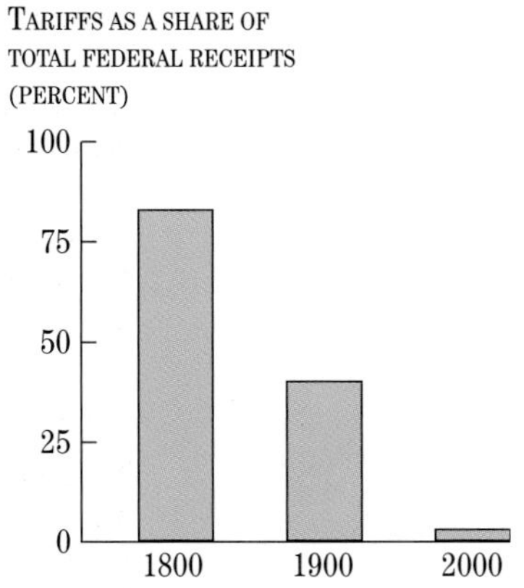

FIGURE 3
Tariffs as a Share of Total Federal Revenue
The first tariff, passed in 1789, represented nearly all of the federal government's revenue; 200 years later, tariff revenues were only about 1 percent of the total.

From the Tariff of Abominations to Smoot-Hawley. Tariffs were high throughout much of U.S. history, rarely going below 20 percent in the nineteenth century. In addition to raising revenue, these tariffs had the purpose of reducing imports of manufactured goods. The tariffs offered protection to manufacturers in the North but raised prices for consumers. Since the South was mainly agricultural and a consumer of manufactured goods, there was a constant dispute between the North and the South over these tariffs.

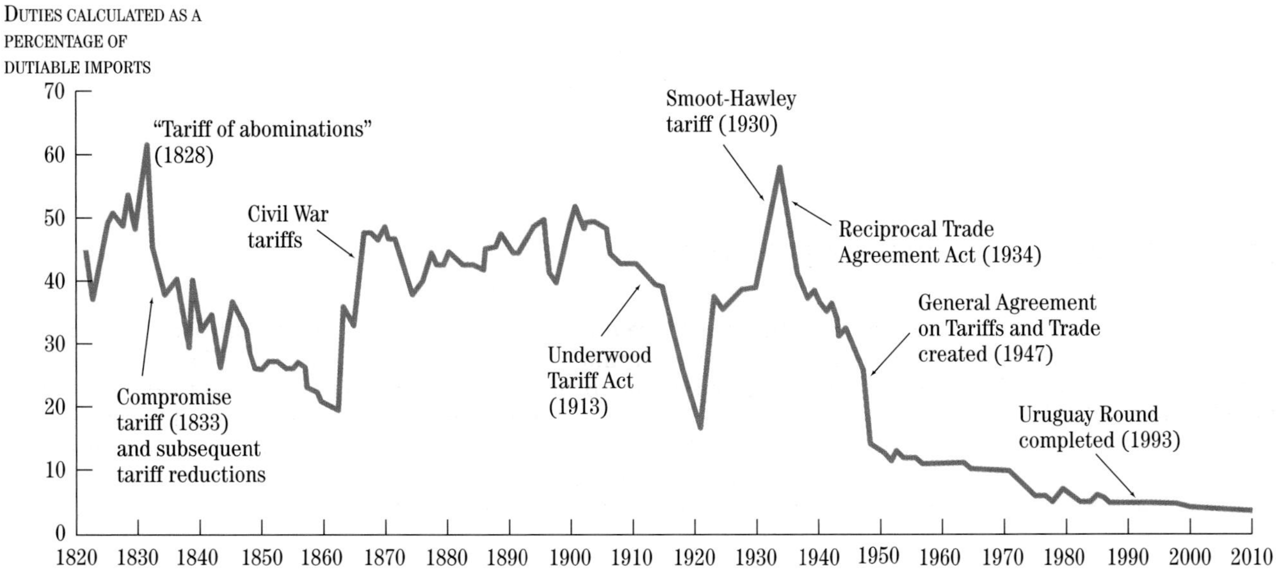

FIGURE 4
History of Tariffs in the United States
The chart shows the ratio of tariff revenues to the value of imports subject to tariffs measured as a percentage. This percentage is a measure of the average tariff excluding goods not subject to any tariff.

The highest of these tariffs was nicknamed the "tariff of abominations." This tariff, passed in 1828, brought the average tariff level in the United States to over 60 percent. The tariff made purchases of farm equipment much more expensive in the southern states. It almost led to a civil war before the actual Civil War, as the southern states threatened to secede. However, because the tariff was so high, it was soon repealed, and for the next 10 years tariffs were relatively low by nineteenth-century standards.

Smoot-Hawley tariff: a set of tariffs imposed in 1930 that raised the average tariff level to 59 percent by 1932.

trade war: a conflict among nations over trade policies caused by imposition of protectionist policies on the part of one country and subsequent retaliatory actions by other countries.

The most devastating increase in tariffs in U.S. history occurred during the Great Depression. The **Smoot-Hawley tariff** of 1930 raised average tariffs to 59 percent. Congress and President Hoover apparently hoped that raising tariffs would help stimulate U.S. production and offset the Great Depression. But the increase had precisely the opposite effect. Other countries retaliated by raising their tariffs on U.S. goods. Each country tried to beat the others with higher tariffs, a phenomenon known as a **trade war.** The Smoot-Hawley tariff had terrible consequences. Figure 5 is a dramatic illustration of the decline in trade that occurred at the time of these tariff increases during the Great Depression. The Smoot-Hawley tariff made the Great Depression worse than it would have otherwise been.

From the Reciprocal Trade Agreement Act to the WTO.

The only good thing about the Smoot-Hawley tariff was that it demonstrated to the whole world how harmful tariffs can be. In order to achieve lower tariffs, the Congress passed and President Roosevelt signed the *Reciprocal Trade Agreement Act* in 1934. This act was probably the most significant event in the history of U.S. trade policy. It authorized the president to cut U.S. tariffs by up to 50 percent if other countries would cut their tariffs on a reciprocating basis. The reciprocal trade agreements resulted in a remarkable

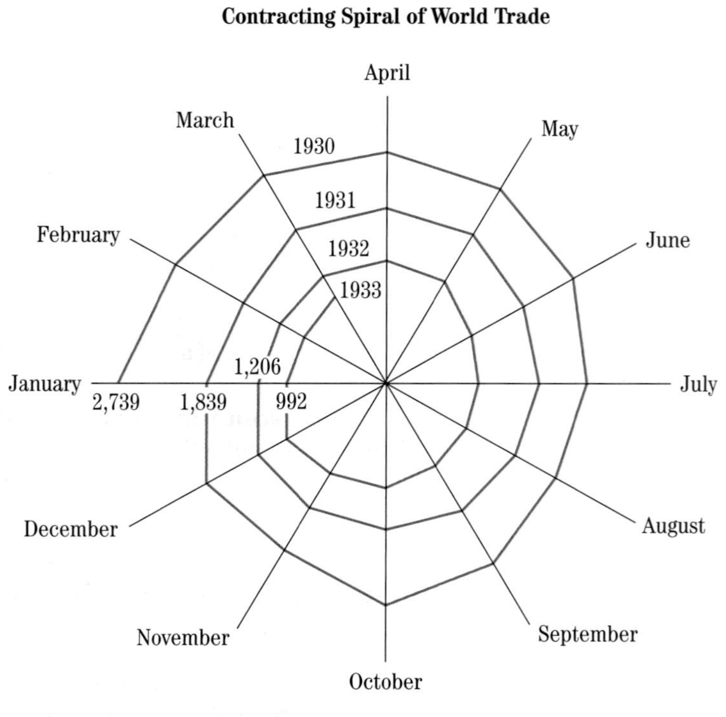

FIGURE 5
Decline in World Trade During the Great Depression
This circular graph, used by Charles Kindleberger of MIT, illustrates how world trade collapsed after tariffs increased during the Great Depression. The distance from the middle of the graph to the point on each spoke is the amount of trade (in millions of dollars) during each month.

reduction in tariffs. By the end of World War II, the average tariff level was down from a peak of 59 percent under Smoot-Hawley to 25 percent. The successful approach to tariff reduction under the Reciprocal Trade Agreement Act was made permanent in 1947 with the creation of a new international organization, the *General Agreement on Tariffs and Trade* (*GATT*). GATT was set up to continue the process of tariff reduction. During the half-century since the end of World War II, tariffs have continued to decline on a reciprocating basis. By 1992, the average U.S. tariff level was down to 5.2 percent.

World Trade Organization (WTO): an international organization that can mediate trade disputes.

In 1993, GATT was transformed into the **World Trade Organization (WTO),** which continues to promote reciprocal reductions in tariffs and other trade barriers. But the WTO also has authority to resolve trade disputes between countries. For example, if the United States complains that Europe is violating a trade agreement by restricting U.S. beef imports in some way, then the WTO determines whether the complaint has merit and what sanctions should be imposed on Europe. This dispute resolution authority has led to complaints, such as those made by the protesters in Seattle in 1999, that the WTO represents a loss of sovereignty for individual countries. On the other side of the argument, by resolving disputes, the WTO can avoid misunderstandings that otherwise can lead to trade wars between countries when trade disputes occur.

antidumping duty: a tariff imposed on a country as a penalty for dumping goods.

Antidumping Duties. No history of U.S. tariffs would be complete without a discussion of antidumping duties. **Antidumping duties** are tariffs put on foreign firms as a penalty for dumping. When a firm sells products in another country at prices below average cost or below the price in the home country, it is called *dumping*. Dumping can occur for many reasons. For example, the firm might want to sell at a lower price in the foreign market than in the home market because the demand in the foreign market is more elastic. If so, consumers in the foreign market benefit. But some people argue that dumping is a way for firms in other countries to drive domestic firms out of business and thereby gain market share and market power. In any case, in the United States and other countries, dumping is illegal; the penalty is a high tariff—the antidumping duty—on the good that is being dumped. Steel is one of the industries protected with antidumping duties in the United States, at a cost to consumers of as much as $732,000 per job protected, about 10 times what a steelworker earns. President Bush's increase in steel tariffs in 2002 provoked retaliation by the European Union and Japan, adding to the deadweight loss caused by trade barriers.

Many economists are concerned that antidumping duties, or even the threat of such duties, are serious restrictions on trade. They reduce imports and raise consumer prices. Moreover, they are frequently used for protectionist purposes. Firms in industries that desire additional protection can file dumping charges and request that tariffs be raised. Frequently, they are successful. Thus, an important issue for the future is how to reduce the use of antidumping duties for restricting trade.

nontariff barrier: any government action other than a tariff that reduces imports, such as a quota or a standard.

The Rise of Nontariff Barriers. As tariffs were being reduced in the post–World War II period, a conflicting trend began to emerge. Some of the other methods of restricting trade—called **nontariff barriers** to trade—grew in popularity. Nontariff barriers include anything from quotas to quality standards aimed at reducing the import of foreign products. Nontariff barriers may have arisen as a replacement for tariffs in response to political pressure for protection of certain industries.

Quality and performance standards are sometimes nothing more than barriers to trade. Some standards may have a good purpose, such as safety or compatibility with other products, but others do not. Consider the Canadian plywood standards for building construction, which keep out U.S. plywood. The Canadians argue that the standards are needed to satisfy building requirements in Canada, but Americans argue that plywood that does not meet the Canadian standards works just as well. A safety restriction against American-made baseball bats in Japan during the 1980s is another example. Most Americans viewed the bats as perfectly safe and viewed the Japanese safety standard as a restriction on trade.

Quality and performance standards, therefore, are a tricky problem because governments can argue that they are for the purpose of improving economic conditions in their own country. The U.S. Food and Drug Administration does not allow untested drugs into the United States even though foreign governments deem them safe. The FDA argues that the restriction is necessary to protect consumers, but foreign governments view it as a trade restriction. Such a standard does seem like a trade barrier, but in reality it is a matter of dispute.

REVIEW

- Tariffs were used by governments to raise revenue long before income taxes were invented.
- Tariffs have also been used for protectionist purposes in several important instances in U.S. history. Manufacturing firms in the North were protected by tariffs at the expense of consumers of manufactured goods, many of whom were in the South.
- The Smoot-Hawley tariff of the 1930s was one of the most harmful in U.S. history. It led to a trade war in which other countries raised tariffs in retaliation.
- Tariffs have come down since the 1930s. However, in recent years, nontariff barriers to trade have gone up.

ARGUMENTS FOR TRADE BARRIERS

Are there any good economic arguments for trade barriers? Let's examine some of the arguments that are typically made.

High Transition Costs

When an industry shrinks as a result of the removal of restrictions on trade, the cost of adjustment in the short run may be quite large, even if other industries grow. Those who lose their jobs in the protected industry, even temporarily, suffer. In the short run, it is difficult to retrain workers. Workers who are laid off as the industry shrinks cannot move easily to another industry. Many have to retire early. Retraining is possible, but it takes time and is difficult for older workers.

Phaseout of Trade Restrictions. Some people argue that these costs are so high that we should not reduce trade barriers. But there is a better approach. These costs of adjustment are a reason for a slow phaseout of trade barriers. *Phaseout* means that trade barriers are reduced a little bit each year. A slow phaseout of trade barriers was part of the North American Free Trade Agreement (NAFTA) between Canada, Mexico, and the United States. This agreement called for a phaseout period of 10 to 15 years, depending on the product. For example, some tariffs were scheduled to be cut by 25 percent in the first year, 50 percent after 5 years, and 100 percent after 10 years. The purpose of the slow phaseout was to allow production to shift from one industry to another slowly. The intention was to adjust the work force through attrition as workers normally retired.

Trade Adjustment Assistance. Another approach is to use *trade adjustment assistance,* which refers to transfer payments to workers who happen to be hurt because of a move to free trade. Unemployment insurance and other existing transfer programs may go a long way toward providing such assistance. However, because society as a whole benefits from free trade, some increased resources can be used to help the workers who bear the brunt of the adjustment. In other words, the extra income that can be obtained by trade may be used to ease the adjustment.

Transition costs are not a reason to avoid free trade. They are a reason to phase out the restrictions on trade gradually and to provide trade adjustment assistance to workers as needed.

The Infant Industry Argument

infant industry argument: the view that a new industry may be helped by protectionist policies.

One of the earliest statements of the **infant industry argument** in favor of trade restrictions was put forth by Alexander Hamilton in 1791 in his *Report on Manufactures.* Hamilton argued that manufacturing firms in the newly created United States should be protected from imports. Once the industries were established, they could compete with foreign imports. But as they got started, they needed protection until they reached a certain scale.

A danger with the infant industry argument is that the protection may last long after it was initially justified. In Latin America, for example, infant industry arguments were used to justify import protection in the 1950s. However, these barriers to trade lasted long after any kind of reasonable infant industry argument could be made.

The National Security Argument

A nation's security is another argument for trade restrictions. The national security argument is that there are certain goods, such as special metals, computers, ships, or aircraft, that the country needs to be able to produce in time of war. If it does not have an industry that produces them, it could be at a severe disadvantage.

However, national security arguments can be used by firms seeking protection from foreign imports. Japanese rice farmers, for example, made national security arguments for protection from rice imports. In fact, the rice restriction has little to do with national security because rice can be imported from many different countries. In the United States, the textile industry has argued on national security grounds that it needs protection because it provides military uniforms made from U.S. textiles.

It is important to examine whether there are alternatives to trade restrictions before applying the national security argument and restricting trade. For example, rather than restricting rice imports, the Japanese could store a large amount of rice in case of a war emergency. Or the United States could store millions of extra uniforms rather than restrict textile imports if it was really thought that uniforms were a national security issue. In fact, the United States does have stockpiles of many rare minerals and metals needed for national defense production.

The Retaliation Argument

Threatening other countries or retaliating against them when they have trade restrictions is another possible reason to deviate from free trade. If the United States threatens the Japanese by saying that it will close U.S. markets, this may encourage Japan to open its markets to the United States. Thus, by retaliating or threatening, there is a possibility of increasing international trade around the world.

However, the retaliation argument can also be used by those seeking protection. Those in the United States who are most vocal about retaliation against other countries are frequently those who want to protect an industry. Many economists worry about threats of retaliation because they fear that other countries will respond with further retaliation, and a trade war will occur.

The Foreign Subsidies Argument

If foreign governments subsidize their firms' exports, does this justify U.S. government subsidies to U.S. firms to help them compete against the foreign firms?

Foreign subsidies to foreign producers are a particularly difficult issue. If foreign subsidies lower the price of U.S. imports, then U.S. consumers benefit. If Europe wants to use taxpayer funds to subsidize aircraft manufacturers, then why not enjoy the lower-cost aircraft? However, foreign subsidies enable industries to thrive more for political reasons than for economic ones. From a global perspective, such government intervention should be avoided, since it hurts consumers by encouraging less economically efficient production and, ultimately, higher prices.

Environment and Labor Standards Arguments

During the 1990s, a new type of argument against reducing trade barriers emerged: that tariffs or quotas should not be removed against countries with weak or poorly enforced environmental protection laws and labor standards, such as child labor laws and workplace safety laws. Because such laws and standards are generally weaker in developing countries than in developed countries, this argument frequently opposes reducing trade barriers to the imports of goods from relatively poor countries. For example, this argument is made by people who are against reducing tariffs on imports of Brazilian oranges into the United States.

Environmental and labor standard arguments are of two main types. First, some argue that holding back on the reduction of trade barriers until countries change their environmental and labor policies is a good way to persuade these countries to change. However, there is an important counterargument: Low trade barriers themselves lead to improvements in environmental and working conditions. History has shown that as their income grows, people become more concerned with the environment and their working conditions; people in deep poverty do not have the time or resources to deal with such issues. Thus, by raising income per capita, lower trade barriers can improve the environment and the workplace. Moreover, more effective and cheaper technologies to improve the environment or increase safety become available through trade.

A second type of argument is that it is difficult for workers and firms in the advanced countries to compete with those in less-developed countries who do not have to pay the costs of complying with environmental protection laws. However, by keeping trade barriers high, income growth may not be sufficient to address the environmental problems in developing countries, so the differences in the law will persist.

The Political Economy of Protection

Firms seek protection from foreign competition simply because the protection raises their profits. But the firms may use any of the above arguments to justify their case. In a famous satire of firms seeking protection from foreign competitors, a French economist, Frédéric Bastiat, wrote more than 150 years ago about candlemakers complaining about a foreign rival—the sun! The candlemakers in Bastiat's satire petitioned French legislators to pass a law requiring the closing of all shutters, curtains, and blinds during the day to protect them from this competition. The behavior Bastiat described seems to apply to many modern producers who seek protection from competition.

One reason that firms seeking protection are frequently successful is that they spend a lot more time and money lobbying the Congress than do the people who would be hurt by the protection. Even though consumers *as a whole* benefit more from reducing trade barriers than firms in the protected industry are harmed, each consumer benefits relatively little, so spending a lot of time and money lobbying is not worthwhile. It is difficult to get enough votes to remove trade barriers when a few firms each have a lot to lose, even though millions of consumers have something to gain.

REVIEW

- Transition costs, environmental and labor standards, national security, infant industry, and retaliation are some of the arguments in favor of trade restrictions. Each has the possibility of being used by protectionists.
- Although many arguments in favor of trade barriers have been put forth over the years, in each case there are better ways to deal with the problems raised. The case for free trade holds up well in the debates when the economic rationale for the gains from trade is applied correctly and understood.

HOW TO REDUCE TRADE BARRIERS

Viewed in their entirety, the economic arguments against trade restrictions seem to overwhelm the economic arguments in favor of trade restrictions. The economic arguments in favor of free trade have been in existence for over 200 years. The recommendation of early economists such as Adam Smith and David Ricardo was simple: Reduce trade barriers.

However, it was not until many years after Smith and Ricardo wrote that their recommendations were translated into a practical trade policy. Then, as now, political pressures favoring protection made the repeal of trade barriers difficult. Hence, a carefully formulated trade policy is needed in order to reduce trade barriers. There are a variety of approaches.

Unilateral Disarmament

One approach to removing trade barriers in a country is simply to remove them unilaterally. Making an analogy with the arms race, we call this policy *unilateral disarmament*. When a country unilaterally reduces its arms, it does so without getting anything in arms reduction from other countries. With unilateral disarmament in trade policy, a country reduces its trade barriers without other countries also reducing their trade barriers. Unilateral disarmament is what Smith and Ricardo recommended for England.

The problem with unilateral disarmament is that some individuals are hurt, if only temporarily, and it is hard to compensate them. Of those who gain, each gains only a little. Of those who lose, each loses a lot. The political pressures that the losers exert are significant. As a result, unilateral disarmament is rarely successful in the developed countries today as a means of reducing trade barriers.

Multilateral Negotiations

multilateral negotiations: simultaneous tariff reductions on the part of many countries.

An alternative to unilateral disarmament is **multilateral negotiations,** which involve simultaneous tariff reductions by many countries. With multilateral negotiations, opposing political interests can cancel each other out. For example, import-competing domestic industries that will be hurt by the reduction of trade barriers, such as textiles in the United States or agriculture in Europe and Japan, can be countered by export interests that will gain from the reduction in trade barriers. Since consumers will gain, they are also a potential counter to protectionism, but they are too diffuse to make a difference, as we just discussed. With multilateral negotiations, interested exporters who gain from the reduction in barriers will push the political process to get the reductions.

Multilateral negotiations also balance international interests. For example, to get less-developed countries to remove their barriers to imports of financial and telecommunications services, the United States had to agree to remove agricultural trade barriers in the United States.

The Uruguay Round. Multilateral trade negotiations have taken place in a series of negotiating rounds, each of which has lasted several years. During each round, the countries try to come to agreement on a list of tariff reductions and the removal of other trade restrictions. There have been eight rounds of negotiations since 1947. The most recent was the **Uruguay Round,** named after the country where the first negotiations occurred in 1986. The Uruguay Round negotiations ended in 1993. Since 2002, the United States has been involved in negotiations for another global trade round, called the **Doha Development Round.** As with all such multilateral negotiations, this round is proving to be long and difficult and is still not finished.

Uruguay Round: a most recent round of multilateral negotiations, opened in 1986 and completed in 1993.

Doha Development Round: the latest round of multilateral negotiations, opened in November 2001 in Doha, Qatar.

The reduction in tariffs through multilateral negotiations under GATT has been dramatic. Tariffs have declined to below 3 percent on average in the United States with the implementation of the Uruguay Round agreement. Recall that this compares with nearly 60 percent in the mid-1930s.

Most-Favored-Nation Policy. Multilateral negotiations are almost always conducted on a *most-favored-nation* (*MFN*) basis. MFN means that when the United States or any other country reduces its tariffs as part of a multilateral trade agreement, it reduces them for everyone. Since the late 1990s, the term *normal trade relations* (*NTR*) has frequently been used in place of MFN because it is a more accurate description of the policy. Today, if a country is not granted MFN or NTR status, the United States imposes very high tariffs on the country. For example, concern about human rights in China has led some to argue that the United States should not grant MFN or NTR status to China. Without MFN or NTR, tariffs on Chinese imports to the United States would be about 60 percent.

Regional Trading Areas

Creating regional trading areas is an increasingly popular approach to reducing trade barriers. For example, NAFTA, the free trade agreement between the United States, Canada, and Mexico, removes all trade restrictions among those countries. An even wider free trade area covering the whole Western Hemisphere has been proposed.

Regional trading areas have some advantages over multilateral approaches. First, fewer countries are involved, so the negotiations are easier. Second, regional political factors can help offset protectionist pressures. For example, the political goal of European unity helped establish grassroots support to reduce trade barriers among the countries of Europe.

trade diversion: the shifting of trade away from the low-cost producer toward a higher-cost producer because of a reduction in trade barriers with the country of the higher-cost producer.

Trade Diversion versus Trade Creation. But there are disadvantages to regional trading areas in comparison with multilateral reductions in trade barriers under GATT. **Trade diversion** is one disadvantage. Trade is diverted when low-cost firms from countries outside the trading area are replaced by high-cost firms within

ECONOMICS IN ACTION

Ending the Corn Laws

Corn laws, recorded as far back as the twelfth century, restricted imports of grains, including wheat, rye, and barley, into England. Adam Smith devoted an entire chapter of his 1776 *Wealth of Nations* to the corn laws, arguing that "the praises which have been bestowed upon the law . . . are altogether unmerited."* But legislation introduced in 1791 raised the grain import tariff even further. The corn laws were unpopular with everyone except landowners and farmers.

The Anti-Corn League, founded in 1839 by Richard Cobden, was the most significant pressure group in nineteenth-century England. The Anti-Corn League used the economic arguments of Smith and Ricardo that the corn laws were an economic disaster and a moral tragedy: The laws impoverished and even starved the working class, constrained the growth of manufacturing, and provided government support to the wealthy. The catalyst was the Irish potato famine of 1845, which raised agricultural prices even further.

Robert Peel was the Tory prime minister from 1841 to 1846. Until 1845, he was against repeal of the corn laws, primarily because of strong support for them from landowners in the Tory party. But under pressure from Cobden and the Anti-Corn League, he changed his position after the potato famine and argued for the repeal of the corn laws.

In February 1846, Peel introduced a package of measures abolishing duties on imported corn over a three-year period. Only a minority of his party supported him, but the package passed. The split in the Tory party ended Peel's career, and the party did not win another election until 1868.

Thus, Peel paid a high political price for his policy of reducing trade protection, a policy that many feel helped make the British economy strong for the rest of the nineteenth century. How do you think he would have fared had he used one of the other methods (such as multilateral negotiations) to reduce protection rather than "unilaterally disarming"?

*Adam Smith, *Wealth of Nations* (New York: Modern Library, 1994), p. 560.

the trading area. For example, as a result of NAFTA, producers of electronic equipment in Southeast Asia have to pay a U.S. tariff, while producers of the same equipment in Mexico do not have to pay the tariff. As a result, some production will shift from Southeast Asia to Mexico; that is viewed as trade diversion from what might otherwise be a low-cost producer. The hope is that **trade creation**—the increase in trade due to the lower tariffs between the countries—will outweigh trade diversion.

trade creation: the increase in trade due to a decrease in trade barriers.

Free Trade Areas versus Customs Unions. There is an important difference between two types of regional trading areas: **free trade areas (FTAs)** and **customs unions.** In both, barriers to trade between countries in the area or the union are removed. But external tariffs are treated differently: Under a customs union, such as the European Union (EU), external tariffs are the same for all countries. For example, semiconductor tariffs are exactly the same in France, Germany, and the other members of the EU. Under a free trade area, external tariffs can differ for the different countries in the free trade area. For example, the United States's external tariffs on textiles are higher than Mexico's. These differences in external tariffs under an FTA cause complications because a good can be shipped into the country with the low tariff and then moved within the FTA to the country with the high tariff. To prevent such external tariff avoidance, *domestic content restrictions* must be incorporated into the agreement. These restrictions say that in order for a product to qualify for the zero tariffs between the countries, a certain fraction of the product must be made within the FTA. For example, under NAFTA, the majority of parts in television sets and automobiles must be manufactured in Canada, Mexico, or the United States in order for the television or car to qualify for a zero tariff.

free trade area (FTA): an area that has no trade barriers between the countries in the area.

customs union: a free trade area with a common external tariff.

REVIEW

- There are many different approaches to removing restrictions on international trade, including unilateral disarmament, multilateral negotiations, and regional trading areas—FTAs and customs unions.
- Of all these approaches, unilateral disarmament is the most difficult politically. Multilateral and regional approaches are both more common and more successful in lowering trade barriers and keeping them low.

CONCLUSION

Very few economists disagree with the proposition that tariffs, quotas, and other trade barriers reduce the economic well-being of a society. In fact, polls of economists show that they disagree less on this proposition than on virtually any other in economics. This unanimity among economists was reflected in the debate over the North American Free Trade Agreement in the United States. Every living Nobel Prize–winning economist endorsed the agreement to eliminate tariffs and quotas among Canada, Mexico, and the United States.

This chapter has shown that despite this unanimity, many restrictions on international trade still exist. There is continued political pressure to erect new trade barriers or prevent the existing ones from being removed.

Thus, the need for good trade policies to reduce trade barriers is likely to increase rather than decrease in the future. The challenge is to develop a means for conducting international trade policy in a world with many sovereign governments, each of which is free to formulate its own policy.

KEY POINTS

1. Despite the economic arguments put forth in support of free trade, there are still plenty of restrictions on trade in the world.
2. Tariffs and quotas are the two main methods of restricting international trade. They are equivalent in their effects on prices and imports.
3. Tariffs were originally a major source of government revenue but are relatively insignificant sources of revenue today.
4. Quotas do not generate any revenue for the government. The quota holders get all the revenue.
5. National security and infant industry are two of the main arguments frequently put forth in support of trade barriers. In most cases, they are overwhelmed by the arguments in favor of reduced trade barriers.
6. Eliminating restrictions on trade unilaterally is difficult because of the harm done to those who are protected by the restrictions.
7. Regional trading areas and multilateral tariff reductions endeavor to reduce trade barriers by balancing export interests against import-competing interests.
8. Free trade areas and customs unions both create trade and divert trade.

KEY TERMS

ad valorem tariff
specific tariff
revenue tariff
Smoot-Hawley tariff
trade war
World Trade Organization (WTO)
antidumping duty
nontariff barrier
infant industry argument
multilateral negotiations
Uruguay Round
Doha Development Round
trade diversion
trade creation
free trade area (FTA)
customs union

QUESTIONS FOR REVIEW

1. In what sense are a tariff and a quota equivalent?
2. Why might a tariff raise the price of the imported product by less than the amount of the tariff?
3. What are some examples of quality standards being used as trade barriers?
4. Why is unilateral disarmament a difficult way to reduce trade barriers?
5. How do multilateral negotiations or regional trading areas make the reduction of trade barriers easier politically?
6. Why might a regional trade agreement cause trade diversion?
7. What is the infant industry argument in favor of trade protection?
8. What are the disadvantages of using retaliation in trade policy?

PROBLEMS

1. Suppose French wine suddenly becomes popular in the United States. How does this affect the price and quantity of imports of French wine? Suppose the U.S. wine industry lobbies for protection. If the government imposes a tariff in order to restore the original quantity of imports, what will happen to the price of French wine in the United States? Show how much tariff revenue the government will collect.
2. Use a supply and demand diagram to show what happens to the price and quantity of sugar in the United States when the quotas on sugar are removed.
3. India has a 70 percent tariff on imported chocolate.
   - **a.** Sketch a diagram to show the impact of this tariff on the price of imported chocolate in India.
   - **b.** Suppose India cuts the tariff to zero but imposes a quota that results in the same high price for imported chocolate. Show this in a diagram.
   - **c.** From the government's perspective, is it better off with a tariff or with a quota? Explain.
4. Suppose that in order to encourage tourism, a Caribbean country subsidizes hotel construction. What impact will this have on the United States? Be sure to identify who the winners and losers will be in the United States as a result of this decision by the Caribbean country.
5. Suppose the president of a nation proposes a switch from a system of import quotas to a system of tariffs, with the idea that the switch will not affect the quantity of goods imported. Who will be in favor of the switch? Who will oppose it?
6. The United States has a very generous system of farm subsidies that supports growers of crops such as corn, soybeans, and peanuts. Explain why countries like Brazil and Ghana, which are large producers of these crops, consider these subsidies to be a form of trade barrier.
7. Suppose the U.S. government has decided that for national security reasons, it must protect the machine tools industry. Name two ways in which the government can accomplish this goal. Which policy would you recommend? Why?
8. Suppose the North American Free Trade Agreement causes the United States to import lumber from Canada instead of from Finland, even though Finland is a lower-cost producer than Canada. Identify and explain this phenomenon.
9. Suppose the United States decides to withdraw most-favored-nation treatment from China. What will happen to the price and quantity of U.S. imports from China? Use a diagram to explain your answer.
10. Assume that several hundred independent farmers in Argentina are the only producers of a rare plant that is used for medicinal purposes around the world. Imagine that you are an economic adviser to the Argentine government. The president asks you to find a way to capture some of the economic rents from the production of this rare plant, so that more profits stay in Argentina. Your job is to design a trade policy that accomplishes the president's goal. Explain verbally what your trade policy would be, how it would affect quantity and price in the market, and how it would affect all the players in this market.

Glossary

ability-to-pay principle the view that those with greater income should pay more in taxes than those with less income. (14)
absolute advantage a situation in which a person or country is more efficient at producing a good in comparison with another person or country. (18)
ad valorem tariff a tax on imports evaluated as a percentage of the value of the import. (19)
adverse selection in insurance markets, a situation in which the people who choose to buy insurance will be the riskiest group in the population; analogous situations apply in other markets. (16)
aggregate demand the total demand for goods and services by consumers, businesses, government, and foreigners. (5)
aggregate demand (*AD*) curve a line showing a negative relationship between inflation and the aggregate quantity of goods and services demanded at that inflation rate. (12)
aggregate hours the total number of hours worked by all workers in the economy in a given period of time. (8)
aggregate supply the total value of all goods and services produced in the economy by the available supply of capital, labor, and technology (also called potential GDP). (5)
antidumping duty a tariff imposed on a country as a penalty for dumping goods. (19)
asset something of value owned by a person or a firm. (10)
asymmetric information different levels of information available to different people in an economic interaction or exchange. (16)
automatic stabilizers automatic tax and spending changes that occur over the course of the business cycle that tend to stabilize the fluctuations in real GDP. (14)

bank a firm that channels funds from savers to investors by accepting deposits and making loans. (10)
balanced budget a budget in which tax revenues equal spending. (14)
budget constraint an income limitation on a person's expenditure on goods and services. (5)
budget deficit the amount by which government spending exceeds tax revenues. (14)
budget surplus the amount by which tax revenues exceed government spending. (14)

capital the factories, improvements to cultivated land, machinery and other tools, equipment, and structures used to produce goods and services. (5)
capital abundant a higher level of capital per worker in one country relative to another. (18)
capital gain the increase in the value of an asset through an increase in its price. (16)
capital income the sum of profits, rental payments, and interest payments. (6)
capital intensive production that uses a relatively high level of capital per worker. (18)
capital loss the decrease in the value of an asset through a decrease in its price. (16)
capitalism an economic system based on a market economy in which capital is individually owned, and production and employment decisions are decentralized. (2)
Cartesian coordinate system a graphing system in which ordered pairs of numbers are represented on a plane by the distances from a point to two perpendicular lines, called axes. (2A)
catch-up line the downward-sloping relation between the level of productivity and the growth of productivity predicted by growth theory. (17)
central bank independence a description of the legal authority of central banks to make decisions on monetary policy with little interference by the government in power. (15)
ceteris paribus "all other things being equal"; refers to holding all other variables constant or keeping all other things the same when one variable is changed. (2)
checking deposit an account at a financial institution on which checks can be written; also called checkable deposit. (10)
choice a selection among alternative goods, services, or actions. (1)
command economy an economy in which the government determines prices and production; also called a centrally planned economy. (1)
commerce clause the clause in the U.S. Constitution that prohibits restraint of trade between states. (18)
comparative advantage a situation in which a group or country can produce one good at a lower opportunity cost than another person or country. (1, 18)
complement a good that is usually consumed or used together with another good. (3)
compound growth applying the growth rate to growth from the previous period; analogous to compound interest. (5A)
consumer price index (CPI) a price index equal to the current price of a fixed market basket of consumer goods and services relative to a base year. (6)
consumption purchases of final goods and services by individuals. (6)
consumption function the positive relationship between consumption and income. (11)
consumption smoothing the idea that although their incomes fluctuate, people try to stabilize consumption spending from year to year. (11A)
controlled experiments empirical tests of theories in a controlled setting in which particular effects can be isolated. (2)
consumption share the proportion of GDP that is used for consumption; equals consumption divided by GDP, or *C/Y*. (7)

Council of Economic Advisers a three-member group of economists appointed by the president of the United States to analyze the economy and make recommendations about economic policy. (2)
countercyclical policy a policy designed to offset the fluctuations in the business cycle. (14)
coupon the fixed amount that a borrower agrees to pay to the bondholder each year. (16)
cross-price elasticity of demand the percentage change in the quantity demanded of one good divided by the percentage change in the price of another good. (4)
crowding out the decline in private investment owing to an increase in government purchases. (7)
currency money in its physical form: coin and paper money. (10)
Current Population Survey a monthly survey of a sample of U.S. households done by the U.S. Census Bureau; it measures employment, unemployment, the labor force, and other characteristics of the U.S. population. (8)
customs union a free trade area with a common external tariff. (19)
cyclical unemployment unemployment due to a recession, when the rate of unemployment is above the natural rate of unemployment. (8)

debt contract a contract in which a lender agrees to provide funds today in exchange for a promise from the borrower, who will repay that amount plus interest at some point in the future. (16)
debt to GDP ratio the total amount of outstanding loans the federal government owes divided by nominal GDP. (14)
deflation a decrease in the overall price level, or a negative inflation rate. (13)
demand a relationship between price and quantity demanded. (3)
demand curve a graph of demand showing the downward-sloping relationship between price and quantity demanded. (3)
demand schedule a tabular presentation of demand showing the price and quantity demanded for a particular good, all else being equal. (3)
demand shock a shift in one of the components of aggregate demand that leads to a shift in the aggregate demand curve. (13)
depreciation the decrease in an asset's value over time; for capital, it is the amount by which physical capital wears out over a given period of time. (6, 16)
developing country a country that is poor by world standards in terms of real GDP per capita. (17)
diffusion the spreading of an innovation throughout the economy. (9)
diminishing returns a situation in which successive increases in the use of an input, holding other inputs constant, will eventually cause a decline in the additional production derived from one more unit of that input. (9)
discount rate an interest rate used to discount a future payment when computing present discounted value. (16A)
discount rate the interest rate that the Fed charges commercial banks when they borrow from the Fed. (15)
discounting the process of translating a future payment into a value in the present. (16A)
discretionary fiscal policy changes in tax or spending policy requiring legislative or administrative action by the president or Congress. (14)
disinflation a reduction in the inflation rate. (13)
dividend yield the dividend stated as a percentage of the price of the stock. (16)
division of labor the division of production into various parts in which different groups of workers specialize. (1)
Doha Development Round the latest round of multilateral negotiations, opened in November 2001 in Doha, Qatar. (19)
dual scale a graph that uses time on the horizontal axis and different scales on the left and right vertical axes to compare the movements of two variables over time. (2A)

earnings the accounting profits of a firm. (16)
economic development the process of growth by which countries raise incomes per capita and become industrialized; also refers to the branch of economics that studies this process. (17)
economic fluctuations swings in real GDP that lead to deviations of the economy from its long-term growth trend. (5)
economic growth an upward trend in real GDP, reflecting expansion in the economy over time. (5)
economic interaction exchanges of goods and services between people. (1)
economic model an explanation of how the economy or part of the economy works. (2)
economic variable any economic measure that can vary over a range of values. (2)
economics the study of how people deal with scarcity. (1)
efficiency wage a wage, higher than that which would equate quantity supplied and quantity demanded, set by employers in order to increase worker efficiency—for example, by decreasing shirking by workers. (8)
efficient market hypothesis the idea that markets adjust rapidly enough to eliminate profit opportunities immediately. (16)
elastic demand demand for which the price elasticity is greater than 1. (4)
employment-to-population ratio the ratio (usually expressed as a percentage) of employed workers to the working-age population. (8)
equilibrium interest rate the interest rate that equates the sum of the consumption, investment, and net exports shares to the share of GDP available for nongovernment use. (7)
equilibrium price the price at which quantity supplied equals quantity demanded. (3)
equilibrium quantity the quantity traded at the equilibrium price. (3)
equilibrium risk-return relationship the positive relationship between the risk and the expected rate of return on an asset, derived from the fact that, on average, risk-averse investors who take on more risk must be compensated with a higher return. (16)
equity contract shares of ownership in a firm; payments to the owners of the shares depend on the firm's profits. (16)

exchange market intervention purchases and sales of foreign currency by a government in exchange markets with the intention to affect the exchange rate. (15)

exchange rate the price of one currency in terms of another in the foreign exchange market. We express the exchange rate as the number of units of foreign currency that can be purchased with one unit of domestic currency. (7)

expansion the period between the trough of a recession and the next peak, consisting of a general rise in output and employment. (5)

expected return the return on an uncertain investment calculated by weighting the gains or losses by the probability that they will occur. (16)

expenditure line the relation between the sum of the four components of spending $(C + I + G + X)$ and aggregate income. (11)

experimental economics a branch of economics that uses laboratory experiments to analyze economic behavior. (2)

exports the total value of the goods and services that people in one country sell to people in other countries. (6)

face value the principal that will be paid back when a bond matures. (16)

factor-price equalization the equalization of the price of labor and the price of capital across countries when they are engaging in free trade. (18)

federal budget a summary of the federal government's proposals for spending, taxes, and the deficit. (14)

federal debt the total amount of outstanding loans owed by the federal government. (14)

federal funds rate the interest rate on overnight loans between banks that the Federal Reserve influences by changing the supply of funds (bank reserves) in the market. (12)

Federal Open Market Committee (FOMC) the committee, consisting of the seven members of the Board of Governors and the twelve presidents of the Fed district banks, that meets about eight times per year and makes decisions about the supply of money; only five of the presidents vote at any one time. (10)

Federal Reserve System (the Fed) the central bank of the United States, which oversees the creation of money in the United States. (10)

final good a new good that undergoes no further processing before it is sold to consumers. (6)

fixed exchange rate policy a policy in which a country maintains a fixed value of its currency in terms of other currencies. (15)

flexible exchange rate policy a policy in which exchange rates are determined in foreign exchange markets and governments do not agree to fix them. (15)

foreign direct investment investment by a foreign entity of at least a 10 percent direct ownership share in a firm. (17)

45-degree line the line showing that expenditure equals aggregate income. (11)

forward-looking consumption model a model that explains consumer behavior by assuming that people anticipate future income when deciding on consumption spending today. (11A)

free trade area (FTA) an area that has no trade barriers between the countries in the area. (19)

freely determined price a price that is determined by the individuals and firms interacting in markets. (1)

frictional unemployment unemployment arising from normal turnover in the labor market, such as when people change occupations or locations, or are new entrants. (8)

gains from trade improvements in income, production, or satisfaction owing to the exchange of goods or services. (1, 18)

GDP deflator nominal GDP divided by real GDP; it measures the level of prices of goods and services included in real GDP relative to a given base year. (6)

government failure a situation in which the government makes things worse than the market, even though there may be market failure. (1)

government purchases purchases by federal, state, and local governments of new goods and services. (6)

government purchases share the proportion of GDP that is used for government purchases; equals government purchases divided by GDP, or G/Y. (7)

gross domestic product (GDP) a measure of the value of all the goods and services newly produced in an economy during a specified period of time. (2)

growth accounting formula an equation that states that the growth rate of productivity equals capital's share of income times the growth rate of capital per hour of work plus the growth rate of technology. (9, 17)

human capital a person's accumulated knowledge and skills. (9)

imports the total value of the goods and services that people in one country buy from people in other countries. (6)

incentive a device that motivates people to take action, usually so as to increase economic efficiency. (1)

income elasticity of demand the percentage change in quantity demanded of one good divided by the percentage change in income. (4)

increasing opportunity cost a situation in which producing more of one good requires giving up an increasing amount of production of another good. (1)

inelastic demand demand for which the price elasticity is less than 1. (4)

infant industry argument the view that a new industry may be helped by protectionist policies. (19)

inferior good a good for which demand decreases when income rises and increases when income falls. (3)

inflation adjustment (*IA*) line a flat line showing the level of inflation in the economy at a given point in time. It shifts up when real GDP is greater than potential GDP, and it shifts down when real GDP is less than potential GDP; it also shifts when expectations of inflation or raw materials prices change. (12)

inflation rate the percentage increase in the overall price level over a given period of time, usually one year. (5)

informal economy the portion of an economy characterized by illegal, unregulated businesses. (17)

innovation application of new knowledge in a way that creates new products or significantly changes old ones. (9)
insider a person who already works for a firm and has some influence over wage and hiring policy. (8)
interest rate the amount received per dollar loaned per year, usually expressed as a percentage (e.g., 6 percent) of the loan. (5)
interindustry trade trade between countries in goods from different industries. (18)
intermediate good a good that undergoes further processing before it is sold to consumers. (6)
International Monetary Fund (IMF) an international agency, established after World War II, designed to help countries with balance of payments problems and to ensure the smooth functioning of the international monetary system. (17)
international trade the exchange of goods and services between people or firms in different nations. (1, 18)
intraindustry trade trade between countries in goods from the same or similar industries. (18)
invention a discovery of new knowledge. (9)
investment purchases of final goods by firms plus purchases of newly produced residences by households. (6)
investment share the proportion of GDP that is used for investment; equals investment divided by GDP, or *I/Y*; sometimes called investment rate. (7)

job rationing a reason for unemployment in which the quantity of labor supplied is greater than the quantity demanded because the real wage is too high. (8)
job search a reason for unemployment in which uncertainty in the labor market and workers' limited information requires people to spend time searching for a job. (8)
job vacancies positions that firms are trying to fill, but for which they have yet to find suitable workers. (8)

Keynesian multiplier the ratio of the change in real GDP to the shift in the expenditure line; the formula is $1/(1 - MPC)$, where MPC is the marginal propensity to consume. (11A)

labor the number of hours people are available to work in producing goods and services. (5)
labor abundant a lower level of capital per worker in one country relative to another. (18)
labor demand curve a downward-sloping relationship showing the quantity of labor firms are willing to hire at each wage. (8)
labor force all those who are either employed or unemployed. (8)
labor force participation rate the ratio (usually expressed as a percentage) of people in the labor force to the working-age population. (8)
labor income the sum of wages, salaries, and fringe benefits paid to workers. (6)
labor intensive production that uses a relatively low level of capital per worker. (18)
labor supply curve the relationship showing the quantity of labor workers are willing to supply at each wage. (8)
law of demand the tendency for the quantity demanded of a good in a market to decline as its price rises. (3)
law of supply the tendency for the quantity supplied of a good in a market to increase as its price rises. (3)
learning by doing a situation in which workers become more proficient by doing a particular task many times. (9)
liability something of value that a person or a firm owes to someone else. (10)
life-cycle model a type of forward-looking consumption model that assumes that people base their consumption decisions on their expected lifetime income rather than on their current income. (11A)
linear a situation in which a curve is straight, with a constant slope. (2A)
liquidity constraint the situation in which people cannot borrow to smooth their consumption spending when their income is low. (11A)

macroeconomics the branch of economics that examines the workings and problems of the economy as a whole—GDP growth and unemployment. (2)
marginal propensity to consume (MPC) the slope of the consumption function, showing the change in consumption that is due to a given change in income. (11)
marginal propensity to import (MPI) the change in imports because of a given change in income. (11A)
market an arrangement by which economic exchanges between people take place. (1)
market economy an economy characterized by freely determined prices and the free exchange of goods and services in markets. (1)
market equilibrium the situation in which the price is equal to the equilibrium price and the quantity traded equals the equilibrium quantity. (3)
market failure any situation in which the market does not lead to an efficient economic outcome and in which there is a potential role for government. (1)
maturity date the date when the principal on a loan is to be paid back. (16)
medium of exchange something that is generally accepted as a means of payment. (10)
microeconomics the branch of economics that examines individual decision-making at firms and households and the way they interact in specific industries and markets. (2)
minimum wage a wage per hour below which it is illegal to pay workers. (4, 8)
mixed economy a market economy in which the government plays a very large role. (2)
moral hazard in insurance markets, a situation in which a person buys insurance against some risk and subsequently takes actions that increase the risks; analogous situations arise when there is asymmetric information in other markets. (16)
monetary policy rule a description of how much the interest rate or other instruments of monetary policy respond to inflation or other measures of the state of the economy. (12)
money that part of a person's wealth that can be readily used for transactions; money also serves as a store of value and a unit of account. (10)

money demand a relationship between the nominal interest rate and the quantity of money that people are willing to hold at any given nominal interest rate. (15)
money supply the sum of currency (coin and paper money) and deposits at banks. (10)
movement along the curve a situation in which a change in the variable on one axis causes a change in the variable on the other axis, but the position of the curve is maintained. (2A)
multilateral negotiation simultaneous tariff reductions on the part of many countries. (19)

national saving aggregate income minus consumption minus government purchases. (6)
national saving rate the proportion of GDP that is saved, neither consumed nor spent on government purchases; equals national saving (*S*) divided by GDP, or *S/Y*. (7)
natural unemployment rate the unemployment rate that exists when there is neither a recession nor a boom and real GDP is equal to potential GDP. (8)
negative slope a slope of a curve that is less than zero, representing a negative or inverse relationship between two variables. (2A)
negatively related a situation in which an increase in one variable is associated with a decrease in another variable; also called *inversely related.* (2)
net exports the value of exports minus the value of imports. (6)
net exports share the proportion of GDP that is equal to net exports; equals net exports divided by GDP, or *X/Y*. (7)
nominal GDP gross domestic product without any correction for inflation; the same as GDP; the value of all goods and services newly produced in a country during some period of time, usually a year. (6)
nominal interest rate the interest rate uncorrected for inflation. (5)
nontariff barrier any government action other than a tariff that reduces imports, such as a quota or a standard. (19)
normal good a good for which demand increases when income rises and decreases when income falls. (3)
normative economics economic analysis that makes recommendations about economic policy. (2)

open market operation the buying and selling of bonds by the central bank. (10)
opportunity cost the value of the next-best forgone alternative that was not chosen because something else was chosen. (1, 18)
outsider someone who is not working for a particular firm, making it difficult for him or her to get a job with that firm even though he or she is willing to work for a lower wage. (8)

peak the highest point in real GDP before a recession. (5)
perfectly elastic demand demand for which the price elasticity is infinite, indicating an infinite response to a change in the price and therefore a horizontal demand curve. (4)
perfectly elastic supply supply for which the price elasticity is infinite, indicating an infinite response of quantity supplied to a change in price and thereby a horizontal supply curve. (4)
perfectly inelastic demand demand for which the price elasticity is zero, indicating no response to a change in price and therefore a vertical demand curve. (4)
perfectly inelastic supply supply for which the price elasticity is zero, indicating no response of quantity supplied to a change in price and thereby a vertical supply curve. (4)
permanent income model a type of forward-looking consumption model that assumes that people distinguish between temporary changes in their income and permanent changes in their income; the permanent changes have a larger effect on consumption. (11A)
political business cycle a business cycle caused by politicians' use of economic policy to overstimulate the economy just before an election. (15)
portfolio diversification spreading the collection of assets owned in order to limit exposure to risk. (16)
portfolio investment investment by a foreign entity of less than a 10 percent ownership share in a firm. (17)
positive economics economic analysis that explains what happens in the economy and why, without making recommendations about economic policy. (2)
positive slope a slope of a curve that is greater than zero, representing a positive or direct relationship between two variables. (2A)
positively related a situation in which an increase in one variable is associated with an increase in another variable; also called *directly related.* (2)
potential GDP the economy's long-term growth trend for real GDP determined by the available supply of capital, labor, and technology. Real GDP fluctuates above and below potential GDP. (5)
present discounted value the value in the present of future payments. (16A)
price the amount of money or other goods that one must pay to obtain the good. (3)
price ceiling a government price control that sets the maximum allowable price for a good. (4)
price control a government law or regulation that sets or limits the price to be charged for a particular good. (4)
price elasticity of demand the percentage change in the quantity demanded of a good divided by the percentage change in the price of that good. (4)
price elasticity of supply the percentage change in quantity supplied divided by the percentage change in price. (4)
price floor a government price control that sets the minimum allowable price for a good. (4)
price level the average level of prices in the economy. (6)
price shock a change in the price of a key commodity such as oil, usually because of a shortage, that causes a shift in the inflation adjustment line; also sometimes called a supply shock. (13)
price-earnings ratio the price of a stock divided by its annual earnings per share. (16)
production function the relationship that describes output as a function of labor, capital, and technology. (5)
production possibilities alternative combinations of production of various goods that are possible, given the economy's resources. (1)

production possibilities curve a curve showing the maximum combinations of production of two goods that are possible, given the economy's resources. (1)
productivity output per hour of work. (9)
productivity curve a relationship stating the output per hour of work for each amount of capital per hour of work in the economy. (9A)
profit sharing programs in which managers and employees receive a share of profits earned by the firm. (16)
property rights rights over the use, sale, and proceeds from a good or resource. (1)

quantity equation of money the equation relating the price level and real GDP to the quantity of money and the velocity of money: The quantity of money times its velocity equals the price level times real GDP. (10)
quantity demanded the quantity of a good that people want to buy at a given price during a specific time period. (3)
quantity supplied the quantity of a good that firms are willing to sell at a given price. (3)
quota a governmental limit on the quantity of a good that may be imported or sold. (18)

rate of return the return on an asset stated as a percentage of the price of the asset. (16)
real business cycle theory a theory of macroeconomics that stresses that shifts in potential GDP are a primary cause of fluctuations in real GDP; the shifts in potential GDP are usually assumed to be caused by changes in technology. (11, 13)
real gross domestic product (real GDP) a measure of the value of all the goods and services newly produced in a country during some period of time, adjusted for changes in prices over time. (5, 6)
real interest rate the interest rate minus the expected rate of inflation; it adjusts the nominal interest rate for inflation. (5)
real wage the wage or price of labor adjusted for inflation; in contrast, the nominal wage has not been adjusted for inflation. (8)
recession a decline in real GDP that lasts for at least six months. (5)
recovery the early part of an economic expansion, immediately after the trough of the recession. (5)
reinflation an increase in the inflation rate caused by a change in monetary policy. (13)
relative price the price of a particular good compared to the price of other things. (2)
rent control a government price control that sets the maximum allowable rent on a house or apartment. (4)
reserves deposits that commercial banks hold at the Fed. (10)
return the income received from the ownership of an asset; for a stock, the return is the dividend plus the capital gain. (16)
required reserve ratio the fraction of a bank's deposits that it is required to hold at the Fed. (10)
revenue tariff an import tax whose main purpose is to provide revenue to the government. (19)

scarcity the situation in which the quantity of resources is insufficient to meet all wants. (1)
scatter plot a graph in which points in a Cartesian coordinate system represent the values of two variables. (2A)
shift of the curve a change in the position of a curve, usually caused by a change in a variable not represented on either axis. (2A)
shortage (excess demand) the situation in which quantity demanded is greater than quantity supplied. (3)
slope a characteristic of a curve that is defined as the change in the variable on the vertical axis divided by the change in the variable on the horizontal axis. (2A)
Smoot-Hawley tariff a set of tariffs imposed in 1930 that raised the average tariff level to 59 percent by 1932. (19)
socialism an economic system in which the government owns and controls all the capital and makes decisions about prices and quantities as part of a central plan. (2)
specialization a concentration of production effort into a single specific task. (1)
specific tariff a tax on imports that is proportional to the number of units or items imported. (19)
spending balance the level of income or real GDP at which the 45-degree line and the expenditure line cross; also called equilibrium income. (11)
stagflation the situation in which high inflation and high unemployment occur simultaneously. (13)
store of value something that will allow purchasing power to be carried from one period to the next. (10)
structural surplus the level of the government budget surplus under the scenario where real GDP is equal to potential GDP; also called the full-employment surplus. (14)
structural unemployment unemployment due to structural problems such as poor skills, longer-term changes in demand, or insufficient work incentives. (8)
substitute a good that has many of the same characteristics as and can be used in place of another good. (3)
supply a relationship between price and quantity supplied. (3)
supply curve a graph of supply showing the upward-sloping relationship between price and quantity supplied. (3)
supply schedule a tabular presentation of supply showing the price and quantity supplied of a particular good, all else being equal. (3)
surplus (excess supply) the situation in which quantity supplied is greater than quantity demanded. (3)

target inflation rate the central bank's goal for the average rate of inflation over the long run. (12)
tariff a tax on imports. (18)
technological change improvement in technology over time. (9)
technology anything that raises the amount of output that can be produced with a given amount of labor and capital. (5, 9)
time inconsistency the situation in which policymakers have the incentive to announce one economic policy but then change that policy after citizens have acted on the initial, stated policy. (15)

time-series graph a graph that plots a variable over time, usually with time on the horizontal axis. (2A)
total amount of saving a measure of the amount of resources a country has for investment, either in its own country or abroad. (6)
trade balance the value of exports minus the value of imports. (6)
trade creation the increase in trade due to a decrease in trade barriers. (19)
trade diversion the shifting of trade away from the low-cost producer toward a higher-cost producer because of a reduction in trade barriers with the country of the higher-cost producer. (19)
trade war a conflict among nations over trade policies caused by imposition of protectionist policies on the part of one country and subsequent retaliatory actions by other countries. (19)
trough the lowest point of real GDP at the end of a recession. (5)

unemployed person an individual who does not have a job and is looking for work (8).
unemployment rate the percentage of the labor force that is unemployed. (5, 8)
unit of account a standard unit in which prices can be quoted and values of goods can be compared. (10)
unit-free measure a measure that does not depend on a unit of measurement. (4)
Uruguay Round the most recent round of multilateral negotiations, completed in 1993. (19)

value added the value of the firm's production minus the value of the intermediate goods used in production. (6)
velocity a measure of how frequently money is turned over in the economy. (10)

working-age population persons over 16 years of age who are not in an institution such as a jail or hospital. (8)
World Bank an international agency, established after World War II, designed to promote the economic development of poorer countries through lending channeled from industrialized countries. (17)
World Trade Organization (WTO) an international organization that can mediate trade disputes. (19)

yield the annual rate of return on a bond if the bond were held to maturity. (16)

Index

Credits

PHOTO AND CARTOON CREDITS

Title page, Part and Chapter Openers: Jeremy Woodhouse/Getty Images.
Chapter 1: p. 3: Michael Newman/PhotoEdit, Inc.; p. 7(left): James D. Wilson/Liason/Getty Images; p. 7 (right): Justin Sullivan/Getty Images; p. 14 (left, top): ©Jim Sulley/ Newscast/ The Image Works; p. 14 (left, bottom): Tim Boyle/Getty Images; p. 14 (center): Andy Sachs/Getty Images; p. 14 (right): Matthew Staver/Bloomberg News/Landov.
Chapter 2: p. 37: AP/Wide World Photos; p. 39: ©Dan Dry.
Chapter 3: p. 53: ©Royalty-Free/Corbis; p. 58 (left): Tim Boyle/Getty Images; p. 58 (center): Topham/The Image Works; p. 58 (right): Tim Boyle/Getty Images.
Chapter 4: p. 100: ©Corbis; p. 101: ©Seth Wenig/Reuters/Corbis; p. 106: Graeme Harris/Getty Images.
Chapter 5: p. 130 (left): Ed Betz/AP Photo; p. 130 (center): Bill Pugliano/ Newsmakers/Getty Images; p. 130 (right): ©Ted Horowitz/Corbis; p. 133: ©Royalty-Free/Corbis.
Chapter 6: p. 145: Adriel Heisey/Getty Images; p. 153 (left): Brooke Slezak/Jupiter Images; p. 153 (right): Jay Dickman/Corbis.
Chapter 7: p. 175: © Raeside; p. 178: David Silverman/Getty Images.
Chapter 8: p. 205 (left): Brent Jones/Stock Boston; p. 205 (center): ©Bob Daemmrich/The Image Works; p. 205 (right): Dana White/PhotoEdit, Inc.
Chapter 9: p. 227 (left): Hulton Archive/Getty Images; p. 227 (right): Royalty Free/Getty Images; p. 228 (left): Lambert/Getty Images; p. 228 (center): The Granger Collection; p. 228 (right): Ed Lane/Index Stock Photo; p. 231 (left): ©Corbis; p. 231 (right): Peter Menzel/Stock Boston.
Chapter 10: p. 247 (left): Wolfgang Kaehler; p. 247 (right): The Granger Collection; p. 249: AP/Wide World Photos; p. 260 (left): Roger Viollet/Getty Images; p. 260 (right): ©Bettmann/Corbis.
Chapter 11: p. 267: ©2005 Dave Carpenter from cartoonbank.com. All rights reserved; p. 271: Jack Spratt/The Image Works; p. 275: © CHAPATTE; p. 279: ©1965 Time Inc./Getty Images.
Chapter 12: p. 303: ©2001 Seattle Post-Intelligencer/Tribune Media Services.
Chapter 13: p. 322: Courtesy of Vikram Madan.
Chapter 14: p. 339: Steve Sack/Star Tribune; p. 348: U.S. Government Printing Office.
Chapter 15: p. 357 (1): ©Bettmann/Corbis; p. 357 (2): James Anderson/SYGMA/Corbis; p. 357 (3): ©Bettmann/Corbis; p. 357 (4): ©R. Mainan/SYGMA/Corbis; p. 357 (5): Jeffrey Markowitz/SYGMA/Corbis; p. 357 (6): Andy Nelson/The Christian Science Monitor via Getty Images; p. 362: Royalty-Free/Fotosearch; p. 373 (left): Ron Chappel/Getty Images; p. 373 (right): Sean Gallup/Getty Images.
Chapter 16: p. 389: ©Ed Quinn/Corbis; p. 393: © Reuter Raymond/SYGMA/Corbis.
Chapter 17: p. 410: Pablo Corral/Corbis; p. 414: © Gerry Penny/epa/Corbis.
Chapter 18: p. 424 (left): © Zack Seckler/Corbis; p. 424 (right): Nathan Benn/Stock Boston; p. 429: ©Bettmann/Corbis.
Chapter 19: p. 445: AP/Wide World Photos.

TEXT AND FIGURE CREDITS

Chapter 1: p. 18, source of feature box material: "Who Needs eBay? For Towns Across U.S. Tradio is the Real Deal" by Reid J. Epstein from the *Wall Street Journal,* 9/11/02. Copyright © 2002 Dow Jones. Reprinted by permission of Dow Jones via Copyright Clearance Center.
Chapter 2: p. 37, source of feature box material: West's Federal Supplement, Vol. 803 (St. Paul, Minn.: West Publishing Company, 1993), pp. 259–337; p. 38, source of feature box material: "The Future of Economics Isn't So Dismal" by David Leonhardt from *The New York Times,* January 10, 2007. Copyright © 2007 The New York Times Co. Reprinted by permission; p. 47, Figure A.8 source: International Monetary Fund, World Economic Outlook.
Chapter 3: p. 68, source of feature box material: "The Big City; By Any Name, a Rose is Dear as a Valentine" by John Tierney from *The New York Times,* 2/11/99, Section B, Page 1. Copyright © 1999 by The New York Times Co. Reprinted by permission.
Chapter 4: p. 90, source of feature box material: "Easing the Burden of School Fees in Africa" by Stephanie Hanes as appeared in *The Christian Science Monitor* online, February 2, 2006.
Chapter 5: p. 118, Figure 1 source: NIPA tables from the Bureau of Economic Analysis; p. 119, Figure 2 source: International Monetary Fund; p. 120: "Good Morning At Last" from *The Economist,* August 3, 2006, www.economist.com. Copyright © 2006 The Economist Newspaper Ltd. All rights reserved. Reprinted with permission. Further reproduction prohibited; p. 125, Figure 4 source: Bureau of Economic Analysis, U.S. Department of Commerce; pp. 126–127, Figures 5, 6, 7, and 8 source: Bureau of Labor Statistics, U.S. Department of Labor; p. 128, Figure 9 source: Board of Governors of the Federal Reserve; p. 132, source of first quote in feature box: Paul Krugman, "Reckonings: After the Horror," *The New York Times,* September 14, 2001; p. 133, source of figures from New York City Chamber of Commerce study in feature box: "Economic Impact Analysis of the September 11th Attack on New York," New York City Partnership and Chamber of Commerce, September 2001; p. 136, Problem 1 Figure source: U.S. Department of Commerce; p. 137, Problem 5 Table source: U.S. Department of Labor.
Chapter 6: p. 158, source of feature box material: "Vigorous Consumer Spending Helped Economy Grow by 3.5% at the End of 2006" by Jeremy W. Peters from *The New York Times,* 2/1/07, section C, page 10. Copyright © 2007 The New York Times Co. Reprinted by permission; p. 160, Figure 6 source: Bureau of Economic Analysis; p. 162, Figure 7 source: U.S. Department of Labor (CPI), Bureau of Economic Analysis (GDP deflator).
Chapter 7: p. 172, Figure 1 source: U.S. Department of Commerce; p. 190, source of feature box material: "Our Currency, Your Problem" by Niall Ferguson. First published in *The New York Times,* March 13, 2005. Copyright © 2005 by Niall Ferguson, permission of The Wylie Agency.
Chapter 8: pp. 199, 200, 201, 204 and 207, Figures 1, 2, 3, 4, and 5 source: U.S. Department of Labor.
Chapter 9: p. 223, Figure 1 source: Angus Maddison, Phases of Capitalist Development (London: Oxford University Press, 1982) and *Economic Report of the President,* 2000; p. 236, source of feature box material: "The Big Economic Worry: Productivity is Slowing," by Robert J. Samuelson from *The Washington Post,* January 3, 2007. Copyright © 2007, *Newsweek* (owned by *The Washington Post*). Reprinted by permission.
Chapter 10: p. 248, source of feature box material: "More Counterfeit Money Changed Hands in '06" by Barbara Hagenbaugh from *USA Today*, February 27, 2007. Reprinted with permission; p. 250, source for Table 1: Board of Governors of the Federal Reserve; p. 259, Figure 4 source: Organization for Economic Cooperation and Development; p. 261, Figure 5 source: J. P. Young, European Currency and Finance, Vol. 1 (Washington, D.C: Government Printing Office, 1925), p. 503.
Chapter 11: p. 268, Figure 1 source: U.S. Department of Commerce; p. 272, source of feature box material: "A Year After Sept. 11, Attacks' Economic Impact Lingers, but Effect is Disparate" by Adam Geller from the Associated Press. Reprinted by permission of the Associated Press; p. 278: Figure 4 source: U.S. Department of Commerce.
Chapter 13: p. 329, source of quote: Christina Romer, "What Ended the Great Depression?" *Journal of Economic History,* Vol. 52, December 1992, pp. 757–784.
Chapter 14: p. 341, Figure 3 source: U.S. Department of Commerce, U.S. Department of the Treasury; p. 342, Figure 4 source: U.S. Department of the Treasury; p. 348, source of feature box material: *The Economic Report of the President* from www.cbsnews.com.
Chapter 15: p. 359, Figure 2 source: A. W. Phillips, "The Relationship Between Unemployment and the Rate of Change of Money Wage Rates in the United Kingdom," from *Economica*. Copyright © 1958 by Basil Blackwell, Ltd. Used with permission. The data period is 1861–1913. Inflation is measured by the rate of change in wages; p. 361, Figure 3 source: Data from Alex Cukierman, Central Bank Strategy, Credibility, and Independence (Cambridge, Mass.: MIT Press, 1992); p. 362, source of feature box material: "Anatomy of a Hump" from *The Economist,* March 8, 2007. Reprinted by permission of *The Economist* via Copyright Clearance Center; p. 369, Figure 6 source: Board of Governors of the Federal Reserve.
Chapter 16: pp. 384–385, source of stock and bond quotes: Reuters; p. 394, source of feature box material: "Ex-Tyco Officers Sentenced" by Ben White from *The Washington Post.* Copyright 2007, *The Washington Post.* Reprinted with permission.
Chapter 17: p. 404, Figure 2 source: Historical Statistics of the United States: Colonial Times to 1970, U.S. Department of Commerce, and State Personal Income, U.S. Department of Commerce; pp. 405, 406, Figures 3 and 4 source: International Comparison Project administered by the United Nations, World Bank, and International Monetary Fund. The data for 1960 are measured in 1985 dollars; p. 408, Figure 5 source: 1990 data from International Comparison Project administered by the United Nations, World Bank, and International Monetary Fund; p. 409, source of Table 1: "Shares of World GDP Produced by

Different Countries" from World Economic Outlook, September 2006, p. 182. Reprinted by permission of the International Monetary Fund.
Chapter 18: p. 422, source of feature box material: "True or False: Outsourcing is a Crisis" by Eduardo Porter from *The New York Times,* June 19, 2005. Copyright © 2005 The New York Times Co. Reprinted by permission; p. 429, source of quotes in feature box: David Ricardo, "On the Principles of Political Economy and Taxation, 1817," pp. 152–153, in The Works and Correspondence of David Ricardo, ed. Piero Sraffa (Cambridge University Press, 1962).
Chapter 19: p. 449, source of feature box material: "Sri Lanka's Revenue from Garment Exports to America Set to Drop 20% as Trade Agreement Expires" from the Associated Press, November 15, 2004. Reprinted by permission of the Associated Press; p. 451, Figure 3 source: Historical Statistics of the United States, Colonial Times to 1957, series Y, 259–260, and Budget of the U.S. Government, 2000; p. 451, Figure 4 source: Historical Statistics of the United States, Colonial Times to 1970, and Statistical Abstract of the United States, 1999; p. 452, Figure 5 source: "Contracting Spiral of World Trade," from Kindleberger, Charles, The World of Depression 1929–39 (Berkeley, California: University of California Press, 1973). Data reprinted by permission from League of Nations, Monthly Bulletin of Statistics, February 1934.